Language Network

Grammar • Writing • Communication

Language Network

- Grammar, Usage, and Mechanics
- Essential Writing Skills
- Writing Workshops
- Communicating in the Information Age

McDougal Littell
A HOUGHTON MIFFLIN COMPANY

Acknowledgments

Cover *top right* © 1997 Ed Bohon/The Stock Market; *bottom left* © 1998 Kevin Laubacher/FPG International; *bottom center* Tabletop by Sharon Hoogstraten; Illustrations by Daniel Guidera.

Table of Contents **viii** *top* Illustration by Daniel Guidera; *bottom* © Copyright 1999 PhotoDisc, Inc.; **x, xi, xii** Illustration by Daniel Guidera; **xiii** © Jim Cummins/FPG International/PNI; **xiv** Illustration by Daniel Guidera; **xv** © Copyright 1999 PhotoDisc, Inc.; **xvi** Corbis/Charles O'Rear; **xvii** Illustration by Daniel Guidera; **xviii** *top* AP/Wide World Photos; *bottom* Illustration by Daniel Guidera; **xix** © Patrick Ingrand/Tony Stone Images; **xxi** Illustration by Daniel Guidera; **xxii** © 1999 Index Stock Imagery; **xxvii** *top, bottom*, **xxviii, xxix** *top left, top right* Illustration by Daniel Guidera; **xxix** *bottom left, bottom right* Courtesy David R. Lee Animal Care Shelter. Photography © Bob Randall. Ad created by Charlie Propsom, copywriter, and Karl Anderson, art director; **xxx, xxxi** *left, right* © Copyright 1999 PhotoDisc, Inc.; **1** Illustration by Daniel Guidera.

McDougal Littell has made every effort to locate the copyright holders for the images and text used in this book and to make full acknowledgment for their use. Omissions brought to our attention will be corrected in a subsequent edition.

Acknowledgments continue on page 685.

ISBN-13: 978-0-395-96739-3 ISBN-10: 0-395-96739-2

2004 Impression.

13 14 15 16 - DCI - 09 08 07 06

Teacher Panels

The teacher panels helped guide the conceptual development of *Language Network*. They participated actively in shaping and reviewing prototype materials for the pupil edition, determining ancillary and technology components, and guiding the development of the scope and sequence for the program.

Cynda Andrews, Western Hills High School, Fort Worth School District, Fort Worth, Tex.
Gay Berardi, Evanston Township High School, Evanston School District, Evanston, Ill.
Nadine Carter-McDaniel, Townview Academic Center, Dallas School District, Dallas, Tex.
Sandra Dean, English Department Chairperson, Kerr High School, Alief School District, Houston, Tex.
Delia Diaz, English Department Chairperson, Rio Grande City High School, Rio Grande City School District, Rio Grande City, Tex.
Cynthia Galindo, Bel Air High School, Yselta School District, El Paso, Tex.
Ellen Geisler, English/Language Arts Department Chairperson, Mentor Senior High School, Mentor School District, Mentor, Ohio
Dr. Paulette Goll, English Department Chairperson, Lincoln West High School, Cleveland City School District, Cleveland, Ohio
Myron Greenfield, Davis High School, Houston School District, Houston, Tex.
Lorraine Hammack, Executive Teacher of the English Department, Beachwood High School, Beachwood City School District, Beachwood, Ohio
James Horan, Hinsdale Central High School, Hinsdale Township High School, Hinsdale, Ill.
Marguerite Joyce, English Department Chairperson, Woodridge High School, Woodridge Local School District, Peninsula, Ohio
Christi Lackey, North Side High School, Fort Worth School District, Fort Worth, Tex.
Jane McGough, Wichita Falls High School, Wichita Falls School District, Wichita Falls, Tex.
Dee Phillips, Hudson High School, Hudson Local School District, Hudson, Ohio
Dr. Bob Pierce, English Department Chairperson, Conroe High School, Conroe School District, Conroe, Tex.
Cyndi Rankin, John Jay High School, Northside School District, San Antonio, Tex.
Mary Ross, English Department Chairperson, Tascosa High School, Amarillo School District, Amarillo, Tex.
Robert Roth, Evanston Township High School, Evanston, Ill.
Carol Steiner, English Department Chairperson, Buchtel High School, Akron City School District, Akron, Ohio
Nancy Strauch, English Department Chairperson, Nordonia High School, Nordonia Hills City School District, MacEdonia, Ohio
Sheila Treat, Permian High School, Ector County School District, Odessa, Tex.
Ruth Vukovich, Hubbard High School, Hubbard Exempted Village School District, Hubbard, Ohio

Content Specialists

Dr. Mary Newton Bruder, former Professor of Linguistics at University of Pittsburgh (creator of the Grammar Hotline Web site), Pittsburgh, Penn.
Rebekah Caplan, High School and Middle Grades English/Language Arts Specialist, New Standards Project, Washington, D.C.
Dr. Sharon Sicinski Skeans, Assistant Professor, University of Houston-Clear Lake, Houston, Tex.
Richard Vinson, Retired Teacher, Provine High School, Jackson, Miss.

Technology Consultants

Dr. David Considine, Media Studies Coordinator, Appalachian State University, Boone, NC (author of *Visual Messages: Integrating Imagery into Instruction*)

Heidi Whitus, Teacher, Communication Arts High School, San Antonio, Tex.

Anne Clark, Riverside-Brookfield High School, Riverside, Ill.

Pat Jurgens, Riverside-Brookfield High School, Riverside, Ill.

Ralph Amelio, Former Teacher, Willowbrook High School, Villa Park, Ill.

Cindy Lucia, Horace Greeley High School, New York, N.Y.

Aaron Barnhardt, Television writer for the *Kansas City Star* and columnist for *Electronic Media,* Kansas City, Mo.

ESL Consultants

Dr. Andrea B. Bermúdez, Professor of Studies in Language and Culture; Director, Research Center for Language and Culture; Chair, Foundations and Professional Studies, University of Houston-Clear Lake, Clear Lake, Tex.

Inara Bundza, ESL Director, Kelvyn Park High School, Chicago, Ill.

Danette Erickson Meyer, Consultant, Illinois Resource Center, Des Plaines, Ill.

John Hilliard, Consultant, Illinois Resource Center, Des Plaines, Ill.

John Kibler, Consultant, Illinois Resource Center, Des Plaines, Ill.

Barbara Kuhns, Camino Real Middle School, Las Cruces, N.M.

Teacher Reviewers

Nadine Carter-McDaniel, Townview Magnet Center, Dallas ISD, Dallas, Tex.

Frances Capuana, Director of ESL, Curtis High School, Staten Island, N.Y.

Lucila A. Garza, ESL Consultant, Austin, Tex.

Dan Haggerty, Drama Department Chair, Lewis and Clark High School, Vancouver, Wash.

Betty Lou Ludwick, Wakefield Senior High School, Arlington, Va.

Linda Maxwell, MacArthur High School, Houston, Tex.

Linda Powell, Banning High School, Wilmington, Calif. (Los Angeles Unified School District)

Cindy Rogers, MacArthur High School, Houston, Tex.

Lynnette Russell, Lewis and Clark High School, Vancouver, Wash.

Joan Smathers, Language Arts Supervisor, Brevard School-Secondary Program, Viera, Fla.

Sharon Straub, English Department Chair, Joel Ferris High School, Spokane, Wash.

Mary Sylvester, Minneapolis North High School, Minneapolis, Minn.

Shirley Williams, English Department Chair, Longview High School, Longview, Tex.

Student Reviewers

Saba Abraham, Chelsea High School

Julie Allred, Southwest High School

Nabiha Azam, East Kentwood High School

Dana Baccino, Downington High School

Christianne Balsamo, Nottingham High School

Luke Bohline, Lakeville High School
Nathan Buechel, Providence Senior High School
Melissa Cummings, Highline High School
Megan Dawson, Southview Senior High School
Michelle DeBruce, Jurupa High School
Brian Deeds, Arvada West High School
Ranika Fizer, Jones High School
Ashleigh Goldberg, Parkdale High School
Jacqueline Grullon, Christopher Columbus High School
Dimmy Herard, Hialeah High School
Sean Horan, Round Rock High School
Bob Howard, Jr., Robert E. Lee High School
Rebecca Iden, Willowbrook High School
Agha's Igbinovia, Florin High School
Megan Jones, Dobson High School
Ed Kampelman, Parkway West High School
David Knapp, Delmar High School
Eva Lima, Westmoor High School
Ashley Miers, Ouachita High School
Raul Morffi, Shawnee Mission West High School
Sakenia Mosley, Sandalwood High School
Sergio Perez, Sunset High School
Jackie Peters, Westerville South High School
Kevin Robischaud, Waltham High School
Orlando Sanchez, West Mesa High School
Selene Sanchez, San Diego High School
Sharon Schaefer, East Aurora High School
Mica Semrick, Hoover High School
Julio Sequeira, Belmont High School
Camille Singleton, Cerritos High School
Solomon Stevenson, Ozen High School
Tim Villegas, Dos Pueblos High School
Shane Wagner, Waukesha West High School
Swenikqua Walker, San Bernardino High School
Douglas Weakly, Ray High School
Lauren Zoric, Norwin High School

Student Writers

Steve Alderson, Springfield High School
Michael Ashkenasi, Whitney Young High School
Laurel Eskra, Evanston Township High School
Laura Hausfeld, New Trier High School
David Lester, Truman High School
Megan McCarville, Evanston Township High School
Jeff Moher, Oak Park River Forest High School
Rashmi Rathor, Naperville Central High School
Christie Sanchez, Yorktown High School
Tom Taylor, Darien High School

Contents Overview

Grammar, Usage, and Mechanics

Essential Writing Skills

Writing Workshops

Communicating in the Information Age

Student Resources

Grammar, Usage, and Mechanics

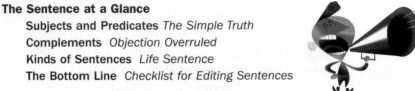

3 Using Phrases

4 Clauses and Sentence Structure

5 Writing Complete Sentences

6 Using Verbs

Alternative Sampler

Hip Hop Mixes

WAR IS OVER!

Quick-Fix Editing Machine

Essential Writing Skills

Jon Krakauer

To:
FROm:
SUBjECT:

16 Revising Sentences

17 Style and Effective Language 379

Writing Workshops

Literary Analysis

20 Response to Literature

Informative Exposition

21 Process Explanation

Narrative/Literary Writing

24 Short Story

Report

25 Research Report

Communicating in the Information Age

Viewing and Representing

Chicago Fireman Rescues Mother and Son At 27th and Western.
Adopt a pet now at the City of Chicago's
David Lee Animal Care Shelter
2741 South Western Avenue
Chicago Streets And Sanitation Crew Picks Up Litter At 27th And Western.
Adopt a pet now at the City of Chicago's
David Lee Animal Care Shelter
2741 South Western Avenue

Viewing and Representing

30 Creating Media

Expanding Literacy

31 Expanding Your Vocabulary

Academic Skills

32 Preparing for Tests

Special Features

Real World Grammar

Grammar in Literature

Power Words: Vocabulary for Precise Writing

Quick-Fix Editing Machine

Grammar, Usage, and Mechanics

Reaching for the Sky

To achieve your dreams, you need to build them on a firm foundation. The tools of grammar give you the power to make your ideas clear and concise. Once you put your dreams into words, who knows what you can build in your life?

The Parts of Speech

Win tickets to see
JAVA
perform live
this Friday.
In 300 words or less, tell us why you think you should be the winner of the two tickets to see this Grammy-winning band.
Deadline: Tuesday, 12:00 midnight
Winners will be announced Friday morning on WGRE.
ADMIT ONE

Theme: Making Music

Music to the Ears

You want to win tickets to see your favorite band perform, but how do you write an essay that will impress the judges? The first two criteria a judge will look for are originality and creativity. Your essay should stand out from all the other entries. Once you have an original, creative idea, the best way to write a winning essay is to choose nouns, verbs, adjectives, adverbs, and other parts of speech that will make your writing memorable and will dazzle the judges.

Write Away: And the Award Goes to . . .
In a short paragraph, write about your favorite musician or musical group. Explain why this person or group is better than anyone else. Save your paragraph in your **Working Portfolio.**

Diagnostic Test: What Do You Know?

Choose the letter of the term that correctly identifies each numbered item.

An extremely unusual (1) blooper happened at the 100th anniversary celebration of The Chicago Symphony Orchestra (2) in 1991. Before the concert, a dinner celebration was held for special donors (3) who had paid $500 or more per person. As a token of its (4) appreciation, the CSO gave the sponsors a gift—a lovely desk clock with an alarm. Little did the staff know that the alarm clocks had not been switched off and were randomly (5) set to go off at different times.

After intermission, the constant beeping began (6). When the disturbances reached a peak, the conductor scornfully addressed his audience, but neither (7) he nor (7) the audience knew that the noise came from the nicely (8) wrapped gifts instead of personal beepers. A staff member (9) finally figured out the problem, and the audience was asked to take the gifts to the lobby. "Wow (10), this is one memorable evening," remarked one of the sponsors.

1. A. adjective
   B. noun
   C. verb
   D. proper noun

2. A. common noun
   B. prepositional phrase
   C. proper noun
   D. adjective

3. A. adverb
   B. noun
   C. interjection
   D. prepositional phrase

4. A. possessive pronoun
   B. preposition
   C. adverb
   D. linking verb

5. A. conjunction
   B. adverb
   C. verb
   D. common noun

6. A. conjunctive adverb
   B. pronoun
   C. verb
   D. preposition

7. A. conjunctions
   B. adverbs
   C. action verbs
   D. linking verbs

8. A. linking verb
   B. indefinite article
   C. pronoun
   D. adverb

9. A. common noun
   B. collective noun
   C. pronoun
   D. conjunction

10. A. conjunction
    B. preposition
    C. interjection
    D. adverb

Nouns

CHAPTER 1

1 Here's the Idea

▶ **A noun is a word that names a person, place, thing, or idea.**

Persons: George Solti, conductor, audience, musicians

Places: theater, Symphony Center

Things: instruments, chairs, podium, music stands

Ideas: inspiration, joy, cooperation, freedom

A **common noun** is a general name for a person, place, thing, or idea. Common nouns are usually not capitalized.

A **proper noun** is the name of a particular person, place, thing, or idea. A proper noun is always capitalized.

Common	guitarist, museum, lake, month
Proper	B.B. King, Rock and Roll Hall of Fame, Lake Pontchartrain, February

A **concrete noun** names an object that can be seen, heard, smelled, touched, or tasted.

An **abstract noun** names an idea, quality, or state.

Concrete	book, bell, flower, sand, apple
Abstract	independence, curiosity, pride, uncertainty, sadness

Nouns may take either a **singular** or **plural** form, depending on whether they name a single person, place, thing, or idea, or more than one.

Singular	stage, city, foot
Plural	stages, cities, feet

For more about spelling plural forms, see p. 637.

All nouns are either common or proper, concrete or abstract, and singular or plural. For example, *drummer* is a common, concrete, and singular noun. *West Indies* is proper, concrete, and plural.

A **collective noun** refers to a group of people or things. Examples include *audience, family, crowd,* and *staff.* A collective noun is singular in form. It can be used to refer to a group either as a single unit or as a number of individuals.

The crew (unit) **prepares the stage for the concert.**

When will the crew (individual) **test the equipment?**

A **compound noun** is made up of two or more words. It may be written as one word, as separate words, or as a hyphenated word.

Compound Nouns	
One word	airplane, sunlight, keyboard
Separate words	rain forest, parking lot, City Hall, Rocky Mountains
Hyphenated word	mother-in-law, runner-up, fade-out

A **possessive noun** shows ownership or relationship. An apostrophe is used with nouns to show possession.

Ownership	the singer's outfit
Relationship	the singer's aunt

PARTS OF SPEECH

2 Why It Matters in Writing

Using proper nouns in place of common nouns often makes writing more realistic and specific. A proper noun can help you picture the person, place, or thing that is referred to in writing.

STUDENT MODEL

DRAFT

When I was ten years old, my mother enrolled me in a **piano class.** While I learned to play **songs** by a famous **composer,** my friends were outside enjoying the long, scorching days of our summer vacation.

REVISION

When I was ten years old, my mother enrolled me in **Mrs. Muffet's Piano School.** While I learned to play **Tchaikovsky's "March" from *The Nutcracker*,** my friends were outside enjoying the long, scorching days of our summer vacation.

3 Practice and Apply

A. CONCEPT CHECK: Identifying Nouns

On your paper, write each noun. Identify it as common or proper, concrete or abstract, and singular or plural.

Preserving Rock's Legacy

1. The Rock and Roll Hall of Fame in Cleveland draws visitors from all over the world.
2. This unusual museum honors musicians for their creativity.
3. The building was designed by I. M. Pei, an architect famous for his strikingly modern designs.
4. Fans can spend days satisfying their curiosity by watching videos and listening to recordings.
5. The public can also view fascinating rock and roll artifacts.
6. One exhibit features the collarless jacket that John Lennon wore while performing with the Beatles.
7. Other famous performers whose costumes can be seen include Tina Turner and David Byrne.
8. A crowd usually gathers around the famous guitars.
9. One of these instruments belonged to Elvis Presley.
10. The guitar, a Martin D-18, was supplied by a private collector.

➜ **For a SELF-CHECK and more practice, see the EXERCISE BANK, p. 584.**

B. REVISING: Using Nouns

Each of the following sentences contains a common noun. Replace each underlined common noun with a proper noun of your own.

A Star Is Born

1. The public's fascination with the life of <u>the singer</u> continues to grow years after his death.
2. <u>The museum</u> promises to bring satisfaction to all of the fans of the singer.
3. Artifacts and memorabilia from early childhood in <u>the hometown</u> will be on display during the month of June.
4. A replica model of the <u>car</u> the singer drove in the movie *Crossroads* will also be included in the exhibits.
5. <u>A friend</u> thinks that this is the best display of an artist's life because it offers personal reflections from family and friends.

Look at your **Write Away** paragraph on page 4 or another draft in your **Working Portfolio** and replace common nouns with proper nouns where necessary.

LESSON 2 Personal and Possessive Pronouns

1 Here's the Idea

▶ **A pronoun is a word used in place of a noun or another pronoun.** The word that a pronoun stands for is called its **antecedent.**

STANDS FOR

Ray said he wanted musical talents to audition for the play.
ANTECEDENT PRONOUN

An antecedent can consist of more than one word, and it may appear in an earlier sentence.

STANDS FOR

Chiyo and I auditioned together. We both got lead parts.
ANTECEDENT PRONOUN

The forms of personal pronouns are shown in the chart below.

Personal Pronouns

	Singular	Plural
First person	I, me (my, mine)	we, us (our, ours)
Second person	you (your, yours)	you (your, yours)
Third person	he, him, she, her, it (his, her, hers, its)	they, them (their, theirs)

Like possessive nouns, **possessive pronouns** show ownership or relationship. In the chart, possessive pronouns are in parentheses.

Sonia delivered her famous monologue.
ANTECEDENT PRONOUN

2 Why It Matters in Writing

Pronouns replace unnecessary or repetitive nouns.

STUDENT MODEL

During a telephone conversation, the composer Leonard Bernstein and the choreographer Jerome Robbins came up with an idea that developed into their ~~Bernstein's and Robbins~~'s hit musical *West Side Story.*

Possessive pronoun helps to avoid repetition.

PARTS OF SPEECH

3 Practice and Apply

A. CONCEPT CHECK: Personal and Possessive Pronouns

On your paper, write each pronoun and tell whether it is personal or possessive.

A Timeless Love Story

1. Bernstein and Robbins convinced the songwriter Stephen Sondheim and the writer Arthur Laurents to work with them.
2. At first, Laurents intended to follow Shakespeare's plot in *Romeo and Juliet* in every respect, but he later changed his mind.
3. The ending of *West Side Story* is slightly different from the ending of the famous tragedy on which it is based.
4. Like *Romeo and Juliet,* the modern play has a bitter feud and an unlikely romance at the center of its plot.
5. In Shakespeare's play, the foes are two feuding families, and in *West Side Story* they are two feuding street gangs.
6. Like Juliet, Maria in *West Side Story* falls in love with her family's enemy.
7. She remains loyal to him as the feud worsens.
8. Tony, the Romeo figure, tries to make peace between the two gangs, but his efforts backfire.
9. Both versions of the tragic story remain popular in our day.
10. Would you rather perform in a production of *West Side Story* or a production of *Romeo and Juliet?*

➜ **For a SELF-CHECK and more practice, see EXERCISE BANK, p. 584.**

B. REVISING: Using Pronouns

Replace any unnecessary or repetitive nouns with personal or possessive pronouns.

***Grease* Is the Word**

In contrast to *West Side Story,* the musical *Grease* offers a light-hearted look at teenage life in the 1950s. The play's setting is Rydell High School, and the play's main characters are Danny Zuko and Sandy Olsson. Danny and Sandy, who shared a special summer romance, are quite surprised when Danny and Sandy find themselves attending the same school. The main obstacle is that Danny is a rebellious fifties-style "greaser," while Sandy seems hopelessly "square." Will the star-crossed teens find true love, or will the star-crossed teens' differences keep the star-crossed teens apart?

CHAPTER 1

LESSON 3

Other Kinds of Pronouns

1 Here's the Idea

Pronouns have many forms and serve different purposes in sentences.

Reflexive and Intensive Pronouns

Reflexive and intensive pronouns are formed by adding *-self* or *-selves* to forms of the personal pronouns.

Reflexive and Intensive Pronouns

	First person	Second person	Third person
Singular	myself	yourself	himself, herself, itself
Plural	ourselves	yourselves	themselves

A **reflexive pronoun** reflects action back upon the subject and adds information to the sentence.

REFLECTS
Donna prepared herself for a long day.
SUBJECT
PRONOUN

An **intensive pronoun** adds emphasis to a noun or pronoun in the same sentence.

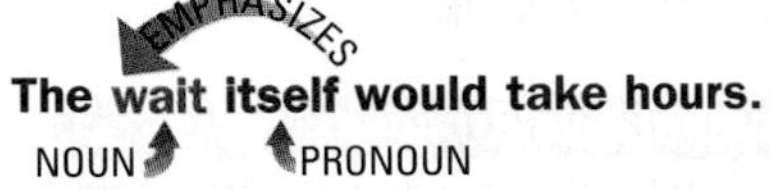
EMPHASIZES
The wait itself would take hours.
NOUN
PRONOUN

WATCH OUT

A reflexive pronoun must have an antecedent. A common error is to use a reflexive pronoun without an antecedent in the sentence.

The planning committee appointed Ted and ~~myself~~. me

Demonstrative Pronouns

Demonstrative pronouns point out specific persons, places, things, or ideas. They allow you to indicate whether the things you are pointing out are relatively near in time or space or farther away. Demonstrative pronouns are *this, these, that,* and *those.*

The people at the front of the line will get better tickets than those at the end, she thought.

PARTS OF SPEECH

Indefinite Pronouns

An **indefinite pronoun** does not refer to a specific person, place, or thing. An indefinite pronoun usually does not have an antecedent.

Many of the fans had arrived at 6 A.M.

Indefinite Pronouns	
Singular	another, anybody, anything, each, either, everybody, everyone, everything, much, neither, nobody, no one, nothing, one, somebody, someone, something
Plural	both, few, many, several
Singular or plural	all, any, more, most, none, some

Some pronouns can also function as adjectives.

Several people had to wait in the rain. (adjective)

Several of the fans waited anxiously in line. (pronoun)

CHAPTER 1

Interrogative and Relative Pronouns

An **interrogative pronoun** is used to ask a question.

What is your favorite song?
INTERROGATIVE PRONOUN (What)

A **relative pronoun** is used to introduce subordinate clauses.

The seats that the students asked for were unavailable.
ANTECEDENT (seats) RELATIVE PRONOUN (that)

Interrogative and Relative Pronouns	
Interrogative	who, whom, whose, which, what
Relative	who, whom, whose, which, that

For more on pronouns, see pp. 180–198.

2 Why It Matters in Writing

Relative pronouns can be used to combine sentences.

STUDENT MODEL

DRAFT

The girl waited for someone to ask her to dance. She decided to ask a boy if he would like to dance with her.

REVISION

The girl, **who** had been waiting for someone to ask her to dance, asked a boy if he would like to dance with her.

3 Practice and Apply

A. CONCEPT CHECK: Other Kinds of Pronouns

Write each pronoun and identify its antecedent if it has one.

Tips on Tickets: The Experts' Advice

1. What is the best way to get good seats for a concert?
2. A long wait in line is an experience that concertgoers are likely to recognize.
3. Someone gets up before dawn in order to be first in line.
4. The seats that go with the tickets turn out to be real disappointments, however.
5. A frustrated fan might well ask himself or herself why this happens.
6. The best way to find out is to ask the ticket sellers themselves.
7. All agree that there is no special advantage to getting to the box office early.
8. Ticket agencies usually give out lottery numbers to determine the customers who get to buy tickets first.
9. As a result, people at the end of the line might get better seats than those at the front.
10. Nothing is more important than luck when people are trying to get good seats.

➔ **For a SELF-CHECK and more practice, see the EXERCISE BANK, p. 585.**

B. REVISING: Relative Pronouns

Combine the following sets of sentences using the relative pronouns in parentheses.

Life on the Road

1. A touring musician's life consists of late nights, fast-food meals, and uneasy rests on tour buses. A musician's life is less romantic than it may seem. (which)
2. Dressing room facilities are often shared by a group of people. Most dressing rooms are not always clean. (which)
3. The audience can vary their response from indifference to ecstasy. The audience's ages range from 16–50. (whose)
4. The music of opening acts may be at odds with your own taste. Some opening acts are unknown to the public. (that)
5. However, there is an energy in music. The music can stir your blood and start your heart pounding. (that)

Verbs

1 Here's the Idea

▶ **A verb expresses an action, a condition, or a state of being.** The two main types of verbs are action verbs and linking verbs.

Action Verbs

An **action verb** expresses action. The action may be physical or mental.

The band marches onto the field. (physical)

The audience expects a great performance. (mental)

When an action verb appears with a direct object (that is, a person or thing that receives the action), it is called a **transitive verb.** When an action verb does not have an object, it is called an **intransitive verb.**

Danny plays the trumpet like a professional.
TRANSITIVE VERB (plays) — OBJECT (trumpet)

He travels around the country with the other musicians.
INTRANSITIVE VERB (travels) — (NO OBJECT)

CHAPTER 1

Linking Verbs

A **linking verb** links the subject of a sentence to a word in the predicate. There are two groups of linking verbs: forms of *to be,* and verbs that express condition.

The instruments are safe in the bus.
LINKING VERB (are)

The students seemed bored during the long trip.
LINKING VERB (seemed)

Forms of *To Be*
is, am, are, was, were, been, being

Verbs that Express Condition
look, smell, feel, sound, taste,
grow, appear, become, seem, remain

Some verbs can be either action or linking verbs.

Verbs	
Action	**Linking**
We **felt** the seat cushions.	They **felt** dry.
We **tasted** the popcorn.	It **tasted** salty.

If you can substitute *is, are, was,* or *were* for a verb, you know it is a linking verb.

Auxiliary Verbs

Auxiliary verbs, also called **helping verbs**, are combined with verbs to form **verb phrases**. A verb phrase may be used to express a particular tense of a verb (that is, the time referred to) or to indicate that an action is directed at the subject.

The stadium is filled to capacity.
AUXILIARY (is) MAIN (filled)

We should save a seat for Jeff.
AUXILIARY (should) MAIN (save)

Common Auxiliary Verbs				
be	have	might	shall	will
can	may	must	should	would

Some of these auxiliary verbs can also be used as main verbs. For example notice how *has* stands alone in the first sentence below and is a helping verb in the second sentence.

Sandra has a pair of Conga drums at home. (main)

She has practiced her drumming all summer. (auxiliary)

② Why It Matters in Writing

Action verbs can create a vivid, interesting picture of a scene. Notice how the verbs create a sense of action even as the character is standing still.

LITERARY MODEL

Hana Omiya **stood** at the railing of the small ship that **shuddered** toward America in a turbulent November sea. She **shivered** as she **pulled** the folds of her silk kimono close to her throat and **tightened** the wool shawl about her shoulders.

—Yoshiko Uchida, *Picture Bride*

CHAPTER 1

③ Practice and Apply

CONCEPT CHECK: Verbs

Write the verbs or verb phrases in each sentence and identify each as an action or a linking verb. Underline any auxiliary verbs. There are 15 in all.

The Big Parade

(1) Every November, bands from across the country visit New York City for the big Thanksgiving Day parade. **(2.)** Even on cold days when strong winds or light rain might scare away spectators, the parade is on schedule. **(3)** The crowd lines the parade route and will stay until the last float has driven out of sight. **(4)** As bands strut down Broadway, drum majors pound their drums, members of color guards rhythmically wave their flags, and baton twirlers toss their batons into the air and catch them as they twirl downward to the ground. **(5)** Meanwhile, giant, colorful cartoon balloons like Betty Boop, Spiderman, and Bart Simpson, and other favorite characters are overhead. **(6)** For young children, the parade remains an eventful experience and becomes a fond memory in their adult lives.

➔ For a SELF-CHECK and more practice, see the EXERCISE BANK, p. 585.

Identify the transitive verbs and write the object of each one.

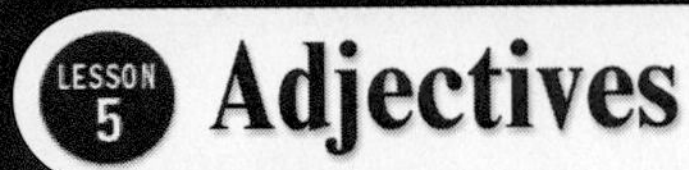

LESSON 5 Adjectives

1 Here's the Idea

An **adjective** modifies or limits the meaning of a noun or pronoun.

We saw the famous singer at the legendary Carnegie Hall.

(MODIFIES → singer; famous: ADJECTIVE) (MODIFIES → Carnegie Hall; legendary: ADJECTIVE)

An adjective tells *what kind, which one, how many,* or *how much.*

Adjectives

What Kind	Which One	How Many	How Much
famous song	**this** star	**one** dollar	**some** music
squeaky noise	**that** way	**three** tenors	**more** room
green light	**these** words	**several** years	**less** energy

Articles

The most common adjectives are the articles *a, an,* and *the. A* and *an* are **indefinite articles** that refer to one of a general group of people, places, things, or ideas. Use *a* before words beginning with consonant sounds. Use *an* before words beginning with vowel sounds. *The* is the **definite article** that usually refers to a specific person, place, thing, or idea.

Articles

Indefinite	Definite
A student volunteered. Jessie brought **an** itinerary.	**The** teacher arrived. Phil borrowed **the** camera from her.

Proper Adjectives

Proper adjectives are formed from proper nouns. They are capitalized and often end in *-n*, *-an*, *-ian*, *-ese*, and *-ish*.

American artists perform in international countries.
Japanese crowds fill Yokohama Stadium.

Proper Nouns	Proper Adjectives
Portugal	Portuguese
Egypt	Egyptian
North America	North American

2 Why It Matters in Writing

Fresh, original adjectives sharpen your writing where dull, overused adjectives like *good* or *great* leave your reader uninterested. Notice how the writer in the following passage describes a concert scene.

STUDENT MODEL

The **boisterous** crowd grew anxious as the band played a few **poignant** ballads. Meanwhile, an **obnoxious** fan ran across the stage wearing a corset and wig.

3 Practice and Apply

CHAPTER 1

A. CONCEPT CHECK: Adjectives

Write each adjective that is not an article in these sentences, along with the word it modifies.

All About Karaoke

1. Karaoke became a major trend in Japan and around the world.
2. The machine is a Japanese invention.
3. The concept is not a new one, however.
4. Years ago, American television featured shows in which people sang along with a chorus.
5. The word *karaoke* means "empty orchestra" in Japanese.
6. Powerful speakers play background music.
7. Meanwhile, the lyrics are displayed on a large screen.
8. Most people enjoy singing along, even those with modest talents.
9. The real purpose is to have fun rather than to give a fabulous performance.
10. In fact, karaoke started in Japan as a way for busy workers to unwind.

➔ **For a SELF-CHECK and more practice, see the EXERCISE BANK, p. 586.**

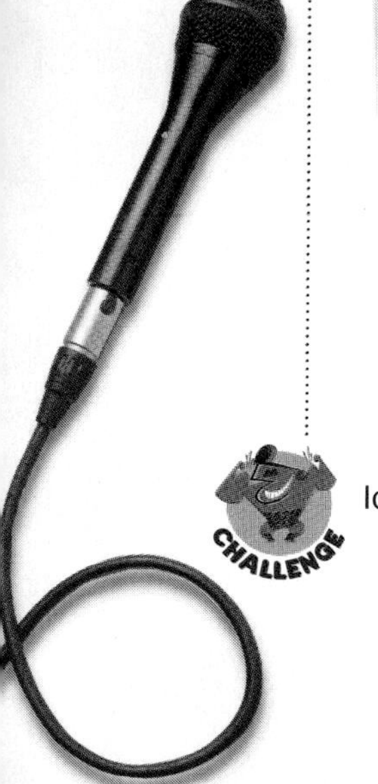

CHALLENGE

Identify the proper adjectives in sentences 1–10.

B. REVISING: Using Strong Adjectives

Replace each underlined adjective with a strong adjective of your own.

Film Music

1. Music has accompanied drama since old times.
2. As a matter of fact, silent films depended on good music to add depth to the visual part of the action.
3. At the time, musical selections were performed live by great pianists who could make smooth transitions within each scene.
4. Silent film music had little, if any, connection to the on-screen action and presented little variation from one scene to the next.
5. The silent film *The Great Train Robbery* is considered a great masterpiece for many reasons, but don't expect the musical selections to resemble the on-screen action.
6. Today music plays a special role in the production of movies.
7. Unlike the small relationship between music and silent films in the past, most movies today depend on music to set the mood.
8. A conductor watches the film closely and cues in music where suspenseful, tragic, dramatic, or funny moments occur in a scene.
9. If you remember Alfred Hitchcock's *Psycho*, then you'll remember the scary music moments before something tragic is about to occur.
10. Can you think of any good movie soundtracks?

C. WRITING: Adding Adjectives

Rewrite the conversation in this cartoon, replacing the words *way cool* in quotations with original adjectives.

9 Chickweed Lane by Brooke McEldowney

PARTS OF SPEECH

Adverbs

1 Here's the Idea

▶ **An adverb modifies a verb, an adjective, or another adverb.**

We instantly recognized Beethoven's Fifth Symphony.
(instantly: ADVERB — MODIFIES — recognized: VERB)

The famous notes rang out quite clearly.
(quite: ADVERB — MODIFIES — clearly: ADVERB)

The orchestra waited until the auditorium grew completely quiet.
(completely: ADVERB — MODIFIES — quiet: ADJECTIVE)

Adverbs	
Where	The student orchestra stopped **here** during a national tour.
When	Will they be returning **soon?**
How	Everyone played **magnificently.**
To what extent	The auditorium was **completely** full.

Many adverbs are formed by adding *-ly* to adjectives. Sometimes the spelling changes because of this addition.

frequent + *-ly* = **frequently**   extreme + *-ly* = **extremely**
true + *-ly* = **truly**   possible + *-ly* = **possibly**

Other Commonly Used Adverbs				
afterward	fast	low	often	today
already	forth	more	slow	tomorrow
also	hard	near	sometimes	too
back	instead	next	still	yet
even	late	not	straight	
far	long	now	then	

An **intensifier** is an adverb that defines the degree of an adjective or another adverb. Intensifiers always precede the adjectives or adverbs they are modifying.

We were rather surprised that classical music is very popular.
(rather: INTENSIFIER — EMPHASIZES — surprised; very: INTENSIFIER — EMPHASIZES — popular)

Intensifiers				
extremely	most	quite	so	truly
just	nearly	rather	somewhat	very
more	only	really	too	

2 Why It Matters in Writing

Adverbs can be used to describe the way things happen. Notice how the highlighted adverbs in the following passage provide a time sequence.

STUDENT MODEL

Recently, many scientists have turned their attention to music and its possible beneficial effects. In one study, researchers conducted an experiment with the help of a group of students. Most students scored significantly higher on an IQ test if they listened to music by classical composer Wolfgang Amadeus Mozart **immediately** before the test, the scientists **subsequently** concluded.

PARTS OF SPEECH

3 Practice and Apply

A. CONCEPT CHECK: Adverbs

For each sentence below, write each adverb.

Beethoven's Triumph

1. Beethoven tirelessly devoted himself to his music.
2. He often worked late.
3. In fact, his nocturnal piano playing made him very unpopular with his more conventional neighbors.
4. The composer was terribly shocked to realize that he was losing his hearing when he was in his late twenties.
5. His condition gradually worsened.
6. It finally became so severe that Beethoven could not hear his own music.

7. No matter how loudly he pounded on the keyboard of his piano, he still could not hear the notes that it produced.
8. Beethoven stubbornly refused to give up, however.
9. He courageously continued not only to compose but also to conduct performances of his works.
10. Would you be very surprised to learn that he composed his greatest works, including the Ninth Symphony, after he had lost his hearing completely?

➜ **For a SELF-CHECK and more practice, see the EXERCISE BANK, p. 586.**

For each adverb above, identify the verb phrase, adjective, or adverb it modifies.

B. REVISING: Using Adverbs

Read the following sentences and replace the words in brackets with an adverb. Write your adverbs on your paper.

Example: [It is surprising] not too many people know that Wolfgang Amadeus Mozart may have been murdered.
Answer: Surprisingly,

The Mozart Murder Mystery

1. [In a rough way] speaking, Beethoven and the great composer Wolfgang Amadeus Mozart were contemporaries.
2. The two crossed paths only [one time] or [two times].
3. This was not because they disliked each other; on the contrary, Beethoven, who was the younger of the two had [at all times] admired Mozart [in a way that is tremendous].
4. [In a way that is tragic] for music lovers, Mozart died at the age of thirty-five.
5. Rumors [in not much time] began to spread that Mozart had [in actual terms] been murdered by a musical rival.
6. [It is alleged], Antonio Salieri, who was a friend of Mozart's and a fellow composer, poisoned the young genius.
7. According to legend, Salieri was [to an extreme degree] jealous of Mozart.
8. Mozart was by all indications one of the most [in a remarkable way] gifted musicians who ever lived.
9. Salieri, by comparison, was only [in a moderate way] talented.
10. The relationship between the two composers is [in a thorough way] explored in a movie called *Amadeus*.

LESSON 7 Prepositions

1 Here's the Idea

A preposition shows the relationship between a noun or pronoun and another word in a sentence.

The sounds of a jazz band filled the kitchen.
The music was coming from a radio.

Commonly Used Prepositions

about	before	during	off	toward
above	behind	except	on	under
across	below	for	onto	underneath
after	beneath	from	out	until
against	beside	in	outside	up
along	between	inside	over	upon
among	beyond	into	since	with
around	by	like	through	within
as	despite	near	throughout	without
at	down	of	to	

Prepositions that consist of more than one word are called **compound prepositions.**

Jazz legend Louis Armstrong sang in addition to playing the trumpet.

When jazz singers perform in a style known as *scatting,* they sing nonsense syllables such as "ba skoodily do" instead of words.

Commonly Used Compound Prepositions

according to	by means of	in place of	on account of
aside from	in addition to	in spite of	out of
because of	in front of	instead of	prior to

PARTS OF SPEECH

Prepositional Phrases

A **prepositional phrase** consists of a preposition and its object, and any modifiers of the object. The **object of a preposition** is the noun or pronoun that follows a preposition. Prepositional phrases often express relationships of location (*by, near*), direction (*to, down*), or time (*before, during*).

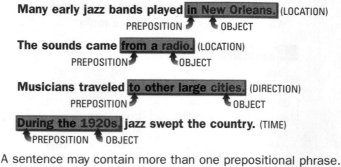

Many early jazz bands played in New Orleans. (LOCATION)
PREPOSITION (in) OBJECT (New Orleans)

The sounds came from a radio. (LOCATION)
PREPOSITION (from) OBJECT (radio)

Musicians traveled to other large cities. (DIRECTION)
PREPOSITION (to) OBJECT (cities)

During the 1920s, jazz swept the country. (TIME)
PREPOSITION (During) OBJECT (1920s)

A sentence may contain more than one prepositional phrase. Each preposition has its own object.

We listened to a solo by Louis Armstrong.

CHAPTER 1

2 Why It Matters in Writing

Prepositional phrases give specific details and often describe a scene or action. Read the following passage without the prepositional phrases, and then read it with the phrases. Notice how the prepositional phrases add importance to the words they describe or relate to.

LITERARY MODEL

How sweet the moonlight sleeps **upon this bank!**
Here will we sit and let the sounds **of music**
Creep **in our ears:** soft stillness and the night
Become the touches **of sweet harmony.**

—William Shakespeare, *The Merchant of Venice*

3 Practice and Apply

A. CONCEPT CHECK: Prepositions

For each sentence below, write each prepositional phrase and underline the preposition. Then circle the object of the preposition.

The Birth of Jazz

1. Jazz is a modern form of music.
2. Many musical styles contributed to its birth.
3. Among these influences are gospel and the blues.
4. Rhythms from West Africa are also part of jazz's heritage.
5. In New Orleans, jazz was often played at funerals.
6. During the early years of the 20th century, jazz became popular as entertainment.
7. People loved the new music because of its bold and innovative sound.
8. Jazz is unique in its use of syncopation and improvisation.
9. Syncopation means the shifting of rhythmic accents within a song or composition.
10. In an improvisation, a musician plays notes of his or her own invention.

For a SELF-CHECK and more practice, see the EXERCISE BANK, p. 586.

PARTS OF SPEECH

B: WRITING: Using Prepositions

Write five sentences that describe the scene below. Use at least one prepositional phrase in each sentence.

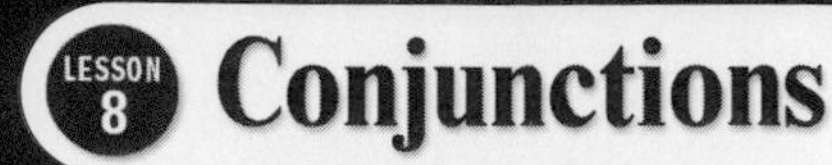

LESSON 8

Conjunctions

1 Here's the Idea

▶ **A conjunction connects words or groups of words.** There are three kinds of conjunctions: coordinating, correlative, and subordinating. Conjunctive adverbs are adverbs that function somewhat like conjunctions.

Coordinating Conjunctions

Coordinating conjunctions connect words or groups of words of equal importance in a sentence.

Sonia and her friends watched the new music video.

The action started out on a beach, but the scene changed quickly.

Coordinating Conjunctions						
and	but	for	nor	or	so	yet

Correlative Conjunctions

Correlative conjunctions are word pairs that serve to join words or groups of words.

You will not only hear your favorite song but also see the performer.

Either the music or the visual images will grab your attention.

Correlative Conjunctions		
both . . . and	neither . . . nor	whether . . . or
either . . . or	not only . . . but also	

Subordinating Conjunctions

Subordinating conjunctions introduce subordinate clauses—clauses that cannot stand alone—and join them to independent clauses.

SUBORDINATE CLAUSE

The band waited while the director checked the lighting.

CONJUNCTION

SUBORDINATE CLAUSE

Although music videos are short, they are expensive to produce.

CONJUNCTION

Subordinating Conjunctions				
after	as though	if	so that	when
although	because	in order that	than	where
as	before	provided	unless	whereas
as if	even though	since	until	while

Conjunctive Adverbs

Conjunctive adverbs are used to express relationships between independent clauses.

The invention of the transistor radio contributed to the rise of rock and roll; similarly, the introduction of cable television helped launch music videos.

Conjunctive Adverbs				
accordingly	consequently	hence	nevertheless	still
also	finally	however	otherwise	therefore
besides	furthermore	instead	similarly	thus

PARTS OF SPEECH

2 Why It Matters in Writing

Conjunctions explain the relationship between ideas and are used to combine two or more short sentences.

STUDENT MODEL

Before music videos were broadcast on cable television, fans had fewer opportunities to see their favorite artists perform. Most people think of music videos as a recent innovation, **but** the concept is not entirely new. The art form can be traced back to the 1920s, **when** a German filmmaker named Oskar Fischinger began making short films to illustrate musical works.

3 Practice and Apply

A. CONCEPT CHECK: Conjunctions

Write the conjunctions and the conjunctive adverbs. If there are none, write *none.*

The Video Revolution

1. The face of the music industry changed when cable television came along and began running music videos twenty-four hours a day.
2. At first, many people predicted that the idea would fail.
3. Either an all-video station would not attract enough viewers, or the producers would never find enough programming to fill all the airtime, they said.
4. These predictions seemed reasonable, but the skeptics turned out to be wrong.
5. Singers and bands began to make more and more videos; consequently, viewers tuned in to watch.
6. Later, while music videos became a major form of entertainment, some critics began to find fault with them.
7. According to critics, performers were creating works that were not only visually but also musically insubstantial.
8. There's some truth to the criticism that many videos are slick and unimaginative; however, there are plenty that are truly striking and innovative.
9. It's been roughly twenty years since videos first appeared.
10. Whether you give them a thumbs-up or a thumbs-down, you must admit that they are here to stay.

For a SELF-CHECK and more practice, see the EXERCISE BANK, p. 587.

B. WRITING: Using Conjunctions

Write the missing conjunctions and conjunctive adverbs.

Early Video History

During the 1940s, jukebox-like machines known as "soundies" showed short films in which famous singers performed hit songs; ______ the popularity of these machines did not last. Musical images did not disappear; ______ other media took the place of soundies. Television variety shows provided entertainers new opportunities to perform; ______, record companies began making short promotional films for records. At the time, ______ producers ______ artists could possibly imagine how important such music films would become.

LESSON 9 Interjections

1 Here's the Idea

An interjection is a word or a phrase used to express emotion. Examples of interjections include *wow, gee, hey, ouch, aha, boy, imagine,* and *unbelievable.* A strong interjection is followed by an exclamation point. A mild interjection is set off by commas.

Yikes! Our project is due tomorrow.

Well, where should we start?

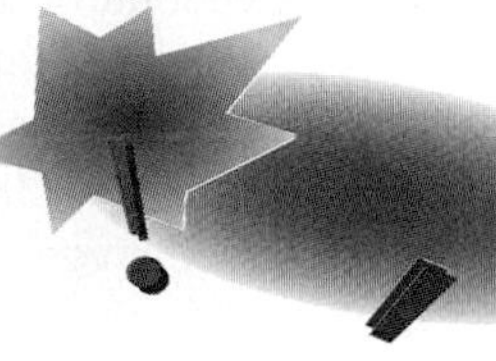

2 Why It Matters in Writing

Interjections add realism to your writing, particularly in dialogue in short stories or essays. Notice the sense of guilt conveyed below by the interjection.

LITERARY MODEL

"If Jim doesn't kill me," she said to herself, "before he takes a second look at me, he'll say I look like a Coney Island chorus girl. But what could I do—**oh,** what could I do with a dollar and eighty-seven cents!"

—O. Henry, "The Gift of the Magi"

PARTS OF SPEECH

3 Practice and Apply

CONCEPT CHECK: Understanding Interjections

For each item, choose the better interjection.

It's a Wrap!

1. (Great!/Oh, no!) We're almost finished with our multimedia presentation.
2. (Wow,/Well,) we still have to choose the background music for the introduction.
3. (Hey!/All right,) I forgot about that!
4. (Here,/Ouch,) listen to this.
5. (Alas! Wow!) I think that's perfect.

For a SELF-CHECK and more practice, see the EXERCISE BANK, p. 587.

Real World Grammar

Music Review

When you write a **music review** for your school newspaper, you express an opinion based on a critical review of a musician's performance and work. For example, if you enjoyed a concert, you will probably praise the musician for his or her rendition. By using various nouns, adjectives, adverbs, and prepositional phrases appropriately, you can express specific details about the performance. Proper nouns can be used in place of common nouns for the artist's name and music. Effective adverbs and adjectives can help support your judgment of the performance.

Times

National Edition

Midwest: Partly cloudy, windy and cooler in the Great Lakes and Ohio Valley. In the Plains, partly to mostly sunny and mild. Weather map and other details appear on page C29.

ONE DOLLAR

Mudd Sisters

Madison Square Garden,
New York, NY
6/25/00

The Mudd Sisters gave a **spectacular** performance last night. These rising stars haven't hit the road since their **widely** successful tour more than a year ago, so the evening proved **quite** satisfying for the more than 20,000 overzealous fans.

The performance began with some of the Sisters' **touching, bittersweet ballads** and built up to their more than rocking, high-energy numbers like **"Get Over It,"** and **"Liberty."** The Sisters were here to please their fans and proved so when they ended the concert with their number one title **"After You."** The explosive applause **from the audience** brought the foursome back **for an encore performance** in which they delighted us and sent us home **with our hearts aching for more.**

—Kendra Cox

Proper noun states the artists' name.

Strong adjective describes the performance.

Adverbs tell the degrees of success and satisfaction.

Adjectives describe the ballads, giving the reader a sense of the music.

Proper nouns name song titles.

Prepositional phrases describe scene and action.

When you write a music review of a concert, you want to provide details that will give your reader the opportunity to understand how you formed your opinion of the musician's work. Here are some of the ways in which the parts of speech can help.

Music Review Checklist

- ✔ Use proper nouns to identify musicians and song titles.
- ✔ Use specific nouns like *bassist, pianist,* and *drummer* to describe band members.
- ✔ Use strong adjectives to describe music, performers, and fans. For music, use words like *mellow, upbeat, playful.* For performers, use words like *outstanding, energetic, invigorating, solid.* For fans, use words like *cheerful, energetic, critical, devoted, animated.*
- ✔ Use effective verbs like *roared, delighted, hypnotized, charmed* to show action.

PRACTICE AND APPLY: Writing

Using the tips above, write a music review of an artist's latest CD. You may use the information below or facts about a real-life artist whose music you are familiar with.

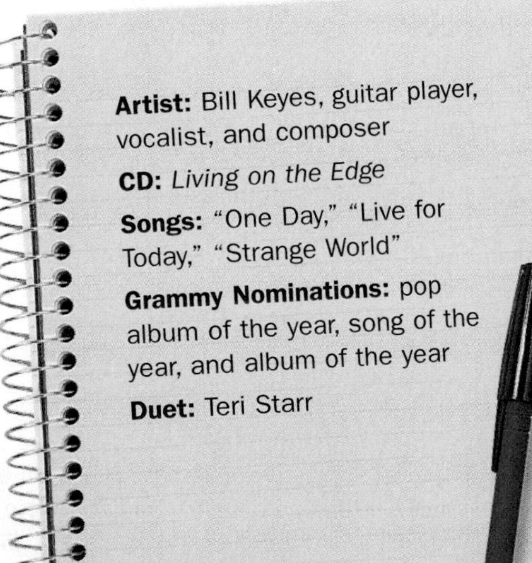

Artist: Bill Keyes, guitar player, vocalist, and composer
CD: *Living on the Edge*
Songs: "One Day," "Live for Today," "Strange World"
Grammy Nominations: pop album of the year, song of the year, and album of the year
Duet: Teri Starr

PARTS OF SPEECH

Mixed Review

A. Nouns, Pronouns, Verbs, and Adjectives Read this passage. Then answer the questions below it.

LITERARY MODEL

(1) I soon found out why old Chong had retired from teaching piano. **(2)** He was deaf. **(3)** "Like Beethoven!" he shouted to me. **(4)** "We're both listening only in our head!" **(5)** And he would start to conduct his frantic silent sonatas.

(6) Our lessons went like this. **(7)** He would open the book and point to different things, explaining their purpose: "Key! Treble! Bass! No sharps or flats! **(8)** So this is C major! **(9)** Listen now and play after me!"

(10) And then he would play the C scale a few times, a simple chord, and then, as if inspired by an old, unreachable itch, he gradually added more notes . . . and a pounding bass until the music was really something quite grand.

—Amy Tan, "Two Kinds"

CHAPTER 1

1. What is the proper noun in sentence 1?
2. Is the verb in sentence 2 an action verb or a linking verb?
3. What are the personal pronouns in sentence 3?
4. Is the noun in sentence 4 common or proper?
5. What are the adjectives in sentence 5?
6. What kind of pronoun is *our* in sentence 6?
7. What kind of verb is *would* in sentence 7?
8. Is *this* in sentence 8 a demonstrative or an interrogative pronoun?
9. What are the verbs in sentence 9?
10. What are the adjectives in sentence 10?

B. Adverbs, Prepositions, Conjunctions, and Interjections In the sentences below, identify each underlined word as either an adverb, preposition, conjunction, or interjection.

Shape Up, Einstein

A newspaper column **(1)** from 1945 relates an amusing anecdote **(2)** about Albert Einstein, the great mathematician **(3)** and physicist. Einstein, **(4)** according to the account, played the violin as a hobby. One day, he invited Artur Schnabel, a famous concert pianist, to join him in some informal music-making. **(5)** While the two were playing a **(6)** technically difficult Mozart sonata, Schnabel became **(7)** quite frustrated. Finally, he could **(8)** neither concentrate **(8)** nor control himself. He stopped playing, banged **(9)** angrily on the keyboard, and exclaimed: "No, no, Albert. **(10)** For heaven's sake, can't you count? One, two, three, four. . . ."

Mastery Test: What Did You Learn?

Write the letter of the term that correctly identifies each underlined item.

<u>What</u> (1) do Frank Sinatra and the Beatles have in common? Both "Old Blue Eyes" and the "Fab Four" have performed at <u>Carnegie Hall</u> (2).

Opened in 1891, Carnegie Hall was originally known as the New York Music Hall. The <u>famous</u> (3) composer Peter Ilich Tchaikovsky was guest conductor <u>during its opening week</u> (4). Since then the hall, which is <u>widely</u> (5) acclaimed for its acoustics, has showcased some of the most famous figures of the 20th century. <u>Not only</u> (6) musicians <u>but also</u> (6) dancers, authors, and political activists <u>have appeared</u> (7) at Carnegie Hall. Jazz composer and bandleader Duke Ellington gave <u>annual</u> (8) concerts there. The writer Mark Twain and the women's rights crusader Emmeline Pankhurst stirred audiences <u>with their impassioned speeches</u> (9). <u>Well</u> (10), we can only guess who will be the next star to grace the great stage at Carnegie Hall.

1. A. relative pronoun
   B. reflexive pronoun
   C. intensive pronoun
   D. interrogative pronoun
2. A. common noun
   B. proper noun
   C. proper adjective
   D. abstract noun
3. A. adjective
   B. adverb
   C. noun
   D. relative pronoun
4. A. prepositional phrase
   B. compound preposition
   C. adverb
   D. demonstrative pronoun
5. A. subordinating conjunction
   B. coordinating conjunction
   C. conjunctive adverb
   D. adverb
6. A. coordinating conjunction
   B. subordinating conjunction
   C. correlative conjunction
   D. conjunctive adverb
7. A. action verb
   B. linking verb
   C. adverb
   D. prepositional phrase
8. A. adverb
   B. adjective
   C. concrete noun
   D. abstract noun
9. A. demonstrative pronoun
   B. reflexive pronoun
   C. prepositional phrase
   D. correlative conjunction
10. A. subordinating conjunction
    B. correlative conjunction
    C. interjection
    D. intensive pronoun

Student Help Desk

Parts of Speech at a Glance

Kinds of Nouns

Unforgettable Nouns

All nouns are either common or proper, concrete or abstract, singular or plural.

The band wrote a song about gratitude for Claudia and her classmates.

band	common, concrete, singular, collective
song	common, concrete, singular
gratitude	common, abstract, singular
Claudia	proper, concrete, singular
classmates	common, concrete, plural, compound

Some nouns are collective or compound.

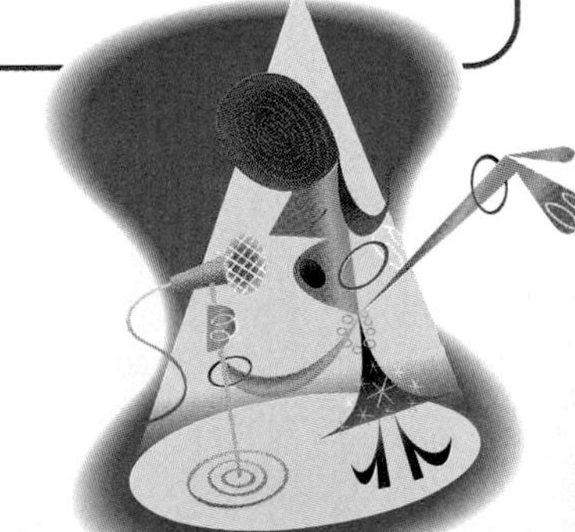

Kinds of Verbs

Playful Verbs

All verbs are either linking verbs or action verbs.

The girls remained calm but then screamed when the band played their music.

remained	linking
screamed	action, intransitive
played	action, transitive

All action verbs are either transitive or intransitive.

Kinds of Adjectives

Shrewd Adjectives

What Kind	**thoughtful** words **sincere** reply
Which One	**that** book **this** song
How Many	**five** albums **several** concerts
How Much	**less** energy **more** sound

The Bottom Line

Checklist for Parts of Speech

Have I . . .

____ chosen precise nouns?

____ used pronouns to avoid repeating nouns?

____ selected specific verbs?

____ added adjectives to identify nouns?

____ used adverbs to describe actions?

____ made good use of conjunctions to link ideas?

____ used prepositions to vary sentence rhythms?

____ used interjections to show character in dialogue?

The Sentence and Its Parts

HELP!
THIS IS AN
STARTED ON A THREE-
HOUR TOUR. THE WEATHER
OUR TINY SHIP, THE MINNOW,
THANKS TO THE
COURAGE OF OUR FEARLESS
CREW
OUR LOCATION IS ROUGHLY
PLEASE BEFORE
IT'S TOO LATE!

Theme: Adventures and Disasters

What's the Message?

The stranded passengers who sent this note were the victims of two disasters: first, a shipwreck, and then—incomplete sentences! Can this note and the passengers still be saved? What information would you add to the message?

Prevent your writing from leading to catastrophe. To communicate your own messages effectively, use **complete sentences**—groups of words that convey complete thoughts.

Write Away: What Else Can Go Wrong?
Disasters aren't always shipwrecks and blizzards. Sometimes a disaster is as simple as a message left on the wrong answering machine or an acne attack before a big date. Write a paragraph about one of your own personal disasters. Save the paragraph in your **Working Portfolio.**

Diagnostic Test: What Do You Know?

Choose the letter of the term that correctly identifies each underlined section.

Have you ever participated in a bicycle race? How fast did you pedal? Hopefully, you weren't clocked at a speed of 190 mph (1). In professional motorcycle road racing, however, riders (2) actually reach this astonishing speed.

Helmets and leather body suits (3) are worn for this sport. Regular motorcycles are purchased and then modified by mechanics. (4) From these modifications emerge lighter and faster bikes. (5) These special bikes are also durable (6). They have to be to endure the 60-mile course! (7)

Racers use a technique (8) called drafting to pass their opponents. As the lead racer pushes against the air, the next rider gets as close as possible. With less wind resistance between the two bikes, the racer on the trailing bike flies right by. The slightest mistake could be a disaster (9). To avoid accidents, riders attend a special school (10).

1. A. simple subject
   B. complete subject
   C. simple predicate
   D. complete predicate

2. A. simple subject
   B. simple predicate
   C. compound subject
   D. compound verb

3. A. simple subject
   B. simple predicate
   C. compound subject
   D. compound verb

4. A. interrogative sentence
   B. imperative sentence
   C. declarative sentence
   D. exclamatory sentence

5. A. inverted sentence
   B. imperative sentence
   C. interrogative sentence
   D. exclamatory sentence

6. A. direct object
   B. indirect object
   C. predicate nominative
   D. predicate adjective

7. A. declarative sentence
   B. imperative sentence
   C. interrogative sentence
   D. exclamatory sentence

8. A. direct object
   B. indirect object
   C. predicate nominative
   D. predicate adjective

9. A. direct object
   B. indirect object
   C. predicate nominative
   D. predicate adjective

10. A. predicate adjective
    B. predicate nominative
    C. direct object
    D. indirect object

Simple Subjects and Predicates

1 Here's the Idea

▶ **Every sentence has two basic parts: a subject and a predicate.**

The **subject** tells whom or what the sentence is about.
The **predicate** tells what the subject is or does or what happens to the subject.

Huge cresting waves	**pound the sailboat.**
SUBJECT	PREDICATE

Hurricane-force winds tear the sails off the mast.
The fragile sailboat is thrown on its side.

Both parts are usually necessary for the meaning of a group of words to be clear. When a subject or a predicate is missing, the group of words is a **sentence fragment.**

For more on fragments, see p. 116–119.

▶ **The basic elements of a sentence are the simple subject and the simple predicate.**

The **simple subject** is the key word or words in the subject.
The **simple predicate** is the verb or verb phrase that tells something about the subject.

Here's How Finding Simple Subjects and Predicates

The violent storm battered the sailboat.

Simple subjects and simple predicates do not include any modifying words, phrases, or clauses.

Simple subject Ask who or what is or does something.	**Simple predicate** Ask what the subject is or does or what happens to it.
What battered the sailboat? **storm**	What did the storm do? **battered**

The violent storm battered the sailboat.

CHAPTER 2

❷ Why It Matters in Writing

If you can't find a simple subject and a simple predicate (verb or verb phrase) in your "sentence," you've created a fragment. The fragment is missing important information. Check your writing to make sure that each sentence expresses a complete thought.

STUDENT MODEL

Teen Rescues Sailboat Crew!

Terri Alvarez showed uncommon courage in the face of nature's fury. The Capland sophomore ^had only a small motorboat to rescue a stranded sailboat crew. ^He ~~B~~battled 20-foot waves and gale-force winds. . . .

The missing verb makes this a sentence fragment.

Who battled? The missing subject would confuse the reader.

SENTENCE PARTS

❸ Practice and Apply

A. CONCEPT CHECK: Simple Subjects and Predicates

Write the simple subject and the simple predicate of each sentence.

Example: The bright Florida sky turned black.
Answer: sky; turned.

Deadly Hurricane Slams into Florida!

1. Hurricane Andrew struck southern Florida in August 1992.
2. This ferocious storm destroyed several communities.
3. The high winds also tore a county zoo apart.
4. Many animals, afraid of the wind, cowered in their cages.
5. Over 150,000 people lost their homes or businesses.
6. Many residents had no water, electricity, or shelter.
7. Relief workers distributed food, clothing, and medicine.
8. Midwesterners sent bottled water to the area.
9. Many Florida residents will remember this storm for the rest of their lives!
10. It was the most costly natural disaster in U.S. history.

➜ **For a SELF-CHECK and more practice, see the EXERCISE BANK, p. 588.**

B. EDITING: Spotting Incomplete Sentences

On a separate sheet of paper, identify each item as a complete sentence (CS) or a fragment (F). For each fragment, tell whether it is missing a subject or a predicate.

Example: The captain and his crew one last trip.
Answer: F; missing a predicate

Courage and Survival at Sea

1. In January 1988, a hurricane struck the Costa Rican coast.
2. Blew a boat with five fishermen out into the Pacific Ocean.
3. Over the next five months, survived by working together.
4. Sharks around the boat all the time.
5. The men watched several ships come close and then sail away.
6. Collected rainwater in canvas bags and old metal containers.
7. Without navigation equipment sailed 4,500 miles.
8. Finally, a Japanese ship rescued the weary crew.
9. Costa Rica a parade and celebration for the men's homecoming.
10. The men had survived an incredible 142 days at sea!

CHALLENGE For each fragment above, add a subject or predicate to make a complete sentence.

Look at your **Write Away** paragraph or another draft from your **Working Portfolio.** Fix any incomplete sentences.

CHAPTER 2

C. WRITING: Creating Disaster Headlines

Simple subjects and simple predicates are used in many headlines ("Warehouse Burns!"). Identify the simple subjects and predicates in Calvin's headlines. Then, with a partner, create three disaster headlines about events in your own lives.

Example: I really messed up my speech.
Answer: *SPEECH BOMBS!*

Calvin and Hobbes by Bill Watterson

Complete Subjects and Predicates

1 Here's the Idea

▶ **The complete subject includes the simple subject and all the words that modify, or tell more about, it.**

▶ **The complete predicate includes the verb and all the words that modify, or tell more about, it.**

Here's How Finding Complete Subjects and Predicates

Disaster movies fascinate nearly everyone.

Complete subject Ask who or what is or does something. What fascinates? **Disaster movies**	**Complete Predicate** Ask what the subject is or does or what happens to it. What do disaster movies do? **fascinate nearly everyone.**

Disaster movies fascinate nearly everyone.

Notice that every word in a sentence is part of either the complete subject or the complete predicate.

SENTENCE PARTS

2 Why It Matters in Writing

Adding details to simple subjects and predicates can help you convey your ideas more clearly to the reader.

STUDENT MODEL

DRAFT

Many of the *Titanic*'s lifeboats were only half full. The crew was worried about the weight. It might break the winch ropes, spilling passengers into the sea.

Were the boats in the water at this point? What about the weight? What is the connection between the first two sentences?

REVISION

Many of the *Titanic*'s lifeboats were **lowered into the water** only half full. The crew was worried about the weight **of full lifeboats**. **The extra weight** could break the winch ropes, spilling passengers into the sea.

Added details clarify meaning and logic.

❸ Practice and Apply

A. CONCEPT CHECK: Complete Subjects and Predicates

On a separate sheet of paper, write the complete subjects of sentences 1–5. Write the complete predicates of sentences 6–10.

Making the Movie *Titanic*

1. James Cameron had been fascinated by the *Titanic* for years.
2. The filmmaker interviewed several survivors of the tragedy.
3. The special-effects crew created tiny models of the ship.
4. The art director copied the *Titanic*'s original furnishings.
5. The real challenge was the re-creation of the death of the ship.
6. The *Titanic*'s final moments were simulated with a computer.
7. Computer-generated "people" fell against computer-generated "propellers" into a computer-generated "sea."
8. Experts on the disaster were fooled by these scenes.
9. Critics asked Cameron about the Blue Heart necklace.
10. Cameron invented the necklace as part of the love story.

For a SELF-CHECK and more practice, see the EXERCISE BANK, p. 588.

On your paper, circle the simple subjects of sentences 1–5 and the simple predicates of sentences 6–10.

CHAPTER 2

B. WRITING: Adding Details

Combine the simple subjects and simple predicates below to form sentences. Add details to each sentence to describe the plot of a disaster movie.

Exchange papers with a partner. Circle the complete subjects and underline the complete predicates on your partner's paper.

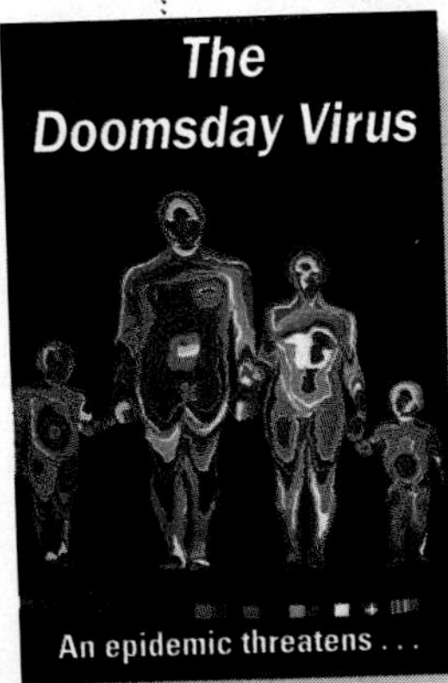

New Disaster Movie

Simple subjects	**Simple predicates**
Virus	appears
People	are contaminated
Epidemic	threatens
Scientist/hero	discovers
Girlfriend/boyfriend	doubts
Truth	is uncovered
Scientist/hero	triumphs
Virus	is killed
People	recover
Enemies	are defeated

Compound Subjects and Verbs

1 Here's the Idea

A sentence can have more than one subject or verb. A sentence part with more than one of these elements is a compound part.

A **compound subject** is made up of two or more subjects that share a verb. The subjects are joined by a conjunction, or connecting word, such as *and, or*, or *but*.

Notice that the subjects can be simple or complete.

CONJUNCTION

Divers and climbers share a love of adventure.

COMPOUND SUBJECT VERB

Extreme danger and exciting challenges are important.

COMPOUND SUBJECT

A **compound verb** is made up of two or more verbs or verb phrases that are joined by a conjunction and have the same subject.

The exhausted diver ached and moaned.

COMPOUND VERB

A **compound predicate** is made up of a compound verb and all the words that go with each verb.

Both groups must be in top physical condition and must be ready for any emergency. ← COMPOUND PREDICATE

SENTENCE PARTS

2 Why It Matters in Writing

Using compound parts can help make your writing more concise and help show relationships between ideas.

STUDENT MODEL

Climbing Mount Fuji was turning into a struggle. ~~I was~~ *Shawn and I were* having trouble breathing the thinner air. ~~So was Shawn.~~ One of the women gave us a canister of oxygen*and* ~~She~~ went on ahead.

Compound subject condenses two sentences into one.

Compound predicate shows the relationship between two ideas.

❸ Practice and Apply

A. CONCEPT CHECK: Compound Subjects and Verbs

Write the compound subject or predicate in each sentence below. Underline the subjects once and the verbs twice.

Example: The brain and heart function differently at high altitudes.

Answer: brain and heart

Your Brain Underwater and at High Altitudes

1. Children and adults can survive frigid water for a long time.
2. Cold water signals the brain and triggers a "diving reflex."
3. The brain slows and needs only half the normal level of oxygen.
4. Electrical activity and chemical actions in the brain keep the body alive.
5. The heart and brain can survive 40 or 50 minutes in this state.
6. Climbers face a different challenge and must adapt to high altitudes.
7. The brain and heart receive up to 30 percent less oxygen.
8. Sometimes fluid accumulates and causes the brain to swell.
9. Climbers can't think or make good decisions.
10. They must get to lower altitudes right away or risk death.

For a SELF-CHECK and more practice, see the EXERCISE BANK, p. 589.

B. REVISING: Improving a Paragraph

Revise the paragraph below, using compound subjects and verbs to combine sentences with similar ideas.

STUDENT MODEL

Hold Your Breath!

Swimmers know ways to stay underwater longer. Divers also know these tricks. You can learn these techniques too. You start out by taking several quick, deep breaths. Your lungs fill with oxygen. Your lungs transport the gas to your bloodstream. Your body tissues absorb oxygen from your blood. They use it to produce the energy they need. Your muscles need a lot of oxygen. You should relax. You should move only as much as necessary. With these techniques you can train yourself to stay underwater for up to four minutes.

Choose a draft from your **Working Portfolio.** How can it be improved by combining sentences?

Kinds of Sentences

1 Here's the Idea

▶ **A sentence can be used to make a statement, ask a question, give a command, or show strong feelings.**

Four Kinds of Sentences

Declarative We've never swum out this far before.
This kind of sentence expresses a fact, wish, intent, or feeling. It always ends with a period.

Interrogative Is that a shark following us?
This kind of sentence asks a question and always ends with a question mark.

Imperative Hide until it leaves. Now swim for shore!
This kind of sentence expresses a command, request, or direction. It usually ends with a period. If the command or request is strong, it may end with an exclamation point.

Exclamatory We almost didn't make it!
This kind of sentence expresses strong feeling. It always ends with an exclamation point.

2 Why It Matters in Writing

Using the four different kinds of sentences can help you

- add variety and interest to your writing
- create realistic dialogue

Notice how natural the use of the four kinds of sentences sounds in this dialogue from the play *The Miracle Worker.*

LITERARY MODEL

Keller. Katie? What's wrong? — INTERROGATIVE

Kate. Look. — IMPERATIVE

(*She makes a pass with her hand in the crib, at the baby's eyes.*)

Keller. What, Katie? She's well; she needs only time to—

Kate. She can't see. Look at her eyes. — DECLARATIVE

(*She takes the lamp from him, moves it before the child's face.*)

She can't *see!* — EXCLAMATORY

—William Gibson, *The Miracle Worker*

❸ Practice and Apply

A. CONCEPT CHECK: Kinds of Sentences

Identify each of the following sentences as declarative, imperative, interrogative, or exclamatory.

Change sentences 6–10 according to the instructions in parentheses.

The Truth About Sharks

1. Did you know that most shark attacks are cases of mistaken identity?
2. Sharks think humans are seals or other prey.
3. Don't dangle your arms and legs over the side of a boat.
4. You can often prevent a shark attack by being aggressive.
5. One diver drove a shark off by punching it in the nose!
6. People once believed that sharks were frenzied killers. (Change to a question.)
7. Are they really just incredibly skilled predators? (Change to an exclamatory sentence.)
8. Keep out of shark waters if you have an open wound. (Change to a declarative sentence.)
9. These hunters can smell even small traces of blood up to a mile away! (Change to a question.)
10. Will they eat exotic items like license plates and inner tubes? (Change to an exclamatory sentence.)

➜ **For a SELF-CHECK and more practice, see the EXERCISE BANK, p. 589.**

B. WRITING: Dialogue

Read the caption of *The Far Side* cartoon and identify the imperative sentences in it. Then write your own dialogue for the cartoon, using the four types of sentences.

THE FAR SIDE by Gary Larson

"Hold still, Omar. . . . Now look up. Yep. You've got something in your eye, all right—could be sand."

Subjects in Unusual Positions

1 Here's the Idea

In most sentences subjects come before verbs. However, on some occasions subjects appear in unusual positions—after verbs or inside verb phrases.

Inverted Sentences

In an inverted sentence the subject comes after the verb or part of the verb phrase. An inverted sentence can be used for emphasis or variety.

Usual Order

The savage storm | came down on the Spanish galleon.

Inverted Order

Down came | the savage storm | on the Spanish galleon.

Usual Order

The sea swept across the deck of the hopeless ship.

Inverted Order

Across the deck of the hopeless ship swept the sea.

Sentences Beginning with *Here* or *There*

Though *here* or *there* may begin a sentence, these words are rarely subjects. In fact, the subject of a sentence that begins with one of these words usually follows the verb.

***Here* is the massive anchor of the galleon.**
***There* lies the great ship, far beneath the ocean.**

Agreement can be tricky in sentences where the subject follows the verb. Identify the subject before choosing the verb form. Singular subjects take singular verbs, and plural subjects take plural verbs.

AGREES WITH

Here is the massive anchor of the galleon.

AGREES WITH

Here are the massive anchors of the galleon.

For more on subject-verb agreement, see pp. 158–169.

SENTENCE PARTS

Questions

▶ **In a question the subject usually comes after the verb or inside the verb phrase.**

Subject After Verb

Was the cargo of the galleon valuable?

Subject Inside Verb Phrase

Did the great ship survive the storm?

Here's How **Finding the Subject**

Was the cargo of the galleon valuable?

1. First change the question into a statement.
   The cargo of the galleon was valuable.
2. Then find the verb and ask *who* or *what.*
   verb: **was** What was? **cargo** = subject

CHAPTER 2

In some questions, words such as *who* or *what* are the subjects and come before the verbs.

Who was aboard the galleon? What happened to the people?

Imperative Sentences

▶ **In an imperative sentence the subject is usually *you.*** In most cases, *you* is not stated; it is understood.

Request: (You) Please read the ancient tale of the galleon.
Command: (You) Beware the wild sea.

2 Why It Matters in Writing

Inverting word order allows you to add variety and to change the emphases in your sentences. In this model, it allows the writer to set the scene before presenting a character.

LITERARY MODEL

In front of the house in a squeaky rocking chair sat Miss Lottie's son, John Burke. . . .

—Eugenia Collier, "Marigolds"

3 Practice and Apply

A. CONCEPT CHECK: Subjects in Unusual Positions

On a separate sheet of paper, write the simple subject and the verb of each sentence below. Be sure to include all parts of each verb phrase.

Example: Have you heard of the destruction of the *Atocha*?
Answer: you; have heard

The Tragedy of the *Atocha*—September 6, 1622

1. There were 28 Spanish ships, including the *Atocha,* on the voyage to Spain.
2. Out of nowhere sprang a fierce storm.
3. From every ship in the fleet came pitiful cries for help.
4. Would the sailors survive this powerful storm?
5. Never doubt the men's skill and bravery.
6. Into the Gulf of Mexico sailed the Spanish vessels.
7. Yet upon a reef crashed the treasure galleon.
8. Who witnessed its destruction and the loss of 260 lives?
9. Here is an important lesson about the power of nature.
10. Remember the misfortune of the great ship and its crew.

➜ **For a SELF-CHECK and more practice, see the EXERCISE BANK, p. 590.**

SENTENCE PARTS

Rewrite sentences 2, 3, 6 and 7 by putting the subjects before the verbs. How do the revisions change the sentences' effects?

B. WRITING: Revising Word Order

Follow the directions in parentheses to change the word order in each sentence.

The Recovery of the *Atocha*'s Treasure—July 20, 1985

1. The skeleton of the *Atocha* sat on the ocean floor. (Invert sentence order.)
2. The galleon and its precious cargo would be discovered. (Make into a question.)
3. The spectacular treasure was found off Florida's Marquesas Keys. (Invert sentence order.)
4. The treasure lay beneath masses of heavy sand. (Begin sentence with *There.*)
5. People should not forget the remarkable recovery of the *Atocha*'s cargo. (Make into a command.)

Subject Complements

❶ Here's the Idea

▶ **Complements are words that complete the meaning or action of verbs.** There are two general kinds of complements: subject complements and objects of verbs.

A **subject complement** is a word that follows a linking verb and identifies or describes the subject. Subject complements may be predicate adjectives or predicate nominatives.

Remember linking verbs? If not, see pp. 14–16.

Predicate Adjectives

A **predicate adjective** describes or modifies the subject.

MODIFIES

The climb had been difficult.

MODIFIES

The explorers felt extremely miserable.

Predicate Nominatives

A **predicate nominative** is a noun or pronoun. It identifies, renames, or defines the subject.

SAME AS

Mount Everest was their destination.

SAME AS

The trip became their worst nightmare.

CHAPTER 2

❷ Why It Matters in Writing

Well-chosen predicate adjectives and predicate nominatives can help you create vivid descriptions and clear definitions. Notice the subject complements in this model.

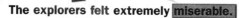

PROFESSIONAL MODEL

From the valleys of Nepal and Tibet, Mount Everest appears a stormy **giant.** Its soaring ridges look so **powerful** that observers feel **humble.** The mountain is at once **beautiful** and **dreadful.**

—Laura Chaveriat

3 Practice and Apply

A. CONCEPT CHECK: Subject Complements

On a sheet of paper, write the subject complement in each sentence, and identify it as a predicate adjective (PA) or a predicate nominative (PN).

Example: The Himalayas are incredibly magnificent.
Answer: magnificent, PA

The Perils of Mount Everest

1. Everest is the highest mountain in the world.
2. Its slopes look risky, even to world-class climbers.
3. Oxygen grows thin beyond the mountain's base.
4. Climbers often become immobile without extra oxygen.
5. Frequently, frostbite becomes a real problem.
6. In such cases the skin appears swollen.
7. Glaciers are great sources of danger.
8. Their surfaces stay slippery because of the constant cold.
9. On the icy ridges, winds become daggers.
10. Mount Everest remains a true test for most climbers.

For a SELF-CHECK and more practice, see the EXERCISE BANK, p. 590.

SENTENCE PARTS

B. REVISING: Replacing Subject Complements

Rewrite each sentence, replacing the subject complement with a more precise word.

Example: The icy trails look bad.
Answer: The icy trails look **dangerous.**

Extreme Experiences

1. With a peak 29,028 feet above sea level, Mount Everest is tall.
2. The climbers feel good during the day.
3. At nightfall, however, they are cold.
4. Snowdrifts become funny shapes.
5. The trails are hard to climb.
6. Winds sound strange to the climbers.
7. Tents feel thin in the weather.
8. Climbers appear different after their experiences.
9. Climbers are happy upon their return.
10. Mount Everest is a strange place.

Objects of Verbs

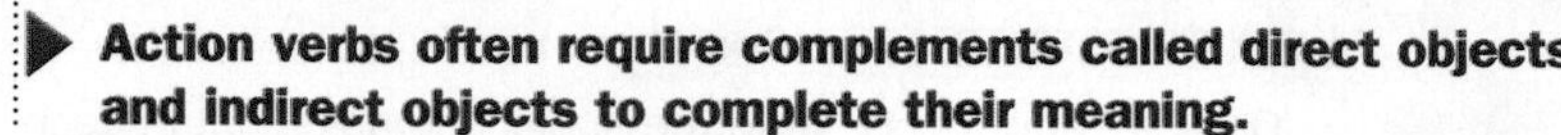

1 Here's the Idea

▶ **Action verbs often require complements called direct objects and indirect objects to complete their meaning.**

Direct Objects

A **direct object** is a word or a group of words that receives the action of an action verb. It answers the question *what* or *whom.*

The climber caught. (Caught *what?* or *whom?*)

The climber caught the nylon rope.

Indirect Objects

An **indirect object** tells to what, to whom, for what, or for whom an action is done. Verbs that often take indirect objects include *bring, give, hand, lend, make, send, show, teach, tell,* and *write.*

The rescue team gives hot food. (Gives food *to* or *for whom?*)

The rescue team gives (*to*) the survivors hot food.

The indirect object is usually between the verb and the direct object.

Here's How **Finding Direct and Indirect Objects**

The survivors told me their dramatic story.

1. Find the action verb in the sentence. ***told***
2. To find the direct object, ask *told what.* told the ***story***
3. To find the indirect object, ask *told the story to* or *for whom.* told (to) ***me*** the story

If the word *to* or *for* appears in the sentence, the word that follows is **not** an indirect object. *Me* is not an indirect object in this sentence: *The survivors told their story to me.*

❷ Why It Matters in Writing

Especially when you are writing dialogue, you need to use objects to convey information and to add important details. Notice the objects in this model.

LITERARY MODEL

"Let's go! Give me the full bottle of oxygen and let's go." But he said, "No, I'm not giving you this bottle."

—Anatoli Boukreev and G. Weston DeWalt, *The Climb*

INDIRECT OBJECT

DIRECT OBJECT

❸ Practice and Apply

A. CONCEPT CHECK: Objects of Verbs

Each sentence below contains at least one complement. Write each complement and identify it as a direct object (DO) or an indirect object (IO).

Mount Everest Expeditions

1. British surveyors calculated the height of Peak XV.
2. In 1865 geographers gave Mount Everest its current name.
3. Irvine lent Mallory a hand in their 1924 expedition.
4. Unfortunately, a sudden ice storm overcame the explorers.
5. In 1953, Hillary and Tenzing showed the world their talents.
6. They conquered the summit of Mount Everest.
7. In 1963, Hornbein and Unsoeld scaled the West Ridge.
8. Their feat earned them praise from professional climbers.
9. On a 1996 expedition fierce blizzards killed 8 climbers.
10. Mount Everest still offers climbers a true challenge.

➜ **For a SELF-CHECK and more practice, see the EXERCISE BANK, p. 590.**

B. WRITING: Filling in Objects

Write each sentence skeleton five times. Add objects as indicated to create different sentences. Add modifiers as needed.

1. One explorer gave (indirect object) a (direct object).
2. Rescuers brought (indirect object) some (direct object).

SENTENCE PARTS

Sentence Diagramming

Watch me for diagramming tips!

Here's the Idea

Diagramming is a way of visually representing the structure of a sentence. It can help you understand how the sentence works by showing how each word functions. Once you understand how diagrams work, you may find yourself diagramming for the fun of it!

Simple Subjects and Verbs

The simple subject and the verb are written on one line and are separated by a vertical line that crosses the main line.

Windows exploded.

Windows | exploded

CHAPTER 2

Compound Subjects and Verbs

For a compound subject or verb, split the main line.

Compound Subject

Windows and clocks exploded.

Windows

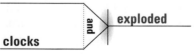

and

exploded

clocks

Because there are two subjects, the left side of the main line is split into two parts.

Compound Verb

Windows shattered and exploded.

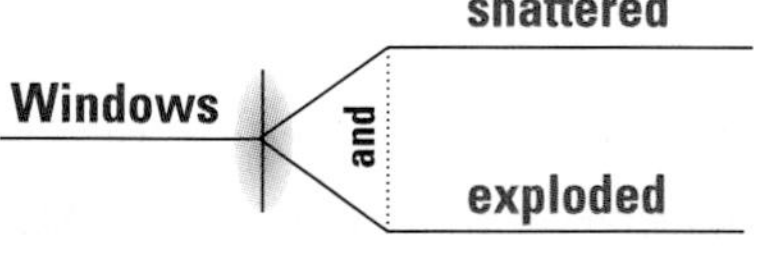

Because there are two verbs, the right side of the main line is split into two parts.

Compound Subject and Verb

Windows and clocks shattered and exploded.

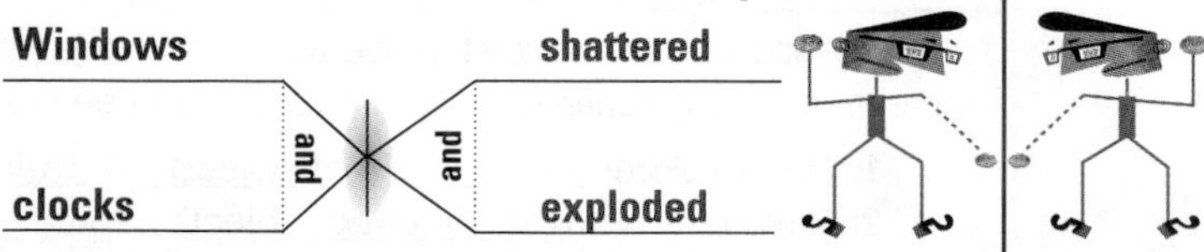

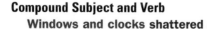

A. CONCEPT CHECK: Subjects and Verbs

Diagram these sentences, using what you have learned.

1. Trees toppled.
2. Trees toppled and fell.
3. Houses and trees swayed and crashed.

Adjectives and Adverbs

Because adjectives and adverbs **modify,** or tell more about, other words in a sentence, they are written on slanted lines below the words they modify.

The atmospheric pressure was falling very rapidly.

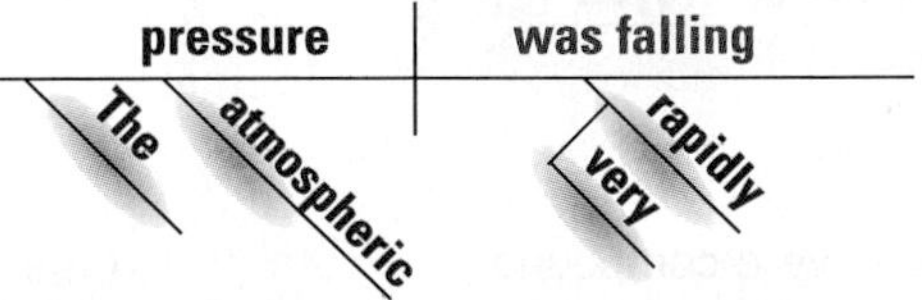

B. CONCEPT CHECK: Adjectives and Adverbs

Diagram these sentences, using what you have learned.

1. The wicked wind whistled wildly.
2. A tornado and a violent rainstorm finally arrived.
3. Roof shingles and tree branches scattered everywhere.

Subject Complements: Predicate Nominatives and Predicate Adjectives

Write a predicate nominative or a predicate adjective on the main line after the verb. Separate the subject complement from the verb with a slanted line that does not cross the main line.

The wind was our enemy. **All residents felt anxious.**

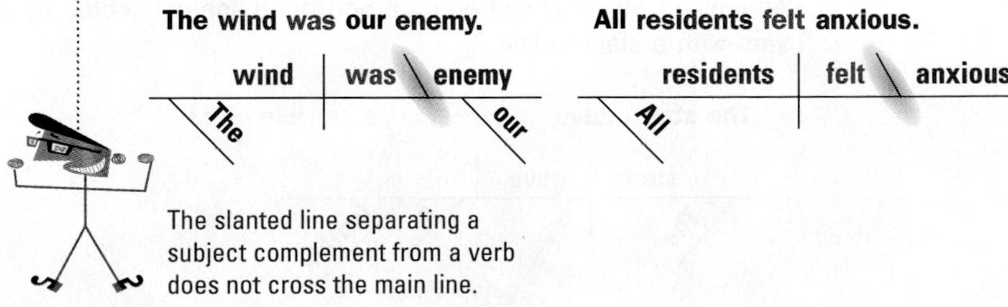

The slanted line separating a subject complement from a verb does not cross the main line.

Direct Objects

A direct object follows the verb on the same line.

The tornado destroyed homes.

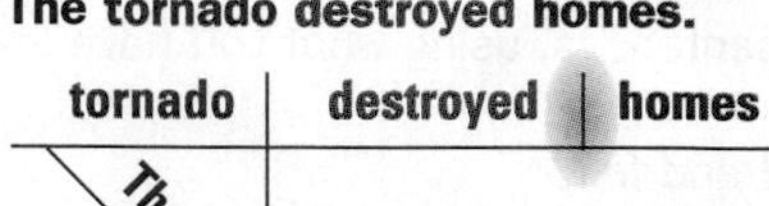

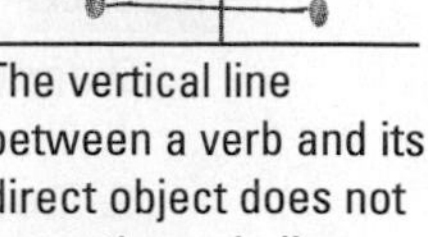

The vertical line between a verb and its direct object does not cross the main line.

Sometimes a sentence has a compound direct object. To diagram this kind of sentence, split the main line and write the parts of the direct object on parallel lines.

The tornado destroyed homes and businesses.

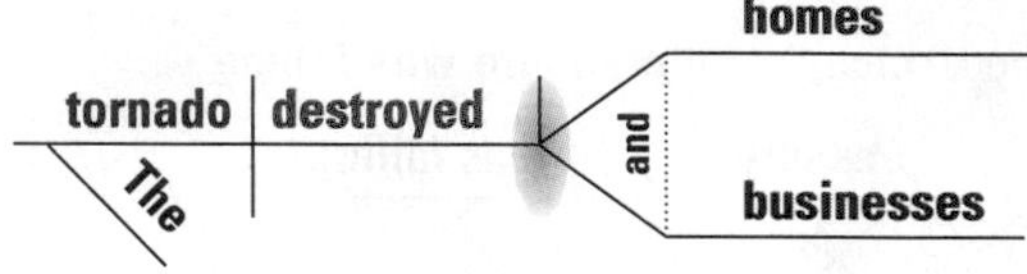

When you have a compound predicate (two verbs, each with its own object), split the line and show the compound parts on parallel lines.

The tornado destroyed homes and changed the landscape.

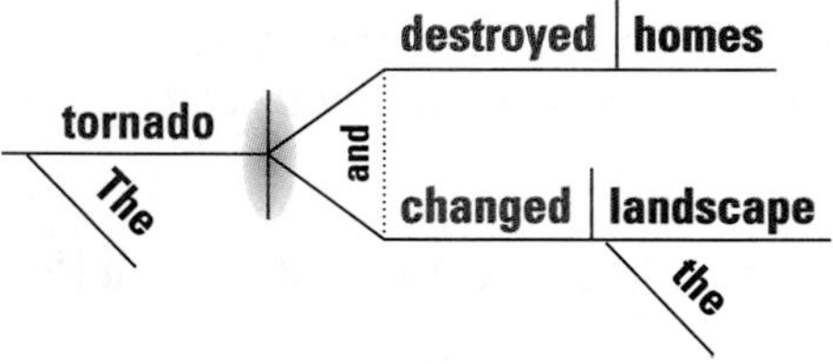

Indirect Objects

An indirect object is written on a horizontal line connected to the verb with a slanted line.

The storm gave townspeople a terrible night.

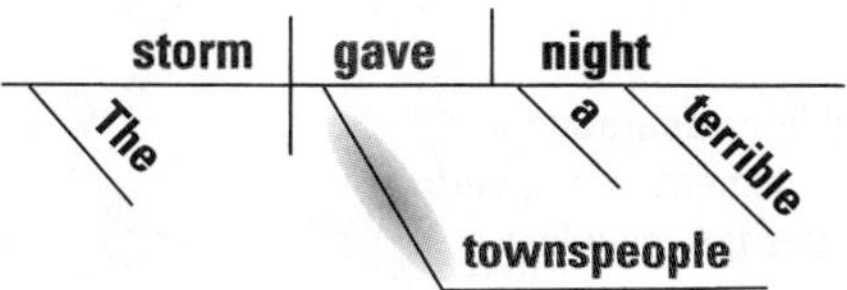

CHAPTER 2

C. CONCEPT CHECK: Subject Complements and Objects of Verbs

Diagram these sentences, using what you have learned.

1. Hurricanes sometimes hit the Gulf Coast and the Atlantic Coast.
2. Most natural disasters are not predictable.
3. Hurricanes give people warning.
4. Floods are often the worst effects.
5. Floods cause homeowners enormous problems.

D. MIXED REVIEW: Diagramming

Diagram the following sentences. Look for all types of complements.

1. Some diseases become international disasters.
2. The 1918 influenza epidemic killed millions.
3. Soldiers and civilians died everywhere.
4. World War I spread the disease.
5. The flu strain was extremely contagious.
6. Soldiers unknowingly gave their buddies the flu virus.
7. Civilians also gave their families the influenza germ.
8. Old people and children caught the disease and died.
9. This global epidemic was universally destructive.
10. Modern scientists still fight such quiet killer diseases.

Mad Mapper

Don't race madly around in circles when a sentence confuses you. Remembering these two simple diagramming patterns can help you get the drift.

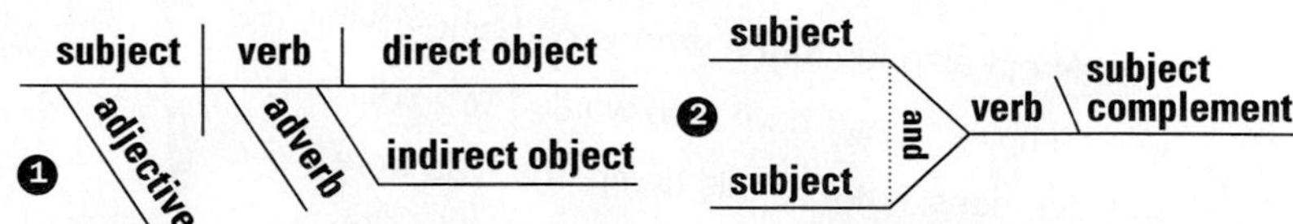

Mother Goose & Grimm by Mike Peters

SENTENCE PARTS

Real World Grammar

Summer-Job Application

Grammar is not just for school. Suppose you find the ultimate summer job. All you have to do is fill out the application and send it in—you and about 500 other applicants!

Other than by your qualifications, how can you stand out? One way is by using your grammar skills to help you present yourself in the best light. Here's one student's first try. She asked her English teacher to comment on her draft.

Adventure Bound!
Day Camp Leaders
Ages 15-18
$300 per month
APPLY NOW!

APPLICATION

Name Avril Brenner **Age** 15

Address 11 South Circle Dr., Marshall, CO

Phone 303-555-4893

Parent or Guardian Patrice and David Brenner

In a paragraph, describe your qualifications.

I believe I am uniquely qualified to be an Adventure Bound! day camp leader. I have taught nature crafts to YMCA kids for three years. During that time, I also led YMCA groups on backpacking and camping trips. I have also worked two summers at Wilderness Trek. At this camp, the kids were taught outdoor skills by the counselors to build self-confidence. We were taught to act as a big sister or brother, and cheerleader, to the kids. I know firsthand what a difference a good leader can make. I believe I can make a real contribution to the lives of children at Adventure Bound!

Combine these skills into one strong sentence.

Say more. What is Wilderness Trek? What was your position?

Show your leadership. Change to action verbs.

Again, say more. Difference to whom?

A good leader communicates well. Let your writing show this quality!

CHAPTER 2

Using Grammar in Writing

Compound parts	Use **compound parts** to combine sentences and present information more concisely. Combining related ideas into one sentence increases their impact on the reader.
Complete subjects and predicates	Use **complete subjects and predicates** to give more information and help your reader understand your meaning. The reader should be able to see clearly why you mention something.
Action verbs	Use **action verbs with their objects** to help you eliminate the passive voice that takes you out of the picture. In an application, you want to state clearly who you are, what you did, and for whom you did it.

REVISED APPLICATION

I believe I am uniquely qualified to be an Adventure Bound! day camp leader. For three years I have taught YMCA kids nature crafts and led them on backpacking and camping trips. For the past two summers I have worked as a camp counselor at Wilderness Trek, an adventure camp for disabled children. As a counselor, I taught the kids outdoor skills to build their self-confidence. I learned how to be a big sister and cheerleader all in one. I know firsthand what a difference a good leader can make in a child's life. I believe I can make a real contribution to the lives of children at Adventure Bound!

Much better! Send it off—Good luck!

SENTENCE PARTS

PRACTICE AND APPLY: Revising

A friend of yours is running for class president and has written the paragraph below for the school newspaper. Your friend asks you to look it over. Use the three writing tips above to revise the paragraph.

Rough Draft

I believe I have the experience to do the best job of serving as class president. Last year, I was treasurer of the student council. I was also captain of the debate team. Student government needs reform. For example, students can't vote on any student council resolutions. Students can't choose their own class projects. A plan for reform was developed by me and my campaign group. Elect someone who will take action!

Mixed Review

A. Subjects, Predicates, and Kinds of Sentences Read the story. Then write the answers to the questions below it.

(1) Luisa took her usual homework break and ambled to her favorite room in the house. **(2)** The overhead light in the kitchen revealed at least 100 mosquitoes on the ceiling. **(3)** Luisa quickly grabbed a weapon and faced the enemy.

(4) "Retreat or die, bugs!"

(5) For nearly three hours, Luisa and her trusty fly swatter slapped mosquitoes and shooed them out an open window. **(6)** The pesky insects feasted on her at every opportunity. **(7)** On and on raged the terrible battle. **(8)** Was there no end to this mosquito invasion? **(9)** Finally, by midnight, there were no more mosquitoes. **(10)** An exhausted Luisa forgot about her essay and wearily crawled into bed.

1. What is the compound verb in sentence 1?
2. What is the simple predicate in sentence 2?
3. What are the simple subject and the verb in sentence 3?
4. What kind of sentence is sentence 4?
5. What are the compound parts in sentence 5?
6. What is the complete subject in sentence 6?
7. What is the complete subject in sentence 7?
8. What kind of sentence is sentence 8?
9. What is the simple subject in sentence 9?
10. What kind of sentence is sentence 10?

CHAPTER 2

B. Subject Complements and Objects of Verbs Identify each underlined word in the following passage as a direct object, an indirect object, a predicate nominative, or a predicate adjective.

PROFESSIONAL MODEL

A solution to a problem isn't always a complete **(1)** success. At one high school in California, many students left the **(2)** campus during school hours. To discourage the practice, administrators installed a **(3)** gate in the student parking lot.

On the first day of school, some officials were understandably **(4)** anxious. They stood by to make sure the system worked smoothly. After several cars passed through the gate, a girl jumped out and handed the **(5)** principal her keys. "Great!" she said. "We finally have valet parking."

—Adapted from "Tales Out of School" by Julia Park, *Reader's Digest,* May 1998

Mastery Test: What Did You Learn?

Choose the letter of the term that correctly identifies each underlined section.

"Rogue waves" are a terrifying hazard (1) at sea. They spring up out of nowhere and destroy everything in their path. (2) These massive waves (3) can tower over 100 feet high. People often don't know that a wave is coming (4). If they are lucky, another ship may radio them (5) a warning.

A rogue wave can flip (6) a boat (7) end over end. Small ships and huge tankers (8) are equally helpless in the face of these monsters. Don't think these waves can be outrun (9). Some travel hundreds of miles an hour. If you're ever hit by a rogue wave, you're in for a terrifying ride! (10)

1. A. predicate nominative
   B. predicate adjective
   C. direct object
   D. indirect object
2. A. declarative sentence
   B. interrogative sentence
   C. imperative sentence
   D. exclamatory sentence
3. A. direct object
   B. simple subject
   C. predicate nominative
   D. simple predicate
4. A. complete subject
   B. predicate nominative
   C. direct object
   D. complete predicate
5. A. direct object
   B. indirect object
   C. predicate nominative
   D. predicate adjective
6. A. simple subject
   B. predicate nominative
   C. simple predicate
   D. complete predicate
7. A. indirect object
   B. simple predicate
   C. direct object
   D. simple subject
8. A. compound object
   B. compound subject
   C. simple predicate
   D. compound complement
9. A. interrogative sentence
   B. inverted sentence
   C. exclamatory sentence
   D. imperative sentence
10. A. exclamatory sentence
    B. declarative sentence
    C. interrogative sentence
    D. imperative sentence

Student Help Desk

The Sentence at a Glance

A sentence has two parts, a subject and a predicate. You should remember that a sentence . . .

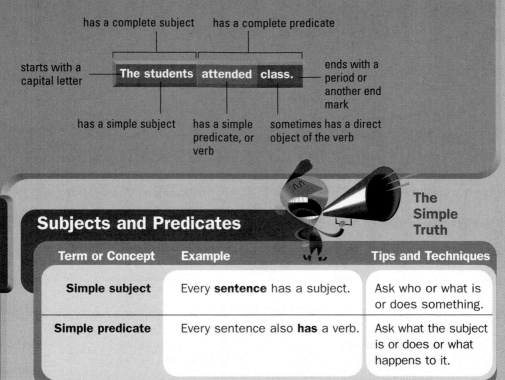

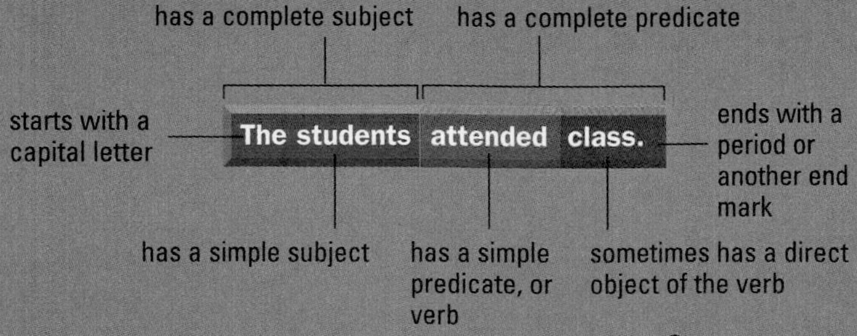

CHAPTER 2

Subjects and Predicates

The Simple Truth

Term or Concept	Example	Tips and Techniques
Simple subject	Every **sentence** has a subject.	Ask who or what is or does something.
Simple predicate	Every sentence also **has** a verb.	Ask what the subject is or does or what happens to it.

Complements

Objection Overruled

Term or Concept	Example	Tips and Techniques
Predicate nominative	This is **grammar.**	Renames the subject
Predicate adjective	It isn't **boring.**	Describes the subject
Direct object	You can use **it.**	Receives the verb's action. Ask, Uses what?
Indirect object	Give **me** a break.	Tells to or for whom the action is done. Ask, Gives what?

Kinds of Sentences

LIFE SENTENCE

Term or Concept	Example	Tips and Techniques
Declarative sentence	This is a declarative sentence**.**	Ends with a period
Interrogative sentence	Is this an interrogative sentence**?**	Ends with a question mark
Imperative sentence	**[You]** Write an imperative sentence now**.**	Ends with a period or exclamation point. Subject (usually *you*) is generally unstated.
Exclamatory sentence	I won't**!**	Ends with an exclamation point
Subjects in inverted sentences	There **goes** my **grade**.	Locate the predicate and ask who or what does that? *Here* and *there* are usually not subjects.

SENTENCE PARTS

The Bottom Line

Checklist for Editing Sentences

Can I improve my writing by . . .

____ correcting any sentence fragments?

____ using compound subjects or predicates to combine sentences with similar ideas?

____ changing a statement into a question or exclamation?

____ changing the position of a subject to emphasize an important point?

____ replacing a complement with a more specific or exciting word?

____ using action verbs and objects to eliminate the passive voice?

Using Phrases

Brothers Reunited After 21 Years in Bowling Alley

Coaches' Criticism of Referees Getting Ugly

Missing Last-Second Shot, Championship Trophy Is Lost

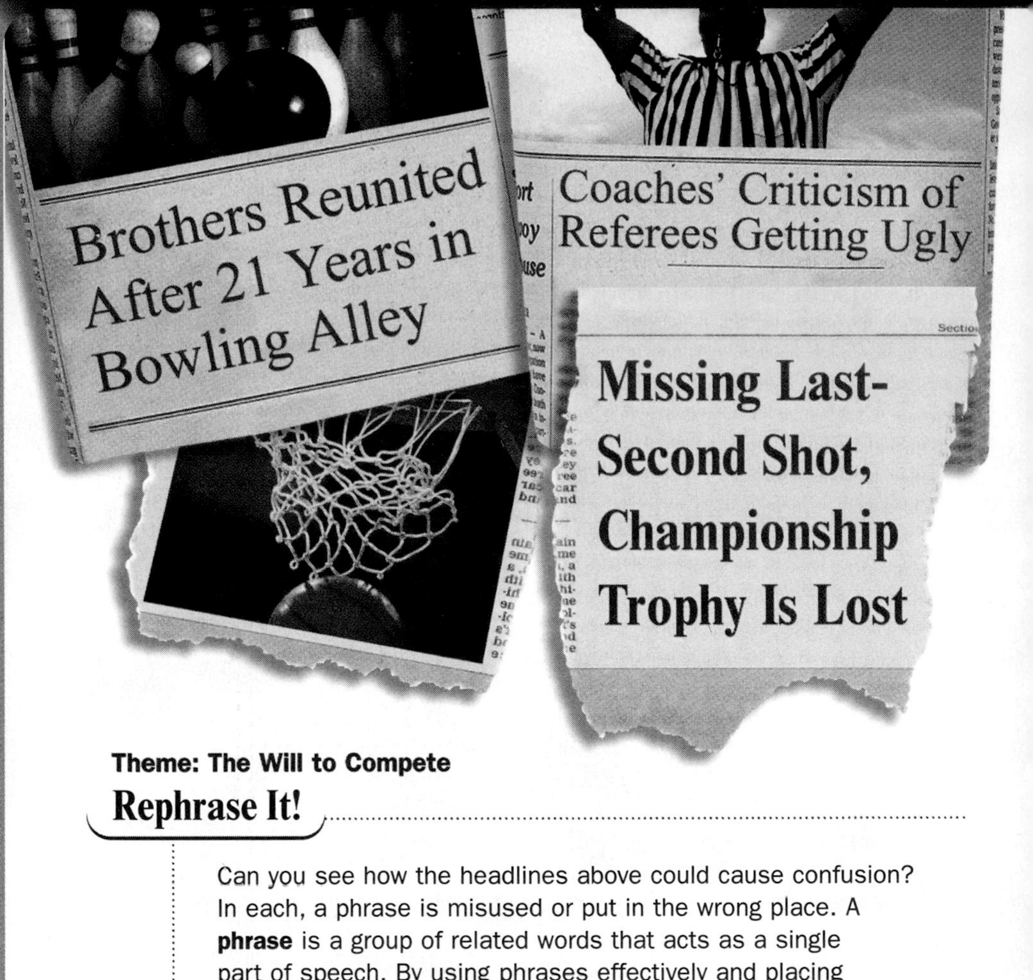

Theme: The Will to Compete

Rephrase It!

Can you see how the headlines above could cause confusion? In each, a phrase is misused or put in the wrong place. A **phrase** is a group of related words that acts as a single part of speech. By using phrases effectively and placing them properly, you can make your writing clearer and more descriptive.

Write Away: Headlining Your Life

Write headlines about three different competitions you have participated in—for example, sports, academic competitions, or music auditions. The headlines should focus on the results of the competitions. Save the headlines in your **Working Portfolio.**

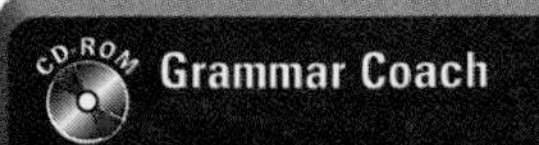

Diagnostic Test: What Do You Know?

Choose the letter that identifies the purpose of each underlined group of words.

Common sense shows that sports, especially professional sports, have a big effect on the American economy (1). The question is, How big? One way to answer is to look at the impact that one sports star has had.

The basketball superstar Michael Jordan (2) made millions by playing. He enriched his team, the Chicago Bulls, by boosting attendance at home games. He also helped send National Basketball Association (NBA) revenues soaring. Greatly increased (3) ticket sales at all of the arenas where the Bulls played were part of the story. NBA television revenues and merchandise sales surged too.

Playing spectacular basketball helped Jordan become one of the most famous persons in the world. He has boosted profits of various companies by endorsing products (4). To measure his economic impact (5), we must also consider sales of sports videos, books, and more. The greatest basketball player in history added billions to the economy.

1. A. acts as a direct object of the verb *have*
   B. acts as a verb
   C. modifies the noun *effect*
   D. modifies the noun *sports*
2. A. acts as a verb
   B. identifies the noun *superstar*
   C. modifies the noun *basketball*
   D. all of the above
3. A. acts as the subject of the verb *were*
   B. modifies the verb *were*
   C. acts as a predicate nominative
   D. modifies the noun *sales*
4. A. acts as the object of the preposition *by*
   B. modifies the noun *companies*
   C. modifies the adjective *various*
   D. none of the above
5. A. acts as a direct object of the verb *must consider*
   B. modifies the verb *must consider*
   C. modifies the noun *sales*
   D. acts as a verb

PHRASES

Prepositional Phrases

❶ Here's the Idea

▶ **A prepositional phrase consists of a preposition, its object, and any modifiers of the object.**

There are many kinds of sports.
PREPOSITION

Some people take a sport to its extreme.
PREPOSITION

In the following excerpt from a well-known story, the author uses prepositional phrases to add details. Notice that a prepositional phrase can function either as an adverb or as an adjective.

LITERARY MODEL

"I've always thought," said Rainsford, "that the Cape buffalo is the most dangerous of all big game."

For a moment the general did not reply; he was smiling his curious red-lipped smile. Then he said slowly: "No. You are wrong, sir. The Cape buffalo is not the most dangerous big game. . . . Here in my preserve on this island," he said, in the same slow tone, "I hunt more dangerous game."

—Richard Connell, "The Most Dangerous Game"

ADVERB PHRASES

ADJECTIVE PHRASE

Adverb Phrases

Like an adverb, an adverb prepositional phrase modifies a verb, an adjective, or another adverb.

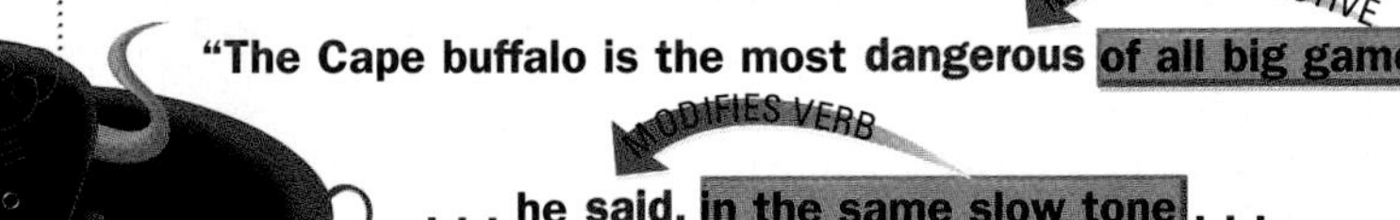

MODIFIES ADJECTIVE
"The Cape buffalo is the most dangerous of all big game."
MODIFIES VERB
. . . he said, in the same slow tone . . .

CHAPTER 3

Adjective Phrases

An adjective prepositional phrase modifies a noun or a pronoun.

MODIFIES NOUN

"Here in my preserve on this island," he said . . .

As you can see in the example above, sometimes an adjective phrase modifies a noun that is part of a different prepositional phrase.

Stringing together too many prepositional phrases can make writing difficult to understand. If you write a sentence that has too many prepositional phrases, check to see if there are any unnecessary details that can be deleted.

Rainsford had fallen off a ship headed from the United States through the Caribbean Sea to the Brazilian city of Rio de Janeiro.

2 Why It Matters in Writing

Inexperienced writers sometimes confuse readers by putting prepositional phrases in the wrong places in their sentences. Think about how the placement of the prepositional phrase affects the meaning of the following sentences.

Brockton Kennels sells retriever puppies to loving families with vaccinations.
(Is it the families who are vaccinated?)

Brockton Kennels sells retriever puppies with vaccinations to loving families.

By placing prepositional phrases closer to what they modify, you can avoid confusing your reader.

Golden retrievers are valued for their eagerness to work by hunters.
(Will a retriever work only when it is next to a hunter?)

Golden retrievers are valued by hunters for their eagerness to work.

③ Practice and Apply

A. CONCEPT CHECK: Prepositional Phrases

Write each prepositional phrase, along with the word it modifies.

The Challenge of Orienteering

1. Orienteering is a popular type of outdoor competition.
2. People who participate in this sport are called orienteers.
3. Orienteers follow a course that leads through a forest or another natural area.
4. Finishing the course in the fastest time is the goal.
5. Using maps and compasses, orienteers find marked points along the course.
6. At each point, they punch a card.
7. The shortest route between points is often not the fastest.
8. When they finish, orienteers return to a timer's table.
9. People with good navigation skills often do well.
10. Many events have courses for both beginners and experts.

➜ **For a SELF-CHECK and more practice, see the EXERCISE BANK, p. 591.**

CHAPTER 3

B. REVISING: Fixing Misplaced Prepositional Phrases

Rewrite these sentences, changing the position of prepositional phrases so that the sentences are no longer confusing. If a sentence is clear already, write *Correct.*

Hunting Dogs

1. Sporting dogs and hounds are the types of dogs for hunting with the most talent.
2. Sporting dogs are mainly used for hunting birds, and hounds are mainly used for hunting rabbits and foxes.
3. The stamina of a Chesapeake Bay retriever allows it to swim when retrieving ducks for a long time.
4. With its water-resistant fur, a hunter is glad to have a Labrador retriever to swim out and bring back ducks.
5. A pointer holds up a front leg at the scent of a quail with the paw pointed down.
6. Irish water spaniels are funny-looking dogs with tufts over their faces of curly hair.
7. People in Hungary used dogs called vizslas for hunting for centuries with falcons.
8. Beagles were faithful pets of people in ancient Rome.
9. Hunters with English foxhounds on horseback track foxes.
10. With their noses close to the ground, rabbits leave a scent that basset hounds are good at tracking.

Appositives and Appositive Phrases

❶ Here's the Idea

▶ **An appositive is a noun or pronoun that identifies or renames another noun or pronoun.** An **appositive phrase** is made up of an appositive plus its modifiers.

The appositive phrase in the sentence below identifies a person.

APPOSITIVE PHRASE

Gail Devers, a champion sprinter, was born in Seattle in 1966.

APPOSITIVE

The appositive phrase in the next sentence identifies a place.

Barcelona, a large city in Spain, hosted the Olympics in 1992.

Essential and Nonessential Appositives

An **essential appositive** is an appositive that provides information that is needed to identify the preceding noun or pronoun. It is sometimes called a restrictive appositive.

ESSENTIAL APPOSITIVE

The American sprinter Gail Devers won an Olympic gold medal in the 100-meter dash in 1992.

Notice that no commas are used with an essential appositive.

A **nonessential appositive** adds information about a noun or pronoun in a sentence in which the meaning is already clear. It is also called a nonrestrictive appositive.

NONESSENTIAL APPOSITIVE PHRASE

Devers, a survivor of Graves' disease, overcame many obstacles to achieve athletic success.

As you can see in the sentence above, a nonessential appositive is set off with commas.

❷ Why It Matters in Writing

Using appositives and appositive phrases offers a concise way of explaining how a person or thing is special or unique.

Devers, also a brilliant hurdler, won the gold medal in the 100-meter dash in 1996.

PHRASES

3 Practice and Apply

A. CONCEPT CHECK: Appositives and Appositive Phrases

Write the appositives and appositive phrases in these sentences, along with the words they rename or identify.

Wilma Rudolph, a True Champion

1. Wilma Rudolph, another champion sprinter, also overcame a disability.
2. Rudolph was born with the disease polio.
3. Her mother, Blanche Rudolph, helped her recover.
4. Rudolph, a determined child, ignored doctors' predictions about never being able to walk again.
5. A basketball star at age 13, she was known for her speed.
6. The coach Edward Temple invited her to a track camp.
7. In 1956, Rudolph, only a 16-year-old, made the U.S. Olympic team.
8. She and three other women, members of the women's 400-meter relay team, won a bronze medal.
9. Four years later, Rudolph achieved her greatest personal triumph, three gold medals in a single Olympics.
10. Rudolph's hometown in Tennessee, Clarksville, honored her with a big parade after the 1960 Olympic Games.

➜ **For a SELF-CHECK and more practice, see the EXERCISE BANK, p. 591.**

B. REVISING: Adding Details

Rewrite each sentence, adding the appositive or appositive phrase shown in parentheses. Include commas if necessary.

The Man Who Won Ten Gold Medals

1. The Olympic athlete also overcame polio. (Ray Ewry)
2. Ewry participated in four Olympics. (A specialist in jumping events)
3. Ewry competed in the standing high jump, the standing long jump, and the standing triple jump. (events not part of today's Olympic Games)
4. Ewry never lost an Olympic event he entered. (the only man to win ten gold medals)
5. He had an advantage over today's athletes: when he competed, four Olympics were held during the nine-year period. (1900–1908)

Verbals: Participial Phrases

A **verbal** is a verb form that acts as a noun, an adjective, or an adverb. There are three types of verbals: participles, gerunds, and infinitives.

❶ Here's the Idea

▶ **A participle is a verb form that acts as an adjective. It modifies a noun or a pronoun.** A **participial phrase** consists of a participle plus its modifiers and complements.

PARTICIPLE

Played for more than 100 years, high school football has a rich tradition.

Large crowds attend games featuring rival schools.

PARTICIPLE

There are two kinds of participles: past participles (*played*) and present participles (*featuring*).

Writers use participles to describe nouns, as in the following excerpt.

LITERARY MODEL

The coach looked like an old gangster: broken **nose,** a scar on his cheek like a stitched **shoestring.**

—Robert Cormier, *The Chocolate War*

PARTICIPLES

Broken modifies *nose*; *stitched* modifies *shoestring.*

In the next excerpt, notice how Robert Cormier uses participial phrases to add details to a description of an injured football player on an autumn afternoon.

LITERARY MODEL

Inhaling the sweet sharp apple air through his nostrils—he was afraid to open his mouth wide, wary of any movement that was not absolutely essential—**he** walked tentatively toward the sidelines, listening to the **coach** barking at the other guys.

—*The Chocolate War*

PARTICIPIAL PHRASES

The first two phrases modify *he;* the third modifies *coach.*

Notice that *coach* is part of a participial phrase and is modified by another participial phrase.

PHRASES

❷ Why It Matters in Writing

Many writers have trouble placing participial phrases in sentences. Putting words in the wrong place can result in a misplaced or dangling phrase that will confuse the reader.

A **misplaced participial phrase** is closer to some other noun than it is to the noun it actually modifies.

STUDENT MODEL

DRAFT

Beginning in the 1890s, Thanksgiving Day was when top high school football teams from different regions paired off in major games.

This sentence makes it sound as if the first Thanksgiving holiday occurred in the 1890s.

REVISION

Beginning in the 1890s, top high school football teams from different regions paired off in major games on Thanksgiving Day.

A participial phrase that begins a sentence should be followed immediately by what it modifies.

A **dangling participial phrase** is one that does not logically modify any of the words in the sentence in which it appears.

STUDENT MODEL

DRAFT

Responding to changes in the rules of football, the forward pass was used more often in high school games in the 1920s.

A forward pass cannot do anything except get caught or hit the ground!

REVISION

Responding to changes in the rules of football, high school coaches began using the forward pass more often in the 1920s.

The coaches were the ones who responded to the rule changes.

Shoe by Jeff MacNelly

3 Practice and Apply

A. CONCEPT CHECK: Participial Phrases

Write the participial phrase in each sentence. Then write the noun modified by the phrase.

A Sport in Decline?

1. In many parts of the country, steadily declining interest has damaged high school football.
2. Preferring soccer or basketball, many students do not sign up for football.
3. Parents concerned about football injuries suggest other sports.
4. Reacting to a lack of interest, school officials have cut football funds.
5. Remaining popular in many urban areas, however, high school football won't be dying out anytime soon.

For a SELF-CHECK and more practice, see the EXERCISE BANK, p. 592.

Write a sentence that expresses your opinion about the value of high school football. Include a participial phrase in the sentence.

B. REVISING: Fixing Dangling and Misplaced Participial Phrases

Read the following paragraph. Rewrite the sentences that contain dangling or misplaced participial phrases, adding or rearranging words to eliminate the errors.

A Star in Two Ways

A high school in Colorado had a homecoming queen who played football. There was a special ceremony at halftime of the homecoming game. Queen Katie smiled for the photographers taking off her helmet. Accepting a white rose, the crowd loudly cheered. Katie enjoyed the ceremony, but she was prouder of her performance on the field. With the game on the line, a field goal sailed through the goal posts kicked by Katie. During her four years on the team, Katie played well without receiving any special treatment. She was tackled by large opposing players kicking extra points. Katie was not ready to give up the game after high school. Determined to play college football, Katie's mother gave her full support.

Verbals: Gerund Phrases

1 Here's the Idea

▶ **A gerund is a verb form that ends in *ing* and acts as a noun.** A **gerund phrase** consists of a gerund plus its modifiers and complements.

GERUND

He loves swimming.

GERUND PHRASE

He loves swimming in the ocean.

LITERARY MODEL

Next morning, when it was time for the routine of **swimming** and **sunbathing**, his mother said, "Are you tired of the usual beach, Jerry? Would you like to go somewhere else?"

—Doris Lessing, "Through the Tunnel"

CHAPTER 3

Like nouns, gerunds and gerund phrases can act as subjects, objects of prepositions, direct objects, indirect objects, and predicate nominatives.

Functions of Gerund Phrases

Function	Example
Subject	**Swimming competitively** requires lots of practice.
Object of a preposition	Jeff got in shape by **swimming at the YMCA**.
Direct object	Mr. Lopez coaches **high school swimming.**
Indirect object	Tameka gave competitive **swimming** a try.
Predicate nominative	Tameka's specialty is **swimming the backstroke.**

2 Why It Matters in Writing

Gerunds can help you make your writing more concise. Sometimes a gerund can replace an entire group of words, as in the student model on the next page.

STUDENT MODEL

~~A person who swims across~~ *Swimming* the English Channel ~~makes~~ *is* an awesome accomplishment. A swimmer must travel at least 21 miles through strong currents. Even the fastest swimmers spend more than seven hours ~~to make the trip across~~ *in crossing* the Channel.

3 Practice and Apply

CONCEPT CHECK: Gerund Phrases

Write the gerund phrase in each sentence. Then indicate whether the phrase functions as a subject (S), an object of a preposition (OP), a direct object (DO), an indirect object (IO), or a predicate nominative (PN).

Pablo Morales, the Swimmer Who Wouldn't Give Up

1. Pablo Morales became known as the comeback kid of Olympic swimming.
2. One of the goals of Morales's mother was having her children learn to swim at an early age.
3. Morales learned quickly, and soon he started winning junior championships.
4. As a student at Stanford University, he attracted attention by winning 11 NCAA championships.
5. Competing in the 1984 Olympics brought him one gold medal and two silver medals.
6. Morales surprised everybody by failing to qualify for the 1988 Olympics.
7. After that, his new goal was earning a law degree.
8. When his mother died in 1991, Morales gave competitive swimming another chance.
9. Having only seven months to prepare made it difficult for him to qualify for the 1992 Olympics, but he did.
10. He touched people's hearts by winning a gold medal in the 100-meter butterfly.

➜ **For a SELF-CHECK and more practice, see the EXERCISE BANK, p. 592.**

Verbals: Infinitive Phrases

1 Here's the Idea

An infinitive is a verb form, usually beginning with the word *to*, that can act as a noun, an adjective, or an adverb. An **infinitive phrase** consists of an infinitive plus its modifiers and complements.

INFINITIVE

More and more women are learning to golf.

INFINITIVE PHRASE

To make a living as a golfer is no easy task.

The following chart shows examples of the different ways in which infinitive phrases can be used in sentences.

Uses of Infinitive Phrases	
Noun	**To win tournaments on the Ladies Professional Golf Association (LPGA) tour** is the goal of top women golfers. (used as subject)
Adjective	In 1998, Se Ri Pak became the youngest player **to win the U.S. Women's Open golf championship.** (modifies *player*)
Adverb	**To become a champion golfer,** Pak spent many hours practicing in her native land of South Korea. (modifies *spent*)

CHAPTER 3

2 Why It Matters in Writing

Using infinitive phrases, you can combine sentences in a way that eliminates unnecessary words and sharpens the relationship between ideas.

STUDENT MODEL

DRAFT

~~Golfers use many different types of clubs during a tournament. Different clubs are needed to hit good shots.~~

REVISION

Golfers use many different types of clubs **to hit good shots** during a tournament.

3 Practice and Apply

A. CONCEPT CHECK: Infinitive Phrases

Write each infinitive or infinitive phrase, indicating whether it acts as an adjective, an adverb, or a noun.

Tiger's Good Works

1. It is a shame that so few sports stars are willing to help people in need.
2. To give something back to society is important to Tiger Woods.
3. Woods was the first person of African-American descent to win a major tournament in men's professional golf.
4. To overcome golf's history of discrimination was no easy task.
5. Woods is determined to help other persons of color become golf stars.
6. To turn his dreams into reality, he founded a charitable organization, the Tiger Woods Foundation, in 1997.
7. It is one of the few golf organizations to work with disadvantaged children.
8. The foundation sponsors clinics to help children learn golf.
9. At the clinics, Woods likes to work with individual kids.
10. His foundation is also working to create new, affordable golf practice facilities around the country.

➔ **For a SELF-CHECK and more practice, see the EXERCISE BANK, p. 593.**

B. REVISING: Combining Sentences

Use an infinitive phrase to combine each pair of sentences.

Example: Hale Irwin has displayed incredible skill. He has won the U.S. Open three times.

Answer: Hale Irwin has displayed incredible skill to win the U.S. Open three times.

A Golfer Who Keeps Winning

1. Hale Irwin must have amazing physical endurance. He has won tournaments for 30 years.
2. He had weeks of outstanding play on the Senior Tour. He earned nearly $3 million in one year.
3. He possesses extraordinary talent. He has dominated a professional sport for so many years.

Placement of Phrases

1 Here's the Idea

A common mistake that writers make is putting phrases in the wrong positions in sentences. This mistake usually involves phrases used as adjectives or adverbs.

Misplaced Phrases

A **misplaced phrase** is a phrase that is placed so far away from the word it modifies that the meaning of the sentence is unclear or incorrect. The types of phrases that are most often misplaced are prepositional phrases and participial phrases.

DRAFT

MISPLACED PREPOSITIONAL PHRASE

The U.S. team in men's indoor volleyball won the most Olympic gold medals during the 1980s.

The sentence above says that the U.S. men's indoor volleyball team won more Olympic gold medals than any other team in any sport. This is not true.

REVISION

The U.S. team won the most Olympic gold medals in men's indoor volleyball during the 1980s.

Dangling Phrases

When the word or words that a phrase should modify are missing from a sentence, the phrase is called a **dangling phrase.** Most dangling phrases are participial phrases or infinitive phrases.

DRAFT

DANGLING PARTICIPIAL PHRASE

Failing to win a gold medal in the 1900s, the Olympic women's indoor volleyball competition has been disappointing.

The sentence above says that a competition won a gold medal.

REVISION

WORDS MODIFIED

Failing to win a gold medal in the 1900s, the U.S. women's indoor volleyball team was disappointing at the Olympics.

CHAPTER 3

2 Why It Matters in Writing

Sentences with phrases that are not placed properly can confuse readers. Such a sentence can end up sounding silly.

To keep their grades up, homework assignments need to take priority over students' athletic activities. (When did homework assignments develop a mind of their own?)

3 Practice and Apply

CONCEPT CHECK: Placement of Phrases

Rewrite these sentences to fix misplaced and dangling phrases. If a sentence has no error, write *Correct.*

Outstanding American Volleyball Players

1. Mike Lambert is one of the top indoor volleyball players in the United States.
2. To become an outstanding all-around player like Lambert, many hours of training are required.
3. Competing for Stanford University, the most-valuable-player trophy at the 1997 NCAA championship was awarded to Lambert.
4. Growing up in Hawaii, soccer was a favorite sport besides volleyball.
5. Lambert joined a professional team after graduating from Stanford in Greece.
6. Holly McPeak is one of the world's best players in women's beach volleyball.
7. Raised in Manhattan Beach, California, few activities were more enjoyable than volleyball.
8. Having won more than $200,000 during her career, her performances include victories in over 20 tournaments.
9. To have success in two-on-two beach volleyball, the right partner must be found.
10. McPeak is especially well-known for her outstanding defensive play by fans.

➜ **For a SELF-CHECK and more practice, see the EXERCISE BANK, p. 593.**

Give two possible answers for items 2 and 8.

Sentence Diagramming

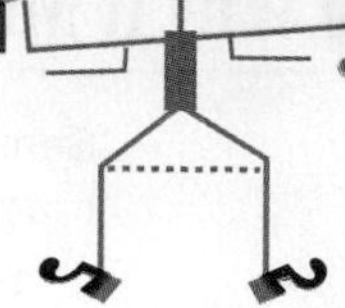

Here's the Idea

Learning how to diagram sentences that contain phrases can help you understand the roles that phrases play in writing.

Watch me for diagramming tips!

Prepositional Phrases

- Write the preposition on a slanted line below the word the prepositional phrase modifies.
- Write the object of the preposition on a horizontal line attached to the slanted line and parallel to the main line.
- Write words that modify the object of the preposition on slanted lines below the object.

Adjective Phrase

Many designers of computer software study artificial intelligence.

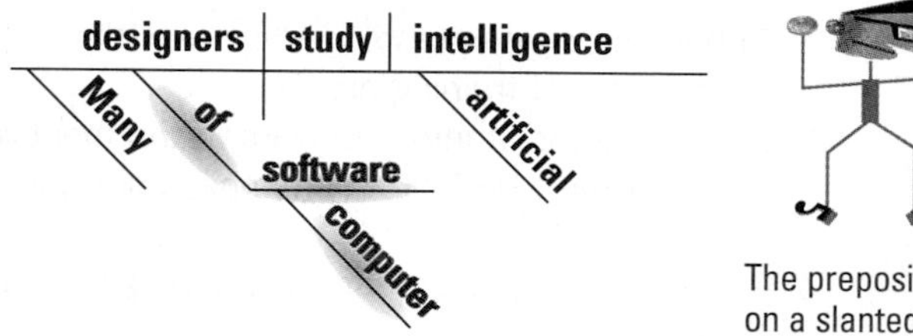

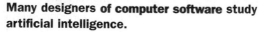

The preposition goes on a slanted line.

Adverb Phrase

These designers program intelligence into computers.

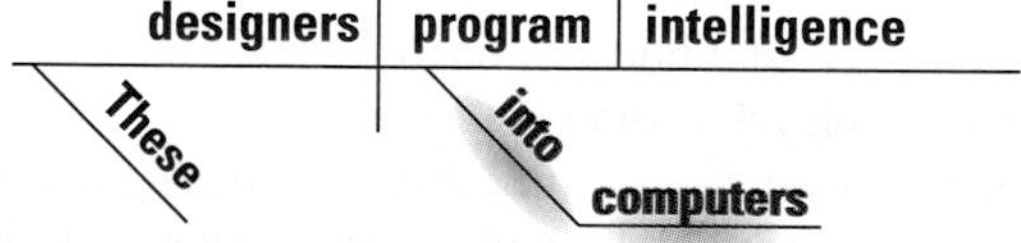

A. CONCEPT CHECK: Prepositional Phrases

Diagram these sentences, using what you have learned.

1. Some computers can play checkers against human opponents.
2. A research team at a Canadian university developed one famous program.

CHAPTER 3

Appositive attitude!

Appositive Phrases

Write an appositive in parentheses after the word it identifies or renames. Attach words that modify the appositive to it in the usual way.

Marion Tinsley, the world champion, played a checkers match against Chinook.

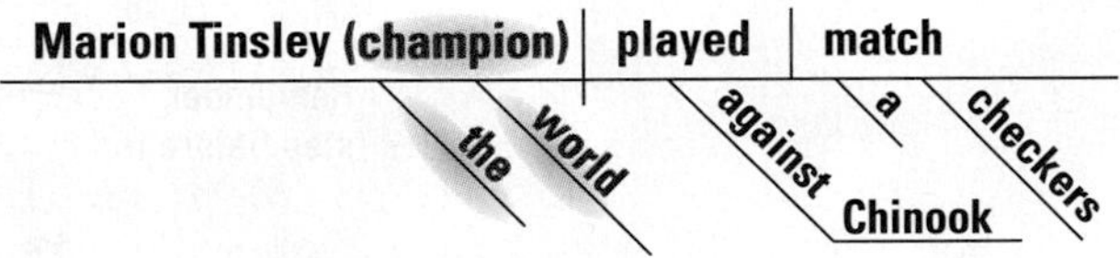

B. CONCEPT CHECK: Appositive Phrases

Diagram the following sentence, using what you have learned.

Tinsley, the best player of all time, beat Chinook in 1992.

PHRASES

Participial Phrases

- The participle curves over an angled line below the word it modifies.
- Diagram an object or a subject complement on the horizontal part of the angled line in the usual way.
- Write modifiers on slanted lines below the words they modify.

Beating other top players brilliantly, Chinook was the new checkers champion.

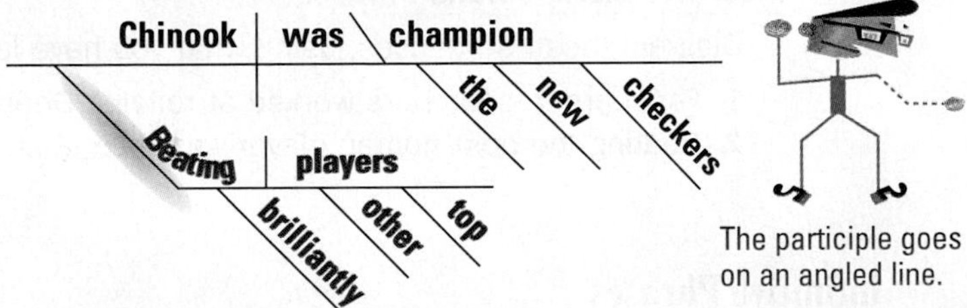

The participle goes on an angled line.

C. CONCEPT CHECK: Participial Phrases

Diagram the following sentence, using what you have learned.

Programmed properly, computers can also play chess expertly.

Gerund Phrases

- The gerund curves over an angled line that looks like a step.
- With a vertical forked line, connect the step to the part of the diagram that corresponds to the role of the gerund phrase in the sentence.
- Complements and modifiers are diagrammed in the usual way.

Gerund Phrase as Subject

Playing chess is the specialty of the program Deep Blue.

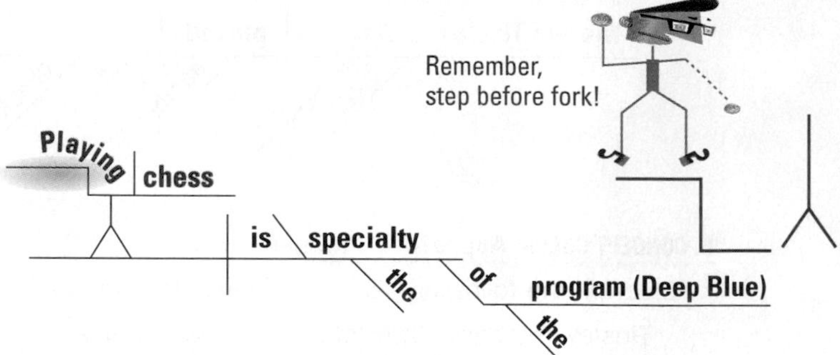

Gerund Phrase as Object of a Preposition

Careful thought is required for winning a game of chess.

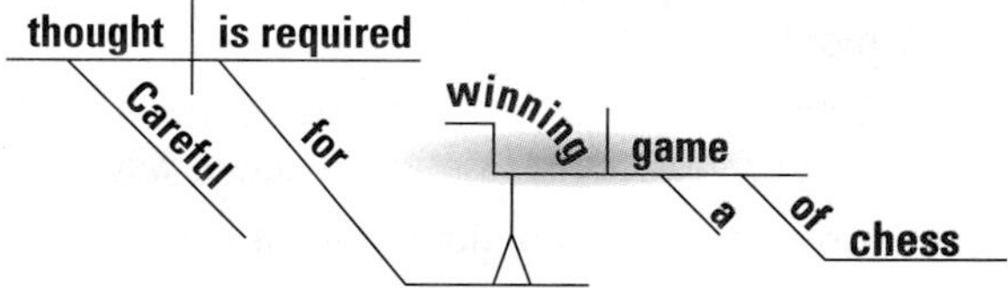

D. CONCEPT CHECK: Gerund Phrases

Diagram these sentences, using what you have learned.

1. For years, researchers worked at refining Deep Blue.
2. Beating the best human player was their goal.

Infinitive Phrases

- Write the infinitive on line, with the word *to* on the slanted part and the verb on the horizontal part.
- If the phrase functions as a noun, use a vertical forked line to connect it to the part of the diagram that corresponds to its role in the sentence.

CHAPTER 3

• If the phrase functions as a modifier, place it below the word it modifies.

Infinitive Phrase as Subject

To defeat top players was the goal of Deep Blue's programmers.

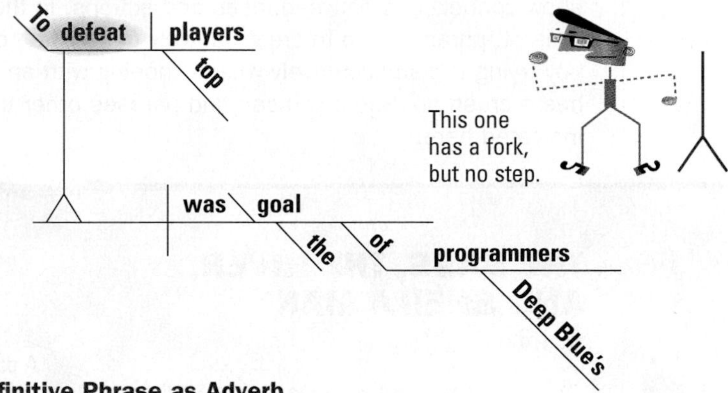

Infinitive Phrase as Adverb

Programmers worked to improve Deep Blue.

E. CONCEPT CHECK: Infinitive Phrases

Diagram these sentences, using what you have learned.

1. Garry Kasparov agreed to play Deep Blue.
2. To defeat Kasparov was the programmers' dream.

F. MIXED REVIEW: Diagramming

Diagram the following sentences. Look for all the types of phrases you have learned about.

1. IBM Corporation developed the computer program Deep Blue.
2. Playing confidently, Garry Kasparov defeated the first Deep Blue.
3. IBM researchers began a project to improve their program.
4. Kasparov and the second Deep Blue met in 1997.
5. Losing the match embarrassed Kasparov.

Grammar in Literature

Adding Detail with Phrases

Writers often use phrases to provide descriptive details and to show connections between ideas and actions. In the following excerpt, phrases help to create a lively description of a 14-year-old boy trying to fish secretively while canoeing with an older girl he has a crush on. See if you can find phrases other than the ones indicated here.

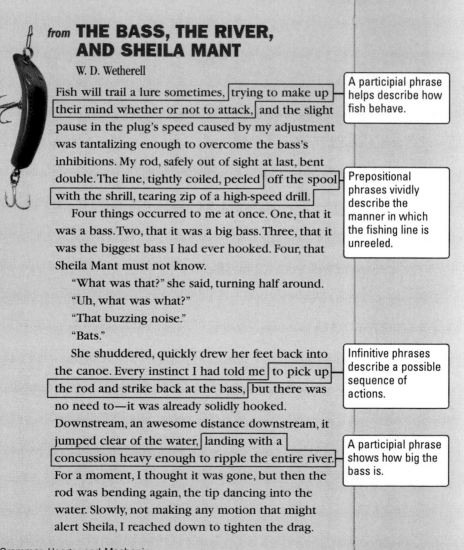

from THE BASS, THE RIVER, AND SHEILA MANT

W. D. Wetherell

Fish will trail a lure sometimes, trying to make up their mind whether or not to attack, and the slight pause in the plug's speed caused by my adjustment was tantalizing enough to overcome the bass's inhibitions. My rod, safely out of sight at last, bent double. The line, tightly coiled, peeled off the spool with the shrill, tearing zip of a high-speed drill.

A participial phrase helps describe how fish behave.

Prepositional phrases vividly describe the manner in which the fishing line is unreeled.

Four things occurred to me at once. One, that it was a bass. Two, that it was a big bass. Three, that it was the biggest bass I had ever hooked. Four, that Sheila Mant must not know.

"What was that?" she said, turning half around.

"Uh, what was what?"

"That buzzing noise."

"Bats."

She shuddered, quickly drew her feet back into the canoe. Every instinct I had told me to pick up the rod and strike back at the bass, but there was no need to—it was already solidly hooked. Downstream, an awesome distance downstream, it jumped clear of the water, landing with a concussion heavy enough to ripple the entire river. For a moment, I thought it was gone, but then the rod was bending again, the tip dancing into the water. Slowly, not making any motion that might alert Sheila, I reached down to tighten the drag.

Infinitive phrases describe a possible sequence of actions.

A participial phrase shows how big the bass is.

CHAPTER 3

Ways You Can Use Phrases in Writing	
Prepositional phrases	Use to express relationships of time, location, or manner
Appositive phrases	Use to identify or specify people, places, things, or ideas
Participial phrases	Use to describe people, places, or events and to give a sense of action to your writing
Gerund phrases	Use to make your writing more concise
Infinitive phrases	Use to add details or explain processes

PRACTICE AND APPLY: Adding Detail with Phrases

In each pair of sentences below, one of the sentences adds detail to the other. Use phrases to combine the sentences, following the directions given in parentheses.

Example: Most sports have rules of conduct. These rules discourage participants from unsporting behavior. (Change the second sentence to a participial phrase that begins with *discouraging.*)

Answer: Most sports have rules of conduct discouraging participants from unsporting behavior.

1. For example, football teams whose players taunt opposing players or criticize officials are penalized 15 yards. The penalty is called unsportsmanlike conduct. (Change the second sentence to a prepositional phrase that begins with *for.*)
2. Sometimes a professional basketball player or coach insults a referee. This can cause the referee to call a technical foul and award the other team a free throw. (Change the first sentence to a gerund phrase by replacing the first part of the sentence with "In basketball, insulting . . . ")
3. Arguing with a baseball umpire is a risk. One risks being thrown out of the game. (Change each sentence to an infinitive phrase, and connect the phrases with the verb *is.*)
4. Rules of conduct are especially strict in golf. Golf is a sport with a long tradition of fair play. (Change the second sentence to an appositive phrase.)
5. A tennis player can be penalized points. Two ways this can happen are if the player argues with the umpire or throws a racket. (Change the second sentence to a prepositional phrase that begins with *for* and contains two gerunds.)

Choose a piece of writing in your **Working Portfolio** and make it more detailed by adding several types of phrases.

PHRASES

Mixed Review

A. Kinds of Phrases Indicate what type of phrase each of the underlined phrases is.

(1) Centuries ago, Alaska's Eskimo peoples began using dogsleds to travel across the snow. **(2)** The dogsled, a reliable means of transportation, later carried gold miners and others along Alaska's trails. **(3)** The invention of the snowmobile changed all that.

(4) Joe Redington, a dedicated dogsledder, wanted to keep dogsledding alive. **(5)** To spark enthusiasm, he organized the first Iditarod Trail Sled Dog Race in 1973. **(6)** Competing for $51,000, 34 mushers (sled drivers) and dog teams raced more than 1,100 miles (1,770 kilometers).

(7) Fascinated by the drama, people around the world follow the annual Iditarod. **(8)** Mushers and dogs must survive subzero temperatures, blizzards, and moose attacks if they hope to win the race. **(9)** Some sled dogs have died, even though most of the dog owners are committed to providing excellent care. **(10)** For this reason, campaigns to end the Iditarod have been launched.

B. Misplaced and Dangling Phrases Proofread the following paragraph for dangling and misplaced phrases. Rewrite the four sentences that contain errors, correcting them.

The 1998 Winter Olympics included a sport that no previous Olympics had included. At that Olympics, medals were awarded for snowboarding for the first time. Snowboarding has come a long way from its beginnings. Once banned at most ski resorts, Americans have made snowboarding the nation's fastest growing winter sport. Two events for men and women, the giant slalom and the halfpipe, were held at the Olympics. In the giant slalom, contestants raced downhill, swerving through gates. To win the halfpipe, spectacular moves had to be made by competitors traveling through a chute of snow. Unfortunately, the U.S. team did not do as well as predicted. Winning only two bronze medals, the 1998 Olympics was a disappointment for the U.S. snowboarders.

Mastery Test: What Did You Learn?

Choose the letter that identifies the purpose of each underlined phrase.

Soccer as we know it gained worldwide popularity <u>in the late 1800s</u>.(1) <u>Embraced by Americans</u>,(2) the game was played at schools and colleges. Soccer clubs were formed for adults wanting to join the fun. By 1900, however, Americans had become more interested in <u>playing football</u>.(3)

Soccer, <u>the world's favorite sport</u>,(4) followed a roller-coaster path in the United States after 1900. The Brazilian soccer star Pelé sparked Americans' interest in the game by playing for a U.S. professional team during the 1970s. <u>To become truly successful</u>,(5) professional soccer needs a larger TV audience. Soccer is most popular among young people. Today millions of American students are happy to spend time on the soccer field.

1. A. acts as a verb
   B. acts as the subject of the verb *gained*
   C. modifies the noun *popularity*
   D. modifies the verb *gained*

2. A. modifies the noun *game*
   B. identifies the noun *schools*
   C. modifies the verb *was played*
   D. all of the above

3. A. acts as the object of the preposition *in*
   B. modifies the noun *Americans*
   C. acts as a predicate nominative
   D. acts as the subject of the verb *had become*

4. A. modifies the verb *followed*
   B. acts as a direct object of the verb *followed*
   C. modifies the noun *path*
   D. none of the above

5. A. acts as the subject of the verb *needs*
   B. modifies the verb *needs*
   C. modifies the noun *audience*
   D. acts as a verb

PHRASES

Student Help Desk

Phrases at a Glance

Kind of Phrase	Functions as	Example
Prepositional phrase	Adjective	The skates **on the floor** are Elena's.
	Adverb	Elena skated **around the rink.**
Appositive phrase	Noun	Mr. Gorski, **the coach,** is here.
Participial phrase	Adjective	Hockey fans **wearing jerseys** waited patiently.
Gerund phrase	Noun	**Rollerblading in the park** is fun.
Infinitive phrase	Noun	Armand loves **to bowl.**
	Adjective	Dropping the ball is something **to avoid.**
	Adverb	Chiang races **to win the match.**

CHAPTER 3

Prepositions

Over the line
Through the hoop

about	before	inside	to
above	behind	into	toward
across	below	near	under
after	beside	of	underneath
against	between	off	until
along	by	on	up
among	down	onto	upon
around	for	out	with
as	from	over	without
at	in	through	

Phrases to Avoid

Modifier Mixups

What It's Called	What's Wrong with It
Misplaced modifier	**It appears to modify something that it doesn't.** **Example:** We sell gasoline to people in plastic jugs.
Dangling modifier	**What it should modify is missing from the sentence.** **Example:** Walking past the kitchen, the fish smelled delicious.

Comma Do's and Don'ts

An Appositive Approach

DO	Example
Use commas with nonessential appositives.	Pedro Martinez, a native of the Dominican Republic, is a pitcher for the Boston Red Sox and one of the best players in baseball.
DON'T	**Example**
Do not use commas with essential appositives.	The Boston Red Sox pitcher Pedro Martinez is one of the best players in baseball.

The Bottom Line

Checklist for Phrases

Have I . . .

____ used phrases to add details and clarity to my writing?

____ used commas with nonessential appositives?

____ placed phrases that act as adverbs or adjectives close to what they modify?

____ avoided stringing together too many prepositional phrases?

PHRASES

Chapter 4

Clauses and Sentence Structure

Theme: Families

It's All in the Family!

Tennis stars Venus and Serena Williams are two of the most famous sisters in sports. If they were your sisters, how would you describe them to someone else? Chances are you'd say something like, "My sisters, *who are really competitive,* love playing against each other." Or "*How they got started in tennis* is a great story."

You've used clauses to add details and to show relationships between ideas. You can use these sentence parts to do the same things in your writing. Although some clauses can stand on their own, many depend on other parts of a sentence for their meaning.

Write Away: Lean on Me

When the going gets tough, whom do you depend on? Write a paragraph about a family member or friend who lends you moral support. Save your paragraph in your **Working Portfolio.**

Diagnostic Test: What Do You Know?

Choose the letter of the term that identifies each numbered part of this passage.

Ursula K. Le Guin, who is one of the world's best science fiction writers (1), creates alien characters and societies that are completely believable (2). As people read her stories (3), they are often amazed at these complex worlds, which she describes in great detail (4). Where her ideas come from (5) might be explained by her family history. Her father was an anthropologist, a scientist who studies human cultures (6). When Le Guin was young (7), she learned about the great variety of customs, languages, and family structures of the world's people. Le Guin's mother, Theodora Kroeber, wrote a famous book about a man called Ishi. (8) He was the last member of his tribe. When Le Guin wanted to create alien people and places (9), she could draw from such material. Le Guin has continued the family tradition of writing about the exotic, and her novels and stories captivate people of all generations. (10)

1. A. independent clause
   B. subordinate clause
   C. adverb clause
   D. noun clause as subject

2. A. noun clause as direct object
   B. adjective clause
   C. independent clause
   D. nonessential clause

3. A. independent clause
   B. noun clause as direct object
   C. adverb clause
   D. adjective clause

4. A. noun clause as subject
   B. essential clause
   C. nonessential clause
   D. adverb clause

5. A. noun clause as subject
   B. independent clause
   C. simple sentence
   D. adverb clause

6. A. essential clause
   B. independent clause
   C. nonessential clause
   D. noun clause as direct object

7. A. noun clause
   B. essential clause
   C. nonessential clause
   D. adverb clause

8. A. compound sentence
   B. complex sentence
   C. simple sentence
   D. compound-complex sentence

9. A. independent clause
   B. adjective clause
   C. noun clause as subject
   D. adverb clause

10. A. simple sentence
    B. compound sentence
    C. complex sentence
    D. compound-complex sentence

CLAUSES

LESSON 1

Kinds of Clauses

1 Here's the Idea

▶ **A clause is a group of words that contains a subject and a verb.**

Your genes carry your family's genetic history.
SUBJECT ↑ ↑ VERB

Independent Clauses

An **independent** (or **main**) **clause** expresses a complete thought. It can stand alone as a sentence.

Genes contain the code for your physical appearance.
INDEPENDENT CLAUSE

CHAPTER 4

Subordinate Clauses

A **subordinate** (or **dependent**) **clause** contains a subject and a verb but does not express a complete thought. It cannot stand alone. Subordinate clauses may be introduced by words like *if, because, even though, how, what, why, that, while, when,* and *since.*

that determines your height
SUBORDINATE CLAUSE

because inherited traits often skip a generation
SUBORDINATE CLAUSE

Creating Complete Sentences

To express a complete thought, a subordinate clause must be combined with, or be part of, an independent clause.

Genes contain the code | **that determines your height.**
INDEPENDENT CLAUSE | SUBORDINATE CLAUSE

SUBORDINATE CLAUSE
Because inherited traits often skip a generation, | **you may resemble your grandparents more than your parents.**
INDEPENDENT CLAUSE

Do not confuse a subordinate clause with a verbal phrase. Unlike a clause, a verbal phrase has no subject.

Verbal Phrase: Driving over the bridge, she sneezed.

Clause: As she was driving over the bridge, she sneezed.

❷ Why It Matters in Writing

Many fragments are actually subordinate clauses. To fix these fragments, join them with independent clauses.

STUDENT MODEL

Clasp your hands together~~. A~~ as the picture shows. Which thumb is on top? If you clasp your hands to position the other thumb on top, it feels wrong. This odd little trait is inherited.

❸ Practice and Apply

CONCEPT CHECK: Kinds of Clauses

Identify the underlined clauses as subordinate or independent.

Your Personality—Is It Inherited?

1. Although you inherit your looks, <u>the origin of your personality is more mysterious</u>.
2. Research on identical twins has fueled <u>what scientists call the "heredity versus environment" debate</u>.
3. The debate focuses on one question—<u>whether personality is mainly inherited or mainly shaped by family and other people</u>.
4. Identical twins raised in separate families showed amazing similarities <u>even though the families were very different</u>.
5. Not only did many of the twins have similar IQs, <u>their body language was also remarkably the same</u>.
6. One set of twins tugged at their hair <u>while they read a book</u>.
7. Although they were raised miles apart, <u>they liked the same school subjects and wore the same kinds of clothes</u>.
8. <u>When separated twins had illnesses</u>, they often had identical illnesses at roughly the same time.
9. <u>Another set of twins really amazed researchers</u> because both once had dogs named Toy and had wives named Betty.
10. <u>Because these similarities are so unlikely to happen by chance</u>, heredity probably plays a role in shaping personality.

➜ **For a SELF-CHECK and more practice, see the EXERCISE BANK, p. 594.**

Adjective and Adverb Clauses

1 Here's the Idea

Subordinate clauses can function as adjectives and adverbs.

Adjective Clauses

An adjective clause is a subordinate clause that is used as an adjective to modify a noun or pronoun. It usually follows the word(s) it modifies. Like adjectives, these clauses answer the questions *which one, what kind, how much,* or *how many.*

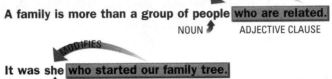

MODIFIES

A family is more than a group of people who are related.

NOUN ADJECTIVE CLAUSE

MODIFIES

It was she who started our family tree.

PRONOUN ADJECTIVE CLAUSE

CHAPTER 4

An adjective clause is introduced by a **relative pronoun** or by a **relative adverb.** These words are called relative because they *relate* adjective clauses to the words they modify.

Words That Introduce Adjective Clauses	
Relative pronouns	who, whom, whose, that, which
Relative adverbs	when, where, why

Families may also include foster children and people who are adopted.

Some people still live in a hunter-gatherer society, where a "family" may have 20 to 200 members.

Essential and Nonessential Adjective Clauses

An **essential** adjective clause provides information that is essential, or necessary, to identify the preceding noun or pronoun.

Someone who is your first cousin is the child of your uncle or aunt.

A **nonessential** adjective clause adds information about a noun or pronoun in a sentence in which the meaning is already clear. The clause can be dropped without changing the sentence's meaning.

Irene, who is your first cousin, was married last fall.

Irene was married last fall. (meaning is still clear)

Notice that a nonessential clause is set off by commas. The commas separate nonessential information from the main idea of the sentence.

That and Which Writers are often not sure whether to use *that* or *which* to introduce essential or nonessential clauses. Follow these guidelines to use these words correctly.

That is used to introduce an essential clause.

The reception was held at a hotel that looks like a castle.

Which is used to introduce a nonessential clause.

The Clarmont Hotel, which looks like a castle, is 100 years old.

CLAUSES

Adverb Clauses

▶ **An adverb clause is a subordinate clause that modifies a verb, an adjective, or an adverb.** It may come before or after the word(s) it modifies. Like adverbs, the clauses tell *where, why, how, when,* or *to what degree* something was done.

MODIFIES

Most children leave home when the time is right.

VERB — ADVERB CLAUSE

MODIFIES

Many young adults think a career is important because it helps them to become independent.

ADJECTIVE — ADVERB CLAUSE

MODIFIES

Many are marrying later in life than their parents did.

ADVERB — ADVERB CLAUSE

Words That Introduce Adverb Clauses

An adverb clause is usually introduced by a subordinating conjunction. A **subordinating conjunction** relates the adverb clause to the word(s) it modifies. The following is a list of the most common subordinating conjunctions.

Commonly Used Subordinating Conjunctions

after	as though	so that	whenever
although	because	than	where
as	before	though	wherever
as if	even though	unless	while
as long as	if	until	
as soon as	since	when	

When you marry, your spouse's family becomes part of your family "in law."

You gain a second mother and father even though you are not related by blood.

Notice that an adverb clause is set off by a comma when it comes *before* the independent clause. When it comes *after* the independent clause, often no comma is needed.

❷ Why It Matters in Writing

Use adjective and adverb clauses to add details, to clarify relationships between your ideas, and to avoid repetition.

STUDENT MODEL

DRAFT

Young adults finish college. Some choose to live with their parents again. These young people are called boomerangers. Boomerangers keep returning home.

REVISION

After they finish college, some young adults choose to live with their parents again. These young people are called boomerangers **because they keep returning home.**

3 Practice and Apply

A. CONCEPT CHECK: Adjective and Adverb Clauses

Write the adjective and adverb clauses in the following sentences. After each clause, write the word or words that it modifies.

Genealogy for Dummies

1. Humans aren't the only ones who have family trees.
2. The crash-test dummy family line started in 1949 when the U.S. Army Air Force bought the first Sierra Sam.
3. Sam was used in ejection seat tests that the army ran.
4. The Sams had sensors so their crashes could be recorded.
5. These dummies were used to test anything that humans could ride, like cars, roller coasters, airplanes, and tanks.
6. When testers needed more models, Sam's family expanded to include Stan, Saul, Sue, Susie, and Sammy.
7. The later Hybrid II dummy worked better than Sierra Sam because it had more flexibility.
8. Crash dummies Larry and Vince, whose TV ads promoted seat belt safety, were probably Hybrid II descendants.
9. The 1976 Hybrid III line was developed because the auto industry needed more accurate crash-test results.
10. Recent additions to the family tree include infant and child dummies that are used to test problems with airbags.

➜ **For a SELF-CHECK and more practice, see the EXERCISE BANK, p. 595.**

B. REVISING: Adding Details

Combine each pair of sentences by changing the italicized one into an adjective or adverb clause. Use the introductory words given.

Example: Childhood can last a lifetime. *Historical records show.* (as)
Answer: Childhood can last a lifetime, as historical records show.

Children or Adults?

1. In old Europe, people had different ideas about parent-child relationships. *The ideas might seem harsh today.* (that)
2. Children couldn't marry or work without permission from their fathers. *Their fathers had authority over their lives.* (who)
3. *Young people married.* (until) They were considered "youths"—not quite children but not adults.
4. *These ideas created two extremes.* (because) You could learn an adult trade at age 7 but still be a "child" at age 30.
5. In some countries, even marriage didn't make a son independent. *He and his family lived with his father.* (if)

Noun Clauses

1 Here's the Idea

A noun clause is a subordinate clause used as a noun. A noun clause can serve the same function as a noun in a sentence.

That my brothers and sisters influence me is obvious.
SUBJECT

They know exactly what drives me crazy.
DIRECT OBJECT

My parents tell whoever is loudest to quiet down.
INDIRECT OBJECT

My sister's or brother's praise is also what inspires me.
PREDICATE NOMINATIVE

We encourage each other in whatever ways we can.
OBJECT OF A PREPOSITION

If you can substitute the word *someone* or *something* for a clause in a sentence, it is a noun clause. (They know *what drives me crazy.* They know *something.*)

Words That Introduce Noun Clauses

A noun clause can be introduced by a **subordinating conjunction** or by a **pronoun.** The chart below lists the most common words that introduce noun clauses.

Words Used to Introduce Noun Clauses	
Subordinating conjunctions	that, how, when, where, whether, why
Pronouns	what, whatever, who, whom, whoever, whomever, which, whichever

How much brothers and sisters argue depends on their ages.

You usually argue most with whoever is closest to your age.

Sometimes the introductory word in a noun clause is omitted. However, you can still substitute *someone* or *something* for the clause to determine whether it is a noun clause.

Most experts say (that) many brothers and sisters become close later in life.

Most experts say something.

2 Why It Matters in Writing

Sometimes a one-word noun won't do. You may need a noun clause to explain something. Notice the difference in the following two paragraphs.

STUDENT MODEL

DRAFT

How children have been raised may depend on the **year**. In the late 1920s, Dr. John B. Watson, a famous psychologist, advised **people** to withhold affection from their children. **This** didn't work. The reason is obvious. Parents found it too hard to follow.

REVISION

How children have been raised may depend on **when they were born**. In the late 1920s, Dr. John B. Watson, a famous psychologist, advised **whichever parents would listen** to withhold affection from their children. **Why this advice didn't work** is obvious. Parents found it too hard to follow.

CLAUSES

3 Practice and Apply

A. CONCEPT CHECK: Noun Clauses

Write the noun clause in each sentence. Then indicate whether it functions as a subject (S), direct object (DO), indirect object (IO), predicate nominative (PN), or object of a preposition (OP).

Are You the Oldest, Middle, or Youngest Child?

1. That birth order influences personality is an intriguing idea.
2. Some evidence shows that first-born children tend to be more conservative and traditional.
3. Yet this fact doesn't explain why many of the greatest inventors are first-born children.
4. Whichever child is born in the middle may become a good negotiator.
5. These negotiating skills could be useful in whatever career the person chooses later.
6. Why the youngest ones are usually risk takers is not hard to understand.
7. Parents may give whoever is the youngest more freedom.

8. Therefore, how parents treat each child also strongly influences personality.
9. People's self-images should not be defined by what some experts say about birth order.
10. Regardless of birth order, people can be whoever they want to be.

➜ **For a SELF-CHECK and more practice, see the EXERCISE BANK, p. 595.**

B. REVISING: Using Noun Clauses

Replace the underlined word in each sentence in the first column with an appropriate noun clause from the second column.

Are You an Only Child?

1. Recent studies show <u>something.</u>
2. For example, <u>someone</u> has his or her parents' undivided love and attention.
3. Also, they don't have to defend their possessions against siblings, so they often discover <u>something</u>.
4. They may have a larger vocabulary depending on <u>something</u>.
5. <u>Someone</u> may dispel the myth that an only child is spoiled.

a. that it's easier to share with others
b. whichever expert you read
c. how much they talk with adults
d. that being an only child has its advantages
e. whoever is an only child

C. WRITING

Have you ever felt like Jason in the cartoon? Write a paragraph about a time when you did something to be accepted by a relative or friend. Use noun clauses in two of your sentences.

Example: *What I did* embarrasses me now. I was convinced *that my parents liked Jeff better*. I decided *that if I learned magic tricks,* I would get their attention.

Foxtrot by Bill Amend

Sentence Structure

Here's the Idea

The structure of a sentence is determined by the number and kind of clauses it contains. Sentences are classified as simple, compound, complex, and compound-complex.

Simple Sentences

A simple sentence consists of one independent clause and no subordinate clauses.

Most TV family shows idealize family life.

A simple sentence may contain a compound subject, a compound verb, and one or more phrases.

COMPOUND SUBJECT

***Leave It to Beaver* and *Father Knows Best* were examples of the "ideal" American family.**

PHRASE

According to TV, parents could understand and solve almost any problem.

SUBJECT COMPOUND VERB

Compound Sentences

A compound sentence consists of two or more independent clauses joined together.

INDEPENDENT CLAUSE INDEPENDENT CLAUSE

The TV father worked, and the TV mother stayed at home with the TV children.

Independent clauses can be joined with a comma and coordinating conjunction, a semicolon, or a semicolon and a comma with a conjunctive adverb.

TV families often owned dogs, but you rarely saw a cat.

Housekeepers were family too; they often gave wise advice.

In 1968, viewers saw their first African-American family *(Julia)* on TV; however, the stories were like those on *Father Knows Best.*

For more on coordinating conjunctions and conjunctive adverbs, see pp. 26–27.

WATCH OUT

Don't use a comma to join two independent clauses. This error—a comma splice—creates a run-on sentence.

CLAUSES

Complex Sentences

A **complex sentence** consists of one independent clause and one or more subordinate clauses.

INDEPENDENT CLAUSE

A 1970s sitcom called *The Brady Bunch* featured a blended family that consisted of two of the original parents, three girls, and three boys. SUBORDINATE CLAUSE

SUBORDINATE CLAUSE

Although it was not as popular as other programs at the time, the show went on to become an enduring classic.

INDEPENDENT CLAUSE

Compound-Complex Sentences

A **compound-complex sentence** consists of two or more independent clauses and one or more subordinate clauses.

INDEPENDENT CLAUSE

On January 12, 1971, *All in the Family* appeared on TV, and audiences saw a show that changed the course of TV comedy. SUBORDINATE CLAUSE

INDEPENDENT CLAUSE SUBORDINATE CLAUSE

Each week the show broke new ground, and, as the actors tackled one sensitive subject after another, the show quickly became the number one program on television.

INDEPENDENT CLAUSE

CHAPTER 4

2 Why It Matters in Writing

Using different sentence structures will help you clarify the relationships between your ideas and add variety to your writing.

STUDENT MODEL

DRAFT

Other black characters had been on TV. *The Jeffersons* was the first show about an affluent black family. The show was a spin-off from *All in the Family.* The show lasted nearly ten years.

REVISION

Although other black characters had been on TV, *The Jeffersons* was the first show about an affluent black family. The show, **which was a spinoff from *All in the Family,*** lasted nearly ten years.

3 Practice and Apply

A. CONCEPT CHECK: Sentence Structure

Identify each sentence as simple (SS), compound (CD), complex (CX), or compound-complex (CC).

Breaking TV Family Taboos

1. Television once had strict codes for family sitcoms.
2. Networks didn't want to offend their viewers, and they had a long list of topics to avoid.
3. *All in the Family* broke most of the TV taboos in its eight years.
4. The show was the first sitcom to deal with topics that previous shows had ignored.
5. For the first time, audiences heard a toilet flush on a sitcom!
6. Archie and Edith Bunker became household names, and the show made stars out of actors Carroll O'Connor and Jean Stapleton.
7. Shows based on minor characters were also hits, which made *All in the Family* even more famous
8. The show opened doors for other sitcoms; in fact, when *The Simpsons* aired, critics called it a cartoon *All in the Family.*
9. Homer, the father on *The Simpsons,* acts like Archie, but Homer is better at avoiding work.
10. When *The Simpsons* tackles a subject, it spares no one.

➜ **For a SELF-CHECK and more practice, see the EXERCISE BANK, p. 596.**

B. REVISING: Using Sentence Variety

Rewrite this paragraph by following the directions below it.

The Brady Bunch: From the 1970s to the 1990s

(1) *The Brady Bunch Movie* shows how out of place the Brady family is in the 1990s. **(2)** They are stuck in the 1970s. **(3)** The family has sack races on the lawn. **(4)** They still wear polyester clothes. **(5)** Middle sister Jan plots to make older sister Marcia look ugly. **(6)** Marcia always remains beautiful. **(7)** The Bradys' neighbor hates them. **(8)** He tries to force them to move. **(9)** The Bradys raise enough money to save their home.

1. Combine sentences 1 and 2 to form a complex sentence by turning sentence 2 into a subordinate clause.
2. Combine sentences 3 and 4 to form a compound sentence.
3. Combine sentences 5 and 6 to form a complex sentence by turning sentence 5 into a subordinate clause.
4. Combine sentences 7, 8, 9 to form a compound-complex sentence, turning sentence 7 into a subordinate clause.

Sentence Diagramming

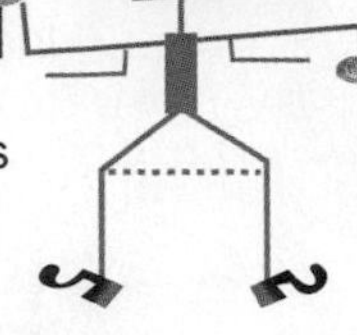

Watch me for diagramming tips!

Here's the Idea

Diagramming is a way to represent visually the parts of a sentence. It can help you understand the sentence structure by showing how the words and clauses in a sentence are related.

Simple Sentences

Simple sentences are diagrammed on one horizontal line, with a vertical line separating subject and predicate. The horizontal line may be split on either side to show a compound subject or a compound verb.

For more on diagramming simple sentences, see pp. 54–56.

Compound Sentences

- Diagram the independent clauses on parallel horizontal lines.
- Connect the verbs in the two clauses by a broken line with a step.

Most children live in nuclear families, but many have extended families too.

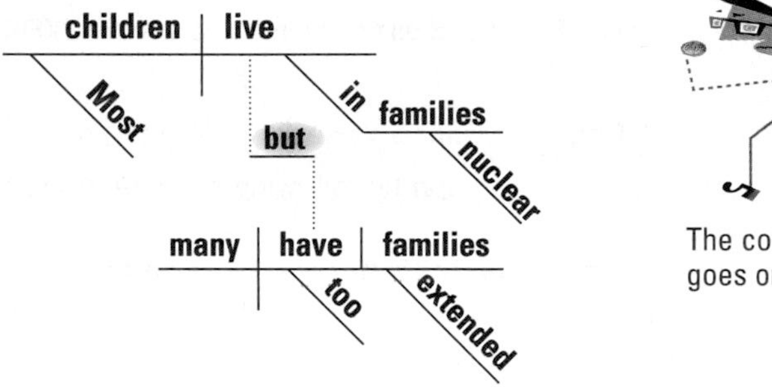

The conjunction goes on the step.

A. CONCEPT CHECK: Simple and Compound Sentences

Diagram these sentences, using what you have learned. For additional help, see pages 54–56.

Family Matters

1. American families have changed over the years.
2. The Census Bureau documents these changes, and it publishes them.
3. The bureau counts a sample population each month, but it tries to count every resident every ten years.

CHAPTER 4

Complex Sentences

Adjective and Adverb Clauses

- Diagram the subordinate clause on its own horizontal line below the main line, as if it were a sentence.
- Use a dotted line to connect the word introducing the clause to the word it modifies.

Adjective Clause Introduced by a Relative Pronoun

The relatives who live with you are your nuclear family.

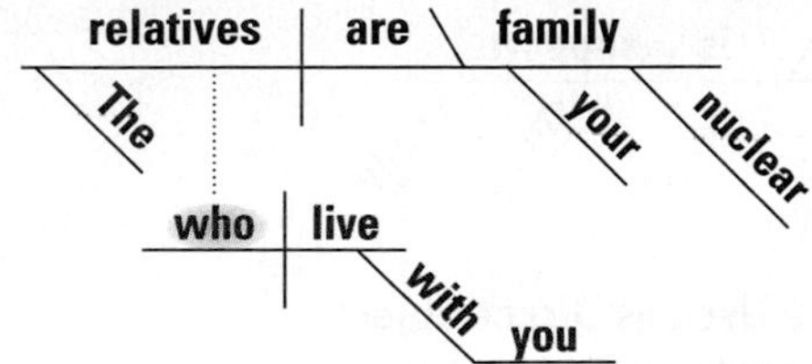

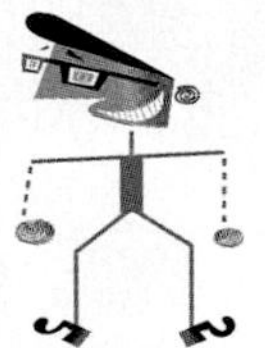

Here, the pronoun introducing the clause is the subject of the clause.

Adjective Clause Introduced by a Relative Adverb

Other relatives may live in the town where you were born.

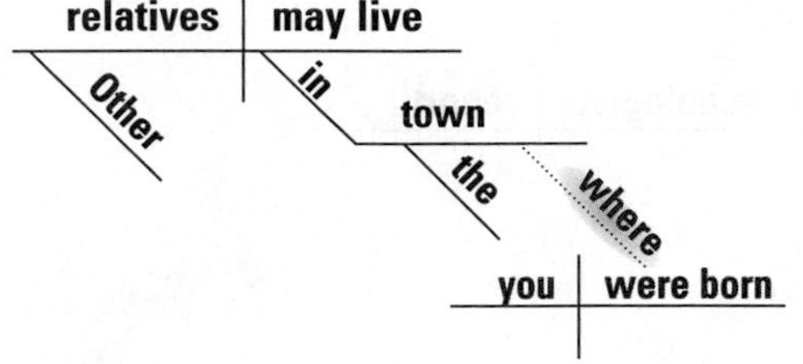

The adverb introducing the clause goes on the dotted line.

Adverb Clause

Because people move so often, families are more scattered.

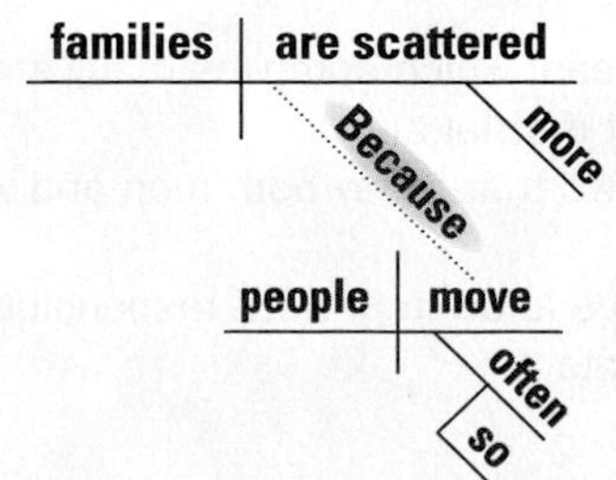

The conjunction goes on the dotted line connecting the verbs in the clauses.

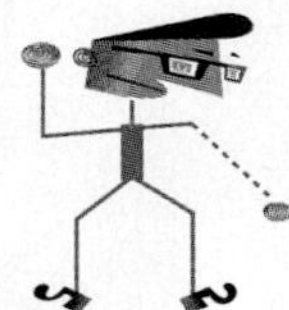

CLAUSES

Noun Clauses

- Diagram the subordinate clause on a separate line that is attached to the main line with a forked line.
- Place the forked line in the diagram according to the role of the noun clause in the sentence.
- Diagram the word introducing the noun clause according to its function in the clause.

Noun Clause Used as Subject

What teenagers need is strong family support.

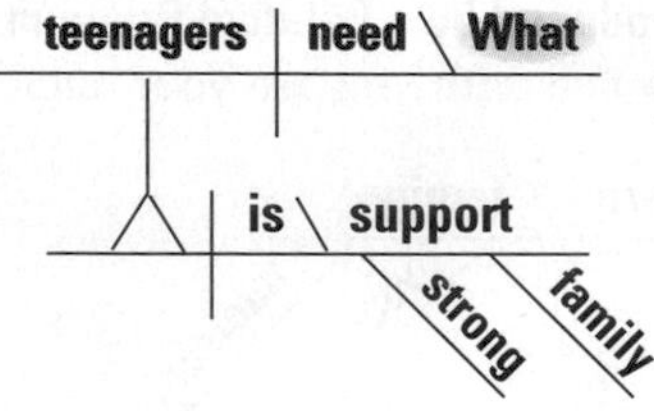

Here, the pronoun introducing the clause functions as a direct object in the clause.

Noun Clause Used as Direct Object

Psychologists report that families handle stress differently.

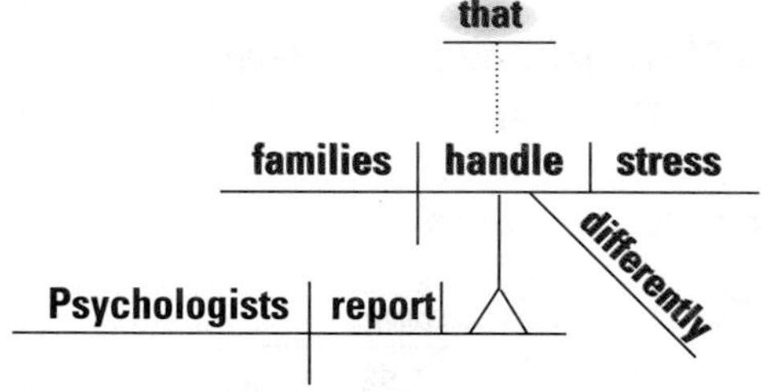

Here, the word introducing the clause is a subordinating conjunction.

CHAPTER 4

B. CONCEPT CHECK: Complex Sentences

Diagram these sentences, using what you have learned.

Wedding Bell Blues

1. The Census Bureau, which compiles many statistics, records people's ages at marriage.
2. The census shows that today both men and women are marrying later.
3. Because marriage is an important responsibility, people shouldn't rush into it.

Compound-Complex Sentences

- Diagram the independent clauses first.
- Attach each subordinate clause to the word it modifies.

Because families are so scattered, many people use e-mail, and grandparents also use computers!

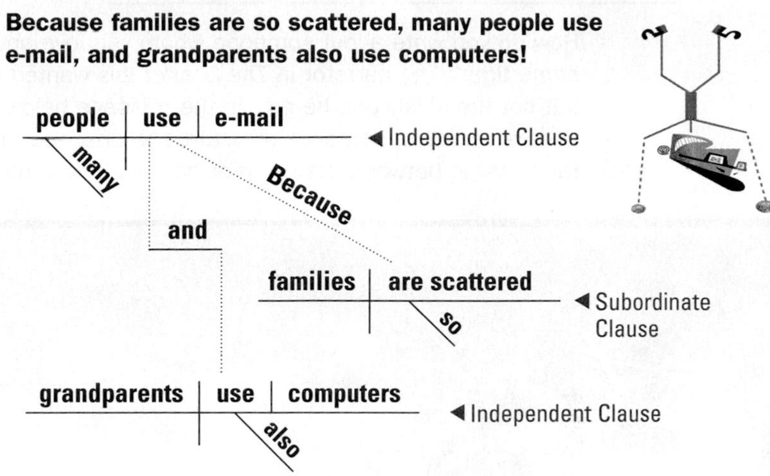

C. CONCEPT CHECK: Compound-Complex Sentences

Diagram these sentences, using what you have learned.

Marry Sooner or Later?

1. Once, a woman married when she was twenty, and she started a family immediately.
2. Attitudes have changed, and today a woman is nearly twenty-five when she first marries.
3. Because they have more choices, many women delay marriage, but most still want a family.

D. MIXED REVIEW: Diagramming

Diagram the following sentences. Look for different types of clauses.

1. Blended families, which include children from each parent's previous marriage, are more common now.
2. When two families merge, the children acquire new siblings.
3. Whether such families are happy depends on how well everyone cooperates.

Grammar in Literature

Sentence Structure and Vivid Writing

How do you write about someone whom you love and resent at the same time? The narrator in *The Scarlet Ibis* wanted a brother—but not the sickly one he got. In the passage below, James Hurst uses a variety of sentence structures to describe the complex relationship between the narrator and his little brother Doodle.

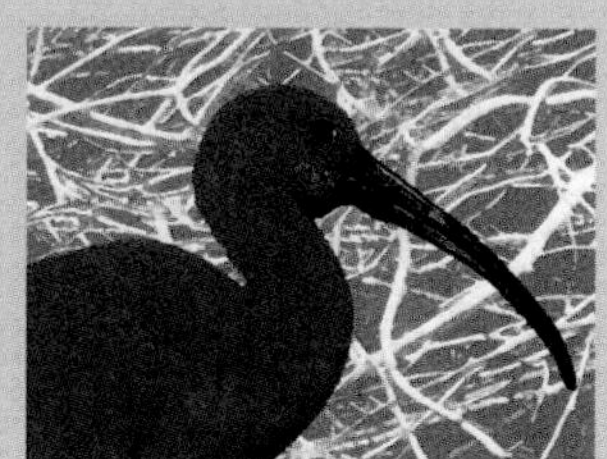

The Scarlet Ibis

James Hurst

Although Doodle learned to crawl, he showed no signs of walking, but he wasn't idle. He talked so much that we all quit listening to what he said. It was about this time that Daddy built him a go-cart and I had to pull him around. At first I just paraded him up and down the piazza, but then he started crying to be taken into the yard, and it ended up by my having to lug him wherever I went. If I so much as picked up my cap, he'd start crying to go with me, and Mama would call from wherever she was, "Take Doodle with you."

He was a burden in many ways. The doctor had said that he mustn't get too excited, too hot, too cold, or too tired and that he must always be treated gently. A long list of don'ts went with him, all of which I ignored once we got out of the house. To discourage his coming with me, I'd run with him across the ends of the cotton rows and careen him around corners on two wheels. Sometimes I accidentally turned him over, but he never told Mama.

Compound-complex sentence contrasts Doodle's disability with his determination.

Compound-complex sentence with **adverb clause** shows Doodle becoming his brother's burden.

Simple sentence bluntly states the narrator's feelings.

Subordinate clauses explain the "burden" in more detail.

Compound sentence contrasts the narrator's roughness with Doodle's loyalty.

Your sentences do more for your writing if you vary their structure.

Revising to Vary Sentence Structure	
Letting an independent clause stand alone	Use simple sentences to focus on a single idea, describe a series of actions, or create a quick, choppy rhythm.
Combining independent clauses	When you need to connect similar or contrasting ideas of equal importance and create a more fluid rhythm, use compound sentences.
Adding subordinate clauses	When you want to build momentum, add details, or show relationships between ideas, use these clauses to form complex or compound-complex sentences.

PRACTICE AND APPLY: Revising Sentence Structure

The paragraph below consists entirely of simple sentences. To improve its clarity and style, try rewriting it, varying the sentence structures. Follow the directions below. After you finish, you might want to try different ways of revising some of the sentences.

(1) Tracing your family tree can be more than just fun. **(2)** It might also help save your life. **(3)** Some serious conditions may be inherited. **(4)** These include diabetes, high blood pressure, cancer, and sickle cell anemia. **(5)** People need to know the facts. **(6)** They may be at risk for these diseases. **(7)** Family documents include medical records. **(8)** These records can show causes of death. **(9)** You know about your family's medical history. **(10)** It can help you safeguard your own health.

1. Combine sentences 1 and 2 to form a compound sentence.
2. Combine sentences 3 and 4 by changing sentence 4 into an adjective clause modifying *conditions.*
3. Combine sentences 5 and 6 by changing sentence 6 into an adverb clause.
4. Combine sentences 7 and 8 by changing sentence 8 into an adjective clause.
5. Combine sentences 9 and 10 by changing sentence 9 into a noun clause.

Choose a draft from your **Working Portfolio,** and revise it by combining sentences in at least three of the ways suggested above.

CLAUSES

Mixed Review

A. Types of Clauses In the sentences below, identify each underlined subordinate clause as an adjective clause, adverb clause, or noun clause.

(1) People of all ages are learning how they can research their family history. **(2)** Whoever has Chinese ancestry may have a more difficult time finding family names, however. **(3)** Because Asian immigration was restricted from 1882 to 1965, many Chinese adopted the names of Chinese families already here. **(4)** An Internet Web site now helps people search cemetery records that might give their ancestors' true names. **(5)** One educator, Albert Cheng, who traced his family back 2,800 years, has helped Chinese-American teenagers find their ancestral villages in China.

B. Kinds of Clauses and Sentence Structure Read the passage. Then write the answers to the questions that follow it.

LITERARY MODEL

(1) Here was a flesh and blood man [poet Walt Whitman], belching and laughing and sweating in poems. **(2)** "Who touches this book touches a man."

(3) That night, at last, I started to write, recklessly, three, five pages, looking up once only to see my father passing by the hall on tiptoe. **(4)** When I was done, I read over my words, and my eyes filled. **(5)** I finally sounded like myself in English!

(6) As soon as I had finished that first draft, I called my mother to my room. **(7)** She listened attentively, as she had to my father's speech, and in the end, her eyes were glistening too. **(8)** Her face was soft and warm and proud. **(9)** "That is a beautiful, beautiful speech, Cukita. **(10)** I want for your father to hear it before he goes to sleep."

—Julia Alvarez, "Daughter of Invention"

1. Is this sentence simple, compound, or complex?
2. What is the function of the noun clause in this sentence?
3. Is this sentence simple, compound, or compound-complex?
4. What verb does the clause "When I was done" modify?
5. Is this sentence simple, compound, or complex?
6. Is this sentence simple, complex, or compound-complex?
7. Is the subordinate clause an adjective, adverb, or noun clause?
8. How would you combine sentence 8 with this sentence: "I looked at my mother's face"?
9. Is this sentence simple, complex, or compound-complex?
10. What is the independent clause in this sentence?

Mastery Test: What Did You Learn?

Choose the letter of the term that identifies each numbered part of this passage.

Many people who attend rock concerts (1) in the Los Angeles area are amazed by one performer, Eloise Baugh. The 83-year-old grandmother introduces the main acts by break dancing and singing rap music. (2) She looks like the main act when she performs (3). She spins on the floor to wild applause; she springs to her feet and hears the crowd roar. (4) That a woman in her 80s can break dance (5) astounds younger people. She usually gives whoever sits in the first row (6) a few "Break Dancin' Grannie" T-shirts. Eloise also writes many of her own rap lyrics, although her granddaughter helps her to select the music. (7) She credits break dancing, which is vigorous exercise (8), for keeping her limber. Whatever else Eloise may do (9), she has proved that "old" doesn't mean "slow." (10)

1. A. adjective clause
   B. adverb clause
   C. independent clause
   D. noun clause

2. A. simple sentence
   B. compound sentence
   C. complex sentence
   D. compound-complex sentence

3. A. nonessential clause
   B. noun clause
   C. essential clause
   D. adverb clause

4. A. simple sentence
   B. compound sentence
   C. complex sentence
   D. compound-complex sentence

5. A. noun clause as predicate nominative
   B. noun clause as subject
   C. noun clause as direct object
   D. noun clause as predicate adjective

6. A. noun clause as subject
   B. nonessential clause
   C. noun clause as indirect object
   D. essential clause

7. A. simple sentence
   B. compound sentence
   C. complex sentence
   D. compound-complex sentence

8. A. independent clause
   B. noun clause as subject
   C. nonessential clause
   D. adverb clause

9. A. subordinate clause
   B. nonessential clause
   C. independent clause
   D. essential clause

10. A. adjective clause
    B. adverb clause
    C. noun clause as predicate nominative
    D. noun clause as direct object

Student Help Desk

Clauses and Sentence Structure at a Glance

A clause is a group of words that contains a subject and a verb. Clauses may be either independent or subordinate. An independent clause can stand alone or be combined with other independent and subordinate clauses.

SIMPLE SENTENCE = independent clause

COMPOUND SENTENCE = independent clause + independent clause(s)

COMPLEX SENTENCE = independent clause + subordinate clause(s)

COMPOUND-COMPLEX SENTENCE = independent clause + independent clause(s) + subordinate clause(s)

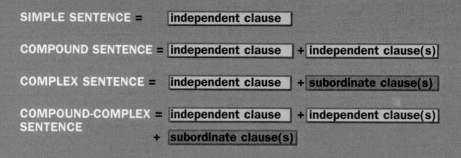

CHAPTER 4

Ties That Bind

Punctuating Clauses

Use a Comma	Example
to join independent clauses with a coordinating conjunction	I am older than my brother**, but** I'm younger than my nephew.
after subordinate clauses that begin a sentence	When I was born**,** my sister's son Jim was four years old.
to set off nonessential adjective clauses	My brother**,** who was born after me**,** is his uncle.
Use a Semicolon	
to join independent clauses without a conjunction	Jim teases me all the time**;** he calls me "old auntie."
Use a Semicolon and a Comma	
to join independent clauses with a conjunctive adverb	People think we're unusual**;** actually**,** we are a little odd.

Subordinate Clauses It's All Relative

Kind of Clause	Function	Example
Adjective clause	Modifies a noun or pronoun	Her family has a coat of arms, **which features a gold lion.**
Adverb clause	Modifies a verb, adjective, or adverb	**When her cousins visited,** she showed it to them.
Noun clause	Acts as a subject, complement, or object of a preposition	She told them **that the lion stands for loyalty.**

Sentence Structure The Variety Show

Kind of Sentence	Structure	Example
Simple sentence	one independent clause	A coat of arms is fascinating.
Compound sentence	two or more independent clauses	It has many symbols, and each one means something.
Complex sentence	one independent clause and one or more subordinate clauses	When a sword appears, it may represent the family's service to the king.
Compound-complex sentence	one or more independent clauses and one or more subordinate clauses	The symbols look complex, but they make sense after you decode them.

CLAUSES

The Bottom Line

Checklist for Clauses and Sentence Structure

Can I improve my writing by . . .

____ making sure that every sentence contains at least one independent clause?

____ using subordinate clauses for details or supporting ideas?

____ combining some simple sentences to avoid repetition or to show relationships between ideas?

____ varying sentence structure?

Writing Complete Sentences

La Cucina Italiana
This restaurant anything but traditional.
Opened in 1996 by Marcelo and Theresa Cellini. Crowds of all ages will enjoy the virtual tour of Italy the tour takes you through
- the romantic city of Venice
- the architecture of Rome
- the busy streets of Florence

After you have walked through the lifelike scenes. Can relax and enjoy an authentic taste of Italian cuisine. Do not pass up any of the pizza creations they offer a taste of Italy you'll want to savor until your next visit. The service excellent in this trendy restaurant

Theme: The Story of Food

Food for Thought

If you were looking for a good place to eat, would this reviewer's notes be helpful? The restaurant sounds great, but if you read closely, you may start to feel confused. Notice how some of the sentences seem to be missing information while others are long and lack coherence.

When you take notes, it's all right to use incomplete sentences or long, rambling sentences. When you write for an audience, however, you should construct sentences that clearly communicate your ideas.

Write Away: Savor the Flavor
Write a paragraph about a combination of foods you've experimented with or would like to create. Save your paragraph in your **Writing Portfolio.**

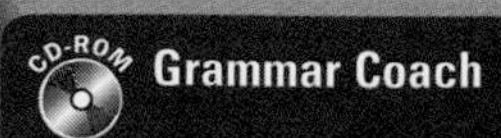

Diagnostic Test: What Do You Know?

For each numbered item, choose the best way to write the underlined section.

Pizza has a long and colorful history that traces back to ancient Rome. Surprisingly, tomatoes a regular ingredient only in the late 1800s. (1) According to legend. The tomato-based pizza got its start in 1889. (2) Then a baker in Naples created a pizza topped with tomatoes, mozzarella cheese, and basil leaves to present to Italy's Queen Margherita. The red, white, and green pizza displayed the colors of the Italian flag and was named Pizza Margherita in honor of the popular monarch.

The first pizza restaurant, or pizzeria, in the United States opened in New York City in 1905. (3) The next milestone in the history of pizza occurred after World War II. Men and women who had acquired a taste for pizza while they were serving in Europe returned home. They continued to eat pizza pizza sales soared. (4) Today pizza is still popular, more than 4 billion fresh pizzas are sold yearly. (5)

1. A. Surprisingly, tomatoes became a regular ingredient. Only in the late 1800s.
   B. Surprisingly, tomatoes a regular ingredient. Only in the late 1800s.
   C. Surprisingly, tomatoes became a regular ingredient only in the late 1800s.
   D. Correct as is

2. A. According to legend, the tomato-based pizza got its start in 1889.
   B. According to legend, the tomato-based pizza its start in 1889.
   C. According to legend, the tomato-based pizza got its start. In 1889.
   D. Correct as is

3. A. The first pizza restaurant, or pizzeria; in the United States opened in New York City in 1905.
   B. The first pizza restaurant, or pizzeria, in the United States in New York City in 1905.
   C. The first pizza restaurant in New York City in 1905.
   D. Correct as is

4. A. They continued to eat pizza sales soared.
   B. They continued to eat pizza. Pizza sales soared.
   C. They continued to eat pizza, pizza sales soared.
   D. Correct as is

5. A. Today pizza is still popular more than 4 billion sold.
   B. Today pizza is still popular 4 billion fresh pizzas are sold yearly.
   C. Today pizza is still popular. More than 4 billion are sold yearly.
   D. Correct as is

SENTENCES

Sentence Fragments

❶ Here's the Idea

▶ **A sentence fragment is part of a sentence that is punctuated as if it were a complete sentence.**

Fragments Caused by Missing Parts

Sometimes a sentence fragment does not express a complete thought because the subject or the verb is left out.

FRAGMENT **In 1853, Native American George Crum served his version of French fries at Moon Lake Lodge. Soon thereafter faced a guest's disapproval.**

Fragment lacks a subject.

SENTENCE **In 1853, Native American George Crum served his version of French fries at Moon Lake Lodge. Soon thereafter he faced a guest's disapproval.**

FRAGMENT **Chef Crum angered by the rejection. Eventually, he created the potato chip.**

Fragment lacks a complete verb.

SENTENCE **Chef Crum was angered by the rejection. Eventually, he created the potato chip.**

Sometimes when writers rush to get several ideas on paper, they not only forget to use subjects or verbs, but they also make punctuation errors that result in sentence fragments. Notice how the writer corrected this error in the following model.

STUDENT MODEL

George Washington Carver created more than 300 products. Which included peanut butter and peanut-butter cookies, from the peanut.

Phrases as Fragments

A **phrase** is a group of words that functions as a part of speech and does not have a subject or a verb. A phrase that stands alone is a fragment.

FRAGMENT **The pretzel has a long and interesting history. Dating back to A.D. 610.**

SENTENCE **The pretzel has a long and interesting history dating back to A.D. 610.**

Participial phrase combined with previous sentence

FRAGMENT **Popular folklore suggests that the pretzel was created. By a medieval Italian monk to reward children.**

SENTENCE **Popular folklore suggests that the pretzel was created by a medieval Italian monk to reward children.**

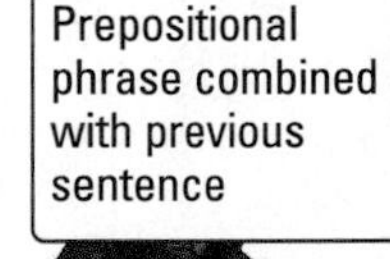

Prepositional phrase combined with previous sentence

FRAGMENT **He shaped the pretzel in the image of children's folded arms in prayer. To motivate them to memorize their prayers.**

SENTENCE **He shaped the pretzel in the image of children's folded arms in prayer to motivate them to memorize their prayers.**

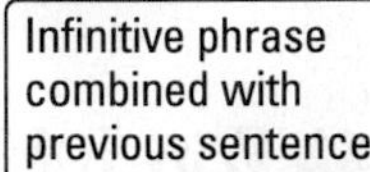

Infinitive phrase combined with previous sentence

Sentence fragments often are used in fiction and in advertisements for emphasis or effect. Don't use fragments in your compositions. Readers might not recognize these fragments as intentional.

For more on phrases, see pp. 66–77.

Subordinate Clauses as Fragments

A **clause** is a group of words that contains a subject and a verb. A clause that cannot stand alone as a sentence is a subordinate, or dependent, clause. Fragments often occur because a subordinate clause is mistaken for a complete sentence.

FRAGMENT **Earl Charles Grey helped abolish slavery throughout the British Empire. Although he is better known for Earl Grey tea.**

SENTENCE **Earl Charles Grey helped abolish slavery throughout the British Empire, although he is better known for Earl Grey tea.**

Clause is combined with the previous sentence.

FRAGMENT **After a British diplomat saved the life of a Chinese government official. The earl received the recipe for the tea as a gift.**

SENTENCE **After a British diplomat saved the life of a Chinese government official, the earl received the recipe for the tea as a gift.**

Subordinate clause is combined with the independent clause.

For more on subordinate clauses, see pp. 92–93.

2 Why It Matters in Writing

If you use a sentence fragment when you speak, your gestures and facial expressions can help convey its meaning. When you write, the reader can't ask you to provide more details, so every sentence has to express a complete thought.

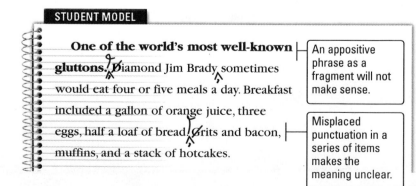

STUDENT MODEL

One of the world's most well-known gluttons. Diamond Jim Brady sometimes would eat four or five meals a day. Breakfast included a gallon of orange juice, three eggs, half a loaf of bread. Grits and bacon, muffins, and a stack of hotcakes.

An appositive phrase as a fragment will not make sense.

Misplaced punctuation in a series of items makes the meaning unclear.

3 Practice and Apply

A. CONCEPT CHECK: Sentence Fragments

Rewrite the numbered fragments as complete sentences. You may add words to the fragments or combine them with sentences.

Rising to Any Occasion

(1) Have been baking bread since prehistoric times. About 4,600 years ago, bakers in Egypt learned how to use yeast. **(2) To make bread rise.** Before that, people made various kinds of breads. **(3) By baking mixtures of water and ground grain on heated stones. (4) Because breads contained no leavening agents.** They did not rise. Today most cultures have their own traditional breads. **(5) Examples of flatbreads from around the world the Mexican tortilla, the Indian chapati, and the Ethiopian injera.** Many cultures serve yeast-risen bread. **(6) Including the Russian black bread and the Danish sourdough bread.** French bakeries make and sell baguettes. **(7) Which are long, thin loaves of white bread with crisp brown crusts.** In Mexico, bakers make a special bread called fiesta bread. **(8) And hide small ornaments within it.** Be sure to check out the selection of breads. **(9) If you find yourself at a large international food market. (10) Won't regret it!**

For a SELF-CHECK and more practice, see the EXERCISE BANK, p. 597.

B. REVISING: Fixing Incomplete Sentences

Rewrite the five fragments in the paragraph below as complete sentences by adding words or combining the fragments with sentences.

A Tasty History

Like corn, the potato, and the tomato. Chocolate originated in the Americas and went on to have a tremendous impact on other parts of the world. Is made from the bean of the cacao tree. The Aztecs used the beans as currency and also roasted and ground them. To make a rich, frothy drink. After the Spanish conquered the Aztec empire in the early 1500s. Chocolate eventually became hugely popular in Europe. The modern chocolate industry was born in 1828. When a Dutch invention revolutionized the processing of cacao beans. People tasted the rich, dark candy, and their craving for chocolate continued to grow! Today, of course, the production of chocolate is a huge international industry.

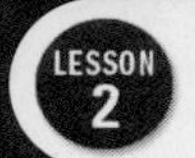

Run-On Sentences

1 Here's the Idea

▶ **A run-on sentence is two or more sentences written as though they were one sentence.**

The Comma Splice

A **comma splice,** or comma fault, occurs when the writer mistakenly uses a comma instead of a semicolon or period.

STUDENT MODEL

For generations, people have enjoyed the ever-popular ice cream as a dessert, historical records show that ice cream was invented by the Chinese around 2000 B.C.

Missing Punctuation or Conjunction

Joining two sentences together without a comma and a conjunction, or without a semicolon, can confuse the reader.

STUDENT MODEL

Historians believe that the Chinese included overcooked rice, milk, and spices in their recipe no one is sure how the recipe spread to Europe.

Separate independent clauses with a period or a semicolon.

2 Why It Matters in Writing

Run-on sentences can cause confusion—and a headache. Your reader can't tell where one idea ends and another begins.

STUDENT MODEL

One popular myth credits Marco Polo with the discovery of this heavenly dessert, yet another tells how a Tuscan confectioner introduced Italians to ice milk and fruit ice.

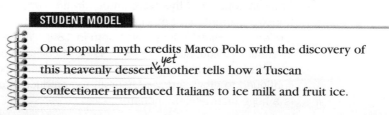

3 Practice and Apply

A. CONCEPT CHECK: Run-On Sentences

Correct the run-ons below. There may be more than one way to fix each run-on. If a sentence is not a run-on, write *Correct.*

Famous Names in Food

1. Julia Child originally had not prepared for a career in the food industry, in fact, she majored in history in college.
2. During World War II, Child served with a secret intelligence agency her assignments took her around the world.
3. After the war, she took courses at a cooking school in Paris there she met two chefs with whom she wrote the book *Mastering the Art of French Cooking.*
4. The book paved the way for Child's television series *The French Chef* eventually Child became a star in the world of cooking.
5. On her show Julia Child shared recipes, demonstrated cooking techniques, and offered good-humored advice.
6. Paul Newman became famous as a movie actor now he is also known for a line of food products.
7. Newman's food company is somewhat unusual, its after-tax profits are donated to educational and charitable causes.
8. The company began on a small scale Newman and writer A. E. Hotchner decided to market the actor's homemade salad dressing.
9. At first they sold the dressing only locally soon orders were pouring in from all over the country.
10. The company so far has donated more than $100 million to the American Red Cross and many other not-for-profit organizations.

➜ **For a SELF-CHECK and more practice, see the EXERCISE BANK, p. 597.**

B. EDITING: Spotting Incorrect Sentences

Reread the reviewer's notes on page 114. Then locate and revise the six fragment and run-on errors. The first one is done for you here.

Fragment: This restaurant anything but traditional.

Revision: This restaurant is anything but traditional.

Real World Grammar

Science Report

Sometimes when you write a paper from notes you have made, you may accidentally use sentence fragments. Whenever you translate notes into more formal writing, remember to check your work for possible fragments.

This edible dish is prepared with fried grasshoppers.

Niabe Gunther
Science 104
2nd Period

Insects as Food for the Future

If you lived in a land where meat was rare, would you eat a fat, juicy spider instead? Many people in Eastern Europe, Asia, Africa, and Latin America wouldn't think twice about it, in these protein-poor regions, insects are a regular part of a daily diet. Only in the Western world do people shudder at the idea of eating insects. bugs as nasty pests. Insects, however, may well become the food of the future. And for good reasons.

Insects are not only among the most plentiful forms of life on earth, they are some of the most nutritious as well in fact, nature's "perfect food." As the table below shows, some popular insect snacks are high in protein, calcium, and iron and lower in fat than lean red meat.

Fix these fragments.

This is really confusing! Fix run-on.

Nutritional Value of Various Insects (per 100 grams)

Insect	Protein (g)	Fat (g)	Carbs (g)	Calcium (mg)	Iron (mg)
Giant Water Beetle	19.8	8.3	2.1	43.5	13.6
Cricket	12.9	5.5	5.1	75.8	9.5
Small Grasshopper	20.6	6.1	3.9	35.2	5.0
Beef (86% lean ground)	25.3	14.0	NA	NA	2.3

Source: *The Food Insects Newsletter,* July 1996 (Vol. 9, No. 2, ed. by Florence V. Dunkel, Montana State University); *Bugs in the System,* by May Berenbaum; and *USDA Handbook,* 8–13, 1990.

CHAPTER 5

REVISED MODEL

If you lived in a land where meat was rare, would you eat a fat, juicy spider instead? Many people in Eastern Europe, Asia, Africa, and Latin America wouldn't think twice about it. In these protein-poor regions, insects are a regular part of a daily diet. Only in the Western world do people shudder at the idea of eating insects, because here bugs are regarded as nasty pests. Insects, however, may well become the food of the future and for good reasons.

Insects are not only among the most plentiful forms of life on earth, they are some of the most nutritious as well. In fact, they are considered nature's "perfect food."

Now that it contains mealworms, this candied apple treat is packed with protein.

PRACTICE AND APPLY

Suppose you had to correct this passage of Niabe's science report. Use the previous lessons in this chapter to help "debug" her sentences.

STUDENT MODEL

Dry-roasted insects can be used in many ways. For instance, crickets can be substituted. For nuts in cookies, breads, brownies, or crispy treats. Usually, live crickets are stored in the refrigerator for a day or two. Because this slows them down and makes them easier to handle. Then the insects are washed and spread on a baking sheet they are baked at 200° F for one to two hours. Usually the legs, wings, and egg sacs are removed after dry roasting, the insects are then crushed and used in a recipe. Like the popular Chocolate Chirpy Chip Cookies.

Mixed Review

A. Fragments and Run-ons Identify each numbered item as a complete sentence, a fragment, or a run-on. Then revise each incorrect item.

Reading *The Dictionary of American Food and Drink* may bring a few laughs or an upset stomach. **(1) Depending on your mood.** Although it may not be surprising, some food names had comic beginnings. **(2) While others happened by accident. (3) Still others originated from religious, artistic, or geographical terms. (4) For example, Buffalo wings have nothing to do with the buffalo, as a matter of fact, they are deep-fried chicken wings served with a side order of hot sauce and blue-cheese dressing.** In 1964 in Buffalo, New York, Teressa Bellisimmo invented this savory snack. **(5) For her son and his visiting friends. (6) Another example, perhaps one that is enjoyed as a mishap, is the origin of German chocolate cake the original recipe appeared in a Texas newspaper in 1957. (7) The recipe called for Baker's German's Sweet Chocolate, the name *Baker* refers to Dr. James Baker, who helped to finance the first chocolate factory in the United States.** The word *German* had nothing to do with the country. **(8) Because it actually refers to the creator of sweet chocolate, Samuel German. (9) Incidentally, French fries probably aren't French either. (10) They have been traced to Belgium in the 19th century, authorities believe they spread to France some time later.**

CHAPTER 5

B. Editing and Revising Read the e-mail message below. Identify and correct any fragments or run-on sentences.

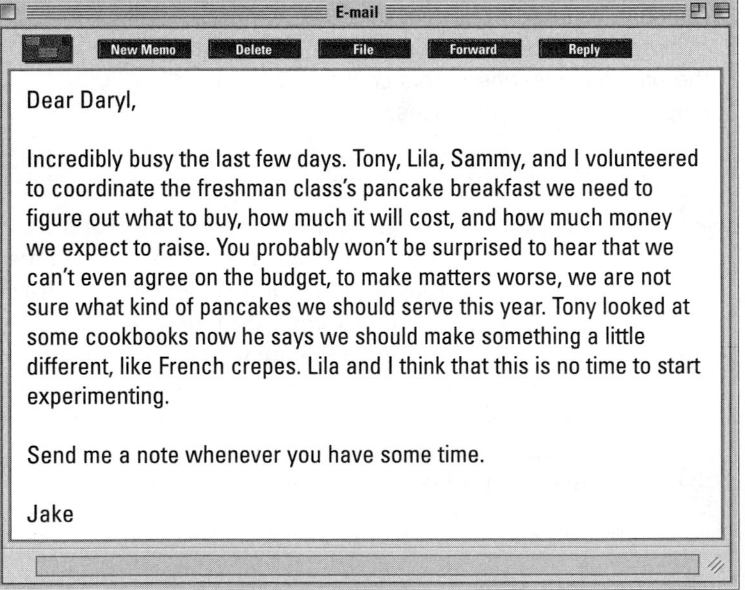

Dear Daryl,

Incredibly busy the last few days. Tony, Lila, Sammy, and I volunteered to coordinate the freshman class's pancake breakfast we need to figure out what to buy, how much it will cost, and how much money we expect to raise. You probably won't be surprised to hear that we can't even agree on the budget, to make matters worse, we are not sure what kind of pancakes we should serve this year. Tony looked at some cookbooks now he says we should make something a little different, like French crepes. Lila and I think that this is no time to start experimenting.

Send me a note whenever you have some time.

Jake

Look at your paragraph from page 114, or another draft from your **Working Portfolio.** Fix any fragments or run-on sentences.

Mastery Test: What Did You Learn?

For each numbered item, choose the best way to write the underlined section.

For centuries, people produced their own sausages and named them after their places of origin. For example, the wiener sausage originated in Vienna, the frankfurter came from Frankfurt. (1) Sometimes, use these names today as alternatives for *hot dog.* (2)

The hot dog can claim Coney Island, New York. As its home. (3) In the early 1890s, Charles Feltman introduced frankfurters, or hot dogs, at this seaside resort. His customers later included Eddie Cantor, a singing waiter, and Jimmy Durante, a piano player. The musicians urged Feltman's delivery boy, Nathan Handwerker. To open his own hot dog stand. (4) His lower-priced, five-cent hot dogs won out over Feltman's. Meanwhile, Cantor and Durante left Coney Island. Both ended up in Hollywood, they became movie stars. (5)

1. A. For example, the wiener sausage originated in Vienna the frankfurter came from Frankfurt.
   B. For example, the wiener sausage originated in Vienna; the frankfurter came from Frankfurt.
   C. For example, the wiener sausage originated. In Vienna, the frankfurter came from Frankfurt.
   D. Correct as is
2. A. Sometimes, people use these names today. As alternatives for *hot dog.*
   B. Sometimes, people use these names today as alternatives for *hot dog.*
   C. Sometimes, people use these names. For the *hot dog.*
   D. Correct as is
3. A. The hot dog can claim. Coney Island, New York, as its home.
   B. The hot dog Coney Island, New York, as its home.
   C. The hot dog can claim Coney Island, New York, as its home.
   D. Correct as is
4. A. The musicians urged Feltman's delivery boy. to open his own hot dog stand.
   B. The musicians urged Feltman's delivery boy. To open his own hot dog stand.
   C. The musicians urged Feltman's delivery boy, Nathan Handwerker, to open his own hot dog stand.
   D. Correct as is
5. A. Both ended up in Hollywood, and they became movie stars.
   B. Both ended up in Hollywood; and became movie stars.
   C. In Hollywood became movie stars.
   D. Correct as is

SENTENCES

Student Help Desk

Fragments and Run-Ons at a Glance

Fragment A part of a sentence that is punctuated as if it were a complete sentence. It cannot stand alone.

Run-On Two or more sentences written as though they were one sentence

Correcting Fragments

Fragment Type	Example	Quick Fix
Missing Subject	Serves more than 15,000 lunches a day.	**The Pentagon** serves more than 15,000 lunches a day.
Missing Verb	A waffle topped with ice cream my favorite breakfast meal.	A waffle topped with ice cream **is** my favorite breakfast meal.
Misplaced Punctuation	For lunch, I can eat two slices of pizza, fries, a hamburger. And a diet soda.	For lunch, I can eat two slices of pizza, fries, a hamburger**, and** a diet soda.
Phrase	It is not healthy to eat. In the middle of the night.	It is not healthy to eat **in** the middle of the night.
Subordinate Clause	If you eat an orange every day. You may avoid getting a cold.	If you eat an orange every day**, you** may avoid getting a cold. **or** You eat an orange every day.

CHAPTER 5

WHEN WILL IT END?

Correcting Run-Ons

Concept	Example	Quick Fix
Comma Splice	Thanksgiving Day meals can include turkey, dressing, potatoes, yams, and pumpkin pie, I usually ask for more.	REPLACE COMMA WITH PERIOD Thanksgiving Day meals can include turkey, dressing, potatoes, yams, and pumpkin pie**.** I usually ask for more.
Missing Conjunction and Punctuation	I dislike most leafy, green vegetables I will eat lettuce.	INSERT COMMA AND CONJUNCTION I dislike most leafy, green vegetables**, but** I will eat lettuce. INSERT SEMICOLON AND CONJUNCTION I dislike most leafy, green vegetables**; however,** I will eat lettuce.

SENTENCES

The Bottom Line

Checklist for Correcting Fragments and Run-Ons

Does each sentence . . .

____ have a subject?

____ have a verb?

____ express a complete thought?

Have I . . .

____ avoided a run-on sentence by adding a conjunction and a comma or a semicolon or a period?

____ corrected any comma splices with a semicolon or a period?

Using Verbs

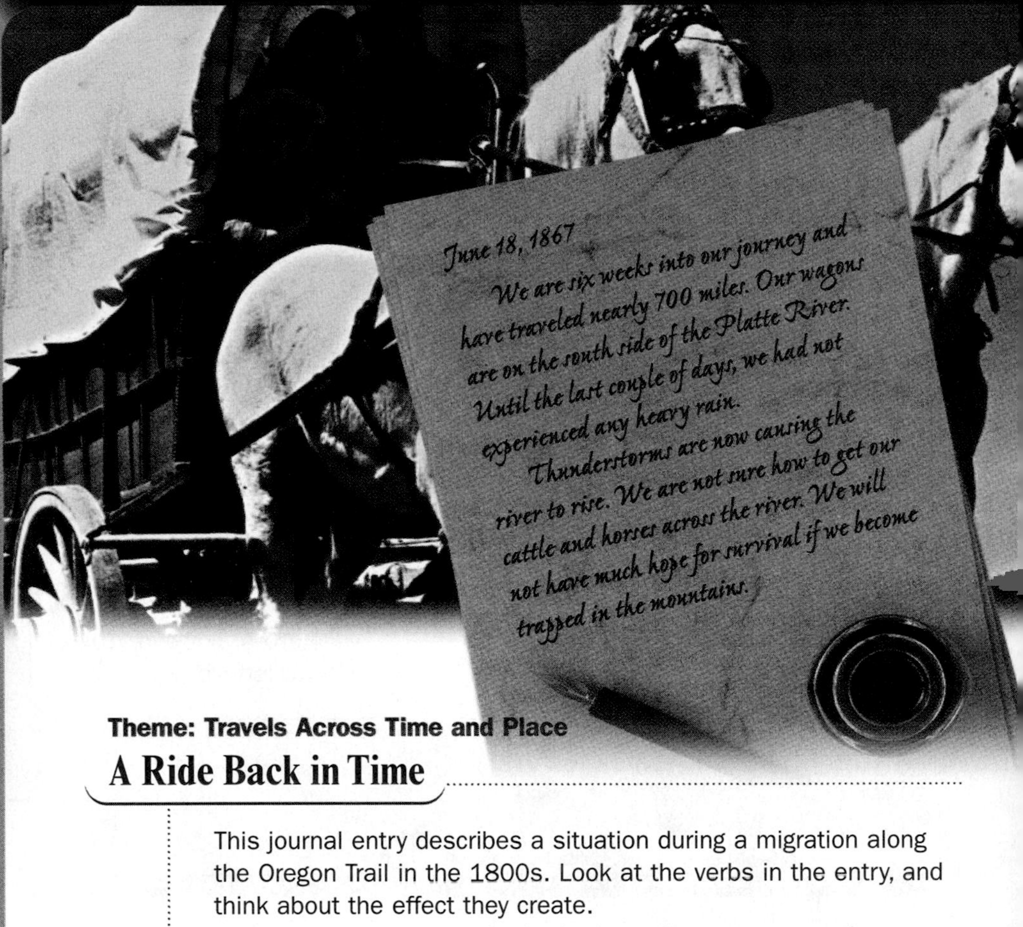

June 18, 1867

We are six weeks into our journey and have traveled nearly 700 miles. Our wagons are on the south side of the Platte River. Until the last couple of days, we had not experienced any heavy rain.

Thunderstorms are now causing the river to rise. We are not sure how to get our cattle and horses across the river. We will not have much hope for survival if we become trapped in the mountains.

Theme: Travels Across Time and Place

A Ride Back in Time

This journal entry describes a situation during a migration along the Oregon Trail in the 1800s. Look at the verbs in the entry, and think about the effect they create.

The present-tense verbs in the journal entry act as a time machine that makes you feel as if you are at the river crossing with the pioneers. The past-tense and future-tense verbs help you understand the sequence of events. You can use verb forms in your own writing to help express relationships among events.

Write Away: A Voice from the Past

Imagine that you are present at an important historical event. Write two or three paragraphs about what is happening. Use different verb tenses in your account. Put your writing in your **Working Portfolio.**

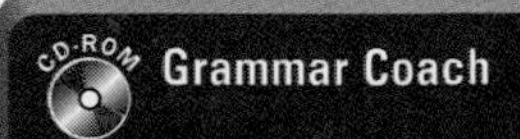

Diagnostic Test: What Do You Know?

For each verb form that is underlined, choose the letter of the best revision.

When Marta and her family taked (1) a vacation in Australia, they are (2) surprised at how the time changed during their airline flights across the Pacific Ocean. When they flied (3) from Los Angeles to Sydney, Australia, they arrived at a time that was nearly 32 hours later than the time when they left. Coming back to Los Angeles, however, they were arriving (4) at a time three and one-half hours *earlier* than when they left Sydney. Did Marta's family fly (5) in a time machine on the way back from Sydney?

The arrival times were so different because the airplanes cross (6) the International Date Line during the flights. The world divides (7) into 24 time zones so that the sun is high in the sky at noon almost everywhere on earth. The International Date Line lays (8) between two time zones in the Pacific Ocean. The time in the first time zone east of the date line is 23 hours earlier than the time in the first time zone to the west. Suppose a person travels around the world and adjusted (9) a watch each time he or she enters a new time zone. If there were (10) no date line, he or she would arrive home with a watch whose date is a day off from everyone else's.

1. A. taken
   B. tooked
   C. took
   D. Correct as is
2. A. will be
   B. were
   C. would be
   D. was
3. A. flown
   B. fly
   C. will fly
   D. flew
4. A. arrived
   B. have been arriving
   C. are arriving
   D. will arrive
5. A. be flying
   B. have flew
   C. have flown
   D. Correct as is
6. A. crossed
   B. will cross
   C. are crossing
   D. was crossing
7. A. divided
   B. is divided
   C. is being divided
   D. has divided
8. A. is laying
   B. lay
   C. lies
   D. Correct as is
9. A. had adjusted
   B. will be adjusted
   C. adjusts
   D. will adjust
10. A. is
    B. was
    C. will be
    D. Correct as is

VERBS

The Principal Parts of a Verb

❶ Here's the Idea

▶ **Every verb has four principal parts: the present, the present participle, the past, and the past participle.** You use the principal parts to make all of a verb's tenses and forms.

The Four Principal Parts of a Verb

Present	Present Participle	Past	Past Participle
look	(is) looking	looked	(has) looked
break	(is) breaking	broke	(has) broken

Here are some examples of how the principal parts are used:

PRESENT
Astronomers use a valuable information collector in space.

PRESENT PARTICIPLE
The Hubbell Space Telescope is providing scientists with new insights about the universe.

PAST
Space agencies decided that a more sophisticated device needed to be sent into orbit.

PAST PARTICIPLE
A number of countries have worked together to build an International Space Station.

When the present participle and the past participle are used to form verbs in sentences, they always take auxiliary verbs.

CHAPTER 6

Regular Verbs

There are two kinds of verbs—regular and irregular. A **regular verb** is a verb that forms its past and past participle by adding *-ed* or *-d* to the present.

PRESENT	PRESENT PARTICIPLE	PAST	PAST PARTICIPLE
look	**(is) look + ing**	**look + ed**	**(has) look + ed**
work	**(is) work + ing**	**work + ed**	**(has) work + ed**

Irregular Verbs

Verbs for which the past and past participle are formed in some other way than by adding *-ed* or *-d* are called **irregular verbs.** The following chart shows you how to form the principal parts of many irregular verbs.

Common Irregular Verbs

	Present	Past	Past Participle
Group 1 The forms of the present, the past, and the past participle are the same.	burst	burst	(has) burst
	cost	cost	(has) cost
	cut	cut	(has) cut
	hit	hit	(has) hit
	hurt	hurt	(has) hurt
	let	let	(has) let
	put	put	(has) put
	set	set	(has) set
	shut	shut	(has) shut
Group 2 The forms of the past and the past participle are the same.	bring	brought	(has) brought
	catch	caught	(has) caught
	get	got	(has) got *or* gotten
	lay	laid	(has) laid
	lead	led	(has) led
	lend	lent	(has) lent
	lose	lost	(has) lost
	make	made	(has) made
	say	said	(has) said
	sit	sat	(has) sat
	seek	sought	(has) sought
	teach	taught	(has) taught
Group 3 The vowel changes from *i* to *a* to *u*.	begin	began	(has) begun
	drink	drank	(has) drunk
	ring	rang	(has) rung
	shrink	shrank	(has) shrunk
	sink	sank	(has) sunk
	spring	sprang *or* sprung	(has) sprung
	swim	swam	(has) swum

A dictionary entry for an irregular verb shows the correct spelling of the verb's past and past participle.

VERBS

Common Irregular Verbs

	Present	Past	Past Participle
Group 4 **The past participle is formed by adding *-n* or *-en* to the past.**	beat break choose lie speak steal tear wear	beat broke chose lay spoke stole tore wore	(has) beaten (has) broken (has) chosen (has) lain (has) spoken (has) stolen (has) torn (has) worn
Group 5 **The past participle is formed from the present—frequently by adding *-n, -en,* or *-ne.***	blow do draw eat give go grow know rise run see take throw write	blew did drew ate gave went grew knew rose ran saw took threw wrote	(has) blown (has) done (has) drawn (has) eaten (has) given (has) gone (has) grown (has) known (has) risen (has) run (has) seen (has) taken (has) thrown (has) written

CHAPTER 6

2 Why It Matters in Writing

If you use incorrect verb forms, you will leave your readers with a poor impression of your writing. Your errors will distract them from your ideas.

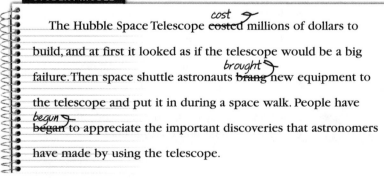

STUDENT MODEL

The Hubble Space Telescope ~~costed~~ *cost* millions of dollars to build, and at first it looked as if the telescope would be a big failure. Then space shuttle astronauts ~~brang~~ *brought* new equipment to the telescope and put it in during a space walk. People have ~~began~~ *begun* to appreciate the important discoveries that astronomers have made by using the telescope.

❸ Practice and Apply

A. CONCEPT CHECK: The Principal Parts of a Verb

Choose the correct form of the verb in parentheses.

A Future Glimpse into the Past

1. The Hubble Space Telescope has (maked, made) astronomers hungry for more information about the universe.
2. They are (seeking, sought) new information about the creation of the universe.
3. NASA has (wanted, want) to send even better telescopes into space.
4. NASA (chose, choosed) four new telescope projects: The Space Infrared Telescope Facility (SIRTF), Space Interferometry Mission (SIM), Next Generation Space Telescope (NGST), and Terrestrial Planet Finder (TPF).
5. By the year 2050, astronomers will have (took, taken) a new look at the universe with the help of the new telescopes.
6. Hubble's replacements will be able to see through the clouds of gas that (gotten, got) in the way before.
7. SIRTF will (detect, detected) infrared light.
8. By the end of its five-year life, SIRTF will have (cut, cutted) through clouds of gases to reveal superplanets and very dim stars called brown dwarfs.
9. SIM will (spot, spotting) individual stars in clusters.
10. Hubble has (brang, brought) us blurry images of clustered stars.

➜ **For a SELF-CHECK and more practice, see the EXERCISE BANK, p. 598.**

B. WRITING: Stellar Events

List the principal parts of the following irregular verbs. Then use any five of the words below to write about an unusual or amazing sky that you have seen in real life or in the movies.

know	set	sink
rise	teach	catch

Look at a recent draft from your **Working Portfolio.** Proofread the draft to correct any errors in the use of principal parts of irregular verbs.

VERBS

Forming Verb Tenses

1 Here's the Idea

▶ **A tense is a verb form that shows the time of an action or a condition.** A verb's tenses are formed from its principal parts.

Simple Tenses

The **present tense** shows that an action or a condition

- occurs regularly or is generally true:

Good stories transport us across time and space.

- is occurring in the present:

I have the new book by Stephen King.

- occurs regularly:

Every night, I read several chapters of this chilling tale.

The **past tense** shows that an action or a condition occurred in the past:

King published *Carrie,* his first novel, in 1974.

The **future tense** shows that an action or a condition will occur in the future:

I will lend you King's new book next week.

Simple Tenses

Tense	Singular	Plural
Present		
First person	I travel.	We travel.
Second person	You travel.	You travel.
Third person	He/she/it travels.	They travel.
Past		
First person	I traveled.	We traveled.
Second person	You traveled.	You traveled.
Third person	He/she/it traveled.	They traveled.
Future *will (shall)* + present		
First person	I will (shall) travel.	We will (shall) travel.
Second person	You will travel.	You will travel.
Third person	He/she/it will travel.	They will travel.

If you want to give special force to a verb, use the emphatic form. You make the emphatic form by adding *do, does,* or *did* to a verb.

I did finish my work!

CHAPTER 6

Perfect Tenses

The **present perfect tense** shows that an action or a condition

- was completed at one or more indefinite times in the past:

  King has published several books under the pen name of Richard Bachman.

- began in the past and continues in the present:

  King has written more than 30 novels in the last 30 years.

The **past perfect tense** shows that an action or a condition in the past preceded another past action or condition:

King had written two novels that were rejected by publishers before he published *Carrie.*

The **future perfect tense** shows that an action or a condition in the future will precede another future action or condition:

By next summer, I will have read half of King's books.

VERBS

Perfect Tenses

Tense	Singular	Plural
Present perfect ***have/has*** **+ past participle**		
First person	I have traveled.	We have traveled.
Second person	You have traveled.	You have traveled.
Third person	He/she/it has traveled.	They have traveled.
Past perfect ***had*** **+ past participle**		
First person	I had traveled.	We had traveled.
Second person	You had traveled.	You had traveled.
Third person	He/she/it had traveled.	They had traveled.
Future perfect ***will (shall) have*** **+ past participle**		
First person	I will (shall) have traveled.	We will (shall) have traveled.
Second person	You will have traveled.	You will have traveled.
Third person	He/she/it will have traveled.	They will have traveled.

Progressive Form

▶ **The progressive form of a verb expresses an event in progress.** Each tense has a progressive form, made by using the corresponding tense of the verb *be* with the present participle.

I am reading this horror story.

A group of friends were camping in the Maine woods.

An escaped convict had been hiding in a nearby cabin.

❷ Why It Matters in Writing

Knowing which verb tense to use can help you make it clear when something happened. Notice how Stephen King uses verb tenses in the following screenplay scene in which a gravedigger is talking to a dead novelist who has just been buried.

LITERARY MODEL

(Exterior view of the grave)

(A groundskeeper pats the last sod into place.) PRESENT

Groundskeeper. My wife says she wishes you'd written a couple more before you had your heart attack, mister. *(pause)* I like Westerns, m'self.

PAST PERFECT

PAST

(The groundskeeper *walks away, whistling.)*

—Stephen King, *Sorry, Right Number*

CHAPTER 6

❸ Practice and Apply

CONCEPT CHECK: Forming Verb Tenses

In each sentence below, the underlined verb is in the incorrect tense or form. Write the verb in the correct tense or form.

Portals to Distant Places

1. Books offer us pleasure and opened doorways to other places and times.
2. Right now, Shay was reading a book.
3. Although she is in the library, her mind had been transported to another time and place.
4. By the end of the day, who knows how far she has traveled.
5. Perhaps Mark Twain invites her on a trip down the Mississippi while she was choosing something to read.
6. As she scanned the shelves, maybe a pioneer family has made room for her on a journey westward.
7. Yesterday she is thinking about ocean voyages.
8. Now she will be following the *Titanic* across the Atlantic.
9. If tomorrow she thinks about circling the globe, undoubtedly she chooses Jules Verne's famous novel.
10. After all, Verne's *Around the World in Eighty Days* had taken many an armchair traveler on an exciting adventure.

➜ **For a SELF-CHECK and more practice, see the EXERCISE BANK, p. 599.**

LESSON 3 Using Verb Tenses

1 Here's the Idea

You can use different verb tenses to describe single events and ongoing actions that are related. Verb tenses are especially helpful when you are writing a story, because they allow you to show how a series of events are related in time.

Writing About the Present

When you are writing about the present, you can use the

- simple present tense
- present progressive form
- present perfect tense
- present perfect progressive form

A Real-Life Adventure

Verb Tenses

I like to read about real-life adventures. I especially enjoy stories in which people struggle against nature.

The simple present shows an action or a condition that is continuously true.

I am reading the book *Back from Tuichi* by Yossi Ghinsberg. The suspense is so intense that I am getting goose bumps.

The present progressive shows action that is now in progress.

So far I have learned that Yossi is a young Israeli man who is on an adventure through the rain forests of Bolivia.

The present perfect shows an action or a condition that began in the past and continues into the present.

I have been trying to resist the urge to skip ahead in the book.

The present perfect progressive shows an action that began in the past and is still in progress.

VERBS

Writing About the Past

When you write about the past, verb tenses can help you show the sequence of events. Describing such a sequence can be very complicated because some events are ongoing and overlap other events. By using correct tenses, you can make it easier for your readers to follow the events.

Yossi Struggles Through the Rain Forest

Passage	Verb Tenses
Yossi Ghinsberg **traveled** to Bolivia in the 1980s. He **explored** the rain forests near the Tuichi River.	The **simple past** shows actions that were completed in the past.
At first Yossi **was traveling** with three men. They **were searching** for a remote Indian village and gold.	The **past progressive** shows actions that continued over time in the past.
After the men **had experienced** difficult travel for several weeks, two of them gave up and headed back to civilization on foot.	The **past perfect** shows an action in the past that came before other actions in the past.
Yossi and the remaining man, Kevin, **had been trying** to raft down a dangerous river when they became separated.	The **past perfect progressive** shows an action that was in progress in the past when another action happened.

CHAPTER 6

Writing About the Future

Future tenses allow you to describe what will happen, what will be happening, or what will have happened in the future.

What Will Happen to Yossi?

	Verb Tenses
When you get to the part where Yossi has been left alone in the rain forest, you will be eager to find out what happens to him.	The **simple future** shows a condition that will occur in the future.
Yossi will be trying to make it out of the jungle with the help of only a few supplies.	The **future progressive** shows an action that will be in progress in the future.
You may wonder if any wild animals will have attacked Yossi before he reaches the nearest village.	The **future perfect** shows an action in the future that will occur before another action.
Yossi will have been causing you to lose a lot of sleep at night before you get to the end of his book.	The **future perfect progressive** shows an action in progress in the future when another action will happen.

VERBS

❷ Why It Matters in Writing

By learning when and how to use verb tenses, you can clearly show actions and conditions occurring one right after another.

PROFESSIONAL MODEL

Suddenly I **understood** where I **was: I had entered** the canyon and **was being swept** swiftly toward the treacherous Mal Paso San Pedro. The raft **bounced** from wall to wall.

—Yossi Ghinsberg, *Back from Tuichi*

❸ Practice and Apply

CHAPTER 6

CONCEPT CHECK: Using Verb Tenses

In each sentence below, the underlined verb is in the incorrect tense. Write it in the correct tense.

A Question of Survival

1. Often I <u>am wondering</u> if I would have the courage to survive in the wilderness.
2. You never <u>knew</u> what you can do until you are put to the test.
3. Yossi Ghinsberg's story was so engrossing that I <u>feel</u> that I was with him in the jungle.
4. He <u>has been traveling</u> with three other men when his personal tale of survival began.
5. The group split up: two headed back to civilization, but Ghinsberg <u>will continue</u> with Kevin.
6. As the two careened down the river on a handmade raft, they <u>run</u> into rapids, rocks, and whirlpools.
7. During one accident, they became separated, and Ghinsberg <u>will find</u> himself alone on the raft.
8. Kevin <u>shouts,</u> "Hang on tight!" just before Ghinsberg plunged over a waterfall.
9. I <u>am gasping</u> for breath as he described the horrible dance of death in the raging waters.
10. He almost drowned, but he finally <u>struggles</u> to the riverbank, about to face even deadlier challenges.

➜ **For a SELF-CHECK and more practice, see the EXERCISE BANK, p. 599.**

Rewrite sentences 1–5 to show the action in the future.

Mixed Review

A. Proofreading Each pair of sentences in the following paragraph contains one error in verb parts or verb tenses. Write the incorrect verb, and then write the correct part or tense for each of the five.

(1) If you are a science fiction fan like me, you have probably read stories about people traveling backward or forward in time. Science fiction authors have wrote about characters using time machines and vortexes to travel through time. **(2)** A vortex is a whirling mass of water or air that sucks everything near it toward its center.

Scientists had studied whether it might actually be possible to travel through time. **(3)** Most of these scientists have used Einstein's theory of relativity as a basis for their research. According to this theory, people experienced time differently depending on where they are and how fast they are moving. **(4)** Suppose a person leaves earth and traveled in a spaceship for many years at a speed close to the speed of light. When the person returns to earth, she or he will not be much older than when she or he left. **(5)** The spacecraft that we have today, however, do not travel fast enough to make much of a difference in the way astronauts age—especially since most space missions last only days or weeks. The technology for ultrafast space travel is not available anytime in the near future.

VERBS

B. Writing Look in your **Working Portfolio** and find the paragraphs you wrote for the **Write Away** activity on page 128. See if you can use different tenses to make your meaning more precise.

Shoe by Jeff MacNelly

Shifts in Tense

1 Here's the Idea

In most cases, use the same verb tense within a sentence to describe events that happen at approximately the same time.

SIMPLE PAST ... SIMPLE PAST

Michiko finished her history assignment and turned on a public television channel.

Some situations require you to shift tenses within a sentence. For example, use a progressive form and a simple tense to describe an ongoing action interrupted by a single event.

PAST PROGRESSIVE

Michiko was watching a nature program about Alaska when she decided to find out more about the state.

SIMPLE PAST

was watching (ONGOING ACTION)

decided (SINGLE EVENT)

When you are describing an event as a point of reference for another event, shift from a perfect tense to a simple tense.

PAST PERFECT ... SIMPLE PAST

Michiko had been at the library for an hour when she found a book about Alaska called *Coming into the Country.*

2 Why It Matters in Writing

Keep verb tenses consistent unless you have a good reason not to. Mixing verb tenses unnecessarily can confuse your readers.

STUDENT MODEL

Long ago a strip of land ~~had~~ connected Alaska with Asia, and Asian peoples ~~are traveling~~ traveled across the strip to settle in Alaska.

3 Practice and Apply

CONCEPT CHECK: Shifts in Tense

For each sentence below, choose the correct verb from the pair shown in parentheses.

Example: After John McPhee (had spent, was spending) several months in Alaska in the mid-1970s, he wrote *Coming into the Country,* a book about his experiences there.

Answer: had spent

A Narrow Escape

1. One day John McPhee was flying a helicopter over Alaska, and he (is seeing, saw) an old plane wreck down below.
2. He (was traveling, travels) with officials who were looking for a site for a new state capital.
3. He learned that the plane was a World War II bomber; it (had crashed, will have crashed) during a training flight.
4. The crew of five (will be conducting, was conducting) some tests when some of the plane's controls broke.
5. Three of the crew members (were, have been) able to parachute out after the plane went into a spin.
6. A search team later found the burned remains of the other two crew members in the crashed plane; they (had failed, were failing) to get out in time.
7. Leon Crane piloted the plane; he (had been, was) the only one of the five who survived.
8. After Crane (had waited, waits) eight days for a rescue team, he set off to search for help.
9. Just as Crane (begins, was beginning) to lose his strength, he reached a cabin that was stocked with food.
10. Crane's story is just one part of McPhee's book; *Coming into the Country* (contains, contained) several other accounts of Alaska.

➔ **For a SELF-CHECK and more practice, see the EXERCISE BANK, p. 600.**

Active and Passive Voice

CHAPTER 6

1 Here's the Idea

▶ **When a verb's subject performs the action expressed by the verb, the verb is in the active voice.**

PERFORMER OF ACTION — VERB

A group of 16 countries constructed the International Space Station.

▶ **When a verb's subject receives the action expressed by the verb, the verb is in the passive voice.**

RECEIVER OF ACTION — VERB

The International Space Station was constructed by a group of 16 countries.

Use the passive voice only when you want to emphasize the receiver of the action or when the performer of the action is not known. Otherwise change passive to active voice as follows:

Here's How Changing Passive Voice to Active Voice

1. Determine the verb and the performer of the action.

   The space station is being lived in by astronauts.

2. Move the performer of the action before the verb and change the verb to the active voice.

   Astronauts is living in the space station.

3. Make sure the verb agrees in number with the new subject.

   Astronauts are living in the space station.

2 Why It Matters in Writing

If you use the passive voice too often, it can make your writing vague and lifeless.

STUDENT MODEL

DRAFT

Skylab 2, one of the first space stations, was launched in 1973.

REVISION

The United States launched *Skylab 2,* one of the first space stations, in 1973.

❸ Practice and Apply

CONCEPT CHECK: Active and Passive Voice

Rewrite each sentence to change the verb from the passive voice to the active voice. Change other words as necessary.

Example: The story of the space station *Mir* was followed by people around the world.

Answer: People around the world followed the story of the space station *Mir.*

Danger at 250 Miles Above the Earth

1. In 1986, the first section of the space station *Mir* was launched by Russia.
2. Years later, another space station was created by Gene Roddenberry for *Star Trek: Deep Space Nine.*
3. Undoubtedly, Roddenberry's station would be preferred by anyone who has ever dreamed of living in space.
4. In 1997 alone, many disasters were suffered by *Mir's* crew members.
5. A science lab was severely damaged by fire.
6. In June 1997, *Mir* was rammed by a 65-ton unmanned cargo ship.
7. A hole was punctured in the hull by the strong impact.
8. Also, a solar panel was destroyed by the crash.
9. The space station was also plagued by computer failures.
10. At one point, departure in the escape capsule had been considered by the frightened crew.

➜ **For a SELF-CHECK and more exercises, see the EXERCISE BANK, p. 601.**

With a partner, discuss whether changing all the sentences from passive to active voice was an improvement. Which sentences might you leave in the passive voice?

Choose a recent draft from your **Working Portfolio.** Revise your work to eliminate any unnecessary use of the passive voice.

VERBS

The Mood of a Verb

❶ Here's the Idea

▶ **The mood of a verb conveys the status of the action or condition it describes.** Verbs have three moods: indicative, imperative, and subjunctive.

Indicative Mood

Use the **indicative mood** to make statements and ask questions. The indicative is the most commonly used mood.

My friend Lisa likes to copy the hairstyles of movie stars.

Why is it that so many people are not happy with who they are?

Imperative Mood

Use the **imperative mood** to make a request or give a command. Notice that the subject, *you,* is omitted.

Be independent. Stop worrying about what others think.

Subjunctive Mood

Use the **subjunctive mood** to express a wish or state a condition that is contrary to fact. In this type of subjunctive expression, use *were* instead of *was.*

I wish I were older, and Grandpa wishes he were younger.

The subjunctive mood also is used in sentences that give a command or make a request. When the subjunctive is used this way, it requires the base form of a verb.

The school requires that students be in homeroom by 8 A.M.

❷ Why It Matters in Writing

The subjunctive mood helps writers express things that are different than they seem to be. Notice how the author of the passage on the next page expresses the feelings of a boy who happens to bump into a girl from school while he is on his paper route.

LITERARY MODEL

And because we stopped we were friends. I didn't know how I could stop, but I didn't hurry on. I stood. There was nothing to do but to act as if I **were walking** on out too. I had three papers left in the bag, and I frantically began to fold them—box them, as we called it—for throwing. We had begun to walk and talk.

—William Stafford, "The Osage Orange Tree"

3 Practice and Apply

VERBS

CONCEPT CHECK: The Mood of a Verb

For each numbered item, identify the underlined verb as indicative, subjunctive, or imperative mood.

A Note from Ida Knowitall, Advice Columnist

Dear Wishful Thinker,

(1) In your letter, you wrote, "I wish I were older." **(2)** Why are you in a hurry? **(3)** If your wish were granted, you would soon want to be younger. What a waste of time! Each person is born in a certain space and time. **(4)** Nothing he or she does will ever change that. **(5)** Don't waste energy wishing for the impossible. **(6)** Spend the time you do have on learning, growing, and enjoying what life has to offer. **(7)** John Adams once said, "Facts are stubborn things; and whatever may be our wishes, . . . they cannot alter the state of facts." **(8)** The fact is that you are the age you are. **(9)** Take full advantage of that fact, and **(10)** use your precious time more wisely.

➔ **For a SELF-CHECK and more practice, see the EXERCISE BANK, p. 601.**

Write your own response to Wishful Thinker, and use verbs in the indicative, subjunctive, and imperative moods.

Commonly Confused Verbs

1 Here's the Idea

Writers often confuse certain pairs of verbs and use one when they should use the other.

lie/lay

The verb *lie* means "to rest in a flat position."

Someday I would like to lie on a beach and watch whales.

The verb *lay* means "to place." It is accompanied by a direct object.

DIRECT OBJECT

Lay your binoculars down here; we'll use them later.

One reason that people often confuse *lie* and *lay* is that the past participle of *lie* is spelled *lay*.

learn/teach

Use the verb *learn* when a person is receiving information. Use *teach* when a person is giving information to someone else.

In biology class we learned about whale migration.

Ms. Rodriguez taught us that whales travel great distances.

raise/rise

Use the verb *raise* when someone or something is lifting someone or something else up. When something is lifting itself up, use *rise*.

A large wave raised the boat high into the air.

Whales must rise up above the water often to breathe.

set/sit

Set means to place something. It requires a direct object. Do not use *set* when you mean *sit*.

DIRECT OBJECT

The captain of the boat set our course for a pod of whales.

We must all sit down in the boat before we can leave.

2 Why It Matters in Writing

Although some verbs are often used incorrectly as part of slang, they should be used correctly in writing.

STUDENT MODEL

My friend Stan took a boat tour that included whale watching. The guide ~~learned~~ *taught* him that when a whale ~~raises~~ *rises* completely up out of the water, it is called breaching.

3 Practice and Apply

CONCEPT CHECK: Commonly Confused Verbs

Choose the correct verb from the pair shown in parentheses.

A Whale of a Time

1. Three boats filled with whale watchers (sit, set) waiting in the still waters of Mexico's San Ignacio Lagoon.
2. A mother gray whale has been (teaching, learning) her newborn calf important whale lessons.
3. The people don't notice that another whale is (laying, lying) in the water behind them.
4. The whale submerges and then (raises, rises) directly in front of them.
5. One woman had (raised, risen) her camera just before the whale's head appeared in the viewfinder.
6. Startled, she (lays, lies) the camera in her lap and strokes the whale affectionately.
7. Sometimes a calf will (rise, raise) from the water on its mother's back.
8. As the gray whales migrate from the Bering Sea to Mexico, whale watchers (set, sit) their sights westward.
9. In San Ignacio Lagoon and elsewhere, whales will sometimes (lie, lay) quietly while humans touch them.
10. No one knows why; maybe someday a scientist will be able to (learn, teach) us.

For a SELF-CHECK and more exercises, see the EXERCISE BANK, p. 602.

Grammar in Literature

Using Verb Tenses to Describe Events

When expert writers are describing a series of events, they use different verb tenses to give a clear picture of when events occurred. By indicating which events happened first and which events were ongoing, writers help their readers understand why things happened as they did.

The following passage was written by Beryl Markham, the first person to make a solo nonstop flight from England to North America. As you read her description of the point during her flight when she reached the eastern coast of Canada, notice how she uses verbs as she recounts the key moments of the flight.

CHAPTER 6

FROM
West WITH THE *Night*
BY BERYL MARKHAM

I saw the ship and the daybreak, and then I saw the cliffs of Newfoundland wound in ribbons of fog. I felt the elation I had so long imagined, and I felt the happy guilt of having circumvented the stern authority of the weather and the sea. But mine was a minor triumph; my swift Gull was not so swift as to have escaped unnoticed. The night and the storm had caught her and we had flown blind for nineteen hours.

I was tired now, and cold. Ice began to film the glass of the cabin windows and the fog played a magician's game with the land. But the land was there. I could not see it, but I had seen it. I could not afford to believe that it was any land but the land I wanted. I could not afford to believe that my navigation was at fault, because there was no time for doubt.

South to Cape Race, west to Sydney on Cape Breton Island. With my protractor, my map, and my compass, I set my new course.

The simple past is used with the past perfect to show how a feeling lasted over time.

The past perfect tells what happened leading up to this part of the story.

The past perfect shows that the author remembers the land even though she can't see it now.

PRACTICE AND APPLY: Using Verb Tenses to Describe Events

Imagine that you are a news writer for a radio station and the year is 1936. You are assigned to write a brief news story about Beryl Markham's historic flight. Your story must be at least 50 words long. You have been provided with a reporter's notes to use for whichever story you choose, but you must put the information into your own words. The information should appear in a logical order.

News story #1 This story will be broadcast the day before Markham takes off on her flight. Include at least two different forms of future-tense verbs in your account.

Beryl Markham is scheduled to take off at 8 P.M. tomorrow, 9/4/36.

She is 33 years old; has worked as a pilot and horse trainer in Kenya.

Born in Leicester, England

Will take off from a military air base in Abingdon, England

She is trying to become the first person to fly solo and nonstop from England to North America.

News story #2 This story will be broadcast as if it were a live account of Markham's takeoff. Use at least two forms of present-tense verbs.

The single-engine Vega Gull plane was built especially for Markham's flight.

The plane has no radio equipment—would add too much weight.

The plane has extra fuel tanks for the long flight across the ocean.

This would be the first solo nonstop flight from England to North America.

As the plane heads down the runway for takeoff, it takes a while for it to lift off the ground—it carries much weight.

But the takeoff is successful, and she is on her way.

News story #3 This story will be broadcast the day after Markham completes her flight. Use at least two forms of past-tense verbs.

Plane crash-landed in a peat bog in the Canadian province of Nova Scotia

Markham suffered minor injuries.

Has become the first person to make a solo nonstop flight from England to North America

Time of flight: 21 hours 25 minutes

Plane did not make it to airport for landing because fuel line froze

Markham to be honored with ticker-tape parade in New York City

VERBS

Mixed Review

A. Revising Incorrect Verb Parts and Tenses For every sentence, write the incorrect verb part or tense, and then write its correct form. If all verbs in a sentence are correct, write *Correct.*

(1) At one time, most people thinked the world was flat. **(2)** To them, the Phoenicians must have been seeming very brave. **(3)** These geniuses of sea travel sailed where no other ancient people had went before. **(4)** No one knows for sure when they begun to make their voyages. **(5)** From their home in Phoenicia, which today was the country of Lebanon, they roamed the seas and established ports. **(6)** For hundreds of years, they lead the world in sea exploration. **(7)** Intrepid Phoenicians sailed around Africa centuries before Vasco da Gama done it. **(8)** Some historians have proposed the theory that the Phoenicians had even sailed to America. **(9)** Imagine an ancient Phoenician voice from beyond the grave saying, "Sorry, Columbus, but we was there first!" **(10)** In fact, the Phoenicians would have beat him by more than 2,000 years.

B. Proofreading for Improper Use of Verb, Voice, or Mood The following passage contains seven errors involving the use of the wrong verb, the unnecessary use of the passive voice, or the use of the wrong mood. Write each error, and then write its correct form.

Do imagine that for some reason you have vanished. Most of your possessions are laying in the hands of your enemies. Because a journal has never been kept by you, there is no record of your daily life, thoughts, and feelings. The only way people can learn about you is by reading what your enemies have written.

In a sense, this is what happened to the Phoenicians. After they were conquered by Alexander the Great, their culture virtually disappeared. Many historians wish they could go back in time and have Phoenicians learn them about Phoenician culture. If a Phoenician was alive today, we could find out if the Phoenicians discovered America. In reality, we can rely only on what was written by the Greeks about the Phoenicians.

C. Writing Write a paragraph describing the events in this time line, using different verb tenses. Write from the point of view of 842 B.C.

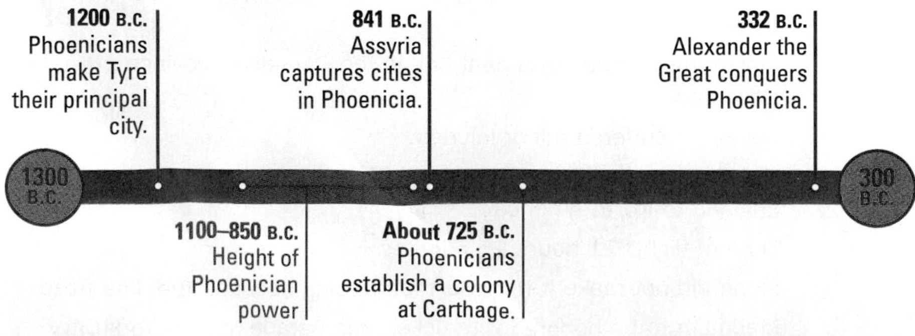

1200 B.C.
Phoenicians make Tyre their principal city.
841 B.C.
Assyria captures cities in Phoenicia.
332 B.C.
Alexander the Great conquers Phoenicia.
1300 B.C.
300 B.C.
1100–850 B.C.
Height of Phoenician power
About 725 B.C.
Phoenicians establish a colony at Carthage.

CHAPTER 6

Mastery Test: What Did You Learn?

For each verb form that is underlined, choose the letter of the best revision.

Courage and determination have took (1) Bill Pinkney to places he had only read about in his youth. In 1992, Pinkney made his dream come true by sailing around the world alone. He had become (2) the first African American to accomplish that feat. For a man who claims to be a terrible swimmer, the trip must have been especially challenging. Pinkney will have said (3), however, that when a person is 5,000 miles from shore, a safety harness was (4) far more important than knowing the backstroke.

Pinkney gone (5) on another adventure in 1999. That voyage retraced the Middle Passage, a route across the Atlantic Ocean that slave ships have used (6) for hundreds of years. He had saw (7) this voyage as an opportunity to draw attention to a period of history that is too often ignored. If Pinkney had been (8) self-centered, he would have traveled alone, but he invited 16 educators to join him. He wanted to learn (9) people about the slave route from Africa to the Americas. Who knows what other goals Pinkney sets (10) for himself in the future?

1. A. take
   B. have taked
   C. have taken
   D. are taking

2. A. becomes
   B. became
   C. was becoming
   D. Correct as is

3. A. will say
   B. is saying
   C. had said
   D. has said

4. A. will be
   B. is
   C. had been
   D. Correct as is

5. A. went
   B. has gone
   C. had been going
   D. is going

6. A. will have used
   B. have been using
   C. use
   D. used

7. A. had seen
   B. will see
   C. seen
   D. Correct as is

8. A. has been
   B. is
   C. was
   D. Correct as is

9. A. be learning
   B. be teaching
   C. teach
   D. Correct as is

10. A. has set
    B. will have been setting
    C. will set
    D. Correct as is

VERBS

Student Help Desk

Verbs at a Glance

Parts
Serve as building blocks for tenses

Voice
Shows whether the subject performs or receives an action

Tense
Indicates when something happened and how events or conditions are related in terms of time

Mood
Indicates a statement, a question, a command, or a condition contrary to fact

Creating Progressive Tenses

Tense or Form	Formula	Example
Present progressive	***am/are/is*** **+ present participle**	We are flying.
Past progressive	***was/were*** **+ present participle**	You were flying.
Future progressive	***will be*** **+ present participle**	They will be flying.
Present perfect progressive	***has/have*** **+** ***been*** **+ present participle**	I have been flying.
Past perfect progressive	***had*** **+** ***been*** **+ present participle**	You had been flying.
Future perfect progressive	***will have*** **+** ***been*** **+ present participle**	They will have been flying.

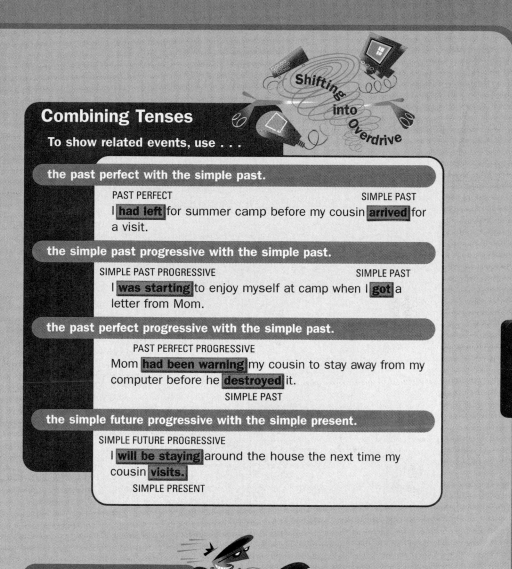

Combining Tenses

To show related events, use . . .

the past perfect with the simple past.

PAST PERFECT — SIMPLE PAST

I **had left** for summer camp before my cousin **arrived** for a visit.

the simple past progressive with the simple past.

SIMPLE PAST PROGRESSIVE — SIMPLE PAST

I **was starting** to enjoy myself at camp when I **got** a letter from Mom.

the past perfect progressive with the simple past.

PAST PERFECT PROGRESSIVE

Mom **had been warning** my cousin to stay away from my computer before he **destroyed** it.

SIMPLE PAST

the simple future progressive with the simple present.

SIMPLE FUTURE PROGRESSIVE

I **will be staying** around the house the next time my cousin **visits.**

SIMPLE PRESENT

The Bottom Line

Checklist for Using Verbs

Have I . . .

- ____ used the right past and past participle of irregular verbs?
- ____ used the correct tenses?
- ____ used progressive forms to show ongoing actions?
- ____ avoided switching tenses unnecessarily?
- ____ avoided unnecessary use of the passive voice?

VERBS

Chapter 7

Subject-Verb Agreement

EVANSTON POLICE DEPARTMENT — SUPPLEMENTARY EVIDENCE TECHNICIANREPORT

INCIDENT: Bank Robbery
LOCATION OF INCIDENT: First Circle Bank
DATE AND TIME PROCESSING: 2/3/20-- 11:54
VICTIM / SUSPECT: X
LOCATION OF PROCESSING: Police Forensics Lab
CASE — NAME: R. L. Marvin
PHONE NUMBER: 555-6868 x403
ADDRESS: Unknown

~~Two~~ One sets of prints are a match with the suspect's fingerprints. Although none of the prints are particularly clear, enough are useful for identification purposes. In particular, the thumbprint match well with prints on record to make a positive identification.

Enough what? And is it one or both thumbprints that match?

Which is it—two sets or one?

RIGHT INDEX FINGER — LEFT THUMBPRINT

Prints recovered from crime scene 2/3/20–
Evidence Technician: J.G. Hughes

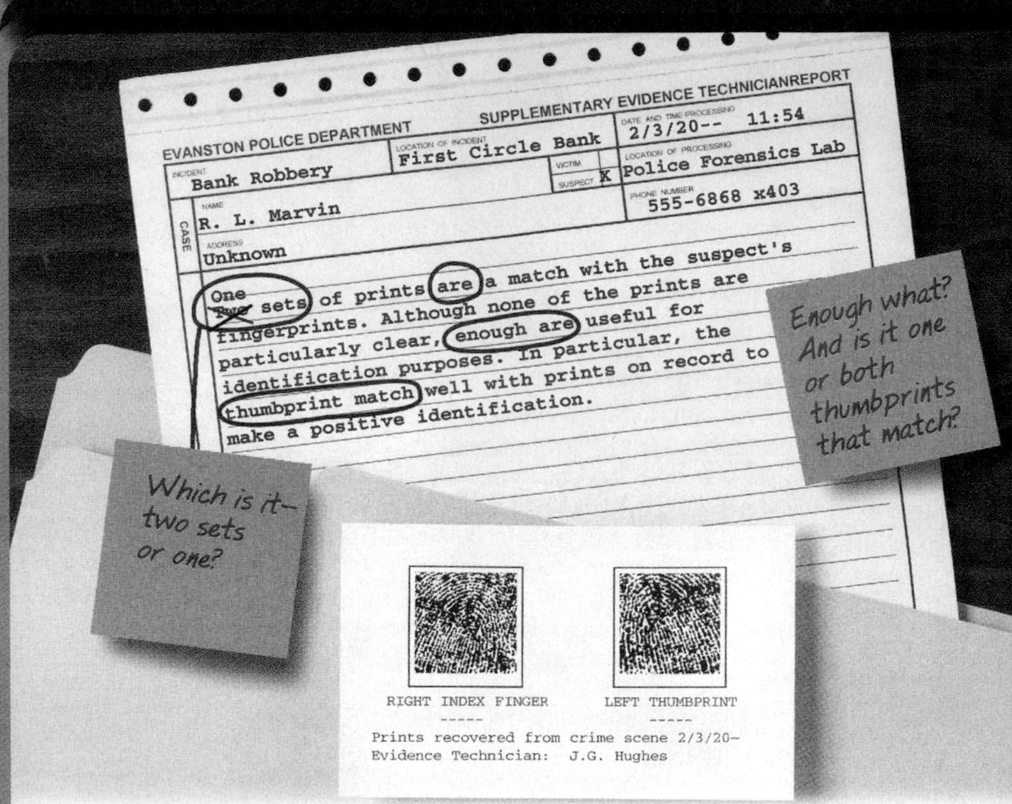

Theme: Mysteries

What's the Crime?

In this case, the first crime is the robbery, but the second "crime" is the writer's carelessness. If you were the district attorney, would you base your case on this report?

Not only does correct subject-verb agreement help your readers understand what you write; it also indicates that you're likely to be careful with your facts.

Write Away: Stop, Thief!
Write a paragraph about a recent crime or trial that fascinated you. What happened, and what was the outcome? Save the paragraph in your **Working Portfolio.**

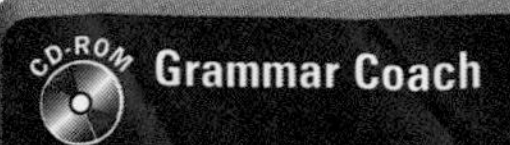

Diagnostic Test: What Do You Know?

Choose the best way to write each underlined section and mark the letter of your answer. If the underlined section needs no change, mark the choice "Correct as is."

Fingerprints have provided a practical and effective method (1) of identification for over a hundred years. Each person's pattern of loops and swirls are unique. (2) No one, not even identical twins, have exactly the same pattern (3) as anyone else. Juan Vucetich and Edward R. Henry was the first to develop efficient methods (4) of classifying fingerprints. Today, the police compare a suspect's fingerprints with thousands of prints stored in computer data banks. A computer can find a match in only a few minutes. From this work comes the facts that prosecutors need for their cases. (5)

1. A. Fingerprints has provided a practical and effective method
   B. Fingerprints has been providing a practical and effective method
   C. Fingerprints was providing a practical and effective method
   D. Correct as is

2. A. Each person's pattern of loops and swirls seem unique.
   B. Each person's pattern of loops and swirls is unique.
   C. Each person's pattern of loops and swirls have looked unique.
   D. Correct as is

3. A. No one, not even identical twins, has exactly the same pattern
   B. No one, not even identical twins, is having exactly the same pattern
   C. No one, not even identical twins, are having exactly the same pattern
   D. Correct as is

4. A. Juan Vucetich and Edward R. Henry is the first to develop efficient methods
   B. Juan Vucetich and Edward R. Henry has been the first to develop efficient methods
   C. Juan Vucetich and Edward R. Henry were the first to develop efficient methods
   D. Correct as is

5. A. From this work has come the facts that prosecutors need for their cases.
   B. From this work is coming the facts that prosecutors need for their cases.
   C. From this work come the facts that prosecutors need for their cases.
   D. Correct as is

SUBJECT-VERB

Agreement in Number

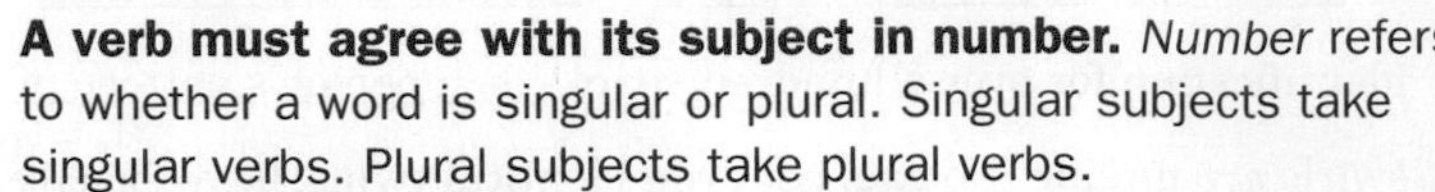

1 Here's the Idea

▶ **A verb must agree with its subject in number.** *Number* refers to whether a word is singular or plural. Singular subjects take singular verbs. Plural subjects take plural verbs.

SINGULAR	***PLURAL***
One early fictional detective was Di Renjie of China.	**Today's detectives are very similar to Di Renjie.**
This book describes ways to analyze evidence of all kinds.	**These books describe ways to examine physical evidence.**

For the most part, agreement problems occur with verbs in the present tense. (The exceptions include sentences with "to be" verbs.) Therefore, pay special attention to subject-verb agreement when you are writing in the present tense.

▶ **In a verb phrase, it is the first helping verb that must agree with the subject.**

In the play *Trifles*, a neighbor has reported a murder.

The officers have been searching for clues.

2 Why It Matters in Writing

Errors in subject-verb agreement can occur when you revise your work. If you change a subject from singular to plural or from plural to singular, don't forget to change the verb to match.

STUDENT MODEL

After a crime, detectives go over the scene inch by inch. Gradually, ~~each clue~~ *the clues* tell~~s~~ the story of the crime.

Clues requires the plural verb *tell.*

CHAPTER 7

3 Practice and Apply

A. CONCEPT CHECK: Agreement in Number

Rewrite the incorrect sentences so that the verbs agree with their subjects. If a sentence contains no error, write *Correct*.

The *Trifles* Crime Scene

1. The play's setting are a farmhouse in the early 1900s.
2. John Wright has been murdered in his own bed.
3. The local sheriff suspect the victim's wife, Minnie.
4. Her motive remain a mystery, however.
5. Two women collects a few belongings to take to Minnie.
6. They piece together the murder from a few "trifles" in the house.
7. Two important clues surface—a broken birdcage and a dead canary.
8. Gradually, these people discovers Minnie's motive for murder.
9. Their next action have surprised many readers.
10. This drama contain some clever twists and turns in the plot.

For a SELF-CHECK and more practice, see the EXERCISE BANK, p. 602.

B. EDITING: Making Subjects and Verbs Agree

Rewrite the following paragraph, changing each singular subject to a plural subject. Be sure to change the verbs to agree with the new subjects.

How to Investigate a Crime

(1) A murder investigation involves several specialists. **(2)** A police officer is usually the first at a crime scene. **(3)** The officer guards the evidence and takes statements from witnesses. **(4)** The homicide squad sends detectives to the scene. **(5)** The medical examiner studies the condition of the body. **(6)** The homicide detective discusses the cause of death with the medical examiner. **(7)** A crime team also arrives at the scene. **(8)** The crime photographer takes pictures of the body and the rest of the crime scene. **(9)** A crime specialist collects physical evidence to study later. **(10)** The homicide detective pieces together all the findings of the various investigators.

Words Between Subject and Verb

❶ Here's the Idea

▶ **The subject of a verb is never found in a prepositional phrase or an appositive phrase.** Don't be fooled by words that come between the subject and verb. Mentally block out those words. Then it will be easy to tell whether the subject is singular or plural.

Prepositional Phrase

AGREE

The files ~~of any computer~~ are vulnerable to electronic-age thieves.

Files takes the plural verb *are.*

AGREE

A computer thief ~~with the right codes~~ controls all the data files.

Thief takes the singular verb *controls.*

Appositive Phrase

AGREE

These thieves, ~~people like the hacker Kevin Mitnick~~, steal government and industry secrets.

AGREE

Mitnick, ~~the most cunning of the thieves~~, was caught by one of his victims, Tsutomu Shimomura.

❷ Why It Matters in Writing

By making sure that a verb agrees with its actual subject, you help the reader understand who or what is responsible for an action.

STUDENT MODEL

Theft by some computer hackers give^s honest hackers a bad name. In fact many hackers help the police catch computer thieves.

The subject is *theft,* not *hackers.*

CHAPTER 7

❸ Practice and Apply

A. CONCEPT CHECK: Words Between Subject and Verb

Correct the subject-verb agreement errors in the sentences below by writing the correct verb forms on a separate sheet of paper. If a sentence contains no error, write *Correct.*

To Catch a Cyber Thief

1. One day in 1994, Kevin Mitnick, one of the country's most wanted computer criminals, makes a critical mistake.
2. Mitnick, already under FBI investigation, break into the home computer of Tsutomu Shimomura.
3. Files of a highly sensitive nature is compromised by Mitnick.
4. Shimomura, a computer expert, vow to catch him.
5. Agents from the FBI joins Shimomura to track down Mitnick.
6. A trail of e-mail messages provide vital clues.
7. Calls from two different locations also help the team.
8. Mitnick, a self-taught expert, believe his calls to be untraceable.
9. Shimomura, with his technical skill, pinpoints Mitnick's exact location in North Carolina.
10. Experts on computer security follows such stories with great interest.

➜ **For a SELF-CHECK and more practice, see the EXERCISE BANK, p. 603.**

B. PROOFREADING: Making Subjects and Verbs Agree

Find the four errors in subject-verb agreement in this paragraph. Change the verbs to agree with their subjects.

Computers on the Case

Private investigators like Kinsey Millhone often uses computers to help solve their cases. In the story "Full Circle" Kinsey is asked to investigate a young girl's death in a car crash. A young man in a blue truck had shot the girl right before the accident. A news photo of the accident scene show the truck parked nearby. The license plate on the vehicle provide Kinsey with her first clue. Computerized records at the Department of Motor Vehicles helps her find the truck's owner. The owner tells her a friend borrowed the truck the day of the murder, providing Kinsey with another lead.

Indefinite-Pronoun Subjects

1 Here's the Idea

An **indefinite pronoun** refers to an unspecified person or thing. Some indefinite pronouns are always singular, and some are always plural. Others can be singular or plural, depending on how they're used.

Indefinite Pronouns	
Singular	another, anybody, anyone, anything, each, either, everyone, neither, nobody, no one, one, someone
Plural	both, few, many, several
Singular or plural	all, any, more, most, none, some

▶ **Singular indefinite pronouns take singular verbs.**

Everyone has heard of Sherlock Holmes and Dr. Watson.

Does anyone know about the detective work of their creator?

▶ **Plural indefinite pronouns take plural verbs.**

Few realize that Arthur Conan Doyle solved real-life cases.

Several were difficult even for a man of Doyle's skill.

▶ **Some indefinite pronouns take singular verbs when they refer to one person or thing. They take plural verbs when they refer to two or more people or things.** To determine whether the pronoun takes a singular or plural verb, find the noun it refers to.

Most of the story takes place in England.

Most of the stories take place in England.

2 Why It Matters in Writing

Mistakes in agreement with indefinite-pronoun subjects are common in writing. Watch for these errors when you revise and proofread.

STUDENT MODEL

All of the suspects deny that they killed the victim. Each claim^s to have been elsewhere.

The writer corrects the verb to agree with the subject.

CHAPTER 7

3 Practice and Apply

A. CONCEPT CHECK: Indefinite-Pronoun Subjects

Correct the subject-verb agreement errors in the sentences below by writing the correct verb forms on a separate sheet of paper. If a sentence contains no error, write *Correct.*

A Case of Night Blindness

1. Many of Arthur Conan Doyle's fans enjoy reading about the real-life cases Doyle solved.
2. One of these cases involve George Edalji, a young man from a small English village.
3. Someone among the villagers are viciously killing animals.
4. Nearly all of the animals are killed at night in open fields.
5. According to the police, most of the evidence point to Edalji.
6. Everyone on the jury find him guilty.
7. Someone writes Doyle, asking him to help Edalji.
8. One of Doyle's tests reveal Edalji's "night blindness."
9. No one with night blindness are able to chase and kill animals in the dark.
10. After hearing Doyle's evidence, all of the commissioners pardons Edalji.

➜ For a SELF-CHECK and more practice, see the EXERCISE BANK, p. 603.

Look at the paragraph you wrote for the **Write Away** on page 156 or another piece in your **Working Portfolio.** Make sure that verbs with indefinite-pronoun subjects agree with those subjects.

B. EDITING: Making Verbs Agree with Indefinite Pronouns

Write the correct verb form for each of the following sentences.

Hercule Poirot: The Belgian Sherlock Holmes

(1) Many of Agatha Christie's stories (feature, features) the Belgian detective Hercule Poirot. **(2)** Almost everyone (agree, agrees) that he and Sherlock Holmes have much in common. **(3)** Both (has, have) a keen knowledge of human nature. **(4)** Neither of the detectives (tolerate, tolerates) deceit or criminal behavior. **(5)** Each (owe, owes) his success to a talent for noticing small details. **(6)** Nobody (fool, fools) these two detectives for long.

Compound Subjects

1 Here's the Idea

A **compound subject** consists of two or more parts joined by a conjunction, such as *and, or,* or *nor*. To decide whether a compound subject takes a singular or a plural verb, follow these guidelines.

Subjects Joined by *And*

▶ **A compound subject whose parts are joined by *and* usually requires a plural verb.**

The Hardy Boys and Nancy Drew are the world's most famous teenage detectives.

These detectives and their fathers have been solving crimes since the 1920s.

Sometimes a compound subject containing *and* refers to a single thing and takes a singular verb.

Spaghetti and meatballs was my favorite takeout food.

Subjects Joined by *Or* or *Nor*

▶ **When the parts of a compound subject are joined by *or* or *nor,* the verb should agree with the part closest to it.**

AGREE

Neither the Hardy Boys nor Nancy is the stay-at-home type.

AGREE

Nancy or the Hardy Boys are always near a crime scene.

2 Why It Matters in Writing

It's important to remember the rules about agreement with compound subjects. You can't just rely on how the singular or plural form of a verb sounds with a compound subject, since the differences between sentences may be very minor.

The office managers and the law intern are guilty.

Either the office managers or the law intern is guilty.

CHAPTER 7

3 Practice and Apply

A. CONCEPT CHECK: Compound Subjects

Write the verb form that agrees with the subject of each sentence.

What's the Verdict on Teenage Detectives?

1. Nancy Drew and the Hardy Boys (has, have) been around for years.
2. Frank and Joe Hardy first (appear, appears) in the 1920s.
3. Neither the two boys nor Nancy (has, have) aged much.
4. Students and even adult fans (continue, continues) to demand more stories.
5. The brothers or Nancy always (show, shows) courage and quick thinking.
6. Unlike the fans, however, critics and parents often (find, finds) fault with the popular detectives.
7. According to the critics, these books and their characters (show, shows) a lack of reality.
8. The average girl or boy (live, lives) in a far different world from the one in the detective books.
9. Neither Nancy nor the brothers (experience, experiences) problems at home or at school.
10. Nevertheless, the detectives' sharp wits and intelligence (inspire, inspires) their readers.

For a SELF-CHECK and more practice, see the EXERCISE BANK, p. 604.

B. PROOFREADING: Making Verbs Agree with Compound Subjects

Write the correct forms of the incorrect verbs in these sentences. If a sentence contains no error, write *Correct.*

Chester Himes: African-American Mystery Writer

(1) Historians and many black writers recognizes Chester Himes as a groundbreaking African-American author. **(2)** Neither mystery fans nor the general reader were exposed to black detectives until Himes's novels appeared. **(3)** Grave Digger Jones and Coffin Ed Johnson are his most famous characters. **(4)** Neither Coffin Ed nor Grave Digger have much use for criminals or corrupt politicians. **(5)** In the movie *Cotton Comes to Harlem,* the two detectives and a criminal gang tries to outwit each other.

SUBJECT-VERB

Other Problem Subjects

1 Here's the Idea

Some subjects, such as collective nouns, singular nouns ending in *s*, and titles can be confusing. Singular or plural—how do you decide?

Collective Nouns

Collective nouns refer to groups of people or things. Common collective nouns include the following:

class	committee	flock	crowd
team	family	staff	police
club	herd	jury	majority

▶ **When a collective noun refers to a group as a unit, it takes a singular verb. When it refers to a group acting as individuals, it takes a plural verb.**

In 1911 a robbery team steals the *Mona Lisa* from the Louvre in France. — The team acts as one unit—the verb is singular.

The team separate after the theft. — The team act as individuals—the verb is plural.

The museum staff argue about what to do. — The staff act as individuals.

Fortunately, the staff alone is not investigating this case. — The staff is considered as one unit.

Nouns Ending in *S*

Some nouns ending in s appear to be plural but are really singular in meaning. Use singular verbs with these words.

mumps	measles	humanities	news
genetics	physics	molasses	

News about fake *Mona Lisa*s appears every week in the papers.

Eventually, forensics is used to help solve the crime.

CHAPTER 7

Titles, Amounts, and Time

▶ **Titles of works of art, literature, and music are singular. Words and phrases that refer to weights, measures, numbers, and lengths of time are usually treated as singular.**

Titles and Amounts		
Titles	Another genuine ***Mona Lisa* has been discovered.**	***The Twelve Chairs* is** a comic mystery story.
Amounts	**Fifty thousand dollars has been raised** to ransom the missing painting.	Over **two-thirds** of the money **comes** from private donations.
Time	**Twelve years is** a long time for an investigation to continue.	**Fifty years was** the maximum sentence for stealing a masterpiece.

Remember that even a plural title (*Mysteries of Sherlock Holmes, 100 Great Detectives*) takes a singular verb.

2 Why It Matters in Writing

Besides occurring in your own writing, these tricky subjects often show up on standardized tests. Knowing the rules of subject-verb agreement can help you choose the right verbs in either situation.

The museum security staff __(1)__ sure that Louvre employees are involved in the *Mona Lisa* theft. Ordinarily, the museum carpenter, Vincenzo Perugia, would be a prime suspect. His right-hand fingerprints are already on record. Forensics __(2)__ little help in this case, however. The police __(3)__ a thumbprint at the crime scene, but it is from Perugia's *left* hand.

1. A. are
   B. is
   C. have been
   D. were
2. A. offer
   B. have offered
   C. offers
   D. is offered
3. A. has found
   B. finds
   C. are finding
   D. find

Answers: 1. B (*Staff* refers to a single unit.) 2. C (*Forensics* is singular.) 3. D (*Police* is a plural collective noun.)

3 Practice and Apply

A. CONCEPT CHECK: Other Problem Subjects

Write the verb form that agrees with the subject of each sentence.

Steal the *Mona Lisa*? Impossible!

1. The usual crowd (begins, begin) to gather at the Louvre Museum on an August day in 1911.
2. The *Mona Lisa* (is, are) not hanging on the wall.
3. The security staff (think, thinks) that the painting is being photographed.
4. Sixty minutes (is, are) all that the robbery and escape took.
5. The robbery team (consists, consist) of a mastermind, a forger, a carpenter, and two accomplices.
6. A million francs (does, do) not even come close to the amount represented by the loss.
7. News of the robbery (break, breaks) slowly.
8. The staff (does, do) not agree about what to tell the press.
9. Forensics (is, are) used to help detect fake *Mona Lisa*s.
10. *The Day They Stole the Mona Lisa* (is, are) a nonfiction book about the robbery and investigation.

➜ **For a SELF-CHECK and more practice, see the EXERCISE BANK, p. 604.**

B. PROOFREADING: Correcting Agreement Errors

Find the subject-verb agreement errors in the following sentences. Write the correct verbs on a separate sheet of paper.

The Story Continues

1. Three minutes are all it takes to remove the painting from the museum wall.
2. *La Joconde,* as the painting is known in France, remain hidden in a shabby apartment across the city.
3. The robbery team argues about selling forgeries of the real *Mona Lisa.*
4. Nearly two million dollars are what the forgeries earn.
5. The French public demand the return of the painting.

Agreement Problems in Sentences

Here's the Idea

In some sentences, the placement of the subject and verb makes it hard to choose the right verb form.

Predicate Nominatives

A verb always agrees with its subject, never with a predicate nominative. A predicate nominative is a noun or pronoun that follows a linking verb and names or explains the subject.

AGREE

The robbers' main target is banks.

Banks are the target.

Inverted Sentences

A subject can follow a verb or come between parts of a verb phrase in the following types of sentences.

Inverted Sentences	
As questions	**Does** the **bank want** the robbers punished?
Beginning with *here* or *there*	Here **is** a **book** about dumb criminals.
Beginning with a phrase	Right by the police **speeds** the **truck**.

There is an easy way to find the true subjects of these sentences.

Here's How Finding the Subject

Out of the bank (come, comes) the two robbers.

1. Turn the sentence around so that the subject comes before the verb.
   The two robbers (come, comes) out of the bank.
2. Determine whether the subject is singular or plural.
   robbers (plural)
3. Make sure the subject and verb agree.
   The two robbers come out of the bank.

For more about subject-verb agreement problems, see p. 47.

2 Why It Matters in Writing

By knowing how to find subjects, you can make sure that verbs agree with their subjects in questions, in sentences beginning with *here* or *there,* and in other inverted sentences. What are the subjects in the following model?

LITERARY MODEL

Mrs. Peters (*crosses right looking in cupboard*). Why, here's a birdcage. (*Holds it up.*) Did she have a bird, Mrs. Hale?

—Susan Glaspell, *Trifles*

3 Practice and Apply

CHAPTER 7

A. CONCEPT CHECK: Agreement Problems in Sentences

Write the subject of each sentence. Then write the verb form that agrees with the subject.

Dumb and Dumber Criminals

1. (Has, Have) you ever heard stories about dumb criminals and their crimes?
2. In the book *Crimes and Misdumbmeanors* (appears, appear) several bungling criminals.
3. Here (is, are) one example of a badly botched robbery.
4. To a large sewing shop (dashes, dash) two police officers.
5. Near a basement window (lies, lie) pieces of broken glass.
6. "(Is, Are) anything missing?" one officer asks.
7. There (is, are) clear evidence that a sewing machine has been stolen.
8. Across the floor of the shop (run, runs) a single bright thread, snagged on a rough floorboard.
9. (Has, Have) the robbers left a trail for police to follow?
10. Out the door, across the alley, and up to the thieves' apartment (goes, go) the police officers, following this "thread of evidence."

➜ **For a SELF-CHECK and more practice, see the EXERCISE BANK, p. 605.**

B. EDITING AND PROOFREADING: Correcting Agreement Errors

Rewrite these sentences, correcting errors in subject-verb agreement. If a sentence contains no error, write *Correct.*

Example: On the hairy legs of one robber is sheer nylon stockings.

Answer: On the hairy legs of one robber **are** sheer nylon **stockings.**

Why the Taos Bank Robbery Failed

1. Does some people have bad luck even in crime?
2. Into the Taos bank walks two robbers, one in women's clothes.
3. There is few things more obvious than a poor disguise.
4. The robbers' main problem are curious onlookers.
5. In one robber's hand gleams a pistol in plain sight!
6. Have someone spread the word to the police?
7. Outside the front door gathers people who know about the robbery.
8. There is only one thing for the robbers to do—run!
9. Has the robbers thought of a getaway plan?
10. There are nowhere to hide after the robbery attempt.

Proofread a piece of writing in your **Working Portfolio** to make sure that subjects and verbs agree.

SUBJECT-VERB

Zits by Scott and Borgman

Real World Grammar

Report

Writing is a lot like private-detective work. In both cases you need to know how to operate within the rules. You need to be thorough. And you need to look after your reputation.

Here are two paragraphs from a student's research report. The comments you see at the sides were made by a trusted friend who caught a few subject-verb agreement errors.

CHAPTER 7

Careers in Forensics

Forensics, the science of crime solving, are an important and exciting field. There is more opportunities within this profession for people with varied backgrounds than you might expect.

Movies and television shows always seem to focus on chemists and doctors working in crime labs and morgues. However, specialists in other branches of science, such as geology and botany, also works on cases, analyzing soil, mud, pollen, and other physical evidence at a crime scene. Psychologists and psychiatrists are also called in to help the police capture or evaluate suspects, especially in cases of murder and other serious crimes. A specially trained photographer records information at a crime scene. Anyone who witnesses a crime talk to forensic artists to help them create pictures of the suspects.

"Forensics" is one of those "ics" words that take singular verbs.

The subject is "opportunities," not "there."

This should agree with "specialists."

You need a singular verb here to agree with the indefinite pronoun "anyone."

Using Grammar in Writing

Agreement in number	Watch out for plural subjects that don't end in *s* (*men, women*) and for collective nouns that refer to groups acting as individuals (*the jury argue*). Watch out for subjects ending in *s* that take singular verbs (*news, physics*).
Words between subjects and verbs	A phrase or clause between a subject and a verb can add important details. Just be sure the verb agrees with its subject.
Sentences beginning with *here* or *there*	Beginning a sentence with *here* or *there* can emphasize the subject, which often follows the verb. (*Here is the pen. There are the fingerprints.*)
Compound subjects	When combining subjects with *or* or *nor,* make sure the verb agrees with the part closest to it. When combining subjects with *and,* make sure the verb is plural.
Indefinite pronouns	When you make a generalization in which the subject is an indefinite pronoun, be sure the verb agrees in number with the pronoun.

SUBJECT-VERB

PRACTICE AND APPLY

Another student interested in forensics has written the letter below. Use the guidelines above to correct the sentences that contain errors in subject-verb agreement.

STUDENT MODEL

Dear Ms. Beck:

Your appearances on *TV Trial* is always a pleasure to watch. In my opinion, your comments and explanations about DNA evidence has been particularly informative. While doing research for a school report on this subject, I recently came across a puzzling question. Here, briefly, is the facts that I do not understand.

On the one hand, according to my reading, identical twins has the same DNA. On the other hand, also according to my reading, identical twins' fingerprints are different. Is this true? If so, how is it possible? Don't our DNA determine our physical characteristics, including our fingerprints?

Any information or research tips you can offer is sure to be helpful. Thank you so much for your time and your advice.

Mixed Review

A. Agreement in Number, Compound Subjects, and Other Problem Subjects Read this passage. Then write answers to the questions below it.

LITERARY MODEL

(1) The final footnote on The Great Taos Bank Robbery was not written until February 4, 1958. **(2)** After the surrender, officers found the two refreshingly frank about their activities. **(3)** In due course, Joe Gomez and Frederick Smith were accused by the U.S. District Attorney of conspiring to violate the provisions of the Federal Banking Act and their case was placed on the winter docket for consideration by the Federal Grand Jury. **(4)** Unfortunately, grand jury proceedings are secret so we will never know exactly what happened when the case was presented. **(5)** We do know that the jury returned a "no bill," which indicates—at the very least—that the jurors could not be convinced that Gomez and Smith took their pistols into the Taos bank with felonious intentions.

—Tony Hillerman, "The Great Taos Bank Robbery"

CHAPTER 7

1. In sentence 1, what verb agrees with the subject *footnote?*
2. In sentence 2, if *found* were in the present tense, would you use *find* or *finds* to agree with the subject?
3. In sentence 3, what is the subject of *were accused?*
4. In sentence 4, what subject does *are* agree with?
5. In summarizing sentence 5, would you say "The jury was not convinced about the intentions of the accused" or "The jury were not convinced about the intentions of the accused"? Explain your choice.

B. Subject-Verb Agreement Write the verb form that agrees with the subject of each sentence.

1. "The Great Taos Bank Robbery" (reveal, reveals) Hillerman's humor.
2. Most of his fiction (seem, seems) more brooding and serious.
3. (Do, Does) the names Joe Leaphorn and Jim Chee sound familiar?
4. Each (is, are) well-known to mystery fans.
5. Both (work, works) for the Navajo police in Hillerman's novels.
6. The Navajo reservation, located in New Mexico, Arizona, and Utah, (cover, covers) a wide territory.
7. All of Hillerman's books (offer, offers) insights into Navajo life.
8. There (is, are) interesting differences between Leaphorn and Chee.
9. (Have, Has) Leaphorn or Chee solved more cases?
10. Almost every year, one of Hillerman's books (make, makes) the bestseller list.

Mastery Test: What Did You Learn?

Choose the best way to write each underlined section and mark the letter of your answer. If the underlined section needs no change, mark the choice "Correct as is.".

Mystery writing is livelier and more varied than ever. A choice of styles ranging from gentle whodunits to nail-biting thrillers keeps (1) fans asking for more. Anyone, no matter how choosy, have (2) only to visit the nearest bookstore to find adventure and intrigue. Writers like Agatha Christie and Arthur Conan Doyle has created (3) great detectives and brain-teasing plots. From America's past comes mysteries (4) written by Edgar Allan Poe and Nathaniel Hawthorne. There is Asian, Hispanic, Native American, and African-American detectives (5)—all with their devoted fans! One hundred and fifty years of mystery writing has produced some of the greatest stories in fiction.

1. A. has kept
   B. is keeping
   C. keep
   D. Correct as is
2. A. Anyone, no matter how choosy, has
   B. Anyone, no matter how choosy, will have
   C. Anyone, no matter how choosy, have had
   D. Correct as is
3. A. Writers like Agatha Christie and Arthur Conan Doyle has been creating
   B. Writers like Agatha Christie and Arthur Conan Doyle have created
   C. Writers like Agatha Christie and Arthur Conan Doyle creates
   D. Correct as is
4. A. From America's past are coming mysteries
   B. From America's past has come mysteries
   C. From America's past come mysteries
   D. Correct as is
5. A. There was Asian, Hispanic, Native American, and African-American detectives
   B. There has been Asian, Hispanic, Native American, and African-American detectives
   C. There are Asian, Hispanic, Native American, and African-American detectives
   D. Correct as is

SUBJECT-VERB

Student Help Desk

Subject-Verb Agreement at a Glance

Verbs should agree with their subjects in number.

A singular subject requires a singular verb.

Plural subjects require plural verbs.

Tricky Cases

Verb phrase The first helping verb should agree with the subject.	**He has been judging** this case. **They have been judging** this case.
Words between subject and verb Block out these words when deciding what verb form to use.	The **facts** in this case **are** clear.
Indefinite-pronoun subject Singular pronouns take singular verbs; plural pronouns take plural verbs. Some pronouns can be singular or plural.	**Everyone wants** to attend the trial. **Many expect** a guilty verdict. **None** of the pie **was stolen.** **None** of the pies **were stolen.**
Compound subject containing *and* Always use a plural verb.	The **lawyer and** the **judge argue** about a point of law.
Compound subject containing *or* or *nor* The verb should agree with the subject closest to it.	Neither the **lawyers nor** the **judge agrees.** Neither the **judge nor** the **lawyers agree.**
Collective noun Can be singular (a unit) or plural (individuals).	The **staff is meeting.** The **staff disagree** about what to say.
Singular noun ending in *s* Often use a singular verb.	The **news is** not good.
Title, amount, time Often use a singular verb.	**Three days is** a long time to deliberate.

CHAPTER 7

Other Agreement Problems

Converted Sentences

Predicate nominative Make sure the verb agrees with the subject, not with the predicate nominative.	The best **evidence is** DNA fingerprints. DNA **fingerprints are** the best evidence.
Question Convert the question into a statement to find the subject.	(Do, does) the fingerprint match the suspect's prints? The **fingerprint does match** the suspect's prints.
Sentence beginning with • ***here* or *there*** • **phrase** Turn the sentence around to find the subject.	There (is, are) no verdict yet. No **verdict is** there yet. Out of the courtroom (come, comes) the suspect and his lawyers. The **suspect** and his **lawyers come** out of the courtroom.

SUBJECT-VERB

The Bottom Line

Checklist for Subject-Verb Agreement

Have I . . .

____ correctly identified the simple subject and predicate in each clause?

____ checked for agreement after changing a subject?

____ checked that *don't* and *doesn't* are used correctly?

____ checked whether indefinite-pronoun subjects are singular or plural?

____ checked that verbs agree with the nearest parts of compound subjects containing *or* or *nor*?

____ checked whether all subjects that end in s are really plural?

____ put questions and other inverted sentences in normal order to check agreement?

____ found the true subjects in sentences beginning with *here* or *there*?

Using Pronouns

If you disappoint me again, I'll put a price on your head so large you won't be able to go near a civilized system for the rest of your short life.
Buzzards will tear your eyes out!

Theme: Heroes and Villains

Good Guys Versus Bad Guys

From the *Odyssey,* to the tales of the knights of the Round Table, and to *Star Wars,* stories about heroes and villains capture our imaginations. Heroes and villains threaten and insult each other and boast about their own greatness, and they all use pronouns to do it. Read the quotations above. Could these characters have threatened their enemies without using pronouns?

Write Away: Threats and Boasts

Use your imagination or memory to write some boasts that a modern hero might make. Add to it some nonviolent threats that might scare a modern enemy. Underline the pronouns you use, and save your work in your **Working Portfolio.**

Diagnostic Test: What Do You Know?

Choose the best way to write each underlined word and mark the letter of your answer. If the underlined section needs no change, mark the choice "Correct as is."

Heroes in stories usually have great strength or speed and carry a powerful weapon with them (1), such as a strong bow or an intergalactic ray gun. Some, like Odysseus or Luke Skywalker, occasionally have a god or another special force working with them (2). However, villains also have physical power and his (3) own weapons. In order to win, heroes have to be smarter than them (4). Heroes must outwit they're (5) enemies. Most of us (6) readers enjoy stories that involve trickery, humor, and contests of wits. We root for the good guys in battles of brains between the villains and they (7). Its (8) the underdog hero, whom (9) has no weapons except their (10) brain, that we like best.

1. A. themselves
   B. him
   C. himself
   D. Correct as is

2. A. him
   B. himself
   C. themselves
   D. Correct as is

3. A. his or her
   B. their
   C. there
   D. Correct as is

4. A. themselves
   B. him
   C. they
   D. Correct as is

5. A. them
   B. their
   C. there
   D. Correct as is

6. A. we
   B. our
   C. his
   D. Correct as is

7. A. theirselves
   B. us
   C. them
   D. Correct as is

8. A. It has
   B. Their
   C. It's
   D. Correct as is

9. A. whoever
   B. who
   C. whose
   D. Correct as is

10. A. theirs
    B. his or her
    C. them
    D. Correct as is

LESSON 1

Pronoun Cases

1 Here's the Idea

▶ **Personal pronouns take different forms depending on how they are used in sentences. The form of a pronoun is called its case.**

There are three pronoun cases: nominative, objective, and possessive. The chart below lists all of the personal pronouns and organizes them by case, number (singular or plural), and person.

Personal Pronouns

	Nominative	Objective	Possessive
Singular			
First person	I	me	my, mine
Second person	you	you	your, yours
Third person	he, she, it	him, her, it	his, her, hers, its
Plural			
First person	we	us	our, ours
Second person	you	you	your, yours
Third person	they	them	their, theirs

2 Why It Matters in Writing

When writers create first-person dialogue in a narrative, they use all forms of pronouns, just as people do when they speak. Notice how many pronouns Odysseus uses when describing his reaction to his archenemy, the Cyclops.

LITERARY MODEL

I would not heed **them** [shipmates] in **my** glorying spirit,
but let **my** anger flare and yelled:
'Cyclops, if ever mortal man inquire
how **you** were put to shame and blinded, tell **him**
Odysseus, raider of cities, took **your** eye:
Laertes' son, **whose** home's on Ithaca!'

—Homer, *Odyssey*

Nominative and Objective Cases

Here's the Idea

Personal pronouns change their case depending on whether they function as subjects or objects.

Nominative Case

Personal pronouns that function as subjects or as predicate nominatives are in the nominative case.

I like the legends of King Arthur. He united the knights.
SUBJECT / SUBJECT

Be particularly careful to use the nominative case when the pronoun is part of a compound subject.

Queen Guinevere and he were wife and husband.
COMPOUND SUBJECT

A **predicate pronoun** also takes the nominative case. A predicate pronoun follows a linking verb and renames the subject of the sentence.

It was he who gathered the knights of the Round Table.
PREDICATE PRONOUN

The following chart shows the nominative form of personal pronouns.

Nominative Pronoun Forms

	First Person	Second Person	Third Person
Singular	I	you	he, she, it
Plural	we	you	they

In conversation, people often use the wrong case for a pronoun in the predicate pronoun position. Make sure you use the nominative case for predicate pronouns in formal writing.

It's her. (INCORRECT)

It's she. (CORRECT)

PRONOUNS

Objective Case

▶ **Personal pronouns that function as direct objects, indirect objects, or the objects of prepositions are in the objective case.**

Merlin the Wizard, Arthur's friend, helped him.
DIRECT OBJECT

Merlin gave him loyalty.
INDIRECT OBJECT

Most of Arthur's knights were also loyal to him.
OBJECT OF PREPOSITION

Also use the objective case of the pronoun when it is part of a compound object construction.

The knights pledged allegiance to both Guinevere and him.
COMPOUND OBJECT OF PREPOSITION

CHAPTER 8

Objective Pronoun Forms

	First Person	Second Person	Third Person
Singular	me	you	him, her, it
Plural	us	you	them

Compound Constructions To make sure you are using the correct case in a compound construction, look at each part separately.

Here's How **Choosing the Correct Case**

Lancelot loved both Arthur and (she, her).
(She, Her) and Arthur both loved Lancelot.

1. Try each pronoun from the compound construction alone in the sentence.

   Lancelot loved she. → **Lancelot loved her.** (objective case correct)

   She loved Lancelot. → **Her loved Lancelot.** (nominative case correct)

2. Choose the correct case for the sentence.

   Lancelot loved both Arthur and her.

   She and Arthur both loved Lancelot.

Always use the objective case after the preposition *between*.

Guinevere's heart was torn between Arthur and him.

❷ Why It Matters in Writing

Most stories have many characters and many opportunities for the misuse of pronouns. Whenever you revise a story, check your pronoun cases.

STUDENT MODEL

For a long time, one chair at King Arthur's Round Table remained empty. Anyone who tried to sit in it died instantly. When Galahad and his servant arrived, Arthur invited ~~they~~ them to sit at the table. Galahad took the empty chair and lived! The chair had been waiting for someone pure in heart, and that person was ~~him~~ he.

❸ Practice and Apply

A. CONCEPT CHECK: Nominative and Objective Cases

Choose the correct form from the pronouns in parentheses.

King Arthur: Legend or History?

1. Although King Arthur is a legendary hero, (he, him) probably existed as a real person as well.
2. While historians think that a real King Arthur existed, (they, them) know little about him.
3. It is (them, they) who say that his legend may be based on a real leader of the fifth or sixth century.
4. The real Arthur may have been a Celtic military leader; (he, him) defended Britain from Anglo-Saxon invaders.
5. So many stories were told about (him, he) that he must have been heroic in real life.
6. The legends that grew from the stories were romances and show (we, us) how people thought knights should behave.
7. In reality, (they, them) were often greedy and violent and used their weapons to get what they wanted.
8. Arthur supposedly brought (they, them) together to improve their morality and the quality of life for citizens.
9. Tales about Arthur were originally oral, but eventually people wrote (they, them) down.
10. Over the course of time, legends grow until (they, them) have little resemblance to the truth.

➜ **For a SELF-CHECK and more practice, see the EXERCISE BANK, p. 606.**

PRONOUNS

B. REVISING: Providing Pronouns

On your paper, write an appropriate pronoun in the correct case for each numbered blank.

Sir Lancelot was one of the most colorful characters in Arthur's Round Table. Not only was **(1)** ________ popular with the ladies, he held quite a war record as well. In one battle **(2)** ________ knocked five knights off their horses and broke the backs of four of **(3)** ________. As **(4)** ________ became angrier, **(5)** ________ knocked off another 28 knights. When a lady led **(6)** ________ to his enemy, **(7)** ________ succeeded in beheading that enemy and freeing 60 of his fellow knights. Lancelot also loved Queen Guinevere. Even though Guinevere was the queen, **(8)** ________ was almost burned at the stake because of her affair with **(9)** ________. Lancelot raced in on his horse; **(10)** ________ rescued **(11)** ________ and returned **(12)** ________ to King Arthur before being banished to France. When **(13)** ________ read the legend of King Arthur, as told in Sir Thomas Malory's *Morte d'Arthur,* **(14)** ________ will think **(15)** ________ are reading a modern adventure story combined with a soap opera.

C. WRITING

The picture at the right shows a tournament in King Arthur's court. Choose one onlooker and write a paragraph describing the scene from that person's point of view. Underline the pronouns you use, and save the paragraph in your **Working Portfolio.**

LESSON 3 Possessive Case

1 Here's the Idea

Personal pronouns that show ownership or relationships are in the possessive case.

Possessive Pronouns			
	First Person	**Second Person**	**Third Person**
Singular	my, mine	your, yours	his, her, hers, its
Plural	our, ours	your, yours	their, theirs

Possessive pronouns can be used in two ways:

1. A possessive pronoun can be used in place of a noun. The pronoun can function as a subject or an object.
   I need a book on Australian myths.
   Can I borrow yours? Mine is at home.
   DIRECT OBJECT (yours) SUBJECT (Mine)

2. A possessive pronoun can be used to modify a noun or a gerund. The pronoun comes before the noun or the gerund it modifies.
   We learned their history through our reading.
   NOUN (their history) GERUND (our reading)

Remember that a gerund acts as a noun. That's why it can be modified by a possessive pronoun.

POSSESSIVE (Our)
Our sailing to Australia was a terrific experience.
GERUND (sailing)

Do not use a possessive pronoun with a participle.

OBJECTIVE (us)
Our friend watched us sailing away.
PARTICIPLE (sailing)

For more information on participles and gerunds, see p. 71–75.

Avoid confusing possessive pronouns with their sound-alike contractions. Read the sentences below to help you understand the difference between these two kinds of words.

You're visiting Australia? [You are]	**Your** book is here.
They're painting a scene. [They are]	**Their** culture is so old.
There's so much to see. [There is]	We have no songs like **theirs.**
It's too bad we can't stay. [It is]	Each landform has **its** story.

PRONOUNS

❷ Why It Matters in Writing

Using pronouns with *-ing* words can be tricky. When you want to stress the **action,** use a gerund with a possessive pronoun: ***His waiting*** *is over.* When you want to stress the **actor,** use the objective form of the pronoun with a participle: *I saw* ***him waiting*** *at the corner.*

STUDENT MODEL

Some rock art of the Australian aborigines is thousands of years old. **My** photographing these symbols was the high point of our trip. At one stop, the guide called me over to look at an unusual image. I saw **him** pointing to a six-fingered handprint!

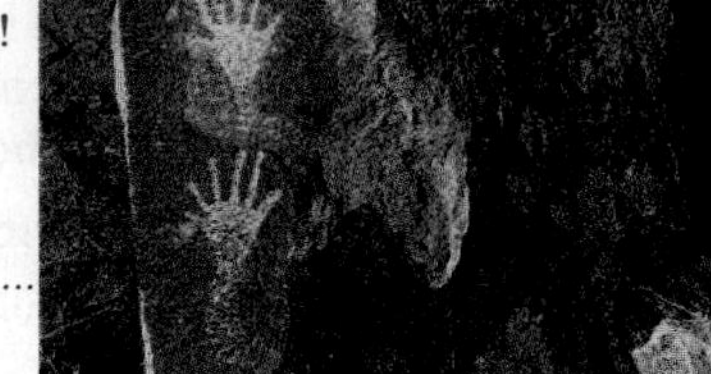

CHAPTER 8

❸ Practice and Apply

A. CONCEPT CHECK: Possessive Case

Write the possessive pronouns in the following sentences.

1. Our Australian friend told us a story from her homeland, the land of the aborigines.
2. She told us about their "dreamtime," a time long ago when our animal ancestors inhabited the earth.
3. People back then talked with the animals, friends of theirs.
4. No people knew how to make fire in those days until their friend Joongabilbil the Chicken Hawk taught them.
5. "Without fire," he said, "your children will starve."

➜ **For a SELF-CHECK and more practice, see the EXERCISE BANK, p. 606.**

B. PROOFREADING: Pronoun Errors

Correct the pronoun errors in each sentence on your paper.

1. Creating a small fire in a tree, he said, "Now take some of my burning branches to you're homes."
2. When they're fires went out, the people came back; and they complaining was noisy.
3. As the people watched his rubbing branches together, Joongabilbil said, "Making fire: this is how its done."
4. "Me replacing your fires daily won't work; you must learn and pass on this knowledge to you're children."
5. This legend of Australia shows that knowledge of fire came from it's unlikely hero, a chicken hawk.

Using *Who* and *Whom*

1 Here's the Idea

▶ **The case of the pronoun *who* is determined by the function of the pronoun in the sentence.**

Forms of *Who* and *Whoever*

Nominative	who, whoever
Objective	whom, whomever
Possessive	whose, whosever

Who and *whom* can be used to ask questions and to introduce subordinate clauses.

Who and *Whom* in Questions

Who is the nominative form of the pronoun. In questions, *who* is used as a subject or as a predicate pronoun.

Who knows the story of Mulan, a heroine of Old China?
SUBJECT

The heroine was who?
PREDICATE PRONOUN

Whom is the objective form. In a question, *whom* is used as a direct or an indirect object of a verb or as the object of a preposition.

Whom did Mulan fool?
DIRECT OBJECT

She told whom the secret of her identity?
INDIRECT OBJECT

Here's How **Choosing *Who* or *Whom* in a Question**

To (who, whom) was the order given?

1. Rewrite the question as a statement.
   The order was given to (who, whom).
2. Figure out whether the pronoun is used as a subject, an object, a predicate pronoun, or the object of a preposition. Then choose the correct form.
   The order was given to whom. (*whom* is the object of the preposition *to*)
3. Use the correct form in the original question.
   To whom was the order given?

PRONOUNS

Who and *Whom* in Subordinate Clauses

One of the trickiest pronoun situations involves using *who* and *whom* in clauses. In such cases, look only at how the pronoun functions within the clause.

▶ **Use *who* when the pronoun is the subject of a subordinate clause.**

SUBORDINATE CLAUSE

It's the rebel chief who is threatening the borders.

SUBJECT

▶ ***Use whom* when the pronoun is an object in a subordinate clause.**

SUBORDINATE CLAUSE

The chief whom we all fear most is a rebel.

DIRECT OBJECT

Here's How Choosing *Who* or *Whom* in a Clause

No one knows (who, whom) wrote the *Ballad of Mulan.*

1. Identify the subordinate clause in the sentence.
   (who, whom) wrote the *Ballad of Mulan*
2. Is the pronoun used as the subject of the clause? Is the pronoun used as the object in the clause? (You may have to rewrite the clause to decide.)
   The pronoun is the subject of the clause. *Who* is the correct choice.
   Who wrote the *Ballad of Mulan?*
3. Choose the correct pronoun for the sentence.
   No one knows who wrote the *Ballad of Mulan.*

Don't assume that *whomever* is correct after the preposition *to.* Choose *whoever* or *whomever* based on the pronoun's function in the subordinate clause.

Give credit to (whoever, whomever) wrote the poem.

Give credit to whoever wrote the poem.

2 Why It Matters in Writing

Writers frequently misuse *who, whom, whoever,* or *whomever* after prepositions, especially in subordinate clauses. What sounds right may not be correct. To avoid mistakes, keep checking the function of the word in the sentence or clause.

Chinese history is filled with stories of invading nomads who caused trouble for whoever was in their way.

3 Practice and Apply

A. CONCEPT CHECK: Using *Who* and *Whom*

Choose the correct pronoun from those in parentheses.

Mulan: The Steel Magnolia

1. The Chinese heroine (who, whom) went to war disguised as a man was portrayed in the popular movie *Mulan.*
2. In the movie, Mulan's father, (who, whom) has fought bravely in the past, is ordered to serve in the army once again.
3. Mulan is afraid that her father, (who, whom) she loves very much, is now too old to go to war.
4. To save his life, she disguises herself and goes in his place so that (whoever, whomever) sees her will think she is a man.
5. During the war, the soldiers discover (who, whom) Mulan really is.
6. (Who, Whom) was the real Mulan?
7. Historians think she was a real person about (who, whom) a famous poem was written more than a thousand years ago.
8. The emperor offered her a reward; but Mulan, (who, whom) wished to go home, accepted only a fine horse.
9. The real Mulan's identity was not discovered until comrades with (who, whom) she had fought visited her at home.
10. For (whoever, whomever) is curious, "Mulan" means "magnolia."

➜ **For a SELF-CHECK and more practice, see the EXERCISE BANK, p. 607.**

B. PROOFREADING: Correcting Errors Using *Who* and *Whom*

Find the sentences in which *who* and *whom* are used incorrectly. Correct each sentence that contains an error.

Women Warriors

(1) Many women in history are known for their bravery in battle. **(2)** One was Raziyya Iltutmish, who ruled Northern India from 1236 to 1240. **(3)** Raziyya's father chose his daughter, who he considered superior to his sons, as his successor. **(4)** Riots protesting a woman ruler broke out, and it was Raziyya herself whom led the troops to restore peace. **(5)** Joan of Arc was the French heroine whom, in 1429, helped to drive the English out of France. **(6)** Joan lived to see the coronation of Charles VII, the man for who she had fought so valiantly. **(7)** Deborah Sampson was the first American woman who we know of that joined an army in combat. **(8)** Like Mulan, Sampson, who fought in the Revolution, dressed as a man to hide her gender.

PRONOUNS

Pronoun-Antecedent Agreement

1 Here's the Idea

▶ **A pronoun must agree with its antecedent in number, gender, and person.** An **antecedent** is the noun or pronoun that a pronoun refers to or replaces.

Agreement in Number

If the antecedent is singular, use a singular pronoun. If the antecedent is plural, use a plural pronoun.

SINGULAR

The *Ramayana* is one of India's greatest epics. It tells stories about heroic characters. Two of them are Rama and Sita, his wife.

PLURAL

Agreement with Compound Subjects Use a plural pronoun to refer to nouns or pronouns joined by *and*.

PLURAL

Rama and Ravana clash when they fight over Sita.

A pronoun that refers to nouns or pronouns joined by *or* or *nor* should agree with the noun or pronoun nearer to it.

REFERS TO

Neither Ravana nor Rama's troops can defeat their foes.

Agreement with Collective Nouns A collective noun, such as *family,* may be referred to by either a singular or a plural pronoun. The number of the collective noun is determined by its meaning in the sentence.

Use a singular pronoun if the collective noun names a group acting as a unit. In the following sentence, *family* refers to the group as a unit and takes a singular pronoun.

REFERS TO

The family finally gives its support to Rama.

Use a plural pronoun if the collective noun shows the members or parts of a group acting individually. In the sentence below, *family* refers to the group as individuals and takes a plural pronoun.

REFERS TO

Rama's family argue over their plans to rescue Sita.

CHAPTER 8

Agreement in Gender and Person

The gender of a pronoun must be the same as the gender of its antecedent. Remember that *gender* refers to the masculine (*he, him, his*), feminine (*she, her, hers*), or neuter forms (*it, its*) of personal pronouns.

Hanuman, the monkey chief, brings his troops to the battle.

Gender-Free Language Don't use only masculine or only feminine pronouns when you mean to refer to both genders. The purpose of gender-free language is to make sure you include everyone.

Here's How Using Gender-Free Language

There are two simple ways to rewrite a sentence such as the following.

Every reader of the *Ramayana* has his favorite tales.

1. Rewrite the sentence to make the pronoun and its antecedent plural.
   Readers of the *Ramayana* have their favorite tales.
2. Use the phrase *his or her* when necessary.
   Every reader of the *Ramayana* has his or her favorite tales.

The person of the pronoun must be the same as the person of its antecedent.

REFERS TO

All you fans should buy your tickets for the latest Rama movie.

2 Why It Matters in Writing

Today's readers are offended by the old-fashioned use of *his* when referring to both males and females. However, *his or her* becomes awkward when used too often. Try making the antecedents and their pronouns plural to avoid awkwardness.

STUDENT MODEL

The **people** of India treasure the *Ramayana* in part because **they** believe that the epic will bring great blessings to **them. They** also adore the characters in the great Indian epic. **Every** Indian child and adult has **his or her** favorite part.

PRONOUNS

3 Practice and Apply

A. CONCEPT CHECK: Pronoun-Antecedent Agreement

Choose the correct pronoun from those in parentheses.

Rama and Ravana: Good Against Evil

1. Rama and Ravana are well known in India because of (his, their) roles as the hero and the villain, respectively, of the *Ramayana*.
2. In the epic, either Rama or his half-brother Bharata must give up (his, their) claim to the throne, and Bharata is made king.
3. Rama, his faithful wife Sita, and his loyal supporter Laksmana leave (his or her, their) home to live in the forest.
4. There, the demon king Ravana and his army kidnap Sita and take her away to (his, their) land.
5. Rama and Laksmana are unable to rescue Sita until a band of talking monkeys and bears offers to help (him, them).
6. At the head of the band is (its, their) leader, the mighty monkey-general Hanuman.
7. In a great battle, neither Ravana nor his demons are easy to defeat because of (his, their) ability to change shapes at will.
8. However, Ravana is defeated by Rama's army through (its, their) incredible feats of strength and bravery.
9. Ravana's army must accept (its, their) defeat.
10. Rama and Sita return to (his or her, their) country's capital, where Rama is finally crowned king.

For a SELF-CHECK and more practice, see the EXERCISE BANK, p. 608.

CHAPTER 8

B. REVISING: Using Gender-Free Language

Use gender-free language to revise the following sentences. Make sure the verbs and other words agree with their subjects.

The *Ramayana* Around the World

1. An Indonesian can cheer for her favorite character in puppet performances of the *Ramayana*.
2. The epic is often performed as a dance-drama; thus, an actor who wants a role must prove that he can dance as well as act.
3. These interpretations are often performed by a character holding a mask in front of her face.
4. A person from South and Southeast Asia will probably see his beliefs reflected in performances of the *Ramayana*.
5. During a festival in our country, an individual could enjoy himself by watching six different performances of the epic.

Indefinite Pronouns as Antecedents

1 Here's the Idea

▶ **A personal pronoun must agree in number with the indefinite pronoun that is its antecedent.**

The number of an indefinite pronoun is not always obvious. Use the chart below when you are trying to determine the number of an indefinite pronoun.

Indefinite Pronouns

Singular		Plural	Singular or Plural
another	much	both	all
anybody	neither	few	any
anyone	nobody	many	more
anything	no one	several	most
each	nothing		none
either	one		some
everybody	somebody		
everyone	someone		
everything	something		

Indefinite pronouns that end in *one, body,* or *thing* are always singular.

Agreement with Indefinite Pronouns

Use a singular pronoun to refer to a singular indefinite pronoun.

REFERS TO

Each myth has its own heroes and villains.

REFERS TO

Everyone has his or her favorite myth.

Notice that the phrase *his or her* is considered a singular personal pronoun.

Use a plural pronoun to refer to a plural indefinite pronoun.

Both of the Viking chiefs have their loyal followers.

Only a few of us brought our mythology books along.

PRONOUNS

Indefinite Pronouns That Can Be Singular or Plural

Some indefinite pronouns can be singular or plural. Use the meaning of the sentence to determine whether the indefinite pronoun is singular or plural.

Use the intervening prepositional phrase to help you decide whether the indefinite pronoun is singular or plural.

None of the mythology has lost its appeal.

Since the noun in the prepositional phrase is singular, the pronoun is singular.

Most of the stories have their origins in tribal myths.

Since the noun in the prepositional phrase is plural, the pronoun is plural.

2 Why It Matters in Writing

If your personal pronouns and their indefinite antecedents don't agree, readers will find your writing confusing.

CHAPTER 8

STUDENT MODEL

During the 700s and 800s, the dreaded Norse Vikings raided the lands around the North Sea in Europe. Some raided villages at night, destroying **most** of ~~it~~ *them* before dawn. **Anyone** spotting a fleet of Viking ships would tell ~~their~~ *his or her* friends to hide in the woods.

Most refers to *villages* and requires a plural pronoun.

Anyone is singular and requires a singular pronoun.

3 Practice and Apply

A. CONCEPT CHECK: Indefinite Pronouns as Antecedents

Choose the correct pronoun from those in parentheses.

Balder and Loki: Norse Hero and Villain

1. In one Norse myth, all of the gods loved Balder, (his, their) gentle partner.
2. Most were upset when (he, they) heard a prophecy that the gentle Balder would soon die.
3. Balder's mother traveled around the world to ask all the beings to give (its, their) promise not to harm Balder.
4. Each gave (its, their) promise, except for the tiny mistletoe plant, which she forgot to ask.
5. Everybody believed that (his or her, their) friend would be protected by his mother's actions.
6. The gods didn't know that (his or her, their) friend was still doomed.
7. Loki, who was jealous because few gave (his or her, their) love to him, made an arrow from the mistletoe plant.
8. The gods were playing a game; each tossed (his or her, their) arrow or stone at Balder, but none hurt him.
9. When Loki gave his mistletoe arrow to one of the gods, (he, they) threw it at Balder and killed him.
10. Balder's death plunged the gods into grief so deep that no one ever gave Loki (his or her, their) forgiveness.

➜ **For a SELF-CHECK and more practice, see the EXERCISE BANK, p. 608.**

B. EDITING: Making Pronouns Agree

Edit the following paragraph by correcting the errors in pronoun-antecedent agreement.

Hero Rabbit

In an Incan fable, the animals in the jungle had a meeting to choose the jaguar or the lion as king. Everyone came to the meeting to cast their vote except the rabbit. Many gave his or her votes to the jaguar, but the same number voted for the lion. To break the tie, someone had to volunteer their services to carry the rabbit to the meeting. The jaguar, thinking that the rabbit would repay the favor by voting for him, volunteered. The rabbit, however, voted for the lion because the lion was more peaceful. The jaguar learned that one who has their ideals well guarded cannot be easily swayed, even if you do him a favor.

PRONOUNS

Pronoun Reference Problems

1 Here's the Idea

▶ **The referent of a pronoun should always be clear.**

Indefinite Reference

Indefinite reference is a problem that occurs when the pronoun *it, you,* or *they* does not clearly refer to a specific antecedent. You can fix this problem by rewording the sentence and eliminating the pronoun or by replacing the pronoun with a noun.

Indefinite Reference

Awkward	Revised
In the "Superheroes" article, **it** discussed only three women.	The "Superheroes" article discussed only three women.
In the article, **they** state that girls aren't interested in superheroes.	The author of the article states that girls aren't interested in superheroes.
In other publications, however, **you** learn that girls are interested.	Other publications, however, claim that girls are interested.

General Reference

A **general reference** problem occurs when the pronoun *it, this, that, which,* or *such* is used to refer to a general idea rather than to a specific antecedent. You can fix the problem by rewriting the sentence.

General Reference

Awkward	Revised
The sidekick is weak and vulnerable, **which** makes the character appealing.	The sidekick's weakness and vulnerability make the character appealing.
Sidekicks don't like dangerous situations. **That** is how most people feel.	Like most people, sidekicks don't like dangerous situations.

Ambiguous Reference

Ambiguous means "having two or more possible meanings." An **ambiguous reference** problem occurs when a pronoun could refer to two or more antecedents. You can eliminate an ambiguous reference problem by rewriting the sentence to clarify what the pronoun refers to.

Ambiguous Reference

Awkward	Revised
Princess Xena and Gabrielle were featured in a 1990s TV show. **She** inspired a series of books as well.	Princess Xena and Gabrielle were featured in a 1990s TV show. Xena inspired a series of books as well.
Xena's allies help her overcome her enemies. **They** usually come from another kingdom.	Xena's allies, who usually come from another kingdom, help her overcome her enemies.

PRONOUNS

2 Why It Matters in Writing

Using indefinite, general, or ambiguous references can make your writing very confusing. Make sure your pronoun references are always clear so they show logical relationships among the ideas in your sentences.

STUDENT MODEL

DRAFT

In an article on the Internet, **it** says that Xena's village was attacked by an evil warlord when she was a young girl. Xena and her mother fought the invaders until **they** were driven out of the village. As a result of the experience, Xena discovered a sense of power in war. **It** inspired her to leave home and begin a life dedicated to waging war.

REVISION

An article on the Internet explains that Xena's village was attacked by an evil warlord when **Xena** was a young girl. Xena and her mother fought the invaders until **the invading forces** were driven out of the village. As a result of the experience, Xena discovered a sense of power in war. **This new feeling** inspired her to leave home and begin a life dedicated to waging war.

3 Practice and Apply

A. CONCEPT CHECK: Pronoun Reference Problems

Rewrite the following sentences to correct indefinite, general, and ambiguous pronoun references. (There may be more than one way to rewrite a sentence.)

Xena's Friends and Enemies

1. Before Xena became a heroine, she honed her warrior skills, but it was her human skills that were lacking.
2. It was for leaving her army; she paid the price by going through the gauntlet.
3. No warriors had survived it before her.
4. It was two lines of warriors clubbing the person—Xena—who ran through.
5. After surviving it, Hercules helped her start becoming a heroine.
6. Xena's archenemy is Callisto the Warrior Queen; her friends include Gabrielle the Amazon Princess and the handsome thief Autolycus.
7. When Gabrielle met Xena, her chief weapons were her quick wit and intelligence.
8. Autolycus enjoys danger, which probably attracts Xena.
9. In one episode, you learned that Xena was responsible for the death of Callisto's parents.
10. This made Callisto vow that she would destroy Xena.

For a SELF-CHECK and more practice, see the EXERCISE BANK, p. 609.

B. REVISING: Eliminating Pronoun Reference Problems

Revise the following paragraph; eliminate any pronoun reference problems.

Wonder Woman

She became the first female superhero when she appeared in comic books in the 1940s. More than 30 years later, you could see Wonder Woman come to life in a TV movie starring Cathy Lee Crosby. Then in 1976, Lynda Carter appeared as the main character in the *Wonder Woman* television series. From episode to episode, they covered everything from hostile alien life forms to a mad scientist to a computerized dating service. The last episode aired in 1979. Nonetheless, it paved the way for shows featuring other superheroines—like Xena.

CHAPTER 8

Other Pronoun Problems

1 Here's the Idea

▶ **Pronouns can be used with an appositive, in an appositive, or in a comparison.** The guidelines in this lesson can help you choose the correct pronoun in each of these situations.

Pronouns and Appositives

An appositive is a noun or a pronoun that follows another noun or pronoun for the purpose of identifying or explaining it.

The cartoonist, my friend, created the popular superhero.
APPOSITIVE (friend)

***We* and *Us* with Appositives** The pronouns *we* and *us* are often used with appositives. The nominative case, *we,* is used when the pronoun is a subject. The objective case, *us,* is used when the pronoun is an object.

We artists dream about creating our own superhero strip.
APPOSITIVE (artists)

Don't tell us beginners that it's impossible.
APPOSITIVE (beginners)

Follow these guidelines to decide whether to use the nominative case or the objective case.

Here's How Using *We* and *Us*

No problem is too hard for (we, us) superheroes.

1. Drop the appositive from the sentence and read the sentence twice, using one of the pronoun choices each time.

   No problem is too hard for we.

   No problem is too hard for us.

2. Often the "sound" will instantly tell you the right choice. Otherwise, determine whether the pronoun is a subject or an object. In this sentence, the pronoun is the object of the preposition *for.*
3. Write the sentence and use the correct case.

   No problem is too hard for us superheroes.

Pronouns in Appositives A pronoun used as an appositive is in the case it would take if the noun were missing.

The publisher paid the students, Mario and him, for the strip.
APPOSITIVE (Mario and him)

PRONOUNS

The pronoun case is determined by the function of the noun it identifies. In this sentence, *students* is the direct object; so the pronoun in the appositive is in the objective case.

Follow these steps to figure out which pronoun case to use in an appositive.

Here's How Using Pronouns in Appositives

The reporters, Clark Kent and (she, her), are working together.

1. Rewrite the sentence with the appositive by itself.

   Clark Kent and (she, her) are working together.

2. Then try each pronoun in the appositive alone. Notice that in this sentence, you have to use a singular verb for each singular pronoun.

   she is working; her is working

3. Determine whether the pronoun is a subject or an object. In this sentence, the pronoun is a subject.

4. Write the sentence and use the correct case.

   The reporters, Clark Kent and she, are working together.

CHAPTER 8

Pronouns in Comparisons

A comparison can be made using *than* or *as* to begin a clause.

Clark Kent is more clumsy than I am.

No one looks as nervous as he does.

When you omit some words from the final clause in a comparison, the clause is called **elliptical.**

I knew she would be braver than I.

If you have trouble determining the correct pronoun to use in an elliptical clause, try filling in the unstated words.

Roger can draw Superman as well as (he, him).

Roger can draw Superman as well as he [can]. (CORRECT)

Roger can draw Superman as well as him [can]. (INCORRECT)

Notice that the meaning you want to express can affect the choice of a pronoun.

I like the hero better than they.

(This sentence means "I like the hero better than they do.")

I like the hero better than them.

(This sentence means "I like the hero better than I like them.")

2 Why It Matters in Writing

Using pronouns correctly in comparisons or with appositives helps your readers understand your meaning better. Proper usage helps identify pronouns as performers or receivers of action.

STUDENT MODEL

Dear Ms. Alvarez,

~~Us~~ We aspiring stuntwomen, **Chin Yau and ~~me~~ I**, showed some of our falls to Peter Bell, who stages action scenes in movies. Our friends, Nat and Bill, showed off for him too. He said that we were more agile than ~~them~~ they!

3 Practice and Apply

A. CONCEPT CHECK: Other Pronoun Problems

Choose the correct pronoun from those in parentheses.

Christopher Reeve: Real-Life Hero

1. (We, Us) movie fans know that the role of Superman in the *Superman* movies was played by Christopher Reeve.
2. When we heard that Reeve had been seriously injured in an accident, it shocked and saddened (we, us) listeners.
3. We sympathized with the whole Reeve family—his wife, his three children, and (he, him).
4. Christopher Reeve says that he used to think heroes were women and men who performed more courageous acts than (we, us) ordinary people.
5. Now he believes that (we, us) ordinary people become heroes when we show the "strength to persevere and endure in spite of overwhelming obstacles."

➜ **For a SELF-CHECK and more practice, see the EXERCISE BANK, p. 610.**

B. WRITING

Find your **Write Away** boasts and threats from page 178 in your **Working Portfolio.** Add two boasts or threats that use pronouns in comparisons.

Real World Grammar

Incident Report

Whether we're talking with friends or testifying in court, we're often asked to report what we saw and heard. Eyewitnesses sometimes write up a report like the one below. Pronouns help clarify who did what. Notice how the writer added and corrected pronouns to clarify the quick draft he had made.

Saturday, June 9, 7 P.M., Clark St. Beach

~~Us~~ *We* guards—Vince and ~~me~~ *I*—were patrolling the beach. About 300 yards offshore were a sailboat and a Jet Ski with a teenaged driver.

Suddenly we heard a loud crack! The Jet Ski had hit the sailboat! *We* ~~S~~aw the sailboat with its mast down, the Jet Ski circling on ~~it's~~ *its* side, and three heads bobbing up and down in the waves. Vince shouted, "*We've* ~~G~~ot to help them!" He plunged into the water and began swimming toward the crash site. I followed. Vince is a faster swimmer than ~~me~~ *I*, but ~~it~~ *he* still took about three minutes of hard swimming to get there. We heard a man, *who* was bobbing in the water, shout for help. *To us,* ~~H~~e screamed, "Find my little girl! *She's* ~~O~~ver there!" Looking at where he pointed, we couldn't see *anyone*. Vince swam in the general direction and dived underwater. When ~~he~~ *Vince* surfaced, the man shouted, "Farther to the right!" Vince swam farther and dived again. *He* ~~S~~tayed down a long time and emerged about 100 yards from where *he* had gone under. Gasping for breath, *he* came up holding a drowned girl *who* looked like a rag doll.

"Jack," Vince said to me, "Get that Jet Ski. *We've* ~~G~~ot to get her to shore." By this time, I had reached the teenager, ~~who's~~ *whose* head was bleeding. The father was clinging to *his* broken sailboat.

It's is a contraction, not a possessive pronoun.

It has no referent.

He is unclear.

Who's is a contraction, not a possessive pronoun.

Using Grammar in Writing	
Unclear reference	Help your readers track the action by making sure that every pronoun clearly refers to one antecedent.
Possessive pronouns	Avoid spelling mistakes! Don't confuse contractions with possessive pronouns.
Pronoun-antecedent agreement	Clarify how many people you're referring to by making sure every pronoun matches its antecedent in number and gender.
Pronoun case	Watch out for appositives and intervening phrases that might cause you to use the wrong case.

PRACTICE AND APPLY: Clarifying with Pronouns

Jack, the eyewitness, didn't have time to finish correcting his draft. Write the pronouns, including *which* and *who,* as well as personal pronouns, that will help him clarify the events in the rest of his report.

I shouted to the teenager, "Stay with the sailboat while Vince takes **(1)** _______ Jet Ski."

I told the dad to stay with the sailboat too. "Vince has got to get **(2)** _______ daughter to shore."

Quickly we got the Jet Ski to Vince, **(3)** _______ climbed on while I held the girl. I handed **(4)** _______ the girl, **(5)** _______ he took to shore immediately.

I swam back to the sailboat, to **(6)** _______ we all clung for support. Within minutes Vince came back. **(7)** _______ told the dad, "Paramedics are there. **(8)** _______ are trying to resuscitate **(9)** _______ daughter. You take this Jet Ski to shore to check on **(10)** _______."

As the dad left, we righted the sailboat and waited for the beach speedboat to pick **(11)** _______ up. By the time **(12)** _______ got to shore, the little girl had been revived. Holding **(13)** _______ dad's hand, she was awake and breathing normally. Her dad hugged Vince and told **(14)** _______, "You saved **(15)** _______ little girl's life! How can I ever thank you?"

Jack and Vince, who saved the lives of three victims, both will receive Citizen Hero Awards.

Dave Cameron
Chief of Police

PRONOUNS

Mixed Review

A. Using Pronouns Read the passage. Then write the answers to the questions below it.

Many have heard of Scheherazade, the legendary storyteller, but **(1)** they may not know her own story. **(2)** She, a heroine in her own right, agreed to marry the cruel King Shahriyar, **(3)** whom other women feared because he used to murder his brides. Anyone who married the king lost **(4)** her life. Neither Scheherazade nor her sister Dunyazad feared for **(5)** her life because they had a plan to save themselves and the other women. The plan was that the night after the wedding, Dunyazad would ask Scheherazade to tell a story. **(6)** She would then start a tale so enchanting that the king, **(7)** who loved stories, would spare her life in order to hear the end the next night . . . and the next, and so on. Scheherazade's stories make up *The Thousand and One Nights.* **(8)** It includes the tales of Sindbad the Sailor and of Aladdin and his magic lamp. Scheherazade's plan worked, because there was no better storyteller than **(9)** she. The tales continued for 1001 nights, during which time Scheherazade had three children. She and all the women knew that **(10)** their lives were safe because Scheherazade's qualities as a wife, mother, and storyteller had made the king fall in love with her and repent his cruelty.

CHAPTER 8

1. What is the antecedent of *they?*
2. Why is the nominative case correct for the pronoun *She?*
3. Why is the objective case correct for the pronoun *whom?*
4. What is the antecedent of *her?*
5. What are the antecedents of *her?*
6. What is the antecedent of *She?*
7. What is the case of *who?* Why would *whom* be incorrect?
8. What is the antecedent of *it?* Why would *they* be incorrect?
9. What case is the pronoun *she?* Why would *her* be incorrect?
10. What are the antecedents of *their?* Why would *her* be incorrect?

B. Pronoun Reference Problems The six italicized words in the passage below have indefinite, general, or ambiguous references. Rewrite the paragraph to eliminate the reference problems. (There may be more than one way to eliminate the problem.)

Penelope, Odysseus' wife, was pretty smart herself. Many suitors wanted to marry her to get Odysseus' wealth, *whom* they assumed was dead. She delayed each suitor for years by saying that she would accept *them* when she finished her weaving. Every night she pulled out what she'd done by day, so she never got anywhere with *it.* She fooled the suitors for three years, and they never caught on to *it.* In the nick of time, before she had to go through with *it,* Odysseus came home and killed *them.*

Mastery Test: What Did You Learn?

Choose the best way to write each underlined word or word group and mark the letter of your answer. If the underlined section needs no change, mark the choice "Correct as is."

<u>We</u> (1) superhero fans also enjoy the not-so-super hero <u>whom</u> (2) is a little smaller than Superman. We've grown to know and love Underdog, Superchicken, and The Tick, even though <u>he</u> (3) can't leap tall buildings in a single bound. Perhaps fans enjoy these characters because they don't take <u>they're</u> (4) lives very seriously. George of the Jungle, for example, is a funny Tarzan type. George's story begins when gorillas raised <u>he</u> (5) from a baby. Now he's become the klutzy king of the jungle <u>whom</u> (6) is crashing from tree to tree. George's best friends are a talking gorilla and an elephant who wishes to be a dog. However, a beautiful woman named Ursula comes between <u>them and he</u> (7). <u>Him</u> (8) is leaving the jungle because of <u>her.</u> (9) George moves to San Francisco, where <u>him</u> (10) and Ursula live hilariously ever after.

1. A. us
   B. our
   C. whoever
   D. Correct as is
2. A. he
   B. they
   C. who
   D. Correct as is
3. A. their
   B. there
   C. they
   D. Correct as is
4. A. themselves
   B. their
   C. them
   D. Correct as is
5. A. it
   B. him
   C. himself
   D. Correct as is
6. A. whomever
   B. who
   C. whoever
   D. Correct as is
7. A. they and him
   B. they and he
   C. them and him
   D. Correct as is
8. A. He
   B. His
   C. Them
   D. Correct as is
9. A. she
   B. hers
   C. anyone
   D. Correct as is
10. A. they
    B. them
    C. he
    D. Correct as is

PRONOUNS

Student Help Desk

Using Pronouns at a Glance

Nominative Case		Objective Case		Possessive Case	
I	we	me	us	my, mine	our, ours
you	you	you	you	your, yours	your, yours
he	they	him	them	his	their, theirs
she		her		her, hers	
it		it		its	

Use this case when
- the pronoun is a **subject**
- the pronoun is a **predicate pronoun**

Use this case when
- the pronoun is the **direct object**
- the pronoun is the **indirect object**
- the pronoun is the **object of a preposition**

Use this case for
- pronouns that show **ownership or relationship**

CHAPTER 8

Pronoun Pitfalls

Who's **Whose**	contraction: Who is possessive form	**Who's** your hero? **Whose** muscles are bigger?
They're **Their**	contraction: They are possessive form	**They're** the bravest women. **Their** speed is amazing.
You're **Your**	contraction: You are possessive form	**You're** extremely talented. **Your** brilliance is known everywhere.

Strictly Singles

Pronouns that end in *-one, -body,* or *-thing* are always singular.

someone	anyone
somebody	anybody
something	anything

Tricks to Fix Pronouns

Pronouns in Comparisons

Example: Superman is stronger than (**he**, him).	**Trick:** Add the missing word or words: than **he** is.

Pronouns and Appositives

Examples: Give (**we**, us) fans an example of your strength. The heroes, Vince and (**I**, me), received awards.	**Trick**: Drop the appositive and figure out how the pronoun works in the sentence: Give **us** an example. **I** received an award.

Pronouns in Compounds

Example: Please save Alana and (I, **me**) from the monster!	**Trick:** Drop the other part of the compound and figure out how the pronoun works in the sentence: Please save **me**!

PRONOUNS

The Bottom Line

Checklist for Using Pronouns

Have I . . .

____ used the nominative case for pronouns that are subjects and predicate pronouns?

____ used the objective case for pronouns that are objects?

____ used the possessive case for pronouns that show ownership?

____ used *who* and *whom* correctly?

____ made sure that all pronouns agree with their antecedents in number, gender, and person?

____ used the correct cases of pronouns in compounds, comparisons, and appositives?

____ made sure the pronoun referent is always clear and correct?

Using Modifiers

Tarantulas: Fact and Fiction

The tarantula is one of the most feared spiders of all and has been the star of several horror films. Yet many people would be surprised to learn that this spider makes a loyal, affectionate pet! It can be more tame than a hamster. The spider will bite only if provoked, and its "deadly" venom is not harmful to humans.

Theme: Animal Legends and Myths

Believe It or Not!

The modifiers in the movie poster *(giant, crawling)* evoke frightening images, but what about the modifiers in the article? Notice how they paint an entirely different picture of this "crawling terror." Used correctly, modifiers can help your readers imagine and feel what you are writing about.

Write Away: Attack of the Killer Goldfish!

Describe a common pet, such as a kitten, rabbit, hamster, or goldfish, in the language of a horror-movie poster. Then write a brief, straightforward description of the animal. Save the work in your **Working Portfolio.**

Diagnostic Test: What Do You Know?

Choose the best way to write each underlined section and mark the letter of your answer. If the underlined section needs no change, mark the choice "Correct as is."

Snakes evoke real strong reactions in many people. (1) Some are terrified of both poisonous and nonpoisonous snakes. Such fears are probably behind some of the far-fetched beliefs about these reptiles.

For example, despite the tales, flying snakes haven't never existed. (2) In fact, snakes don't even soar good. (3) They just fall gracefully out of trees. They can even fall from great heights without being hurt, and this ability can help them escape predators.

An even more sillier tale states that if you cut a snake into pieces, it can put itself back together. (4) This is totally untrue. A sliced-up snake is as dead as any corpse. (5)

1. A. Snakes evoke real stronger reactions in many people.
   B. Snakes evoke real strongly reactions in many people.
   C. Snakes evoke really strong reactions in many people.
   D. Correct as is

2. A. For example, despite the tales, flying snakes haven't never, ever existed.
   B. For example, despite the tales, flying snakes have never existed.
   C. For example, despite the tales, no flying snakes have never existed.
   D. Correct as is

3. A. In fact, snakes don't even soar real good.
   B. In fact, snakes don't even soar well.
   C. In fact, snakes don't even soar real well.
   D. Correct as is

4. A. An even sillier tale states that if you cut a snake into pieces, it can put itself back together.
   B. An even most silly tale states that if you cut a snake into pieces, it can put itself back together.
   C. An even more silliest tale states that if you cut a snake into pieces, it can put itself back together.
   D. Correct as is

5. A. A sliced-up snake is as dead as a corpse.
   B. A sliced-up snake is as dead as any other corpse.
   C. A sliced-up snake is as dead as corpses.
   D. Correct as is

MODIFIERS

Using Adjectives and Adverbs

Here's the Idea

Modifiers are words that give information about, or modify, the meanings of other words. Adjectives and adverbs are common modifiers.

For a review of adjectives and adverbs, see pp. 17–22.

Using Adjectives

▶ **Adjectives modify nouns and pronouns.** They answer the questions *which one, what kind, how many,* and *how much.* In the revision below, the writer adds adjectives to give the reader more specific information.

STUDENT MODEL

DRAFT

In England, people believed that carrying a spider in a pouch around the neck would prevent sickness.

REVISION

In **medieval** times, **many English** people believed that carrying a **small, harmless** spider in a **cloth** pouch around **their** necks would prevent **dreadful** sicknesses.

Proper adjectives are capitalized.

More than one adjective can be used with the same noun or pronoun.

Most adjectives come before the words they modify.

Words classified as other parts of speech can be used as adjectives.

Words Used as Adjectives	
Nouns	**cloth** pouch, **silk** shirt
Possessive pronouns	**their** necks, **her** head, **your** idea
Demonstrative pronouns	**this** house, **that** road, **these** hills, **those** people
Participles	**living** spider, **dreaded** plague

CHAPTER 9

A **predicate adjective** follows a linking verb and modifies the subject of a clause.

The spider looked harmless and small.

Using Adverbs

▶ **Adverbs modify verbs, adjectives, and other adverbs.** They answer the questions *where, when, how,* and *to what degree.* Adverbs such as *so, very, most, more,* and *ever* intensify the meanings of the words they modify.

STUDENT MODEL

A Cherokee story explains how Spider **very cleverly** steals the sun. Half the world is **always** dark, and the other half **always** light. Spider travels **far** to save her people.

Tells how Spider does something—*very* stresses the cleverness

Indicate when and where

Notice that an adverb can be placed before or after a verb it modifies.

Place modifiers like *only* and *even* next to the words they modify. Changing their positions will change the meanings of sentences.

Only she stole the sun. (No one else did it.)

She only stole the sun. (She merely stole it; she didn't destroy it.)

She stole only the sun. (She didn't steal anything else.)

2 Why It Matters in Writing

How important are modifiers? Read the following passage without the highlighted words. What critical information would be missing?

STUDENT MODEL

Certain poisonous spiders have a **well-deserved** reputation for being **dangerous.** If you **ever** see a **black** spider with a **red hourglass** mark on **its** belly, move **away quickly! Its** bite is **poisonous.**

❸ Practice and Apply

A. CONCEPT CHECK: Using Adjectives and Adverbs

On a separate sheet of paper, write each italicized word in these sentences, then indicate whether it is used as an adjective or as an adverb.

Spider Lore

1. Around the world, *superstitious* beliefs about spiders *still* persist.
2. *Some* people say that if you *accidentally* step on a spider, rain will come.
3. If *this* idea were true, it would be raining *everywhere,* all the time.
4. In Tahiti, people see the *web-spinning, lowly* spider as a shadow of the gods.
5. They teach children, *big* or *small, never* to harm any spider.
6. *South Sea* islanders say that if you see a spider drop *down* in front of you, you will receive a present.
7. Find a *tiny* spider on your clothes and you'll *soon* receive money.
8. In *Ozark folk* belief, discovering a web with your initials in it near a door brings you good luck *forever.*
9. Spiders have *often* been used in *traditional* medicine.
10. One *interesting* remedy involves rolling a *live* spider in butter and swallowing it!

➜ **For a SELF-CHECK and more practice, see the EXERCISE BANK, p. 611.**

B. WRITING: Creating Captions

Read the cartoon below and identify the modifiers the author uses. Then substitute and add your own modifiers to make the images more frightening or less frightening. For example, you might write "The *small gray* octopus, *alone* and *scared,* oozes *slowly* across the beach."

Calvin and Hobbes by Bill Watterson

LESSON 2

Problems with Modifiers

1 Here's the Idea

Writers may confuse an adjective with an adverb, use a double negative, or add an extra *here* or *there*. Can you find the five mistakes this writer made with modifiers?

STUDENT MODEL

(1) My grandmother tells urban myths real well. **(2)** Most people can't hardly tell if they're true or not. **(3)** She said that once a koala in a zoo felt badly after eating too many oily eucalyptus leaves. **(4)** This here koala was so full of oil that his fur caught fire when he sat on a heater! **(5)** You won't find no proof of this story, though.

Answers: (1) *really well,* not *real well;* (2) *can hardly,* not *can't hardly;* (3) *felt bad,* not *felt badly;* (4) *This koala,* not *This here koala;* (5) *won't find any,* not *won't find no*

Read on to find out how you can avoid these mistakes.

Adverb or Adjective?

It's easy to confuse adjectives and adverbs. For example, you might think all words that end in *ly* are adverbs, but some *ly* words—such as *lonely* and *lowly*—function as adjectives.

The lonely scientist turned a lowly insect into a radioactive terror.

Many words have both adjective and adverb forms. If you're not sure which form of a word to use, look at the word that it modifies. If the modified word is a noun or pronoun, use the adjective form. If it's a verb, adjective, or adverb, use the adverb form.

Some stories about real people are really strange.

Some words can function as either adjectives or adverbs depending on how they are used.

A weird tale may appear in the daily newspaper. (ADJECTIVE)

I read the newspaper daily. (ADVERB)

Two pairs of modifiers in particular cause writers problems: *good/well* and *bad/badly.*

Good = Adjective

A good urban myth has some truth to it. (*what kind* of myth? *good* myth)

The koala feels good today. (It feels happy.)

Well = Adjective or Adverb

Animals eat well in the zoo. (eat *how?* eat *well*)
ADVERB

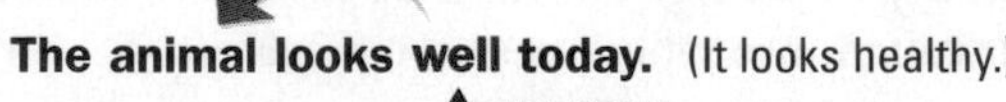

The animal looks well today. (It looks healthy.)
ADJECTIVE

Bad = Adjective

A bad myth is too phoney to be true. (*what kind* of myth? *bad* myth)

The koala felt bad after eating. (It felt sick or unhappy.)

Badly = Adverb

He tells stories badly. (tells stories *how? badly*)

Never write "He feels badly" or "She looks badly" when referring to someone's state of mind or health. You are saying the person literally *feels* (touches things) poorly or *looks* (sees things) poorly.

Double Negatives

In school and business writing, avoid the use of **double negatives**—two negative words in a single clause. Use only one negative word to express a negative idea.

NONSTANDARD: **I can't hardly believe that people flushed pet alligators into the sewers.**

STANDARD: **I can hardly believe . . .**
I can't believe . . .

NONSTANDARD: **You won't find no proof for this story.**

STANDARD: **You won't find any proof for this story.**
You will find no proof for this story.

The words *hardly, barely,* and *scarcely* often appear as parts of double negatives. When you use one of these words, make sure that there are no other negative words in the same clause.

This, That, These, Those

This, that, these, and *those* are demonstrative pronouns that can be used as adjectives. There are only three rules you need to remember when using these words as adjectives.

1. They must agree in number with the words they modify.

These kinds of myths stem from half-truths. (PLURAL)

This kind of myth stems from half-truths. (SINGULAR)

2. Never use *here* or *there* with demonstrative adjectives. The adjective already points out which one; it doesn't need any help.

NONSTANDARD: **This here sewer worker saw an alligator.**

STANDARD: **This sewer worker saw an alligator.**

3. Never use the pronoun *them* as an adjective in place of *these* or *those.*

NONSTANDARD: **Them people have written a book about urban myths.**

STANDARD: **These people (Those people) have written a book about urban myths.**

2 Why It Matters in Writing

In many real-world situations, such as applying for a job, the use of double negatives, *here* or *there* with demonstrative adjectives, or *them* as an adjective could make you appear less qualified.

STUDENT MODEL

Job Application—draft

I ~~can't~~ can hardly believe how this job matches my experience with kids ages 7 to 10. For the past year, I've been a volunteer at a skating rink, working with these ~~here~~ grade-school kids.

3 Practice and Apply

A. CONCEPT CHECK: Problems with Modifiers

For each sentence, write the correct choice of the words in parentheses.

Dog Catches Intruder!

1. Urban myths appear (frequent, frequently) in newspapers.
2. One example of (this type, these type) of story concerns a choking guard dog.
3. A woman comes home, and her dog is choking (bad, badly).
4. She (quick, quickly) takes the dog to a veterinarian and leaves it there.
5. She (hasn't, has) scarcely returned home when the phone rings.
6. The vet has found three fingers lodged (firm, firmly) in the dog's throat.
7. The vet shouts, "Don't waste (no, any) time! Get out of the house!"
8. The woman calls the police, who drive (rapid, rapidly) to her home.
9. They search the house (good, well) for intruders.
10. They find a (real, really) scared burglar hiding in the closet—with three fingers missing!

➜ **For a SELF-CHECK and more practice, see the EXERCISE BANK, p. 611.**

B. EDITING AND PROOFREADING: Correcting Errors

Rewrite these sentences, correcting errors in the use of modifiers.

Track of the Cougar

(1) Haven't you never heard of the cougar attacks in several Western towns? **(2)** These type of stories sound like urban myths, but they're true! **(3)** In recent years, people have been moving steady into cougars' mountain territories. **(4)** A few joggers have been injured real bad by the big cats, who think people are prey. **(5)** For this reason, people and cougars can't live together very good.

C. WRITING: Revising Paragraphs

Look over the **Write Away** pieces in your **Working Portfolio** and correct any modifier errors you find.

CHAPTER 9

LESSON 3

Using Comparisons

1 Here's the Idea

Have you ever said something like "I think horror films are better than mysteries"? If so, you have used a modifier to compare two or more things. Adjectives and adverbs have two forms that can be used to make comparisons: the comparative form and the superlative form.

Making Comparisons	
An adjective or adverb modifies a word and makes no comparison.	In most legends, Coyote is a **smart** trickster.
The **comparative** compares two persons, places, or things.	Coyote is **smarter** than Wolf at outwitting people.
The **superlative** compares three or more persons, places, or things.	Coyote is the **smartest** of all the animals.

MODIFIERS

Regular Comparisons

Most modifiers are changed in regular ways to show comparisons.

Regular Comparisons

Rule	Comparative	Superlative
Add *-er* or *-est*		
• to a one-syllable word	tough**er**	tough**est**
• to many two-syllable words	happi**er**	happi**est**
Use *more* or *most*		
• with some two-syllable words to avoid awkward sounds	**more** helpless (*not* helplesser)	**most** helpless (*not* helplessest)
• with words of more than two syllables	**more** important	**most** important
• with adverbs ending in *ly*	**more** quickly	**most** quickly

Never use the superlative form when comparing only two things.

NONSTANDARD: **Of the two stories, which was the most exciting?**

STANDARD: **Of the two stories, which was the more exciting?**

Irregular Comparisons

Some modifiers have irregular comparative and superlative forms.

He thinks storytelling is good and practical jokes are better, but tricks to get rich are the best of all.

Common Irregular Forms

Adverb or Adjective	Comparative	Superlative
good	better	best
well	better	best
far	farther, further	farthest, furthest
bad	worse	worst
much	more	most
many	more	most
little	less, lesser	least

CHAPTER 9

2 Why It Matters in Writing

Understanding the differences between comparative and superlative forms can help you choose the correct forms in your work. You'll avoid mistakes like those in the model below.

STUDENT MODEL

Ranchers and wildlife experts are learning that coyotes are better at surviving than wolves ever were. For instance, of the two animals, coyotes are ~~the smartest~~ smarter at finding new sources of food. However, the most important~~est~~ factor may be that whenever people kill coyotes, the survivors have more pups than usual. There are more coyotes today than there were 100 years ago!

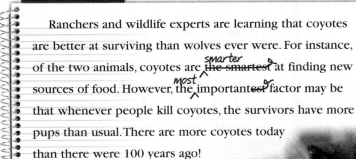

3 Practice and Apply

A. CONCEPT CHECK: Using Comparisons

For each sentence, write the correct comparative or superlative form.

Coyote, Iktome, and the Rock (from a Sioux Story)

1. Coyote and his friend Iktome discovered the (most remarkable, remarkablest) rock.
2. "I think this rock has power," Coyote said. He gave it his (better, best) blanket to keep it warm in the chill weather.
3. As they traveled on, the weather became (worse, worser).
4. Iktome was cold, but Coyote was (colder, coldest).
5. "That rock has (less, least) feeling than I do. I'm going to get my blanket back. Stupid rock—why does it need a cover?"
6. However, the more Coyote pulled, the (harder, hardest) the rock held on to the blanket.
7. Coyote finally yanked it off and ran, every step taking him (fartherest, farther) away from the rock.
8. Behind him, he heard a rumbling sound getting (louder, loudest) every moment.
9. The rock squashed Coyote (flatter, flattest) than a rug and wrapped itself in the blanket again.
10. The (best, better) advice is "If you have something to give, give it forever."

For a SELF-CHECK and more exercises, see the EXERCISE BANK, p. 612.

B. WRITING: Interpreting Graphs

Home on the Range
This graph compares animal ranges in 1850 and 1990. For each blank in the sentence below, write a comparative or superlative form of *many* or *few*.

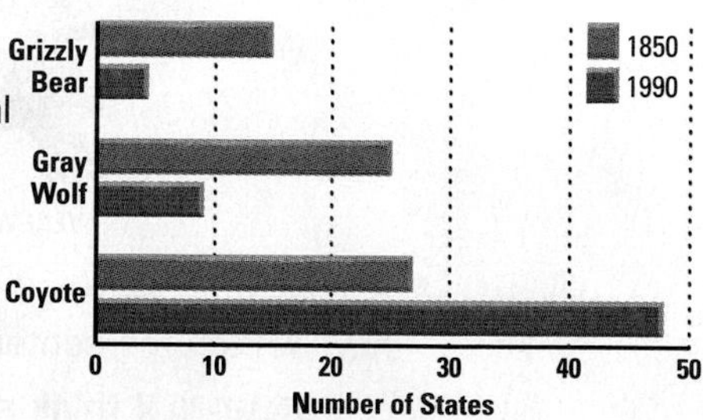

Source: *The Nature of North America,* 1998.

1. In 1850 gray wolves lived in _______ states than grizzly bears.
2. In 1990 gray wolves could be found in far _______ states than in 1850.
3. Of the three animals, coyotes live in the _______ states.
4. Grizzly bears can be found in the _______ states.

MODIFIERS

Problems with Comparisons

1 Here's the Idea

When using modifiers to compare two or more things, writers may commit two errors: double comparisons and illogical comparisons.

Double Comparisons

▶ **Do not use both *-er* and *more* to form a comparative. Do not use both *-est* and *most* to form a superlative.** Double comparisons are always incorrect.

NONSTANDARD: **The actor's eyes were more yellower than a wolf's.**

STANDARD: **The actor's eyes were yellower than a wolf's.**

NONSTANDARD: **He wears the most hairiest makeup I've ever seen.**

STANDARD: **He wears the hairiest makeup I've ever seen.**

Illogical Comparisons

▶ **When you are comparing something that is part of a larger group to the group itself, use *other* or *else* to avoid an illogical comparison.** In the following sentence, the writer meant to compare the werewolf to other monsters. But is that what the sentence says?

NONSTANDARD: **I think a werewolf is more mysterious than any monster.**

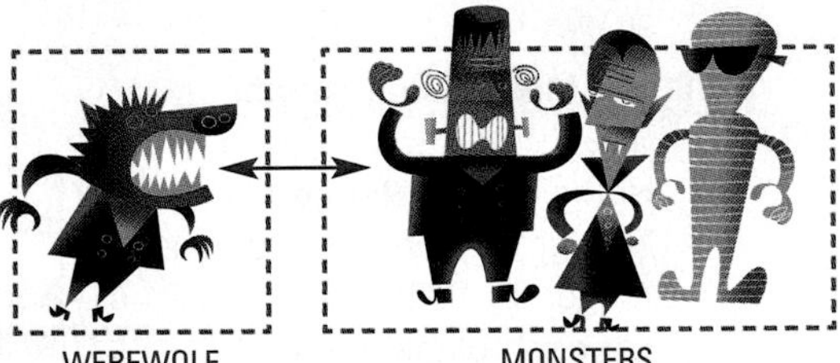

Because the werewolf is a kind of monster, too, the writer should have written the sentence this way:

STANDARD: **I think a werewolf is more mysterious than any other monster.**

2 Why It Matters in Writing

Correct comparisons help the reader understand what you are comparing and to what degree.

STUDENT MODEL

Modern filmmakers have created ~~more~~ scarier and *more* realistic werewolves than filmmakers in the past. The ~~better~~ *best* of the werewolf films is *An American Werewolf in London*. It won an Oscar in 1982 for makeup. I think it was more frightening than any *other* film of the year.

MODIFIERS

3 Practice and Apply

CONCEPT CHECK: Problems with Comparisons

Correct the illogical and double comparisons in the following sentences. If a sentence contains no error, write *Correct.*

How to Make a Werewolf

1. *The Wolf Man* (1941) was the most scariest film of its time.
2. The movie made Lon Chaney, Jr., more popular than any actor in his family.
3. In those days, film had fewer special effects than modern movies have.
4. Filmmakers created special effects with a far more slower technique, called stop-motion photography.
5. The technique involved shooting footage one frame at a time, in a process more time-consuming than any special effect.
6. The most easiest way to create a werewolf was to apply fake hair a little at a time, shooting a few frames at each stage.
7. The actor looked hairier than anyone on the movie set.
8. In modern werewolf movies, computers and robotics are used to create more better monsters.
9. *An American Werewolf in London* had the most wildest makeup, including extra long fangs on the werewolf.
10. The transformation looked stranger than in earlier movies.

For a SELF-CHECK and more exercises, see the EXERCISE BANK, p. 612.

Grammar in Literature

Setting the Scene with Modifiers

Modifiers help writers
- create a vivid image of a person, place, or thing
- provide key details and information in only a few words
- compare two or more people, places, or things

In the following excerpt, the author uses modifiers to describe a dog's reaction to extreme cold.

CHAPTER 9

To Build a Fire

Jack London

At the man's heels trotted a dog, a big native husky, the proper wolf dog, gray-coated and without any visible or temperamental difference from its brother, the wild wolf. The animal was depressed by the tremendous cold. It knew that it was no time for travelling. Its instinct told it a truer tale than was told to the man by the man's judgment. In reality, it was not merely colder than fifty below zero; it was colder than sixty below, than seventy below. It was seventy-five below zero. Since the freezing point is thirty-two above zero, it meant that one hundred and seven degrees of frost obtained. The dog did not know anything about thermometers. Possibly in its brain there was no sharp consciousness of a condition of very cold such as was in the man's brain. But the brute had its instinct. It experienced a vague but menacing apprehension that subdued it and made it slink along at the man's heels, and that made it question eagerly every unwonted movement of the man as if expecting him to go into camp or to seek shelter somewhere and build a fire.

Adjectives paint a vivid picture of the dog.

Comparisons are used to tell how cold it was and to contrast the dog's feeling about the conditions with the man's.

Adjectives and adverbs describe the dog's reaction to the conditions.

Using Modifiers to Provide Key Information

Adjectives	In descriptions, it's better to use a few selected adjectives than to pile them up and slow your readers down *(big native husky* versus *big, handsome, steel-eyed native husky).*
Adverbs	Words that intensify, such as *very, so,* and *extremely,* can be overused. For example, instead of using *very often,* choose a more precise modifier, such as *frequently.*
Comparisons	With just a word or two ("... it was *colder* than sixty below, ...") you can quickly convey differences between people or things.

PRACTICE AND APPLY: Choosing Effective Modifiers

Read the following passage. Then choose modifiers from the list to fill in the blanks.

golden	precious	ancient Greek
this	several	brilliantly
one-eyed	jealously	always

(1) In (what kind?) legends, the griffin (how?) guards a treasure of jewels and gold. **(2)** (which one?) fabulous beast has the head and wings of an eagle and the body of a lion. **(3)** His only enemies are the (what kind?) fighters known as the Arimaspians. **(4)** These warriors are (when?) after the griffin's (what kind?) treasure. **(5)** In some stories, (how many?) griffins pull the chariot of the sun across the sky. **(6)** Their (what kind?) wings shine (how?) as they fly high above the earth.

Mixed Review

A. Adjectives and Adverbs Read the following passage. Then answer the questions below it.

LITERARY MODEL

(1) The country Fox and the city Cat were chatting one day. **(2)** The Fox bragged forever about all his tricks. **(3)** "I am so good! No matter what the danger, I have one hundred tricks to save myself." **(4)** The humble Cat said, "I have only one trick—climbing a tree. If it fails, I'm lost." **(5)** "One trick?" that proud Fox sneered. **(6)** "What if an eagle swoops down on you? **(7)** I must say, you are really stupid." **(8)** Suddenly a pack of baying hounds burst upon the two startled animals. **(9)** The Cat dashed so quickly up a tree he almost reached the top. **(10)** The unlucky Fox tried all his clever tricks but was caught by the hounds anyway.

—*Aesop's Fables*

CHAPTER 9

1. What nouns are used as adjectives in sentence 1?
2. Which word in sentence 2 is an adverb?
3. Is the word *good* in sentence 3 an adjective or an adverb?
4. What are the two adjectives in sentence 4?
5. What kind of adjective is the word *that* in sentence 5?
6. What question does the adverb *down* answer in sentence 6?
7. Which word in sentence 7 is a predicate adjective?
8. What participles are used as adjectives in sentence 8?
9. What are the adverbs in sentence 9?
10. In sentence 10, what questions do the adjectives *unlucky, all,* and *clever* answer?

B. Using Comparisons If an underlined word or phrase contains an error, write the correct word or phrase. If there is no error, write *Correct.*

There **(1)** isn't no other animal as mysterious as the cat. In the countries formerly known as Burma and Siam, cats were held in the **(2)** most highest regard. **(3)** Those kind of feelings were probably based on ancient beliefs about the animal's magical powers. Temple cats, in particular, were cared for really **(4)** good. People treated them better than **(5)** any cat. **(6)** Them cats were the guardians of the people who had died. Some were even **(7)** more holier because they were buried alive in the tombs of royalty. Of course, their **(8)** biggest challenge was to escape through holes in the tombs. Once they did, **(9)** those here cats were taken back to the temple. They were given **(10)** real expensive food and treated like gods and goddesses!

Mastery Test: What Did You Learn?

Choose the best way to write each underlined section and mark the letter of your answer. If the underlined section needs no change, mark the choice "Correct as is."

<u>Some people are afraid of the most tiniest housefly.</u> (1) Imagine, then, how frightening a fly the size of a car would be. <u>Makers of horror films take them scary prospects seriously.</u> (2) <u>Their insect fright movies are more terrifying than many horror films.</u> (3)

In *Them!* atomic testing is blamed for enormous ants roaming the New Mexico desert. <u>The ants are defeated in a real big battle in the Los Angeles sewer system.</u> (4) In *Beginning of the End,* radioactivity creates a plague of giant locusts. <u>At first, authorities can't hardly believe that everyone in Ludlow, Illinois, has vanished.</u> (5) Then a huge swarm of locusts heads for Chicago. The situation seems hopeless until the hero lures the locusts into Lake Michigan, where they drown.

1. A. Some people are afraid of the tinier housefly.
   B. Some people are afraid of the most tinier housefly.
   C. Some people are afraid of the tiniest housefly.
   D. Correct as is

2. A. Makers of horror films take this scary prospects seriously.
   B. Makers of horror films take these scary prospects seriously.
   C. Makers of horror films take these here scary prospects seriously.
   D. Correct as is

3. A. Their insect fright movies are more terrifying than many other horror films.
   B. Their insect fright movies are more terrifying than horror films.
   C. Their insect fright movies are more terrifying than any films.
   D. Correct as is

4. A. The real ants are defeated in a big battle in the Los Angeles sewer system.
   B. The ants are defeated in a really big battle in the Los Angeles sewer system.
   C. The ants are real defeated in a big battle in the Los Angeles sewer system.
   D. Correct as is

5. A. At first, authorities can't scarcely believe that everyone in Ludlow, Illinois, has vanished.
   B. At first, authorities can hardly believe that everyone in Ludlow, Illinois, has vanished.
   C. At first, authorities can't never believe that everyone in Ludlow, Illinois, has vanished.
   D. Correct as is

Student Help Desk

Using Modifiers at a Glance

	Modifier	Comparative	Superlative
Adjectives			
tell which one, what kind, how many, how much	green	greener	greenest
	gigantic	more gigantic less gigantic	most gigantic least gigantic
Adverbs			
tell when, where, how, to what extent	greedily	more greedily less greedily	most greedily least greedily

CHAPTER 9

Crafty Comparisons

	Comparative Form	Superlative Form
One-syllable words	Add *-er.*	Add *-est.*
Two-syllable words	Add *-er* or *more.*	Add *-est* or *most.*
Words with more syllables	Add *more.*	Add *most.*

Remember . . .

- Never use *-er* and *more* (*more higher*) or *-est* and *most* (*most highest*) together.
- Never use *-est* or *most* to compare only two things.
- Always use *else* or *other* when comparing one member of a group to the whole group.

Frank and Ernest by Thaves

Adjective or Adverb?

Modifier Mania

Adverb really, badly, well	They drive **badly.** He **really** wants to go. She plays **well.**
Adjective real, good, well, bad	It's a **real** story. I made a **bad** mistake. That's a **good** idea. They feel **good** (happy). She looks **well** (healthy). I feel **bad.**

Use the adverb form if . . .
the word modifies a verb, an adjective, or another adverb and tells how, when, where, or to what degree: **Crow behaved badly.**

Use the adjective form if . . .
the word modifies a noun or pronoun and tells which one, what kind, how much, or how many: **He stole food from his good friends.**

OR

the word follows a linking verb and refers to the subject: **He felt bad about what he did.**

MODIFIERS

The Bottom Line

Checklist for Using Modifiers

When I use modifiers, do I . . .

____ place them close to the words they modify?

____ choose the correct adverb or adjective forms?

____ avoid double negatives?

____ avoid using *them* for *these* or *those?*

____ avoid using *here* or *there* with demonstrative pronouns used as adjectives?

When I make comparisons, do I . . .

____ always use *-er* or *more* when comparing only two things?

____ avoid double comparisons and illogical comparisons?

Capitalization

If you're a STAR TREK fan, come and meet other "TREKKERS"; enter the costume contest for best ferengi, romulan, or vulcan; and learn to speak klingon at the world's biggest star trek convention.

Theme: Unusual Events

Calling All Trekkers!

Red alert! The person who wrote this ad needs to brush up on the rules of capitalization. Why do you think it's important to capitalize some letters and not others? For example, what is the difference in meaning between the words *Enterprise* and *enterprise?* between the words *Federation* and *federation?*

Write Away: An Event to Remember

Write a paragraph describing a memorable event from the last school year. It might be an unusual event or simply one that you found enjoyable. Save your paragraph in your **Working Portfolio.**

Diagnostic Test: What Do You Know?

For each underlined group of words, choose the letter of the correct revision.

Are you a follower of *The Next Generation*, deep space nine, *Voyager*, or the original *Star Trek* (1) series with captain James T. Kirk as commanding officer (2) of the starship *Enterprise?* If so, you may be interested in conventions sponsored by Starfleet: The International Star Trek Fan Association (3). if you're thinking, "That would be interesting," (4) I would like to tell you about some contests held at such conventions. You might enter a paper-airplane contest in which each plane must be made by its Captain and must carry one United States penny during flight (5). You might enter a costume contest for the best-dressed Starfleet officer, alien, or Greek god (6). Instead of attending a convention, you might prefer to take courses in literature, history, or other subjects at Starfleet academy (7), which has "campuses" all over the world, including Officer's Command college (8) in Harbord, new south Wales, Australia (9). You could even attend the Vulcan Academy of Science (vas) and take courses such as thermodynamics, Volcanology I, and logic (10).

1. A. Follower
   B. *The next generation*
   C. *Deep Space Nine*
   D. Correct as is
2. A. Captain
   B. james t. kirk
   C. Commanding Officer
   D. Correct as is
3. A. international
   B. fan
   C. association
   D. Correct as is
4. A. If you're thinking
   B. that
   C. Interesting
   D. Correct as is
5. A. captain
   B. Penny
   C. Flight
   D. Correct as is
6. A. Officer
   B. Alien
   C. God
   D. Correct as is
7. A. Literature
   B. History
   C. Academy
   D. Correct as is
8. A. officer's command college
   B. officer's
   C. College
   D. Correct as is
9. A. harbord
   B. New South Wales
   C. new South Wales
   D. Correct as is
10. A. VAS
    B. Thermodynamics
    C. Logic
    D. Correct as is

People and Cultures

Here's the Idea

People's names and titles, the names of the languages they speak, and the religions they practice are all proper nouns and should be capitalized.

Names and Initials

Capitalize people's names and initials.

Toni Morrison
Franklin Delano Roosevelt
R. L. Stine
Lyndon B. Johnson
Sandra Cisneros
B. B. King

Personal Titles and Abbreviations

Capitalize titles and abbreviations of titles that are used before names or in direct address.

Professor Stevens
Dr. Martin Luther King, Jr.
Chief Justice William H. Rehnquist
Lt. Col. Eileen Collins

Sgt. Kaspar escorted Ambassador Nakamora to the dinner.

Capitalize abbreviations of titles even when they follow names.

Emilio Estefan, Jr.
Stephen Baker, C.E.O.
Michelle Phillips, Ph.D.

Capitalize a title of royalty or nobility only when it precedes a person's name.

Queen Elizabeth I

Sir Winston Churchill

King Henry VIII

Count Victor

The poetry reading was attended by Sir Robert.

The audience included the prince and princess.

Family Relationships

▶ **Capitalize words indicating family relationships only when they are used as parts of names or in direct address.**

Aunt Ruth　　Uncle Ed　　Grandma Johnson

When my mother and Aunt Betty were children, did you read poetry to them, Grandfather?

In general, do not capitalize a word referring to a family relationship when it follows a person's name or is used without a name.

Ben, my brother, likes writing poetry.

The Pronoun *I*

▶ **Always capitalize the pronoun *I*.**

My friends and I had never been to a poetry slam before.

CAPITALIZATION

Ethnic Groups, Languages, and Nationalities

▶ **Capitalize the names of ethnic groups, races, languages, and nationalities, along with adjectives formed from these names.**

English　　Spanish　　Cherokee
Chinese　　Swahili　　German

Religious Terms

▶ **Capitalize the names of religions, religious denominations, sacred days, sacred writings, and deities.**

Religious Terms	
Religions	Christianity, Judaism, Islam
Denominations and sects	Sunni, Baptist, Methodist
Sacred days	Ramadan, Easter, Passover
Sacred writings	Bible, Koran, Torah
Deities	Allah, God

Do not capitalize the words *god* and *goddess* when they refer to gods of ancient mythology.

Athena was the Greek goddess of wisdom.

2 Practice and Apply

A. CONCEPT CHECK: People and Cultures

Identify and rewrite the words that contain capitalization errors in the following sentences.

Poetry Slam!

1. A poetry slam is a competition in which readers perform original poems that are rated by a panel of Judges.
2. "The difference between a slam and a traditional poetry reading," reports ms. malaika fisher, "is the level of energy."
3. Love, hate, death, Religion, and other topics about which people feel strongly are typical subjects of the poems.
4. Anyone is welcome to read at a slam, from your Dentist to your Grandmother.
5. All poets are welcome, from beginners to distinguished poets such as linda gregg, a teacher at a prestigious university.
6. If there is ever a poetry slam in my area, i plan to attend it.
7. Poetry slams take place in more than 100 american cities.
8. Now they are being held in other countries as well, with poets reading in languages such as german and swedish.
9. As Marc k. Smith, the Father of the poetry slam, says, "The performance of poetry is an art—just as much an art as the art of writing it."
10. Because of his role in originating and popularizing the poetry slam, smith has been nicknamed slampapi.

➜ **For a SELF-CHECK and more practice, see the EXERCISE BANK, p. 613.**

B. REVISION: Capitalization Errors

Identify and correct all capitalization errors in this family tree.

LESSON 2

First Words and Titles

1 Here's the Idea

First words in sentences, most lines of poetry, quotations, and outline entries are capitalized. Greetings and closings in letters and important words in titles are capitalized.

Sentences and Poetry

▶ **Capitalize the first word of every sentence.**

Many people enjoy reenacting historical events.

▶ **Capitalize the first word in every line of traditional poetry.**

LITERARY MODEL

Listen, my children, and you shall hear
Of the midnight ride of Paul Revere,
On the eighteenth of April, in Seventy-five;
Hardly a man is now alive
Who remembers that famous day and year.

—Henry Wadsworth Longfellow, "Paul Revere's Ride"

Modern poets often choose not to begin each line with a capital letter. You also have this choice in writing your own poems.

Quotations

▶ **Capitalize the first word of a direct quotation if it is a complete sentence.** Do not capitalize a direct quotation if it is a fragment of a sentence.

The e-mail said, "Is anyone interested in reenacting a battle?"

One player says reenactments are "the closest we can get to time travel."

▶ **In a divided quotation, do not capitalize the first word of the second part unless it starts a new sentence.**

"We have the costumes," the e-mail continued, "but we need history experts."

"Join our group," the writer said. "**Y**ou'll have fun."

CAPITALIZATION

Parts of a Letter

▶ **In a letter, capitalize the first word of the greeting, words such as *Sir* or *Madam*, and the first word of the closing.**

May 20, 200-

Civil War Reenactors
1800 W. Wheeling St.
Boston, MA 02124

Dear **S**ir:

I would be very interested in joining your group. I've read a lot about American history, and I've always wanted to take part in a reenactment. Please send me more information.

Yours truly,
Ellen Hobson

CHAPTER 10

Outlines

▶ **Capitalize the first word of each entry in an outline, as well as the letters that introduce major subsections.**

I. **H**istorical reenactments
  A. **R**eenactments of events in American history
    1. **F**amous battles
    2. **N**onmilitary events

Titles

▶ **Capitalize the first word, the last word, and all other important words in a title. Do not capitalize conjunctions, articles, or prepositions of fewer than five letters.**

Titles	
Books	*The **C**atcher in the **R**ye, The **O**ld **M**an and the **S**ea*
Plays and musicals	*The **D**evil and **D**aniel **W**ebster, **W**est **S**ide **S**tory*
Short stories	"The **G**ift of the **M**agi," "To **B**uild a **F**ire"
Magazines and newspapers	***P**eople, **N**ational **G**eographic, **N**ew **Y**ork **T**imes*
Movies	*The **P**hantom **M**enace, **G**one with the **W**ind*
Television shows	*The **S**impsons, The **T**oday **S**how*
Works of art	*The **T**hinker, **O**phelia*
Poems	"**M**y **P**apa's **W**altz," "The **R**oad **N**ot **T**aken"

2 Practice and Apply

A. CONCEPT CHECK: First Words and Titles

Identify and rewrite the words that contain capitalization errors in the following sentences.

Reenact It

1. each year, Civil War reenactors gather at Gettysburg, Pennsylvania, to reenact the battle that took place there.
2. One reenactment takes place at the Yingling Farm, where the movie *gettysburg* was filmed.
3. If you ask a participant, "are you an actor?" he or she may reply, "no, I'm a reenactor."
4. Newspapers like the *Civil War news* and magazines like *Camp Chase gazette* provide information for reenactors.
5. reenactors are not professional actors, but people who get together to reenact historical events.
6. "some groups specialize in reenacting battles," explained the tour guide.
7. The poem "Concord hymn," by Ralph Waldo Emerson, commemorates the first battle of the American Revolution, a good subject for a reenactment.
8. another kind of reenactment occurs at Renaissance fairs.
9. If you go to a Renaissance fair, people will be dressed like characters from Shakespeare's *Twelfth night* and *the Tempest.*
10. You might see a Shakespeare reenactor as he composes the line "shall I compare thee to a summer's day?"

➜ **For a SELF-CHECK and more practice, see the EXERCISE BANK, p. 614.**

B. EDITING AND PROOFREADING: Capitalization Errors

Find and correct 15 capitalization errors in this letter.

dear mr. oliver,

I thought you would like to know that I did something educational this summer! last week we went to a Renaissance fair. The whole fair is a dramatization of a day when Queen Elizabeth I leads a procession through an English village. everyone talks and dresses like characters out of *romeo And juliet*. A girl dressed as a lady-in-waiting said to us, "give ye good day, my lords and ladies," and we answered,"'Tis a passing fair day." there were jugglers, tumblers, and dancers; there were musicians playing and singing songs like "greensleeves" and "o mistresse mine."

sincerely,

Julia

CAPITALIZATION

Places and Transportation

1 Here's the Idea

The names of specific places, celestial bodies, landmarks, and vehicles are capitalized.

Geographical Names

▶ **In geographical names, capitalize each word except articles and prepositions.**

Geographical Names	
Divisions of the world	**A**rctic **C**ircle, **N**orthern **H**emisphere
Continents	**S**outh **A**merica, **A**ustralia, **A**frica
Bodies of water	**P**acific **O**cean, **S**nake **R**iver, **L**ake **M**ichigan
Islands	**W**est **I**ndies, **L**ong **I**sland, **C**anary **I**slands
Mountains	**M**ount **R**ainier, **A**lps, **A**llegheny **M**ountains
Other landforms	**G**rand **C**anyon, **M**ohave **D**esert, **R**ock of **G**ibraltar
Regions	**E**astern **E**urope, **S**candinavia, **L**atin **A**merica
Nations	**S**pain, **S**audi **A**rabia, **C**zech **R**epublic
States	**M**aine, **T**exas, **S**outh **C**arolina
Counties and Townships	**A**lameda **C**ounty, **M**iddlebury **T**ownship
Cities and towns	**H**ouston, **S**an **F**rancisco, **E**vanston
Roads and streets	**F**ifth **A**venue, **L**ake **S**hore **D**rive, **M**ain **S**treet

Directions

▶ **Capitalize the words *north*, *south*, *east*, and *west* when they name particular regions of the country or world or are parts of proper names.**

Interesting festivals are held all over the country, from the **W**est **C**oast to the **E**ast **C**oast, in the **N**orth and in the **S**outh.

Each year, the Apple Butter Festival is held in **W**est Virginia.

Do not capitalize words that indicate general directions or locations.

To get to the fair, drive north on Route 17.

Bodies of the Universe

▶ **Capitalize the names of planets and other specific objects in the universe.**

Halley's Comet   Venus   Pleiades

▶ **Do not capitalize *sun* and *moon.* Capitalize *earth* only when it is used with other capitalized astronomical terms. Don't capitalize *earth* when it is preceded by the article *the* or when it refers to land or soil.**

Of all the inner planets, only Earth and Mars have satellites.

The earth is rich in nutrients.

Buildings, Bridges, and Other Landmarks

▶ **Capitalize the names of specific buildings, bridges, monuments, and other landmarks.**

Washington Monument   Empire State Building

London Bridge   Gateway Arch

Pat sent me a postcard of the Golden Gate Bridge.

Planes, Trains, and Other Vehicles

▶ **Capitalize the names of specific airplanes, trains, ships, cars, and spacecraft.**

Vehicles	
Airplanes	*Flyer* (the Wright brothers' first successful airplane)
Trains	*Super Chief, City of New Orleans*
Ships	U.S.S. *Constitution, Half Moon*
Cars	Civic, Mustang
Spacecraft	*Sputnik 1,* space shuttle *Columbia*

CAPITALIZATION

❷ Practice and Apply

A. CONCEPT CHECK: Places and Transportation

For each sentence, write correctly the words that should be capitalized. If a sentence is correct, write *Correct.*

Flip That Flapjack!

1. Every year in liberal, kansas, in the united states of america, one day a year is designated International Pancake Day.
2. Liberal is in seward county, in southwestern Kansas.
3. On the other side of the atlantic ocean, in the british isles, the people of olney hold a similar celebration.
4. Olney is located in a county called buckinghamshire.
5. Women in Liberal compete against women in Olney in a race that is the only official one of its kind on the earth.
6. The race begins on pancake boulevard in liberal and at the market square in Olney.
7. You will not find a similar race in continental europe or in any other town in the united states.
8. The tradition began in 1445, even before Columbus's *Niña*, *pinta*, and *santa maría* set sail.
9. In a town in england, a woman who was making pancakes heard the church bells ringing and, not wanting to be late, ran to the church with skillet in hand.
10. Whether you come from the east or the west, visit liberal and celebrate Pancake Day with friends and family.

➜ **For a SELF-CHECK and more practice, see the EXERCISE BANK, p. 615.**

B. EDITING AND PROOFREADING: Capitalization Errors

Identify and correct ten capitalization errors in this paragraph.

The Festivals of Texas

The state of texas may have the most unusual festivals in the United States. For example, the city of san antonio starts off each year by draining the river and inviting residents to roll in the mud or throw mud at photos of their city council members. The world's biggest rattlesnake roundup takes place in sweetwater, where Texans collect about 6,000 pounds of rattlers and fry thousands of pounds of rattlesnake steaks. In shamrock, Texas, on St. Patrick's Day, everyone adds *O'* to his or her name. People in this town gather to kiss a slab of the Blarney Stone imported from cork, ireland. In dublin, Texas, festivals feature Irish dancers and an Irish stew cook-off. San Antonio dyes the river green and renames it the river shannon.

LESSON 4 Organizations and Other Subjects

1 Here's the Idea

Capitalize the names of organizations, historical events and documents, and months, days, and holidays.

Organizations and Institutions

▶ **Capitalize all important words in the names of organizations, institutions, stores, and companies.**

University of New Mexico

National Association of Manufacturers

Madison Township Middle School

Bernard's Fine Foods

Chicago Public Library

Kansas Department of Agriculture

Do not capitalize words such as *school*, *company*, *church*, *college*, and *hospital* when they are not used as parts of names.

Abbreviations of Organization Names

▶ **Capitalize abbreviations of the names of organizations and institutions.**

ABA (American Bar Association)

UCLA (University of California, Los Angeles)

OAS (Organization of American States)

USAF (United States Air Force)

Historical Events, Periods, and Documents

▶ **Capitalize the names of historical events, periods, and documents.**

The League of Nations was formed after World War I.

Historical Events, Periods, and Documents	
Events	American Revolution, Civil War
Documents	Declaration of Independence, Bill of Rights
Periods	Middle Ages, Roaring Twenties

CAPITALIZATION

Time Abbreviations and Calendar Items

▶ **Capitalize the abbreviations B.C., A.D., B.C.E., C.E., A.M., and P.M.**

According to Roman legend, Rome was founded in 753 **B.C.**

The restaurant is open from 7:00 **A.M.** to 10:00 **P.M.**

▶ **Capitalize the names of months, days, and holidays but not the names of seasons.**

March	summer	Memorial Day
Thanksgiving	Friday	spring

The activities will begin on Saturday, April 17, at 9 **A.M.**

When the name of a season is used in the title of a festival or celebration (Winter Carnival), capitalize it.

Special Events, Awards, and Brand Names

▶ **Capitalize the names of special events and awards.**

Super Bowl	Olympic Games
Newbery Medal	Academy Awards

The Chilean poet Pablo Neruda won the Nobel Prize for literature in 1971.

▶ **Capitalize the brand names of products but not common nouns that follow brand names.**

Strongstik adhesive tape	Power Pack batteries

School Subjects and Class Names

▶ **Capitalize the names of school subjects only when they refer to specific courses.** (Do, however, capitalize proper nouns and adjectives in all such names.)

geometry	American history
French	American History I

▶ **Capitalize the word *freshman, sophomore, junior,* or *senior* only when it is used as part of a proper noun or in a direct address.**

The Senior Council will meet next Thursday.

Please take your seats, Freshmen.

CHAPTER 10

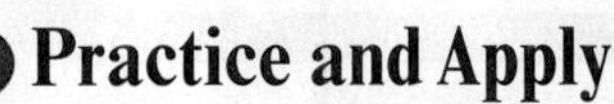

2 Practice and Apply

A. CONCEPT CHECK: Organizations and Other Subjects

For each sentence, write correctly the words that should be capitalized. If a sentence is correct, write *Correct*.

Bug Watch

1. Every april, purdue university plays host to an unusual event called the bug bowl.
2. This curious spring carnival was originated by Tom Turpin, an entomology professor.
3. Turpin, who teaches entomology 105, sees the event as a way to help people understand insects better.
4. One part of the weekend-long happening is a parade of cars decorated to look like different kinds of bugs.
5. A highlight is the cockroach race, the winner of which receives an award called the old open can—a bronzed garbage can with a cockroach on top.
6. In bug bowl 98, penn state challenged purdue to a Big Ten Spit-Off to see who would hold the cricket-spitting record.
7. People have eaten insects since before the stone age, and those attending can taste foods made with insects.
8. In 1995 the carnegie foundation for the advancement of teaching declared Turpin the "indiana professor of the year."
9. The award was presented by the council for advancement and support of education, or case for short.
10. The bug bowl is part of springfest, which offers nearly 100 activities and events.

CAPITALIZATION

➡ **For a SELF-CHECK and more practice, see the EXERCISE BANK, p. 615.**

B. MIXED REVIEW: Capitalization Errors

Rewrite the following newspaper ad, correcting all capitalization errors.

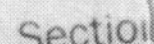

Section

LAKE CENTRAL HIGH SCHOOL CLASS OF '91 REUNION

Date	friday, september 7, 2001	saturday, september 8, 2001
Time	7:00 p.m. - 1:00 a.m.	1:00 p.m. - whenever
Event	alumni dinner and dance	old gold picnic
Location	springfield country club 2080 w. jefferson rd.	lincoln park

Real World Grammar

Itinerary

At some point, you may have the responsibility of creating an itinerary. An **itinerary** is a written record, schedule, or account of a journey. An itinerary should include the date, time, and location of each stop, highlights of the attractions, and other important information related to your trip. When you capitalize words appropriately, you help your reader distinguish general terms from specific names.

ITINERARY

DATE: Friday, june 29
EVENT: Uptown Poetry Slam
LOCATION: Old Mill Books, Chicago, Illinois
HIGHLIGHTS: Reading by class member callie ortiz at 8:00 P.M.

DATE: Saturday, June 30
EVENT: Pioneer Days
LOCATION: Utica, Illinois, outside of Starved Rock state park
HIGHLIGHTS: Craft displays, reenactment of the battle of starved rock

DATE: Sunday, July 1
EVENT: Bristol Renaissance faire
LOCATION: 12550 120th avenue, Kenosha, Wisconsin
HIGHLIGHTS: medieval games at 11:00 A.M., parade at 1:00 P.M.

Capitalize:

names of months

people's names

national and state parks

names of historical events

events

names of streets

names of historical periods

CHAPTER 10

PRACTICE AND APPLY: Creating an Itinerary

Your science club is planning a field trip to the East Coast for March 19–25. Use the following information about tourist attractions to create an itinerary like the one on the preceding page. Be sure to capitalize words appropriately.

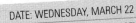

DATE: WEDNESDAY, MARCH 22

ATTRACTION: CAPE COD MUSEUM OF NATURAL HISTORY

LOCATION: ROUTE 6A
BREWSTER, MASSACHUSETTS

HIGHLIGHTS: SEAL CRUISE ABOARD *BEACHCOMBER,* WORKING BEEHIVE AT 9:30 A.M., WHALE EXHIBIT, WILDFLOWER GARDEN

DATE: FRIDAY, MARCH 24

ATTRACTION: PHILADELPHIA INSECTARIUM

LOCATION: 8046 FRANKFORD AVENUE
PHILADELPHIA, PENNSYLVANIA

HIGHLIGHTS: WORLDWIDE BUTTERFLY COLLECTION, EXOTIC BEETLE COLLECTION, LIVE TERMITE TUNNEL, CAMOUFLAGE INSECTS

Mixed Review

A. Capitalization Read the following passage. On a separate sheet of paper, explain why each underlined word or phrase is capitalized.

Who is Punxsutawney Phil? Does **(1)** Groundhog Day ring a bell? Punxsutawney Phil is the official groundhog weather prognosticator who makes an appearance once a year on **(2)** Gobbler's Knob in **(3)** Punxsutawney, Pennsylvania. The official celebration is traced back to **(4)** February 2, 1886, when Clymer Freas wrote in the **(5)** *Punxsutawney Spirit*, **(6)** "Today is Groundhog Day and up to the time of going to press the beast has not seen its shadow." Groundhog Day is rooted in a tradition associated with the holiday of **(7)** Candlemas. On February 2, halfway through winter, people would wait for the sun to come out. If the day turned out to be sunny, they would expect six more weeks of wintry weather. In 1993 **(8)** Columbia Pictures released the comedy **(9)** *Groundhog Day*, starring Bill Murray. Although it was filmed in Woodstock, Illinois, some names of Punxsutawney businesses, including **(10)** The Smart Shop and Stewart's Drug Store, were used in the movie. Whether you believe in Phil's forecast or not, he's been right about 39 percent of the time.

B. Editing and Proofreading Rewrite the ad below, using the capitalization rules presented in this chapter.

If you're a STAR TREK FAN, come and meet other "TREKKERS"; enter the costume contest for best ferengi, romulan, or vulcan; and learn to speak KLINGON at the opening of this attraction.

C. Revision For each capitalization error, write the word correctly.

Chocolate, Sweet Chocolate!
Oakdale Chamber of commerce
590 north Yosemite avenue
Oakdale, california 95361

dear Sir or madam:

I understand you are looking for interesting, mouthwatering chocolate concoctions to feature at the Oakdale Chocolate Festival to be held may 15 and 16. I am the author of The Chocolate lover's Guide and teach chocolate 101 at Calorie college, and I have a few recipes that might interest you. I recently exhibited my creations at the International Festival Of Chocolate in london.

Please send me information about the festival in Oakdale.

Sincerely Yours,
c. Barr

Mastery Test: What Did You Learn?

For each underlined group of words, choose the letter of the correct revision.

On a quiet Sunday in a cabin on the slopes of the volcano kilauea, (1) the first things Sonny Ching saw when he woke up were the trophies. (2) His students had won both the women's and the men's competition in the annual Merrie monarch Festival (3) hula competition. The festival, a celebration of traditional Hawaiian culture, is named for the last Hawaiian king, king david kalakaua, (4) who worked to preserve his people's rich heritage of music and dance. It is held in the city of Hilo, on the island of hawaii (5) in the state of Hawaii. Each Spring, (6) at the festival, groups of dancers compete and are rated by judges, but as the 1995 miss aloha hula, (7) Tracy Vaughan, said, "I didn't come here to win. I came to show how much i love the hula (8)." Before the competition, dancers honor the ancient fire Goddess Pele and her sisters (9). "Hula is the language of the heart," the king once said, "And therefore the heartbeat of the Hawaiian people (10)."

1. A. sunday
   B. volcano
   C. Kilauea
   D. Correct as is
2. A. sonny
   B. ching
   C. Trophies
   D. Correct as is
3. A. merrie
   B. Monarch
   C. merrie monarch festival
   D. Correct as is
4. A. King David Kalakaua
   B. king David Kalakaua
   C. King david kalakaua
   D. Correct as is
5. A. hilo
   B. Island of Hawaii
   C. Hawaii
   D. Correct as is
6. A. State of Hawaii
   B. each spring
   C. Each spring
   D. Correct as is
7. A. Miss Aloha Hula
   B. miss Aloha Hula
   C. Miss
   D. Correct as is
8. A. i didn't come here to win
   B. i came to show
   C. how much I love the hula
   D. Correct as is
9. A. goddess pele
   B. goddess Pele
   C. Sisters
   D. Correct as is
10. A. King
    B. "and therefore the heartbeat . . ."
    C. hawaiian
    D. Correct as is

CAPITALIZATION

Student Help Desk

Capitalization at a Glance

People and Cultures
First Words and Titles
Places and Transportation
Organizations and Other Subjects

CHAPTER 10

To Capitalize or Not to Capitalize: Nouns

Common	Proper
college	Smith College
island	Easter Island
hall	Orchestra Hall
mountains	Rocky Mountains
war	Civil War
club	Chess Club
museum	Metropolitan Museum of Art

Capitalization Tips Do Capitalize

The first word of a sentence	Who wrote the poem "Annabel Lee"?
The first word in every line of a traditional poem	It was many and many a year ago, In a kingdom by the sea, —Edgar Allan Poe, "Annabel Lee"
A family word used as a name or in direct address	Susan saw the parade with Uncle Ed.
The first and last words and other important words in a title	*To Kill a Mockingbird*
The name of a particular person, place, planet, event, brand, or the like	Professor Jones plans to take his geography class on a trip to the Grand Canyon.

Capitalization Pitfalls

Don't Capitalize

The first word in every line of some modern poems	I am fourteen and my skin has betrayed me —Audre Lorde, "Hanging Fire"
A family word used as a common noun	My uncle competed for the city record in the pie-eating contest.
The name of a season used as a common noun	Every spring, people demonstrate their wacky talents in the festival.
A class name used as a common noun	She is a senior.
A compass direction not used as a proper noun	The festival is held on Route 41, just south of North Shore Avenue.

CAPITALIZATION

The Bottom Line

Checklist for Capitalization

Have I capitalized . . .

____ people's names and initials?

____ personal titles before names?

____ names of ethnic groups, races, languages, and nationalities?

____ names of religions and other religious terms?

____ names of bodies of the universe?

____ names of monuments, bridges, and other landmarks?

____ names of planes, trains, and spacecraft?

____ names of historical events, periods, and documents?

____ names of special events, awards, and brands?

Punctuation

PRINCIPAL

Want your Mascot
back? Go To the quick
mart past the Chicken Shack
left to the gas Station and look
in the red truck

Theme: Games and Hobbies

A Treasure Hunt

You're trying to figure out where a rival school's team has left your school mascot. Is it "Go to the Quick Mart, (then) past the Chicken Shack" or "Go to the Quick Mart (that is) past the Chicken Shack"? Without proper punctuation marks, this message makes no sense.

Write Away: Return It or Else!
If you were one of the students whose school mascot was stolen by the rival school, how would you respond to the ransom note? Write a short letter to the editor of your school newspaper, giving your opinion about the playing of pranks on rival schools. Save your writing in your **Working Portfolio.**

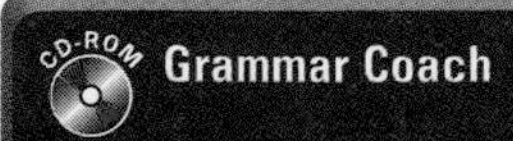
CD-ROM
Grammar Coach

Diagnostic Test: What Do You Know?

For each numbered item, choose the letter of the best revision.

Can you imagine the popularity the game of chess has had over the years. (1) For some, people (2) chess is more than a competitive game. In Marostica Italy, (3) a ceremony takes place every other year to celebrate a game of chess. The townspeople dress up as chess pieces in festive colorful costumes (4) and act out the game. The origin of this event goes back to the 15th century, when two rival suitors; (5) challenged each other to a game of chess; each wanted to marry the local lord's daughter. (6) To emphasize the importance of the challenge (7) the game was played in front of an audience. Today the town "reenacts" (8) this 15th-century duel on a giant chessboard (9) while an announcer calls out the moves from a tower. . . (10)

1. A. Can you imagine?
   B. Can you imagine the popularity the game of chess has had over the years?
   C. Can you imagine the popularity; the game of chess has had over the years?
   D. Correct as is
2. A. For some people,
   B. For some people:
   C. For some people—
   D. Correct as is
3. A. Marostica, Italy,
   B. Marostica—Italy,
   C. "Marostica Italy,"
   D. Correct as is
4. A. festive colorful, costumes
   B. festive, colorful costumes
   C. festive colorful—costumes
   D. Correct as is
5. A. two rival suitors:
   B. two rival suitors'
   C. two rival suitors
   D. Correct as is
6. A. the local, lord's daughter
   B. the local lords daughter
   C. the local lords' daughter
   D. Correct as is
7. A. To emphasize the importance of the challenge,
   B. To emphasize the importance, of the challenge
   C. To emphasize the "importance" of the challenge
   D. Correct as is
8. A. re—enacts
   B. re enacts
   C. reenacts
   D. Correct as is
9. A. "chess board"
   B. chess—board
   C. chess-board
   D. Correct as is
10. A. tower?
    B. tower!
    C. tower.
    D. Correct as is

PUNCTUATION

Periods and Other End Marks

1 Here's the Idea

Periods, question marks, and exclamation points—together known as **end marks**—are used to indicate the end of sentences. Periods are also used in several other ways.

Periods

▶ **Use periods at the end of all declarative sentences and most imperative sentences.**

Declarative Sentence
Chess is a strategic game.

Imperative Sentence
Follow the rules.

▶ **Use periods at the end of most sentences containing indirect questions.** An indirect question tells what someone has asked without giving the exact wording.

The student asked how chess is played.

Other Uses of Periods

▶ **Use periods after initials and after most abbreviations.**

Gen. George Washington   3 lb. 10 oz.
Dr. Michael C. Scott

▶ **Use a period after each number or letter in an outline or list.**

Outline
I. Traditional games
  A. Board games
    1. Chess
    2. Backgammon
  B. Tile games

List
1. Board games
2. Tile games
3. Target games
4. Card games

Question Marks

▶ **Use a question mark at the end of an interrogative sentence.**

Do you know who has won the most championships?

Exclamation Points

▶ **Use an exclamation point to end an exclamatory sentence or after a strong interjection (a word that shows feeling or imitates a sound).**

Hurrah**!** We won the game**!** What a game**!**

Don't overuse exclamation points. They lose their effectiveness if used too frequently, as in the sentences below.

Chess is the most competitive game! It requires skill and concentration! Tension mounts as each player attacks the enemy king!

2 Practice and Apply

CONCEPT CHECK: Periods and Other End Marks

Write these sentences, inserting periods, question marks, and exclamation points where needed.

Chess Geniuses

1. Can a child learn to play chess at three years of age
2. Bobby Fischer, the first American to win the world championship, learned the moves of chess at the age of six
3. Many people wonder why Fischer lost his title in 1975
4. He simply refused to play the Russian challenger Anatoly Karpov under federation rules
5. Anatoly Karpov won the title by default. Amazing
6. Karpov, a child prodigy, learned to play chess at the age of four
7. How did Karpov dominate world competition from the mid-1970s to the mid-1980s
8. In 1985, he lost the championship title to Gary Kasparov
9. Kasparov became the youngest champion in the history of the game, and in 1996 he defeated a powerful chess computer
10. If you want to write a report on chess, follow this outline:

    I History of chess
      A Ancient precursors
        1 Persia
        2 Europe
      B Modern chess

➔ **For a SELF-CHECK and more practice, see the EXERCISE BANK, p. 616.**

Commas in Sentence Parts

1 Here's the Idea

Commas can make the meaning of sentences clearer by separating certain sentence elements. However, using too many commas can cause more confusion than leaving them out.

Commas in Series

- **In a series of three or more items, use a comma after every item except the last one.**

Bungee jumping has joined the ranks of **surfboarding**, **skateboarding**, and **sky surfing** as an extreme sport.

A person who wants to bungee jump can go to professional sites and jump from **bridges**, **hot-air balloons**, and **tall buildings.**

- **Use commas after *first, second,* and so on when they introduce items in a series.**

Participants are asked to follow three simple rules: **first**, secure the bungee cord for safety; **second**, do not attempt to hold on to anything; and **third**, have fun.

- **Use commas between adjectives of equal rank that modify the same noun.**

A **young**, **adventurous** man jumped off a 300-foot bridge.

To tell whether a series of adjectives requires a comma, place the word *and* between the adjectives. If the sentence still makes sense, replace *and* with a comma. Likewise, if you can change the order of the adjectives without changing the meaning of the sentence, place a comma between them.

Commas with Introductory Elements

▶ **Use a comma after an introductory word or a mild interjection such as *oh* or *well.***

Oh, bungee jumping is not for the faint-hearted.

However, if you are a thrill-seeker, then this is the perfect hobby.

▶ **Use a comma after an introductory prepositional phrase that contains one or more other prepositional phrases.**

At the beginning of the jump, a person feels a rush of emotions.

▶ **Use a comma after an infinitive phrase, a participial phrase, or an adverb clause that begins a sentence.**

PARTICIPIAL PHRASE

Taking a deep breath, the jumper prepares for the dive.

ADVERB CLAUSE

When the jump is over, the exhilaration remains.

Commas with Interrupters

▶ **Use commas to set off words that interrupt the flow of thought in a sentence.**

Bungee jumping, **by the way,** can be done in groups.

A seven-person team, **for example,** has jumped in a specially designed basket.

Common Interrupters

however	I suppose	by the way	of course
therefore	moreover	in fact	furthermore
for example	I believe	after all	nevertheless

▶ **Use commas to set off nouns of direct address.** A noun of direct address names the person or people being spoken to. Nouns of direct address can be either proper nouns or common nouns, as these examples show.

David, do you know anyone who has gone bungee jumping?

If you want to learn more about bungee jumping, **ladies and gentlemen,** try a search on the Internet.

PUNCTUATION

Use commas to set off nonessential appositives. An appositive is a word or phrase that identifies or renames a noun or pronoun. A nonessential appositive adds information about a noun or pronoun in a sentence in which the meaning is already clear.

NONESSENTIAL

Paul, **my brother,** has gone bungee jumping in Australia.

An essential appositive provides information that is needed to explain the preceding noun or pronoun. It requires no commas.

ESSENTIAL

His friend **Sheila** will jump from a hot-air balloon in August.

Without the appositive the word *friend* could refer to any friend.

2 Practice and Apply

CONCEPT CHECK: Commas in Sentence Parts

Write the words that should be followed by commas. If no commas are necessary in a sentence, write *None.*

An Ancient Ritual or a Modern Craze?

1. Bungee jumping has been called the human yo-yo the brain-squasher and the leap of faith.
2. Although bungee jumping is a recent invention the craze has already spread around the world.
3. Bungee jumping is a must-do activity for people visiting or living in places like France Australia and Mexico.
4. However this sudden craze is nothing new to the people of Pentecost Island in the South Pacific.
5. Our modern hobby is their version of an ancient tribal ritual that tests manhood.
6. The men it is said leap from towers 50 to 80 feet high, attached by just enough vine for their heads to barely touch the ground.
7. No this ritual is not a make-believe story.
8. In 1979 members of Oxford University's Dangerous Sports Club heard stories about the ritual and decided to test their own courage with a jump.
9. Wearing tuxedos and top hats they jumped off the 245-foot Clifton Bridge in Bristol, England.
10. A. J. Hackett a New Zealander brought bungee jumping to public attention when he jumped from the Eiffel Tower.

For a SELF-CHECK and more practice, see the EXERCISE BANK, p. 617.

LESSON 3

More Commas

1 Here's the Idea

Commas to Avoid Confusion

▶ **Use a comma whenever readers might misinterpret a sentence without it.**

UNCLEAR: Before the rodeo cowboys competed against one another for fun.

CLEAR: Before the rodeo, cowboys competed against one another for fun.

Commas with Quotations

▶ **Use commas to separate direct quotations from explanatory words like *he said, Greg replied,* and *Sheila asked.*** If the explanatory words precede the quotation, insert a comma before the quoted words.

Mr. Cruz said, "The rodeo was born during the era of the cattle industry, in the 1860s and 1870s."

If the explanatory words interrupt a quotation, insert a comma inside the quotation marks before the explanatory words and another comma after the explanatory words.

"Cowboys would gather together," **Mr. Cruz said,** "and compete against one another in steer roping and bronco riding."

If the explanatory words follow a quotation, insert a comma inside the quotation marks before the explanatory words.

"Today cowboys compete against each other for monetary awards," **added Mr. Cruz.**

Commas in Compound Sentences

▶ **Use a comma to separate independent clauses joined by a conjunction in a compound sentence.**

Rodeos are held in many parts of the United States, **but** they are also popular in Mexico, Canada, and Australia.

Do not use a comma to separate the parts of a two-part compound predicate.

Many Western regions claim to be the birthplace of the rodeo and hold annual exhibitions to celebrate the Old West.

PUNCTUATION

Commas with Nonessential Clauses

▶ **Use commas to set off nonessential clauses.** A nonessential clause adds extra information to a sentence but is not necessary to the meaning of the sentence.

> Trick riding and fancy roping**, which are virtually unknown to rodeo fans today,** were popular events during the 1920s and 1930s.

Essential clauses are necessary to the meaning of sentences and are not set off with commas.

> Fancy roping originated among those Mexican horsemen who are known as *charros*.

Commas in Letters, Place Names, and Dates

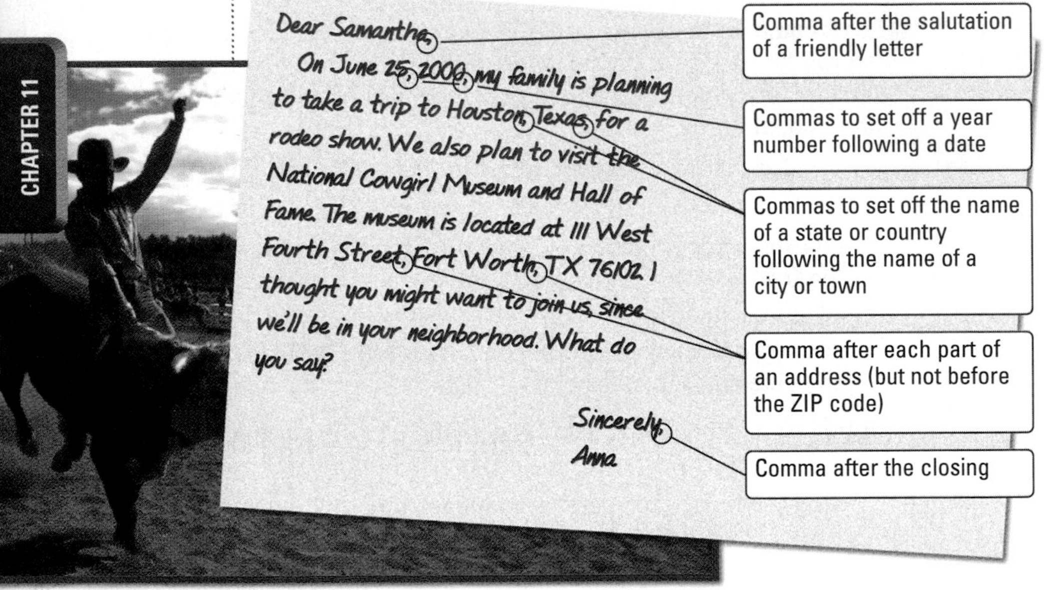

Dear Samantha,

On June 25, 2000, my family is planning to take a trip to Houston, Texas, for a rodeo show. We also plan to visit the National Cowgirl Museum and Hall of Fame. The museum is located at 111 West Fourth Street, Fort Worth, TX 76102. I thought you might want to join us, since we'll be in your neighborhood. What do you say?

Sincerely,

Anna

Comma after the salutation of a friendly letter
Commas to set off a year number following a date
Commas to set off the name of a state or country following the name of a city or town
Comma after each part of an address (but not before the ZIP code)
Comma after the closing

Peanuts by Charles Schulz

I WONDER IF THEY HAVE FRACTIONS IN HEAVEN..
NO FRACTIONS, SIR..NO DECIMALS, EITHER...
HOW ABOUT COMMAS?
© 1993 United Feature Syndicate, Inc.
THERE HAVE TO BE COMMAS, SIR.. WE CAN'T AVOID THEM
11-29
ETERNITY'S GOING TO BE LONGER THAN I THOUGHT..
SCHULZ

2 Practice and Apply

A. CONCEPT CHECK: More Commas

Write the words that should be followed by commas in these sentences. If a sentence is correct, write *Correct.*

College for Cowboys

1. Scottsdale Arizona is home to the Arizona Cowboy College.
2. In 1989, Lloyd Bridwell started his own college after watching some commercials for trade schools.
3. Bridwell offers his course up to eight times a year and accepts up to eight students per course.
4. The course which lasts a week teaches students basic cowboy skills.
5. Not only do students wake before sunrise and cook over campfires but they also learn about cattle grazing, branding, and roping.
6. Before leaving students gain an understanding of the demands of life on a ranch.
7. In a recent interview one of Bridwell's students said "This has completely changed my life."
8. Bridwell's appreciation of the cowboy way of life comes from his father who once competed in rodeos.
9. After high school Lloyd worked as a ranch hand and cowboy for four years before going off to college and in 1986 he opened an equestrian training center.
10. Anyone who is interested in taking Bridwell's course should be prepared to work hard.

➜ **For a SELF-CHECK and more practice, see the EXERCISE BANK, p. 617.**

B. PROOFREADING: Adding Commas

Proofread the following letter for punctuation errors. Write the words that should be followed by commas in the letter.

Dear Chris

On August 25, 2000 a few of us got together to visit the Cowboy Hall of Fame in Oklahoma City Oklahoma. Its museum has a great art exhibit devoted to the American West. You would have loved it!

The museum has works by Frederic Remington who was born in Canton New York and Charles Russell from St. Louis. If you find yourself in Oklahoma City, visit the museum. Its address is 1700 NE. 63rd St. Oklahoma City OK. I hope you enjoy the postcard.

Sincerely
Julie

PUNCTUATION

Semicolons and Colons

1 Here's the Idea

A semicolon marks a break in a sentence; it is stronger than a comma but not as strong as a period. A colon indicates that a list, a quotation, or some form of explanation follows.

Semicolons

Use a semicolon to join the parts of a compound sentence if no coordinating conjunction is used.

The first recorded Olympics took place in 776 B.C. in Olympia, Greece; only one athletic event was held that year—a footrace of about 193 meters (210 yards).

Use a semicolon before a conjunctive adverb that joins the clauses of a compound sentence. Conjunctive adverbs include *therefore, however, otherwise, consequently,* and *moreover.* These usually function as introductory words and need to be followed by commas.

The first 17 ancient Olympics featured only footraces and ended in one day; **however,** the program changed in the 18th Olympics, when wrestling and the pentathlon were added.

When commas occur within parts of a series, use semicolons to separate the parts.

The first modern Olympics were held in Athens, Greece; the second in Paris, France; and the third in St. Louis, Missouri.

Colons

Use a colon to introduce a list of items. Colons often follow words like *these* or *the following.*

The pentathlon included the following events: **discus throw, long jump, javelin throw, running, and wrestling.**

Never use a colon after a verb or a preposition.

The spectators watched wrestling, boxing, and chariot races.

Use a colon between two independent clauses when the second explains or summarizes the first.

Before the games the athletes had to affirm their eligibility to compete: **they swore a solemn oath to Zeus.**

CHAPTER 11

▶ **Use a colon to introduce a long or formal quotation.**

Before the athletes were allowed to begin their two-day march to Olympia, the judges gave a few words of caution: **"If you have practiced hard for Olympia and if you have not been lazy or done anything dishonorable, then go forward with confidence. But if you have not trained yourselves this way, then leave us and go where you choose."**

The following chart shows other uses of colons.

Uses of Colons	
Greetings of business letters	Dear Sir or Madam: Dear Ms. McDonough:
Times of day	12:00 A.M. 9:30 P.M.
References to some holy books	Psalms 23:7 Qur'an 75:22

PUNCTUATION

2 Practice and Apply

CONCEPT CHECK: Semicolons and Colons

Write each word that should be followed by punctuation, indicating whether the punctuation should be a semicolon or a colon. If a sentence is correct, write *Correct.*

The Olympics: A Heroic Tradition

1. The pentathlete was the most admired athlete in ancient Greece athletes in Athens and Sparta began their training at a young age.
2. Although the style and grace of an athlete were important, winning was more important athletes who took first place were regarded as heroes.
3. Historical records show that statues were built as a tribute to the winners however, these statues were destroyed.
4. Lists of Olympic winners were compiled by several writers Hippias of Elis, the Greek philosopher Aristotle, and the Roman historian Sextus Julius Africanus.
5. Today a first-place athlete gets a gold medal a second-place one, a silver medal and a third-place one, a bronze medal.

➜ **For a SELF-CHECK and more practice, see the EXERCISE BANK, p. 618.**

Quotation Marks

Here's the Idea

Quotation marks are used to indicate that a statement made by another person is being quoted word for word.

▶ **Use quotation marks at the beginning and at the end of a direct quotation.**

Bill **said,** "My favorite sport is baseball."

Quotation marks are not used with an indirect quotation—that is, a retelling of what a person said, thought, or wrote.

Bill **said that** his favorite sport is baseball.

▶ **Use single quotation marks around a quotation within a quotation.**

"President Franklin D. Roosevelt once said, 'Major league baseball has done as much as any one thing in this country to keep up the spirit of the people,' " stated Mr. Pennebaker.

When both quotations end at the same place, include both single and double closing quotation marks.

CHAPTER 11

Divided Quotations

Sometimes a direct quotation is divided into two or more parts by explanatory words (*he said, she exclaimed, they reported*). In such cases use quotation marks before and after each part of the quotation.

"The first baseball game between two organized teams," **Mr. Pennebaker explained,** "was in Hoboken, New Jersey, on June 19, 1846."

Commas separate explanatory words from the quotation.

When the second part of a divided quotation is a new sentence, use a capital letter. If the sentence is not new, do not capitalize the second divided quotation.

"In 1845 Alexander Cartwright started the Knickerbocker Base Ball Club of New York," **Mr. Pennebaker told us.** "He is known as the father of organized baseball for his contribution."

Long Quotations

If one speaker's words continue for more than a paragraph, each paragraph should begin with a quotation mark. However, a closing quotation mark should not be used until the end of the entire quotation.

Sonia said, "Who do you think has the record for the most home runs in a season? Is it Babe Ruth, Joe DiMaggio, Sammy Sosa, or Mark McGwire?

"Babe Ruth is my favorite."

No quotation mark at the end of first paragraph

Quotation Marks with Other Punctuation

Punctuation Guide

Mark	Inside or Outside Closing Quotation Mark?
Period or comma	**inside** He told us, "The Cincinnati Red Stockings were the first professional baseball team."
Question mark or exclamation point	**inside if the quotation itself is a question or exclamation** "You know that baseball is considered the national pastime, don't you**?**" he asked. **outside if the sentence containing the quoted material is a question or explanation** Do you think anyone here knows the song "Take Me Out to the Ball Game"**?**
Colon or semicolon	**outside** Baseballs used from the mid-1800s until about 1920 were "dead"**;** when hit, they didn't travel as far as those used today.

PUNCTUATION

Dialogue

Dialogue is conversation between two or more people. Begin a new paragraph each time the speaker changes, and use a separate set of quotation marks for each speaker's words.

LITERARY MODEL

"I'm playing outfield," she said. "I don't like the responsibility of having a base."

"Yeah, I can understand that," I said, though I couldn't. "There's a band in Dixford tomorrow night at nine. Want to go?"

—W. D. Wetherell, "The Bass, the River, and Sheila Mant"

Titles

CHAPTER 11

Use quotation marks around the titles of magazine articles, chapters, short stories, TV episodes, essays, short poems, and songs.

"One Throw" (SHORT STORY)

"Baseball and Softball: A Comparative Study" (ESSAY)

"Picking Dandelions in the Outfield" (POEM)

2 Practice and Apply

A. CONCEPT CHECK: Quotation Marks **Answers in column.**

Write the following sentences, inserting quotation marks (and commas) where necessary. If a sentence is correct, write *Correct.*

Baseball Legends

1. Whoever wants to know the heart and mind of America one famous educator wrote had better learn baseball.
2. Most young Americans learn about this game, and they delight in stories about legendary players like Babe Ruth and Joe DiMaggio said my teacher, Mr. Richards.
3. Babe Ruth once daringly pointed to center field while at bat and then smashed the next ball over the center-field fence.
4. If I'd missed that homer after calling it Babe Ruth later told a sportswriter I'd have looked like an awful fool.

5. Another time Ruth was reported as saying All I can tell 'em is I pick a good one and sock it. I get back to the dugout and they ask me what it was I hit and I tell 'em I don't know except it looked good.
6. In 1941 Joltin' Joe DiMaggio hit safely in 56 consecutive games.
7. His nerves are steady as his bat the sportswriters declared.
8. During the 56 games of the streak, DiMaggio's batting average was .408.
9. Ernest Hemingway even mentioned him in the book *The Old Man and the Sea;* its main character says I would like to take the great DiMaggio fishing.
10. As long as baseball is the national pastime Mr. Richards exclaimed we will continue to hear about great baseball players who make history!

For a SELF-CHECK and more practice, see the EXERCISE BANK, p. 619.

B. PROOFREADING: Adding Quotation Marks

On your paper, write the sentences that require quotation marks, inserting the needed punctuation.

PROFESSIONAL MODEL

I am one of the few people I know who hate sports. I can confess to having never watched the Super Bowl. Furthermore, it baffles me how anyone can remember which baseball teams are in the National League and which are in the American League. I do, however, enjoy humorous stories and quotations about baseball, particularly the remarks of Yogi Berra, the former New York Yankees catcher. Once a reporter asked Yogi, How did you like school when you were growing up, Yogi? Yogi replied, Closed. Another time Yogi commented, You can't think and hit at the same time. I also like humorous books about baseball, especially Joe Garagiola's *Baseball Is a Funny Game.* One Detroit Tigers pitcher is quoted as saying, All the fat guys watch me and say to their wives, See, there's a fat guy doing okay. Nothing, however, has made me want to go see a baseball game in person. If the people don't want to come out to the park, Yogi once observed, nobody's going to stop 'em.

PUNCTUATION

Other Punctuation

1 Here's the Idea

Other punctuation marks include hyphens, apostrophes, dashes, and parentheses. Like commas, semicolons, and colons, these punctuation marks help clarify your writing.

Hyphens

Use a hyphen if part of a word must be carried over from one line to the next.

Ancient stargazers were intrigued and fascinated by the movements of the planets and other heavenly bodies.

Only divide words of two or more syllables. Never divide one-syllable words like *growl* or *weight,* and do not leave a single letter at the end or beginning of a line. For instance, these divisions would be wrong: *e-lection, cloud-y.*

Use hyphens in compound numbers from twenty-one to ninety-nine.

eighty-eight constellations   twenty-five astronomers

Use hyphens in fractions.

one-third of the students   three-fourths of the course

Use hyphens in certain compound nouns.

cross-references   great-grandfather

Use a hyphen between words that function as a compound adjective before a noun.

The Milky Way is a much-studied galaxy.

Such a compound is not usually hyphenated when it follows the noun it modifies.

The Milky Way galaxy has been much studied.

Do not use a hyphen between an adverb ending in *-ly* and the adjective it modifies.

Over the years many people have conducted carefully timed observations of comets.

CHAPTER 11

Use a hyphen after the prefixes *all-*, *ex-*, or *self-* (as in *all-around*, *ex-president*, and *self-employed*). If in doubt, use the dictionary to check hyphenation.

Apostrophes

- **Use apostrophes to form the possessive forms of nouns.**

  Singular noun + 's: student**'s**, instructor**'s**, writer**'s**

  Use an apostrophe and *s* even if the singular noun ends in *s*: *Carlos's*.

  Plural noun + ': boys**'**, books**'**, Smiths**'**

  Plural nouns that do not end in *s* take an apostrophe and *s*: *women's, children's*.

Add only an apostrophe to a classical name ending in *s*: *Jesus', Moses', Zeus'*.

- **To form the possessive of an indefinite pronoun, use an apostrophe and *s*.**

  everybody + **'s** = everybody**'s**

  someone + **'s** = someone**'s**

  Do not use apostrophes in possessive personal pronouns: *hers, ours, yours, its, theirs*. Do not confuse the possessive form *its* with the contraction *it's* (*it is*).

  It's fun to watch the space show in the planetarium.

  Compared with **its** tail, a comet's nucleus is extremely small.

- **Use an apostrophe and *s* to form the plural of a letter, a numeral, or a word referred to as a word.**

  ABC**'s** two *n***'s**
  three 4**'s** *yes***'s** and *no***'s**

- **Use an apostrophe to show the omission of numerals in a date.**

  the summer of '99 (the summer of 1999)

  If it is not clear what century is intended, write out the entire year number.

PUNCTUATION

Use an apostrophe in a contraction. In a contraction words are joined with one or more letters left out. An apostrophe shows where the letter or letters have been omitted.

they're = they are shouldn't = should not

Dashes

Use dashes to signal an abrupt change of thought or set off an idea that breaks into the flow of a sentence.

Stargazing and comet tracking **—two of the oldest pastimes—** are not just for astronomers.

Use a dash after a series to indicate that a summary statement follows.

Halley, Encke, and Klemola—each of these people had a comet named after him.

Do not overuse dashes, especially in formal writing. They can make your writing appear too casual. Also, do not use dashes to replace semicolons or periods.

CHAPTER 11

Parentheses

Use parentheses to set off material that is loosely related to the sentence or paragraph in which it occurs.

Ancient stargazers created the constellations **(such as Orion, the great hunter, and Leo, the lion)** by connecting the bright stars with imaginary lines.

If a complete sentence enclosed in parentheses stands alone, it is punctuated and capitalized like any other sentence.

Constellations were named for gods, people, animals, and objects. **(Actually, this is how we got the zodiac.)**

When a parenthetical sentence occurs within another sentence, it does not begin with a capital letter. An end mark is included only if the parenthetical sentence is a question or exclamation.

On clear, dark nights you can see up to 3,000 stars with the naked eye **(can you believe it?)**, but only a few comets are are bright enough to be seen with the naked eye.

2 Practice and Apply

CONCEPT CHECK: Other Punctuation

Proofread the following draft for punctuation errors. Write the underlined passages, inserting or deleting hyphens, apostrophes, dashes, and parentheses where necessary. If an underlined passage is correct, write *Correct.*

STUDENT MODEL

The Curse of Halley's Comet

For centuries, people believed that comets **(1)** heavenly bodies that move in large elliptical orbits about the sun were omens of catastrophe. Though the moon, the sun, and the stars were familiar, **(2)** a comets characteristics were unknown. To some people, a comet's tail resembled a woman's unbound hair **(3)** a traditional sign of mourning. Others thought the tail resembled a sword **(4)** an omen of death and war. Several historical documents point to massive chaos when a comet made **(5)** it's appearance. In 1066 **(6)** Halleys comet was first sighted in April and remained visible for two months **(7)** long enough to cause both the English and the Normans great distress. According to historians, the **(8)** intensely-feared comet was blamed for **(9)** Englands' defeat in the Battle of Hastings. Halley's return in 1456 created such a stir that people believed that the comet caused illness, a **(10)** mysterious red-rain, and the births of **(11)** two headed animals.

Although the physical structure of comets was clearly known by the 1900s, **(12)** scientific observations—at the time—aroused new fears. Astronomers at the **(13)** University of Chicago's Yerkes Observatory discovered a poisonous gas within the tail of Halley's comet. Within days, newspaper headlines warned people of the "danger." Before Halley's return in 1910, some people constructed **(14)** gas-proof rooms, while others purchased an assortment of gimmicks **(15)** comet pills, inhalers, comet insurance, and conjure bags to protect themselves against disaster. Finally, in 1986 (Halley's final appearance in the 20th century) some people had comet parties, while others thought that the comet would crash into the North Pole and end life.

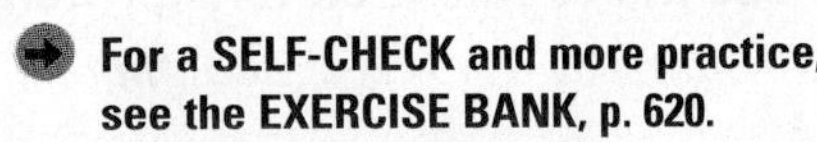

For a SELF-CHECK and more practice, see the EXERCISE BANK, p. 620.

Ellipses and Italics

1 Here's the Idea

Ellipses indicate that material has been left out. **Italics** (represented by underlining in handwritten or typewritten material) are used to set off certain words, phrases, and titles.

Ellipses

Use an ellipsis (. . .) to indicate an omission of words or an idea that trails off. If you use an ellipsis at the end of a sentence, make sure you include a period before it.

PROFESSIONAL MODEL

Although marathon runners are admired for their perseverance, they are also considered a bit insane. . . . The thought of the striking midday sun beaming its rays into our bodies at 97° is enough to make some of us sit in front of an icebox all day long. But what about those individuals who run . . . out of necessity?

CHAPTER 11

Do not omit words from a quoted passage if doing so changes the passage's meaning.

UNCLEAR: The article says, "The athlete would be in great shape . . . to run the marathon."

CLEAR: The article says, "The athlete would be in great shape—in about a year or so after rebuilding physical stamina—to run the marathon."

Italics

Use italics to set off letters referred to as letters and words referred to as words.

Do you know where the word ***marathon*** originated?

Can you write a paragraph that contains no ***e***'s?

Use italics to set off foreign words and phrases.

au revoir ***ad infinitum***

Words and abbreviations that have become part of the English language, however, are not italicized: faux pas, gringo, etc., et al.

▶ **Use italics to set off the titles of books, newspapers, magazines, plays, movies, television series, book-length poems, long musical compositions, and works of art.**

Romeo and Juliet (PLAY) ***Road Rules*** (TV SERIES)

2 Practice and Apply

A. CONCEPT CHECK: Italics

Write these sentences, underlining words that should be italicized. Also, indicate which words, if any, are incorrectly italicized.

Marathon Tidbits

1. According to *The World Book Encyclopedia,* the word marathon refers to a footrace of about 26 miles (42 kilometers).
2. In Runner's World, Owen Anderson wrote that a person training for a marathon should have fun and enjoy the workout—the health benefits will inevitably follow.
3. You've probably heard of the *Boston Marathon,* but did you know that marathons are run in Chicago, New York, Los Angeles, and many other cities around the world?
4. In World-Class Marathoners, Nathan Aaseng wrote about Abebe Bikila, a first-time marathoner who shocked the world by running barefoot in the 1960 *Olympics.*
5. If you are looking for a list of marathon champions, you may want to read the ESPN Information Please Sports Almanac, which is published annually.

➔ **For a SELF-CHECK and more practice, see the EXERCISE BANK, p. 621.**

B. REVISING: Using Ellipses

Write this passage, using ellipses to cut it to four lines.

PROFESSIONAL MODEL

Hundreds of hours, hundreds of miles, and now I'm here, with hundreds, thousands of regular people like me. We are packed together on a downtown Los Angeles avenue, a throbbing swarm of gel soles, mesh shirts, and digital watches. An unspoken but persistent question hovers over most of the 19,000 racers: Will I make it?

—Michael Konik, "Marathon Man," *Men's Fitness*

Real World Grammar

Business Letter

Business letters require complete clarity, since they often contain important dates, order numbers, addresses, and lists of items. When you write a business letter, always proofread your draft for punctuation errors that can lead to miscommunication and can delay a reply.

Hang Gliding
ADVENTURES
Your source for hang gliding information

1400 Green Street
San Francisco CA 94133
May 27 2001

Hang Gliding Adventures
2552 North Canal St.
San Francisco CA 94166

Dear Sir or Madam,

About two weeks ago I called your 800 number and asked for some information about your training centers, particularly Hang Gliding Adventures I. The literature I received covered the basics lessons safety hang-gliding locations and equipment. I am now requesting additional information. Do you have a list of shops where I can find a beginners glider, or can I buy a used glider over the Internet.

Please call me at (415) 555-5512 between 3:00 P. M. and 5:00 P. M. with the information I requested. Thank you for your assistance.

Sincerely
Erica Springfield

Insert commas in addresses and in the date.

Use a colon after the salutation of a business letter.

Use a colon to introduce a list of items.

Insert commas between items in a series.

Insert an apostrophe in a possessive noun.

Use an appropriate end mark.

Insert a comma after the closing.

PRACTICE AND APPLY: Proofreading

Proofread this letter for incorrect or missing commas, periods, colons, and parentheses. Rewrite the letter correctly.

3155 W Orchard St
Boulder CO, 80304
June 15 2001

Omega Corporation
4636 State Street
Seattle WA, 98107

Dear Sir or Madam

On April 20 I ordered pairs of your Omega 2000 running shoes Omega Silver Series aerobic shoes and Omega Gold Star in-line skates through your advertisement in *Runner's Guide.* The advertisement stated that if I purchased a pair of Omega 2000 serial #2345 and Omega Silver Series serial #2346 before May 29 I would receive a $40 refund. However your company failed to give me a refund when I received the bill.

I am enclosing a copy of the dated check for your records. Please send me my refund as soon as you clear up the misunderstanding

Sincerely

Sarah G Collins

Buy Direct and Save
Omega athletic shoes and in-line skates
Omega Corporation
$40 Rebate
When you purchase
2 pairs of shoes from
the Omega Series
SEE DETAILS BELOW

PUNCTUATION

Mixed Review

A. Punctuation: Comma, Hyphen, Quotation Marks, End Marks For each numbered item, explain why the highlighted punctuation is used.

LITERARY MODEL

(1) "Perhaps," said General Zaroff, "you were surprised that I recognized your name. You see, I read all books on hunting published in English, French, and Russian. I have but one passion in my life, Mr. Rainsford, and it is the hunt."

(2) "You have some wonderful heads here," said Rainsford as he ate a particularly well cooked filet mignon. "That Cape buffalo is the largest I ever saw."

"Oh, that fellow. Yes, he was a monster."

(3) "Did he charge you?"

"Hurled me against a tree," said the general. "Fractured my skull. But I got the brute."

"I've always thought," said Rainsford, "that the Cape buffalo is the most dangerous of all big game."

For a moment the general did not reply; he was smiling his curious **(4)** red-lipped smile. Then he said slowly: "No. You are wrong, sir. The Cape buffalo is not the most dangerous big game."

—Richard Connell, **(5)** "The Most Dangerous Game"

Look at the letter you wrote for the **Write Away** on page 248 or another piece from your **Working Portfolio.** Proofread the piece for punctuation errors.

B. Proofreading Write the underlined groups of words, inserting the correct punctuation.

How would you feel if you were trapped inside **(1)** a ring a bullring, to be precise with a ferocious bull that weighed 1,000 pounds **(2)** 450 kilograms or more? In countries such as **(3)** Spain Portugal Mexico and France, bullfighting is a traditional pastime. **(4)** The bullfighter called a *matador* is considered a national hero. The matador is accompanied by assistants called **(5)** *banderilleros* these assistants provoke the bull with a cape that is magenta on one side and yellow on the other. **(6)** Since the bull is colorblind it can only detect the movement of the cape. If the matador performs gracefully **(7)** actually, when he endangers himself enough to give the spectators a thrill the crowd will applaud and shout, **(8)** Ole! If the **(9)** matadors efforts have been moderately successful, the *presidente,* usually a local official, rewards him with one of the **(10)** bull's ears an exceptional performance merits two ears.

Mastery Test: What Did You Learn?

For each numbered item, choose the letter of the best revision.

How much do you think an empty glass bottle (1) is worth or, better yet, (2) how much would you be willing to pay for an empty bottle? The average person might say, "Empty bottles have no value." (3) However (4) to an antique-bottle collector, a bottle can be worth hundreds, even thousands, of dollars.

Richard Rushton-Clem of Lewisburg Pennsylvania (5) purchased an unusual, pickle bottle (6) (more commonly known as a pickle jar) for $3. Clem—a former (7) antique-shop owner, had an idea that the bottle was worth more than $3, but he never imagined it was worth thousands of dollars. He decided to sell it over the Internet to the highest bidder; the reserve price was set at $275. An interested buyer: (8) confirmed that the bottle was a rare 11-inch amber Willington pickle bottle (9). In the end, there were about 57 bids. A Pennsylvania doctor purchased Mr. Clems (10) $3 bottle for $44,100.

1. A. empty, glass bottle
   B. empty glass-bottle
   C. empty glass, bottle
   D. Correct as is

2. A. worth, or better yet
   B. worth or better yet,
   C. worth, or, better yet,
   D. Correct as is

3. A. The average person might say, "empty bottles have no value."
   B. The average person might say: empty bottles have no value.
   C. The average person might say, "Empty bottles have no value?"
   D. Correct as is

4. A. However—
   B. However:
   C. However,
   D. Correct as is

5. A. Lewisburg, Pennsylvania
   B. Lewisburg-Pennsylvania
   C. Lewisburg, Pennsylvania,
   D. Correct as is

6. A. unusual pickle bottle
   B. unusual-pickle bottle
   C. unusual pickle, bottle
   D. Correct as is

7. A. Clem,—a former
   B. Clem: a former
   C. Clem, a former
   D. Correct as is

8. A. An interested buyer,
   B. An interested buyer—
   C. An interested buyer
   D. Correct as is

9. A. "11 inch" amber Willington pickle bottle
   B. 11-inch amber, Willington pickle, bottle
   C. 11-inch, amber, Willington, pickle, bottle
   D. Correct as is

10. A. Mr. Clems'
    B. Mr. Clem's
    C. Mr. Clems's
    D. Correct as is

Student Help Desk

Punctuation at a Glance

CHAPTER 11

Hyphenating Compound Adjectives

Join Us

Tips to Remember	
Always use a hyphen after the prefix *all, ex,* or *self.*	George is very **self-reliant.**
Never use a hyphen if each adjective could be used separately.	His performance showed a **trendy '90s** style.
Never use a hyphen when one of the words ends in *-ly.*	Sonia showed off her **lovely rare** watch.
Never hyphenate a compound containing the words *very* and *most.*	This is the **most anticipated** movie of the year.

Apostrophes

Little Marks That Make a Big Difference

Type of Word	Possessive
singular noun school, girl, Tess	school's, girl's, Tess's
plural noun ending in s teachers, cars, Joneses	teachers', cars', Joneses'
plural noun not ending in s children, women, people	children's, women's, people's
indefinite pronoun everyone, anybody	everyone's, anybody's

Punctuating Titles

Names Up in Lights

Quotation Marks

Magazine article	"America's Pastime Returns in the Summer of '98"
Chapter title	Chapter 1, "Fast-Pitch Softball—No Speed Limits"
Short story	"One Throw"
Essay	"Baseball and Softball: A Comparative Study"
Short poem	"Picking Dandelions in the Outfield"
Song	"Take Me Out to the Ball Game"

Italics

Book title	*The Adventures of Huckleberry Finn*
Newspaper	*Chicago Sun-Times*
Magazine	*Newsweek*
Play	*A Midsummer Night's Dream*
Movie	*The Silence of the Lambs*
TV series	*The X-Files*
Work of art	*The Night Café*
Book-length poem	*Paradise Lost*
Long musical composition	*The Nutcracker Suite*

The Bottom Line

Checklist for Punctuation

Have I . . .

____ ended every sentence with the appropriate end mark?

____ used commas to separate items in series?

____ used semicolons to separate independent clauses in compound sentences whose parts are not joined with conjunctions?

____ used a dictionary to verify hyphenated words?

____ used apostrophes in possessive nouns?

____ used parentheses to enclose material that is loosely related to what surrounds it?

____ used italics and quotation marks correctly to set off titles of books, magazine articles, stories, artworks, and songs?

PUNCTUATION

Quick-Fix Editing Machine

You've worked hard on your assignment. Don't let misplaced commas, sentence fragments, and missing details lower your grade. Use this Quick-Fix Editing Guide to help you recognize grammatical errors and make your writing more precise.

QUICK FIX

Fixing Errors

Improving Style

1 Sentence Fragments

What's the problem? Part of a sentence has been left out.
Why does it matter? A fragment doesn't convey a complete thought.
What should you do about it? Find out what is missing and add it.

What's the Problem?	Quick Fix
A. A subject is missing. Disappeared into cyberspace.	**Add a subject.** **My homework** disappeared into cyberspace.
B. A verb is missing. Something strange on my disk.	**Add a verb.** Something strange **is** on my disk.
C. A helping verb is missing. My friends saying that I couldn't lose it.	**Add a helping verb.** My friends **were** saying that I couldn't lose it.
D. Both a subject and a verb are missing. Somewhere on the hard drive.	**Add a subject and a verb to make an independent clause.** **I'll** probably **find** it somewhere on the hard drive.
E. A subordinate clause is treated as if it were a sentence. Because I spent two hours on my homework.	**Combine the fragment with an independent clause.** **I'm frustrated** because I spent two hours on my homework. **OR** **Delete the conjunction.** ~~Because~~ I spent two hours on my homework.

For more help, see Chapter 5, pp. 116–119.

2 Run-On Sentences

What's the problem? Two or more sentences have been run together.

Why does it matter? A run-on sentence doesn't show where one idea ends and another begins.

What should you do about it? Find the best way to separate the ideas or to show the proper relationship between the two.

What's the Problem?	Quick Fix
A. The end mark separating two complete thoughts is missing. I practice the violin every day the dog always howls.	**Add an end mark and start a new sentence.** I practice the violin every day**. The** dog always howls.
B. Two sentences are separated only by a comma. Singing dogs may be funny on TV**,** in real life they can drive you crazy.	**Add a coordinating conjunction.** Singing dogs may be funny on TV, **but** in real life they can drive you crazy. **OR** **Change the comma to a semicolon.** Singing dogs may be funny on TV**;** in real life they can drive you crazy. **OR** **Replace the comma with an end mark and start a new sentence.** Singing dogs may be funny on TV**. In** real life they can drive you crazy. **OR** **Make one of the independent clauses into a subordinate clause.** **Although singing dogs may be funny on TV,** in real life they can drive you crazy.

For more help, see Chapter 5, pp. 120–121.

QUICK FIX

3 Subject-Verb Agreement

What's the problem? A verb does not agree with its subject in number.

Why does it matter? Readers may regard your work as careless.

What should you do about it? Identify the subject and use a verb that matches it in number.

What's the Problem?	Quick Fix
A. A verb agrees with the object of a preposition rather than with the subject. The animation of **cartoons are** fascinating.	**Mentally block out the prepositional phrase and make the verb agree with the true subject.** The **animation** ~~of cartoons~~ **is** fascinating.
B. A verb agrees with a word in a phrase that comes between the subject and the verb. I, as well as my **friends, are** the first in line for animated films.	**Mentally block out the phrase and make the verb agree with the true subject.** **I**, ~~as well as my friends,~~ **am** the first in line for animated films.
C. A verb doesn't agree with an indefinite-pronoun subject. **Each** of us **plan** to make cartoons our life.	**Decide whether the pronoun is singular or plural and make the verb agree with it.** **Each** of us **plans** to make cartoons our life.
D. A verb in a contraction doesn't agree with its subject. **It don't** seem like a waste of time to us.	**Use a verb in a contraction that agrees with the subject.** **It doesn't** seem like a waste of time to us.
E. A singular verb is used with a compound subject that contains *and*. **Celeste and Jono wants** to open a studio someday.	**Use a plural verb.** **Celeste and Jono want** to open a studio someday.

For more help, see Chapter 7, pp. 158–171.

What's the Problem? / Quick Fix

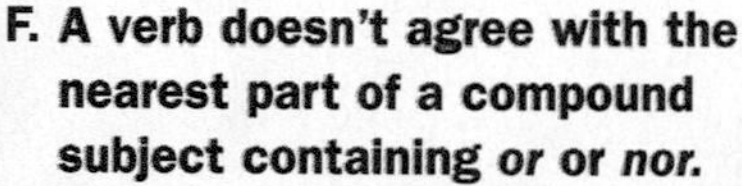

What's the Problem?	Quick Fix
F. A verb doesn't agree with the nearest part of a compound subject containing *or* or *nor*.	**Use a verb that agrees with the subject closest to the verb.**
Neither my friends nor **my teacher think** animation is a boring topic.	Neither my friends nor **my teacher thinks** animation is a boring topic.
G. A verb doesn't agree with the true subject of a sentence beginning with *here* or *there*.	**Mentally turn the sentence around so that the subject comes first, and make the verb agree with it.**
There is many new techniques in animated films.	There **are** many new **techniques** in animated films.
H. A singular subject ending in *s*, *es*, *or ics* is mistaken for a plural.	**Watch out for these nouns and use singular verbs with them.**
Mathematics are useful in learning those techniques.	**Mathematics is** useful in learning those techniques.
News of the techniques **were featured** in several magazine articles.	**News** of the techniques **was featured** in several magazine articles.
I. A collective noun referring to a single unit is treated as plural (or one referring to individuals is treated as singular).	**If the collective noun refers to a single unit, use a singular verb.**
Our **group are** working on a storyboard.	Our **group is** working on a storyboard.
J. A period of time isn't treated as a single unit.	**Use a singular verb whenever the subject refers to a period of time as a single unit.**
Two weeks aren't enough time to learn how to draw!	**Two weeks isn't** enough time to learn how to draw!

For more help, see Chapter 7, pp. 158–171.

4 Pronoun Reference Problems

What's the problem? A pronoun does not agree in number or gender with its antecedent, or an antecedent is unclear.

Why does it matter? Lack of agreement or unclear antecedents can cause confusion.

What should you do about it? Find the antecedent and make the pronoun agree with it, or rewrite a sentence to make the antecedent clear.

What's the Problem?	Quick Fix
A. A pronoun doesn't agree with an indefinite-pronoun antecedent. **Each** of the team members cast **their** vote.	**Decide whether the indefinite pronoun is singular or plural, and make the pronoun agree with it.** **Each** of the team members cast **his or her** vote.
B. A pronoun doesn't agree with the nearest part in a compound subject joined by *nor* or *or*. Neither the doctor nor the **nurses** hurt **herself** when I dropped the tray of glasses.	**Find the nearest simple subject and make the pronoun agree with it.** Neither the doctor nor the **nurses** hurt **themselves** when I dropped the tray of glasses.
C. A pronoun doesn't have an antecedent. In the handbook **it** says to put safety first.	**Rewrite the sentence to eliminate the pronoun.** The handbook says to put safety first.
D. A pronoun's antecedent is vague or indefinite. I guess **they** knew I was coming.	**Change the pronoun to a specific noun.** I guess **the supervisor** knew I was coming.
E. A pronoun could refer to more than one noun. The **supervisor** and the **nurse** talked, and **she** assigned me to pillow duty.	**Substitute a noun for the pronoun to make the reference specific.** The supervisor and the nurse talked, and **the supervisor** assigned me to pillow duty.

For more help, see Chapter 8, pp. 190–198.

5 Incorrect Pronoun Case

What's the problem? A pronoun is in the wrong case.

Why does it matter? Readers may regard your writing as sloppy and careless, especially if your writing is supposed to be formal.

What should you do about it? Identify how the pronoun is being used and replace it with the correct form.

What's the Problem?	Quick Fix
A. A pronoun that follows a linking verb is in the wrong case. The funniest student in school is **him.**	**Always use the nominative case after a linking verb.** The funniest student in school is **he.** **OR** **Reword the sentence.** **He is** the funniest student in school.
B. A pronoun used as the object of a preposition is not in the objective case. Geoff tries his jokes out on Marie and **I.**	**Always use the objective case when a pronoun is the object of a preposition.** Geoff tries his jokes out on Marie and **me.**
C. The wrong case is used in a comparison. Not even Drew Carey is funnier than **him.**	**Complete the comparison and use the appropriate case.** Not even Drew Carey is funnier than **he (is).**
D. *Who* or *whom* is used incorrectly. When we need a laugh, **who** do we call? Geoff!	**Use *who* if the pronoun is a subject, *whom* if it is an object.** When we need a laugh, **whom** do we call? Geoff!
E. A pronoun followed by an appositive is in the wrong case. **Us students** even laugh when Geoff is being serious.	**Mentally eliminate the appositive to test for the correct case.** **We** ~~students~~ even laugh when Geoff is being serious.

For more help, see Chapter 8, pp. 181–189.

QUICK FIX

6 *Who* and *Whom*

What's the problem? A form of the pronoun *who* or *whoever* is used incorrectly.

Why does it matter? The correct use of *who, whom, whoever,* and *whomever* in formal situations gives the impression that the speaker or writer is careful and knowledgeable.

What should you do about it? Decide how the pronoun functions in the sentence to determine which form to use.

What's the Problem?	Quick Fix
A. *Whom* is incorrectly used as a subject. **Whom is making** noise in the basement?	**Use *who* as the subject of a sentence.** **Who is making** noise in the basement?
B. *Who* is incorrectly used as the object of a preposition. **With who** will you go to check out the noise?	**Use *whom* as the object of a preposition.** **With whom** will you go to check out the noise?
C. *Who* is incorrectly used as a direct object. **Who could I ask?**	**Use *whom* as a direct object.** **Whom could I ask?**
D. *Whomever* is incorrectly used as the subject of a sentence or a clause. **Whomever is** in the basement, come out now!	***Whomever* is used only as an object. Use *whoever* as the subject of a clause.** **Whoever is** in the basement, come out now!
E. *Who's* is incorrectly used as the possessive form of *who*. **Who's** house could be this scary?	**Always use *whose* to show possession when the possessive form of *who* is needed.** **Whose** house could be this scary?

For more help, see Chapter 8, pp. 187–189.

7 Confusing Comparisons

What's the problem? The wrong form of a modifier is used when making a comparision.

Why does it matter? Incorrectly worded comparisons can be confusing and illogical.

What should you do about it? Use wording that makes the comparison clear.

What's the Problem?	Quick Fix
A. ***Both -er* and *more* or *-est* and *most* are used in making a comparison.**	**Eliminate the double comparison.**
Jamilla is **more luckier** than I.	Jamilla is ~~**more**~~ **luckier** than I.
I used to think I was the **most unluckiest** person on the planet.	I used to think I was the ~~**most**~~ **unluckiest** person on the planet.
B. The word *other* is missing in a comparison where it is logically needed.	**Add the missing word.**
I had more bad luck than any student at school.	I had more bad luck than any **other** student at school.
C. A superlative form is used where a comparative form is needed.	**When comparing two things, always use the comparative form.**
I'm not sure who has the worst luck—Lorenzo or I.	My luck never improves; it gets **worse** than Lorenzo's every day.
D. A comparative form is used where a superlative form is needed.	**When comparing more than two things, use the superlative form.**
Of the five kids in my family, I am the **more** unfortunate.	Of the five kids in our family, I am the **most** unfortunate.

For more help, see Chapter 9, pp. 217–221.

QUICK FIX

8 Verb Forms and Tenses

What's the problem? The wrong form or tense of a verb is used.

Why does it matter? Readers may regard your work as careless or confusing.

What should you do about it? Replace the incorrect verb with the correct form or tense.

What's the Problem?	Quick Fix
A. The wrong form of a verb is used with a helping verb. A thief in the park **had stole** a woman's purse.	**Always use a past participle with a helping verb.** A thief in the park **had stolen** a woman's purse.
B. A helping verb is missing. Agent Lance **seen** the incident happen.	**Add a helping verb.** Agent Lance **had** seen the incident happen.
C. An irregular verb form is spelled incorrectly. Unfortunately, Lance had not **wore** his glasses.	**Look up the correct spelling and use it.** Unfortunately, Lance had not **worn** his glasses.
D. A past participle is used incorrectly. The thief got away long before Lance **seen** him.	**To show the past, use the past form of a verb.** The thief got away long before Lance **saw** him. **OR** **Change the verb to the past perfect form by adding a helping verb.** The thief got away long before Lance **had seen** him.
E. Different tenses are used in the same sentence without a valid reason. Lance **lost** his chance because he **forgets** his glasses.	**Use the same tense throughout the sentence.** Lance **lost** his chance because he **forgot** his glasses.

For more help, see Chapter 6, pp. 134–139.

QUICK FIX

9 Misplaced and Dangling Modifiers

What's the problem? A modifying word or phrase is in the wrong place, or it doesn't modify any other word in the sentence.

Why does it matter? The sentence can be confusing or unintentionally funny.

What should you do about it? Move the modifying word or phrase closer to the word it modifies or add a word for it to modify.

What's the Problem?	Quick Fix
A. The adverb *even* or *only* is not placed close to the word it modifies. Bats **only** frighten me. I'm afraid of **even** things that look like bats.	**Move the adverb to make your meaning clear.** **Only** bats frighten me. I'm **even** afraid of things that look like bats. **OR** Bats frighten **only** me. Bats don't scare my friends.
B. A prepositional phrase is too far from the word it modifies. During our freshman year **in Kentucky** we went to one of the huge **caves.**	**Move the prepositional phrase closer to the word it modifies.** During our freshman year we went to one of the huge **caves in Kentucky.**
C. A participial phrase is too far from the word it modifies. **Flying near the ceiling,** our class watched the bats.	**Move the participial phrase closer to the word it modifies.** Our class watched the bats **flying near the ceiling.**
D. A participial phrase does not relate to anything in the sentence. **Peering through binoculars,** hundreds of bats were visible.	**Reword the sentence by adding a word for the participial phrase to refer to.** **Peering through binoculars, we** observed hundreds of bats.

For more help, see Chapter 3, pp. 78–79, and Chapter 9, p. 211.

10 Missing or Misplaced Commas

What's the problem? Commas are missing or are used incorrectly.

Why does it matter? Incorrect use of commas can make sentences hard to follow.

What should you do about it? Determine where commas are needed and add or omit them wherever necessary.

What's the Problem?	Quick Fix
A. A comma is missing before the conjunction in a series. Too many TV talk shows are crude, offensive and depressing.	**Add a comma.** Too many TV talk shows are crude, offensive, and depressing.
B. A comma is incorrectly placed after a closing quotation mark. "These shows are simply a means to show the depressing side of life", noted one TV critic.	**Always put a comma before a closing quotation mark.** "These shows are simply a means to show the depressing side of life," noted one TV critic.
C. A comma is missing after an introductory phrase or clause. Although these shows are about people's problems the problems are rarely solved.	**Find the end of the phrase or clause, and add a comma.** Although these shows are about people's problems, the problems are rarely solved.
D. Commas are missing around a nonessential phrase or clause. Other talk shows which feature entertainers are simply a means to promote various entertainment products.	**Add commas to set off the nonessential phrase or clause.** Other talk shows, which feature entertainers, are simply a means to promote various entertainment products.
E. A comma is missing from a compound sentence. Talk shows waste my time and most of them disgust me.	**Add a comma before the coordinating conjunction.** Talk shows waste my time, and most of them disgust me.

For more help, see Chapter 11, pp. 252–257.

11 Using Active and Passive Voice

What's the problem? The use of a verb in the passive voice makes a sentence weak.

Why does it matter? Sentences written in the active voice are more interesting to readers than are sentences with verbs in the passive voice.

What should you do about it? Rewrite sentences, and use the active rather than the passive voice.

What's the Problem?	Quick Fix
A. The passive voice makes a sentence dull.	**Use the active voice to revise the sentence.**
Twisters **are tracked** and **chased** by tornado watchers.	Tornado watchers **track** and **chase** twisters.
B. The passive voice takes the emphasis away from the people performing an action.	**Change the voice from passive to active.**
Storm sightings **are** immediately **plotted** on maps by these eager followers.	These eager followers immediately **plot** storm sightings on maps.
C. The passive voice makes a sentence wordy.	**Change the voice from passive to active.**
The unpredictable tornado **has been followed** closely by storm chasers.	Storm chasers **followed** the unpredictable tornado closely.

For more help, see Chapter 6, pp. 144–145, and Chapter 16, pp. 374–375.

QUICK FIX

Note: The passive voice is effective in the following situations:

to emphasize the receiver of an action or the action itself

This site for the next vacation **was chosen** to avoid tornadoes.

to make a statement about an action whose performer does not have to be specified or is unknown

No tornadoes **have been spotted** in this area since 1995.

12 Improving Weak Sentences

What's the problem? A sentence repeats ideas or contains too many ideas.

Why does it matter? Empty or overloaded sentences can bore readers and weaken the message.

What should you do about it? Make sure that every sentence contains a substantial, clearly focused idea.

What's the Problem?	Quick Fix
A. An idea is repeated.	**Eliminate the repeated idea.**
Elizabeth enjoys the best of two worlds because she is bilingual **and speaks two languages fluently.**	Elizabeth enjoys the best of two worlds because she is bilingual~~, and speaks two languages fluently~~.
B. A single sentence contains too many weakly linked ideas.	**Divide the sentence into two or more sentences while using subordinate clauses to show relationships between ideas.**
In Montreal, Canadians speak French and English, and Elizabeth's home was in Montreal, and Elizabeth learned both languages, so that she spoke both fluently when her family moved to the United States five years ago.	In Montreal, where Elizabeth was born, both French and English are spoken. When her family moved to the United States five years ago, Elizabeth spoke both languages fluently.
C. Too much information about a topic is crammed into one sentence.	**Divide the sentence into two or more sentences, and use subordinate clauses to show relationships between ideas.**
The official language spoken in Montreal is still controversial because many French people settled there, although Canada was once controlled by the British, so some people want French to be Quebec's official language, and some want English.	Although Canada was once controlled by the British, many French people settled in Montreal. A controversy continues about whether French or English should be the official language of Quebec.

For more help, see Chapter 16, pp. 366–367.

13 Avoiding Wordiness

What's the problem? A sentence contains unnecessary words.

Why does it matter? The meaning of wordy sentences can be unclear to readers.

What should you do about it? Use concise terms and eliminate extra words.

What's the Problem?	Quick Fix
A. A single idea is unnecessarily expressed in two ways.	**Delete the unnecessary words.**
At 7:00 A.M. **in the morning**, we were waiting at the cold, drafty bus stop.	At 7:00 A.M. ~~**in the morning**~~, we were waiting at the cold, drafty bus stop.
B. A sentence contains words that do not add to its meaning.	**Delete the unnecessary words.**
What I mean to say is that the four of us were desperately trying to keep warm.	~~**What I mean to say is that**~~ The four of us were desperately trying to keep warm.
C. A simple idea is expressed in too many words.	**Simplify the expression.**
The bus was late **on account of the fact that** it had a flat tire.	The bus was late **because** it had a flat tire.
D. A clause is used when a phrase would do.	**Reduce the clause to a phrase.**
The bus driver, **who is** a ten-year veteran, arrived a half-hour late with a brand-new tire and cups of hot cocoa.	The bus driver, ~~**who is**~~ a ten-year veteran, arrived a half-hour late with a brand-new tire and cups of hot cocoa.

For more help, see Chapter 16, pp. 364–365.

14 Varying Sentence Beginnings

What's the problem? Too many sentences begin the same way.

Why does it matter? Lack of variety in sentence beginnings makes writing dull and choppy.

What should you do about it? Reword some sentences so that they begin with prepositional phrases, verbal phrases, or subordinate clauses.

What's the Problem?	Quick Fix
Too many sentences in a paragraph start with the same word. My little sister loves attention. She charms the adults. She flashes her toothless smile. She blows bubbles, and they think she's darling.	**Start a sentence with a prepositional phrase.** My little sister loves attention. **With her toothless smile,** she charms the adults. She blows bubbles, and they think she's darling.
	OR
My older brother also loves attention. He entertains his friends. He does tricks. He does pratfalls, and they think he's hilarious.	**Start a sentence with a verbal phrase.** My older brother also loves attention. **Entertaining his friends with tricks and pratfalls is a favorite activity because they think he's hilarious.**
	OR
My cousin is rather quiet. She stays in her room for hours. She writes poetry there. She lives in our house, but we sometimes forget she exists.	**Start a sentence with a subordinate clause.** My cousin is rather quiet. **When she writes poetry, she stays in her room for hours.** We sometimes forget that she lives in our house.

For more help, see Chapter 3, pp. 66–77 and Chapter 4, pp. 92–100.

15 Varying Sentence Structure

What's the problem? A piece of writing contains too many simple sentences.

Why does it matter? Similarity in sentence structure makes writing dull and lifeless.

What should you do about it? Combine or reword sentences to create different structures.

What's the Problem?

The use of too many simple sentences leads to dull or choppy writing.

Members of the school band set a record last Saturday. They raised a thousand dollars. The money was for charity.

They held a "playathon." It was a musical marathon. It lasted 12 hours.

The marathon came to an end. The band members collapsed on the gym floor. The volunteers handed out lip balm, bandages, and refreshments.

For more help, see Chapter 16, pp. 368–373.

Quick Fix

Combine the sentences to form a compound sentence.

Members of the school band set a record last Saturday**, and** they raised a thousand dollars ~~The money was~~ for charity.

OR

Combine the sentences to form a complex sentence.

They held a "playathon," a musical marathon, **that lasted 12 hours.**

OR

Combine the sentences to form a compound-complex sentence.

When the marathon came to an end, the band members collapsed on the gym floor**, and** volunteers handed out lip balm, bandages, and refreshments.

QUICK FIX

16 Adding Supporting Details

What's the problem? Unfamiliar terms aren't defined, and claims aren't supported.

Why does it matter? Undefined terms and unsupported claims weaken an explanation or persuasive writing.

What should you do about it? Add supporting information to clarify statements and reasons.

What's the Problem?	Quick Fix
A. A key term is not defined. As more people use e-mail, the problem of **UCE** grows.	**Define the term.** As more people use e-mail, the problem of UCE **(unsolicited commercial e-mail)** grows.
B. No reason is given for an opinion. The flood of electronic junk mail is bad.	**Add a reason.** The flood of electronic junk mail is bad **because it slows down the e-mail system.**
C. No supporting facts are given. Consumers must be careful.	**Add supporting facts.** **The Federal Trade Commission reports that a lot of the junk mail is fraudulent; therefore,** consumers must be careful.
D. No examples are given. Consumers should arm themselves with information.	**Add examples.** Consumers should arm themselves with information**, such as the tips from the "Internet Fraud Watch" Web site.**

For more help, see Chapter 15, pp. 354–357.

17 Avoiding Clichés and Slang

What's the problem? A piece of formal writing contains clichés or slang expressions.

Why does it matter? Clichés do not convey fresh images to readers. Slang is inappropriate in formal writing.

What should you do about it? Reword sentences to replace the clichés and slang with clear, fresh expressions.

QUICK FIX

What's the Problem?	Quick Fix
A. A sentence contains a cliché. After a morning of packing and stacking boxes of goods for the hurricane victims, the volunteers **were so hungry they could have eaten a horse.**	**Eliminate the cliché and use a fresh description or explanation.** After a morning of packing and stacking boxes of goods for the hurricane victims, the volunteers **swooped down on the donated lunches like ravenous vultures.**
B. A sentence contains inappropriate slang. Everyone agreed that working for the hurricane relief effort was **way cool.**	**Replace the slang with more appropriate language.** Everyone agreed that working for the hurricane relief effort was **a rewarding and uplifting experience.**

For more help, see Chapter 17, pp. 384–389.

18 Using Precise Words

What's the problem? Nouns, modifiers, or verbs are not precise.

Why does it matter? Writers who use vague or general words do not engage their readers' interest.

What should you do about it? Replace general words with precise and vivid ones.

What's the Problem?	Quick Fix
A. Nouns are too general.	**Use specific nouns.**
The **group** unloaded the **equipment** and marched into the **building.**	The **four members of the Kingpins** unloaded their **bowling bags and uniforms** and marched into the **Shady Lanes Bowling Alley.**
B. Modifiers are too general.	**Use more precise or vivid adjectives and adverbs.**
Today they would be facing their **biggest** opponent, the Splits. "We're going to beat the Splits," Ivan said.	**In a few hours,** they would be facing their **fiercest and most feared** opponent, the Splits.
C. A sentence tells about what happens rather than shows it.	**Use precise verbs and modifiers to describe the actions.**
The Kingpins **were** tense as they **headed** for lane 21. "We're **going** to beat the Splits," Ivan said. "**Let's** warm up," Frank **replied.**	Ivan, the team captain, **scanned** the lane numbers. "Well, today's the day we'll **destroy** the Splits' winning streak," he said, his voice **quivering unconvincingly.** Frank **lurched** forward. "Let's just find lane 21 and do our warm-ups," he **snapped.**

For more help, see Chapter 17, pp. 382–383.

19 Using Figurative Language

What's the problem? A piece of writing is lifeless or unimaginative.

Why does it matter? Lifeless writing bores readers because it doesn't help them form mental pictures of what is being described.

What should you do about it? Add figures of speech to make the writing lively and to create pictures in readers' minds. Do not, however, combine figures of speech that have no logical connection.

What's the Problem?	Quick Fix
A. A description is dull and lifeless.	**Add a simile.**
The first Sunday dinner I ever prepared was a failure. Aunt Lydia inspected each forkful.	The first Sunday dinner I ever prepared was a failure. Aunt Lydia inspected each forkful **like a picky shopper examining damaged goods.**
OR	**OR**
I couldn't tell if Uncle Lou liked the dinner.	**Rewrite the sentence, adding a metaphor.** Uncle Lou was **a statue at our dinner table.** He ate his meal stiffly and silently but never revealed his thoughts.
B. Figures of speech that have no logical connection have been used together.	**Delete one of the figures of speech.**
However, my brother, **always as hungry as a great white shark,** was **a human steam shovel,** scooping up great mounds of food and dumping them in his mouth.	However, my brother, ~~**always as hungry as a great white shark,**~~ was **a human steam shovel,** scooping up great mounds of food and dumping them in his mouth.

For more help, see Chapter 17, pp. 386–389.

QUICK FIX

20 Paragraphing

What's the problem? A paragraph contains too many ideas.

Why does it matter? A long paragraph doesn't help to signal new ideas and discourages readers from continuing.

What should you do about it? Break the paragraph into smaller paragraphs, each focusing on one main idea. Start a new paragraph whenever the speaker, setting, or focus changes.

What's the Problem?

A. Too many ideas are contained in one paragraph.

Every morning the towering figure of Principal Douglas Mulder stands guard in the hallway. His booming voice has stopped many mischief-makers in their tracks. Few students would guess that Principal Mulder has a hobby that contrasts with his ex-Marine image. Mulder has always loved creating figurines out of glass. Back in his office, Principal Mulder shows off his collection of glass figurines to a new substitute teacher, Mr. Kravitz. Many have admired them, but few knew their origin. "Mr. Mulder, these are impressive!" "I've loved glass-blowing ever since my grandmother first taught me the craft."

For more help, see Chapter 14, pp. 342–345.

Quick Fix

Every morning the towering figure of Principal Douglas Mulder stands guard in the hallway. His booming voice has stopped many mischief-makers in their tracks.

Start a new paragraph to introduce a new idea.

Few students would guess that Principal Mulder has a hobby that contrasts with his ex-Marine image. Mulder has always loved creating figurines out of glass.

Start a new paragraph to change the setting or place.

Back in his office, Principal Mulder shows off his collection of glass figurines to a new substitute teacher, Mr. Kravitz. Many have admired them, but few knew their origin.

Start a new paragraph whenever the speaker changes.

"Mr. Mulder, these are impressive!"

"I've loved glass-blowing ever since my grandmother first taught me the craft."

What's the Problem?

B. An essay is treated as one long paragraph.

Have you ever watched a movie with great special effects and wondered, How did they do that? Many people might be surprised to learn that special efffects involve just a few basic techniques. Some special effects rely on the use of models and miniatures. The shark in *Jaws,* for example, was really depicted by three different mechanical models designed to be used in different scenes. Some of the most complex special effects involve a process called composite photography. For instance, the cartoon characters' actions in the film *Who Framed Roger Rabbit?* were drawn and photographed on one piece of film; the live actors' movements were photographed on another. The two pieces of film were then combined so that the cartoon characters and the humans looked as if they were on screen together. The next time you watch a movie, you won't have to ask how they did that. You'll already know.

For more help, see Chapter 14, pp. 342–345.

Quick Fix

Have you ever watched a movie with great special effects and wondered, How did they do that? Many people might be surprised to learn that special efffects involve just a few basic techniques.

Start a new paragraph to introduce the first main idea.

Some special effects rely on the use of models and miniatures. The shark in *Jaws*, for example, was really depicted by three different mechanical models designed to be used in different scenes.

Start a new paragraph to introduce another main idea.

Some of the most complex special effects involve a process called composite photography. For instance, the cartoon characters' actions in the film *Who Framed Roger Rabbit?* were drawn and photographed on one piece of film; the live actors' movements were photographed on another. The two pieces of film were then combined so that the cartoon characters and the humans looked as if they were on screen together.

Start a new paragraph to give the conclusion.

The next time you watch a movie, you won't have to ask how they did that. You'll already know.

Essential Writing Skills

A Total Experience

The writing process begins before you put pen or pencil to paper or input words on a computer. It may start with a word or a conversation, a sound or an image. In any case, you'll draw upon most of the skills presented in this chapter to move from ideas to a piece of writing that you can share.

Power Words
Vocabulary for Precise Writing

stimulus

origin

In the Beginning

Do you yearn to create something new? You'll need an inventive vocabulary to describe the process of going from idea to finished product.

One Percent Inspiration

What is the **source,** the **origin,** or the **genesis** of an idea? What **creative impulse** sparked its **inception?** What **stimulus** provoked it? Did you have a sudden **inspiration, revelation,** or **epiphany?** Did your **intuition** tell you what line of thought to pursue?

Ninety-Nine Percent Perspiration

You're not satisfied with just an idea—you want to develop it. You will need **stick-to-itiveness** (yes, that's an actual word), **persistence, perseverance,** and **tenacity.** You must be **determined, firm, resolved, unwavering, resolute, steadfast, tenacious,** and **unflagging** in your efforts. Once you have your idea worked out, you will want to **improve** it, **enhance** it, **refine** it—in fact, **perfect** it!

epiphany

Your Turn Mother of Invention

Invent something unusual. After imagining your creation in some detail, draw a picture of it. Use labels to show how this invention works (you don't have to obey the laws of mechanics or physics). If you prefer, you can describe your invention in a few paragraphs.

inspiration

Chapter 12

Writing Process

THE FAR SIDE by Gary Larson

"I don't know where my ideas come from. . . . The idea for any cartoon (my experience, anyway) is rarely spontaneous. Good ideas usually evolve out of pretty lame ones, and vice versa. . . . Some cartoons spring forth from just staring stupidly at a blank sheet of paper and thinking about aardvarks or toaster ovens or cemeteries or just about anything, and others come out of 'doodles' that I continually enter into a sketchbook."

—Gary Larson, *The Prehistory of The Far Side*

Proceed with a Process

Writing, like drawing, is a creative process that begins with an idea. How do you turn an idea into a piece of writing? Do you start off with one idea and then replace it with something better? Maybe you stay with the same idea and gradually craft it into something special. In any case, at some point you must put your idea on paper. Having a good system for getting ideas from brain to paper will make your life as a writer much easier.

Write Away: Putting the Plan into Action

Use the strategies in this chapter to complete your next writing assignment. These strategies work for any type of writing. Put your completed assignment in your **Working Portfolio.**

LESSON 1 Prewriting

Prewriting is the stage during which you explore key aspects of writing—why you are writing, whom you are writing for, what you need to say, and how you need to say it. Where do you start?

1 Asking Questions

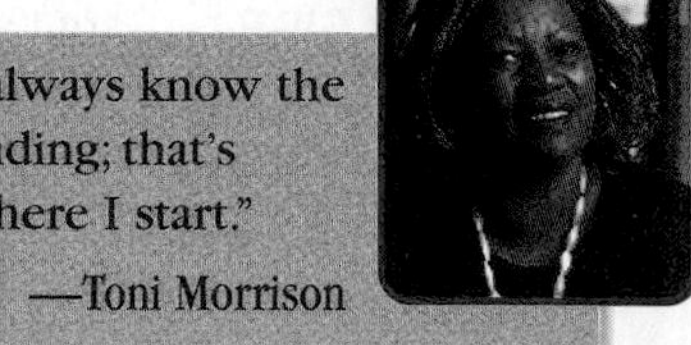

"I always know the ending; that's where I start."

—Toni Morrison

You can use the following questions to help you get started. Don't worry; you don't have to know all of the answers before you begin to develop a topic. As you work through the writing process, you'll probably change your mind about some things. You can always revisit these questions to see whether your writing is accomplishing what you want it to.

Questions to Ask Yourself	
Purpose	Why am I writing this piece? Am I writing to entertain, inform, or persuade? What personal need does it fulfill? What effect do I want to have on my readers?
Topic	Is my topic assigned, or can I choose it? What would I be interested in writing about? What do I already know about my topic?
Audience	Who is my audience? What might they already know about my topic? What do they need to know? What about the topic might interest them? What approach and language might they respond to best?
Form	What form will work best? Which of the following formats would be most suited to my purpose, topic, and audience? • essay • poem • script • letter • research paper • short story • news article • review • speech

"Many of my story ideas come from my life, but in many cases I use something interesting that has happened to me as a 'trigger' for my imagination."

—Judith Ortiz Cofer

❷ Exploring a Topic

Sometimes you're assigned a topic to write about. Sometimes you choose your own. In either case, explore your topic to find a fresh, unique way to write about it. You might use one of these methods.

Freewriting

Freewriting is a way of discovering what you know or think about a topic by writing rapidly, without stopping.

Here's How Freewriting

- Focus on a topic.
- Set a time limit—for example, ten minutes.
- Write as quickly and continuously as you can. Then read what you wrote.
- Circle the best ideas, and freewrite about them for a few more minutes.

Listing

If you find yourself with a lot of ideas about a topic, the fastest way to get them down is by listing them. Jot down phrases or even just words. When you are done, see which item on the list strikes you as the most interesting. You can then make a second list of ideas related to the item you selected.

WRITING PROCESS

Clustering

If you like to use graphic organizers to explore ideas, try clustering. Write your idea in the center of a piece of paper and circle it. Outside the circle, write related ideas. Circle these and draw lines connecting them to your topic.

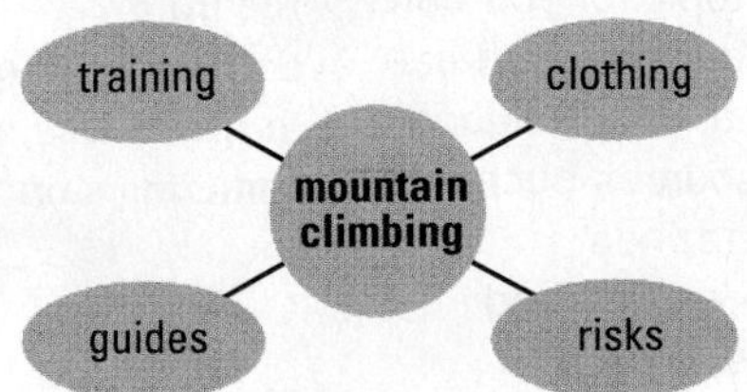

❸ Refining a Topic

Once you've explored your topic, you'll want to see if it's a manageable size. Choose from the following options when you need to refine your topic.

- Create a rough outline about your topic to get an idea of how much information you will need to cover. If there is too much material, look for a narrower topic within your outline.
- Ask yourself what aspect of your topic your readers would be most interested in.
- Check books about your topic to see how information is arranged in the tables of contents. See if there is a subheading that fits your topic.

❹ Gathering and Organizing Ideas

Before you start writing, you'll need to spend some time gathering and organizing ideas. Your search for information may lead you to an interview with an expert or to a magazine article that raises new questions about your topic.

Developing Research Questions

CHAPTER 12

Suppose you decided to write about Sherpas, guides for mountain climbers in Nepal and Tibet. To help focus your search for information, make a list of questions that you want answered.

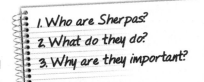

1. Who are Sherpas?
2. What do they do?
3. Why are they important?

Finding and Organizing Ideas

You can find ideas about your topic in a number of ways. You can draw on any of your personal experiences that are related to the topic, or you can do research. Your research can include personal observations or secondary sources such as books and magazines.

When you have finished gathering ideas, you can organize them by using such graphic devices as Venn diagrams, flow charts, or outlines.

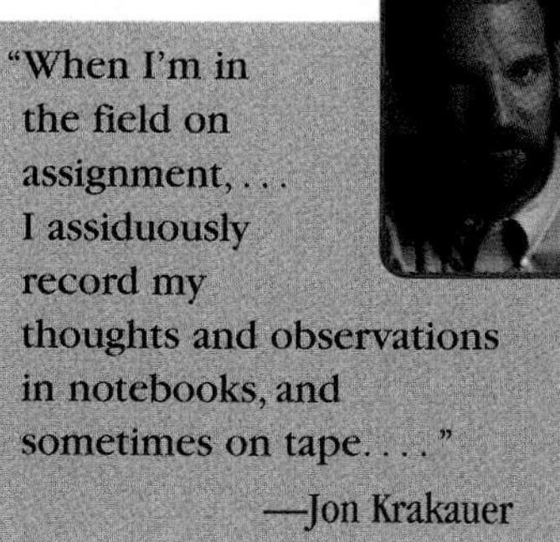

"When I'm in the field on assignment, . . . I assiduously record my thoughts and observations in notebooks, and sometimes on tape. . . ."

—Jon Krakauer

LESSON 2 Drafting

There is no right or wrong way to turn prewriting ideas into a first draft. Some writers write freely to get ideas on paper. Others work from a detailed outline. Either way, don't worry about errors at this stage. It's more important to start writing!

"I'm free, with white sheets of paper before me, and a head full of wild ideas, ideas that excite me."

—Richard Wright

1 Drafting to Discover

Drafting to discover means that you use your first draft to explore ideas, developing the topic along the way with no set plan or structure. Review the ideas you produced during your prewriting, and then simply begin writing. You may be surprised by how absorbed you get in your topic.

2 Drafting from a Plan

If you know ahead of time that your ideas have to be arranged in a certain way, you may find drafting from a plan useful. There are several plans or outlines to choose from. You may decide to use a formal outline that actually spells out each main point and the supporting details in the order they will be presented. Or you may decide on a modified outline that gives you a rough idea of the points you want to cover. A modified outline might look like the one below.

STUDENT MODEL

Jon Krakauer and Mount Everest

Jon's early interest in climbing
- —Family friend was a climber
- —Climbed 9,000-foot mountain at age nine

How he became a writer
- —No formal training
- —Hired by *Outside* magazine

The Everest climb
- —Assignment for magazine
- —Disastrous blizzard

The success of *Into Thin Air*
- —Praise from critics
- —Bestseller for many months

WRITING PROCESS

The following is the first paragraph based on the outline on the previous page.

STUDENT MODEL

DRAFT

Jon Krakauer was born in 1954. A family friend, Willi Unsoeld, encouraged Jon's interest in climbing. Willi had climbed Mount Everest using a very difficult route. When Jon was nine, Willi and the Krakauers climbed a 9,000-foot mountain. This was Jon's first test of climbing to such a height.

3 Using Peer Response

Except for journals, nearly all of your writing will be addressed to one or more readers. It makes sense, then, to test your writing on an audience. One such audience is a **peer group,** or a group of your classmates. Here are some tips for working with peer groups.

As a writer, do these things

- Have a copy of the draft for each member of the group.
- Indicate whether you are more interested in feedback about your ideas or your presentation of them.
- Ask questions or let readers respond on their own. (For a list of questions, see page 317.)
- Give readers time to think.
- Encourage readers to be honest.

As a reader, do these things

- Offer positive reactions first.
- Respect the writer's feelings.
- Use "I" statements. For example, say "I think this is . . ." rather than "This is . . ."
- Give specific feedback. Don't say, "I don't understand." Say, "Can you tell me more about . . ."
- Suggest changes, but do not rewrite.

CHAPTER 12

LESSON 3 Revising

The revising stage allows you to polish your draft, making changes in its content, organization, and style. You may not need to revise as many times as Amy Tan, but you will probably revisit your writing several times before you're satisfied with it.

"I probably revise about a hundred times before I turn anything in [to a publisher]."

—Amy Tan

1 Six Traits of Effective Writing

The following six traits may be used to evaluate any piece of writing.

Six Evaluation Traits	
Ideas and content	Make sure ideas are clear, focused, and supported with relevant details.
Organization	Arrange your ideas in a logical order to help the reader move easily through the text.
Voice	Express your ideas in a way that shows an individual style and personality.
Word choice	Use language that is precise, powerful, and engaging.
Sentence fluency	Create an interesting rhythm and flow by using varied sentence lengths and structures.
Conventions	Use correct grammar, spelling, and punctuation.

WRITING PROCESS

Evaluating Ideas

Troubleshooting Problems with Content

Problem	Solution
Main idea not clear	Make sure the main idea appears in the introduction and is mentioned elsewhere.
Not enough details	Add more facts and examples that support your ideas.
Ideas hard to understand	Use simpler vocabulary and more examples.
Weak introduction	Begin with an anecdote, a surprising statement, or a quotation.
Weak conclusion	Restate your main idea in powerful language, or recommend a course of action.

Evaluating Organization

Here's How **Evaluating Organization**

- Each topic sentence is related to the main idea.
- The details in each paragraph support its topic sentence.
- Paragraphs flow smoothly from one to the next through the use of transitional words and phrases, such as *first, as a result,* and *similarly.*
- Ideas appear in a logical order.

It's not unusual to do a formal outline after you've written a first draft. At this point, the outline can help you see how well you've organized your ideas and how thoroughly you've covered them.

"As a writer, . . . I'm in every song . . . I inject my thoughts and my humor and my concerns and things that I think about into these songs. That's the genesis of creation, if there is one." —Michael Stipe

CHAPTER 12

Evaluating Style

Voice in writing is the unique way in which a writer expresses himself or herself on paper. It is based on all aspects of writing, but especially vocabulary, sentence structure, and figurative language. Notice the difference in voice in the following excerpts.

LITERARY MODEL

I took from their sconces two flambeaux, and giving one to Fortunato, bowed him through several suites of rooms to the archway that led into the vaults. I passed down a long and winding staircase, requesting him to be cautious as he followed. We came at length to the foot of the descent and stood together on the damp ground of the catacombs of the Montresors.

—Edgar Allan Poe, "The Cask of Amontillado"

LITERARY MODEL

At 6:30, as the last of the daylight seeped from the sky, I'd descended to within 200 vertical feet of Camp Four. Only one obstacle now stood between me and safety: a bulging incline of hard, glassy ice that I would have to descend without a rope. Snow pellets borne by 70-knot gusts stung my face; any exposed flesh was instantly frozen. —Jon Krakauer, *Into Thin Air*

Word choice has a major effect on how a reader understands your writing. You can adjust your writing style by choosing from the following kinds of language, depending on your audience and purpose.

- Figurative language
- Technical terminology
- Slang and idioms
- Sound devices

Sentence fluency is the flow and rhythm writers create when they effectively build sentences into paragraphs. You can create sentence fluency by varying the length and structure of your sentences.

STUDENT MODEL

DRAFT

Jon Krakauer climbed Mount Everest in 1996. He was on a magazine assignment. He had difficulty climbing back down the mountain. A blizzard hit. His oxygen ran out. He barely made it to camp. Nineteen people were trapped in the blizzard. Eight died.

The paragraph above lacks fluency because all of the sentences are short, with no variety in structure or length.

STUDENT MODEL

REVISION

For a magazine assignment, Jon Krakauer climbed Mount Everest in 1996. He ran into difficulty. While he was climbing back down the mountain, a blizzard hit. Then his oxygen ran out, and he barely made it back to camp. Nineteen people were trapped in the blizzard; eight died.

LESSON 4

Editing and Proofreading

Editing and proofreading are the final steps you take to make sure you have followed the rules of writing. Mistakes in mechanics or grammar can distract readers from your message. Take time to read your work carefully so that you can eliminate careless errors.

1 Editing and Proofreading Techniques

Here are some tips that will help you focus on little details—those mechanical errors that could make a difference in your final product.

Here's How **Editing and Proofreading**

1. If possible, don't begin proofreading after you've just finished writing. Put your work away for at least several hours. You'll find more errors if you take a break.
2. Read your work slowly—one sentence at a time.
3. Look for the kinds of mistakes that you have often made before, as well as other kinds of mistakes.
4. Use a dictionary to check spelling.
5. Ask a family member or friend to read your work.

Use the checklist below to help you correct some of the most common errors writers make.

Checking Usage and Mechanics

- ✔ Have I avoided nonstandard words or expressions?
- ✔ Have I corrected any errors in subject-verb or pronoun-antecedent agreement?
- ✔ Have I double-checked for errors in confusing word pairs, such as *it's/its, than/then, too/to*?
- ✔ Have I corrected all of the run-on sentences and sentence fragments?
- ✔ Have I followed the conventions for correct capitalization?
- ✔ Have I used punctuation marks correctly?
- ✔ Have I checked the spellings of all unfamiliar words in the dictionary?

The spell check feature on a computer is helpful, but it won't catch the error if a word is misspelled as a different word, as in the following poem.

Eye halve a spelling checker.
It came with my pea see.
It plainly marks four my revue
Miss steaks eye kin knot sea.

Eye half run this poem threw it.
Eye em shore yore pleased two no.
Its letter perfect awl the weigh.
My checker tolled me sew.

2 Using Proofreading Marks

The following chart lists and explains the most commonly used proofreading marks.

Proofreading Marks			
∧	Add letters or words.	⌒	Close up.
⊙	Add a period.	¶	Begin new paragraph.
∧,	Add a comma.	≡	Capitalize a letter.
#	Add a space.	/	Use lowercase.
ℓ	Delete letters or words.	∾	Switch the positions of letters or words.

Notice how the marks are used to make revisions and corrections.

STUDENT MODEL

Jon didn't start out as a writer. ~~But~~ [B]because[#]he liked climbing and being outdoors[,] he [accepted] ~~excepted~~ a job [as a writer] for a magazine called *Outside.* he wrote many articles about dangerous adventures. As he continued to write for the magazine, he realize[d]~~s~~ how much he loved writing. Critics have said that his writing places you at the scene of an adventure. Jon says that he recie ved his training as [a] writer just by doing it.

WRITING PROCESS

LESSON 5

Publishing and Reflecting

1 Sharing Your Writing

The writing process can be difficult, so it is important to have the sense of accomplishment that comes from sharing your finished work. Here are some ways you might publish your work.

> "I do enjoy being a writer. The truth is, there's nothing I'd rather do with my life, but writing is 'fun' in the same way lifting weights is fun. It's hard and it hurts."
>
> —Sue Grafton

Print Media

- Submit your work to your school newspaper or literary magazine or to a community newspaper. Weekly newspapers are often likely to print students' work. Letters to the editor are especially well received.
- Send your work to a magazine.
- Get a copy of *Writer's Market* or *Market Guide for Young Writers* at a local library to find information about where you can send your work.
- Enter your work in a contest sponsored by a community organization or a magazine.

Electronic Media

- Send your writing, via e-mail, to a friend or relative.
- Put your writing on a school Web site.
- Submit your work to an online journal or Internet site for student writing.

Before you submit material to a magazine, a Web site, or an online journal, become familiar with its rules for submitting manuscripts.

Performances

- Dramatize an original poem, story, or monologue in class.
- Present a persuasive or an opinion essay as a speech.
- Participate in a readers' circle or a writing exchange group with friends or classmates, in or out of school.

For more publishing options, visit the McDougal Littell Web site: mcdougallittell.com

2 Reflecting on Your Writing

If you reflect on your writing process, whether the end product is a song or an essay, not only can you learn more about yourself, but you may be able to make improvements as a writer.

Questions to Ask about Your Writing Process
✔ Am I becoming more or less of a planner/explorer than I used to be? Is this good or bad, and why?
✔ Which parts of the process did I find easiest? Which parts were more difficult?
✔ What was the biggest problem I faced during the writing process? How did I solve the problem? Could I use that solution again in some future work?
✔ What changes have occurred in my writing style?
✔ Have I noticed any features in the writing of my peers that I can apply to my own work?

Using Portfolios

You can keep your reflections about your writing as well as your writing pieces in portfolios like the ones described below.

Working Portfolio You can keep all of your writing here, no matter what stage it's in. You may revise some pieces later.

Presentation Portfolio The pieces in this portfolio represent your best work. They are ready for presentation or publication.

Student Help Desk

Writing Process at a Glance

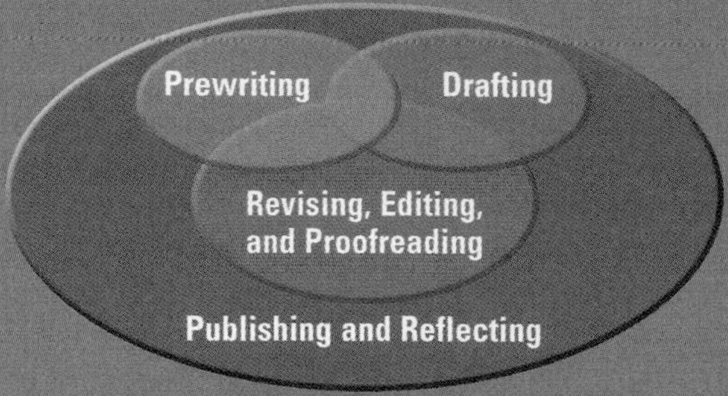

Prewriting

Drafting

Revising, Editing, and Proofreading

Publishing and Reflecting

Jump Start

Prewriting Strategies

Browse	Look through magazines, newspapers, and online bulletin boards for ideas.
Freewrite	Write down anything that comes into your head.
Brainstorm	In a group, come up with as many ideas as you can without stopping to critique them.
Discuss	Meet with someone to discuss your ideas so far. Perhaps interview someone who knows a lot about the subject area.
Question	Ask "what if" questions.
Go graphic	Use word webs, pro and con charts, Venn diagrams, flow charts, or other graphic organizers.
Get sense-able	Use your five senses to enrich your descriptions.
Take a hike	Take a walk, making notes as you go.
See the setting	Revisit a place that you are thinking of using as a setting.
You do say	Listen to conversations.

Friendly Feedback

Questions for Your Peer Reader

- Was this piece of writing easy to follow, or did you find yourself getting lost?
- What point do you think I was trying to make?
- How can I make my introduction more appealing?
- Which part of my writing worked best for you? Can you tell me which words or phrases you found striking or interesting?
- What would you like to know more about?

Calvin and Hobbes by Bill Watterson

The Bottom Line

Checklist for Writing Process

Have I . . .

____ presented clear and well-focused ideas?

____ organized the ideas so that the connections between them are clear and logical?

____ used words that are specific, precise, and appropriate to my audience and purpose?

____ written sentences that are varied and flow together smoothly?

____ used correct punctuation, grammar, capitalization, and spelling?

WRITING PROCESS

Power Words
Vocabulary for Precise Writing

hamlet

Bright Lights, Big City

Do the words "bright lights, big city" come to mind at the mention of New York City? There are many words for large cities and for small towns that can help you set the scene for your next narrative.

This Great Hive, the City!

The community you live in might be **urban, suburban** (even **exurban**), or **rural.** You might be a tiny atom in a very large **metropolis, megalopolis,** or **conurbation** or a gigantic molecule in a small **village** or an even smaller **hamlet.**

Greater Than the Sum of Its Parts

Towns and cities are divided in different ways into **districts, quarters, wards,** and **precincts.** New York City consists of five **boroughs,** the only such city in the United States. A city usually has an **uptown,** a **midtown,** and a **downtown;** an **inner** (or **central**) **city;** and lots of different **neighborhoods.** A town usually has a downtown, a **commercial district,** several **residential areas,** and **outskirts.**

Smaller Than Most Parts

There are many terms for towns, some of them more flattering than others. You may live in the **'burbs,** a **burg,** a **boom town,** a **hick town,** a **cow town,** a **one-horse town,** a **whistle stop,** or a **bedroom community.**

▶ Your Turn Town Meeting

What word would you use to describe the place you live in? Would your classmates use the same word? With a group of them, discuss the word you chose along with the aspects of your community that prompted your choice.

megalopolis

cowtown

uptown

Chapter 13

Sentences to Paragraphs

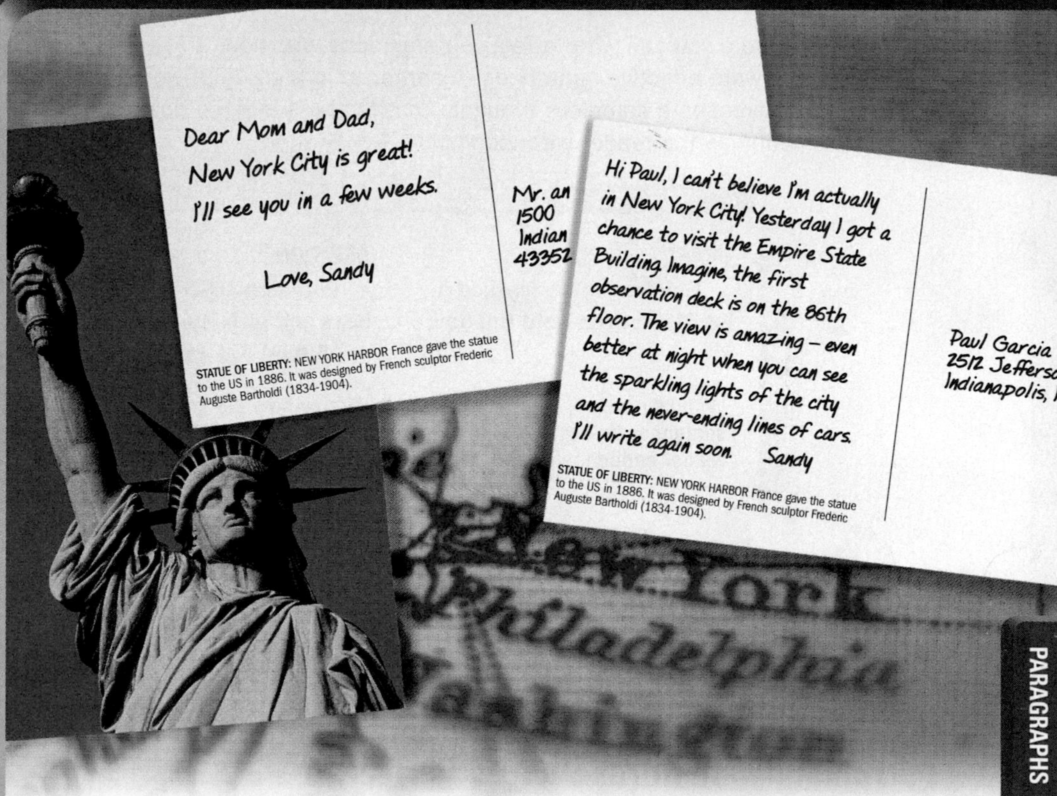

Dear Mom and Dad,
New York City is great!
I'll see you in a few weeks.
Love, Sandy
Mr. an
1500
Indian
43352
STATUE OF LIBERTY: NEW YORK HARBOR France gave the statue to the US in 1886. It was designed by French sculptor Frederic Auguste Bartholdi (1834-1904).
Hi Paul, I can't believe I'm actually in New York City! Yesterday I got a chance to visit the Empire State Building. Imagine, the first observation deck is on the 86th floor. The view is amazing – even better at night when you can see the sparkling lights of the city and the never-ending lines of cars. I'll write again soon. Sandy
Paul Garcia
2512 Jefferson
Indianapolis, IN
STATUE OF LIBERTY: NEW YORK HARBOR France gave the statue to the US in 1886. It was designed by French sculptor Frederic Auguste Bartholdi (1834-1904).
New York
Philadelphia

PARAGRAPHS

Getting the Message Across

What makes New York City "great"? After reading the first postcard, would you know? What additional details does the second postcard give? The postcards show that although you can express an idea in a single sentence, you usually need a paragraph to develop your idea.

Write Away: An Extraordinary Place

Write a paragraph about a place you have visited (for example, a museum, a park, or an interesting city). Describe why you think this place is amazing. What details would interest your readers? Save your paragraph in your **Working Portfolio.**

LESSON 1 Building Effective Sentences

1 Expressing Thoughts Effectively

Before you can write effective paragraphs, you need to know how to write effective sentences. A sentence is a group of words that expresses a complete thought. An effective sentence doesn't confuse the reader with incomplete information.

STUDENT MODEL

DRAFT

Children once worked a lot. Many even held full-time jobs.

Without context, these sentences do not give the reader enough information.

REVISION

Between 1890 and 1910, boys and girls under the age of 15 held full-time jobs.

Notice how the missing information answers the questions a reader might have.

Don't think that an effective sentence has to be long! Short sentences can also give the right amount of information.

This morning I awoke to the sound of sirens instead of the blare of my alarm clock. I had overslept again!

CHAPTER 13

2 Making Your Words Picture Perfect

Specific details and effective word choice can replace boring, lifeless words and make your sentences more interesting. Notice how this sentence changes as more details are added.

The smell woke people up.

The scent rose to stir the household.

Use more specific verbs and nouns.

The warm scent rose to stir the boarders, the aunts, the uncles, the visiting cousins.

Add adjectives and replace *household* with specific nouns.

The warm scent of batter rose in the drafty halls to stir the boarders, the aunts, the uncles . . . , in their rooms.

Add prepositional phrases.

—Ray Bradbury, *Dandelion Wine*

③ Cutting Out the Fluff

When you add details, make sure they relate to your sentence and provide necessary information. Unnecessary details can make your sentences lengthy and complicated. Look what happens when a sentence has too many details.

STUDENT MODEL

DRAFT

I believe that in order for teenagers to become responsible at home they should have several duties, although too many duties wouldn't be fair, either.

Unnecessary details clutter the sentence.

REVISION

In order for teenagers to become responsible at home, they should have several duties.

Here's How **Revising for Unnecessary Details**

1. Determine what information your readers need to know.
2. Eliminate any unimportant or unrelated details.
3. Delete empty sentences that repeat ideas.

PRACTICE **Writing Effective Sentences**

Revise the following sentences by following the directions in parentheses.

1. The girl drives a car. (Describe the girl. How does she drive? What kind of car does she drive?)
2. We will plant a tree. (Who will plant a tree? Where will the tree be planted? What kind of tree is it?)
3. Everyday I walk to school and see the 100-year-old church when I walk in the morning and afternoon. (Remove repetitive ideas.)
4. During the month of August, we visit my cousins in California because we enjoy visiting them. (Remove unimportant details.)

Writing Effective Paragraphs

1 What Is a Paragraph?

A **paragraph** is a group of sentences that work together to develop a single main idea. A paragraph may stand alone, as in a one-paragraph answer to a test question, or it may be part of a longer piece of writing. A well-organized, well-developed paragraph has the following characteristics:

- **Unity**—Each sentence supports the main idea.
- **Coherence**—All sentences relate to one another.

The four main kinds of paragraphs are **descriptive**, **narrative**, **informative** (or expository), and **persuasive**.

2 Descriptive Paragraphs

When you write a **descriptive** paragraph, you create a picture of a person, place, event, or object. You want your reader to experience—see, hear, feel, taste, and smell—whatever you are describing. Notice how the narrator describes a childhood memory of her hometown.

CHAPTER 13

LITERARY MODEL

When I think of the home town of my youth, all that I seem to remember is dust—the **brown, crumbly** dust of late summer—**arid, sterile** dust that gets into the eyes and makes them water, gets into the throat and between the toes of **bare brown** feet. I don't know why I should remember only the dust. . . . And so, when I think of that time and that place, I remember only the **dry September** of the **dirt roads** and **grassless yards** of the **shanty-town** where I lived.

—Eugenia Collier, "Marigolds"

First sentence introduces the setting.

Modifiers "paint a picture."

Effective word choice and details show instead of tell.

PRACTICE A **Writing a Descriptive Paragraph**

Write a descriptive paragraph about the picture shown here. You might want to describe the setting (for example, the soccer game, the players, the location, and so forth) using sensory details.

❸ Narrative Paragraphs

A narrative paragraph tells a story or relates an event. It may be based on fact, on imagination, or on both. It has a clear sequence—a beginning, a middle, and an end. The following paragraph tells how the narrator forces her mother to give up the idea that her daughter will become a child genius.

LITERARY MODEL

So now on nights when my mother presented her tests, I performed listlessly, my head propped on one arm. I pretended to be bored. And I was. I got so bored I started counting the bellows of the foghorns out on the bay while my mother drilled me in other areas. . . . **The next day,** I played a game with myself, seeing if my mother would give up on me before eight bellows. **After a while** I usually counted only one, maybe two bellows at most. **At last** she was beginning to give up hope.

—Amy Tan, "Two Kinds"

Narrative begins.

Transitions tell the order of events.

Narrative ends.

PRACTICE B **Writing a Narrative Paragraph**

Write a narrative paragraph telling the events in a scene from your favorite movie, story, music video, novel, or television show.

PARAGRAPHS

④ Informative Paragraphs

An **informative** paragraph, also called an **expository** paragraph, presents facts or examples, explains ideas, or defines terms. For example, you can use an informative paragraph to answer an essay question, write a research paper, or explain how something works.

STUDENT MODEL

How many of your friends suffer from stress? Stress is defined as a state of extreme difficulty that causes mental or physical tension. In a recent study, teenagers were shown to experience stress as often as adults. According to the study, the most common stressors include divorce of parents, death of a loved one, loneliness, moving to a new neighborhood, and having difficulty in a social environment.

Writer gets the reader's attention.

Difficult term is defined.

Series of examples support implied topic sentence.

PRACTICE C **Writing an Informative Paragraph**

Look at the diagram shown here of a simplified grazing food chain. Then write an informative paragraph that explains the process of this food chain.

Secondary Consumers
animals that eat other animals.
Primary Consumers
animals that feed directly on plants.
Producers
plants and organisms that use the sun's energy to make their own food.

❺ Persuasive Paragraphs

A **persuasive** paragraph gives logical reasons to support an opinion. You can use this type of paragraph to convince the reader to hold a certain opinion or to act in a particular way. Once you have clearly defined your opinion, consider who you are writing for and then choose appropriate language and details that will appeal to your audience.

STUDENT MODEL

How would you like to work 10 extra hours every week and not get any money for the time and effort you put in? We students who spend an average of 10 hours or more on extracurricular activities should receive some kind of academic credit. Most students who are involved in sports, music, journalism, or theater activities are actively learning on a daily basis. We attend practice and events and participate regularly as we do in class. Furthermore, our participation in these activities helps us become more responsible and disciplined students.

- First sentence captures the reader's attention.
- Writer clearly states opinion in a respectful tone.
- Facts support opinion.
- Final sentence gives an additional reason.

PARAGRAPHS

PRACTICE D **Writing a Persuasive Paragraph**

Choose one of the topics below and write a persuasive paragraph that either defends or opposes the statement.

1. Air pollution is/is not a serious issue.
2. The school year should be/should not be extended.
3. Television has a beneficial/harmful effect on young children.

Paragraph Unity

1 Understanding Unity

A paragraph has **unity** when all the sentences support the topic sentence or the implied topic sentence. The following paragraph shows how unrelated sentences can confuse the meaning of a paragraph.

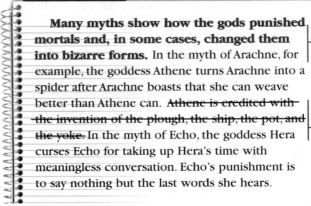

STUDENT MODEL

Many myths show how the gods punished mortals and, in some cases, changed them into bizarre forms. In the myth of Arachne, for example, the goddess Athene turns Arachne into a spider after Arachne boasts that she can weave better than Athene can. ~~Athene is credited with the invention of the plough, the ship, the pot, and the yoke.~~ In the myth of Echo, the goddess Hera curses Echo for taking up Hera's time with meaningless conversation. Echo's punishment is to say nothing but the last words she hears.

Topic sentence states main idea.

Writer removes unrelated details.

CHAPTER 13

2 Topic Sentence

To achieve unity, a writer may use a **topic sentence** to state the main idea, or topic, of the paragraph. Usually the topic is stated in the first sentence so that the reader knows what to expect. Notice how the topic sentence is used in this model.

LITERARY MODEL

My father was a master storyteller. He could tell a fine old story that made me hold my sides with rolling laughter and sent happy tears down my cheeks, or a story of stark reality that made me shiver and be grateful for my own warm, secure surroundings. He could tell stories of beauty and grace, stories of gentle dreams, and paint them as vividly as any picture with splashes of character and dialogue.

—Mildred D. Taylor, *Roll of Thunder, Hear My Cry*

Topic sentence introduces the main idea.

Each detail supports topic sentence.

❸ Implied Topic Sentence

The topic sentence is not always stated. For example, some paragraphs have an **implied topic sentence** rather than a directly stated topic sentence.

PROFESSIONAL MODEL

After a year and a half in Hong Kong, we moved to Malaysia. . . .There I learned to swim in the lovely warm waters of the tropics and fell in love with the sea. On land I was a cripple; in the ocean I could move with the grace of a fish. I liked the freedom of being in the water so much that many years later, when I was a graduate student in Hawaii, I became greatly enamored with a man just because he called me a "Polynesian water nymph."

—Sucheng Chan, "You're Short, Besides!"

Notice how every sentence supports the implied main idea: *Swimming gives Chan a sense of freedom.*

Here's How **Revising for Unity**

1. Determine whether each sentence supports the topic sentence or the implied topic sentence.
2. Remove or rewrite any sentence that does not clearly relate to or support the topic sentence.
3. Add information or details that clearly support the topic sentence.

PRACTICE **Revising for Unity**

Identify the topic sentence. Then revise the paragraph for unity.

He was born Ehrich Weiss in 1874. As a young child, he taught himself to make small items appear and disappear. Because Ehrich's family was quite poor, he went to work for a locksmith at the early age of 12. Most children of poor families worked to help support the family. Before long, Ehrich knew how to pick almost any lock in existence. Thus began the career of Harry Houdini—one of the most remarkable magicians of all time.

PARAGRAPHS

LESSON 4

Coherence

A paragraph is **coherent** when all its sentences are related and flow logically from one to the next. You can achieve coherence by using an appropriate pattern of organization and effective transitions. Five types of paragraph organization are described: **sequential, spatial, cause and effect, comparison and contrast,** and **order of degree.**

1 Sequential Order

Use **sequential order** to tell a story or relate historical events in the order they occurred, or chronologically. Also use it to describe the step-by-step order of a process or procedure. Transitional words help to show time relationships: *after*, *first*, *next*, *then*, and *finally*.

LITERARY MODEL

Soon the biggest of the boys poised himself, shot down into the water, and did not come up. The others stood about, watching. . . . **After a long time,** the boy came up on the other side of a big dark rock, letting the air out of his lungs in a sputtering gasp and a shout of triumph. **Immediately** the rest of them dived in.

—Doris Lessing, "Through the Tunnel"

Transitions show sequence of events.

2 Spatial Order

Use **spatial order** to arrange details according to their position in space (for example, front to back, or near to far). Spatial order is effective in descriptive paragraphs.

LITERARY MODEL

Below, the canyon was shut in. There was no view. The walls leaned together abruptly and the canyon ended in a chaos of rocks. **Up the canyon** rose far hills and peaks, the big foothills, pine-covered and remote. **And far beyond,** like clouds upon the border of the sky, towered minarets of white where the Sierra's eternal snows flashed austerely the blazes of the sun. —Jack London, "All Gold Canyon"

Transitions show spatial order.

Here's How **Using Spatial Order**

- Picture a person, a place, or a thing you want to describe.
- Choose a vantage point—the position from which you will "look" at the subject.
- Choose the most appropriate method of organization: *top to bottom, outside to inside, left to right, or side to side.*
- Use transitional words and phrases, such as *above, in front of,* and *near.*

For more transitional words and phrases, see p. 333.

3 Cause and Effect

Use **cause-and-effect** paragraphs to tell why something happened, why certain conditions exist, or what resulted from an action. A **cause** is something that brings about a result. An **effect** is the result of a cause.

STUDENT MODEL

The San Francisco earthquake of 1906 is one of the strongest ever recorded. The earthquake shook at about 5:15 A.M. on April 18, with a magnitude of 7.8 on the Richter scale. It lasted only a minute, but the destruction spread over a large area. Blazing fires devastated the city for nearly three days, leaving thousands of people homeless.

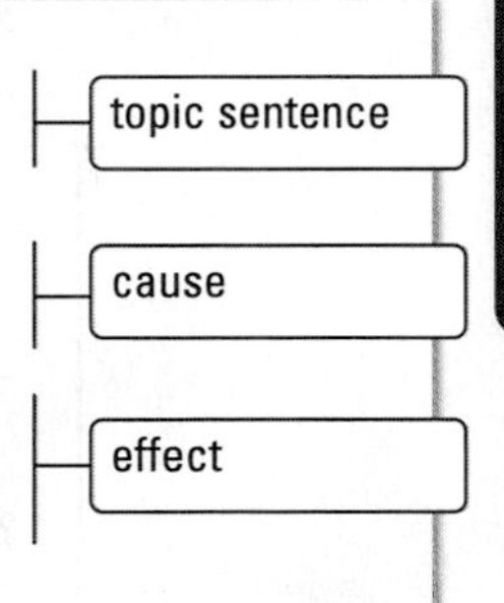

Here's How **Using Cause and Effect**

- Clearly state the cause-and-effect relationship.
- Present facts in a logical order.
- Use facts, examples, and other details to show each cause and effect.
- Use transitions (*because*, *since*, and *therefore*) effectively.

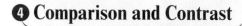

❹ Comparison and Contrast

Use **comparison and contrast** to discuss the similarities and the differences between two or more subjects. In the following model, Maya Angelou uses a subject-by-subject organization.

LITERARY MODEL

The girls often held hands and no longer bothered to speak to the lower students. There was a sadness about them, as if this world was not their home and they were bound for higher ground. The boys, **on the other hand,** had become more friendly, more outgoing. . . . Now they seemed not ready to give up the old school, the familiar paths and classrooms.

—Maya Angelou, *I Know Why the Caged Bird Sings*

Subject 1: reactions of graduating girls

Transitional phrase signals the contrast.

Subject 2: reactions of graduating boys

Here's How **Using Comparison and Contrast**

1. Identify the subjects that are being compared and contrasted.

   Subject 1: Girls **Subject 2: Boys**

2. Use a graphic device to investigate the similarities and the differences of the subjects.

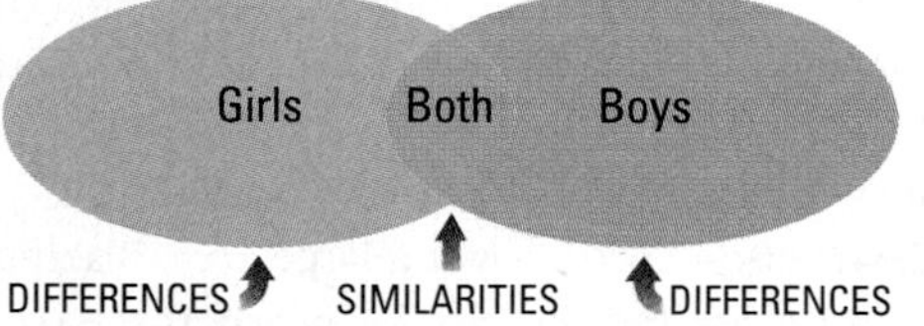

3. Choose a pattern of organization for each example.

Subject by Subject

Girls	Boys
• Attitude	• Attitude
• Action	• Action

Feature by Feature

Attitude	Action
• Girls	• Girls
• Boys	• Boys

4. Use transitional words and phrases for **comparison** (*also, likewise,* and *similarly*) and for **contrast** (*although, however,* and *yet*).

Make sure you have enough details to support your topic. You can't prove two things are alike or different if you only find one example.

5 Order of Degree

Order of degree is a way of organizing supporting details from **least to most** or **most to least.** Details can be grouped according to their usefulness, familiarity, or importance. Notice how Twain uses order of importance to describe the characteristics of a steamboat pilot.

LITERARY MODEL

A [steam]boat pilot must have a **memory:** but there are two much higher qualities which he must also have. He must have good, quick judgment and decision, and a cool, calm courage that no peril can shake. Give a man the merest trifle of **pluck** [courage] to start with, and by the time he has become a pilot he cannot be unmanned by any danger a steamboat can get into; but one cannot quite say the same for judgment. **Judgment** is a matter of brains, and a man must start with a good stock of that article or he will never succeed as a pilot.

—Mark Twain, *Life on the Mississippi*

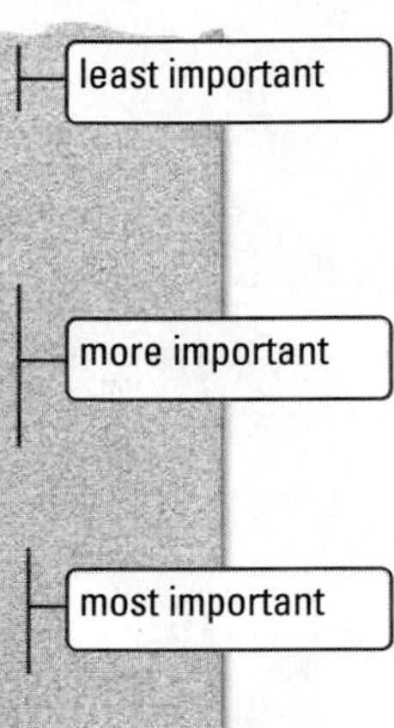

To build your reader's interest or to create a strong persuasive argument, begin with the least important item and proceed to the most important.

Here's How Using Order of Degree

1. Arrange your details according to their usefulness, familiarity, or importance.
   - least important
   - more important
   - most important

   or

   - most familiar
   - less familiar
   - unfamiliar
2. Use transitions like *first, furthermore,* and *last.*

PRACTICE Patterns of Organization

Read the following topics and determine which pattern of organization is the most appropriate.

1. A view from a high-rise building in downtown Chicago
2. Changes in the environment, school, or home
3. Two versions of the same movie

Student Help Desk

Sentences to Paragraphs at a Glance

An effective sentence
- expresses ideas clearly
- does not confuse the reader
- answers questions the reader may have

An effective paragraph
- has a topic sentence or an implied topic sentence
- shows unity
- is coherent
- uses an appropriate pattern of organization

Ways to Go

Types of Paragraphs

Type	Definition	Uses
Descriptive	Creates a picture of a person, place, event, or object	Stories and novels; travel writing; biographies; book, music, and restaurant reviews; character sketches
Narrative	Tells a story or relates an event	True-life adventure stories, anecdotes, biographies, autobiographies, memoirs, novels, stories, speeches
Informative/ Expository	Defines terms, gives directions, or explains a process or procedure by presenting facts and examples	History reports, science lab reports, speeches, essay questions, research papers, newspaper and magazine articles, "how to" manuals
Persuasive	Uses logical reasons to convince a reader to hold a certain opinion or to act in a particular way	Editorials, speeches, letters to the editor or political proposals

Patterns of Organization

Does It Follow?

Pattern	Transitions
Sequential	afterward, at once, before, during, finally, first, immediately, meanwhile, next, then, today, soon, until
Spatial	above, before, between, below, here, inside, nearby, over, there, through, under
Cause and effect	as a result, because, consequently, since, therefore, thus
Comparison and contrast	also, and, besides, in addition, likewise, moreover, similarly, although, but, in spite of, in contrast, on the other hand, unlike
Order of degree	first, second, finally, last, mainly, then, to begin with, ultimately

Topic Sentences

Support Your Topic Sentence

Do all your sentences support the topic sentence or main idea?

Where Does It Go?

The topic sentence can go in the beginning, the middle, or the end—depending on your purpose and the effect you want.

Get the Point?

The main idea can be implied, but each sentence must advance and add to the main idea.

PARAGRAPHS

The Bottom Line

Checklist for Sentences

Does each sentence . . .

____ express a complete thought?

____ use strong, effective words?

____ have enough details?

Checklist for Paragraphs

Does the paragraph . . .

____ have unity—each sentence supporting the main idea?

____ have sentences that relate to one another and flow logically?

____ organize the information appropriately?

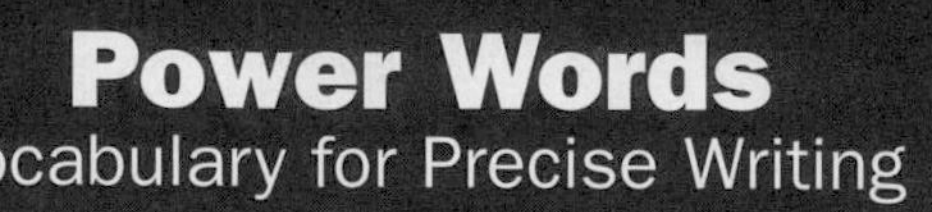

Power Words
Vocabulary for Precise Writing

chasm

Bridge Over Troubled Waters

Bridges help people get from one place to another—traveling the distance between two points. Here are some words you can use to talk about all kinds of bridges.

Bridging the Gap

Bridges cross rivers, **traverse** streams, and **span** divides. They **link, connect,** or **unite** that which is physically separated. You want to **bridge a gap,** but you definitely don't want to **burn your bridges behind you.**

Who builds bridges? Architects and engineers create the modern ones: **suspension bridges, girder bridges,** even floating **pontoon bridges.** However, every civilization that lives near gorges, valleys, and rivers has created its own bridges—from **covered bridges** to **rope bridges** that hang precariously over **chasms** and sway when you cross them. Even medieval folk had **drawbridges** to close when enemies were attacking. Romans built **viaducts,** which are bridges over land, and **aqueducts,** bridges that transport water.

People are always trying to shorten the distance, **cut corners,** or get somewhere using the most direct route—**as the crow flies.** When bridges don't work, **tunnels** might get you there. If not, **flues** or **underground passageways** might be your best option.

traver

viaduct

▶ **Your Turn** Building Bridges

Think about your town. In what place would a bridge make it easier to get from one part to another? Sketch a map to show the location of the bridge you would build. Compare maps with classmates, and explain why you chose that location to build your bridge.

rope bridge

Chapter 14

Paragraphs to Compositions

COMPOSITIONS

The Structure of a Composition

How do you think engineers go about creating a structure as big and complicated as this bridge in Normandy, France? Do they just start building and hope for the best?

Creating a bridge that has the proper support and balance requires careful planning. Much smaller projects, such as a composition, also require careful planning. When you create a composition, you need to connect your ideas properly so that the composition doesn't collapse when you're halfway through.

Write Away: A Big Buildup

What is the most interesting structure you have ever seen, either in person or in a picture? In a few sentences, explain what makes the structure interesting and what its parts are. Put your writing in your **Working Portfolio.**

LESSON 1

What Is a Composition?

What's the Idea?

A **composition** is a longer piece of writing that consists of at least several paragraphs. Like a paragraph, a composition has an overall purpose, which may be to describe, to tell a story, to explain, or to persuade. This chapter focuses on one type of composition—expository. **Expository** writing explains ideas and processes.

The chart below compares a paragraph and a composition. Notice the similarities and differences.

Comparing Paragraphs and Compositions

A paragraph has	A composition has
• a topic sentence	• an introductory paragraph with a thesis statement
• sentences with supporting details	• body paragraphs that support the thesis statement
	• a concluding paragraph

The Three Parts of a Composition

CHAPTER 14

A composition has three parts—an introduction, a body, and a conclusion.

The **introduction** begins the composition and tells what the composition is about. The most important part of the introduction is the thesis statement. Like a topic sentence in a paragraph, the thesis statement of the composition gives the purpose.

The **body** presents ideas that support and expand on the thesis statement. For example, in a composition about a process, the body might list the steps in the process.

The **conclusion** winds up the composition. It might restate the main idea, state the significance of the topic, or call on readers to take a course of action.

In the following expository composition, a student describes the factors that led to the independence of Texas. Notice how the body of the composition presents ideas chronologically, or in the order that they happened.

Before the Alamo

Many people know that the Battle of the Alamo contributed to Texas's declaring its independence from Mexico. But most do not realize that the battle was only the last in a long chain of events. **The conflicts between Mexico and the United States that led to Texas's independence stemmed not only from political differences but from religious and geographical ones as well.**

The Texas conflict began with the Louisiana Purchase of 1803, which put Roman Catholic Mexicans in contact with Protestant Americans. Then, in 1819, the Adams-Onis Treaty made Spanish Florida part of the United States. The treaty also put the boundary between the United States and Spain's Mexican territory at the Sabine River. U.S. settlers soon built dwellings right along the river.

The next stage of the conflict resulted from Mexico's allowing U.S. citizens to settle in Texas. Mexican officials hoped that doing this would create a neutral zone between Mexico and the United States. Mexico, which had gained its independence from Spain in 1821, required the U.S. settlers to become Mexican citizens and members of the Roman Catholic Church. The settlers refused.

The Mexican government was unable to enforce the requirements, however, because the settlers lived so far away from the Mexican capital, Mexico City. As the Texans grew in number and economic strength, the conflict worsened. In 1836, the year of the Battle of the Alamo, the U.S. settlers declared Texas to be a republic that was independent of Mexico. Texas became a state in 1845. The United States supported the settlers and defeated Mexico in a war that ended in 1848.

Texas's long history with Mexico has produced shared cultures and traditions that are still evident today. Texans enjoy food, festivals, music, and many other things connected with their Mexican heritage. Although at one time Texans and Mexicans lived in conflict, they now are peaceful neighbors with close economic and cultural ties.

INTRODUCTION
This section explains the purpose for writing and presents the **thesis statement.**

BODY
The **topic sentence** in each paragraph describes a different set of events that contributed to Texas's independence.

CONCLUSION
The final paragraph states the significance of Mexico's influence on Texas history.

LESSON 2

Creating a Thesis Statement

The most important part of your composition is your **thesis statement.** A thesis statement is a sentence that tells your purpose for writing. It also may reveal your point of view. A thesis statement can appear anywhere in the first two paragraphs of a composition, but it usually appears at the start of the first paragraph.

PROFESSIONAL MODEL

The rain forests are vanishing. By some estimates, nearly half of the rain forests that existed a century ago have already been cut down, and more are being destroyed, at a rate of 43,000 square miles (111,000 sq km) per year, an area roughly half the size of Pennsylvania. Within half a century, there may be no rain forests left at all. And for every square mile of rain forest that is removed, untold thousands of plants are killed, and an important animal habitat is lost.

—Christopher Lampton, *Endangered Species*

Writing a Thesis Statement

The first step in writing a thesis statement is developing a **controlling idea**—a sentence or two that you write for yourself to explain what you want your composition to accomplish.

Here's How Developing a Controlling Idea

1. Decide on a purpose for your composition.

   I want to find out what is being done to try to stop the destruction of the rain forests.

2. Think about what angle of your topic you would like to explore.

   I would like to focus on rain forests in South America.

3. Jot down a sentence that summarizes what you want to say. This is your controlling idea.

   I will write about several groups that are working to save the Amazon Rain Forest.

Once you have your controlling idea, you can focus it to create a thesis statement. The thesis statement will appear in your composition, so it should be more polished than your controlling idea. Avoid thesis statements that are too broad or too narrow.

Draft

The South American rain forests have been around for millions of years.

The thesis statement above is too broad. If you used it as a thesis statement for a composition, you would have to write a very long composition that explains the entire history of the rain forests.

Draft

Rain forests cover about 40 percent of Brazil's total area.

This thesis statement is too narrow, because it would be hard to write more than a couple of paragraphs about such a specific piece of information.

Revision

Several groups are working with the Brazilian government to try to stop the destruction of the Amazon Rain Forest.

The third thesis statement is the right scope for an expository composition because the topic can be covered in a page or two with the support of several key ideas.

As you are writing the rest of your composition, you may need to revise your thesis statement. Your focus may change as you take a closer look at the key ideas for your topic.

PRACTICE **Properly Focused Thesis Statements**

Identify the sentence in each group that makes the best thesis statement, and explain why.

1. **a.** Bridge designs have become more imaginative over the past few decades.
b. Bridges are interesting to look at.
c. San Francisco's beautiful Golden Gate Bridge was completed in 1937.

2. **a.** Texas history has been the subject of countless movies and books.
b. Movies and books have portrayed the battle of the Alamo in several different ways.
c. John Wayne directed and starred in a 1960 film called *The Alamo.*

COMPOSITIONS

LESSON 3

Effective Introductions

Engaging the Reader

An **introduction** should present the thesis statement and capture your reader's attention. The best way to engage the reader depends on who the audience is and on your purpose for writing.

Start with an Anecdote

Would the following sentence capture someone's interest?

It is sometimes difficult to get along with your neighbors.

One way to make an introduction more engaging is to start with an anecdote. An **anecdote** is an interesting or amusing brief story, usually about an individual.

PROFESSIONAL MODEL

A man in Cambridge, Mass. took his neighbor to court because the neighbor hadn't cut his grass in fourteen years. This is the kind of story that interests me. There are something like sixty million single family homes in the United States and I'll bet ninety percent of the people living in those houses are having some kind of trouble with their neighbors.

—Andrew A. Rooney, "Neighbors"

CHAPTER 14

Use a Quotation

How could you make this introductory sentence more interesting?

Young people are America's hope for the future.

You might consider using a **quotation,** which is simply a repetition of someone else's exact words.

STUDENT MODEL

"I have faith in young people," said Barbara Jordan, **"because I know the strongest emotions which prevail are those of love and caring and belief and tolerance."** High school students can take these words to heart as they make difficult decisions about who they are and what they want out of life.

Make a Surprising Statement

Another effective introduction is a **surprising statement** that grabs your reader's attention. Compare the professional model below with this much less interesting beginning.

Black widow spiders are found in many places.

PROFESSIONAL MODEL

I hunt black widow. When I find one, I capture it. I have found them in discarded wheels and tires and under railroad ties. I have found them in house foundations and cellars, in automotive shops and toolsheds, in water meters and rock gardens, against fences and in cinderblock walls. I have found them in a hospital and in the den of a rattlesnake, and once on the bottom of the chair I was sitting in.

—Gordon Grice, "The Black Widow"

Ask a Question

Starting with an engaging **question** involves the reader immediately by requiring at least a mental answer. Notice how the student model improves on the following sentence.

Junk mail is harmful to the environment.

STUDENT MODEL

How can you help to prevent the waste of 28 billion gallons of water and 320 million tax dollars? You can join the effort to reduce the amount of junk mail. Many of us throw away junk mail without even opening it. The manufacturing of paper products takes precious resources from the environment and creates disposal problems that are costly to taxpayers.

PRACTICE **Writing Introductions**

Use one of the techniques in this lesson to improve the introduction in a piece of writing from your **Working Portfolio.**

COMPOSITIONS

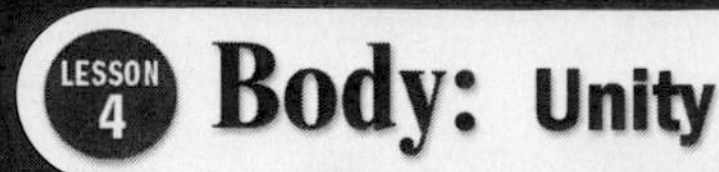

Body: Unity

A composition has **unity** when ideas appear in separate paragraphs and all of the ideas support the thesis statement.

1 Achieving Unity

A good way to make sure your composition has unity is to start with a graphic organizer. After you have selected a type of graphic organizer, fill it in by using the following steps.

Here's How Achieving Unity

1. Write your thesis statement.
2. List your key ideas, along with supporting details for each one.
3. Check to see that each key idea supports the thesis statement.
4. Check that each supporting detail supports the appropriate key idea.

See how a student used an outline to establish unity before writing the essay on page 337.

Before the Alamo

Thesis statement—Religious and geographical factors—not just political ones—led to the independence of Texas.

I. Origins of Texas independence
   - A. Louisiana Purchase
   - B. Adams-Onis Treaty
   - ~~C. Missouri Compromise~~

This detail doesn't support the key idea it appears under.

II. Rising conflict with Mexico
   - A. U.S. settlers move into Mexico
   - B. Settlers refuse to become Mexican citizens or Catholics

~~III. Heroes of the Alamo~~

This idea isn't related to the thesis statement.

III. Achieving independence
   - A. Distance from Mexican capital makes settlers hard to control
   - B. Settlers declare independence
   - C. War with Mexico results in Texas statehood

❷ Creating Topic Sentences

Once you have checked your graphic organizer to make sure your key ideas have unity, turn each idea into a topic sentence.

Key idea from outline
Origins of Texas Independence

⬇

Topic sentence for body of composition
The Texas conflict began with the Louisiana Purchase of 1803, which put Roman Catholic Mexicans in contact with Protestant Americans.

For more details about writing topic sentences, see pp. 326-327.

❸ Paragraphing

Jumbling ideas together in one long paragraph weakens unity. Use the following guidelines to break up long paragraphs.

- **Look for changes in focus.** When a new idea appears or the topic changes, begin a new paragraph.
- **Look for events or steps.** When you are describing a series of events or the steps in a process, begin a new paragraph for each major event or important step.
- **Look for unnecessary information.** Sometimes a paragraph is too long simply because it contains unrelated or repeated ideas.

COMPOSITIONS

PRACTICE **Supporting the Thesis Statement**

Read each thesis statement. Then decide which one of the lettered sentences does not support the thesis statement.

1. *Thesis statement* **A good horror story has several key elements.**

a. The suspense should increase during the story.
b. Some horror stories are based on real-life events.
c. There should be at least one terrifying event.
d. The characters should be interesting.

2. *Thesis statement* **Edgar Allan Poe had a difficult life.**

a. Poe's mother died in 1811, when he was an infant.
b. Poe spent much of his life in poverty and ill health.
c. Poe's wife died in 1847.
d. Poe was born in 1809.

LESSON 5

Body: Coherence

Achieving Coherence

A composition has **coherence** when its parts appear in a logical order and flow smoothly from one to the next. To make the paragraphs in the body of your composition flow smoothly, you can use the three types of transitional expressions described below.

Transitional Words and Phrases

Transitional words and phrases help connect ideas by showing relationships of time and place. The following passage about an injured female eagle shows relationships of time.

LITERARY MODEL

Far up on the opposite hill I see her, flapping and hopping. . . . Even at two hundred yards, I can feel her binocular vision zeroing in; I can feel the heat of her stare.

Later, I look through my binoculars at all sorts of things. I'm seeing the world with an eagle eye. . . .

That night I dream about two moons. One is pink and spins fast; the other is an eagle's head, farther away and spinning in the opposite direction.

—Gretel Ehrlich, "Spring"

Repeated Phrases

When a key phrase from one paragraph is repeated in the next, it helps create a transition.

STUDENT MODEL

The Verrazano-Narrows Bridge is the **longest bridge** in the United States. It is a suspension bridge that connects the boroughs of Brooklyn and Staten Island in New York City.

The main section of the bridge is nearly a mile long. When the bridge was completed in 1964, it was the **longest bridge** in the world. Since then, several countries have built longer ones.

The next **longest bridge** in the United States is the Golden Gate Bridge. It is San Francisco's most famous landmark.

Transitional Sentences

You can also link paragraphs by using **transitional sentences.**

PROFESSIONAL MODEL

Civic devotion is the most noticeable characteristic of San Francisco residents; indeed, it is one of the few matters upon which they unanimously agree. The city is comparatively young, yet seldom is there found a greater passion for preservation of the past with all its colorful legends and architecture. This spirit is evident in the preservation of historic buildings as well as the famous cable cars.

Combined with this love of the city is the great **determination** and courage that rebuilt the city not once but seven times after devastating fires. Six of them came within a period of two boomtown years; the last one, which destroyed four-fifths of the town, blazed for days after the 1906 earthquake broke the water mains and rendered the firefighting equipment useless.

The phrase "this love of the city" refers to the civic devotion described in the first paragraph.

Possibly it is the beauty of San Francisco's setting that commands such loyalty. Varying in altitude from sea level to 929 feet, the city rests on 40 hills at the tip of a narrow peninsula, bounded on one side by the Pacific Ocean and on the other by San Francisco Bay, one of the largest landlocked harbors in the world.

The phrase "such loyalty" refers to the determination described in the second paragraph.

—"San Francisco and Vicinity,"
AAA Tour Book: California and Nevada

COMPOSITIONS

PRACTICE **Improving Coherence**

Find a composition in your **Working Portfolio** and exchange it with a partner's. Read your partner's composition, and find two examples of transitional expressions. If you cannot find two, identify places where transitional expressions could be added to improve coherence.

Writing the Conclusion

1 Purpose of Conclusions

Your strongest memory of a person is often based on the last time you saw him or her. The **conclusion** of your composition leaves a final impression with a reader. Notice how the following conclusion leaves a strong impression.

LITERARY MODEL

Each of us has the right and the responsibility to assess the roads which lie ahead, and those over which we have traveled, and if the future road looms ominous or unpromising, and the roads back uninviting, then we need to gather our resolve and, carrying only the necessary baggage, step off that road into another direction. If the new choice is also unpalatable, without embarrassment, we must be ready to change that as well.

—Maya Angelou, "New Directions"

CHAPTER 14

2 Types of Conclusions

Writers most often conclude their compositions in one of three ways: they restate the main idea, they issue a call for action, or they state the significance of the topic.

Restate the Main Idea

This type of conclusion acts as a mini-summary of the composition.

STUDENT MODEL

Dinosaurs ruled the earth for 150 million years, but 65 million years ago their reign ended. Although there are still questions about what caused them to become extinct, it seems clear that changes in climate played a role. **The failure of the dinosaurs to adapt to a new climate brought about their downfall.**

Call for Action

This type of conclusion urges someone to do something about an issue. The following conclusion comes from an article that urges people in the fashion industry not to make fur coats.

PROFESSIONAL MODEL

Just this once, look away from the profit margins and mirrors and catwalks and fashion glossies, and give a little thought to the animals. The world is bigger than New York, Paris, and Milan, full of strange and wonderful creatures, and they are not doing "just fine."

—Matthew Scully, "The Last Gasps of the Fur Trade"

State the Significance

In this type of conclusion, the writer emphasizes the importance of the topic. The following conclusion is from a piece about Susan B. Anthony's arrest for voting in an election in 1872, when women did not have the right to vote.

LITERARY MODEL

True to her promise, Susan paid the legal expenses for the three inspectors. With the help of contributions from sympathetic admirers, she paid the costs of her own trial. But she never paid that one-hundred-dollar fine. **Susan B. Anthony was a woman of her word as well as a woman of courage.**

—Margaret Truman, "The United States vs. Susan B. Anthony"

Some people find it easier to write a composition if they write the conclusion or the body before the introduction.

PRACTICE **Writing Conclusions**

Choose a composition from your **Working Portfolio,** and rewrite the conclusion using a different approach. Use one of the three approaches discussed in this lesson.

COMPOSITIONS

Student Help Desk

Compositions at a Glance

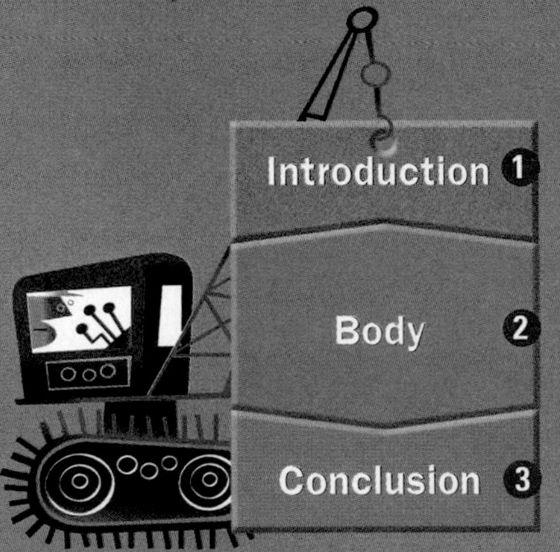

1. Lay a strong foundation for your composition by capturing the reader's interest and writing a strong thesis statement.

2. Build an impressive structure by supporting your thesis statement and creating smooth connections between sections.

3. Put the finishing touches on your composition with a memorable ending.

Types of Introductions

Rope 'Em In

Question	How can learning to write good expository compositions be of any use to high school students in the future?
Surprising Statement	Learning to write good essays can help you win lots of money in contests.
Anecdote	Laura Overland, a college student in Missouri, received $5,000 for winning first prize in an essay contest sponsored by the Elie Wiesel Foundation for Humanity in New York City.
Quotation	"I can think of no better tool for success in college than learning to write well," said Ethel Wilkinson, a guidance counselor at a city college in Chicago.

CHAPTER 14

Fox Trot by Bill Amend

Transitional Expressions

Go with the Flow

Time	before, by, finally, first, meanwhile
Place	above, around, beneath, down, here, there
Order of importance	first, second, mainly, more important, most important
Cause and effect	as a result, because, consequently, for, so, therefore
Contrast	but, however, in contrast, on the other hand, unlike, yet
Comparison	as, in the same way, likewise, similarly, than

Types of Conclusions

Out with a Bang

Call for Action

Our information-based economy requires good communication skills. Improve your writing and improve your chances of getting a good job.

State the Significance

You are going to have to write many essays in high school. How well you write them will have a big impact on your grades.

Restate the Main Idea

Becoming a good composition writer will not only help you in high school. It can bring you success in college and the workplace as well.

COMPOSITIONS

The Bottom Line

Checklist for Compositions

Have I included . . .

- ____ a thesis statement with a main idea that is carried through the composition?
- ____ an engaging introduction?
- ____ unified paragraphs that support the thesis statement?
- ____ coherent organization with clear transitions?
- ____ a memorable conclusion?

Power Words
Vocabulary for Precise Writing

People Who Like People

What if the fun-loving companion in the ad on the next page were a person? There are many words besides *friendly* that you could use to describe him or her.

A Friend Indeed. . .

The number of words for *friendly* is a testimonial to how highly this quality is valued: **sociable** and **gregarious** people like to be with other people; **agreeable, amiable, amicable, affable, sympathetic, companionable,** and **genial** people are friendly, warm, and pleasant to be with.

Merry, jolly, jovial, hearty, and **convivial** folk are especially fine for the fun-loving (and good-feasting) set. And if you find someone **congenial,** that person is particularly well-suited for *you*.

People who make you feel welcome in their homes and in their lives are to be treasured. They are **generous, warm-hearted,** and **open-handed;** they are **receptive, neighborly, cordial, gracious,** and **hospitable.**

Your Turn Opposites Attract

With a partner, start a list of antonyms for the word *friendly.* (Hint: The prefixes "un-" or "dis-" can be added to a few of the words above. Look these words up in a thesaurus and find any others.)

Chapter 15

Elaboration

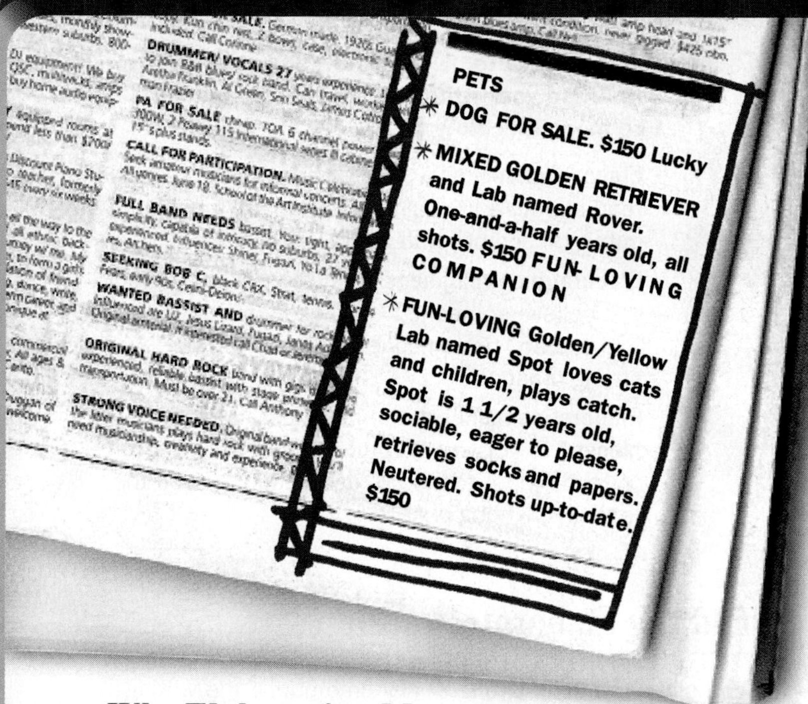
PETS

*DOG FOR SALE. $150 Lucky

*MIXED GOLDEN RETRIEVER and Lab named Rover. One-and-a-half years old, all shots. $150 FUN-LOVING COMPANION

*FUN-LOVING Golden/Yellow Lab named Spot loves cats and children, plays catch. Spot is 1 1/2 years old, sociable, eager to please, retrieves socks and papers. Neutered. Shots up-to-date. $150

Why Elaboration Matters

Compare these three ads from a local paper. Which one would you find most helpful if you were in the market for a new dog? Why?

The third ad includes the most relevant information. The writer won't get a lot of calls from people who want a puppy or a poodle. Readers who own cats can tell right away that the dog would fit into their households.

The relevant information included in the third ad is an example of elaboration. **Elaboration** is the addition of supporting details and explanations to develop a description, a narration, or an argument. You can improve almost any type of writing by asking—and answering—the question, What else does the reader need to know?

Write Away: Preowned but in Good Condition

Think of something you have that would be of value to others. Try writing a classified ad to sell that item. Keep the ad short, but carefully choose details that give relevant information to potential customers. Keep your ad in your **Working Portfolio.**

LESSON 1

Why Elaborate?

1 What's the Idea?

Before you write, as you draft, and especially while you revise your writing, keep asking yourself, Could I be more specific?

- **Elaboration makes a story exciting.** Would you rather read about "a lion fighting" or about "an injured lion in mortal combat with a pack of hyenas"?
- **Elaboration strengthens persuasive writing.** Would you believe someone who argued by saying "I told you so" or someone who gave you three strong reasons?
- **Elaboration makes directions clear.** "Attach the pieces" is not very helpful. On the other hand, "Attach side A to side B, using tab C" gives the reader a fighting chance.

2 When Should You Elaborate?

You can elaborate your writing at any time during the writing process. As you draft, think about specific details and supporting information your readers will need to know. Then read over your draft, looking for places where you were too hurried or too vague. Use the following techniques to add more details.

Elaboration Techniques	
Focus	When you're writing a poem or story, focus on smaller details. Once you describe the bug on the nose of the toad in the garden, your readers will be with you.
Show, don't tell	Use concrete details in place of, or in support of, generalizations. Instead of just saying that a man was distracted, describe how he stumbled on the bottom stair.
Answer questions	Anticipate questions your readers might ask, and satisfy their curiosity in advance. Ask and answer the reporters' questions: *who, what, why, when, where,* and *how.*
Complete the picture	Look for gaps in the logic of an argument or the completeness of a description. Fill those gaps with new information you discover through research.

CHAPTER 15

❸ How Can You Elaborate?

Elaboration has many uses. By elaborating, you can provide specific details, brief explanations, or full-scale illustrations. Here are some common types of elaboration and their purposes.

- **Sensory details** enrich descriptive and narrative writing.
- **Facts and statistics** back up opinions and arguments.
- **Incidents (anecdotes)** bring descriptions to life.
- **Specific examples** enrich descriptive and informative writing.
- **Quotations** illustrate ideas and lend authority to opinions.
- **Charts, graphs, and other visuals** present information visually.

STUDENT MODEL

Even though dolphins have no vocal cords, they can produce a variety of sounds, including clicks, groans, and whistles. Scientists believe that dolphins make these sounds by blowing air through spaces in their heads and then out their blowholes. One reason dolphins make these noises is to find food. The sound waves bounce off objects and produce echoes, helping the dolphins find fish to eat. Dolphins also use sounds to communicate with one another. For example, if a dolphin is beached and needs help, it signals its trouble to other dolphins by whistling. Dolphins in captivity can learn to imitate human sounds and obey certain commands. Because dolphins have this ability, scientists hope that we might someday learn to communicate with this intelligent species.

FACT

SENSORY DETAILS

DESCRIPTIVE DETAILS

EXPLANATION

EXAMPLE

EXPLANATION

PRACTICE **Writing a Paragraph**

Add details to build a paragraph around one of these sentences.

- The girl wore interesting blue jeans.
- To make a simple pizza, start with an English muffin.
- Everyone should play at least one sport.

Take another look at the ad you wrote on page 351 for your **Working Portfolio.** Add a detail that will help you clinch the sale.

LESSON 2 Supporting Details

1 Elaborating with Sensory Details

Sensory details are bits of information that you can collect through your five senses. Such details are especially valuable in making narrative and descriptive writing convincing. Here is an observation chart showing sensory impressions you might collect at a deli.

Observation Chart

Sense	Details
Sight	steam rising, waiters moving quickly, dozens of customers coming in and sitting, dog tied up outside
Hearing	orders called out, dishes rattling, sizzle of frying food, buzz of conversation
Touch	smooth hard-plastic seats, soft old cloth napkins, squishy rye bread, cold drink
Taste	sour cream, pickles, roast beef, cream cheese, coffee, cabbage soup
Smell	frying bacon, baking bread, perfume, smoke

In the following example, sensory details are used to elaborate a scene in a narrative. The writer chose details that describe color, texture, and taste and convey a warm feeling.

LITERARY MODEL

She fried thick pink slabs of home-cured ham and poured the grease over sliced red tomatoes. Eggs over easy, fried potatoes and onions, yellow hominy and crisp perch fried so hard we could pop them in our mouths and chew bones, fins and all.

—Maya Angelou, *I Know Why the Caged Bird Sings*

PRACTICE A **Observing Details**

Without looking at your feet, picture the shoes you are wearing today. On a piece of paper, list all the details you can think of about those shoes. Now look at them. Can you add more details? Describe specific creases, scratches, markings, and features you had not remembered. What might the shoes tell someone about you?

❷ Elaborating with Facts and Statistics

Facts are statements that can be proved, and **statistics** are facts expressed in numbers. Facts and statistics make good additions to your writing, especially when you want to inform or persuade your readers.

Facts	
Statements that can be proved by observation, experience, or research	Americans buy more vanilla ice cream than any other flavor.
Statistics	
Numerical data, such as measurements or percentages	The average American consumes 16 pounds of ice cream a year.

Look at the two versions of a paragraph below. Notice how facts and statistics make the revised paragraph more informative.

STUDENT MODEL

DRAFT

The Panama Canal is an impressive engineering feat, extending across Central America. It took ten years to build. In 1913, thousands of people worked on the canal at one time.

REVISION

The Panama Canal is among the greatest engineering achievements in the world. **Linking the Atlantic and Pacific oceans,** it extends **51 miles across Panama. Begun in 1904,** it took ten years to build. By 1913 more than **43,400** workers were employed on the canal.

PRACTICE B **Using Facts**

Write a paragraph, using the details listed below and this opening statement: "Roller coasters have features that provide death-defying thrills."

- no engine
- open cars
- speeds up to 100 mph
- hills as tall as a 20-story building
- loops in which cars travel upside down

Incidents, Examples, and Quotations

1 Elaborating with Incidents

An **incident,** or **anecdote,** is a brief account of a single event. Writers use incidents to show character traits and to illustrate points. Often such incidents are humorous.

PROFESSIONAL MODEL

Show business tradition holds that whatever happens, "the show must go on." Often performers are called upon to make enormous sacrifices to achieve this end. For example, once flutist James Galway was performing in an outdoor concert at Ravinia, just north of Chicago. At one point in the show, when Galway opened his mouth to take a breath, a large bug flew into it. For a moment, he stopped playing and considered what he might do. Then realizing that the show must go on, he took a great gulp and continued with his playing.

—Bob Shepherd, "The Show Must Go On"

PRACTICE A **Relating an Incident**

Think of a simple statement, such as "Younger brothers and sisters can be dangerous." Write a paragraph about an incident from your own experience that illustrates the statement. Share your paragraph with a group of your classmates.

CHAPTER 15

2 Elaborating with Specific Examples

A **specific example** is something that can be used to illustrate a general statement or to show the characteristics of a group. Examples are especially useful in writing definitions. It is easier to illustrate the idea of a tree by pointing to oak, pine, and maple trees than by trying to describe the characteristics of trees in general. Writers of both fiction and nonfiction use examples to fill in the picture. In the model on the next page, the second sentence provides an example that supports the statement in the first sentence.

PROFESSIONAL MODEL

The insurance industry has been burned recently by earthquakes, hurricanes, and tornadoes. Florida's Hurricane Andrew alone bankrupted nine insurance companies.

—John F. Ross, "Risk: Where Do Real Dangers Lie?"

PRACTICE B **Analyzing Examples**

Read five or six news articles and editorials in a newspaper, circling the examples that the writers used to elaborate their writing. Then think about what purpose each example serves.

3 Elaborating with Quotations

Quotations are records of people's exact words. In fiction, elaboration with quotations takes the form of dialogue. Character traits and background can be conveyed through the characters' words. In nonfiction, a quotation can be used to support an opinion or point of view, as in the following example.

ELABORATION

STUDENT MODEL

The author Ambrose Bierce knew how to put people in their place. In his humorous dictionary, he defined *edible* as "good to eat and wholesome to digest, as a worm to a toad, a toad to a snake, a snake to a pig, a pig to a man, and a man to a worm."

Keep quotations short and to the point. Remember that a quotation supports your main idea; it doesn't replace it.

PRACTICE C **Recording Quotations**

Read a newspaper report, and write down the exact words of a person quoted in the article. Then write a paragraph about the news story, using your quotation as elaboration.

LESSON 4

Elaborating with Visuals

1 Illustrating a Definition

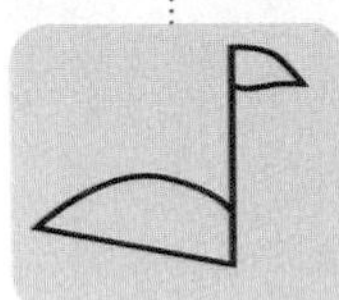

In some ancient writing, the written word for a bird looked like a bird. As time went on, writing became more and more abstract, and today's words don't resemble the things they refer to. One of the best ways to elaborate writing, therefore, is to add pictures.

You can clarify a definition by including a sketch of your own or a picture downloaded from the Internet.

kettledrum: a large copper or brass hemispherical drum with a parchment head that can be tuned by adjusting the tension.

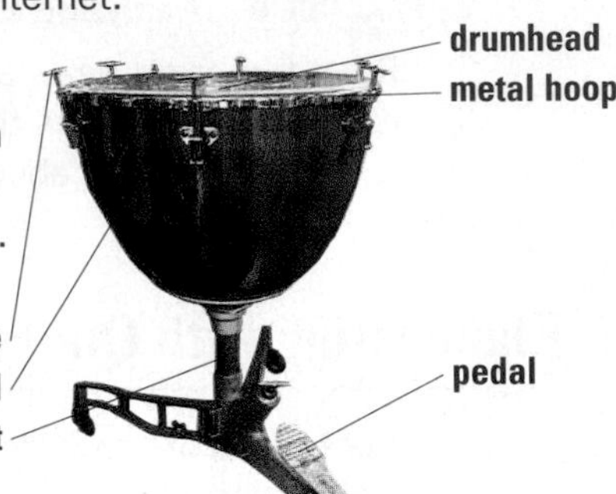

2 Illustrating a Process

You can clarify a set of directions by adding pictures. The following sketches show the process of tie-dyeing a T-shirt. Notice how simple written instructions can be if you include illustrations.

1. Start with a plain T-shirt.

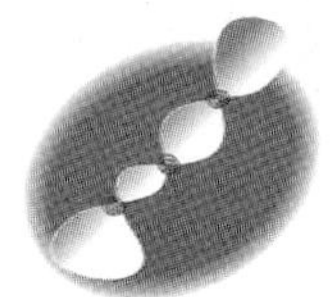

2. Crumple up the shirt and wrap rubber bands around it.

3. Dip the shirt in one or more buckets of fabric dye, depending on how many colors you want.

4. Let the shirt dry, and take off the rubber bands. Now you have a unique shirt!

PRACTICE A **Illustrating Directions**

Work with a partner to write a set of illustrated directions for making a paper airplane. Make a sketch for each step.

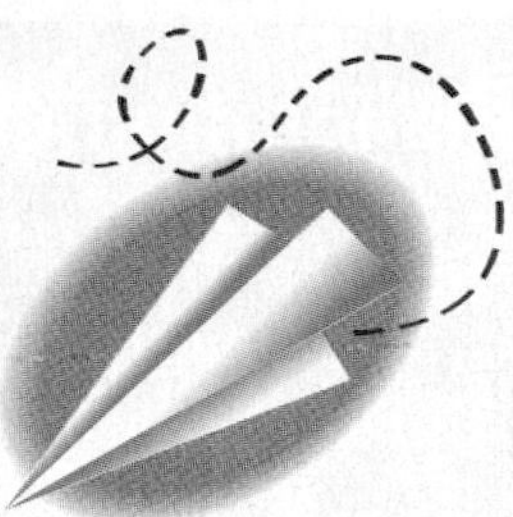

❸ Creating a Visual Display of Information

You can convey information economically in a chart or graph. Such a visual can also, like the bar graph below, help you show the relationship between data.

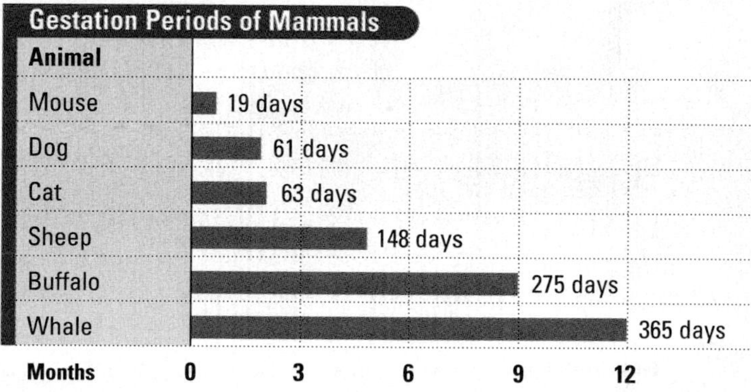

There are many kinds of charts and graphs to choose from.

- **Bar graphs** compare quantities.
- **Line graphs** show changes over time.
- **Pie graphs** show parts of wholes.
- **Time lines** show sequences of events.
- **Flow charts** show steps in processes.

Choose a visual display that makes the information easier to understand. Then tell the reader what it means.

PRACTICE B **Surveying and Charting**

Ask five people in your class to estimate the number of pizza slices they ate last month. Determine the average number per person and the range, or difference between the highest and lowest numbers. Create a visual display of the data you have collected, using a graphic form appropriate to the information.

ELABORATION

Student Help Desk

Elaboration at a Glance

- **Focus** Look, listen, and zero in on the smallest details.
- **Show, Don't Tell** Use concrete, specific words.
- **Answer Questions** Give your reader the whole scoop: who, what, why, when, where, and how.
- **Complete the Picture** Fill any gaps in information.

Elaboration Pizzeria

How will you elaborate your plain ideas? Just as if you were adding your favorite ingredients to a pizza, choose your favorite ways of elaborating from this menu.

Illustrate with Words

Clinch your arguments or round out your descriptions with one of the following.

Add Flavor

Incident (anecdote) or joke	a special seasoning to interest and involve your readers
Examples	sprinklings of specifics that give your general statements muscle
Quotations	dashes of people's exact words to personalize your writing

Add Visual Aids

Spice It Up

Sometimes graphic aids are needed. Choose from **charts and graphs, tables, diagrams,** and **time lines** to provide a feast for the eyes and convey a lot of information in a little space.

Pizza Preferences

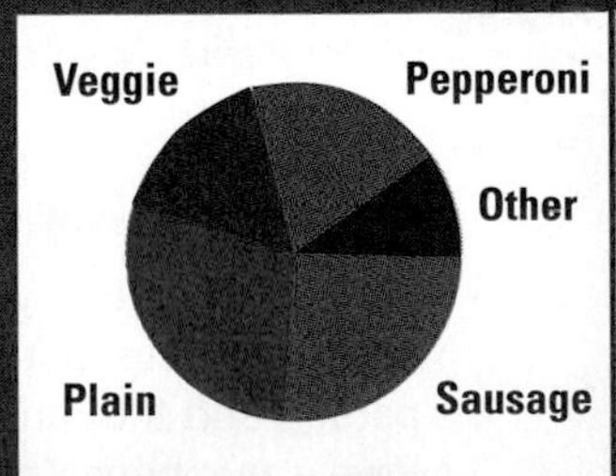

CHAPTER 15

Hot Toppings

Supporting Details

Provide spicy support for your stories and arguments. Use some of these ingredients to elaborate.

Sensory Details

a spicy helping of details from each of the senses: sight, hearing, touch, taste, and smell

Spicy pepperoni and salty anchovies stung my mouth and made my eyes water.

Facts and Statistics

a hearty serving of information that can be proved, expressed in either words or numbers

One ounce of mozzarella cheese contains 80 calories, 170 milligrams of sodium, 15 milligrams of cholesterol, and 8 grams of protein.

Explanations

a rich blend of reasons and details that explain statements

Pizza is nutritious. In one dish, it combines several food groups: protein in meat and cheese, dairy products in cheese, vegetables in tomato sauce and toppings, and bread in crust.

The Bottom Line

Checklist for Elaboration

Can I improve my writing . . .

____ by adding details that appeal to the five senses?

____ by adding facts and statistics?

____ by adding an anecdote to highlight a specific character trait or make a specific point?

____ by using a quotation to support an opinion?

____ by adding specific examples to support general statements or definitions?

____ by adding pictures to clarify a definition or process?

____ by using a chart or graph to make information easier to understand?

Power Words
Vocabulary for Precise Writing

More than Plenty

The person shown on the next page has too much stuff. Certain words can come in handy for describing the condition of her suitcase—and in other cases in which there is more than plenty.

Bag and Baggage!

Can she fit everything into those two suitcases? Although one is **large** (**ample, generous,** even **capacious**) it's already **stuffed;** in fact, it's **over-stuffed!** It's **jammed, crammed, jam-packed, chock full,** and **chock-a-block.** It is **swollen** and **bulging,** ready to **burst at the seams.**

Too Much Stuff!

She has an **abundance** of clothing: **tons** of T-shirts, **scads** of scarves, a **surplus** of suits, an **excess** of accessories, a **surfeit** of socks, a **plethora** of pants, an **oversupply** of underwear, a **myriad** of mod belts, and a general **extravagance** of extras.

Over the Top!

There are more words for excess, many of which start with *over-*. Try ***overstock, overage, overload, overflow, overgrowth,*** and ***overextension.***

Your Turn Stuff It!

It's time to clean your closet, your school locker, or the space under your bed (if there actually is space!). Take an inventory of your belongings. List them, using some of the words above.

Revising Sentences

What a Mess!

You're leaving for adventure camp today. Your favorite accessories are a tangled mess. You've overloaded one suitcase and you don't have anything in another. Worse yet, your bus leaves in two hours. Can you take out the right amount of items from one suitcase and fill another? Can you untangle those belts and make it to the bus station in time?

Revising sentences is a lot like packing for a trip. You have to leave out what you don't need, combine similar ideas, and separate what doesn't belong together. You have to streamline your writing so the reader can understand your message.

Write Away: Hey, Wait for Me!
Write a paragraph telling how and what you would pack for a two-week summer trip. Save your paragraph in your **Working Portfolio.**

Empty and Padded Sentences

1 Filling Empty Sentences

Empty sentences provide little or no information. Some simply repeat ideas, while others make statements without supporting them with facts, reasons, or examples. Suppose you wrote the following sentences about surfing the Internet.

STUDENT MODEL

DRAFT

I like surfing the Net because it's enjoyable. Many of the Web sites are educational.

Like and *enjoyable* convey the same idea. The second sentence needs an example that explains why Web sites are educational.

REVISION

I like surfing the Net. Many of the Web sites **give information about places I'd like to visit.**

Here's How **Revising Empty Sentences**

- Eliminate repeated ideas or words.
- Add supporting details, such as facts, reasons, or examples.

2 Cutting the Fat from Padded Sentences

Padded sentences have more words than are needed to communicate an idea. What unnecessary words could you take out of the following sentence without changing its meaning?

STUDENT MODEL

DRAFT

What I want to say is that surfing the Net is a great way to learn about the world on your own.

REVISION

Surfing the Net is a great way to learn about the world on your own.

Here's How Eliminating Unnecessary Words

1. Look for unnecessary words and phrases that add no helpful information.
2. Either cut them out or use more concise versions.

Unnecessary Phrases	Better
• because of the fact that	because, since
• on account of the fact that	because, since
• in spite of the fact that	although
• what I want to say is	(Just say it.)
• what I mean is	(Just say it.)

Don't use empty or padded sentences simply to make your piece of writing meet a required length. Instead, give the reader more details about your topic.

See "Personal Trainer for Sentences," p. 376.

PRACTICE Empty and Padded Sentences

Follow the instructions in parentheses to revise these sentences.

(1) Colorado is a great state. (Add a reason or fact.) **(2)** You can visit winter ski areas, such as Breckenridge and Copper Mountain, where you can ski all winter. (Eliminate repeated ideas.) **(3)** Our family drove along Trail Ridge Road on account of the fact that we wanted to see Rocky Mountain National Park. (Use a shorter version of a wordy phrase.) **(4)** Great Sand Dunes National Monument is very educational. (Add a reason or fact.) **(5)** What I mean to say is that Colorado is by far my favorite state. (Eliminate unnecessary words.)

Apply what you have learned about empty and padded sentences by revising your Write Away paragraph or another draft from your **Working Portfolio.**

REVISING

Peanuts by Charles M. Schulz

Stringy and Overloaded Sentences

1 Untangling Stringy Sentences

A **stringy sentence** contains too many ideas loosely connected by the word *and.* Writers often create sentences like the one shown in the draft below, in which four ideas are strung together.

STUDENT MODEL

DRAFT

My family and I visited the Coyote Point Museum last summer **and** we learned about the habits of the California condor **and** we also stayed at a dude ranch **and** I rode a horse for the first time.

REVISION

My family and I visited the Coyote Point Museum last summer. We learned about the habits of the California condor. We also stayed at a dude ranch, **where** I rode a horse for the first time.

The first two ideas are separated. The conjunction shows how the second two ideas are related.

CHAPTER 16

Here's How **Revising Stringy Sentences**

1. Begin by listing each idea in the sentence separately.
2. Ask yourself how the ideas are related. By time? As cause and effect?
3. Decide which ideas can be combined and which should remain separate.
4. Decide on the best connecting words to use, such as *but, or, if, because, where,* or *which.*
5. Rewrite the sentence as two or more sentences.

If you write stringy sentences, you may also write run-on sentences. Watch for comma splices or sentences that run together with no punctuation separating them.

For more about run-on sentences, see pp. 120–121.

2 Overloaded Sentences

An **overloaded sentence** contains too much information about a single topic. The reader barely grasps one idea before another is presented, as in the draft on the next page.

STUDENT MODEL

DRAFT

The California condor once ruled the skies over the western coastlands of the continent, but by 1988 it was nearly extinct, because only about 20 condors survived, all of them in zoos.

REVISION

The California condor once ruled the skies over the western coastlands of the continent, but by 1988 it was nearly extinct. Only about 20 condors survived, all of them in zoos.

The first two ideas are combined in one sentence for effect. A second sentence separates the last fact from the others.

Here's How Revising Overloaded Sentences

1. Begin by breaking the overloaded sentence into smaller sentences, each containing only one or two facts or ideas.
2. Decide which facts or ideas can be combined and which should remain separate.
3. Choose the best connecting words to use, such as *only, however, and, but, because, which,* or *where.*
4. Rewrite the sentence as two or more sentences.

Here's a quick way to spot a stringy or an overloaded sentence. Read it aloud without taking a breath. If you turn blue before you finish the sentence, you may need to revise your work!

PRACTICE Revising Stringy and Overloaded Sentences

Rewrite the following paragraph by revising the stringy sentence and the overloaded sentence.

I had never ridden a horse in my life, and we decided to try riding at this dude ranch, and we had to saddle the horses ourselves! When you saddle a horse, you have to make sure the saddle is on tight because the horse can puff out its stomach as you put the saddle on and then afterwards it lets the air out, and when you try to get on the horse, the saddle will be too loose and will dump you on the ground.

REVISING

LESSON 3

Combining Sentences

1 Why Combine Sentences?

Which of the following drafts do you find more interesting and easier to read? Why?

STUDENT MODEL

DRAFT 1

My great-grandfather was from Zamora, Spain. His name was Jorge de la Hoz. In the early 1900s he went to the Philippines. He married my great-grandmother Pilar Luisa.

DRAFT 2

My great-grandfather Jorge de la Hoz was from Zamora, Spain. In the early 1900s he went to the Philippines and married my great-grandmother Pilar Luisa.

Draft 2 combines several short sentences from Draft 1. By combining sentences, you can create writing that flows more smoothly, makes more sense, and is more interesting to read.

CHAPTER 16

2 Combining Whole Sentences

Use a **coordinating conjunction** (*and, so, for, but, yet, or*) to join similar or contrasting ideas.

DRAFT

My great-grandfather Jorge was born in Zamora, and his older brother was born in Madrid.

In those days, families might have several sons, but only the oldest son inherited the family fortune.

Coordinating Conjunctions	
to combine similar ideas	and, so, for
to combine contrasting ideas	but, yet, or

Always use a comma before a coordinating conjunction that joins two independent clauses.

Sometimes, you may join two sentences whose ideas are not equally important. Use a **subordinating conjunction,** such as *although* or *because,* to make the less important sentence a subordinate clause. Then combine it with an independent clause to create a complex sentence.

DRAFT

Jorge decided to go to the Philippines. ~~O~~pportunities were better there. ~~H~~e didn't know anyone. ~~H~~e found work right away.

because / Although / h (handwritten edits)

Subordinating conjunctions show clearly the relationship between the main idea and the less important idea.

Subordinating Conjunctions	
Time or Sequence	when, after, before, until, while, as long as
Cause-effect	since, because
Condition	although, though, unless, if, whether

3 Combining Sentence Parts

Two sentences may share the same subject or the same predicate. Use a coordinating conjunction to combine the sentences by creating a **compound subject** or **compound predicate.**

Compound Subject

DRAFT

He hoped to meet someone at a dance. Pilar Luisa hoped to meet someone there too.

REVISED

He and **Pilar Luisa** both hoped to meet someone at a dance.

Compound Predicate

DRAFT

They were married that year. They moved to Manila.

REVISED

They **were married that year** and **moved to Manila.**

When combining subjects, make sure the new compound subject agrees in number with the verb in the sentence.

REVISING

❹ Combining with *That, Which, Who*

You can combine sentences by turning one sentence into a clause beginning with *that, which* or *who.* These clauses add details about a person, place, or thing.

STUDENT MODEL

DRAFT

Their oldest son Carlos was an outstanding athlete. He became a champion swimmer. He competed in the Pan Asian Games. These games were held in Manila. He won the silver cup. It sits on our fireplace mantel.

REVISED

Their oldest son Carlos was an outstanding athlete **who** became a champion swimmer. He competed in the Pan Asian Games, **which** were held in Manila. He won the silver cup **that** sits on our fireplace mantel.

Using Commas with *That, Which, Who* Clauses

The word *that* is used to add essential details, so no commas are needed.

I have an old picture that shows him in the pool.

The word *which* is used to add nonessential details. Set off the details with commas.

He set a 100-meter record, which stood for years.

The word *who* can be used to add essential or nonessential details. Use commas when the details are nonessential.

His mother, who was excitable, went to one race.

It was she who shouted from the stands, "Carlos, get moving!"

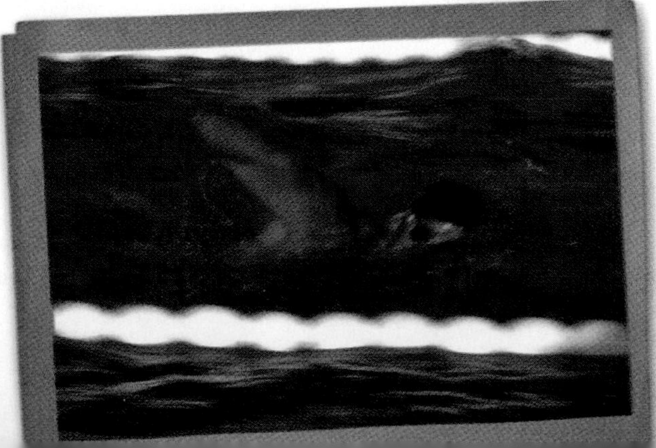

CHAPTER 16

Using Parallel Structure

When you combine sentences, make sure the combined parts are equal, or **parallel,** in structure.

Carlos liked soccer. He also liked to play baseball.

NOT PARALLEL: **Carlos liked soccer and to play baseball.**
(*soccer* is a noun; *to play baseball* is a phrase)

PARALLEL: **Carlos liked soccer and baseball.**
(*soccer* and *baseball* are both nouns)

He wanted to join the swim team. He also wanted to be a high diver. He asked about swimming in relays.

NOT PARALLEL: **He wanted to join the swim team, to be a high diver, and swimming in relays.**
(*to join* and *to be* are infinitives; *swimming* is a participle)

PARALLEL: **He wanted to join the swim team, to be a high diver, and to swim in relays.**
(*to join, to be,* and *to swim* are all infinitives)

PRACTICE **Combining Sentences**

Follow the instructions in parentheses to combine the following pairs of sentences.

1. I tried out for the swim team. I wanted to be like my grandfather Carlos. (Use a subordinating conjunction.)
2. We had to dive into the pool. Then we had to swim to the far end. (Use a compound predicate.)
3. My arms thrashed like windmills. My legs kicked like a frog's. (Use a coordinating conjunction.)
4. The other kids were laughing at my style. The coach was laughing too. (Use a compound subject.)
5. Luckily, the coach thought I could be a good swimmer. It turned out to be true. (Use *which*.)
6. The coach taught me how to kick. He also taught me stroking. (Use parallel structure.)
7. I practiced every day after school. I really wanted to improve. (Use *because*.)
8. The next tryout went so well. It surprised even me. (Use *that*.)
9. I was nervous at the start. I swam like a dolphin. (Use a coordinating conjunction.)
10. I made the team. I felt as if my grandfather were watching. (Use a subordinating conjunction.)

REVISING

Inserting Words and Phrases

1 Combining with Words and Phrases

Sometimes two sentences are used to express one idea, even though the second sentence adds only a small bit of additional information. A more efficient way to express the idea is to insert the additional information into the first sentence. Notice how the following sentences are combined.

Inserting Single Words

Connie Williams led the annual parade. She is our mayor.

Mayor Connie Williams led the annual parade.

Inserting Words That Change Form

Sometimes the form of a word must be changed before it is added to another sentence. You may need to add an ending such as *-n, -y, -ed, -ing,* or *-ly.*

We loved the marching band. It was from Australia.

We loved the Australian marching band.

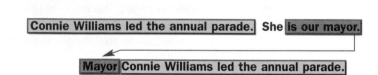

The town solved the problem of too many parades.
Its solution was clever.

The town cleverly solved the problem of too many parades.

Inserting Phrases

Everyone heard the children.
They were giggling throughout the procession.

Everyone heard the children giggling throughout the procession.

For more about phrases, see pp. 71–77.

CHAPTER 16

❷ Combining with Appositives

An **appositive** is a noun or noun phrase that identifies or explains a noun or pronoun. When two sentences give information about the same noun or pronoun, you can often combine them by changing one of the sentences into an appositive.

The mayor met with Frank Battaglia.
Mr. Battaglia is the parade grand marshal.

The mayor met with Frank Battaglia, the parade grand marshal.

Mr. Battaglia introduced Ms. Jacob at a special awards breakfast.
Ms. Jacob is a float designer.

Mr. Battaglia introduced Ms. Jacob, a float designer, at a special awards breakfast.

For information about using commas with appositives, see pp. 69–70.

PRACTICE **Inserting Words and Phrases**

Follow the instructions in parentheses to combine the following pairs of sentences.

1. Most people around the world eat when they wake up. They eat breakfast. (Insert a word.)
2. Around the world, breakfast foods are varied. They're as varied as the languages people speak. (Insert a phrase.)
3. More people around the world are eating breakfast cereals and pastries. These are foods that come from America. (Insert a word that changes form.)
4. A favorite breakfast dish in Japan is nori and rice. Nori is a seaweed. (Insert an appositive.)
5. In Mexico, a typical breakfast includes three foods. These are chicken tacos, eggs, and refried beans. (Insert a phrase.)

REVISING

Using Active and Passive Voice

You can make your sentences more effective by choosing verbs in the appropriate voice. The **active voice** emphasizes who or what is doing the action. The **passive voice** emphasizes the receiver of the action or the action itself.

Active: Rebecca Lobo sparked the second-half rally.
EMPHASIZES SUBJECT

Passive: The second-half rally was sparked by Rebecca Lobo.
EMPHASIZES RECEIVER

For more about active and passive voice, see p. 144.

1 Using Active Voice

In the following passage, the active voice makes it clear who urged and invaded.

LITERARY MODEL

Susan **urged** all her followers in Rochester to register. The next day, a dozen women **invaded** the Eighth Ward barbershop. . .

—Margaret Truman, "The United States vs. Susan B. Anthony"

CHAPTER 16

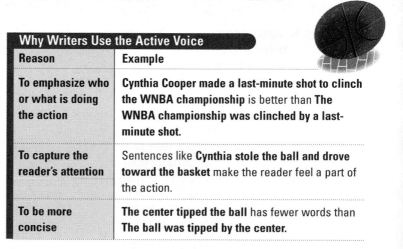

Why Writers Use the Active Voice

Reason	Example
To emphasize who or what is doing the action	**Cynthia Cooper made a last-minute shot to clinch the WNBA championship** is better than **The WNBA championship was clinched by a last-minute shot.**
To capture the reader's attention	Sentences like **Cynthia stole the ball and drove toward the basket** make the reader feel a part of the action.
To be more concise	**The center tipped the ball** has fewer words than **The ball was tipped by the center.**

❷ Using Passive Voice

In most of your writing, use the active voice. However, the passive voice also has its uses, as the model below shows.

LITERARY MODEL

We **had been given** "free" exercise time and **had been ordered** by our P.E. teacher, Mr. DePalma, to "keep moving."

—Judith Ortiz Cofer, "American History"

The passive voice is used to emphasize the receiver of the action.

Why Writers Use the Passive Voice

Reason	Example
To emphasize the receiver of the action or the action itself	**Four runners were chosen for the Olympic track team** emphasizes who was chosen, not who did the choosing.
To indicate that the performer of the action is unknown or not important	**The modern Summer Olympics have been held since the late 1800s.** *Who* held the Olympics is not important to the meaning.
To create a passive, timeless mood or tone	**The soccer field was marked by the feet of every team in the Olympics.**

Use the passive voice if you're writing about the results of a science experiment. By doing so, you will emphasize the procedures and results instead of the person doing the experiment.

PRACTICE **Using Active and Passive Voice**

Revise the sentences below according to the instructions in parentheses.

(1) Left-handed people are called southpaws by many writers. (Use active voice.) **(2)** The word *southpaw* was invented by a Chicago sportswriter around 1890. (Use active voice.) **(3)** During the 1940s, baseball fans were amazed at the play of the one-armed southpaw Pete Gray. (Use active voice.) **(4)** Left-handed players have earned many honors in baseball. (Use passive voice.) **(5)** For instance, two home-run records were set by the left-handers Babe Ruth and Roger Maris. (Use active voice.)

REVISING

Student Help Desk

Revising Sentences at a Glance

A Good Sentence is . . .

Not too skinny, not too fat
It states an idea clearly and uses supporting details when necessary.

Not stringy or overloaded
It doesn't contain too many ideas.

A pair of ideas
It uses conjunctions such as *and, but, or, although,* and *because* to combine whole sentences and sentence parts with similar or contrasting ideas.

Usually active but sometimes passive
It often uses the active voice to emphasize the doer of the action.

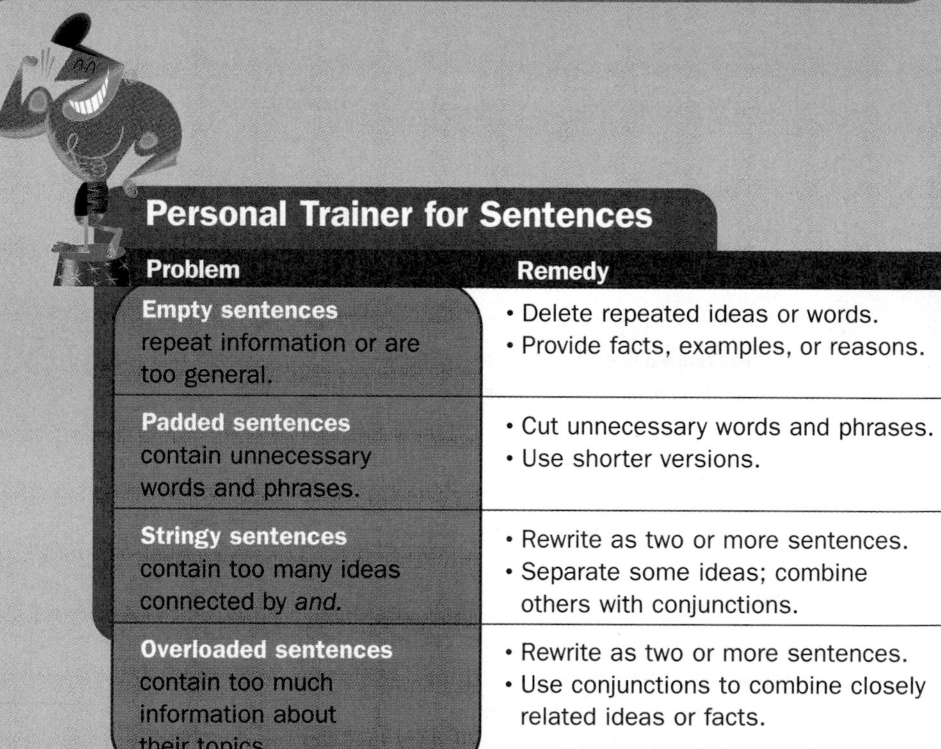

Personal Trainer for Sentences

Problem	Remedy
Empty sentences repeat information or are too general.	• Delete repeated ideas or words. • Provide facts, examples, or reasons.
Padded sentences contain unnecessary words and phrases.	• Cut unnecessary words and phrases. • Use shorter versions.
Stringy sentences contain too many ideas connected by *and.*	• Rewrite as two or more sentences. • Separate some ideas; combine others with conjunctions.
Overloaded sentences contain too much information about their topics.	• Rewrite as two or more sentences. • Use conjunctions to combine closely related ideas or facts.

Mixing It Up

Ways of Combining Sentences

Technique	Example
Using conjunctions	I bought two root beers. Erin wanted a root beer too. I bought two root beers **because** Erin wanted one too.
Using compound subjects and verbs	I'm going to the basketball game tonight. Tamiko is going too. **Tamiko and I** are going to the basketball game tonight.
Using clauses beginning with *who, which,* or *that*	The coach sent in Tom Einsen. He made the game-winning shot. The coach sent in Tom Einsen, **who** made the game-winning shot.
Inserting words or phrases from one sentence into another	I have a new bicycle. It is a ten-speed. I have a new **ten-speed** bicycle.
Using an identifying phrase from one sentence as an appositive phrase in another	Dr. Alma Wilson is the best doctor we ever had. Dr. Alma Wilson is our family dentist. Dr. Alma Wilson, **our family dentist,** is the best doctor we ever had.

REVISING

The Bottom Line

Checklist for Clear, Concise Sentences

Can I improve my sentences by . . .

____ adding details that give examples or reasons?

____ taking out unnecessary words or phrases?

____ dividing stringy sentences into shorter ones?

____ cutting down on the number of ideas in overloaded sentences?

____ combining sentences by using conjunctions, inserting words and phrases, or using compound subjects and predicates?

____ changing the voice to active or passive?

Power Words
Vocabulary for Precise Writing

metamorphosis

I've Got a New Attitude!

Just as a caterpillar has changed into this butterfly, the teen on the next page has also made changes in his appearance. There are many words to describe this process.

Quick Change

You can **alter** your look; you can **revamp** your whole wardrobe. Your hairstyle may **differ** from day to day. You may **vary** your interests from time to time.

More Than a New Do!

If you did everything in the previous paragraph all at once, you would be going through a **transformation** or **metamorphosis**—more complete changes in appearance and character. Hopefully, you won't **mutate** or turn into the frog you studied in biology!

For Better or Worse

For a change from something relatively ordinary to something absolutely radiant, you might use **transfigurement;** into something grotesque, **transmogrification.** For change in a positive direction, use **progress** or **evolution;** in a negative direction, use **degeneration** or **devolution.**

alter

mutate

transform

Your Turn Style Profile

Think about the way you dress (or would like to), wear your hair (or would like to), etc. What are you trying to tell the world about yourself with these choices? Write a paragraph describing your style.

Chapter 17

Style and Effective Language

STYLE

What's Your Style?

How does each style of clothing change your impression of this person? Which style would you choose for yourself? Would it depend on what you were doing?

Your personal style—the way you dress, move, talk—is created by the many choices you make. Likewise, your writing **style** is a combination of the words and images you choose, your tone, and the types of sentences you write. Like the person in the picture, you can change your style to match your purpose and audience.

Write Away: They've Got It!

Freewrite for five minutes about someone you know or a famous person whose style you admire. Remember that *style* can mean how a person talks, sings, dances, or plays a sport or a musical instrument. Save your writing in your **Working Portfolio.**

LESSON 1 What Is Style?

1 Recognizing Style

Style is not only *what* a writer says but, more importantly, *how* the writer says it. In the cartoon below, the writer uses two different styles to create two versions of a math word problem.

Calvin and Hobbes by Bill Watterson

- As you read the two versions, what emotions do you feel?
- Which version contains more images or more colorful language?
- How do the word choices differ in each version?
- How do the length and structure of the sentences differ?
- What is the writer's tone, or his attitude toward the subject?

Your answers to these questions will suggest some of the qualities that make up a writer's style.

2 Describing Style

Here are some of the terms used in talking about style.

Word Choice

Depending on the subject, writers may prefer to use concrete words or abstract words, specific words or general words, technical words or everyday words. **General:** man **Specific:** private eye

CHAPTER 17

Varieties of Language

Formal writing is carefully composed. **Informal writing** is more relaxed and has the quality of everyday speech. Most writing falls somewhere between these extremes. **Informal:** Two saps, Jack and Joe, drive toward each other.

Imagery and Figures of Speech

Imagery consists of sensory words that help the reader imagine what the writer is describing. Figurative language includes **similes** and **metaphors,** which compare one thing to another. **Simile:** Questions pour down like rain.

Tone

Tone is a writer's attitude toward a subject as expressed by word choice, imagery, and formal or informal language. Tone can be humorous, angry, ironic, critical, serious, or sarcastic.

Sentence Structure

A writer may use sentences of varying lengths and complexity to create particular effects.

PRACTICE **Identifying Style**

Read the two models. Working in pairs or in a small group, discuss or write the answers to the questions on the previous page. What are the characteristics of each author's style?

STYLE

LITERARY MODEL

Miss Adela Strangeworth came daintily along Main Street on her way to the grocery. The sun was shining, the air was fresh and clear after the night's heavy rain, and everything in Miss Strangeworth's little town looked washed and bright.

—Shirley Jackson, "The Possibility of Evil"

LITERARY MODEL

Then my eyes focus. There he is! The Wonder Horse! At the end of the glade, on high ground surrounded by summer green. He is a statue. He is an engraving. . . .

Eyes flashing. Tail waving active defiance. Hoofs glossy and destructive. Arrogant ruler of the countryside.

—Sabine R. Ulibarrí, "My Wonder Horse"

Word Choice

1 Choosing Precise Words

The precise noun, verb, or modifier can help bring your writing to life. Instead of general or abstract words, you can choose specific, concrete ones.

GENERAL: **The man saw a car.**

SPECIFIC: **The patrol officer spotted a blue convertible.**

How much difference can word choice make? Compare the paragraph below with the literary model that follows it.

I **brought** my attention back to the road in front of me. The **car** ahead **moved quickly** back into the fast lane, **touched** the rear of a third **car,** then hit the center divider and **moved** directly into my path. I **put my foot on** my brakes, **fear going** through me as I tried to control my **car's movements.**

General words provide few sensory details or actions.

LITERARY MODEL

I **snapped** my attention back to the road in front of me. The **white compact veered abruptly** back into the fast lane, **clipped** the rear of the **red Porsche,** then hit the center divider and **careened** directly into my path. I **slammed on** my brakes, **adrenaline shooting** through me as I fought to control the **VW's fishtailing rear end.**

—Sue Grafton, "Full Circle"

Concrete nouns, action verbs, and precise modifiers create vivid sensory details.

Precise nouns and verbs also can be used to replace a string of words and modifiers. "The car shifted from lane to lane through traffic." "The car zigzagged through traffic."

PRACTICE A **Be Specific**

Read the paragraph below, then substitute more specific, concrete words for the words in dark type.

Anne **gave** me the **ball**, and I **went** down the field toward the goalie. With **little time** left, I **put** the ball between the goal posts and **got** the **last** point. I **was happy.**

2 Denotative and Connotative Meanings

The **denotative** meaning of a word or phrase is simply its dictionary definition. The **connotative** meaning of a word refers to the emotions that arise when someone hears or reads the word. For example, *cheap, inexpensive,* or *economical* all mean about the same thing, but their connotative meanings are very different.

Connotations

Example	Connotation	Explanation
That car is really **economical.**	Positive	The price is low and the car may save you money by running efficiently.
That car is really **inexpensive.**	Neutral	The car's price is low.
That car is really **cheap.**	Negative	The price is low and the car is poorly made.

Connotative meanings are important in persuasive writing when you are trying to influence your readers' emotions. If you were campaigning against drunk driving, for instance, you could be more effective if you described accidents as "deadly" or "gruesome," and not just as "bad."

STYLE

PRACTICE B **Say What You Mean**

Explain how each pair of sentences differs in meaning.

1. Solange perfume has a **smell** he won't forget!
   Solange perfume has a **fragrance** he won't forget!
2. She sounded very **confident** after the game.
   She sounded very **smug** after the game.
3. That was a **mistake.**
   That was a **stupid thing** to do.

Look at your **Write Away** paragraph or another draft from your **Working Portfolio.** Can you replace any general words with more precise ones?

Varieties of Language

1 Matching Language to Audience and Purpose

You're answering an ad for volunteers at a local animal rescue center. You say to yourself, "All that pet-sitting I've done has paid off—this job is made for me." You say in your letter, "I believe my experience in caring for other people's pets has prepared me to be a volunteer at the rescue center."

You have just matched your language to your audience and purpose. For most school and business communication, you will use **standard English**, which conforms to accepted grammar and usage rules. Standard English ranges from formal to informal language.

2 Formal and Informal Language

Formal language contains more complex vocabulary and sentence structure, uses standard punctuation, and avoids contractions. **Informal language** contains everyday words and expressions, uses contractions, and often uses simpler sentence structure.

Compare the levels of language in the following student models. The student wrote the first film review to a friend. He wrote the second review for the school newspaper.

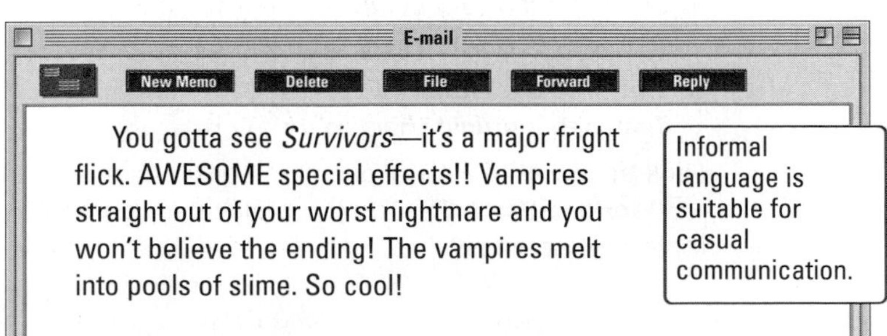

You gotta see *Survivors*—it's a major fright flick. AWESOME special effects!! Vampires straight out of your worst nightmare and you won't believe the ending! The vampires melt into pools of slime. So cool!

Informal language is suitable for casual communication.

1999 Sectio

Survivors is a film for serious horror fans only. The special effects crew used plasticine and robotics to create some of the most frightening vampires on film. The fiery ending should shock even hardened horror fans.

A published review requires more formal language and sentence structure.

3 Varieties of Informal Language

The following types of expressions are commonly used in informal language.

Idiom

An idiom is a common expression whose real meaning is different from its literal meaning. You can use idioms when you are writing to friends, giving an informal talk, or creating dialogue for characters.

Examples: He's **itching to play.** I'll **try my hand** at computer chess.

Slang

Slang includes words or phrases made up by members of a special group, such as teenagers, musicians, technicians, and others. Slang is colorful, but goes out of style quickly. Use slang only in informal writing—e-mails, letters to friends—and in fiction.

Examples: Don't **have a cow, dude.** He's just **yanking your chain.**

Jargon

Jargon is specialized language used in a business or a profession. Use jargon only when you are writing for an audience who understands it.

Example: The **server** couldn't locate the **URL** for the Web site.

STYLE

PRACTICE **Dress It Up**

Rewrite the following application letter to make it more formal.

Dear Ms. Towers,

I read your newspaper ad for a volunteer helper in the Animal Rescue Center. I'm totally ready for this job!! There isn't nothing about dogs and cats I can't handle—I've raised three golden retrievers and even trained them myself! I'm dying to work there, so let me know when we can talk about the job.

LESSON 4 Imagery and Figures of Speech

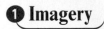

1 Imagery

crisp, cold air
dazzling light
crowds huddled
getting BIG air!
shredding slopes
scent of new snow

Imagery refers to words that help readers imagine they can see, hear, feel, taste, and smell what is being described. Here is a brief example from a student writer.

STUDENT MODEL

The **crisp winter day** with its **dazzling light** and **scent of new snow** was a **perfect setting** for the women's halfpipe competition. The **densely packed** crowd **huddled together** for warmth and tried to avoid sliding on the **slippery, steep slope.** The competitors **whizzed by, shredding the slopes, inches from the spectators.** What an exciting day!

A list or a chart, like the one below, can help you generate images to describe a scene.

Sight	Sound	Taste	Touch	Smell
dazzling light	cheers	hot cocoa	huddled crowd	new snow

PRACTICE A **You're in the Picture**

Suppose you are the snowboarder in the picture above. Or think about a scene you see everyday on the way to school. Write a few sentences using imagery to bring the scene to life for your readers.

CHAPTER 17

❷ Figures of Speech

Figures of speech, or **figurative language,** communicate ideas beyond the ordinary, literal meaning of the words.

LITERARY MODEL

Somehow the country dark had always been **a friend, like a warm bed and being tucked in and being hugged and kissed good night.**

—Nash Candelaria, "The Day the Cisco Kid Shot John Wayne"

The dark is not literally a friend or a warm bed or a hug. The figurative language, however, shows how comforting the country dark feels to the author.

The three most common forms of figurative language are **simile, metaphor**, and **personification**.

Simile

A **simile** is a comparison that uses *like* or *as*. Use similes to help readers visualize or understand something better by comparing it with something else. The two examples below show how similes make the scene from James Hurst's story more vivid.

Without Similes

. . . then a gum tree ahead of us was shattered by a bolt of lightning.

The drops stung my face.

. . . [the rain] fell straight down in parallel paths.

LITERARY MODEL

. . . then, **like a bursting Roman candle,** a gum tree ahead of us was shattered by a bolt of lightning.

The drops stung my face **like nettles. . . .**

. . . [the rain] fell straight down in parallel paths **like ropes hanging from the sky.**

—James Hurst, "The Scarlet Ibis"

STYLE

Metaphor

A **metaphor** directly compares one thing with another. The words *like* or *as* are not used in metaphors. Notice the difference between the simile and the metaphor below.

SIMILE: Lightning is *like* nature's Roman candle.

METAPHOR: Lightning *is* nature's Roman candle.

In your writing, use metaphors to create an even more vivid picture or impression in the reader's mind than a simile might create. In the example below, Richard Wright uses the metaphor of a runaway train to describe the path his life was taking.

LITERARY MODEL

> . . . Without my knowing it, the **locomotive** of my heart was rushing down a dangerously steep slope, heading for a **collision,** heedless of the **warning red lights** that blinked all about me, the **sirens** and the **bells** and the **screams** that filled the air.
>
> —Richard Wright, *Black Boy*

Every image after "locomotive" builds the metaphor.

Personification

Personification is a figure of speech that gives human qualities to ideas, objects, or animals. In the model below, Susan Doro uses personification to present a poem as a main character.

LITERARY MODEL

> But tonight the poem saw that she was having a good time, joking with her "buddies." It was an hour and a half later when the poem looked in again.
>
> —Susan Doro, "The Cultural Worker"

PRACTICE B **Picture This**

Follow the instructions in parentheses.

Example: He walks like . . . (Use a simile.) He walks **like a penguin**.

1. I'm walking in the hot sun and getting thirsty . . . (Use imagery.)
2. My room looks like . . . (Use a simile.)
3. Fireworks are . . . (Use a metaphor.)
4. When I sing, I sound as weird as . . . (Use a simile.)
5. I think video games are . . . (Use a metaphor.)

PRACTICE C **They're Almost Human**

Think of an object you use everyday (a computer, a hot comb, a toaster, a CD player) or an animal you know. Write a paragraph that uses personification to describe how the object or the pet acts.

Example: My computer was making those "I'm not talking to the printer today" noises. . .

Avoiding Clichés

A **cliché** is an overused, worn-out expression. Every cliché starts out as an original image, but over the years, it loses all trace of freshness and originality. Here are a few examples:

I was **green with envy.**

That remark was really **off the wall.**

They haven't a clue about how to win.

The science assignment is **over my head.**

Here's How Avoiding Clichés

1. Try to find a fresh image for what you want to say.
2. Connect with the feeling you want to convey and try to associate a word or an image with that feeling. For instance, how does envy feel? Does it gnaw, bite, cut, burn?
3. If you cannot think of something fresh, then simply use ordinary language. It's better to state something clearly than to put a tired cliché in your sentence.

Another reason to avoid clichés is that they don't really say anything. For instance, what does "over my head" or "off the wall" actually mean? When you have to explain something in more detail, you're beginning to use your own words to express yourself.

PRACTICE D **Get Fresh!**

Replace the clichés in boldface type with more original language.

1. I'm **dead meat** now. *(in real trouble)*
2. You'll have to **bite the bullet.** *(accept something painful or difficult)*
3. The principal was **really ticked off**. *(very angry)*
4. It's better to be **safe than sorry**. *(act cautiously beforehand)*
5. All we need to do is **wrap it up**. *(take care of some final details)*

STYLE

LESSON 5

Tone and Voice

1 Creating Tone

Tone is an expression of a writer's attitude toward a subject, revealed by word choice, sentence structure, and imagery. As a writer, you can choose the tone that best expresses your attitude—serious, sarcastic, humorous, angry. Identify the tone of the passages below.

PROFESSIONAL MODEL

Age-Appropriate Chores

. . . Working builds skills, makes [children] feel useful, and teaches appreciation for the work that needs to be done and for those who do it. It may be tempting for parents to do everything themselves, thinking it is easier and will get done "properly." When parents take that attitude, they deprive their kids of opportunities to learn cooperation and responsibility.

—Jane Nelsen, Lynn Lott, Stephen Glenn, *Positive Discipline A-Z*

More formal diction, complex sentence structure, and lack of sensory words and images create a serious tone.

Adulthood

. . . Any teenager who has been dragooned [forced] into doing the dishes knows . . . that the stuff at the bottom of the strainer is toxic waste—deadly poison—a danger to health. In other words about as icky as icky gets. One of the very few reasons I had any respect for my mother when I was 13 was because she would reach into the sink with her bare hands—BARE HANDS—and pick up that lethal gunk and drop it in the garbage.

—Robert Fulghum, *Chicken Soup for the Teenage Soul*

Informal language and punctuation, precise sensory words, and exaggerated images create a humorous tone.

PRACTICE A **It's All About Attitude**

Think about something you either like to do or hate to do (eating fudge ice cream versus washing windows). Write a paragraph that describes the activity and shows your attitude toward it.

Exchange papers with a partner and identify the tone of the paragraph. Underline the words and images that support your choice.

CHAPTER 17

❷ Recognizing Your Own Voice

When your friends call, you usually recognize their voices not only by the tone but by the words and expressions they use. Writers also have a **voice,** which is the "sound" of their work that readers "hear" in their minds as they read.

Voice is based on the writer's vocabulary, sentence structure, and figurative language. For example, notice how different Ernest Hemingway's voice is from that of Truman Capote.

LITERARY MODELS

. . . We came out through the first-floor dining room to the street. A waiter went for a taxi. It was hot and bright. Up the street was a little square with trees and grass where there were taxis parked.

—Ernest Hemingway, *The Sun Also Rises*

Hemingway uses short, simple sentences, ordinary language, and few images. His voice sounds like a reporter's.

Here, there, a flash, a flutter, an ecstasy of shrillings remind us that not all the birds have flown south. Always, the path unwinds through lemony sun pools and pitch-black vine tunnels.

—Truman Capote, "A Christmas Memory"

Capote uses complex vocabulary (*ecstasy, shrillings*) and vivid images. His voice sounds like a poet's.

STYLE

PRACTICE B **How Do You Sound?**

Take the paragraph you wrote for Practice A and exchange papers with a partner. To identify your partner's voice, ask these questions.

- Is the writer's vocabulary simple or complex—or a mix of both?
- Does the writer use imagery and figurative language or prefer plain description?
- Does the writer use short, direct sentences; longer, more complex ones; or a variety of sentence structures?
- Does the writer's voice sound closer to Hemingway's or to Capote's?

Student Help Desk

Style and Effective Language at a Glance

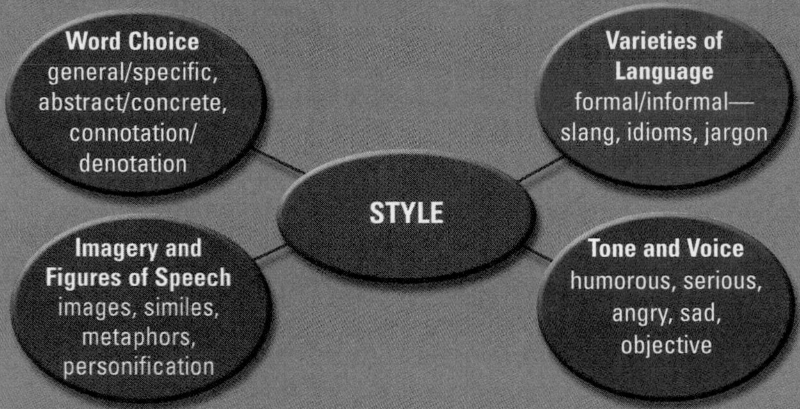

CHAPTER 17

Word Choice — Lay Them to Rest

Leave clichés like these in the verbal graveyard.

easier said than done
down in the dumps
happy as a lark
face the music
needle in a haystack
pretty as a picture
better late than never
walking on air
grin and bear it
leave well enough alone
pushing up daisies
stubborn as a mule

Dress It Up . . .

Formal and Informal Language

Formal	Idiom	Slang
discuss	talk it up	rap
observe	take a look	scope it out
stolen	lifted	ripped off
children	kids	rugrats

. . . Or Down!

Images and Figures of Speech

Bring Them to Life!

- **List words or phrases that describe what a person, place, or thing feels, looks, tastes, smells, or sounds like.** "Air shriveled and dry, dusty smell, sun hammering down, insects dive-bombing my face"

- **Use comparisons to describe the condition of the person, place, or thing.** "Throat like raw hamburger, tongue a dry sponge, face stretched tight as spandex, eyelids are sandpaper"

- **Try to think of human qualities that might bring the subject more to life.** "Thirst stalked me from the first mile."

STYLE

The Bottom Line

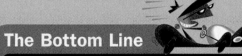

Style Checklist

Have I . . .

____ matched my level of language to my audience and purpose?

____ chosen the best words for my meaning?

____ used images and figures of speech where appropriate?

____ avoided clichés?

____ expressed my attitude toward my subject?

____ tried to let my own "voice" come through?

Writing Workshops

Getting in the Groove

The sky's the limit for your imagination. To bring your ideas down to earth where they can engage and move readers, you'll need to use different types of writing. Learn how each type works, and you can take your readers anywhere.

Personal Narrative

Learn What It Is

Why are television talk shows, human interest stories, and biographies so popular? It's because stories of dramatic events in other people's lives fascinate us. You may have an interesting story to tell about your own life. In fact, putting your **personal narrative** on paper may help you understand the meaning of certain events in your life or in the life of someone you know.

Basics in a Box

PERSONAL NARRATIVE AT A GLANCE

Beginning	Middle	End
Introduces the incident, including the people and place involved	• Describes the event using descriptive details and possibly dialogue • Makes the significance of the event clear	• Tells the outcome or result of the event • Presents the writer's feelings about the experience

RUBRIC

Standards for Writing

A successful narrative should

- focus on a clear, well-defined incident
- make the importance or significance of the event clear
- show clearly the order in which events occurred
- use descriptive details that appeal to the senses to describe characters and setting
- use dialogue to develop characters
- maintain a consistent tone

See How It's Done: *Personal Narrative*

Student Model
Megan McCarville
Evanston Township High School

RUBRIC IN ACTION

Mind Games

"Swimmers . . . Take your marks . . . GO!" I heard the nasal voice of the official as I flew from my position bent over at the starting block into the water.

The water was a cold slap in my face as I thought, "I hate this race."

My thoughts ran to trying to cheer myself up as I flipped my turn into the second lap of my five hundred freestyle race.

"It's only a five-hundred. Twenty lengths! Come on, you can do it! You do more than this every day in practice. Anyway, it's not as if you're expected to win, so there's no reason to worry about losing. You're in lane six, the worst one."

As I swam, wishing the race were over, I stared at the grimy bottom of the pool, wondering how often it was cleaned. I thought about how tired I would be before the race was over.

When I came to the end of the pool, before my turn I glanced at the board with my number seven on it in large black print that my counter was holding in the water.

"Only thirteen more lengths," I told myself. "See, it isn't that bad. It's been going by pretty quickly." This was a lie. My arms felt like they were going to fall off, and I couldn't take breaths fast enough.

Every time I took a breath I saw my teammates and coaches standing at the edge of the pool yelling, "GO! Come on, GO!"

I wondered irritably why they were cheering so loudly; it wasn't as if I was going to win.

But, then again, maybe I was winning. After all, I couldn't really tell where my opponents were. At this thought, I realized how much energy I had and began to pick up the pace. I wondered what it would be like to actually win a race and felt myself go even faster.

❶ This writer focuses on one event and starts at the beginning of the incident.

Other options:
- Start in the middle.
- Start with background information.

❷ Uses writer's thoughts as a form of "dialogue" to describe the event and develop her character

❸ Uses swim-lap numbers to show clearly the order in which events occur

❹ Maintains a consistent tone through the reactions of the narrator

NARRATIVE

"This is so cool," I thought, seeing my counter push down the number seventeen. "Just three more lengths to go, and I must be winning."

It was funny how I hadn't realized how quickly the numbers were passing. I hadn't remembered seeing number thirteen.

❺ Foreshadows the event to come

"Just one more length," I thought triumphantly as I made the last turn.

I swam the last length as hard as I could and touched the end of the pool rejoicing. I popped my head out of the water to look around. I was breathing hard, and my face was burning hot.

❻ Uses descriptive details

"Gee," I thought, "no one else has finished yet."

Glancing up at the scoreboard, I wondered for a moment why my time hadn't registered but then decided it was most likely a problem with the timing system.

To my surprise, a white-outfitted official walked up to my lane and knelt down to talk to me.

"Young lady," he said, "I'm afraid you've been disqualified."

❼ Uses dialogue to show the outcome of the event

"Well, how?" I asked. "You can't do anything wrong with a freestyle stroke."

"We just found out your counter skipped a number," the official said. "You really had two more lengths to swim. You've already moved away from the wall, so you can't continue swimming."

I looked up and saw the apologetic faces of my teammates looking down at me and my coaches hollering at my counter. Unexpectedly, I started to laugh. My mind had experienced enough drama for one day.

❽ Presents the writer's reaction to the experience

Do It Yourself

Writing Prompt Write a **personal narrative** about your own experience or something that happened to someone you know.

Purpose To entertain or inform

Audience Your classmates, friends, or family

1 Prewriting

Pick a story. Think about incidents that happened to you or someone you know. Think of interesting or unusual things that are funny, sweet, exciting, or sad. You might recall family stories that have been told over and over. Once you've chosen an event, use the following questions to help you focus your ideas.

- **Why is the event meaningful?** Try to decide why the event stands out in your mind.
- **What is your purpose and who is your audience?** Think about what you want your narrative to do: amuse? teach a lesson? evoke strong emotion?
- **How will you tell it?** Let your memory of the event recall sensory details and dialogue that help you show instead of tell.

2 Drafting

Decide where to begin. You might begin with a colorful, dramatic event. You could also begin by introducing a character or by describing the setting or giving background information.

Keep a time line in mind. You might organize your narrative by the order of events. Or you might begin your draft with an exciting event or dialogue. Just be sure that your reader can follow what is happening. Use transitions to clarify the order and duration of events.

Use descriptive details. Allow your reader to see, hear, and feel what is happening through the words you use.

Keep the same tone. Don't start off being amusing and then shift to a lecture. Decide on the feelings you want to convey and try to stick to that tone.

Wrap it up. Don't leave readers wondering what happened or why it was important to you. Make the outcome clear in your ending.

For information about getting feedback from your peers, see p. 403.

NARRATIVE

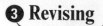

3 Revising

TARGET SKILL ▶Elaborating with Dialogue You can use dialogue to show rather than tell about characters and action. Read your dialogue aloud to make sure that it sounds natural. For more help with revising, review the rubric on page 396.

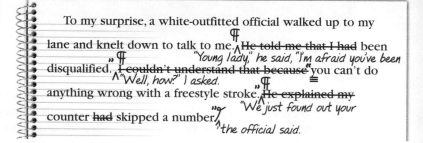

To my surprise, a white-outfitted official walked up to my lane and knelt down to talk to me. ¶ ~~He told me that I had~~ "Young lady," he said, "I'm afraid you've been disqualified." ¶ ~~I couldn't understand that because~~ "Well, how?" I asked. ¶ "You can't do anything wrong with a freestyle stroke." ~~He explained my~~ "We just found out your counter ~~had~~ skipped a number," the official said.

4 Editing and Proofreading

TARGET SKILL ▶Correcting Run-on Sentences When writing about personal incidents, you may create run-on sentences. You can fix run-on sentences by rewriting them as two sentences or by joining them with a semicolon or a coordinating conjunction.

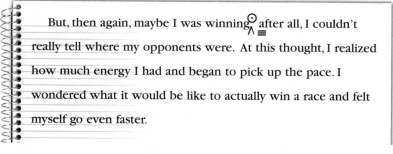

But, then again, maybe I was winning. After all, I couldn't really tell where my opponents were. At this thought, I realized how much energy I had and began to pick up the pace. I wondered what it would be like to actually win a race and felt myself go even faster.

For more on run-on sentences, see pp. 120-121.

5 Sharing and Reflecting

Share your personal narrative with your classmates or family once you're satisfied with the work.

For Your Working Portfolio What did you learn about your experience or about your writing process? Attach your answer to your finished work. Save your narrative in your **Working Portfolio.**

Real World Personal Narrative

When you hear someone telling his or her story, you are hearing a personal narrative. Celebrities and public figures often tell about their experiences in books and TV interviews. You might keep a diary or a journal of important events in your life. People with personal stories to tell have many outlets:

- Autobiographies
- Comedy monologues
- Documentaries
- Diaries
- Magazine profiles
- Letters
- Photographic journals

VIDEO

A Production of Home Box Office and the United States Holocaust Memorial Museum

ONE SURVIVOR REMEMBERS

39 min.

License Copy

VHS

direct cinema limited

Specialized Magazine

Section

Kris Schultz
Twins Magazine

The Sound of My Name

I heard something last week that touched me in a way no one would understand unless they had lived my life. It was not a philosophical anecdote or a piece of advice from a wise elder. It was much more simple than that.

It was my name. Someone said my name.

For the complete text of the article, see MODEL BANK, pp. 622-623.

NONFICTION BOOK

Freedom's Children

Ellen Levine

MAGAZINE ARTICLE

A RACCOON NAMED T65

This ring-tailed home wrecker taught us a few things about life

By Bob Noonan

"Somethin' in the road!" yelled four-year-old Robert from the back seat of our car. We stopped and got out to take a closer look.

No bigger than a quart milk container, the fuzzy gray animal was mostly head and feet. A pair of shiny, alert eyes were set in a black face mask, and a short ringed tail stuck out from under its rump. "It's a young raccoon," I told Robert and his two-year-old brother, Paul.

I picked the animal up cautiously—rabies wasn't the serious

87

NARRATIVE

Student Help Desk

Personal Narrative at a Glance

Beginning	Middle	End
Introduces the incident including the people and place involved	• Describes the event using descriptive details and possibly dialogue • Makes the significance of the event clear	• Tells the outcome or result of the event • Presents the writer's feelings about the experience

Idea Bank

These memory joggers may help you find a good topic for your personal narrative.

I learned a good lesson when . . .

That was the most satisfying . . .

I was so scared when . . .

I really learned how ____ felt about ____ when . . .

What changed my mind about ____ was when . . .

A day that was especially fun for me was when . . .

I've often wondered what happened after . . .

Reading someone else's personal narrative may also inspire ideas. Read a narrative such as Maya Angelou's personal narrative, *I Know Why the Caged Bird Sings* (*Language of Literature,* Grade 9).

Publishing Options

Print Create a display in your school with narratives by you and your classmates.

Oral Communication Read your narrative aloud to a selected audience. Use gestures and voice volume and pitch to convey actions and emotions. Ask your audience to give you feedback about the effectiveness of your presentation.

Online Visit **mcdougallittell.com** for more publishing options.

Friendly Feedback

Questions for Your Peer Reader

- What did you like best about my narrative?
- Which details seemed strong and interesting?
- What seemed significant about the narrative?
- What tone did I use? Was there a place where the tone changed?
- Which parts may need more details?

The Bottom Line

Checklist for Personal Narrative

Have I . . .

___ chosen a clear, well-defined event?

___ made the significance of the event clear?

___ maintained a clear order in the narrative?

___ used descriptive sensory details to describe characters and setting?

___ used dialogue to advance the story or develop characters?

___ used the same tone throughout?

NARRATIVE

Character Sketch

Learn What It Is

A good **character sketch** makes a person come alive for the reader. It allows the reader to draw conclusions from a vivid portrayal of the person's physical attributes, personality, and actions.

Basics in a Box

CHARACTER SKETCH AT A GLANCE

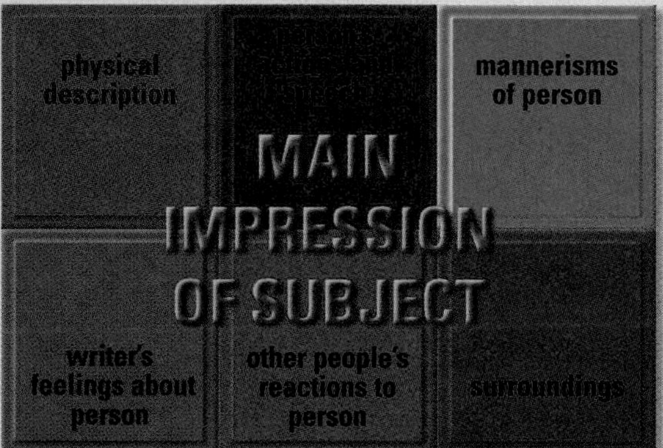

RUBRIC

Standards for Writing

A successful character sketch should

- present a vivid picture of the personality and physical appearance of a person
- establish a dominant, or main, impression of the person
- include dialogue, accounts of mannerisms, descriptions, and other devices that show what the person is like
- reveal the writer's response to the person
- place the person in a context that contributes to the reader's understanding of him or her
- have a clear organizational structure and a strong conclusion

See How It's Done: *Character Sketch*

Student Model
Rashmi Rathor
Naperville Central High School

RUBRIC IN ACTION

A Fly in the House

"I am India," she said. Thinking I misinterpreted her, she repeated the statement. The second time, she pointed her wrinkled finger to her heart and pronounced a single word, "I." As if she was contemplating her word choice, she paused in the middle of the sentence. I hoped that, for once, she forgot what she wanted to say and that I could escape the torture of listening to her drone on incessantly.

❶ Presents a vivid image that captures the mannerisms of the person

She reminds me of a fly. Like the annoying bug that never leaves the house once it has entered, she circled my home, dusting imaginary particles, organizing the desk she just cleaned two minutes before. The only way to force the bug to leave is to slam its life out with a fly swatter. Unfortunately, ridding the house of Aaji is not as easy as killing the fly. My thoughts were interrupted as, all of a sudden, Aaji whispered the word "India" in a thick Indian accent. . . . I realized she longed to return to her home twelve thousand miles away. . . .

❷ This writer clearly states his reaction to the person.

Another option:
- Imply a reaction without stating it directly.

I never wanted to live with Aaji. My dad worked on assignment in Taiwan, my mom found a job in New Jersey, and I inhabited an empty house. Before my parents left, they decided to leave me in the Aaji's care. Though my parents invited Aaji to live with me, she was an intruder in my life.

Every day around five o'clock, Aaji would stand at the foot of the stairs and, in Marati, yell, "Rashoooo, what do you want for dinner?"

❸ Places the person in a context that contributes to the reader's main impression of her.

I thought of my favorite vegetables that my mom made when she lived at home. "Lima beans, spinach, and potatoes," I said. "Any of those suffice." Around seven o'clock, I smelled the spices as they wafted up the stairs. . . . I leaped down the stairs to the kitchen table. Lifting the lid of the steel pot, I saw the steam rise into the air. Before the cloud dissipated, I realized this was not my favorite vegetable. Instead, Aaji prepared the dish that I liked the least: kidney beans. Consumed with hunger, I angrily swallowed the food without moaning to my grandmother about her deceit. In the following days, Aaji always asked me what I wanted for dinner, but each time she would ignore my selection and make something worse than the day before. . . .

Every day for dessert, Aaji prepared *shira.* She always asked, "Rashoooo, do you like it? Does it taste like your mom's *shira?*"

Wanting to wipe the cheerful smile off her face, I always responded, "No, Aaji." Her *shira,* along with the rest of her cooking, was not at all similar to my mom's food. In fact, she was not like my mom in any way. . . . She stands four feet nine inches tall, whereas my mom is five feet three inches. My mom wears pants and skirts, not just dull brown, orange, or blue saris. My mom would not color her hair the shade of tar if she was naturally a brunette. My mom does not wear dentures, and if she did, she would not leave them soaking next to the sink for all the world to see.

My grandmother failed to understand the irritation I felt when she compared herself to my mother. . . . Once, I began to tell my grandmother that she annoyed me. As expected, she interrupted and taught me a lesson about patience. "If you lose your temper," she said, "Laxmi will not bless your family with her presence." She told me that Laxmi, the goddess of wealth and prosperity, enters only quiet, peaceful homes. . . .

My grandmother blessed me with her presence for a short time because, within a year, she returned to India. For the first time, when she was leaving, I embraced both her and her ideas. Once again, I am living in the house with my parents. However, something seems amiss because I do not hear the "buzzzz" of the fly circling my house.

❹ Presents mannerisms and dialogue to show what the person is like

❺ Presents contrasting details to tell more about the person's physical appearance

❻ Ends with a strong conclusion

Do It Yourself

Writing Prompt Choose someone you know or admire, and write a character sketch of that person.

Purpose To depict the personality and appearance of a person

Audience Student magazine, classmates, or people who know the individual

1 Prewriting

Pick a subject. Write the names of all the people that come to mind. You'll probably find it easier to write about someone you know well, but you don't have to. You may choose to write about someone you observe regularly, such as a vendor selling hot dogs on a busy street corner.

Focus on a main impression. Try to decide what your audience most needs to know. How do you feel about the person? What tone will you use to show your feelings? What is the main impression that you want to give?

Pick a setting. If you use a specific incident to reveal your subject's personality, the setting will be determined by the incident. If your sketch covers a longer span of time, you may have to decide which setting will best show the person's traits.

Decide which details contribute to your main impression. Make a list or chart like the following to record specific details.

Physical Appearance	Voice	Mannerisms	Emotions
• bushy beard • lined face	• deep • raspy	• tugs at hat	• friendly • laughs constantly

2 Drafting

You may want to start with an anecdote or a quotation that conveys your subject's personality. You can also just begin writing and let his or her character emerge. You can always refine the beginning later.

As you write, keep thinking, How can I show that? Include dialogue, descriptive details, action scenes, or other elements that show, rather than tell, what your subject is like.

For information about getting feedback from your peers, see p. 411.

DESCRIPTION

3 Revising

TARGET SKILL ▶ Varying Sentences To make your work interesting, avoid including too many sentences of the same length or structure. For more help with revising, review the rubric on page 404.

I leaped down the stairs to the kitchen table. ~~I lifted~~ Lifting the lid of the steel pot, I saw the steam rise into the air. Before the cloud dissipated, I realized this was not my favorite vegetable.

4 Editing and Proofreading

TARGET SKILL ▶ Pronoun-Antecedent Agreement Each pronoun you use should agree with its antecedent in person, number, and gender.

My mom would not color her hair the shade of tar if ~~it~~ she were naturally a brunette. My mom does not wear dentures, and if she did, she would not have ~~it~~ them soaking next to the sink for all the world to see.

For more on pronoun-antecedent agreement, see pp. 190-191.

CHAPTER 19

5 Sharing and Reflecting

Review and revise your character sketch until you're satisfied with it, then **share** it with an audience.

For Your Working Portfolio After you get feedback from your audience, **reflect** on what you learned about writing a character sketch. Did the way you felt about your subject change as you were writing the sketch? If you were starting to write it again, would you choose a different writing strategy or a different approach to the person? Attach your answers to your finished work. Save your character sketch in your **Working Portfolio.**

Real World Character Sketch

Character sketches are easy to find. If you've ever read a magazine article about your favorite celebrity, you've found one. Novels and stories are filled with information about their characters. Obituaries in newspapers sometimes include short character sketches of people. Character sketches can be found in

- newspaper articles
- documentary TV shows
- radio programs

Jacques Cousteau not only spent his life documenting and cataloguing the oceans in books, television and film, but he also made invaluable contributions to the science and technology of underwater studies. Born in Saint-Andre-de-Cubzac, France in 1910, he was named president of the French Oceanographic Campaigns in 1950. In that same year, he took command of the ship Calypso. Seven years later he became director of the Oceanographic Museum of Monaco. Among his inventions were the aqualung diving apparatus and a process for underwater television work. He applied these as head of the Conshelf Saturation Dive Program, in which men lived and worked at extreme depths along the continental

Newspaper Obituary

Sadie Delany, Witness to a Century

Sarah (Sadie) Delany, who died recently at the age of 109, was the oldest survivor of one of America's most remarkable families, the daughter of a man who had been born a slave, and the first colored woman—the term she preferred—ever permitted to teach home economics in white New York City schools.

Miss Delany and her younger sister, Dr. A. Elizabeth (Bessie) Delany, were always celebrated in Harlem, where they lived and flourished from 1916 to 1957, after leaving their native Raleigh, N.C.

For the complete text of the obituary see MODEL BANK, pp. 624-625.

DESCRIPTION

Student Help Desk

Character Sketch at a Glance

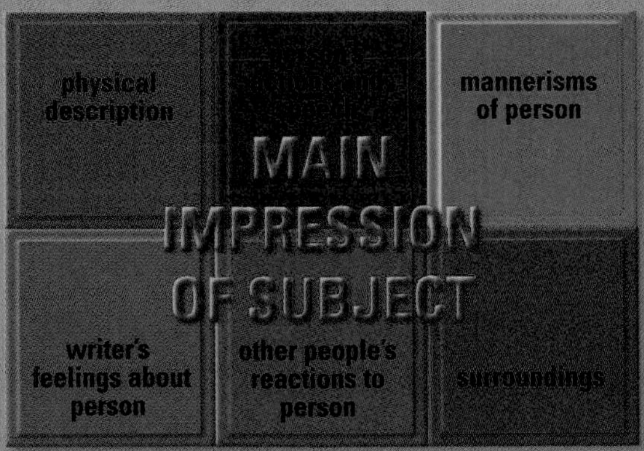

Idea Bank

Where Do I Start?

Look at photographs at home or school.

Make a list of personality traits, such as *sad, funny, bitter, lonely, happy,* or *sweet.* Try to match a person with each word.

List people that you see frequently: your boss and fellow workers (if you have a job) and people that you see regularly at school, at your favorite restaurant, and so on.

Reread a story like "A Christmas Memory" by Truman Capote (*The Language of Literature*, Grade 9). Write a sketch about one of the characters.

CHAPTER 19

Zits by Scott and Borgman

Publishing Options

Print Compile a collection of sketches written by you and your classmates and submit them to a teen or student-writing publication. If possible, group together sketches about similar kinds of people, such as school characters, neighborhood characters, and family members.

Oral Communication Tape-record a reading of your character sketch. Practice reading the sketch several times before recording it. Use different tones and inflections to convey your feelings about the person to your listeners.

Online Visit **mcdougallittell.com** for more publishing options.

Friendly Feedback

Questions for Your Peer Reader

- How would you describe my subject?
- How do you think I feel about the person?
- How does the setting help show the person's traits?
- Which details are most vivid?
- What details are not useful?
- Where should there have been more detail?

The Bottom Line

Checklist for Character Sketch

Have I . . .

___ presented a clear picture of my subject's personality?

___ presented a clear picture of the person's physical appearance?

___ conveyed a main impression of the person?

___ shown how I feel about the person?

___ used devices that show rather than tell?

___ used a setting that contributes to an understanding of the person?

___ used a clear organizational scheme?

___ included a strong conclusion?

Response to Literature

Learn What It Is

How do you feel after you read a book or see a movie? Do you think about the message? Do you identify with a character? Writing a personal **response to literature** essay can help you clarify your feelings about a story or poem. It may also help you gain some insights into your own life as well as the world around you.

Basics in a Box

RESPONSE TO LITERATURE AT A GLANCE

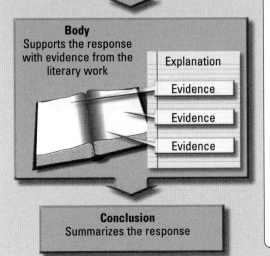

Introduction
Introduces the literary work and includes a clear thesis statement that introduces the response

Body
Supports the response with evidence from the literary work

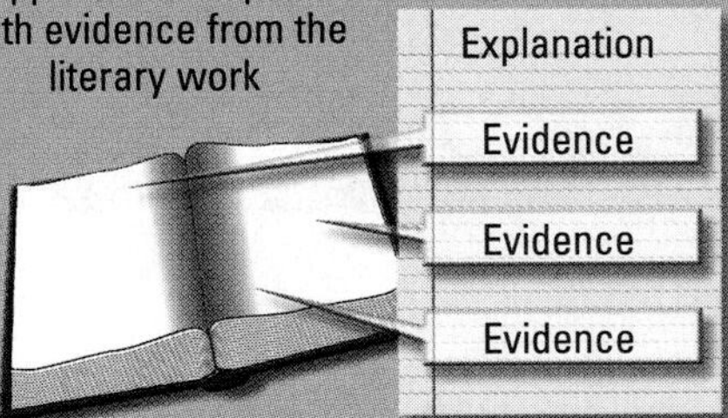

Explanation

Evidence

Evidence

Evidence

Conclusion
Summarizes the response

RUBRIC

Standards for Writing

A successful response to literature should

- include an introduction that identifies the literary work and clearly states your overall response to it
- tell enough about the literary work so that readers can understand your response
- contain clearly described, specific responses to the literary work
- support your statements with quotations and details
- use language and details that are appropriate for your audience

See How It's Done: *Response to Literature*

Student Model
Laura Hausfeld
New Trier High School

RUBRIC IN ACTION

Personal Response to "The Necklace"

In the short story "The Necklace" by Guy de Maupassant, Mme. Loisel, a middle class woman, longs to be rich but finds out that trying to appear rich comes as a wasted sacrifice. When she and her husband get the opportunity to attend a high-class reception, she goes to a friend, Mme. Forestier, to borrow a beautiful diamond necklace. Unfortunately, when Mme. Loisel returns from the reception, the necklace is gone. After she and her husband search everywhere without success, they decide they must replace the necklace. They borrow money from friends and money lenders to pay a jeweler 36,000 francs for a new necklace, which they return to Mme. Forestier.

❶ Identifies the title, author, and main characters of the literary work in the introduction

The couple spend the next ten years working off their debts. Mme. Loisel does heavy housework and her husband works evenings to balance a tradesman's accounts. After the ten years of struggle, Mme. Loisel sees Mme. Forestier and explains what she had done in order to pay for the replacement diamond necklace. It is then that Mme. Forestier informs Mme. Loisel that the necklace was not diamond, but only cut glass.

❷ Tells enough about the story so that readers can understand writer's response

While reading this story I felt great sorrow and sympathy for Mme. Loisel and her husband. I also felt that the story carries two important lessons.

❸ Describes personal response to the story

One of the lessons shown in "The Necklace" is that we should appreciate what we have. Although Mme. Loisel is actually pretty fortunate, she does not appreciate it.

> She grieved incessantly, feeling that she had been born for all the little niceties and luxuries of living. She grieved over the shabbiness of her apartment, the dinginess of the walls, the worn-out appearance of the chairs, the ugliness of the draperies.

Mme. Loisel does not stop to think of all the things she does have but instead thinks of what she does not have—and what is wrong with what she does have: "She would dream of silent chambers, draped with Oriental tapestries and lighted by tall bronze floor lamps, and of two handsome butlers." When the Loisels are paying for the necklace, though, she experiences "the horrible life the needy live." After Mme. Loisel works for ten years, she probably feels she would do anything to have her old life back.

❹ Supports statements with quotations and details

The second lesson is that it is better to be truthful and honest than to lie and hide something. When the Loisels discover the necklace is gone, they decide to cover up for what had happened. Instead of going to Mme. Forestier and explaining, they choose to lie about it. It turns out that if they had told the truth, they could have saved themselves from ten long years of hard work. In the end Mme. Forestier says, "Why, at most it was only worth five hundred francs!" This was a small amount to pay compared to the 36,000 francs the Loisels had spent for the diamond necklace.

"The Necklace" reminded me of a time in my own life when I thought that an alternate plan was preferable to telling the truth. Luckily the consequences of my actions weren't as severe as the ones felt by the Loisels. The story proves in a very powerful way that no matter how much anger or pain it causes, telling the truth is usually the best route to take in solving a problem.

❺ This writer concludes by describing some of her thoughts about life generated by the story.

Another option: Explain how your response changed after careful consideration of the story.

Do It Yourself

Writing Prompt Write a **personal response** to a short story or a poem.

Purpose To explain your reaction to the story or the poem

Audience Your classmates, friends, or teacher

1 Prewriting

As you read, take notes on passages that affect you. Does the story or poem have a theme that reminds you of your own experience? Do you identify with any of the characters? Include page numbers for your future reference.

Decide on a focus for your essay. It may be a character or the setting or the plot. Reread the story or poem to find details and quotations that support your response.

Identify your audience. How much will you need to explain to your audience about the work? Will they know the work? What will they need to know to understand your response?

2 Drafting

Let your reactions to the story or poem shape your writing. In addition, use the following chart in two ways: as a guide for formatting your draft and as a checklist for revision.

Personal Response to Literature

Introduction	Body	Conclusion
• Include the author and title of the work. • Summarize important information such as a story's characters, plot, and setting, or a poem's theme, language, and imagery.	• Begin by stating your general response to the piece of literature. Then explain why you felt as you did. • Quote or summarize specific details and passages to elaborate on your response. You could also include personal experiences that affected your reading.	• Summarize your overall response. OR • Draw a conclusion about the work's significance to you or about its influence on your own life. OR • Explain how your response has changed after careful consideration of the story.

For information about getting feedback from your peers, see p. 419.

3 Revising

TARGET SKILL ►Incorporating Quotations You can make your writing more interesting and more convincing by adding quotations to support the general statements. Look for places in your response where you might ask "Such as what?" or "Why?" Reread the literary piece to find quotations that help you answer those questions. Try to incorporate the quotations smoothly into your own writing. For more help with revising, review the rubric on page 412.

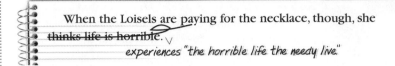

When the Loisels are paying for the necklace, though, she ~~thinks life is horrible~~. experiences "the horrible life the needy live."

4 Editing and Proofreading

TARGET SKILL ►Subject-Verb Agreement Reread your writing sentence by sentence to check that the subject and the verb agree in every case. Be careful when a sentence begins with the word *there.* In that case, look for the subject that follows the verb to decide whether to use a singular or a plural verb.

There ~~is~~ are also two important life lessons that ~~is~~ are told through the story. First, you should appreciate what you have. Second, truth and honesty ~~is~~ are better than lying and hiding something.

For more on subject-verb agreement, see p. 280.

CHAPTER 20

5 Sharing and Reflecting

After you have read your piece of writing several times and checked to see that it is just the way you want it, **share** it with a group of classmates who have read the same story or poem. Compare your ideas.

For Your Working Portfolio Decide on whether writing about the story or poem helped you to understand it better. **Reflect** on how your writing changed your first impressions of the literary work. What might you do a different way the next time you write a response to a story or a poem? Attach your answer to your finished essay. Save them in your **Working Portfolio.**

Real World Response to Literature

Responses to books and stories pop up in many different places. Web sites display book reviews written by readers and critics alike. Many magazines and newspapers have sections devoted to current literature. All you have to do is look.

- Magazines
- Internet
- Book review sections in newspapers
- Essay collections
- TV book discussions and author interviews
- Book clubs

BOOK COVER

SCALE THE HIGHEST PEAKS WITH THE WORLD'S YOUNGEST CLIMBER

within reach
MY EVEREST STORY

Book Review

WITHIN REACH: MY EVEREST STORY

by Mark Pfetzer and Jack Galvin

In May 1996, Mark Pfetzer at age 16 was the youngest climber on Mount Everest to reach 26,000 feet, and his gripping autobiography focuses exclusively on his mountain climbing achievements. Recounted in diary format, Pfetzer's dense but taut story opens during the 1996 Everest expedition, then jumps back to a 1992 advanced camping trip, when his passion for climbing first ignited.

For the complete text of the review, see MODEL BANK, p. 626.

MAGAZINE BOOK REVIEW

The Horn Book Magazine

THE ONLY OUTCAST
Julie Johnston

spent the summer a
Canadian lakesid
1904. Johnston's
out his bare-bo
concerned with
excursions, and
create an endearir
fictional charac
Dickinson we c
humiliated by hi
tendency to stu
expires from
when he acciden
swandive in fro
(and spends n
deeply and h
with her); an
mightily fro
belittling co
"nerves," immaturity, and weak-
ness of character. Contrary to his
... young man—sensitive, self-

INTERNET BOOK REVIEW

L-Net

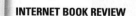

Back | Forward | Reload | Home | Images | Print | Security

Location: http://www.bookreview.com

Soldier's Heart:
Being the Story of the Enlistment and Due Service of the Boy Charley Goddard in the First Minnesota Volunteers
by Gary Paulsen 1998
Ages 12 and up

Thinking war to be an exciting adventure, 15-year-old Charley Goddard lies to get into the Union Army. His first experience with battle brings an immediate change of heart..."Make it stop now!"

Gary Paulsen spares no detail describing the physical horrors, mental anguish turmoil and each battle fought. Charley returns at the age of 20 an old man with a "Soldier's Heart."

RESPONSE TO LIT.

Student Help Desk

Response to Literature at a Glance

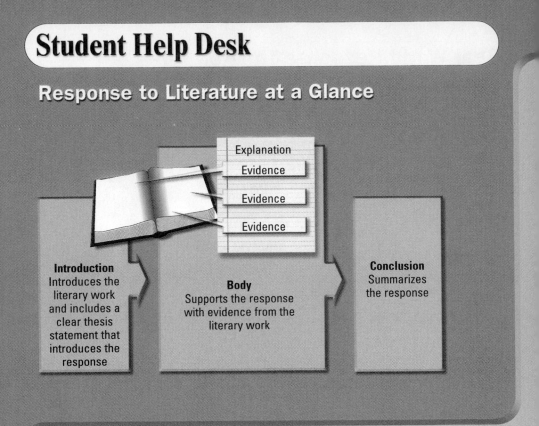

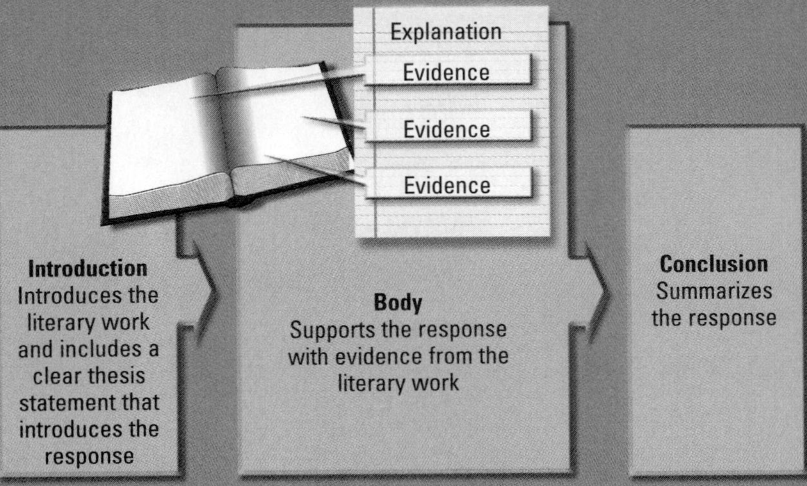

Explanation
Evidence
Evidence
Evidence
Introduction
Introduces the literary work and includes a clear thesis statement that introduces the response
Body
Supports the response with evidence from the literary work
Conclusion
Summarizes the response

Idea Bank

Keep a journal of your reactions to literary works that you have read both in and out of school. Choose one that you had a particularly strong reaction to and write a response essay.

Take another look at a story or a poem that you didn't like or didn't understand. Discuss it with someone who has a different viewpoint. Then write to explore your new understanding of the work.

Reread a story such as "American History" by Judith Ortiz Cofer (*Language of Literature,* Grade 9). Write a response essay that explores the meaning you find in the story.

Publishing Options

Print With a group of classmates, create a dust jacket for a novel that each person has read recently. Collaborate on the artwork for the front cover and a summary of the story for the inside panel. Write sentences for use as quotations for the back cover.

Oral Communication To help you understand a difficult literary work, hold a book or story discussion group with several classmates in which you identify and analyze the artistic elements within the text. Allow each member of the group to share likes and dislikes and any insights or misunderstandings about characters, plot, theme, and so on.

Online Visit **mcdougallittell.com** for more publishing options.

Friendly Feedback

Questions for Your Peer Reader

- How did my piece make you feel about this literary work?
- How would you summarize my general reaction to this literary work?
- What additional details would have helped you understand my response?
- What information was unnecessary?
- How did my response influence your own reactions to this work?

The Bottom Line

Checklist for Response to Literature

Have I . . .

____ identified the type of literature, author, and title?

____ clearly stated my overall response?

____ told enough about the work in the introduction?

____ given specific personal reactions?

____ supported all my points with details and quotations?

____ summarized my response in the conclusion?

Process Explanation

Learn What It Is

Have you ever followed a recipe? Or pressed the Help key on a computer to find out how to complete a task? If so, you've read a process explanation. A **process explanation** tells the reader how to do something or how something works. Each step must be correct and each step must be included, or the results may be disappointing.

Basics in a Box

PROCESS EXPLANATION AT A GLANCE

Part 1
Presents purpose and topic, provides background information, and lists necessary equipment or materials

Part 2
Describes all steps in the process in logical order using transitional words and phrases

Part 3
Summarizes the process and describes the end result or final product

RUBRIC

Standards for Writing

A successful process explanation should

- begin with a clear statement of the topic and your purpose
- explain to readers how to do something or how something works
- present the steps of the process in logical order
- define any unfamiliar words or phrases and provide background information that is essential to the reader's understanding
- use precise language and transitional words to describe each step clearly
- when appropriate, use diagrams or other visuals to help clarify the explanation

See How It's Done: *Process Explanation*

Student Model
Michael Ashkenasi
Whitney Young High School

RUBRIC IN ACTION

How to Paint Drops for a Theatrical Production

When you attend a theater production, your reaction to each scene may be affected by the drop. A drop is a large piece of painted fabric, preferably scrim or muslin. The scrim is raised or lowered at the back of the stage to set the mood of the scene—a backdrop. If the drop is not done well, the success of the play may be at stake. Here are guidelines for creating good-looking drops that will enhance each scene.

❶ Provides background information and defines an unfamiliar term

❷ This writer gives a clear statement of the topic and his purpose after providing background.

Another option: Begin the essay with the topic and purpose.

Creating the drops usually requires a crew of workers. Before starting to plan the drops, find out what kind of crew you will be working with. Discuss the number of hours people can work, the skills needed to do the work, and the actual time available to create the drops. Decide how many drops to use. (This may be affected by the time and talent you have.) Then set up a schedule and assign certain portions of each drop to certain crew members.

Next, measure out the space where the drops will be used and order the scrim. At the same time you can order the other materials you will need: grommets for attaching the drop to a piece of pipe, paints, brushes, pans, drop cloths, and cleaning materials.

❸ Presents the steps of the process in a logical order; lists materials needed

The next two processes will go on at the same time. One process is to design the drops. In designing, the first step is to figure out the tone of the play. Is it cheerful? Sad? Think through the mood of each scene. Choose a color scheme for the drops that fits the mood of that part of the play.

<u>Now,</u> sketch out a picture of what you want each scene to look like. Remember when you were little and you used to try to draw inside the lines? Well, now you're going to have to draw the lines as well. Do a few preliminary sketches, then plot your design on a graph. Draw a picture of what you want it to look like when it's done, colors and all.

❹ Uses transitional words to describe the sequence of each step clearly

At the same time the design process is going on, a scrim must be prepared for each drop. Make sure someone is hemming the drop on all four sides. The bottom must have a pocket for the insertion of a conduit piece that will weigh it down and make it hang properly. The conduit piece will probably be an extremely long, circular piece of metal that is the length of the stage. At the top of the drop, have small slits cut at a foot apart and grommets hammered into the material. These small, metal eyelets will be used to attach the drop to a pipe that will lift and lower the drop during the play. Then, using a special primer paint, prime the drop so it is ready for painting.

❺ Explains fully how to carry out the step

Now you are ready to paint the drop. Attach it to the pipe with some kind of string going through the grommets and tied around the pipe. Lift the pipe to a certain level so you can paint different parts of the drop. Sketch the basis lines and measure out the crucial lines and angles. Try to stay focused and work on large areas of the drop. Don't spend too much time on details. Worry about those later. Take care of the BIG tasks! The little ones will be easier later.

After the paint has dried, go back to touch up the details and make any final adjustments.

Finally, sit back and relax. Your work is done. Enjoy the show!

❻ Concludes by restating the end result

Do It Yourself

Writing Prompt Write a process explanation to show how to do something or how something works.

Purpose To inform or explain

Audience People who are interested in the process

1 Prewriting

Choose a subject you know well. Perhaps you have a special skill or hobby that someone has asked you about. Or you may want to learn a particular process. Once you've chosen your topic, the steps below can help you plan your explanation.

For more help in picking a topic, see the Idea Bank, p. 426.

- **What do you need?** Think through how much information you already have and how much more you will need. Make a list of any materials needed.
- **Who wants to know?** Think about how much your audience will already know. Consider what special terms should be defined and whether any background information will be required.
- **What are the steps?** It may be helpful to make a list of the steps in sequential order before you begin your draft.

2 Drafting

Writing a process explanation is a good way to communicate your enthusiasm for a process you know well. Here are some strategies to make the writing clear and interesting.

Set the stage. Tell your readers what you will be explaining and why it is important.

Be complete. Include all the steps described with enough details for the readers to carry out the steps. List any equipment or materials needed to carry out the process.

Picture it. Use drawings, photographs, diagrams, maps, or other graphic aids to help your readers follow the process.

For more on using illustrations, see "Making Good Graphics," p. 426.

Say when. Use transitional words such as *next, after, before,* or *during* to help your readers understand when each step occurs.

For information about getting feedback from your peers, see p. 427.

PROCESS

3 Revising

TARGET SKILL ▶Considering Audience When writing your process explanation, keep your audience in mind. Are your readers already familiar with the process or do they need explanations of unfamiliar terms? Writing for a general audience may be the best choice. Then you will need to explain technical terms clearly. For more help with revising, review the rubric on p. 420.

> When you attend a theater production, your reaction to each scene may be affected by the drop. *A drop is a large piece of painted fabric, preferably scrim or muslin. The scrim is raised or lowered at the back of the stage to set the mood of the scene—a backdrop.* Here are the guidelines for creating good-looking drops.

4 Editing and Proofreading

TARGET SKILL ▶Parallel Structure Parts of a sentence that serve a similar function should be parallel in structure. Keeping similar ideas parallel helps you present your ideas clearly and logically.

> Discuss ~~how many~~ *the number of* hours people can work, *the* skills *needed to do the work*, and the *actual* time available to create the drops.

For more on parallel structure, see p. 371.

CHAPTER 21

5 Sharing and Reflecting

One way to **share** your process explanation is to have someone read it and actually try to complete the process. Or you might have someone repeat the process to you in his or her own words. In turn, you will find out how successful you were in explaining it.

For Your Working Portfolio After someone has attempted to complete the process that you have explained, **reflect** on what you learned in writing your explanation. What was most difficult about the writing assignment? What was most satisfying? What did you learn about the subject or the process? Attach your answers to your finished work. Save your process explanation in your **Working Portfolio.**

Real World Process Explanation

When you buy a new game, the instructions tell you how to play. Do-it-yourself books provide step-by-step guides for building or fixing things. An article in the encyclopedia shows you the stages of digestion. All of these are process explanations.

- How-to books
- Science magazines
- Instruction manuals
- Package instructions
- Do-it-yourself guides
- Recipes

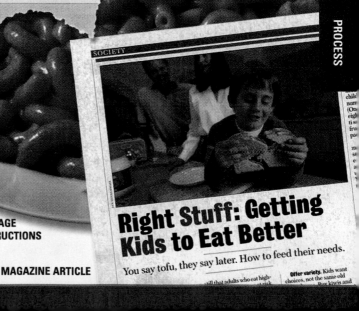

INSTRUCTIONS

VCR Programming

Note: If the VCR does not respond to the remote control POWER button, press ALT on the VCR and try again.

Programming function allows you to pre-set the VCR to record at a later time and date. You can program the VCR to record on up to 12 separate dates and up to a year in advance.

1. Press the SET TIMER button to display the "PROGRAM" screen.
2. Turn the Shuttle Wheel to select "TIME/DATE SET", then press ENTER.
3. In the "TIME/DATE SET" screen, use the Shuttle Wheel and the ENTER button to select the following in the appropriate fields:
   - DATE
   - START TIME
   - STOP TIME
   - CHANNEL

Sunday Magazine Article

Troy Corley
Parade Magazine

Discover Your Family Tree

Finding the roots of your family tree has never been easier than with today's technological tools, ranging from computer programs to genealogy Web sites. Here's how to get started:

Learn what's involved

• Join a genealogy society, take a class, or start with one of the sources below. . . .

Talk with relatives

• Write down family stories that relatives tell you. If they have articles, obituaries, or letters, photocopy them. If they won't part with the documents, write everything down . . .

For the complete text of the article, see MODEL BANK, pp. 627-628.

PREMIUM
Macaroni & Cheese
DINNER

EASY COOK DIRECTIONS:
TOP OF STOVE
- BRING 6 cups water to a rapid boil. Stir in macaroni. Boil uncovered 7 to 10 minutes, stirring occasionally.
- DRAIN. DO NOT RINSE. Return to pan.
- ADD 1/4 cup butter or margarine, 1/4 cup milk and contents of cheese packet; stir well. Makes 3 cups.

PACKAGE INSTRUCTIONS

Right Stuff: Getting Kids to Eat Better

You say tofu, they say later. How to feed their needs.

MAGAZINE ARTICLE

PROCESS

Student Help Desk

Process Explanation at a Glance

Part 1	Part 2	Part 3
Presents purpose and topic, provides background information, and lists necessary equipment or materials	Describes all steps in the process in logical order using transitional words and phrases	Summarizes the process and describes the end result or final product

Idea Bank

Watch someone.	Observe a person in the process of cooking a meal, painting a picture, or some other action.
Talk it through.	With a friend, take turns thinking of a daily activity and describing the steps involved.
Make a list of subjects.	Write down words that would complete this sentence: This is how a _______ works.
Make a list of activities.	Write words or phrases that would complete this sentence: This is how to _______.
Read a selection.	"To Build a Fire" (*Language of Literature*, Grade 9) includes a process explanation. You may get ideas on how to make your own explanation more lively.

CHAPTER 21

Making Good Graphics

A graphic can sometimes show a step more clearly than it can be described in words. However, the graphic must be clear and complete.

- Give the graphic a title.
- Clearly label any rows or columns.
- Identify parts of drawings or photos as needed.
- Use arrows to show directions or to point out features.
- Make sure the graphic will reproduce clearly.

Publishing Options

Print Share your process explanation with a person who shares your interest and who wants to try it.

Oral Communication Demonstrate the process to an audience. Use drawings or actual items to show how the process is done or what the finished result looks like.

Online Visit **mcdougallittell.com** for more publishing options.

Friendly Feedback

Questions for Your Peer Reader

- What is the purpose of my explanation?
- What are the main steps in my process?
- What was the most helpful part of the explanation for you?
- What steps were hard to understand or incomplete?
- What parts seemed unnecessary?

The Bottom Line

Checklist for Explaining a Process

Have I . . .

____ clearly stated the topic and the purpose in the introduction?

____ explained how to do something or how something works?

____ presented the steps of the process in a logical order?

____ defined any unfamiliar words or phrases?

____ provided background information where needed?

____ used precise language and appropriate transitions to describe each step clearly?

Comparison-Contrast Essay

Learn What It Is

You probably have definite preferences in movies, in clothing, and even in friends and pets. You might make a decision between one shoe brand and another by thinking about the differences between the two. Writing a **comparison-contrast essay** can help you evaluate two products, candidates, opinions—any two related subjects—by exploring their similarities and differences.

Basics in a Box

COMPARISON-CONTRAST ESSAY AT A GLANCE

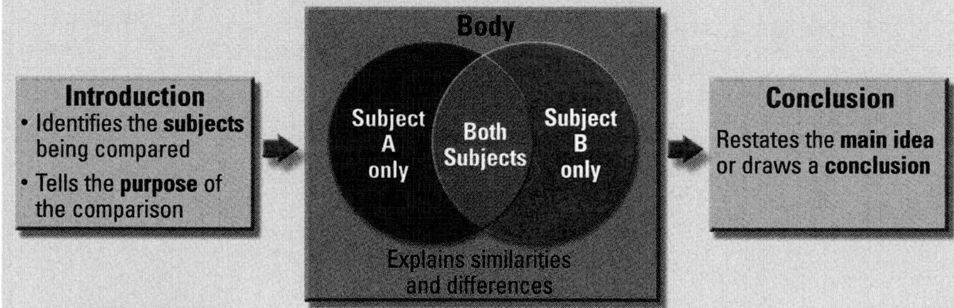

Introduction
- Identifies the **subjects** being compared
- Tells the **purpose** of the comparison

Body

Subject A only | Both Subjects | Subject B only

Explains similarities and differences

Conclusion

Restates the **main idea** or draws a **conclusion**

RUBRIC

Standards for Writing

A successful comparison-contrast essay should

- identify the subjects being compared
- establish a clear purpose for the comparison
- include both similarities and differences, and support them with specific examples and details
- have a clear organizational plan
- contain transitional words and phrases that make relationships between ideas clear
- summarize the comparison in the conclusion

See How It's Done: *Comparison-Contrast Essay*

Student Model
Jeff Moher
Oak Park River Forest
High School

RUBRIC
IN ACTION

Cats versus Dogs

Dogs and cats are both popular household pets, yet people differ drastically in their feelings about these two species. Why do some people say they are "cat people," and others "dog people"? It may be that one animal has a clear advantage over the other. Let's find out.

❶ Identifies the subjects being compared and establishes a clear purpose for the comparison

There is one similarity between the two species—they're both pets. Major differences exist between the two species in intelligence, maintenance, and the level of companionship that each provides.

❷ Clearly identifies the features being compared

First, there is a definite difference in intelligence. As a dog fan, I am sad to say that dogs fail to win this category. Dogs—with a few minor exceptions, such as poodles—are not the brightest of creatures. For example, most cats can be let out of the house to wander the streets and will return home; a dog, on the other hand, would probably chase a skittering leaf into the middle of the street (or at least mine would) and then get lost. Also, cats have the ability to think about something other than food and walks for 24 hours a day. Therefore, I think cats easily win the intelligence test.

❸ This writer uses a feature-by-feature organizational plan, first discussing intelligence in both species.

Another option:

- Use a subject-by-subject plan, first discussing all the characteristics of one subject, then all the characteristics of the other.

Second, there is a definite difference in maintenance. Dogs must be fed, walked, played with, groomed, and petted constantly. However, cats take care of all of this on their own (including petting, because if they want to be petted, they will jam their face into your hand). A cat can be left alone when its owner leaves for a few days, but dogs can't be left alone. They can't regulate their eating, because they're pigs, and there aren't any litter boxes for dogs yet! It is obviously a lot more work to take care of a dog. On the other hand, it is a lot of fun. You can't walk a cat for a mile on a spring night. This is not an easy call, but I say dogs have at least an emotional advantage over cats for maintenance.

COMPARISON

So at this point cats have one point and dogs have one point. The final comparison will be the deciding one.

The third and final comparison is companionship. Both dogs and cats bring pleasure to their owners. Still, although I may get some argument, I think dogs are by far the victor in this one. Most dogs are happy almost all the time, with that dumb-yet-lovable stare on their faces. Dogs greet you at the door, tails in motion, and they will play with you all day. Cats, on the other hand, prefer to be on their own most of the time and with a few exceptions don't usually like a steady diet of people. They interact with people only on their own schedules, which are unpredictable.

Considering all this information, and with apologies to cat people, I think that dogs make better pets than cats. Dogs are truly more fun to have around and are better companions. Why else would they be known as people's best friends? Dogs may be dumb and harder to take care of, but when you come home to a dog who has been waiting for you the whole day and is now wagging his tail at about 100 miles an hour, having a dog is the best experience there can be.

❹ Makes a clear transition to another feature—companionship

❺ Supports the general statement about companionship with evidence—details about how dogs and cats respond to and interact with people

❻ Concludes by summarizing the differences and giving an opinion based on the comparison

Do It Yourself

Writing Prompt Select two subjects and write a **comparison-contrast essay** to show how they are similar and how they are different.

Purpose To clarify or explain

Audience Anyone interested in your subjects

1 Prewriting

Gather ideas for a topic. If you think about the sorts of comparisons you make in everyday life, some ideas should immediately come to mind. Which candidate will you choose in a school election? Do you need to evaluate two products before deciding which one to buy? Should you spend money to see a concert, or should you just buy a recording of the live performance?

For more topics, see the Idea Bank, p. 434.

Choose an organizational pattern. Before deciding which pattern to use, you might want to make a chart similar to the one below. You will also need to decide whether you're going to discuss similarities, then differences, or the other way around.

Subject-by-Subject		*Feature-by-Feature*	
Subject A	*Cats*	*Feature 1*	*Intelligence*
Feature 1	*Intelligence*	*Subject A*	*Cats*
Feature 2	*Maintenance*	*Subject B*	*Dogs*
Subject B	*Dogs*	*Feature 2*	*Maintenance*
Feature 1	*Intelligence*	*Subject A*	*Cats*
Feature 2	*Maintenance*	*Subject B*	*Dogs*

2 Drafting

You can begin writing even if you haven't fully planned out your essays. Writing will help you think your topic through.

In your **introduction,** clearly identify the subjects you are comparing and indicate your purpose for making the comparison. In the body of the essay, include specific details and examples to support the comparison. Be sure to include **transitional words** as you shift from point to point. Summarize your main points in the **conclusion.**

For information about getting feedback from your peers, see p. 435.

③ Revising

TARGET SKILL ►Transitions Use transitional words and phrases to show connections between the ideas in your comparison. Transitions that signal similarities include *in the same way, also, both,* and *similarly.* Transitions that signal differences include *yet, while, on the other hand, in contrast,* and *however.* For more help with revising, review the rubric on page 428.

For example, most cats can be let out of the house to wander the streets and will return home; a dog, on the other hand, would probably chase a skittering leaf into the middle of the street (or at least mine would) and then get lost.

④ Editing and Proofreading

TARGET SKILL ►Sentence Fragments It will be hard for readers to follow your points if you leave sentence fragments in your essay. Be sure that every sentence has a subject and a predicate so that readers will know just what is being discussed.

Dogs must be fed, walked, played with, groomed, and petted constantly. However, cats take care of all of this on their own (including petting, because if they want to be petted, they will jam their face into your hand).

For more on sentence fragments, see pp. 116–117.

CHAPTER 22

⑤ Sharing and Reflecting

There are several ways for you to **share** your essay with others. Depending on its subject, you might use the essay as support in a debate or as the basis of a science, history, or consumer report.

For Your Working Portfolio As you **reflect** on your planning and writing, consider what other points you might have made. Did you change your mind as you gathered information? Could you have supported the other side of an argument? Was your comparison true and convincing? Attach your answers to your finished work. Save your essay in your **Working Portfolio.**

Real World Comparison-Contrast Essay

When you look in the sports section of a newspaper, you may see teams' records weighed against one another. In an advertisement, one car's price may be compared with another's. Newspaper articles may contrast the views of political candidates. Comparisons and contrasts can also be found in

- Consumer magazines
- Scientific articles
- TV commercials
- Movie reviews

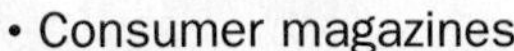

CONSUMER MAGAZINE

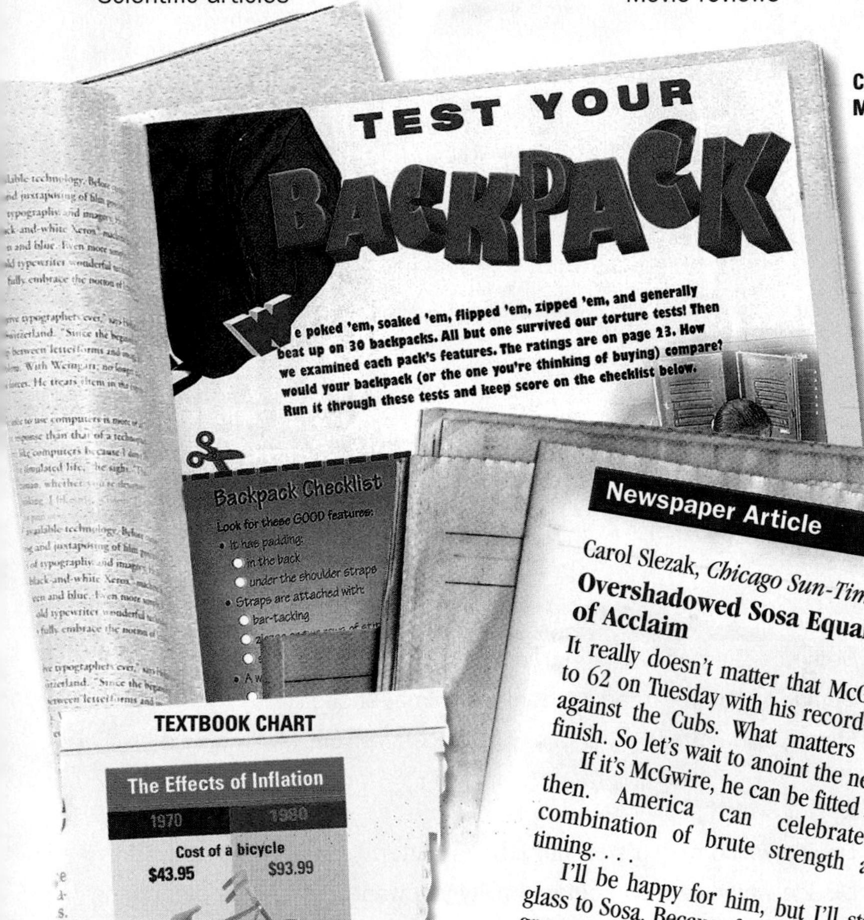

TEST YOUR BACKPACK

We poked 'em, soaked 'em, flipped 'em, zipped 'em, and generally beat up on 30 backpacks. All but one survived our torture tests! Then we examined each pack's features. The ratings are on page 23. How would your backpack (or the one you're thinking of buying) compare? Run it through these tests and keep score on the checklist below.

Backpack Checklist

Look for these GOOD features:

- It has padding:
  - in the back
  - under the shoulder straps
- Straps are attached with:
  - bar-tacking

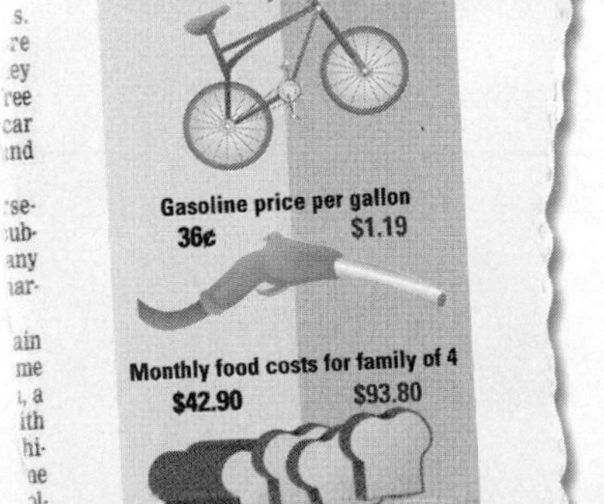

Newspaper Article

Carol Slezak, *Chicago Sun-Times*

Overshadowed Sosa Equally Worthy of Acclaim

It really doesn't matter that McGwire beat Sosa to 62 on Tuesday with his record-breaking blast against the Cubs. What matters is where they finish. So let's wait to anoint the new king.

If it's McGwire, he can be fitted for his crown then. America can celebrate his rare combination of brute strength and precise timing. . . .

I'll be happy for him, but I'll still raise my glass to Sosa. Because from the beginning of the great chase to wherever it might end, only Sosa has unfailingly demonstrated the meaning of grace under pressure.

For the complete text of the article, see MODEL BANK, pp. 629-630.

TEXTBOOK CHART

The Effects of Inflation

	1970	1980
Cost of a bicycle	$43.95	$93.99
Gasoline price per gallon	36¢	$1.19
Monthly food costs for family of 4	$42.90	$93.80

Sources: *The Value of a Dollar; Statistical Abstract of the United States,* 1971, 1976, 1980, 1982–83

Student Help Desk

Comparison-Contrast Essay at a Glance

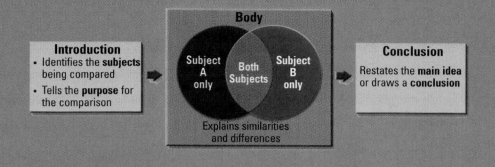

Introduction
- Identifies the **subjects** being compared
- Tells the **purpose** for the comparison

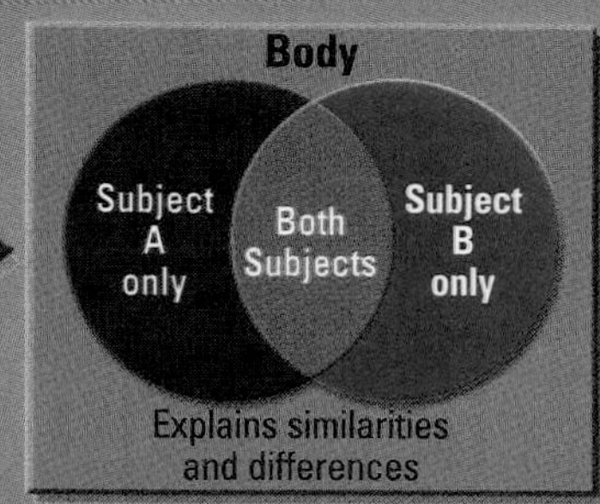

Conclusion

Restates the **main idea** or draws a **conclusion**

Idea Bank

Need a topic for a comparison-contrast essay? Try these ideas.

- Compare the original version of a movie with a recent remake.
- Decide which pet to adopt from an animal shelter.
- Identify the better of two possible places for your family's next vacation.
- Decide which pair of jeans to buy.
- Decide which of two summer jobs is better.
- Decide which extracurricular activity you want to participate in during the school year.
- Decide the best way to raise money for a worthy cause.

Publishing Options

Print With your classmates, assemble a consumer guide of goods and services based on the class's comparison-contrast essays. Keep the guide on file in your school library or media center.

Oral Communication Read your essay to your classmates or anyone else interested in your topic. Use a chart or Venn diagram to make your comparison clear.

Online Visit **mcdougallittell.com** for more publishing options.

Friendly Feedback

Questions for Your Peer Reader

- Is my purpose for comparing these two subjects clear?
- What is the most important similarity between the subjects?
- What is the most important difference?
- What parts of my essay did you find most and least interesting? Why?
- Is my conclusion convincing? Why or why not?

The Bottom Line

Checklist for Comparison-Contrast Essay

Have I . . .

____ identified the subjects being compared?

____ explained why I am making the comparison?

____ included both similarities and differences?

____ supported each point with details and examples?

____ used a clear organizational plan?

____ provided a summary in the conclusion?

COMPARISON

Opinion Statement

Learn What It Is

Have you ever felt that a rule or a situation was unfair? Did the issue move you to express an opinion? Maybe you just shared your feelings with a friend. Another way to make sure your voice is heard, though, is through an **opinion statement,** a written statement in which you express a point of view and back it up with reasons and facts. An effective opinion statement can actually influence how your readers feel about an issue.

Basics in a Box

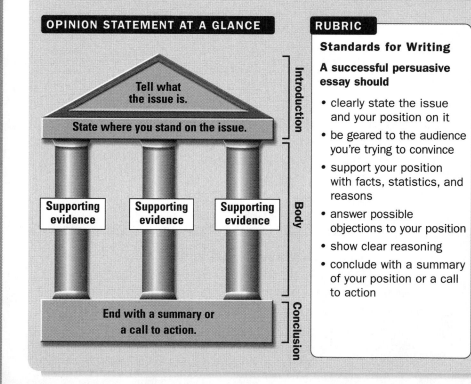

OPINION STATEMENT AT A GLANCE

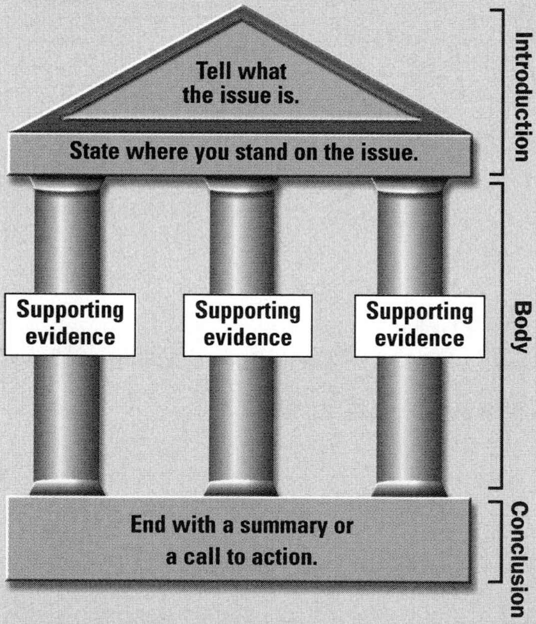

Introduction
- Tell what the issue is.
- State where you stand on the issue.

Body
- Supporting evidence
- Supporting evidence
- Supporting evidence

Conclusion
- End with a summary or a call to action.

RUBRIC

Standards for Writing

A successful persuasive essay should

- clearly state the issue and your position on it
- be geared to the audience you're trying to convince
- support your position with facts, statistics, and reasons
- answer possible objections to your position
- show clear reasoning
- conclude with a summary of your position or a call to action

See How It's Done: *Opinion Statement*

Student Model
Laurel Eskra
Evanston Township High School

RUBRIC IN ACTION

Why I Need a Later Curfew

Dear Mom and Dad,

Now that I'm in high school and my friends are staying out later, I feel very strongly that my curfew should be extended to 1:00 A.M. I know that we've talked about this before, but please take a minute to consider my reasons again.

❶ States the topic and her position on it

On weekdays, I spend 12 hours—almost half of every day—at school because of before- and after-school sports. My only free time is on the weekends, and Saturday and Sunday are barely enough time to relax before the next school week begins. Since I can't ask you to change the length of the weekend, I'm asking you to rethink my curfew.

❷ This writer begins with a strong reason for her appeal.

Other options:
- Quote authorities.
- Cite statistics.

It seems to me that the only reason my curfew is at 11:30 is because you don't want to have to drive me home or be awake any later than that. I appreciate those reasons, but consider how the whole scenario has changed now that my friends can drive me home. You argue that the streets get dangerous late at night because there are not as many cars around, but I see the lack of cars as an advantage. Since there's so much less congestion late at night, it should be much easier to avoid accidents then. I do realize that it's very difficult for you to sleep when I'm out late, but you need to trust that I'll be home when I say I will be—and give me the chance to prove it.

❸ Tailors her writing to her audience

Another objection you've had to an extended curfew is that I don't get enough sleep. Although it's true that I need more sleep than I'm getting, I feel that I'm mature and responsible enough to at least decide my own sleeping schedule. I'm a happy and healthy kid who just wants to live her life. And remember, a 1:00 A.M. curfew means that's the latest I can come home. It doesn't mean that I'll never be home earlier.

❹ This writer states each objection to her position and then answers it.

Other option:
- State all the reasons supporting your opinion and then answer the objections.

"But don't forget the law," your voices warn me. I

know that the law forbids me to be out past midnight because I'm under 17. However, the police crack down on kids who are out walking around, and they don't usually bother those who are driving and on their way home. You know I wouldn't just cruise around until 1:00 A.M. I guarantee that I will be off the streets and at a friend's house by midnight and then come home by 1:00. Since the police seem to accept this situation, I think you should too.

Teachers say that high school is all about preparing kids for college. Though they mean it strictly academically, it also applies socially. I think that kids need to learn to handle freedom before going off on their own. One way they can get this experience is by scheduling their own time. You already know that I'm a fairly responsible kid, and you need to trust me to act sensibly and honor my curfew; otherwise, we can never be totally close and honest with each other.

You're truly wonderful parents, and I hope you'll consider my arguments and agree to extend my curfew.

Your loving daughter,

Laurel

5 Shows clear reasoning

6 Ends with a powerful reason that shows the long-term importance of the issue

7 This writer concludes with an emotional appeal to her parents.

Other options:
- Summarize your main points.
- Issue a call to action.

Do It Yourself

Writing Prompt Write an **opinion statement** in which you explain your stand on an important issue.

Purpose To influence people's beliefs and actions

Audience Anyone interested in or affected by the issue

1 Prewriting

Pick a topic that matters. The most important thing about writing an opinion statement is choosing an issue that you care enough about to stand up and fight for. But also make sure it's an issue that affects others, too. The following activities can help you zero in on your topic.

- **Get the bugs out** Think about situations in your family, school, or community that "bug" you and that you'd like to change.
- **And in this corner** With several friends, brainstorm a list of issues that you argue about.
- **On everybody's mind** Read the Letters to the Editor in your local and school newspapers to find out what issues people care about.
- **Analyze your opinion** Why do you feel the way you do about the issue? What facts or other evidence support your opinion?
- **Gather information** What additional evidence do you need to support your opinion? Will you need to do library research or interview others who have the same opinion?

For more help, see the Idea Bank, p. 444.

Analyze your audience. For an opinion statement to be effective, it has to convince your readers that your opinion is valid. To analyze your audience, ask yourself questions like these.

- What do they already know about your topic?
- What are their positions on it?
- How might you address any opposing views?
- What reasons might they find convincing?

Consider the tone of your statement. Would a humorous or serious tone be more effective with your audience? Which approach would you be more comfortable using?

2 Drafting

Pull it together. Here are two ways to present your arguments and respond to possible objections.

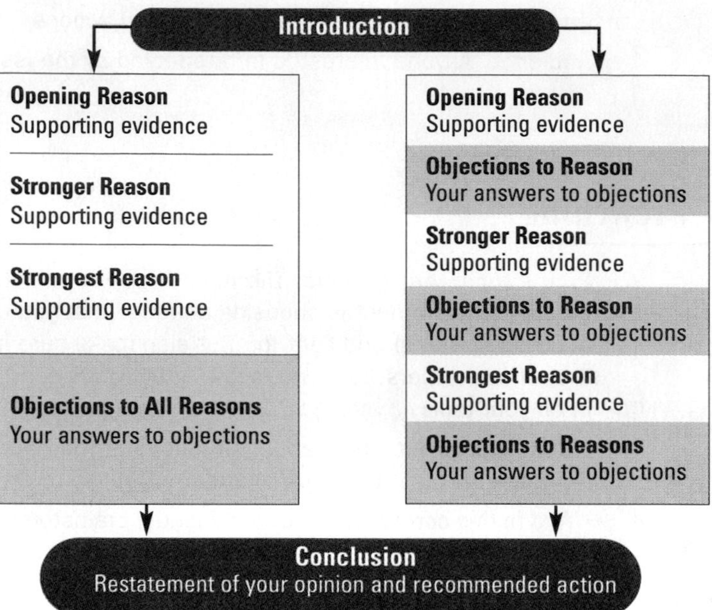

Support your arguments. To get your readers to support your cause, you need to elaborate your statements with convincing evidence.

Ways to Support Your Arguments	
Facts	statements that can be proved by consulting a reference work or an authority
Statistics	facts that are stated in numbers
Examples	specific instances that prove your point
Observations	events or situations you have seen personally
Anecdotes	brief stories that illustrate your point
Quotations	statements from authorities

For more on elaboration, see pp. 354–357.

Watch your language. Beware of using biased language and faulty reasoning.

- **Loaded Language** Use with caution. Be aware of the emotional connotations of words. ("John is clever" versus "John is sly.")
- **Facts and Opinions** Don't confuse them. Opinions are personal beliefs that need to be supported by facts. (Fact: "Chocolate is a source of carbohydrates." Opinion: "Chocolate tastes good.")
- **Vague Statements** Avoid using words such as *good, bad, right,* and *wrong* unless you can accompany them with logical reasons.

Avoid Illogical Arguments

Circular reasoning	Don't try to prove a statement simply by repeating it in different words. ("Passing this law is essential because we need it.")
Overgeneralization	Don't make a statement that is too broad to prove. ("Everybody likes pizza.")
Either/or fallacy	Don't state that there are only two alternatives, when there are many. ("Either we raise taxes or the schools will close.")
Cause-and-effect fallacy	Don't assume that because one event follows another, the second event caused the first. ("It rained because we washed the car.")

For information about getting feedback from your peers, see p. 445.

3 Revising

TARGET SKILL ►Revising for Clarity For your arguments to be persuasive, they must make sense. Be sure that connections between your statements are clear. Include transitional words such as *although, since,* and *for that reason* to help readers make the right connections. For more help with revising, review the rubric on page 436.

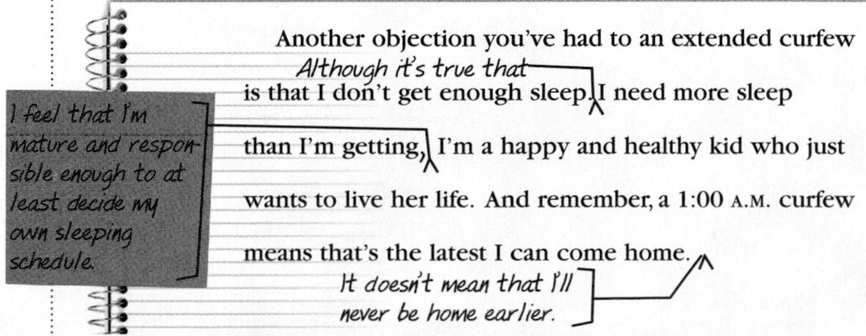

Another objection you've had to an extended curfew
Although it's true that
is that I don't get enough sleep. I need more sleep
than I'm getting, I'm a happy and healthy kid who just
wants to live her life. And remember, a 1:00 A.M. curfew
means that's the latest I can come home.
It doesn't mean that I'll never be home earlier.
I feel that I'm mature and responsible enough to at least decide my own sleeping schedule.

OPINION

4 Editing and Proofreading

TARGET SKILL ▶Sentence Fragments In an opinion statement, your arguments must be complete, and so must your sentences. As you edit, look for incomplete sentences, or fragments. Combine sentence fragments with whole sentences. Be sure to change capitalization and punctuation marks as needed.

You argue that the streets get dangerous late at night. Because there are not as many cars around. But I see the lack of cars as an advantage. Since there's so much less congestion late at night. It should be much easier to avoid accidents then. I do realize that it's very difficult for you to sleep. When I'm out late. But you need to trust that I'll be home when I say I will be.

For more on fragments, see pp. 116–117.

5 Sharing and Reflecting

You might present your opinion statement as a speech. Or you might **share** your views in a roundtable discussion with other classmates who have opinions on the same topic. You might also design a poster that summarizes the main idea of your statement.

For Your Working Portfolio After you present your opinion, **reflect** on what you learned about writing, about your topic, and about yourself. Did your opinion change as you wrote your essay? How was your position strengthened or weakened by your readers' responses? What would you do differently next time? Attach your answers to your finished work. Save your opinion statement in your **Working Portfolio.**

Real World Opinions

Persuasive messages are everywhere you look. You may read a letter to the editor in a newspaper, or you may write one yourself. Your school newspaper may print opinion pieces about important school issues. Some of the places you can find persuasive writing in the real world include the following.

- school and community newspapers
- magazine articles and advertisements
- junk mail advertisements
- Internet
- newsletters
- public service posters

PUBLIC SERVICE AD

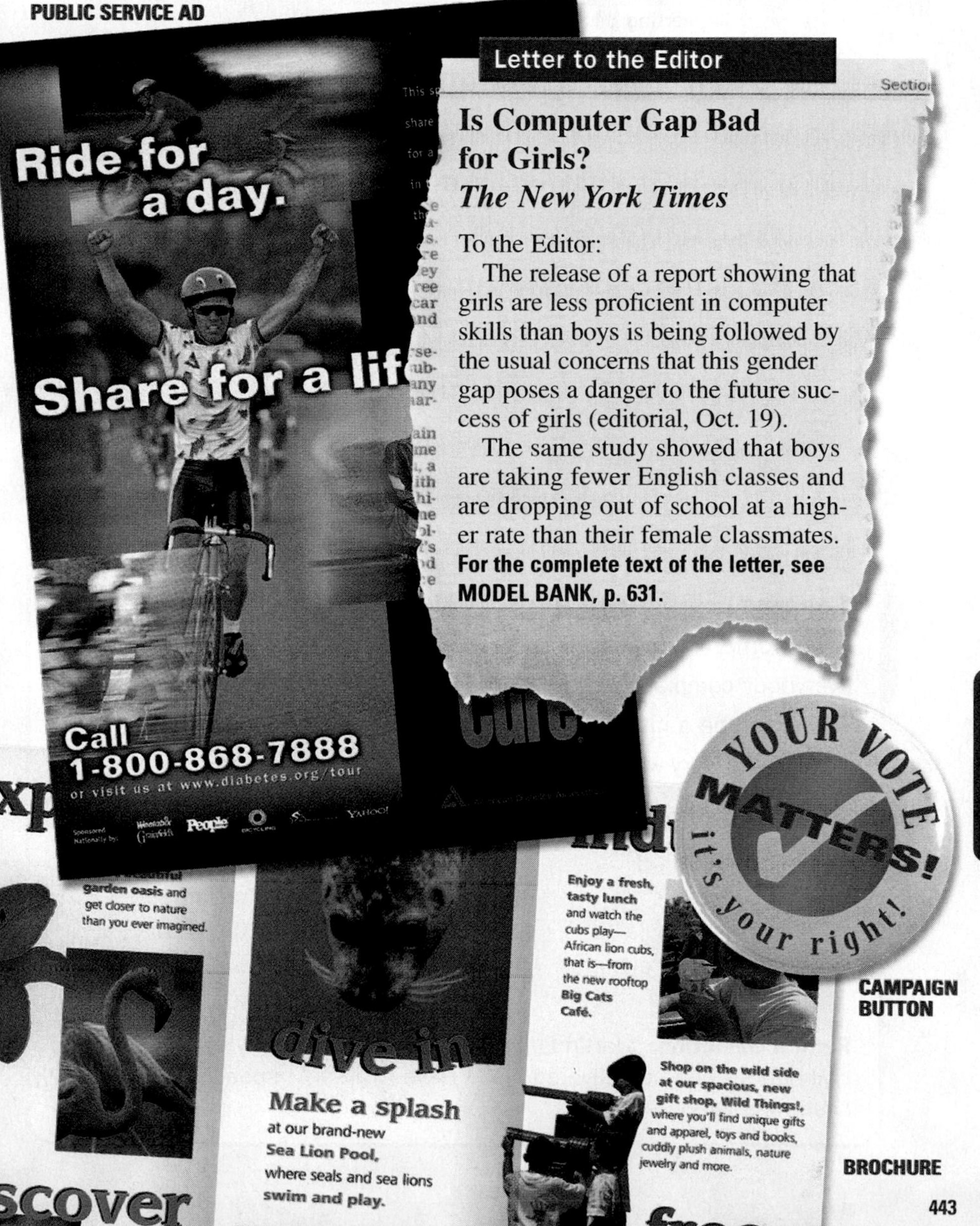

Ride for a day.
Call 1-800-868-7888
or visit us at www.diabetes.org/tour
YOUR VOTE MATTERS! it's your right!
garden oasis and get closer to nature than you ever imagined.
dive in
Make a splash at our brand-new Sea Lion Pool, where seals and sea lions swim and play.
Enjoy a fresh, tasty lunch and watch the cubs play— African lion cubs, that is—from the new rooftop Big Cats Café.
Shop on the wild side at our spacious, new gift shop, Wild Things!, where you'll find unique gifts and apparel, toys and books, cuddly plush animals, nature jewelry and more.
free

Letter to the Editor

Is Computer Gap Bad for Girls?

The New York Times

To the Editor:

The release of a report showing that girls are less proficient in computer skills than boys is being followed by the usual concerns that this gender gap poses a danger to the future success of girls (editorial, Oct. 19).

The same study showed that boys are taking fewer English classes and are dropping out of school at a higher rate than their female classmates.

For the complete text of the letter, see MODEL BANK, p. 631.

CAMPAIGN BUTTON

BROCHURE

Student Help Desk

Opinion Statement at a Glance

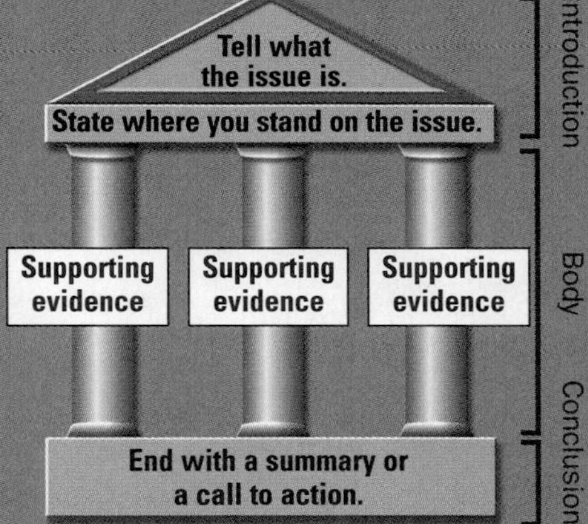
Tell what the issue is.
State where you stand on the issue.
Supporting evidence
Supporting evidence
Supporting evidence
End with a summary or a call to action.
Introduction
Body
Conclusion

Idea Bank

How Do I Get Started?

Fill in the Blanks. Completing these sentences might trigger some topic ideas.

If we don't do something about ____________ soon, ____________________.

What worries me most is ______________________________________.

Everybody complains about ____________________________________.

This would be a much better world if ____________________________.

I get really angry when I think about ____________________________.

Try It on for Size. See if one of these issues bothers you enough to write about.

school dress	speed limits	racism
homeless people	gang activity	the media
rights of in-line skaters	censorship of music	water pollution
global warming		

Read a Selection. Martin Luther King, Jr., shared many opinions about civil rights when he delivered his "I Have a Dream" speech (*Language of Literature,* Grade 9).

CHAPTER 23

Publishing Options

Print Submit your opinion statement to your school or local newspaper.

Oral Communication Present your opinion statement in a debate with a classmate who has an opposing view regarding the same issue.

Online Visit **mcdougallittell.com** for more publishing options.

Friendly Feedback

Questions for Your Peer Reader

- Which of my points were most convincing?
- Which statements need more explanation?
- What other arguments can you think of that support my position?
- How would you argue against me?
- What did you learn from reading my opinion statement?

OPINION

The Bottom Line

Checklist for Opinion Statements

Have I . . .

____ clearly stated the topic and my position on it in the introduction?

____ taken my audience's knowledge and needs into account?

____ supported my opinion with facts and other evidence?

____ answered possible objections?

____ used logical reasoning?

____ summed up my reasons and called for action in the conclusion?

Short Story

Learn What It Is

Creative writing can take different forms, depending on what you want to emphasize—plot, characters, mood, language—or what you think will best communicate your ideas. This chapter will concentrate on the short story, but it will also show how ideas can be expressed through poetry and drama.

A **short story** is meant to entertain, but it may also explore ideas such as truth, right or wrong, or loyalty. You will find stories everywhere: in magazines, videos, ballads, books, and television.

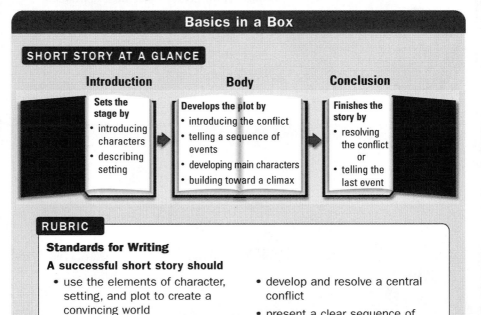

Basics in a Box

SHORT STORY AT A GLANCE

Introduction

Sets the stage by
- introducing characters
- describing setting

Body

Develops the plot by
- introducing the conflict
- telling a sequence of events
- developing main characters
- building toward a climax

Conclusion

Finishes the story by
- resolving the conflict

or
- telling the last event

RUBRIC

Standards for Writing

A successful short story should
- use the elements of character, setting, and plot to create a convincing world
- use vivid sensory language, concrete details, and dialogue to create believable characters and setting
- develop and resolve a central conflict
- present a clear sequence of events
- maintain a consistent point of view

See How It's Done: *Short Story*

Student Model
Tom Taylor
Darien High School

RUBRIC IN ACTION

Frank and the Guy From Planet 20

Frank found it hard to concentrate on his homework with a fleet of Craxans chasing after them at just over Warp 37. Q-11 was a great pilot, but the Craxans were great marksmen, and the ship rocked with their laser fire.

❶ Immediately introduces characters and setting

"Are you sure we're not going to get killed?" Frank asked, bending over to pick up his pencil. Trying to finish his homework neatly in Q-11's XP-38 was even more impossible than trying to finish it on the bus.

"Don't worry," Q-11 said. "We're just two light-years from the wormhole. The Craxans won't follow us through there. That's good, because this wormhole will take us back to our galaxy in about a third of the time it would take under normal hyperspace."

❷ Uses dialogue to advance the plot

Other options:
- Use more sensory language.
- Develop characters more extensively.

"Oh." Frank still didn't get half of what Q-11 said, but he liked him, and he liked spending his lunchtime with Q-11 like this.

The ship rumbled, and Frank broke the tip off his pencil. "Rats. Are we in trouble?"

"Naw, not really. We just lost 10% engine efficiency. We might be slightly late for class."

That was OK. History was the first class after lunch, and kids were usually late for it. Frank looked out the window and saw a blue spiraling cloud with millions of white dots being sucked into it. "Is that our wormhole?"

"Yep," said Q-11. "Sorry, you Craxan dopes! Time for me to hand in my history homework!"

❸ Develops a central conflict

They were swirling into the blue cloud. The world outside the ship stretched itself into a single ray of light that shot off into the distance. They rode this ray at a staggering speed.

❹ Plot builds to a climax.

Q-11 spun in his chair. "Was that fun or what?"

"Yeah, it was fun," Frank said. "It's always fun." Things had quieted to a point where he might get

STORY

some work done. "Give me a hand. I forget what she means when she says, 'Manifest Destiny.'"

"It's like when American settlers moved west and conquered the Indians who were in their way. Survival of the fittest, as the Craxans would say."

Frank looked up when he was finished writing. "How come you're so good at history?"

"I like learning about your planet. It's interesting. Earth's history is a lot more complicated than Planet 20's history."

"What?" Frank asked. "You guys have been around eons longer than us."

"Yeah, that's true, but we're a lot less complicated. On Planet 20 there is only one culture, so our history is much simpler. But on your own small planet—"

Frank shot a frown at Q-11. "Hey, watch that. It's bigger than Venus!" Frank realized that that wasn't saying much. "Shut up. I like my planet."

Q-11 sighed. "I like it too. I'm saying that you've got a heck of a lot to see on that one tiny planet."

"I'll accept that," Frank said.

Ten minutes later they were in orbit around Earth. Frank waved his right arm in frustration. "What time is it? My watch stopped in that time tunnel."

"Wormhole," Q-11 said. "In town, it's 12:34."

"Cool!" Frank said. He looked at Q-11. "I still don't get how we can spend a day playing in space and still get back to Earth about half an hour after we left."

"Don't worry," Q-11 said. "It's science."

"Geeze," said Frank. "What isn't?"

The two friends got into the transporter and appeared behind a group of trees in the schoolyard thirty seconds before the bell rang. They ran inside and handed in their homework to Mrs. Travers.

5 Resolves events of plot clearly

Do It Yourself

Writing Prompt Write a **short story** based on a conflict.

Purpose To entertain

Audience Your classmates and friends

1 Prewriting

Find a story idea. Can you elaborate on something unusual that happened to you or to someone else? Can you build a story around something you overheard at a shopping mall or a sports event?

Expand on the idea. Whatever idea you choose, your story will be more believable if you can provide many details about characters, setting, and plot. Use the following suggestions to help you develop your idea into a story:

- **Think who (narrator, characters).** Who will be telling the story? What other characters are needed? Who is the main character?
- **Think where (setting).** What is the setting of the story? How will the setting affect the plot?
- **Think feeling (mood).** Is your story scary? funny? sad? bitter?
- **Think when (time, organization).** What happens first? next? last?
- **Think what and why (plot).** What is the problem? Why did it occur? What will solve it?

2 Drafting

A short story often begins by introducing the characters and setting and then leads to a conflict. However, you may want to begin in the middle of the action and focus on your characters a bit later. No matter how you choose to develop your ideas, it's important to begin writing. Then you can see where the story takes you. As you write, use the suggestions below to make your characters, setting, and plot seem real to the reader.

Use sensory language. Don't just say that the day was hot. Tell how it felt on your characters' skin or how it affected their spirits.

Use dialogue. Make a character's speech fit the individual—stuffy, slangy, prissy, sour, cheerful—and let the characters' words show their actions and feelings.

Use description. Use details that help show what is happening in the story. For example, a broken window may reveal a break-in, or a missing button on a coat may be evidence of a struggle.

For information about getting feedback from your peers, see p. 455.

3 Revising

TARGET SKILL ▶Consistency in Point of View Once you have chosen a narrator and a point of view, be careful not to change them in the middle of your story. For example, the author of this short story used the third-person limited point of view; that is, the story is seen through Frank's eyes. Readers can be told Frank's thoughts, but not those of other characters. For more help with revising, review the rubric on page 446.

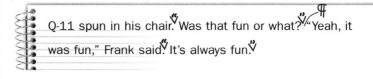

"Oh." Frank still didn't get half of what Q-11 said, but ~~I~~ he liked him, ~~Q-11 liked Frank, too~~ and he liked spending his lunchtime with Q-11 like this.

4 Editing and Proofreading

TARGET SKILL ▶Punctuating Dialogue When you are writing dialogue, remember to use quotation marks and to start a new paragraph each time the speaker changes.

Q-11 spun in his chair. "Was that fun or what?" ¶ "Yeah, it was fun," Frank said. "It's always fun."

For more about punctuating dialogue, see p. 262.

CHAPTER 24

5 Sharing and Reflecting

Find an appropriate audience for your story and read it to them. Use the tone of your voice to establish the emotions of the characters. You can also use your voice to slow the action of your story or speed it up. Have your peers analyze how this technique affected your presentation.

For Your Working Portfolio After this sharing, **reflect** on what you have learned in writing the story. Did any of the reactions of the audience surprise you? What about your writing process? Did you find yourself reshaping the characters or the mood of the story as you got into it? Did your plot take an unexpected twist as you wrote your first draft? Attach your answers to your finished work. Save your short story in your **Working Portfolio.**

Learn What They Are: *Poems and Dramatic Scenes*

Short stories are not the only kind of creative writing you can do. Two other possibilities are poems and dramatic scenes. Each of these forms calls upon your skills of language and imagination, but each form has its own unique demands.

Basics in a Box

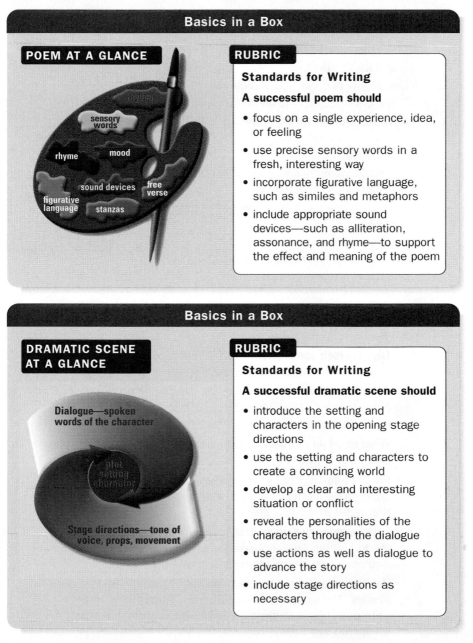

POEM AT A GLANCE

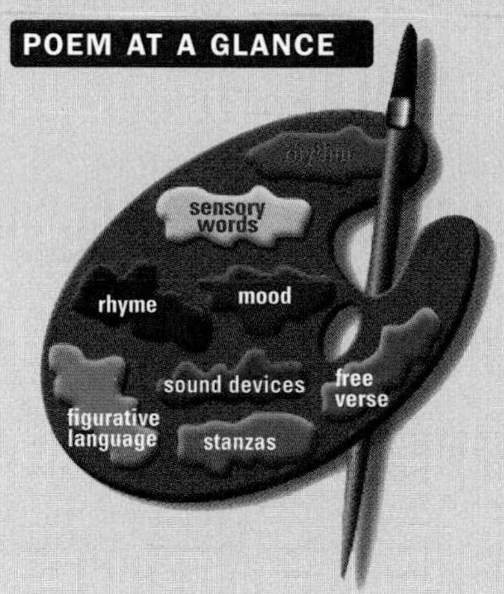

RUBRIC

Standards for Writing

A successful poem should

- focus on a single experience, idea, or feeling
- use precise sensory words in a fresh, interesting way
- incorporate figurative language, such as similes and metaphors
- include appropriate sound devices—such as alliteration, assonance, and rhyme—to support the effect and meaning of the poem

Basics in a Box

DRAMATIC SCENE AT A GLANCE

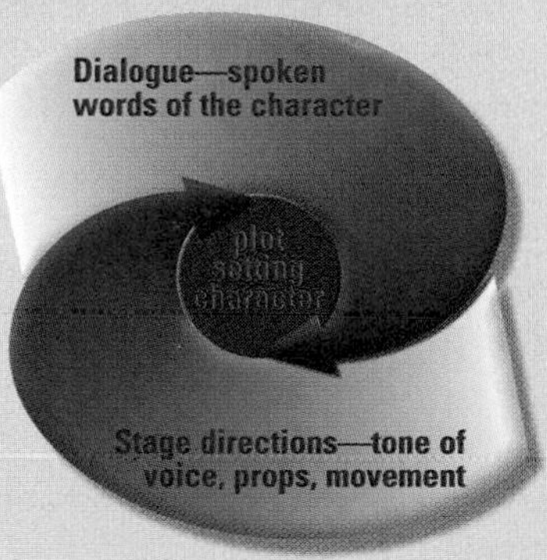

RUBRIC

Standards for Writing

A successful dramatic scene should

- introduce the setting and characters in the opening stage directions
- use the setting and characters to create a convincing world
- develop a clear and interesting situation or conflict
- reveal the personalities of the characters through the dialogue
- use actions as well as dialogue to advance the story
- include stage directions as necessary

See How They're Done

Poem
Christie Sanchez
Yorktown High School

Abuela

Quiet buzzing of a rotating fan,
Saturday afternoon
spreads the aroma thickly around the house—
of yellow rice, chicken, and chorizo.
Spanish soap opera in the room adjacent.
A quiet laundry machine spins humble dignity—
in the back room.
The woman works like a bee—
sister, grandmother, wife, but always mother.
The savor on the hot stove
is wafted out the window into a hot tropical summer,
with her jabbering nonstop talk—
always there, yet becoming more distant,
carrying lost memories far away.

GUIDELINES IN ACTION

❶ Focuses on a single experience—Saturday afternoon

❷ Appeals to senses (smell and sound)

❸ Uses figurative language (personification)

❹ Uses alliteration (**w**afted, **w**indow) and assonance (h**o**t, tr**o**pical)

Tips for Writing a Poem

- **Give yourself some quiet time.** Let memories, songs, and emotions run through your mind. Reflect on your ideas.
- **Jot down ideas.** Write as much as you can about the ideas that come to mind. Read what you've written, and circle any interesting subjects or details that might lead to a poem.
- **What mood do you want to express?** Do you feel happy or sad about the topic? What images could help you show that mood?
- **Choose a focus.** Choose an interesting detail or image from your notes to be the focus of your poem. You might consider using that detail in the first line.
- **Experiment with sounds.** Use devices such as **alliteration** (**f**elt the **f**ury of the **f**ire) and **assonance** (p**ou**nd on the gr**ou**nd) to add rhythm to your poem and help enhance the mood.
- **Use figurative language.** Describe your topic in new ways with **similes** (The woman works like a bee), **metaphors** (His eyes were sparkling blue pools), and **personification** (The sea whispered sad tales).

Dramatic Scene (excerpt)
David Lester
Truman High School

GUIDELINES IN ACTION

On the Road Again

Characters: Jeff, *a charming, irresponsible fellow;* **Lucinda,** *sixteen, energetic and aggressive;* **Luke,** *thirteen, the shy youngest of the family.*
Scene: *The kitchen in a small apartment.*

Jeff. Good meal, as always. It's a perfect intro to my wonderful news. (*The two others freeze.*) I've got a chance for a swell deal in a great new business.
Lucinda. (*suspiciously*) Where's this deal going to be?
Jeff. That's the very best part, honey. Sunny California!
Lucinda. (*pounding her fists on the table*) No! I'm not going! Not this time! I love this school and I'm not leaving till I graduate! (*She runs from the room.*)
Jeff. (*startled, but recovering quickly*) Chee! Well, she'll get over it when we're rich. How about you, Luke? Doesn't California sound great . . . (*he realizes Luke is crying*) What's the matter, son?

1. Introduces characters and setting in the opening stage directions
2. The characters' names are set off, and actions are shown, in parentheses.
3. Develops a clear and interesting conflict
4. Uses action as well as dialogue to advance the story

Tips for Writing a Dramatic Scene

- **Develop your characters.** Give your characters names, ages, physical characteristics, speaking styles, and personalities.
- **Choose a setting.** When and where does the scene take place?
- **Sketch out the plot.** What is going to happen in the entire play? What will the sequence of events be in this scene?
- **Create clear stage directions.** What kind of lighting and props are needed? How will the characters speak and move on stage?
- **Write the dialogue.** In a dramatic scene, dialogue is the main device for moving the story along. It is also the main device through which you show characters' personalities and attitudes.
- **Plan the action.** Actions are also needed to advance the plot. You may need to have characters carry out certain actions while on stage or have them leave the stage.

Student Help Desk

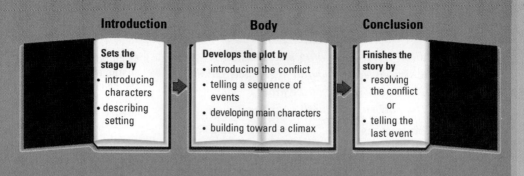

Short Story at a Glance

Introduction	Body	Conclusion
Sets the stage by • introducing characters • describing setting	**Develops the plot by** • introducing the conflict • telling a sequence of events • developing main characters • building toward a climax	**Finishes the story by** • resolving the conflict or • telling the last event

Idea Bank

- **Start with a conflict.** Invent your own conflict, pick one from the headlines, or think of conflicts among the people you know.
- **Let something special inspire you.** Think about a person, pet, or object that you care about. Pick one to write a story about.
- **Make a "what if" list for your story.**
  —What if you got the starring role in a play?
  —What if your family lost everything overnight?
  —What if your pet started talking?
  —What if you found a million dollars in an old trunk in the park?
- **Read literature.** Read a short story such as "The Open Window" by Saki (*Language of Literature,* Grade 9) to see how one author uses characters, setting, dialogue, and details to develop the plot.

Publishing Options

Print Submit your short story to your school's literary magazine.

Oral Communication Read your story aloud to a small group. Or turn it into a dramatic scene and ask friends to help you act it out for an audience.

Organize a class or school poetry slam, a competition in which poetry is read or performed and evaluated by a panel of peer judges.

Online Visit **mcdougallittell.com** for more publishing options.

Friendly Feedback

Questions for Your Peer Reader

- How would you define the mood of this story?
- Which character seemed most real?
- What part of the story needed to be shown through dialogue or action scenes?
- What do you think of the way the story begins? How might the beginning be improved?
- What part is not clear to you?

STORY

The Bottom Line

Checklist for a Short Story

Have I . . .

____ used techniques such as vivid sensory language, concrete details, and dialogue to create believable characters and setting?

____ developed and resolved a central conflict?

____ presented a clear sequence of events?

____ maintained a consistent point of view?

____ used the elements of character, setting, and plot to create a convincing world?

Research Report

Learn What It Is

Writing a **research report** gives you an opportunity to learn about a topic in depth by investigating a question or an idea. To write this kind of report, you must gather information from a variety of sources and then present what you've learned clearly and accurately.

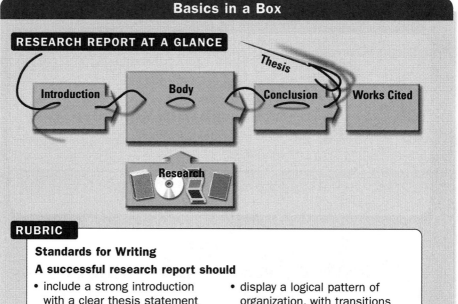

Basics in a Box

RESEARCH REPORT AT A GLANCE

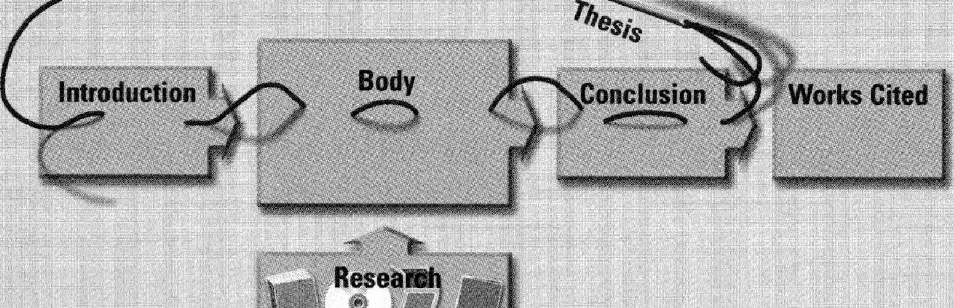

RUBRIC

Standards for Writing

A successful research report should

- include a strong introduction with a clear thesis statement
- present evidence from primary and/or secondary sources to develop and support ideas
- credit the sources of information
- display a logical pattern of organization, with transitions between ideas
- conclude with a satisfying summary of ideas
- include a correctly formatted Works Cited list at the end

See How It's Done: *Research Report*

Alderson 1

Steve Alderson

English I

Mr. Wilder

14 April 2000

Softball: A Game as Exciting as Hardball

Take me out to the ball game
Take me out to the crowd.

If someone took you out to a ball game and the crowd wasn't packed into a stadium that held 40,000 people or more, there is a good chance that you were taken to a softball game. When an attempt was made to reestablish a professional softball league in 1997, the opening game was played in a stadium that held just over 2,000 people (Kennedy). The media have never given the attention to softball that they have to hardball, and many people think of softball as an inferior type of baseball. In reality, though, it is played by far more people than hardball. In the magazine Sporting Goods Business, Marianne Bhonslay reported that in 1997 there were 13.3 million registered baseball players and 22.1 million softball players. In fact, in its "fast pitch" form, softball is every bit as exciting, competitive, and tough as its older cousin.

❶ This writer opens with familiar song lyrics that instantly evoke baseball.

Other options:

- Tell an anecdote.
- Present a startling fact.
- Introduce the topic immediately by presenting the thesis statement.

❷ Includes a clear thesis statement

Although major-league baseball began in 1876, the game itself "was not invented; it evolved" (Thorn and Palmer 5). On the other hand, we know exactly when, where, and how softball began. According to The Worth Book of Softball, on Thanksgiving Day in 1887 a small group of young men were gathered in a boat club's gymnasium in Chicago. They were listening to a series of telegrams giving the score of the football game between Harvard and Yale. At one point, one man threw a boxing glove across the gym and another

❸ Supports ideas with information from credited sources

REPORT

Alderson 2

picked up a broom handle and hit it back. A reporter named George Hancock then yelled, "Let's play ball," and they did (Dickson 46-47).

This beginning suggests that the greatest similarity between softball and baseball is the fundamental fact that the rules are much the same. A person who knows how to play baseball knows how to play softball, and vice versa. In fact, the differences between the games are so minor that Joe Brinkman and Charlie Euchner maintain that "any baseball umpire can become a good softball umpire" (161).

❹ Uses a clear comparison-contrast organizational plan

❺ Cites a primary source

Alderson 4

Works Cited

Bhonslay, Marianne. "Bases Loaded: Growth in Baseball and Softball Equipment Sales." Sporting Goods Business 10 June 1998: 40.

Brinkman, Joe, and Charlie Euchner. The Umpire's Handbook. Lexington: Greene, 1985.

Chiarella, Tom. "The Real Summer Game." Esquire May 1998: 119-25.

Dickson, Paul. The Worth Book of Softball: A Celebration of America's True National Pastime. New York: Facts On File, 1994.

Kennedy, Kostya. "On an Idyllic Night, a Women's Pro Softball League Made a Historic Pitch." Sports Illustrated 9 June 1997: 31.

"Softball." The Columbia Encyclopedia. 5th ed. 1993. Infoplease Encyclopedia. 6 April 2000 <http://www.infoplease.com/ce5/CE048504.html>.

Thorn, John, and Pete Palmer, eds. Total Baseball. 4th ed. New York: Viking, 1995.

Works Cited List

- Identifies all sources of information credited in the report
- Presents entries in alphabetical order
- Gives complete publication information
- Contains correct punctuation in entries
- Is double-spaced throughout
- Follows an accepted style, such as the MLA style

Do It Yourself

Writing Prompt Investigate a topic that interests you, and write a research report about it.

Purpose To share information about your topic

Audience People interested in the topic, classmates, or your teacher

1 Developing a Research Plan

When you investigate a subject in depth, you need to consult a wide range of sources. The research takes time; therefore, planning ahead is a major priority.

Defining Information Needs

Whether your topic is one that you've been assigned or one that you've chosen yourself, it's important to find an "angle" on it—a focused and fresh perspective. Suppose, for example, you have an interest in baseball. After skimming books and looking through magazines, you may decide that softball, a similar game, may provide you with your angle.

You don't know yet what you want to write about softball. You just know that the topic seems interesting. You might make a list of questions to help you explore different aspects of the game.

- *How did the game of softball get started?*
- *Who started it and why?*
- *How does softball differ from baseball?*
- *Why is softball popular?*
- *What if the media covered softball as thoroughly as baseball?*

For more ideas on finding a research topic, see p. 470.

Developing Research Questions

As you begin to find answers to your initial questions, you will be able to refine and focus the topic of your report. You will then need to develop another list of questions to guide your research. The writer of the report on softball decided to focus on the differences between baseball and softball and to prove that softball can be as exciting as baseball. These were two of his questions.

- What are the similarities and differences between the two games?
- What aspects of each game appeal most to fans?

REPORT

Good questions can help you write an effective report. You might evaluate each of your questions by asking yourself,

- Is the question interesting? relevant to my topic?
- Will answering the question give me insight into my topic?
- Can I find a source that will answer the question?

Finding and Prioritizing Sources

There are two basic kinds of information sources. A **primary source** gives firsthand information. **Secondary sources** provide interpretations of, explanations of, and comments on material from other sources.

Research Resources

	Characteristic	Examples
Primary source	Provides direct, firsthand knowledge	Letters, journals, diaries, original manuscripts, questionnaires, interviews
Secondary source	Provides information gathered from primary and other secondary sources	Encyclopedias, textbooks, newspapers, magazines, biographies and other nonfiction books

Evaluating Sources

Not all sources are equally valuable. Ask yourself the following questions to **evaluate** each source you find.

- **Is the source up-to-date?** The more recent the source, the better, especially for rapidly changing fields like science and medicine.
- **Is the source reliable?** Is the author from a respected university, business, or other institution? Is the author recognized as an expert on your particular subject?
- **What are the author's viewpoint and biases?** Does the author seem to have a political, ethnic, gender, or other bias? How might it affect his or her objectivity?

Using a good mix of sources will help you present a range of ideas and thus make your report more interesting. It is, of course, vitally important that your facts be correct.

For more help, see Finding Information, pp. 475-487.

❷ Using and Documenting Sources

Making Source Cards

Skim your sources to see which ones you might use for your report. If a source seems useful, record all the relevant information about it on an index card. You will need this information when you prepare your Works Cited list. Be sure to number each source card so that you can use the number as a reference when you take notes and add documentation in your report. For a library book it is useful to include the call number.

Here's How Making Source Cards

Follow these guidelines when you make source cards.

- **Book** Write the author's or editor's complete name, the title, the name and location of the publisher, and the copyright date.
- **Magazine or Newspaper Article** Write the author's complete name (unless the article is unsigned), the title of the article, the name and date of the publication, and the page number(s) of the article.
- **Encyclopedia Article** Write the author's complete name (unless the article is unsigned), the title of the article, and the name and copyright date of the encyclopedia.
- **World Wide Web Site** Write the author's or editor's complete name (if available), the title of the document, publication information for any print version of it, the date of the document's electronic publication (if available), the name of any institution or organization responsible for the site, the date when you accessed the site, and the document's electronic address (in angle brackets).

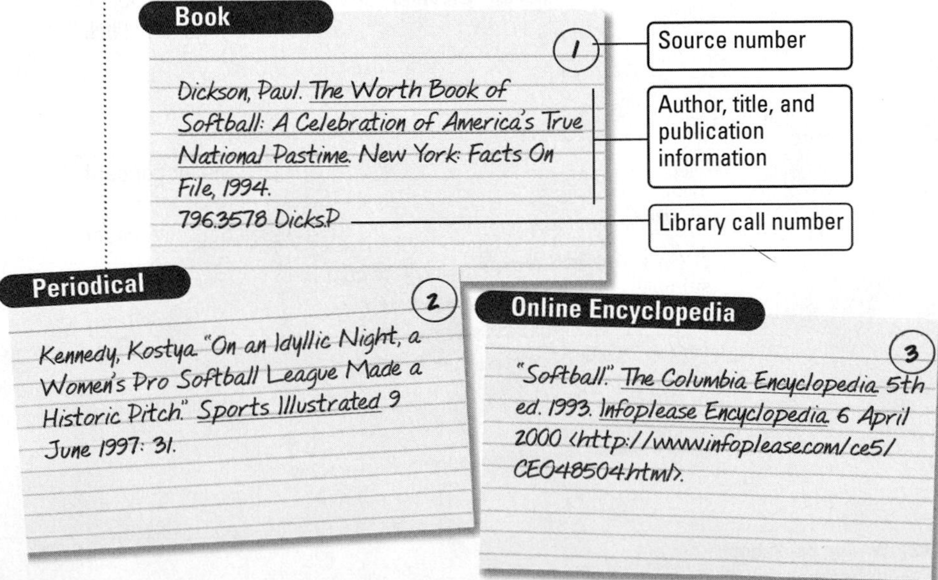

Book
1
Dickson, Paul. The Worth Book of Softball: A Celebration of America's True National Pastime. New York: Facts On File, 1994.
796.3578 DicksP
Source number
Author, title, and publication information
Library call number
Periodical
2
Kennedy, Kostya. "On an Idyllic Night, a Women's Pro Softball League Made a Historic Pitch." Sports Illustrated 9 June 1997: 31.
Online Encyclopedia
3
"Softball." The Columbia Encyclopedia. 5th ed. 1993. Infoplease Encyclopedia. 6 April 2000 <http://www.infoplease.com/ce5/CE048504.html>.

Taking Notes

Review your sources, and when you find material that answers your research questions, take notes. Good notes are key to crafting a good research report. You should include information paraphrased from your sources, as well as quotations that will support your ideas and make your paper interesting.

Here's How **Taking Notes**

Follow these guidelines as you take notes.

- **Use a separate index card** for each piece of information.
- **Write a heading** on each card, indicating the subject of the note.
- **Write the number of the corresponding source card** on each note card.
- **Put direct quotations in quotation marks.**
- **Record the number of the page** in the source where you found the material.

Paraphrasing

When you paraphrase, you restate someone else's idea in your own words. If you use any of the original author's words or phrases, put them in quotation marks.

PROFESSIONAL MODEL

There was the overflow crowd at 2,006-seat Durham Athletic Park, the gaggles of glove-clutching girls, the letter of good wishes from President Clinton and the tautly played softball that kept onlookers riveted to the end.

—Kostya Kennedy, "On an Idyllic Night, a Women's Pro Softball League Made a Historic Pitch"

CHAPTER 25

Paraphrase

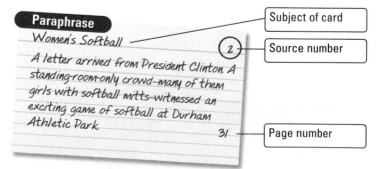

Women's Softball (2)

A letter arrived from President Clinton. A standing-room-only crowd—many of them girls with softball mitts—witnessed an exciting game of softball at Durham Athletic Park.

31

Subject of card

Source number

Page number

Quoting

Always be sure to use quotation marks to distinguish quotations from paraphrases. Avoid using a lot of direct quotations—especially lengthy ones—in your report. Include quotations only when sources

- express extremely important ideas
- express ideas in unusually concise language
- express ideas in lively, original language

Avoiding Plagiarism

Plagiarism means passing off someone else's work as your own. It is dishonest. Obviously you have plagiarized if you have borrowed, bought, or stolen someone else's paper. But it is also plagiarism to "borrow" words without identifying their source, as in the example below.

ORIGINAL

The organizers of Women's Professional Fastpitch (WPF) softball will always recall opening night in Durham, a balmy and breezeless evening when all was as right as a perfect game.

PLAGIARIZED VERSION

Everyone who was there will always remember the first night of Women's Professional Fastpitch softball, in Durham, North Carolina, on May 30, 1997, because it was such a balmy and breezeless evening with everything as right as a perfect game.

In this case, the writer did change much of the original text, but that still wasn't enough. Below is a version that acknowledges the source. (Note that because the Works Cited list gives the page number of Kennedy's one-page article, no page reference is needed in this sentence.)

STUDENT MODEL

According to Kostya Kennedy, the first night of Women's Professional Fastpitch softball will always be remembered as "a balmy and breezeless evening when all was as right as a perfect game."

Information is attributed to its source.

Distinctive language of the author is put in quotation marks.

REPORT

❸ Crafting a Good Thesis Statement

Let's suppose you have gathered all the information that you can. How do you begin to get it all on paper? Perhaps the best way to start is to create a thesis statement—a statement of a central idea that is supported by the information you have gathered.

Your thesis statement should convey your point of view, and it should be a statement that can be supported with various kinds of evidence. Here are some sample thesis statements for research papers.

- Laser technology has had its most important effects in the field of medicine.
- We may never know whether the events described in the *Odyssey* are just stories and legends or things that really happened, but an exploration of the issue can lead to a greater understanding of this classic story.

Here is a checklist to help you develop a good thesis statement for a research report.

Thesis Statement Checklist

- ✔ Is the thesis sufficiently limited and sharply focused?
- ✔ Have I stated it concisely in a sentence that my readers will understand?
- ✔ Do I have the time and resources to do justice to my thesis?
- ✔ Will my thesis allow me to write a paper that will fulfill my assignment?

For more on thesis statements, see pp. 338-339.

❹ Organizing and Outlining

After researching your topic, taking notes, and developing a thesis, you will need to choose an organizational pattern and outline your paper.

Choosing an Organizational Pattern

You can begin organizing your research information by arranging your note cards according to their key ideas. Try several arrangements, such as sequential order and comparison-contrast order, to see which works best. You may want to use different forms of organization in different parts of your report. Then create an outline, using the key ideas as the main entries.

For the report about softball vs. baseball, comparison-contrast organization was an obvious choice. Here is the beginning of the outline that the writer of that report used.

Softball: A Game as Exciting as Hardball

Thesis Statement: *In its "fast pitch" form, softball is every bit as exciting, competitive, and tough as its older cousin.*

I. *Introduction*

II. *History of the games*

   A. *Baseball*

   B. *Softball*

III. *Similarities in the rules*

IV. *Differences between the sports*

   A. *Playing-field dimensions*

   B. *Size of ball*

Once you have an outline, you can group your index cards according to the entries in it. Keep in mind, however, that an outline is meant to guide you, not to limit you. You can change it at any time as you draft.

You may be tempted to try to write a research paper without using an outline. This may work for you on some occasions, but an outline will almost always help you write a better paper.

5 Drafting

Gather together your note cards and your outline and begin writing. You may want to begin with the section you understand best or are most interested in and then continue your report. Or you may choose to begin with the introduction and move sequentially through the outline. You don't have to follow any formula. It is best to write in the way that is most comfortable for you.

Make sure that you write one or two paragraphs for every entry in your outline and that you put your paragraphs in order before you review your writing and begin your revision. Remember to incorporate your own ideas into the report. Your major goal will be to support your thesis statement.

Integrating Your Notes into Your Paper

The writer of the softball report knew from playing the game how hard it is to hit a well-pitched softball. But, of course, he had to prove this. Then he read that softball pitchers had struck out two of the greatest baseball players of all time.

Babe Ruth 1937 (1)

Babe Ruth was struck out by Johnny "Cannonball" Baker on three pitches. Ruth was umpiring a softball game and was to put on a hitting demonstration after the game. This was in 1937. 78

Babe Ruth 1938 (1)

Ruth was struck out by another softball pitcher in 1938, again on three straight pitches. 79

Ted Williams (1)

In Waterbury, Conn., in 1962, with 18,000 people watching, Ted Williams missed 38 of 40 pitches thrown by Joan Joyce, a great fast-pitch hurler. (Her fastball had been clocked at over 100 mph.)

101-102

Ted Williams (continued) (1)

Williams got one hit and one foul in the 1962 exhibition. "He did not touch another pitch."

101-102 (quote from 101)

To confirm how good a hitter Ted Williams was, Steve looked up his records in *The Baseball Encyclopedia.*

Ted Williams (6)

He has the sixth-best batting average (.344) in major league history.

To show how talented softball pitchers can be, and how effective against great baseball players, Steve wove some of these facts into a single paragraph in the final version of his report.

STUDENT MODEL

In 1937, Babe Ruth promised to put on a hitting demonstration after umpiring a softball game, but he failed to do so, because a softball pitcher struck him out on three straight pitches. A year later, he tried again, with the same result (Dickson 78-79). Even more embarrassing was the fate of Ted Williams, who in 1962, with 18,000 people looking on, faced 40 pitches from the rifle arm of Joan Joyce, perhaps the greatest female fast-pitch softball pitcher of all time. Williams, one of the best hitters in major-league history, fouled off one pitch and got a single hit. He failed to even touch the other 38 pitches (Dickson 101-02).

Share Your Own Ideas and Interpretations

When you write a report, do more than just restate the information you found. Make inferences, analyze and interpret evidence, and draw your own reasonable conclusions. Of course, you will need to use facts, examples, and other evidence to back up your ideas. Make sure that your statements and conclusions are accurate and well supported.

Calvin and Hobbes by Bill Watterson

Documenting Information

Parenthetical documentation is the most common way of crediting sources in the body of a research report. In this method of record documentation, a detailed record of sources appears at the end of the report, in a Works Cited list. Brief references in parentheses within the body of the report allow readers to locate the complete information about the sources in the Works Cited list. You should credit the source of each quotation, paraphrase, or summary you use.

REPORT

Here's How **Guidelines for Parenthetical Documentation**

- **Work by One Author** Give the author's last name and the page number in parentheses: **Over several decades Eddie Feigner led a four-man team to many victories over nine-man teams (Dickson 101).**
  If you mention the author's name in the sentence, give only the page number in parentheses: **According to Paul Dickson, over several decades Eddie Feigner led a four-man team to many victories over nine-man teams (101).**
- **Work by More than One Author** Give the authors' last names and the page number in parentheses: **(Thorn and Palmer 16)** If a source has more than three authors, give the first author's last name followed by *et al.* and the page number: **(Brown et al. 27)**
- **Work with No Author Given** Give the title (or a shortened version of it) and the page number: **(Baseball Encyclopedia 2274)**
- **One of Two or More Works by the Same Author** Give the author's last name, the title or a shortened version of it, and the page number: **(Dickson, Worth Book 98)**
- **Two or More Works Cited at the Same Place** Use a semicolon to separate the entries: **(Brown 42; Zinsser 28)**
- **Electronic Source** Give the author's last name, or if no author is named, give the title: **("Softball")**

Preparing a Works Cited List

With all your source cards handy, read through your report and put a check mark on the card for every work that you have cited. Put the other cards aside. (A Works Cited list documents only the works that you have actually referred to in your report.) Then alphabetize the checked cards according to the authors' last names. Alphabetize anonymous works by the first words (except *A, An,* or *The)* in their titles. Follow the instructions below when typing the list.

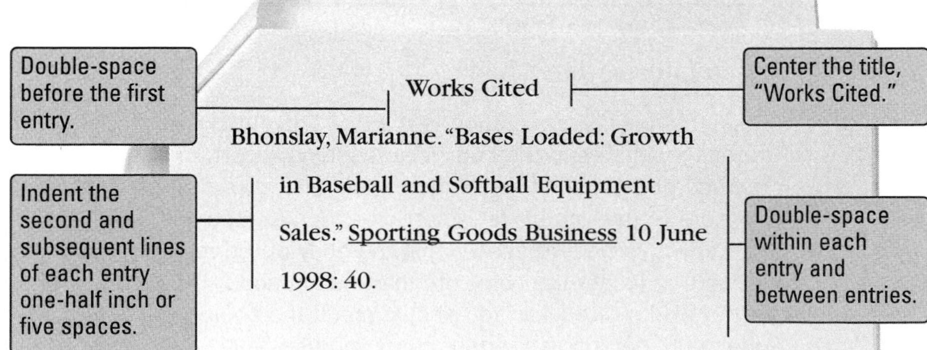

Double-space before the first entry.
Works Cited
Center the title, "Works Cited."
Bhonslay, Marianne. "Bases Loaded: Growth
in Baseball and Softball Equipment
Sales." Sporting Goods Business 10 June
1998: 40.
Indent the second and subsequent lines of each entry one-half inch or five spaces.
Double-space within each entry and between entries.

For more help, see the MLA citation guidelines on pp. 648–655.

6 Revising

TARGET SKILL ►Effective Word Choice In the rush and heat of writing a draft, it is likely that you will have chosen some lazy or hazy words that could profitably be replaced. Look for such words and think of more exact and vivid substitutes.

the longest measured home run ~~went~~ *soared* 643 feet. By contrast, the longest softball home run ~~went~~ *traveled* 510 feet.

7 Editing and Proofreading

TARGET SKILL ►Using Parenthetical Documentation Follow the guidelines for parenthetical documentation when you cite sources in your paper. Remember, when you mention an author's name or the name of an anonymous source in the body of the paper, put only the page reference in parentheses.

In fact, the differences between the games are so minor that Joe Brinkman and Charlie Euchner maintain that "any baseball umpire can become a good softball umpire" (~~Brinkman and Euchner~~ 161).

8 Sharing and Reflecting

After you have revised and polished your research report, find an interested audience to **share** it with.

For Your Working Portfolio After you have shared your report, **reflect** on what you learned in writing it. Do you have a deeper appreciation of your topic? Are there steps in the process you think you could do more quickly the next time? Are there still things you want to learn about your topic? Attach your answers to your finished report and save it in your **Working Portfolio.**

Student Help Desk

Research Report at a Glance

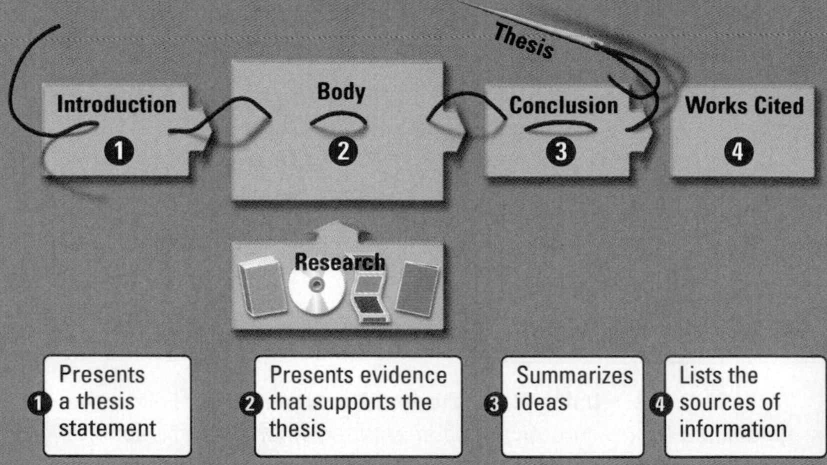

1 Presents a thesis statement	2 Presents evidence that supports the thesis	3 Summarizes ideas	4 Lists the sources of information

Idea Bank

Brainstorm. List hobbies, current events, special interests—things you are curious about. Think up questions about each item on your list. Circle the question that holds the most interest for you.

Go exploring. Browse magazines, encyclopedias, and the Internet for answers to your question. Follow leads that branch into other areas of interest. Through this process you will likely discover areas you want to explore more closely.

Don't let an assigned subject slow you down. You may not be excited about the Civil War, but the splits that occurred in families as a result may be an interesting topic to pursue. Look for ways to find a specific aspect of the subject that you want to explore.

Read literature. Think of authors you have been studying, such as Edgar Allan Poe, Maya Angelou, or Sandra Cisneros. What would you like to know about them or about the subjects they explore in their writing?

Publishing Options

Print If you researched a topic of local interest, check to see if your community newspaper will publish an excerpt from your report. Gather reports from your classmates to make a class notebook for all to read.

Oral Communication Turn your report into an oral presentation. If possible, bring in drawings or photographs to extend the explanations in your report. Or use hypertext software to create a multimedia presentation. **See pp. 539-549 for help with multimedia products.**

Online Visit **mcdougallittell.com** for more publishing options.

Friendly Feedback

Questions for Your Peer Reader

- What did you like best about my report?
- What is my thesis?
- What evidence needs to be strengthened?
- What information might be cut?
- What part of my report is confusing?
- What did you learn that you did not know before?

The Bottom Line

Checklist for Research Report

Have I . . .

- ____ included a strong introduction with a clear thesis statement?
- ____ used evidence from primary and/or secondary sources?
- ____ credited my sources of information?
- ____ used an appropriate organizational pattern?
- ____ used transitions between ideas?
- ____ summarized my ideas in a satisfying conclusion?
- ____ provided a properly formatted Works Cited list at the end of the report?

REPORT

Communicating in the Information Age

Reach Out and Touch

In our high-tech world, communication is just a click away. To send information into cyberspace, however, you'll need a firm understanding of communication skills and technical resources. Likewise, you'll need critical thinking skills to evaluate and interpret the messages that you receive.

Power Words
Vocabulary for Precise Writing

drowning in data?

turmoil?

inundated?

Information Anxiety

Searching for that special word to describe your feelings when you're faced with too much information? You've come to the right place.

Under a Strain?

Are you **drowning** in data? Are you **flooded** with facts? **swamped, deluged,** and **inundated** with information? **besieged, bombarded, blitzed,** and **barraged** by bulletins? Are you totally **saturated** with news reports and firsthand accounts?

Overwhelmed?

Do you find yourself **overwhelmed** by countless Web site links? **anxious** and **agitated? distraught** or **overwrought?** in **turmoil? at sea? fazed, flustered,** and **frazzled? confused, confounded,** and **disconcerted** by a list of over 200 books on the same subject? **baffled** and **bewildered? rattled** and **ruffled? upset** and **unsettled?** Mix and match the appropriate adjectives, and join the legions of others who suffer from information anxiety!

overwhelmed?

▶ Your Turn Design a Word

What word best expresses your feelings about information overload? Write or draw the word in a way that captures its meaning. Display your word whenever you feel that way.

Chapter 26

Finding Information

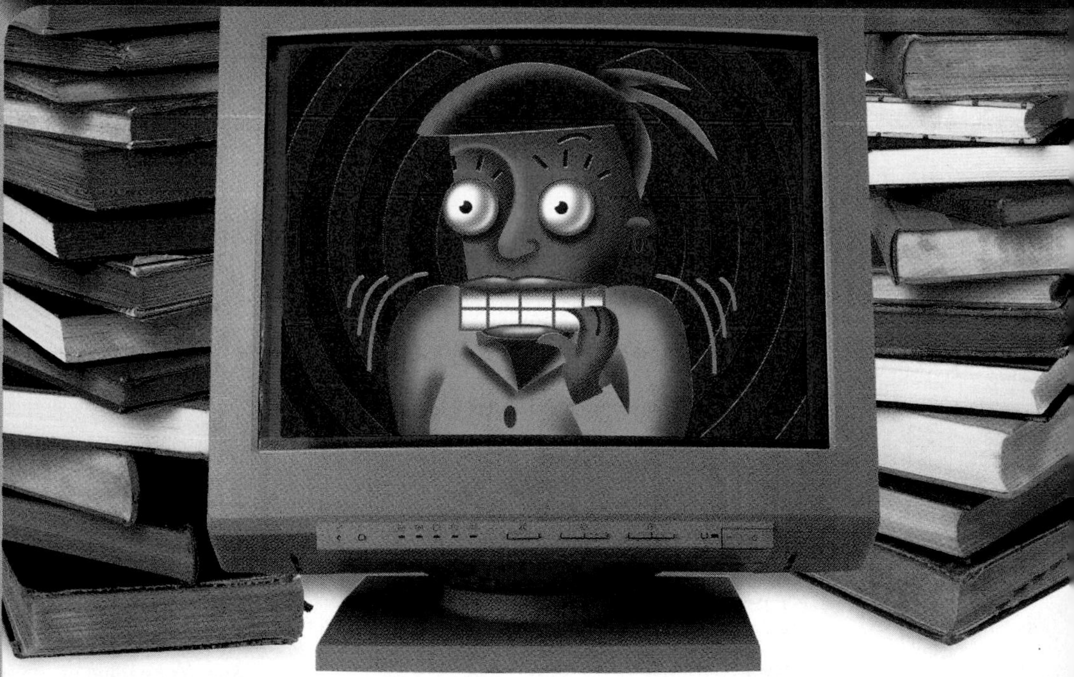

Chill Out!

Don't lose your cool every time you do research. We live in the information age, so we have a wealth of resources to choose from. However, too much information can give even the most seasoned researcher a bad case of information anxiety.

Smart researchers understand that finding and using information in today's world is a lifelong learning process. They learn the basics and then stay on top of changes in the ways information is accessed. This chapter introduces you to the wealth of print and electronic resources available and gives tips and strategies for using them effectively.

Write Away: Off Ramps on the Information Highway
Most people have favorite information sources. Make a list of the reference books, computer databases, Web sites, and other sources that you usually use to find information. Save your list in your **Working Portfolio.**

INTERNET ClassZone at mcdougallittell.com

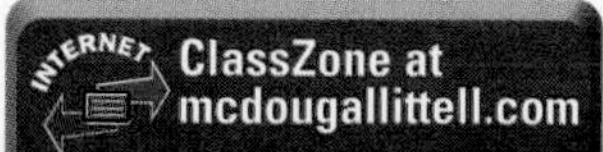

The Library and Media Center

Think of the library or media center as an information center for almost any topic you can imagine. Whether you're investigating consumer reports on CD players, figuring out how to fix a bike, or doing a research report on forensic sciences, the library can provide the answers to your questions.

1 Using Catalogs

The library's catalog provides a complete listing of books, periodicals, media, and other materials available in the library system. Although some libraries still maintain a catalog on 3″ x 5″ cards, most libraries now have their catalogs on computer, complete with on-screen prompts and information to direct your search.

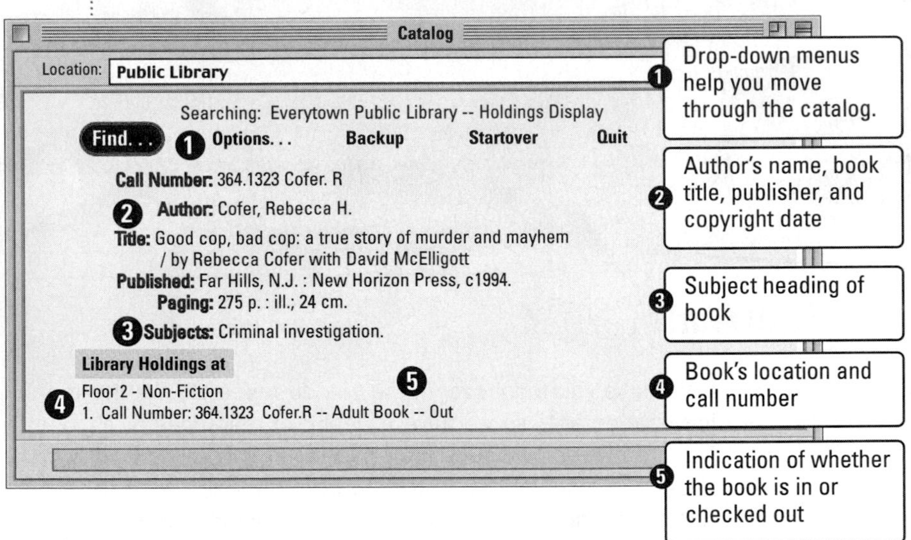

2 Special Services

Don't overlook the librarian when you're trying to find information on a particular topic. Librarians are highly trained information specialists. Reference librarians can answer questions and tell you where to search for more in-depth information on your topic.

Many libraries also offer telephone reference services. You simply call the library, ask for the reference desk, and then ask your question.

Some libraries also sponsor book groups, storytelling events, films, and special-interest lectures on such topics as travel or health. They may also have special sections on genealogy, local history, and fine arts.

❸ The Library Collection

Library materials are organized into sections, which are standard among U.S. libraries. Becoming familiar with the sections of the library will make your research more efficient.

Sections of the Library	
Stacks	Fiction, nonfiction, biography and autobiography, oversize folios (large books that do not fit on the shelves with other books)
Search Tools: Catalogs and Indexes	Library card catalog and online computer indexes containing information about library materials and their locations
Reference	Encyclopedias, dictionaries, almanacs, chronologies, and atlases
Periodicals	Newspapers, magazines, and journals
Audiovisual	Films, CDs, tapes, videos, and records
Children and Young Adults	Fiction, nonfiction, and reference books written for children and young adults
Computer Lab	Computers with basic software programs, such as word processing (may have access to the Web and other Internet sources)
Microfiche and Microfilm	Collections of older issues of newspapers and periodicals reproduced on film

Fiction and Nonfiction

Along the library's shelves, books are generally categorized as fiction and nonfiction. Fiction includes novels and short-story collections, arranged in alphabetical order by the author's last name.

Nonfiction books are classified into subject categories. The groupings are made according to either the **Dewey decimal** classification or the **Library of Congress** classification system.

For a guide to the classifications, see the Student Help Desk, p. 486.

Using Reference Works

❶ Using Print References

The library stocks a variety of reference works in a special reference section. Reference works are useful collections of all kinds of information. To use reference works effectively, you need to know what kinds of information are in them and how they're organized.

Library Reference Materials

Reference Work	Kinds of Information	How Organized
Almanacs and Yearbooks	Facts and statistics	By topic or category
Atlases	Maps	By region or topic
Encyclopedias	General articles	Alphabetically by topic
Biographical Dictionaries and Encyclopedias	Information about famous people, past and present	Alphabetically by last name
Dictionaries	Word meanings, origins, spellings, and pronunciations	Alphabetically by word entry
Chronologies	Historical events	By date or time period
Indexes	References to articles and essays in newspapers and magazines	By topic or author
Vertical Files	Pamphlets, booklets, catalogs, handbooks, and clippings	By topic

❷ Using Databases

In addition to magazines, periodicals, and newspapers, many libraries have electronic collections of these materials as well. Electronic collections are large databases that allow you to search for articles on any number of topics.

Often the library will subscribe to a database service, such as *InfoTrac, NewsBank,* or *SIRS Researcher,* so that the information is updated regularly. These databases may be available on CD-ROM or online and can be found in the library.

You will find that different databases provide different services. Some databases might provide

- **Indexes** to articles in newspapers, magazines, journals, and reference books
- **Full-text articles,** sometimes with illustrations, charts, and maps
- **Daily updates** that provide the most current news

3 Using Electronic References

Many reference materials are also available in an electronic format. One of the most popular electronic products is the CD-ROM encyclopedia. Many entries have articles with links to animation, film footage, and audio files.

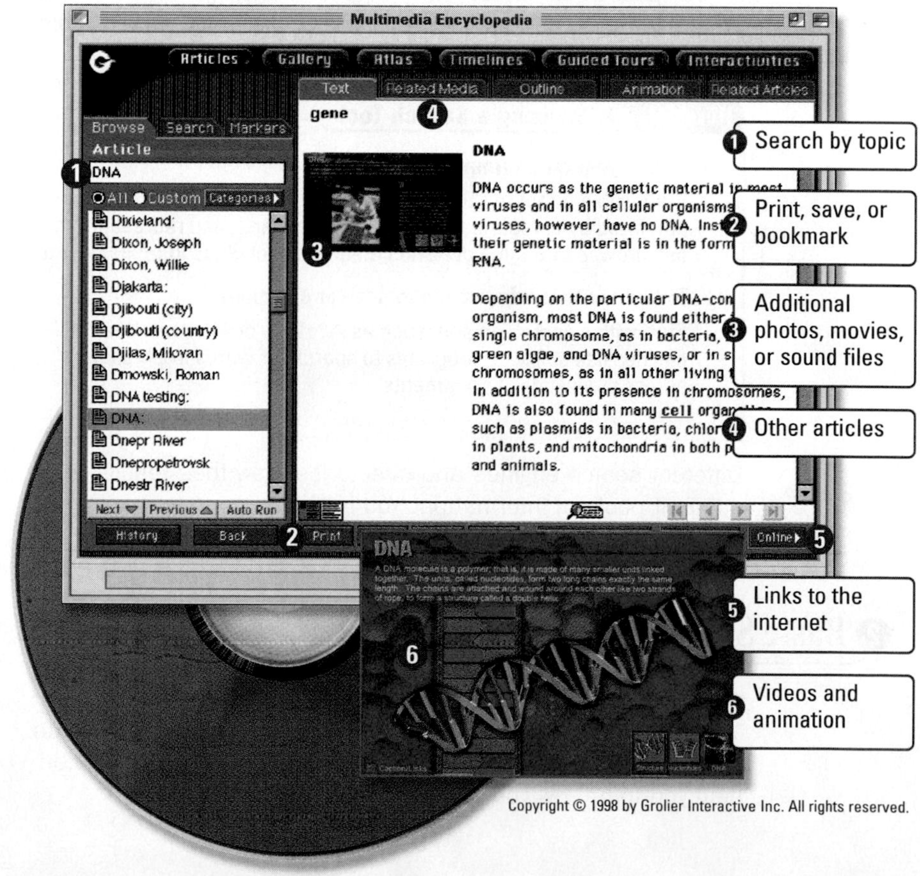

1 Search by topic
2 Print, save, or bookmark
3 Additional photos, movies, or sound files
4 Other articles
5 Links to the internet
6 Videos and animation

Searching the Web

The World Wide Web has changed forever the way we access and use information. On the Web, you can click into late-breaking news, scan the articles of professional magazines, and ask questions of experts on the other side of the world. Be careful out there! Don't get lost on the information highway. Learn some basic Web skills to become a savvy traveler.

Go to ClassZone at mcdougallittel.com for a complete tutorial on using the Web for research.

1 Using Search Tools

The Web connects millions of documents through a system of linked "pages" or "sites." To find general and specific information on the Web, you can use one or more of the many search tools available.

Here's How **Choosing a Search Tool**

1. To find **general information** about your topic:
   Start with a directory, such as *Yahoo!* or *StudyWeb*. Directories are organized by categories, such as business, arts, and recreation. You can browse through a general category to get ideas to refine your topic.
2. To find **specific information** to answer questions:
   Start with a search engine, such as *AltaVista* or *Infoseek*. Search engines use software programs to search for words or phrases across thousands of documents.

Different search engines and directories draw their results from different pools of information. You may have to try out several of these tools to find what you are looking for.

2 Basic Search Strategies

Everyone has his or her own process for searching on the Web. There are a few steps you can take to tune up your own results. If you are using a search engine, the tips on the next page can help you to narrow your search.

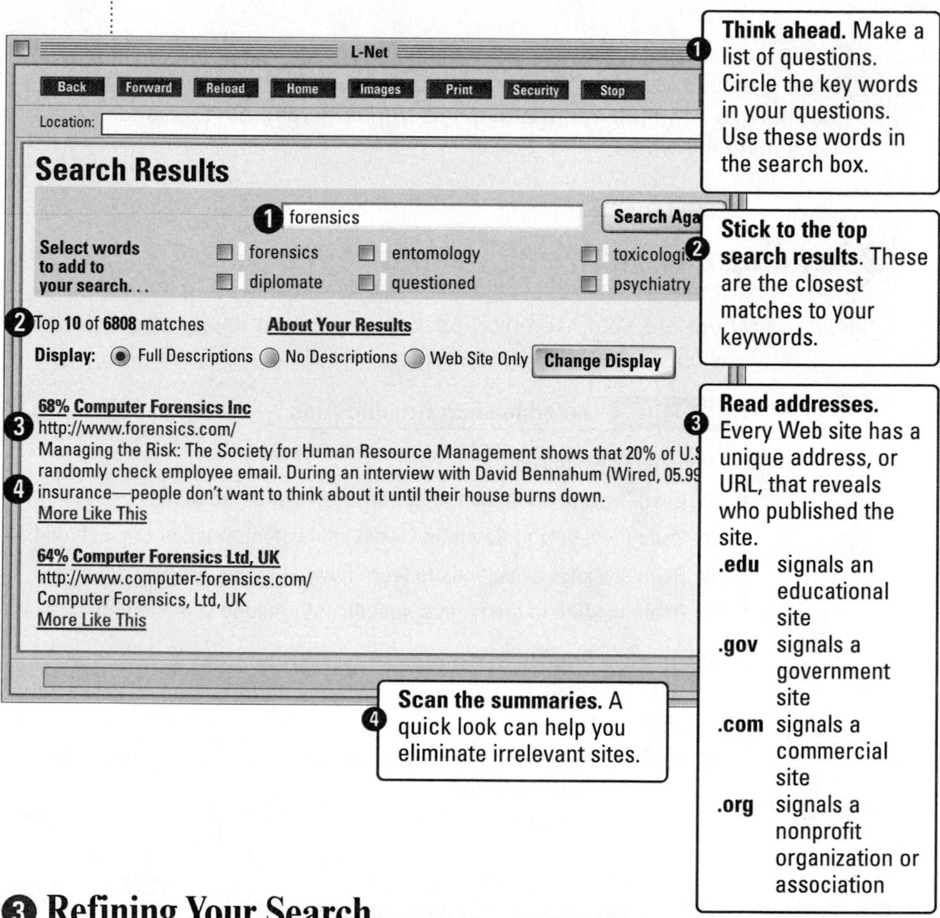

3 Refining Your Search

If you get too many sites, use the *Help* or *Search Tips* feature of each search engine to narrow your search further.

Common Search Tips	
Use " "	Double quotation marks define an exact phrase or proper noun, such as **"baltimore orioles"**.
Use +	The plus sign signals that each word or phrase must be included. **baltimore +orioles**
Use –	The hyphen or minus sign signals that a word or phrase must not be included. **baltimore +orioles -baseball**

If you find too few sites, go back to your keywords and think of more general words to search—for example, **orioles +birds.**

Charts and Diagrams

Charts, tables, graphs, maps, and diagrams present information in pictures. These graphic aids can make complex information easier to understand. Use them to compare information, see trends across time, or understand how something works.

1 Reading and Analyzing Graphic Aids

There are some common strategies you can use to understand any chart, graph, or diagram.

Here's How Understanding Graphic Aids

Reading Graphic Aids

1. Read the title or caption to get an overview of the topic.
2. Read the labels to determine what kinds of information are included.
3. Read any keys or legends to learn how colors or symbols are used.
4. Read the data to learn what specific information is presented.

Interpreting Graphic Aids

5. Think about the big picture first. What patterns or general impressions do the data suggest?
6. Ask questions about the information. Where are the extremes? Are there any holes or gaps?

2 Types and Purposes of Graphic Aids

Each type of graphic aid has a different structure and purpose. **Diagrams** are drawings that show the parts of something or explain how something works. For example, this diagram shows the three basic patterns of fingerprints.

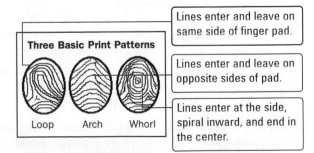

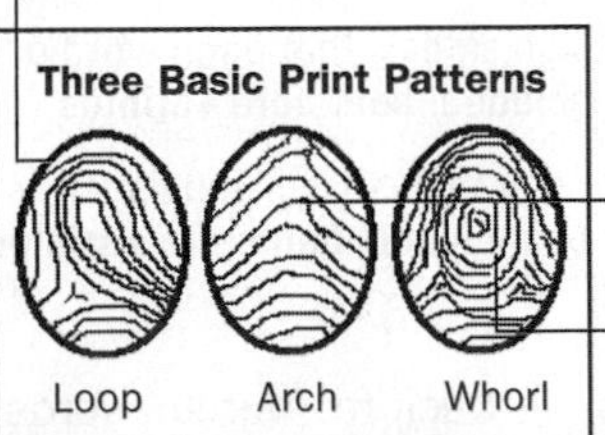
Three Basic Print Patterns
Loop
Arch
Whorl
Lines enter and leave on same side of finger pad.
Lines enter and leave on opposite sides of pad.
Lines enter at the side, spiral inward, and end in the center.

CHAPTER 26

Line graphs show patterns of change, or trends in data over time.

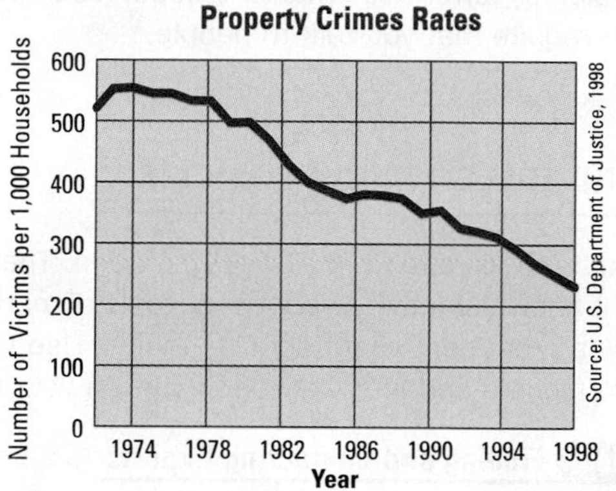

Circle or pie graphs let you compare the parts of a whole with each other and with the whole. The full circle represents 100 percent, or the whole, of an amount. The sections of the circle represent parts that make up the whole.

Kinds of Property Crimes

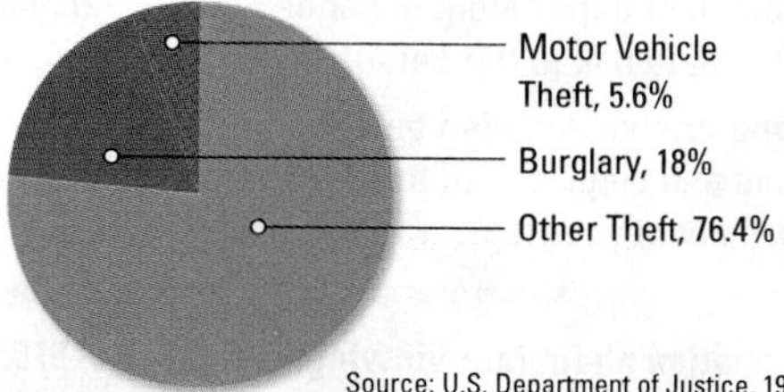

A circle graph can be misleading if the whole is a very small set of data. Suppose, for example, you ask three people, "Should we hire more police?" Two say yes and one says no. Your circle graph would show that 66 percent responded favorably to your question—but that represents only two people!

The Duplex Glenn McCoy

Interviews and Surveys

Sometimes you need information that you just can't find in books or online. Projects exploring current community issues, local history, or a special event often require that you talk to people.

1 Contacting and Interviewing Experts

Think about the kinds of information you need. Then ask yourself who might know something about your topic. Experts are people who know a great deal about specific topics. Use these guidelines to help you locate and interview an expert on your topic.

Here's How Finding and Contacting Experts

1. **List all the people and organizations that might be helpful.** Use the phone book and professional directories to find out how to contact these people or organizations.
2. **Rehearse what you will say.** Remember to tell who you are, what you want to find out, and why you are doing research.
3. **When you call an organization, be specific about your needs.** Ask what person or department might be able to help you. Make an appointment to talk to the person.
4. **For phone interviews, plan before you call.** Prepare a list of questions and be prepared to follow up on any new information you learn about your topic.

For more information about interviewing, see pp. 514–515.

2 Using Surveys

Sometimes you want to collect information from a group of people. A survey allows you to gather and compare information about opinions, preferences, and beliefs across a large group of people.

Planning the Survey

The results of your survey are only as good as the questions you ask. Carefully plan what you will ask and how you will ask it.

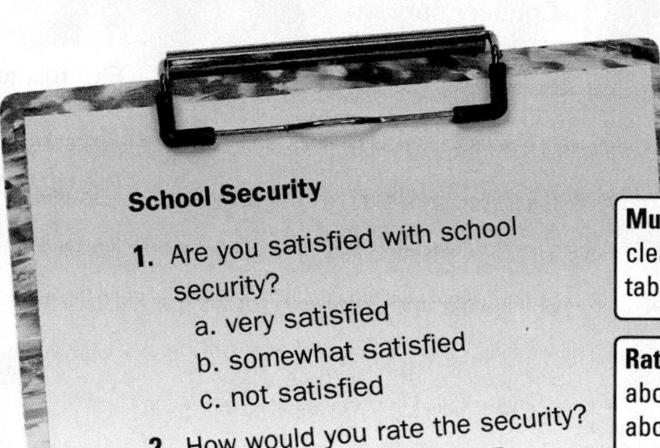

School Security
1. Are you satisfied with school security?
a. very satisfied
b. somewhat satisfied
c. not satisfied
2. How would you rate the security?
1 2 3 4 5
POOR FAIR EXCELLENT
3. Should we have security cameras in the halls?
yes no
4. What changes in school security would you recommend?

Multiple Choice: gives clear choices; easy to tabulate answers

Rating Scale: gives data about how people feel about something

Yes/ No: requires people to make a choice; easy to tabulate answers

Open-Ended: allows new issues to surface; hard to tabulate answers

Giving the Survey

The next step is to select a group of people, or sample population, for your survey.

1. Decide who should be included in your survey. For the survey above, would you include the whole community or only your school's students and faculty? Remember, your results will reflect the thinking only of your survey population.
2. Administer the survey in the same way to each person.

Interpreting Survey Results

After you compile the answers to your survey questions, think about what the information tells you.

- Do the results show a clear preference?
- Do the results show that certain groups of people think one way while other groups think another way?
- Are you surprised at any results?

Student Help Desk

Finding Information at a Glance

Types of Information

Facts or statistics
General information
Technical information
News articles
Personal accounts
Maps

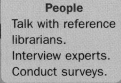

People
Talk with reference librarians.
Interview experts.
Conduct surveys.

Electronic Media
Use key words to search databases.
Use CD-ROMs.

Videos and Films
Search references for videos and films.
View and take notes.

Print Media
Use indexes to find topics and sources. Take notes on materials.

Sources

Nonfiction Classifications

There are two systems used to assign classifications and call numbers to nonfiction materials. Some libraries use the Dewey decimal classification, and others use the Library of Congress classification.

Dewey Decimal System

000–099	General Works
100–199	Philosophy, Psychology
200–299	Religion
300–399	Social Sciences
400–499	Language
500–599	Science, Mathematics
600–699	Applied Technology
700–799	Fine Arts
800–899	Literature
900–999	History, Geography

Library of Congress System

A	General Works
B	Philosophy, Psychology, Religion
C	Auxiliary Sciences of History
D	General History
E–F	American History
G	Geography, Anthropology, Recreation
H	Social Sciences
J	Political Science
K	Law
L	Education
M	Music
N	Fine Arts
P	Language and Literature
Q	Science
R	Medicine
S	Agriculture
T	Technology
U	Military Science
V	Naval Science
Z	Library Science and Information Resources

CHAPTER 26

Evaluating Information Sources

Has the expert

1. an educational background in the subject?
2. published anything on the subject?
3. worked in an industry related to the subject?
4. had personal experiences related to the subject?

Does the Web site

1. present material written by a reliable organization or expert?
2. have a current date?
3. contain a bibliography or links to other Web sites?
4. contain information based on fact or opinion?

Doing Research on the Web

Use the Help tool in a search engine for specific strategies on conducting a search. In general, connect terms you are searching with:

and	to retrieve pages in which *all* the keywords appear. This strategy narrows your search. **(cats and dogs)**
or	to retrieve pages containing *any* one of the keywords. This strategy expands your search. **(cats or dogs)**
and not	to retrieve pages containing *one* keyword and not the other. Use this strategy when you have a keyword that has more than one meaning. **(cats and not dogs)**

The Bottom Line

Checklist for Finding Information

Have I . . .

____ clearly identified what I need to know?

____ used library catalogs and databases to find sources?

____ worked with the reference librarian to find specific information?

____ used general references to help define and narrow my topic?

____ focused my research on the Internet to find what I need?

____ evaluated the reliability of both print and online resources?

FINDING INFO.

Power Words
Vocabulary for Precise Writing

buy this now!

Product Lines

Are you being pressured to buy a CD player for the car you don't have? The following words describe a range of persuasive tactics used to influence consumers.

The Come-On

Does the ad try to **soft-soap, sweet-talk,** or **fast-talk** us? Does it go for the **hard sell** or **soft sell?** What's the **hook?** the **pitch?** the **line?** Is it all a big **con,** just so much **hype?** Are they doing a **snow job** on us?

Buy This (or Else)!

Those using the hard sell do not merely **urge** us to buy, they insistently **pressure—press** and **push, exhort** and **importune.** A little **browbeating** and **arm-twisting** never hurt a sale, they say. **Hucksterism** (the use of aggressive and flashy sales techniques) is the name of their game.

cajole

Gentle Persuasion

Some prefer the softer sell, a gentler approach. They **tempt, lure,** and **entice;** they **coax** and **wheedle;** they **cajole** and **blandish** and **inveigle.** After all, why should they pressure us when they can so easily **captivate, beguile,** and **intrigue** us, **enchant, mesmerize,** and **enthrall** us with their wondrous wares?

temptation!

▶ Your Turn Sell, Sell, Sell!

Invent a product, high-tech or otherwise, and write ad copy for it. You may want to illustrate your ad as well.

importune

Chapter 27

Analyzing and Evaluating Ideas

Don't be left out.
Buy the revolutionary, temperature-controlled Comfort Strider. Your feet stay cool when it's hot, and toasty when it's not.
68°

Do You Buy It?

Would you buy the high-tech shoe shown in the drawing? What kind of information might convince you to get a pair? Every day you are bombarded with thousands of pieces of information, including news reports, school lessons, and conversations with friends, as well as sales pitches. To make sense of all this information, you must become a smart consumer of ideas.

Critical-thinking skills can help you sort through all of the information you read and hear each day. **Critical thinking** is the process of analyzing, evaluating, and interpreting ideas effectively.

Write Away: Getting Pitched

Think about an occasion when someone tried to persuade you to buy something. Write two or three paragraphs about this incident, describing what the person said in his or her attempt to convince you to buy. Explain why the sales pitch did or did not work. Add your writing to your **Working Portfolio.**

Separating Facts from Opinions

Have you heard the saying, "Don't believe everything you read"? Whether you're buying a CD player or researching a report topic on the Internet, you'll have to decide which pieces of information you discover are accurate and reliable.

1 Proving Facts

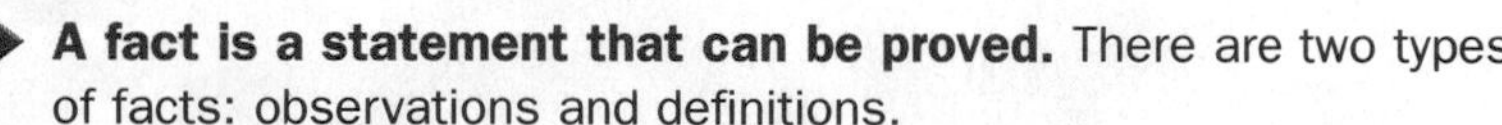

A fact is a statement that can be proved. There are two types of facts: observations and definitions.

Types of Facts	
Observations	A basketball is larger than a baseball.
	Each year, there are more than 1 million divorces in the United States.
Definitions	High-tops are athletic shoes that lace up to the ankle.
	A kilometer is 1,000 meters.

Observations can be either firsthand or secondhand. Firsthand observations are those you make yourself. Secondhand observations are made by other people—for example, the information you can find by looking in books or talking with people.

A statement is not a fact unless you can prove it. Here are some ways you can prove a statement.

Ways to Prove a Statement

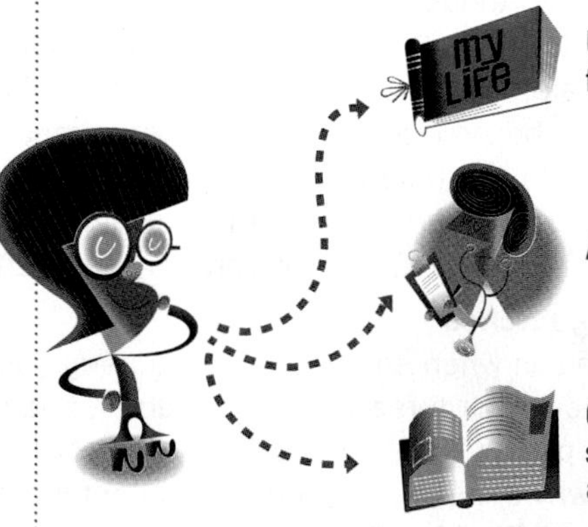

Use your experiences or make firsthand observations.

Ask a recognized expert.

Consult an authoritative written source, such as an encyclopedia, an atlas, an almanac, or a dictionary.

2 Evaluating Opinions

▶ **An opinion is a statement that tells what a person thinks, believes, or feels about a subject.** Unlike a fact, an opinion can't be proved.

You can determine if a statement is an opinion in the following ways:

- Look for adjectives or adverbs that involve judgments—for example, *bad* or *good, better* or *worse, excellent* or *terrible.*
- Look for words that tell someone's beliefs about what needs to happen—for example, *ought* or *should.*
- Look for information that cannot be proved by using observations, experiences, or an authoritative written source or an expert.

To decide whether an opinion is worth considering, you should determine whether it is unsupported or informed.

Unsupported opinions often consist of exaggerations or strongly worded judgments. They are not backed up by factual evidence.

> **Our town's recreation program is worthless.**

Informed opinions are supported with facts.

> **Our town's recreation program is worthless because there are no after-school programs and the sports leagues are disorganized.**

A statement that you agree with or that makes sense to you is not necessarily a fact.

PRACTICE **Fact or Opinion?**

Identify each statement as a fact or an opinion. If the statement is a fact, explain how you might prove it. If it is an opinion, tell how you could support it.

1. Tallahassee became the capital of Florida in 1824.
2. This new Kickturn Deluxe skateboard is excellent.
3. A modem is a device that converts data from one form into another.
4. Mariah Carey has had several platinum albums.
5. The Rampager sport utility vehicle is the best car on the market for handling both wet and icy roads.

ANALYZING IDEAS

Logical Relationships

Being able to judge the value of a single statement is not enough to make you a skilled consumer of information. You also must be able to use **logic**—the science of reasoning—to judge relationships between statements.

1 Cause and Effect

A **cause** is an event or action that directly brings about another event. An **effect** is the direct or logical outcome of an event or action. Words that signal a cause-and-effect relationship include *because, therefore, so,* and *since.* Recognizing causes and effects can be especially helpful to you in studying history and science.

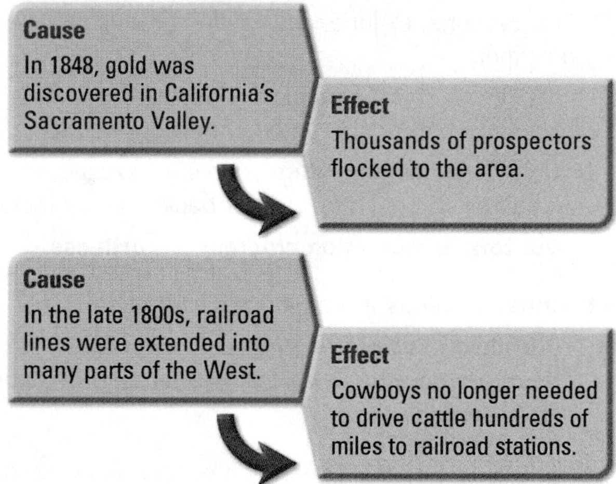

Cause
In 1848, gold was discovered in California's Sacramento Valley.
Effect
Thousands of prospectors flocked to the area.
Cause
In the late 1800s, railroad lines were extended into many parts of the West.
Effect
Cowboys no longer needed to drive cattle hundreds of miles to railroad stations.

When one event follows another, be careful not to assume that the first event caused the second. An event that has nothing to do with an event that follows it is called a **false cause.**

First Event
On July 4, 1776, the Continental Congress approved the Declaration of Independence.

Second Event
On July 12, 1776, a large fleet of British warships arrived in New York Harbor.

It is wrong to conclude that the first event was a cause of the second event just because the ships arrived soon after the Declaration was approved. In fact, Britain had decided to attack New York before it learned about the Declaration.

❷ Comparison and Contrast

A **comparison** shows how two or more things—people, places, events, ideas, or objects—are alike. Some words that point to similarities are *also, both, in the same way,* and *likewise.* A **contrast** shows how two or more things differ. Words that indicate differences include *but, however, on the other hand,* and *unlike.*

Using comparison and contrast can help you understand the relationship between two topics. The Venn diagram below compares and contrasts the Northern and Southern American colonies in the late 1700s.

Northern Colonies

farms: small farms

crops: varied crops

exports: basic goods

slavery: not important

cities: small towns and larger ports

Both

origin of immigrants: most came from England

imports: finished goods

type of government: representational

Southern Colonies

farms: large farms and plantations

crops: single cash crop per farm

exports: crops

slavery: important

cities: a few large towns

To analyze this type of comparison, ask yourself the following questions.

- **Are all of the main categories covered?** For example, the creator of the Venn diagram might also have included a transportation category.
- **Are the same sorts of things compared across categories?** Notice how both sides of the Venn diagram focus on foreign trade rather than on domestic trade.
- **Is the information presented in an unbiased way?** The Venn diagram does not portray either the North or South in a positive or negative way.

Using comparison and contrast can help you make decisions by providing you with a way to evaluate an issue's strengths and weaknesses.

3 Analogy

An **analogy** shows a type of relationship between two things. You can use analogies to help explain unfamiliar concepts by comparing them to other, more well-known concepts.

For many Americans, the Great Depression of the 1930s was like a long nightmare. It seemed to go on and on, with no way out of the suffering.

You can also use analogies when you are trying to persuade other people to agree with your opinion. Analogies are especially useful when you want to refute an argument.

Blaming President Hoover for the Great Depression is like blaming President Kennedy for the Vietnam War.

Although analogies can be used to persuade or explain, they can also be misused to support a weak argument or explanation. A **false analogy** is a comparison that is unfair, exaggerated, or otherwise illogical.

Having a closed campus is like keeping students in jail.

To evaluate whether an analogy is valid, ask yourself the following questions:

- Are the situations being compared really similar?
- Are the situations of equal importance?
- Is the analogy being used to hide a weak argument?

PRACTICE **Evaluating Analogies**

Indicate whether each analogy is valid or invalid.

1. Trying to find a summer job is like participating in a competition.
2. Many battles in the Civil War were like mass slaughter.
3. Our governor is the Abraham Lincoln of the 21st century.
4. Studying for a test at the last minute is like trying to eat a pizza in 30 seconds.
5. Getting the highest score on a video game is like winning an Olympic medal.

LESSON 3 Interpreting Facts

Sometimes you have to interpret what you read or hear. Three strategies that can help you interpret facts and details are making inferences, drawing conclusions, and forming generalizations. Learning these strategies can help you in many situations—from buying a product to solving a difficult problem.

1 Making Inferences

An **inference** is a logical guess based on facts and common sense. To make an inference, you "read between the lines," using facts and details and drawing on your own knowledge and experience to figure out what isn't stated directly.

STUDENT MODEL

Prehistoric paintings of deer and horses have been found on cave walls in France and Spain. Cave paintings in Lascaux, France, are believed to be as much as 15,000 years old. **FACTS AND DETAILS**

The paintings are so lifelike that it would have been impossible for people to have painted the animals without ever having seen them. **KNOWLEDGE AND EXPERIENCE** So we can infer that deer and horses lived in France and Spain in prehistoric times. **INFERENCE**

When making an inference, check to be sure that it doesn't contradict any of the facts you've been given.

PRACTICE A **Making Inferences**

Study the photograph. Use the visual clues that are given and your own knowledge and experience to infer what might be made from these ingredients.

❷ Drawing Conclusions

Like a detective making sense of clues, you draw a **conclusion** by reviewing a number of facts and details and using your prior knowledge to make a logical statement about a topic. Unlike the process of making inferences, drawing conclusions requires you to read *beyond* the lines. Conclusions are more than guesses; they are explanations based on evidence.

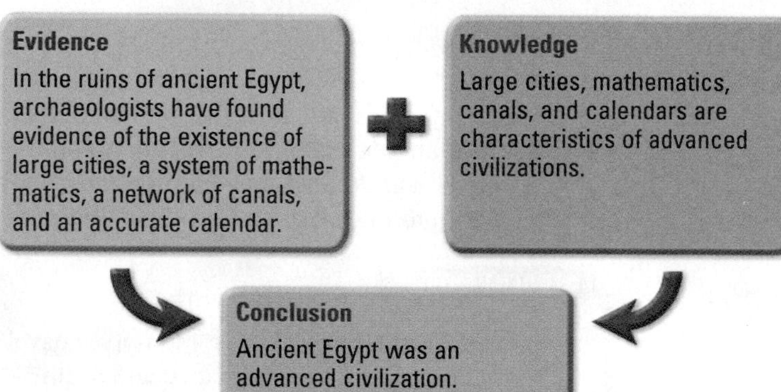

Evidence
In the ruins of ancient Egypt, archaeologists have found evidence of the existence of large cities, a system of mathematics, a network of canals, and an accurate calendar.
Knowledge
Large cities, mathematics, canals, and calendars are characteristics of advanced civilizations.
Conclusion
Ancient Egypt was an advanced civilization.

A **valid conclusion** is an explanation that is reasonable and consistent with the evidence. An **invalid conclusion** is an explanation that is not consistent with known facts and details. Here's an invalid conclusion drawn from the facts and details given in the diagram.

Ancient Egypt had a system of government similar to ours.

Sometimes a set of evidence can lead to more than one valid conclusion.

PRACTICE B Valid Conclusions

Read the following groups of statements. For each group, choose the conclusion that is valid.

1. An exhibit of Vincent van Gogh's paintings opens at the art museum Monday. Van Gogh exhibits always attract large crowds.
   a. Van Gogh was a famous Dutch painter who lived in the 1800s. **b.** Everybody loves van Gogh's paintings. **c.** Many people will be at the art museum on Monday.
2. Chanika is one of the most talented members of the photography club at school. All of her photographs deal with people. The club had a competition, and the winning entry was a photograph of a setting sun.
   a. Chanika should become a professional photographer.

b. Chanika did not win the club's competition. **c.** The most talented photographers take photographs of people.

3. Constantin Brancusi became famous for his polished bronze and marble sculptures. These sculptures were unusual because they used simple forms to represent people or animals.
   a. Some of Brancusi's sculptures were made of bronze and had simple forms. **b.** Brancusi's sculptures appear in many famous museums. **c.** Brancusi has had a great deal of influence on modern art.

❸ Forming Generalizations

A **generalization** is a broad statement that is made based on many specific, related examples or events.

Events
Julius Caesar conquered Gaul in 51 B.C.
+
Octavian conquered Egypt in 30 B.C.
+
Claudius conquered Britain in A.D. 43.
+
Trajan conquered Dacia in A.D. 106.
Generalization
Roman leaders conquered much territory.

A **valid generalization** is a general observation based on a wide range of characteristics, usually using a qualifying word such as *few, generally, many, most,* or *some.*

Many successful artists struggled to overcome poverty.

An **overgeneralization** is a generalization that doesn't take every example into account and may include a word such as *all* or *none.*

All successful artists struggled to overcome poverty.

When you make generalizations, avoid **stereotyping**—making broad, inaccurate statements about members of a particular political, social, racial, ethnic, or religious group.

Avoiding Errors in Reasoning

Sometimes an idea at first appears to make sense but fails to stand up to close examination because it is based on a **fallacy.** A fallacy is an error in logic. There are several types of fallacies, including false causes, false analogies, and overgeneralizations. Two of the most common kinds of fallacies are the either/or fallacy and circular reasoning.

1 The Either/Or Fallacy

A writer who states that there are only two choices when there are actually many more is using an **either/or fallacy.** The following excerpt from a letter to the editor in a school newspaper concludes with an either/or statement.

STUDENT MODEL

Since last year, lunch in the cafeteria has gotten worse and worse. First, most of the food served isn't fresh. Vegetables and fruit are usually canned or frozen. Second, the cafeteria rarely serves popular foods like pizza. Some students have to buy snacks from the vending machine just so they aren't starving all day. Finally, I think the lunch menu is too limited. We can only choose between two meat dishes and two or three side dishes. **Either** students should be allowed to leave school to have lunch at nearby fast-food restaurants, **or** they should be allowed to choose the cafeteria menu.

The student who wrote the letter focuses on two options but leaves out other alternatives for solving the problem, such as the following.

- Student representatives could meet with the cafeteria managers and an assistant principal to try to work out a compromise.
- Students could be allowed to vote on what foods they would like to have served for lunch. Some of their choices could be added to the menu on a regular basis.
- A private company could be hired to run the school cafeteria.

2 Circular Reasoning

The attempt to prove a statement by simply repeating it in different words is called **circular reasoning.** In the following sentence, the second part of the statement repeats the information given in the first part.

Teenagers should avoid fad diets, because it is important for adolescents to stay away from quick weight-loss plans.

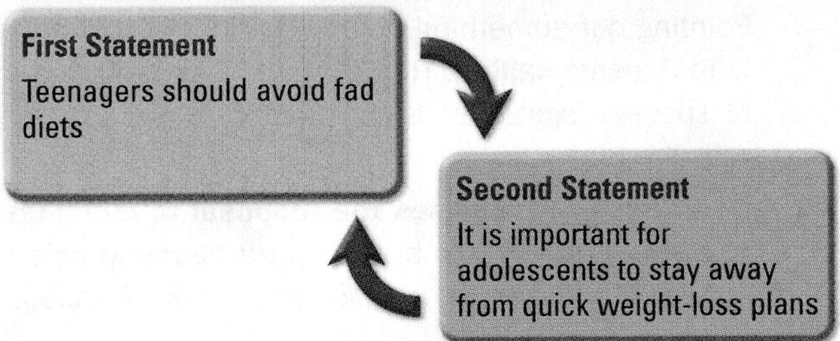
First Statement
Teenagers should avoid fad diets
Second Statement
It is important for adolescents to stay away from quick weight-loss plans

The sentence does not provide any facts or details to support the writer's argument. The second part of the sentence needs to be replaced with something more meaningful.

Teenagers should avoid fad diets, because their bodies are still growing and need nutrients that fad diets lack.

PRACTICE **Eliminating Errors in Reasoning**

For items 1–2, write an alternative to the two choices suggested. For items 3–5, rewrite the sentence to eliminate circular reasoning and provide a supporting detail.

1. Either schools should have vending machines with candy bars, or students should be allowed to go to convenience stores during their free period.
2. Either teenagers must eat less fast food, or they will not be as healthy as they could be.
3. Improving physical fitness is an important goal because being physically fit has many benefits.
4. Obesity is a serious problem in the United States because many Americans are overweight.
5. Reading labels to learn what ingredients are in a product is important because knowing what is in the food you eat is helpful.

Misusing Emotional Appeals

Emotional appeals use language that stirs up people's emotions. An emotional appeal can be an effective means of persuading people to do something. Sometimes, however, emotional appeals are misused to support flawed opinions. Learning about the following types of emotional appeals can help you see through weak arguments.

1 Name-Calling

Pointing out something negative about a person to discredit an idea is **name-calling.** Rather than discussing the idea, the writer or speaker expresses a low opinion of the person who came up with the idea.

Mayor Craig opposes the proposal to clean up an abandoned lot and turn it into a town park because he's close-minded. *(Mayor Craig might not like some new ideas, but why does he oppose the plan?)*

When you contradict or dispute someone's ideas, use facts and logical reasoning instead of name-calling.

2 Bandwagon Appeals and Snob Appeals

In old-time political campaigns, politicians traveled from place to place on elaborately decorated parade wagons, urging citizens to "jump on the bandwagon," or join the crowd and vote for them. **Bandwagon appeals** use the argument that a person should believe or do something because everyone else does. They take advantage of people's desire to be socially accepted by other people.

"More and more people are making the switch to Discountline long-distance service."

The logic in the statement above is weak because it gives no reasons for following the crowd.

Snob appeals urge you to do something because an elite group of people are doing it.

Both bandwagon and snob appeals are used in advertising.

3 Loaded Language

A word's dictionary definition is its denotation. The emotions and attitudes suggested by the word create its connotations. **Loaded language** consists of words with strongly positive or negative connotations, like those listed in the chart.

Comparing Word Connotations

Positive	Negative
determined	stubborn
economical	stingy
honest	blunt
leader	boss
freedom	chaos
confidently	arrogantly

When used properly, loaded language adds an emotional charge to persuasion. When misused, however, loaded language can cloud factual information, disguise poor reasoning, or unfairly manipulate people's emotions for the purpose of influencing attitudes or shaping opinions.

Senator Wilson is an honest family man who has led the crusade to protect our freedom.

For more information about connotations, see p. 383.

PRACTICE **Recognizing the Misuse of Emotional Appeals**

Identify the type of misused emotional appeal—name-calling, bandwagon appeal, snob appeal, or loaded language—in each sentence.

1. Chuck Dale still clings to old-fashioned views on crime prevention.
2. People have started to realize that this candidate is completely wrong for the job.
3. Informed citizens are voting for Sylvia Johnson for city council.
4. Governor Maria Jimenez has been a fearless leader in the fight to keep our pristine mountains out of the hands of greedy strip miners.
5. Mark shouldn't be given the job of class treasurer because he's a slick liar.

Student Help Desk

Evaluating Ideas at a Glance

Learning how to analyze and evaluate ideas effectively can help you find the reliable information you need for making good decisions.

Reliable information should

- include facts or informed opinions
- present logical relationships, such as cause-and-effect
- help you draw valid inferences, conclusions, or generalizations
- not include errors in reasoning, such as the either/or fallacy or circular reasoning
- not include improper emotional appeals, such as name-calling

Separating Facts from Opinions

Facts	Opinions
can be proved	can't be proved

Ways of Proving Statements

- Personal observation
- Firsthand experience
- Information from a recognized expert
- Information from an authoritative written source

Characteristics of Informed Opinions

- Factual support
- Logical reasoning
- Consideration of opposing viewpoints

Don't Get Led Astray

Types of Flawed Reasoning

To sort through information effectively, you need to be on the lookout for the types of flawed reasoning listed below.

Bandwagon appeal implies that you should do or believe something because everyone else does.

Circular reasoning repeats the same statement in different words.

An either/or fallacy asserts that there are only two alternatives in a given situation when there are many.

A false analogy compares two things that do not have essential features in common.

A false cause is an event that happened before another event but did not cause it.

Loaded language uses words with strong negative or positive connotations.

Name-calling attacks a person's character to try to discredit his or her ideas.

Overgeneralization is a broad statement that does not apply to all the things it describes.

The Bottom Line

Checklist for Analyzing and Evaluating Ideas

Have I . . .

____ correctly identified facts and opinions?

____ figured out logical connections between ideas?

____ identified valid inferences, conclusions, and generalizations?

____ recognized errors in reasoning?

____ avoided being influenced by appeals to emotions?

Power Words

Vocabulary for Precise Writing

inattentive

listless

Send In the Clowns

Need to write a review of a speech, a circus, or a concert? Try some of these words that describe how people receive messages.

Know Your Audience

Whether they're your **following,** your **market,** your **constituency,** or an **assembly, spectators,** or **onlookers,** you'll want to please them.

On a Good Day

If you're lucky, before you even open your mouth, the audience will be **well-disposed, welcoming,** and **receptive;** both **sympathetic** and **empathetic.** They will recognize how terrific you are, since they are so **perceptive,** so **discerning** and **discriminating,** so **insightful** and **astute.**

discerning

On a Bad Day

Although you may be at the top of your form your audience may be **hostile** and **antagonistic** and generally **ill-disposed.** Or, they may be **bored, indifferent,** and **inattentive; lethargic, listless,** and **apathetic;** both **passive** and **impassive.**

astute

CHAPTER 28

Your Turn Yeah, Right!

Suppose you're trying to persuade your parents to let you attend a concert on a school night. What words would you use to describe your parents' reaction to your argument?

receptive

Chapter 28

Oral Communication

These clowns aren't listening to me....
FUNNYSIDE UP
SALES

Is Anybody Listening?

Do you think this group is going to pay attention to whatever the speaker has to say? If she were dressed as a clown, would her audience be more interested in her message?

Effective **oral communication** occurs when the audience understands a message the way the speaker intends it. You can make your communication more effective by learning more about your role as a speaker and as a listener.

Write Away: Speak Out!

Think about a time when a speaker or storyteller held you spellbound. Did the person use vivid examples or a compelling tone of voice? Write a paragraph describing what you found so fascinating. Put your paragraph in your **Writing Portfolio.**

Effective Communication

1 What Is Communication?

Oral communication requires three elements: the **speaker,** the **message,** and the **audience.** Oral communication can be either one-way or two-way.

In **one-way communication,** the speaker delivers a message to an audience. The audience is either unable to respond or doesn't need to respond. News programs, movies or other entertainment, and announcements are examples of one-way communication.

In **two-way communication,** the speaker delivers a message to the audience, and the audience gives feedback to the speaker. Some types of two-way communication include group discussions, interviews, and conversations.

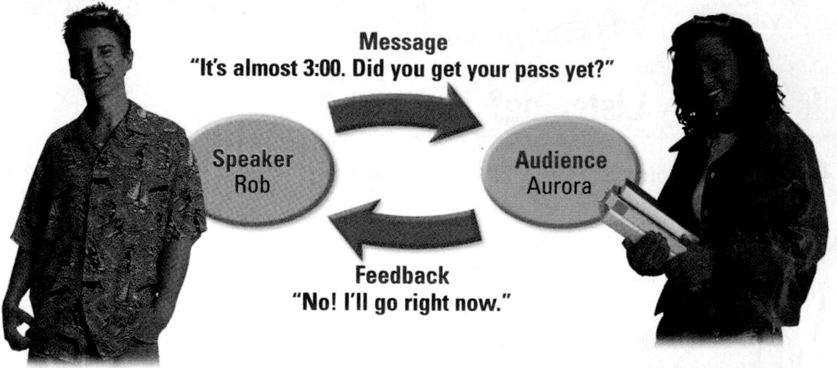

Message
"Pick up your movie passes by 3:00 today."
"It's almost 3:00. Did you get your pass yet?"
Speaker
Rob
Audience
Aurora
Feedback
"No! I'll go right now."

For oral communication to be effective, the **purpose** of the message has to be appropriate to the **occasion** that prompted it and the **audience** who receives it.

In the examples above, each audience understands what the speaker is saying and how to react to the message.

❷ Communication Barriers

As you're listening to a speaker, a passing siren drowns out his words. Or, maybe the room is too crowded, too hot or too cold, too dim or too bright. These **external barriers** can cause communication to fail. Likewise, both the speaker and audience may create **internal barriers** that can distort or block a message, as shown below.

THE FAR SIDE by Gary Larson

What we say to dogs
Okay, Ginger! I've had it! You stay out of the garbage! Understand, Ginger? Stay out of the garbage, or else!
What they hear
blah blah GINGER blah blah blah blah blah blah blah blah GINGER blah blah blah blah blah...

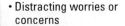

Speaker  **Audience**

Speaker

- Distracting appearance—hair, clothes, jewelry
- Annoying mannerisms—tugging at hair, clearing throat, etc.
- Obvious prejudice or lack of knowledge about the topic
- Tone of voice, nonverbal gestures conflict with the spoken words

Audience

- Distracting worries or concerns
- Daydreaming
- Prejudice, lack of interest and/or knowledge about the topic
- Physical discomfort—headache, hunger, illness

The next time you give a talk or listen to one, think about the communication barriers listed above. How could you keep them from interfering with your communication?

LESSON 2

Active Listening

Did you know that you can listen to about 400 spoken words a minute? That's a lot of words, but there's a catch. Of those words, you'll probably remember only about 25 percent. There's another catch. How much of what you hear can you believe? To become a more active listener—and to learn how to analyze a spoken message—follow these strategies.

1 Listening for Information

Listening for information is one of the most important types of listening you do as a student. Whether you're listening to a class discussion or a formal speech, how do you get the most out of what you hear?

Prepare to listen

- Learn what the topic is beforehand.
- Think about what you know or want to know about the topic.
- Have a pen or pencil and paper or a laptop computer to take notes.

Identify the main ideas

- Listen for the speaker's purpose (usually stated at the beginning), which alerts you to main ideas.
- Listen for words or phrases that signal important points, such as *to begin with, in addition, most importantly, finally, in conclusion.*
- Listen for ideas that are repeated for emphasis.

Take notes

- Write down only the most important points.
- If possible, use an outline or list format to organize main ideas and supporting points.
- Use phrases, abbreviations, and symbols to keep up with the speaker.
- After the presentation, ask questions to clear up any points.
- Review your notes right away to fill in details and reinforce understanding.

Suppose a guest speaker talks to your English class about some of the financial skills that high school students must learn to be independent after they graduate. One way to take notes on such a presentation is to use an outline format. See the example on the next page.

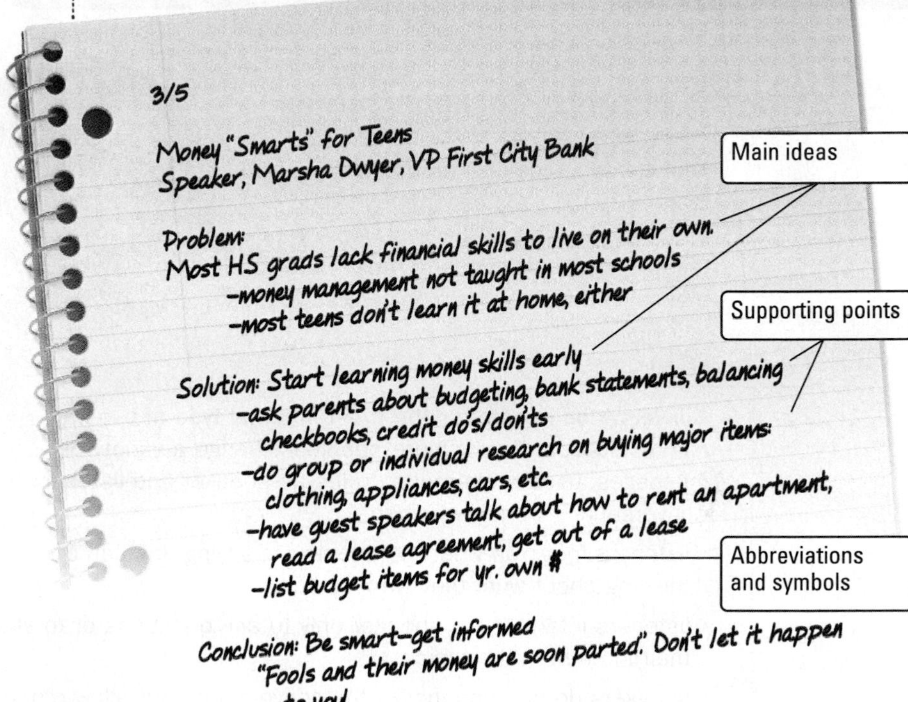

3/5
Money "Smarts" for Teens
Speaker, Marsha Dwyer, VP First City Bank
Main ideas
Problem:
Most HS grads lack financial skills to live on their own.
-money management not taught in most schools
-most teens don't learn it at home, either
Supporting points
Solution: Start learning money skills early
-ask parents about budgeting, bank statements, balancing
checkbooks, credit do's/don'ts
-do group or individual research on buying major items:
clothing, appliances, cars, etc.
-have guest speakers talk about how to rent an apartment,
read a lease agreement, get out of a lease
-list budget items for yr. own #
Abbreviations
and symbols
Conclusion: Be smart-get informed
"Fools and their money are soon parted." Don't let it happen
to you!

2 Critical Listening

Critical listening involves examining and analyzing a spoken message to judge its accuracy and reliability. Every day, you listen to messages from advertisers, politicians, lecturers, and others. No matter how dynamic or persuasive these speakers may be, you should evaluate their messages using the guidelines below.

Here's How Listening Critically

Detect faulty reasoning. "We offer the best car deals in town." On what evidence is this claim based? Always listen for supporting facts before you accept a statement.

Consider the source. Think about the background, viewpoint, and possible motives of the speaker. Speakers often slant information to persuade you to buy a product, accept an idea, or watch a program.

Observe nonverbal messages. Ideally, a speaker's gestures, facial expressions, and tone of voice should reinforce the message. If not, you should doubt the speaker's sincerity and the message's reliability.

ORAL COMM.

LESSON 3

Informal Speaking

Types of Informal Communication

You've been speaking informally since you learned to talk. You can improve your informal speaking skills, however, if you follow certain guidelines to make sure your message is clearly communicated.

Conversation

Conversation is perhaps the most informal type of two-way communication. Two or more people exchange a variety of messages, usually alternating roles as speaker and listener. Conversations work best when

- listeners focus on what the speaker is saying, instead of thinking about what they want to say
- listeners interrupt the speaker only to ask questions or to show their interest in the topic
- speakers do not monopolize the conversation but allow others to participate
- both listeners and speakers respect one another's opinions and viewpoints
- both listeners and speakers maintain eye contact and give appropriate feedback

Introductions

An **introduction** is one-way communication whose purpose is to give listeners information about someone they are meeting for the first time. For example, you may want to introduce a new student to your friends or a friend to members of your family. Introductions are most helpful when

- speakers provide the full names or the names and titles (Grampa Isley, Mrs. Vargo) of everyone present
- speakers tell something about the background of the person they are introducing ("Carla just moved here from Arizona.")
- speakers mention something that the new person might have in common with the others
- listeners pay close attention to people's names and to the background information provided

Announcements

An **announcement** is one-way communication that provides an audience with important details about a topic or event. Sometimes, however, an announcement requires participation from the listeners. They have a responsibility to ask questions if they don't understand the message. Oral announcements convey a clear message when

- they answer the basic questions *who, what, where, when, why,* and *how*
- they include all necessary details
- listeners know exactly what to do after hearing the message

Storytelling

Storytelling is one-way communication meant to entertain an audience or to illustrate a certain point. You might use storytelling to relate a personal anecdote to a friend or to tell others about a story you've heard or read. Good storytelling is an art. You know this is true if you've ever stifled a yawn halfway through someone's rambling, long-winded anecdote.

Here's How Telling a Good Story

- **Use vivid details, but don't use too many.** Choose your details to paint a clear picture of time, place, setting, and characters, but don't get too detailed. You want to describe the forest, not every tree.
- **Use nonverbal language to heighten interest**. Use your facial expressions, voice, and gestures to convey the different characters, emotions, and actions.
- **Make the point, or theme, of your story clear.** The end of a story is a good place to reinforce the purpose ("So, after that, I learned never to . . . ").
- **Stay in contact with your audience.** Be aware of their reactions. If you notice the audience is getting restless, pick up the pace of your story.

ORAL COMM.

Group Communication

Have you ever been part of a group in which none of its members could agree? Have you ever witnessed a group that seemed to accomplish the impossible? Whether at school, at play, or later at work, you are likely to spend a lot of time in groups. Knowing a few guidelines and strategies for making this form of two-way communication successful can help you now and in the future.

1 Roles in Groups

Successful groups assign roles to each member, such as chairperson, recorder, and participants. These roles distribute responsibility among the members and help keep discussions focused.

Chairperson

- Introduces topic
- Explains goal or purpose
- Participates in discussion and keeps it on track
- Helps resolve conflicts and maintain fairness
- Helps group reach goal

Recorder

- Takes notes on discussion
- Reports on suggestions and decisions
- Organizes and writes up notes
- Participates in discussion

Participants

- Contribute facts or ideas to discussion
- Respond constructively to others' ideas
- Reach agreement or vote on final decision

2 Group Dynamics

Every group has a different **dynamic**—the energy and activity created by its members. Some groups are eager to talk, make plans, and get things done. Other groups can't even get started. Because everybody has different perspectives and experiences, group members have two major challenges: managing discussions and reaching agreement on ideas and actions.

By learning a few guidelines and strategies, you can help create a more cooperative atmosphere. This in turn can produce a high-energy, take-charge group dynamic.

Guidelines for Discussion

- Be informed about the topic.
- Make sure everyone participates.
- Don't talk while someone else is talking.
- Support statements and opinions with facts and examples.
- Listen attentively; be courteous and respectful of others' viewpoints.
- Work toward the goal; avoid getting sidetracked by conflicts or unrelated topics.

Strategies for Achieving Agreement

- Each side gives a little to reach a compromise.
- The group members brainstorm various solutions until they find one agreeable to everybody.
- The group postpones a decision so that members can get more information or calm down.
- The group asks an outside counselor or adviser to help settle conflicts and reach an agreement.

Conducting an Interview

An interview is a formal type of two-way conversation with a definite purpose and goal. To get the most out of the experience, follow these guidelines for preparing, conducting, and following up an interview.

1 Preparation

Thorough preparation can help you be mentally and emotionally ready for the interview. The following example shows how you might plan an interview with a former used-car salesperson.

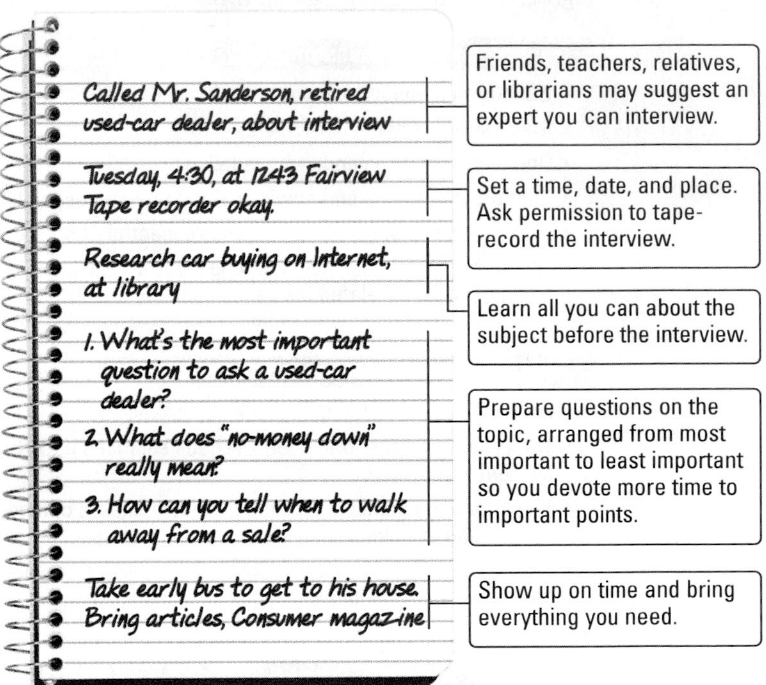

Called Mr. Sanderson, retired used-car dealer, about interview
Friends, teachers, relatives, or librarians may suggest an expert you can interview.
Tuesday, 4:30, at 1243 Fairview
Tape recorder okay.
Set a time, date, and place. Ask permission to tape-record the interview.
Research car buying on Internet, at library
Learn all you can about the subject before the interview.
1. What's the most important question to ask a used-car dealer?
2. What does "no-money down" really mean?
3. How can you tell when to walk away from a sale?
Prepare questions on the topic, arranged from most important to least important so you devote more time to important points.
Take early bus to get to his house.
Bring articles, Consumer magazine
Show up on time and bring everything you need.

Make sure that you have fresh batteries and a new tape in your recorder.

CHAPTER 28

❷ During the Interview

Once you arrive at the interview, use these strategies to help you get the information you need.

Strategy: Conducting an Interview

1. **Ask questions that encourage a detailed response instead of a "yes" or "no" answer.** "Please describe how you first got interested in . . . " or "What do you think is important about . . . ?"
2. **Listen carefully to what the person says. Ask follow-up questions to clarify any points or to pursue an interesting comment.** "Would you explain what you mean by . . . ?" or "Could you say more about . . . ?"
3. **Repeat or summarize important points to make sure you've understood them.** "So, you're saying that . . . " or "What I hear you saying is . . . "
4. **Listen or watch for nonverbal cues (tone of voice, gestures). Encourage the person to say more.** "You sound as if that made you sad."
5. **When the person gets off the subject, gently guide him or her back.** "That's a good point, but let's get back to . . . "
6. **Even if you tape an interview, take notes on important points. You might want to go back to those points later.**
7. **Always thank the person for the interview and ask if you can call with any follow-up questions. You may also send a thank-you note to the person in appreciation for his or her time and effort.**

❸ Follow-up

While the interview is still fresh in your mind, follow these steps:

1. Rewrite your notes or make a written copy of the tape recording as soon as possible. Often you will see gaps or inconsistencies that you may not have noticed before.
2. If any points are unclear or if information is missing, call and ask more questions while the person is still available.
3. Select the most appropriate quotes to support your ideas. Decide what information you might want to summarize in your own words.

Make sure that when you quote someone you don't misrepresent what they say or take the quote out of context. To be on the safe side, have the person review your work for accuracy.

ORAL COMM.

LESSON 6

Formal Speaking

Does the idea of giving a formal speech in front of an audience terrify you? Don't worry; many people feel the same way. You can learn to manage your fears by following the four R's of public speaking—Recognize, Research, Rehearse, and Relax.

1 Recognize Occasion, Purpose, and Audience

Remember, for communication to succeed, the purpose of your message has to be appropriate to the occasion that prompts it and the audience who will hear it.

Suppose the students in your English class are assigned to give a 10-minute speech on a life skill, such as buying clothes or managing money. You decide to talk about how to buy a car. Use this chart to help you focus on what you want to say, how you want to say it, and who your audience is.

Analyzing Occasion, Purpose, and Audience

Occasion	**What is the occasion for this speech?** A 10-minute talk in English class about a life skill we should know: buying a car.
	What interests me about this topic? What do I think others would like to know? I want to get a car someday. Do's and don'ts about buying a car—how to talk to dealers, private owners, and how to protect yourself.
Purpose	**Do I want to inform, persuade, or entertain?** Mainly inform, but in an interesting way. Maybe include slides, lists of questions to ask.
Audience	**Who is the audience?** classmates
	What do they know about the topic? Some know a lot, others almost nothing. So focus on how to buy a car—skip most technical details about engines and mechanics.

Because you have only 10 minutes, you decide to narrow your topic to how to buy a used car from a private owner.

❷ Research and Write

As you gather information from various sources, jot down ideas for illustrations or graphic aids. For example, you can include pictures of different used cars and a list of key questions for each one that a buyer should ask a private owner. Like a research paper, your speech will contain an introduction, a body, and a conclusion.

Introduction: Tell them what you're going to say.
Attention-grabbing opener: startling fact, thought-provoking question, unusual statistic. This introduces the topic and purpose of the speech.

"So you want to buy a used car. What's the one question most people forget to ask the owner?"

Body: Say it.
Facts and examples to support the main idea and purpose of the speech, illustrated by graphic aids or other props

"Ask for all the car's paperwork. Don't kick the tires—it shows you don't know what you're doing."

Conclusion: Tell them what you said.
Restatement of main points and purpose—can end with a memorable fact, statistic, or quote

"The more you ask, the more you know. The more you know, the less you pay in the long run."

Speech Format Often, your teacher will tell you whether you can give your speech from a manuscript, an outline, or note cards.

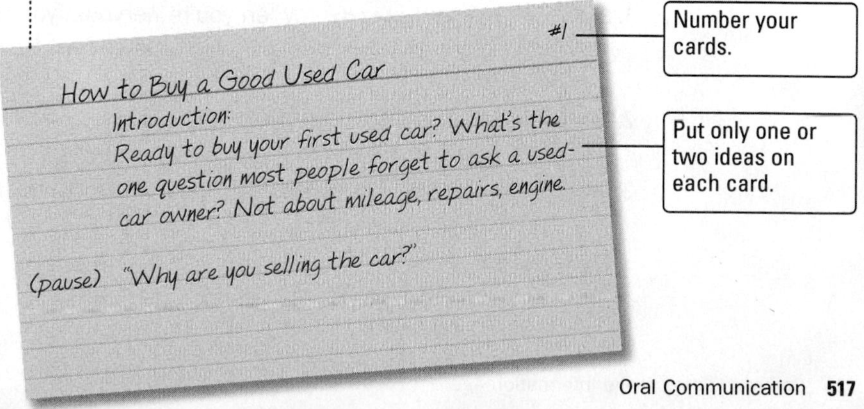

#1
How to Buy a Good Used Car
Introduction:
Ready to buy your first used car? What's the one question most people forget to ask a used-car owner? Not about mileage, repairs, engine.
(pause) "Why are you selling the car?"
Number your cards.
Put only one or two ideas on each card.

ORAL COMM.

3 Rehearse the Speech

Rehearsing the speech will help you become familiar with the material and comfortable presenting it. You can practice in front of a mirror or with an audience of friends or family.

Rehearsing a Formal Speech

- Videotape or tape-record your practice sessions.
- Make sure your speech fits the allotted time.
- Practice using your visual aids so they fit smoothly into your talk.
- Practice making eye contact with your audience.
- Vary the pitch and rhythm of your voice to avoid a monotone delivery.
- Vary the pace—pausing for effect, slowing down to make a point.
- Make notes on your speech that point out where to pause, speak louder or softer, use a graphic, or any other item you need to remember.

If you can, rehearse in the room where you will give the speech. Practice using equipment before your speech.

4 Relax—and Deliver

Before Your Speech The secret to relaxing is based on a simple truth: *it's impossible to be physically relaxed and emotionally terrified at the same time.* To relax, follow these three steps:

1. **Breathe deeply and slowly**—This tells your body that the speech is not a life-threatening crisis.
2. **Move around**—Movement helps to burn up the stress hormones pumping through your system.
3. **Get support**—Arrange to make eye contact with a supportive friend in the audience.

During the Speech As you talk, keep these guidelines in mind.

1. **Speak slowly and clearly**—When you're nervous, you tend to talk faster. By slowing down, you'll sound just right to your audience.
2. **Make eye contact with the audience**—Glance up from your notes often and look people in the eye.
3. **Watch the audience for responses**—If they start fidgeting or yawning, speak a little louder, skip a graphic or two, or get to your conclusion a little sooner.

❺ Evaluating Speakers

Learning how to evaluate someone else's speech can improve both your listening and speaking skills. Use this chart as an evaluation guide.

Evaluating Content

- What was the purpose of the speech? Did the speaker accomplish it?
- Did the speech match the audience's level of interest and knowledge?
- Did the introduction capture the audience's attention?
- Were the main idea and supporting details clear from the beginning?
- Did the conclusion sum up the main points?

Evaluating Delivery

- Did the speaker seem prepared?
- Were visual aids helpful and presented well?
- Did the speaker make eye contact with the audience?
- Was the speaker's voice loud enough? Did the pitch, rhythm, and pace vary enough?
- Did gestures and facial expressions reinforce the message or distract from it?

Giving Verbal Feedback At times you will be asked to give direct feedback to a speaker. Here's how to give constructive suggestions for improvement.

1. **Be specific**—Don't make blanket statements like "Your charts need work." Offer concrete suggestions, such as "Make the type size bigger so we can read the poster from the back of the room."
2. **Discuss only the most important points**—Don't overload the speaker with too much feedback about too many details. Focus on important points such as these:
    - Is the topic too advanced for the audience?
    - Are the supporting details well organized?
    - Is the conclusion weak?
3. **Give balanced feedback**—Tell the speaker not only what didn't work but what did: "I'd drop the last two slides, since you already covered those points earlier. But I really liked the first two slides. They got my attention, and I learned a lot."

Student Help Desk

Oral Communication at a Glance

For communication to succeed, the **purpose** of a message must be appropriate to the **occasion** that prompts it and the **audience** who will hear it.

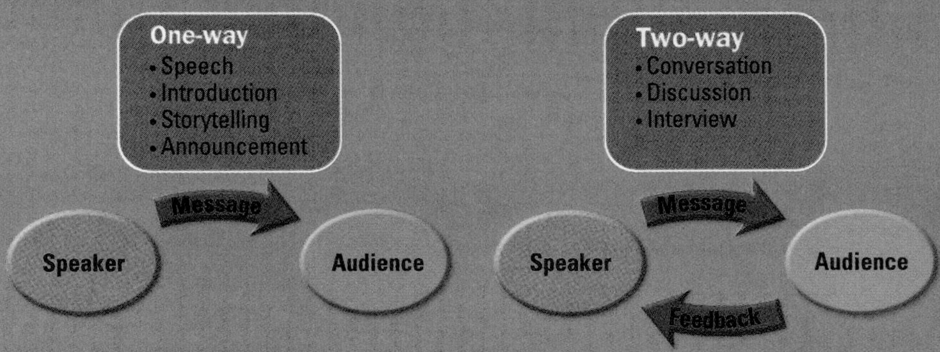

Tips for Active Listening

Now HEAR This!

To listen for information

- Learn what the topic is.
- Think about what you know and want to know about the topic.
- Concentrate on what the speaker says.
- Identify main points and supporting details.
- Take notes.

To listen critically

- Listen for supporting evidence.
- Consider how the speaker's background, viewpoint, and motives affect the message.
- Check to see if the speaker's nonverbal messages match the spoken message.

Tips for Formal Speaking

Speaker's Tricks

Breathe slowly and deeply; move around; get support from friends.

Before your talk, don't drink milk or eat chocolate; they thicken your voice.

Fear dries out your mouth, so keep a glass of water on hand for your talk.

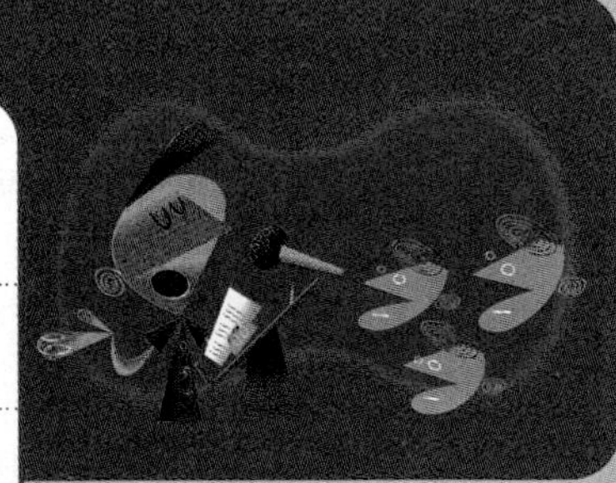

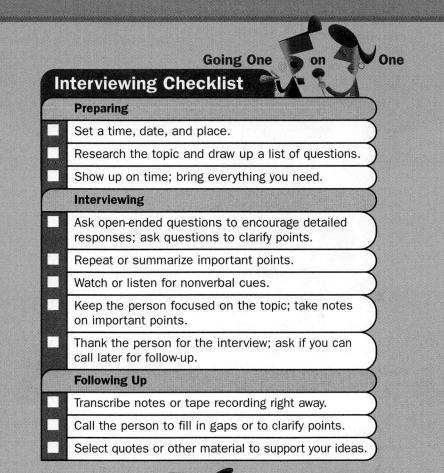

Going One on One

Interviewing Checklist

Preparing

- ☐ Set a time, date, and place.
- ☐ Research the topic and draw up a list of questions.
- ☐ Show up on time; bring everything you need.

Interviewing

- ☐ Ask open-ended questions to encourage detailed responses; ask questions to clarify points.
- ☐ Repeat or summarize important points.
- ☐ Watch or listen for nonverbal cues.
- ☐ Keep the person focused on the topic; take notes on important points.
- ☐ Thank the person for the interview; ask if you can call later for follow-up.

Following Up

- ☐ Transcribe notes or tape recording right away.
- ☐ Call the person to fill in gaps or to clarify points.
- ☐ Select quotes or other material to support your ideas.

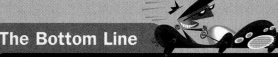

The Bottom Line

Checklist for Giving a Formal Speech

Have I . . .

____ matched my purpose to the occasion and the audience?

____ marked my speech for pacing, voice, visual aids, etc.?

____ opened with an attention-grabbing question, fact, or statement?

____ stated the purpose and main ideas clearly?

____ supported the main ideas with facts and examples?

____ used visuals or other aids to illustrate the main points?

____ concluded by restating main ideas?

____ maintained eye contact and matched nonverbal language to my message?

Power Words

Vocabulary for Precise Writing

Sensory Overload

Media messages come at us from all sides, all day long, on TV and radio. There's no escape. But don't run away from these sensory words. They can be scene-stealers in your next description.

In Our Ears

We have a number of words for **noise,** especially loud, *unpleasant* noise: **din, dissonance, caterwauling,** and **cacophony.** And we have lots of words for **loud,** especially for *too* loud: **noisy, deafening, earsplitting, piercing, booming, thundering, clamorous,** and **clangorous.**

And In Our Eyes

Everywhere you look you see **images** and **countenances** on billboards and buses. You may be overwhelmed and bombarded with **tableaux** on the street and **tabloids** on the newsstand. You may witness a **spectacle** or a **phantasmagoria.**

Your Turn Rock the House

Think about your favorite radio station. Describe it from your parents' point of view. Would you use any of the words above?

Chapter 29

Understanding the Media

Media Blitz

You are exposed to hundreds of images and messages every time you watch television, listen to the radio, or read a newspaper or magazine. When you watch a TV commercial, do you stop to think about the effect it has on you? Does it influence the way you think, feel, act, or even dress? Understanding how different types of media work and the role that they play will help you become more informed about the choices you make in response to the media.

Write Away: Media Messages

Think of a commercial, magazine or billboard advertisement, or radio announcement that caught your attention. In a short paragraph, describe the message and tell why it grabbed your interest. Save your paragraph in your **Working Portfolio.**

THE MEDIA

Characteristics of Media

The term *media* refers to means of communication intended to reach a large number of people. Three types of media are print, broadcast, and the Internet. The more you know about each medium, the easier it will be to understand how the media influence your thoughts, attitudes, and actions.

1 Print

Print media convey information by means of printed words, images, or symbols. Some forms of print media are books, newspapers, magazines, advertisements, newsletters, brochures, billboards, posters, and photographs. The chart below describes the purpose and characteristics of different types of print media.

Newspaper	
Examples	*Chicago Tribune, The New York Times, The Miami Herald*
Purpose	To inform and/or persuade
Characteristics	• Covers feature stories; editorials; sports; and local, regional, or national news • No video images or sounds • Relies on advertising and customer subscription to cover costs, but maintains lower subscription rates than other print media • Aimed mainly toward adults • May contain special weekly features to attract certain audiences
Magazine	
Examples	*Newsweek, National Geographic, Teen People*
Purpose	To entertain and/or inform
Characteristics	• Often has a specialized focus: fashion, news, sports, special interest • Presents content through words, graphics, and photographs • Relies heavily on advertising and mass-mailing subscription offers to cover costs • Audience varies depending on focus of magazine

❷ Broadcast and Film Media

Broadcast media include two of the most important media inventions of the 20th century—television and radio. The medium of television is so popular that in the average American household, the TV is on for at least seven hours a day. **Film media** include movies, videotapes, videodiscs, and DVDs.

Radio	
Examples	*Sports Talk, Mornings with Grace and Mike*
Purpose	To entertain, inform, and/or persuade
Characteristics	• Unlimited access • Presents a wide variety of talk shows, music programs, and news broadcasts • Uses sound, music, and voice-overs to present message; no visual images • Relies on selling airtime to advertisers to cover costs • Public radio relies on contributions from listeners

Film	
Examples	*Titanic, Grease, Glory*
Purpose	To entertain and inform
Characteristics	• Access may be limited, depending on availability of film • Presents message through images, sound effects and music, actors' performances • Depends on ticket sales and video rentals to cover costs • Appeals to a wide audience

Television	
Examples	*Dateline, Saturday Night Live, Friends*
Purpose	To entertain, inform, and/or persuade
Characteristics	• Unlimited access • Features entertainment, education, sports, and news programs • Uses video, music, special effects, graphics, and images to bring topics to life • Relies heavily on advertising to cover costs • Type of audience depends on program

3 Internet

Many computer users access the **Internet** to learn more about topics that interest them or to communicate with others. Web sites, like other media forms, have some unique characteristics.

Web sites	
Examples	individual pages; e-zines; corporate, government, and university sites; search engines
Purpose	To inform, persuade, and entertain
Characteristics	• Can provide in-depth coverage of news and special-interest topics • Presents content through words, graphics, video and sound clips, and interactive features • Includes links to other sites with related information • Many Web site owners rely on advertising to support their sites, and are paid for the number of hits, or visits, the site receives

WATCH OUT Some information on the Internet may be inaccurate or outdated. Use more than one source to check for accuracy.

PRACTICE **Media Coverage**

Choose a current political, environmental, or social issue, such as television ratings for children. Then find three examples of appropriate coverage of this issue by different forms of media—print, broadcast, film, or the Internet. Create a chart like the one below and compare the ways in which the message is presented.

	Article	6 o'clock news	Web
Text			
Images			
Sound			
Other			

LESSON 2 Influences on the Media

You already know that the media have a powerful influence on people. Some wake up to the sound of their radios, others read the paper first thing in the morning, and others turn on the television every day. Did you know, however, that people also have a strong influence on the media?

1 Owners

Some forms of media are independently owned, whereas others are part of a corporate family, in which each medium is like one of the children. Think about who makes the decisions in your household. In most families, the parent or parents make decisions for the well-being of the family. Similarly, some media rely on their parent companies to make decisions about what programs, news stories, music, and so forth will be featured.

Many parent companies own several different kinds of media. For example, a parent company may own three radio stations, five newspaper or magazine publications, a publishing company, and a small television station.

2 Target Audience

Whenever you read a magazine, watch a television program, or buy a pair of shoes you saw in an advertisement, you become a member of a target audience. **Target audiences** are a part of the entire population that share similar characteristics. Companies spend millions of dollars to target a particular audience and get its support. Look at the characteristics of three groups of people on the following page. These characteristics reflect an effort by the media and society to define a particular group of people and to target their needs.

THE MEDIA

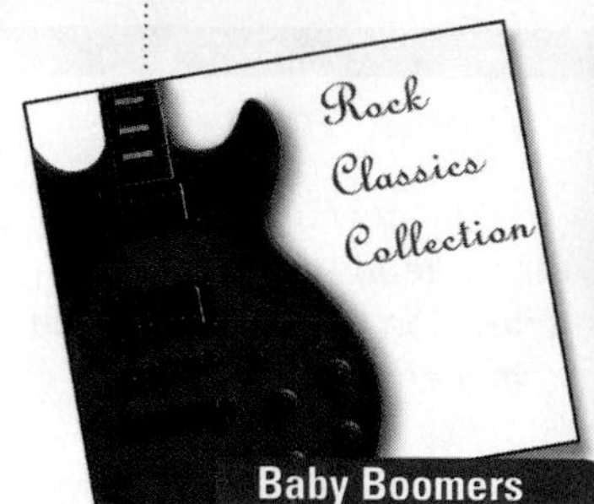

Baby Boomers

Born (1946–64)

Population:
76 million

Characteristics:
wealthiest generation of the 20th century; overworked; fearful of aging; shaped by Vietnam War

Popular shows (1950s–1960s): *The Honeymooners, I Love Lucy, Bonanza, American Bandstand*

Generation X

Born (1965–77)

Population:
55 million

Characteristics:
self-reliant and independent; risk-taking, competitive

Popular shows (1970s–1980s): *All in the Family, M*A*S*H, The Brady Bunch, Fame, The Cosby Show, Cheers*

Generation Y

Born (1978–94)

Population:
60+ million

Characteristics:
computer and media savvy; quick-paced mentality; optimistic; environmentally conscious

Popular shows (1990s): *ER, NYPD Blue, Seinfield, The Simpsons, Friends*

The shared characteristics of a particular group are often referred to as **demographics**—statistical data about age, gender, profession, level of income, level of education, ethnic background, and so forth. The media are directly influenced by demographics. They research the behavior of their target audience and think of ways to attract them. For example, toy manufacturers know that many children watch Saturday morning cartoons. Therefore, to reach this audience, they sell child-oriented TV commercials to Saturday morning shows.

When you use a certain medium, think about to whom it is targeted and what it says about the demographics of that group.

PRACTICE A **Generations to Come**

In a group, list characteristics and relationships that define your generation. You might want to list a few of your favorite TV shows, books, or Web sites. Also, think about the major events and trends that have had an impact on your generation. How are these characteristics and relationships represented in various media?

3 Advertisers

Each year advertisers spend billions of dollars to reach as vast an audience as possible. Company sponsors buy television or radio airtime or magazine, newspaper, or billboard advertising. They pay top dollars to air commercials on programs with high ratings. Since selling time and space to advertisers generates much of the income the media need to function, the media need advertising as much as advertisers need the media. Therefore, the media will work hard to attract the audiences that advertisers want.

The biggest day of the year for advertisers is the Sunday the annual Super Bowl football game is played. The following statistics show the importance of Super Bowl Sunday.

Super Bowl XXXIII
Number of viewers: More than 127.5 million people
Average cost of 30-second spot commercials: $1.6 million+
Number of commercials: 51

Because companies invest so much money in advertising, they are selective about the types of media they use. Often, they will support a specific TV program or magazine that has a wide target audience. The media, in turn, will do their best to accommodate advertisers. For example, a television series with controversial issues that might offend its viewers is not likely to attract advertisers. If the show loses favor with advertisers and the public, it will be canceled.

PRACTICE B **Becoming Media Savvy**

Think about a television series, talk show, radio program, or game show that was canceled. In a group, discuss some of the reasons why you think it was cancelled. Did it have low ratings? limited audience appeal? controversial issues? Record your thoughts.

Messages in the Media

The media not only reflect the values, ideas, and opinions of culture but they also influence culture.

1 Reflection of Culture

What do the media say about you? What do they say about your family or your friends? The media try to reflect who we are, what we believe in, how we view things, and what values we hold. For example, the two pictures below portray women as they were reflected in the media in the 1950s and 1990s.

Women in the 1950s

Happy Homemaker

Women in the 1990s

Working Mom

What do the two images say about the way society viewed women at the time?

Another way the media reflect culture is through their coverage of the current social or political concerns. In the 1960s, the Vietnam War influenced how the media portrayed culture. Magazine covers showed strong images of war and violence. Front page headlines of newspapers focused on a country torn by the effects of war.

PRACTICE **Culture Through the Decades**

For each decade, the media forms an image of pop culture—what is popular in our culture at a given time. For example, the 1950s and 1960s were influenced by rock-n-roll, the 1970s by disco, the 1980s by punk rock, and the 1990s by hip-hop. In a group, discuss how the media reflect pop culture today. What changes in fashion, hairstyles, music, and so forth are characteristic of this decade?

❷ Influence on Culture

Media messages are carefully thought out and researched in order to effectively influence audiences. How many times have you purchased a magazine because of its cover or a newspaper because of its catchy headlines? People employed by the media will think of clever ways to make you think you need a certain product. The next time you see, listen to, or read something, keep in mind that the media have the power to positively or negatively influence the way you think, feel, or act.

Reality Versus Fantasy

The media provide an escape from reality for many people. Television, for example, provides an outlet for people to forget about their problems and relax before returning to their daily routine. As a media consumer, you should be aware that the media may purposely distort reality even though many of the situations they present are portrayed realistically. Examine some of the ways in which the media influence your perception of reality.

Stereotypes

- Some films and TV programs feature one-dimensional characters—the fearless hero, the mad scientist, the ditsy blond, the bratty teen—who might be comical or who might possess dramatic appeal but who have little in common with real people.
- Many lead characters on television or in films are doctors, lawyers, or police officers.

- Most women on the pages of fashion magazines are pencil-thin models who represent an unrealistic body type.
- Most people on television are wealthy, lead glamorous, interesting lives, and are rarely shown performing mundane tasks.

Violence

- Media often glamorize violence.
- The hero usually prevails and the villain pays for the crime.
- In most cases, a violent act can be resolved in a one-hour TV episode or a two-hour film.
- A jail sentence can be as brief as five to ten minutes.

Time

- Several years can seem to pass in a few days.
- One day can be stretched over several weeks.

LESSON 4

Evaluating Media

1 Analyzing Purpose in Media

Every message you receive from the media has a core purpose. To discover that purpose, think about why its creator paid for and produced the message. An ad might entertain you with its humor, but its core purpose is to persuade you to buy something. Often, multiple purposes are attached to the core purpose in order to reach wider audiences or to boost ratings. As a consumer, your job is to analyze messages or ideas so that you can make informed decisions. The first task is to identify the core purpose of a message.

Here's How Identifying the Core Purpose

1. Look for elements that are added to the core purpose to create multiple purposes. For example, a morning news show might feature such live entertainment as musical performances, interviews with actors, or wacky antics to entertain its audience.
2. Analyze each element and ask why and how it is used. Such elements might include humor, special effects, music tracks, slogans, comic skits, and graphics.
3. Mentally subtract the added elements and focus on the core purpose of the message. Is the purpose to inform, persuade, or entertain? In this example, the morning news show provides entertainment, but its core purpose is to inform.

PRACTICE A **Analyze This!**

Using the strategies listed above, think about the messages in these ads and determine their core purpose.

Chicago Fireman
Rescues Mother and Son
At 27th and Western.
Adopt a pet now at the City of Chicago's
David Lee Animal Care Shelter
2741 South Western Avenue
Chicago Streets And Sanitation
Crew Picks Up Litter At
27th And Western.
Adopt a pet now at the City of Chicago's
David Lee Animal Care Shelter
2741 South Western Avenue

2 Evaluating Content

Being able to respond critically to media images and messages will help you evaluate the reliability of the content and make informed decisions. To evaluate the content of media messages, ask yourself the following questions:

Here's How Evaluating Media Content

- **What is the core purpose?** Review the core purpose of the message. Think about who created the message and why it was created.
- **Who is the target audience?** What age group, ethnic group, gender, and/or profession is the message targeting? How does the message relate to you?
- **Is the message based on reliable information?** Think about the reliability of the source. An informative article in a newsmagazine or newspaper provides information based on fact. A tabloid, on the other hand, is often unreliable.

Once you have evaluated the message using the questions above, you should look at the message critically for a deeper meaning. Use the following guidelines to help you understand the message that lies beneath the surface.

- **Ask yourself if you agree with the message.**
- **Determine what the message says about American culture.** Does it reflect any current political or social concerns? What does it say about pop culture? Is the message based on reality or fantasy? Does it include stereotypes?
- **Think about the values that are expressed.** Do they go against your values or the values of society in general?
- **Look for bias.** A reliable source should present all sides of an issue. It should not reflect a certain slant or point of view.
- **Look for persuasive techniques that are used to sway your opinion.** For example, does it use bandwagon appeal ("Everyone's buying it")?
- **Recognize logical fallacies.** For example, does it use circular reasoning ("It's a good idea to buy it because it's a smart purchase") or overgeneralization ("No one should be without it")?

For more on persuasive techniques and logical fallacies, see pp. 490–501.

❸ Evaluating Presentation

Different types of media use visual and verbal elements to achieve a desired effect. Visual elements include symbols, printed text, color, photographs, camera angles, and special effects.

- **Printed text** Big headlines show the significance of a story and grab your attention.
- **Design** Color, symbols, logos, photographs, and images focus your attention on an idea and set a mood.
- **Film techniques** Camera angles, lighting, special effects, and other techniques influence your perception of reality.

Which visual devices in the following magazine article grab your attention? Keep in mind that the designer or editor planned the visual elements to appeal to your emotions and sense of logic.

Dark red background connects the reader to the word "Pain" in article title.

Cover Story

CONQUERING PAIN

New discoveries and treatments offer hope

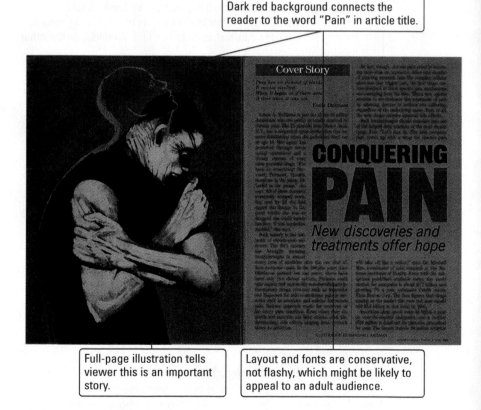

Full-page illustration tells viewer this is an important story.

Layout and fonts are conservative, not flashy, which might be likely to appeal to an adult audience.

In addition to visual elements, verbal elements are used to convey media messages and to attract your attention and help you recall what is being communicated.

Verbal elements include music, spoken words and tone of voice, and sound effects.

- **Music** Different types of music can create a mood and offer clues about the content. For example, dramatic violin music might intensify feelings of suspense.
- **Spoken words and tone** Word choice and tone of voice create a formal or informal impression of the speaker.
- **Sound effects** Canned applause, laugh tracks, and other sound effects add to the humor, emphasize a point, or contribute to the mood.

The next time you watch a commercial, pay attention to the music. Advertisers want you to associate their products or services with a catchy jingle or a popular song.

When evaluating media, think about how visual and verbal effects bring media messages to life. Different media will use multiple visual and verbal elements to hook your interest and draw you in.

Here are some questions to consider as you evaluate media messages for presentation:

- Is the information current, original, and interesting?
- How are the photographs and illustrations used? Do they relate to the written content and provide visual information? Are they used simply to decorate the page? Do they grab your attention?
- Is there a connection between the scene and the music? Does the music contribute to the mood?
- Are the special effects useful, or do they confuse the story line?
- Are the sound effects realistic? Are they effective?

PRACTICE B Understanding Messages

Record a series of commercials at home or at school, using the library equipment. Pick your favorite or one that grabs your attention. Evaluate and critique the persuasive techniques of the media message by answering the following questions: Who is the target audience? What message is being sent? What effects are created by the verbal and visual elements? How might others interpret the commercial? Finally, rate the effectiveness of the commercial based on your evaluation.

Student Help Desk

Understanding Media at a Glance

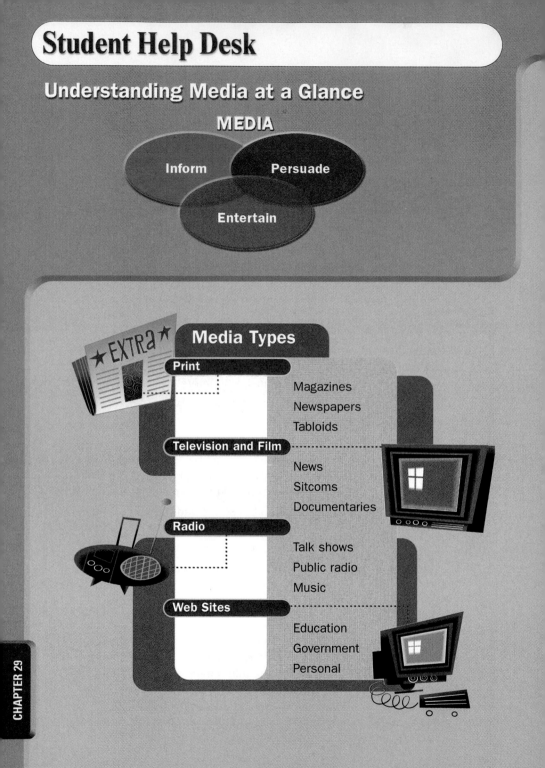

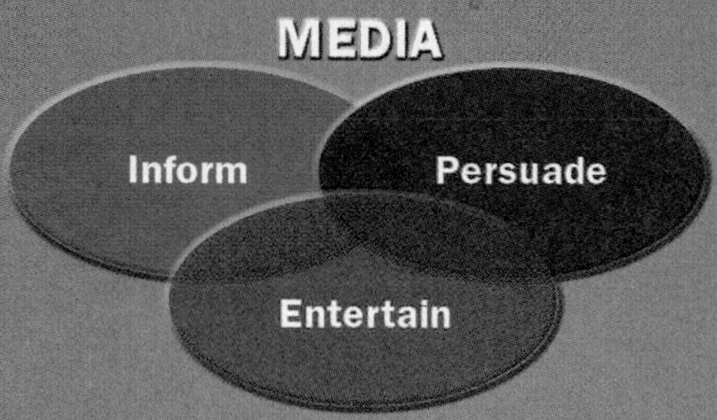

Media Types

Print
- Magazines
- Newspapers
- Tabloids

Television and Film
- News
- Sitcoms
- Documentaries

Radio
- Talk shows
- Public radio
- Music

Web Sites
- Education
- Government
- Personal

CHAPTER 29

Evaluating Media

- Who created this message?
- Who is the target audience?
- Are there multiple purposes? What is the core purpose?
- What does the message say about American culture?

Are the Media Watching You

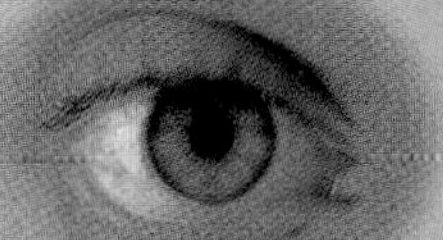

or Are You Watching the Media?

- Is the message based on reality or does it distort reality?
- Does it use any persuasive techniques to sway your opinion?
- Does it use any visual or verbal elements? What is their effect?

The Bottom Line

Checklist for Evaluating Media Messages

Have I . . .

____ identified the creator of the message, its core purpose, and its target audience?

____ recognized the influence of media owners, consumers, and advertisers?

____ evaluated the content of a media message?

____ considered how the message both reflects and influences culture?

____ analyzed the verbal and/or visual devices used to convey the message?

THE MEDIA

Power Words
Vocabulary for Precise Writing

panoramic

The Eye of the Artist

"Great shot!" Do people say that about your pictures? With the words below, you can tell how you achieved those great photographs.

zoom

photomontage

Get the Picture?

To get the best picture, choose your subject, select a **point of view,** then **frame** your shot to find the best **composition.** You look through the **viewfinder** to decide on a **close-up** or a **panoramic** shot. For a manual camera, you'll want to set the lens **aperture,** or **f-stop,** and the **shutter speed** for the right **exposure.** If you have a **telephoto** lens, you can **zoom** in for a close-up. Indoors, you might need a **flash attachment** for better **contrast.**

See What Develops

You could have your own **darkroom** for developing film. Or, you could use **digital** cameras, whose images can be processed on computers. **Film** is printed first as **proofs** or **contact sheets.** An individual picture can be **enlarged, reduced, cropped,** or made a **halftone.** You can combine pictures into a **photocollage,** an **assemblage,** or a **photomontage.**

Your Turn My Viewpoint

Create a photocollage about a person, place, or thing that interests you. Use some of the words above to discuss the images you chose and the effect you were trying to create.

f-stop

Chapter 30

Creating Media

Lights! Camera! Information!

Imagine you were asked to create a video yearbook. How would you present the information? Would you include highlights of all academic, sports, and social events? Would you interview student leaders, athletes, teachers, and parents? Would you show humorous still shots of class members or feature background music?

Creating a media product, such as a video documentary, a multimedia presentation, or a Web page, is not as difficult as it may appear. As long as you plan your steps carefully, research your topic and audience, and produce the necessary images and sounds, you can create an effective, attention-grabbing media product.

Write Away: Momentous Moments

Think about all the events and special occasions of your life during the past year. Make a list of those you would want to highlight in some medium. Save your list in your **Working Portfolio.**

CREATING MEDIA

LESSON 1

Using Media

A few decades ago, the standard method for making a formal presentation before a live audience was to stand behind a podium and talk for an hour or more, occasionally displaying a poster or slide. Today computers and other high-tech equipment offer presenters a number of alternatives.

1 Media Options

As you prepare to create your media product, you will need to examine the various types of media available. Each medium has its own advantages. Your job is to choose the one that is most appropriate for your message and purpose. The following chart explains three types of media options.

When to Use a Specific Media Option

Option	Best Use
Video	• To capture live action • To present information that has a strong narrative element, like a story, a process, or historical information
Multimedia Presentation	• To give a high-interest presentation to a group of people • To present complex instructional information or research (e.g., science projects and history reports) that can be conveyed more effectively through sound or images
Web Site	• To communicate with a broad audience including people outside your local area • To present information that needs to be updated frequently • To interact with others who have similar interests

2 Targeting Your Audience

Before you choose a media product, you should define your target audience. Do you want to reach the students in your school, people in your community, business owners, state legislators? Knowing your audience will help you choose a medium that suits their interests, age, and/or education.

CHAPTER 30

For example, if you were trying to teach children the dangers of smoking, you might create a puppet video with a strong script to get your message across. But, if you were trying to present the same topic to a panel of judges at a science fair, you might prepare a multimedia presentation using real-life photos of lung disease.

3 Choosing a Medium

The medium you choose will depend on your message, audience, and purpose. Your goal should be to deliver your message most effectively. The following example shows three different ways in which a subject could be presented.

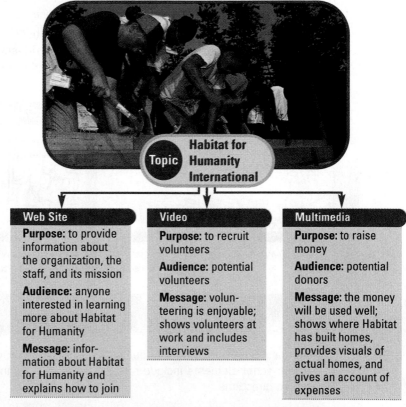

Topic Habitat for Humanity International

Web Site	Video	Multimedia
Purpose: to provide information about the organization, the staff, and its mission	**Purpose:** to recruit volunteers	**Purpose:** to raise money
Audience: anyone interested in learning more about Habitat for Humanity	**Audience:** potential volunteers	**Audience:** potential donors
Message: information about Habitat for Humanity and explains how to join	**Message:** volunteering is enjoyable; shows volunteers at work and includes interviews	**Message:** the money will be used well; shows where Habitat has built homes, provides visuals of actual homes, and gives an account of expenses

Don't forget that print media also can engage specific audiences and deliver your message effectively. You can use anything from a print ad to a cereal box to get your message across.

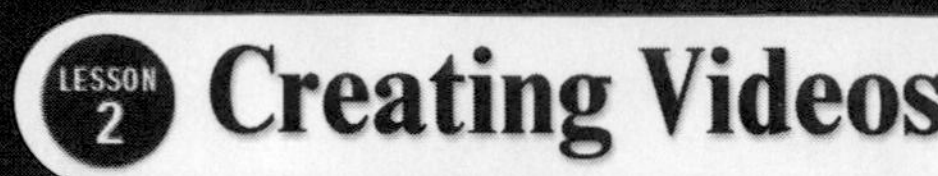

LESSON 2 Creating Videos

A video allows you to experiment with audio, visual, and verbal media elements. Here are just a few of the video projects you can create.

- music video
- documentary
- talk show
- campaign announcement
- news program
- narrative film

1 Preproduction

The first stage in video production is much like the prewriting process for a paper. First you create a treatment. Then you develop a script and/or a storyboard to flesh out the details.

Treatment A **treatment,** or overview, is a brief written statement that defines the video's goals, purpose, audience, and message.

Storyboard A **storyboard** is a series of pictures outlining the sequence of shots in your video. Each scene and camera angle has to have its own panel and simple sketch. Below is a sample storyboard.

Script A **script** is a text that guides the entire video production. Basic script elements include narration, dialogue, sound, and stage directions.

Before you begin to shoot your video, review the following checklist:

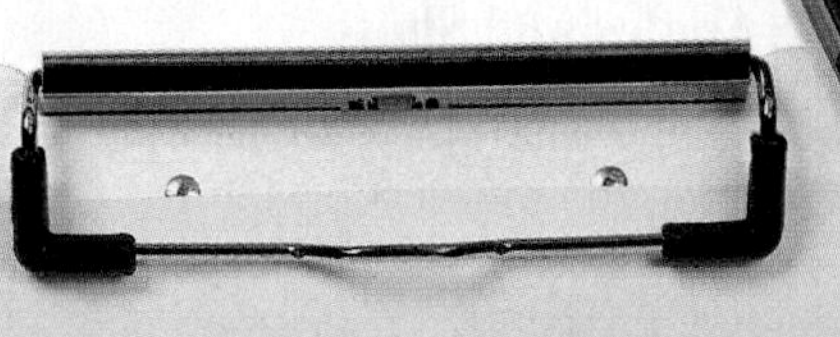

- ✓ **Cost** Do you have a budget to cover the cost of your project? Have you asked people you know to volunteer their services and equipment for free?
- ✓ **Site** Have you visited the location and determined where the action will take place and where the equipment will go? If you are filming outside, do you have an alternate location and/or date if weather conditions are not favorable? Did you check the noise level?
- ✓ **Crew and Talent** Do you know who will act in scenes, narrate the video, and serve as part of the technical crew (camera, lighting, sound)?
- ✓ **Equipment** Do you have cameras, sound and lighting equipment, props, microphones, video, tape, batteries, and tripods?

2 Production

After you've completed the planning stage, you are ready to begin videotaping. Your script and/or storyboard will guide you through each step in the production stage. At this point, you should know whether you will work alone or in a group. As you begin the actual shoot, you should decide ahead of time who will be responsible for each of the following steps:

- **Ensure the props are set up** as needed.
- **Check lighting** for both indoor and outdoor scenes. If you are shooting inside, bring additional lighting to give your subject a natural look.
- **Check sound equipment and microphones** for volume. If you are shooting outside, make sure you can control the noise level.

- **Direct the talent** by telling them how you want them to say their lines and where you want them to stand, sit, or move.
- **Shoot titles, credits, and graphics** to add when you edit.
- **Choose appropriate camera angles and shots** by experimenting with different angles for different effects.

Experiment with Angles and Shots

How you choose to shoot your video piece will depend on the subject matter, the mood you wish to create, and your personal style. As you direct your shoot, experiment with different camera techniques. For example, a close-up shot allows the audience to focus on tiny details, and it also creates a feeling of intimacy; a long or distant shot sets the scene.

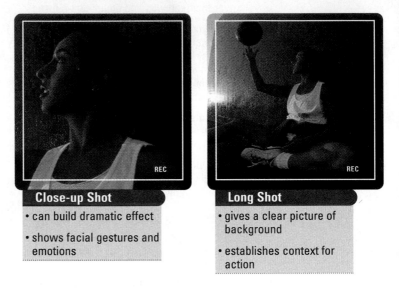

Close-up Shot
- can build dramatic effect
- shows facial gestures and emotions

Long Shot
- gives a clear picture of background
- establishes context for action

If you are creating a video of a news program, an interview, or a talk show, you should try to get a few reaction shots of your audience. Reaction shots can include people laughing, nodding in agreement, or listening intensely.

Do not zoom in and out. Zooming can make your video appear unprofessional. Instead, use a tripod to keep the camera steady and focused.

CHAPTER 30

❸ Postproduction

The postproduction stage gives you a chance to edit your video. Editing involves

- arranging scenes in logical sequence
- cutting out slow or lengthy scenes
- adding reaction shots as needed
- adding sound effects, music, and special effects
- ensuring that sound and image are matched properly
- adding graphics, titles, and credits

Three important concepts in editing are pace, continuity, and purpose.

Pace Consider the pace of your video. Short, quick cuts create a fast pace in a story; long cuts slow down a story.

Continuity Each shot should blend into the next without any abrupt cuts. Also, make sure your props, talent, and other visual elements do not change from one scene to the next unless they're supposed to.

Purpose Edit each scene to advance the story. Try to avoid long interviews by choosing relevant sound bites and inserting reaction shots and cutaways—shots of related objects, such as photos, mementos, and other personal objects.

❹ Evaluating and Revising

Hold a sneak preview before the big release! This will allow you to get initial reactions to your piece from a sample audience. Here are some questions to ask as you reflect critically on your media product.

- Was the story or message clear?
- Is the video interesting?
- Is the organization effective?
- Are the visuals in focus and is the sound clear?

With this information you can revise and improve your video. You may have to change music, narration, or sequence shots.

For more on video projects in the classroom, see "Media Focus: Analyzing and Producing Media."

Planning Multimedia Presentations

A multimedia presentation allows you to provide information in an interactive way by combining a variety of media—text, graphics, sound, and video—using a computer. With the help of such tools as HyperStudio, PowerPoint, or Claris Slide Show, you can create a multimedia presentation.

1 Planning and Organizing

After you have gathered enough background on your topic, determine which information you want to include and how you want to arrange it. A flow chart can help you figure out how to organize your information and link each screen.

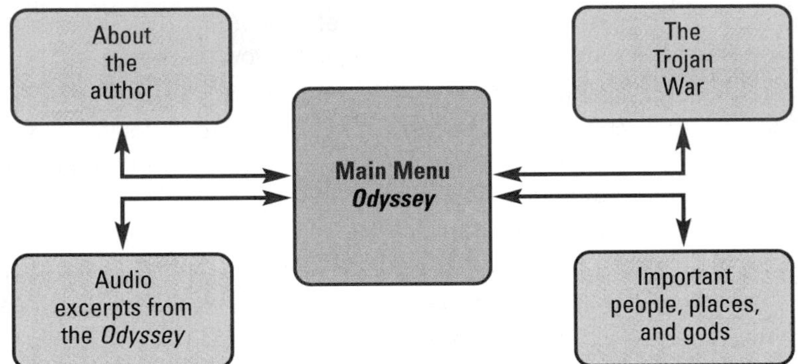

After you have mapped out the individual screens and determined how they will link to each other, you can draw a storyboard for each screen. Each storyboard should show the text, visuals, links, and audio and video buttons necessary for that page.

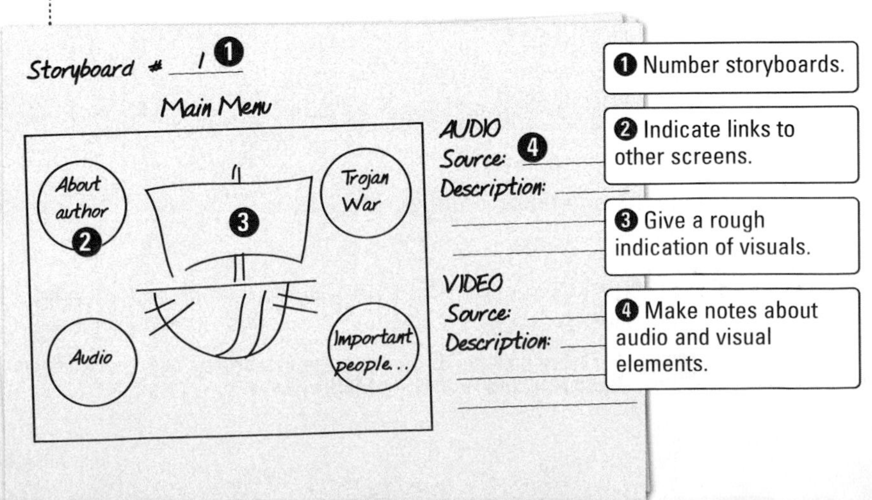

CHAPTER 30

❷ Developing the Presentation

Once you are satisfied with your storyboards, you can begin to create the media components that will fit into each screen. Use the following tips to guide you in the process:

Text Avoid long paragraphs. Instead, bullet important information and use phrases to convey main points.

Graphics Use charts, diagrams, maps, time lines, photos, and drawings to present information that is better described by pictures rather than words.

Audio Use music, voice-over narratives, and sound effects to emphasize a point or to connect one screen to the next.

Video clips Use clips to show real-life or simulated action.

If you plan to download video clips, visual images, or audio clips from the Internet, make sure they are copyright-free. If they aren't, you will need to get permission to use them.

❸ Evaluating and Revising

Test your work on a group of friends or peers before you give the formal presentation. Ask the following questions to help you understand the strengths and weaknesses of your presentation:

- Was the message delivered clearly? Were any parts confusing?
- Do you feel better informed about the subject? If not, why?
- Which parts of the presentation were most interesting?
- Were all images interesting and appropriate?
- Was the text readable?

Use the feedback from your audience to make changes to your presentation if necessary.

Before running your presentation, be sure you know how to use the equipment. You may want to rehearse several times until you are comfortable with the flow of the presentation and the equipment.

LESSON 4 Creating a Web Site

Creating a Web site is no longer a complicated, difficult project. With the help of readily available software programs you can design a Web site based on your own needs, personality, and style. The success of your Web site depends on the planning and organization of the site's content and design.

1 Planning the Site

Like other multimedia products, a Web page combines a number of media components, including text, visuals, audio elements, and interactive features.

Here's How Planning for Content and Design

1. Choose your topic, purpose, and target audience.
2. Research your topic.
3. Decide which information you will include as text and which you will include as visuals and audio.
4. Determine the layout and the number of pages you will need to cover the content and design elements.
5. Create a flow chart and storyboards to show how your information will be presented and how each screen will be linked.

The flow chart shows how the pages are connected. Be sure to include a link back to your home page on each screen. The home page serves as the starting point and introduces the site's subject.

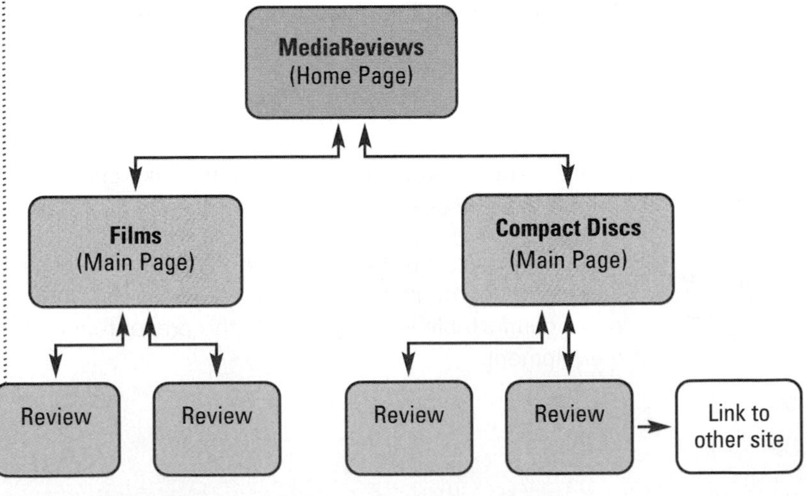

❷ Developing the Web Site

After you have planned your site, you can begin to develop the Web pages by using a software program or hypertext mark-up language (HTML). The Web page illustrated below shows some of the elements you'll need to include.

❸ Evaluating and Revising

Ask a friend or classmate to visit your Web site and have them respond to the following questions:

- Does the Web page provide substantial information?
- Is it visually interesting?
- Is the site easy to navigate and explore, or did you experience problems?
- Do the links work?

Use the feedback from your audience to make changes to your presentation if necessary.

Student Help Desk

Media at a Glance

Media products include documentaries, video yearbooks, interviews, educational or government Web sites, reports, and instructional videos.

Use the following steps as a guide to create your media product:

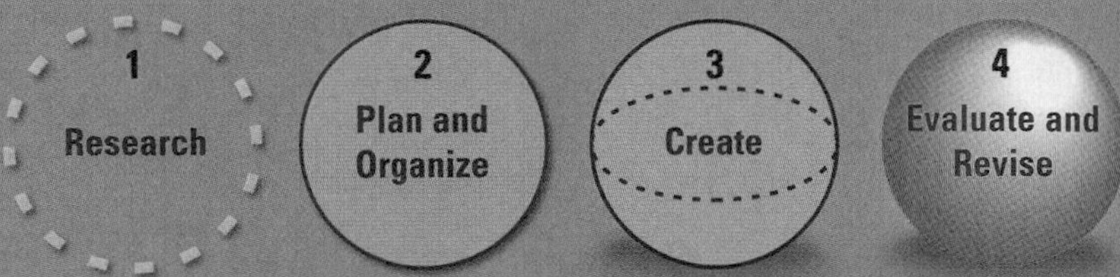

Lights, Camera, Action

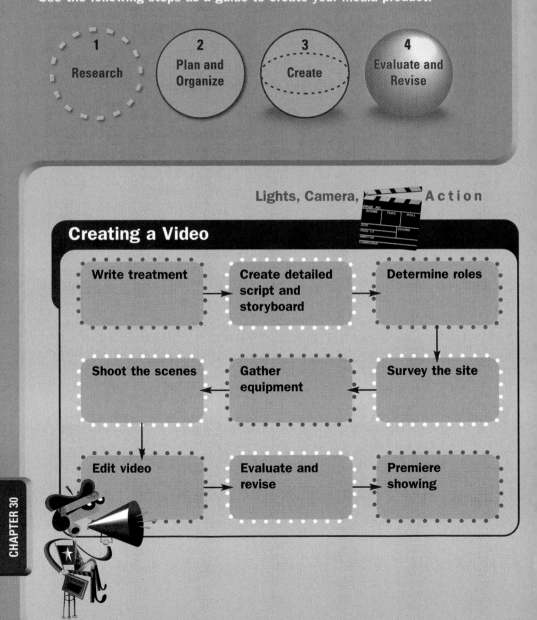

Creating a Video

Write treatment → Create detailed script and storyboard → Determine roles → Survey the site → Gather equipment → Shoot the scenes → Edit video → Evaluate and revise → Premiere showing

Calvin and Hobbes by Bill Watterson

LOOK, HOBBES, I CUT A PIECE OF CARDBOARD TO MAKE A TV SCREEN.
SEE, I JUST HOLD IT UP AND IT'S LIKE I'M ON TV.
WOW, YOUR OWN SHOW!
TOO BAD I CAN'T REALLY FORCE MY WAY INTO MILLIONS OF PEOPLE'S HOMES EACH DAY.
BUT ON THE OTHER HAND, NO ONE IN *THIS* HOME CAN TURN ME OFF!
© 1990 Universal Press Syndicate

Web Site Checklist

Do's and Don'ts

Do

- Use search engines to help create Web sites by using the key words "creating Web pages"
- Include relevant information about your topic
- Create links to other sites with relevant information
- Get yourself listed on commonly used search engines

Do Not

- Borrow copyrighted graphics from any site—hundreds of Web sites offer free clip art with full copyright clearance
- Use fancy graphics or large photos that clutter the page and make it time-consuming to download
- Include any personal information

The Bottom Line

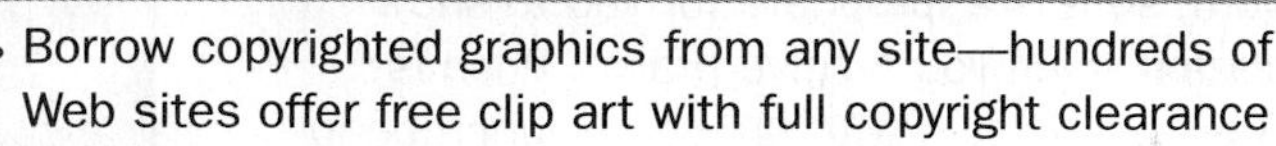

Checklist as You Create a Media Product

Have I . . .

____ defined the topic, purpose, and audience?

____ chosen a media product to match my message?

____ included various multimedia components?

____ edited the final product for organization and clarity?

____ obtained audience feedback for final revisions?

CREATING MEDIA

Power Words
Vocabulary for Precise Writing

A Pat on the Back

plaudits!

Compliments are sometimes hard to come by. The following words can help you give someone a much-needed morale boost.

PLEASE APPLAUD WITH HANDS ONLY

acclaim!

Many Words of Praise

Plaudits and **accolades; commendation, acclamation, laudation, approbation; acclaim** and **homage**—these words for enthusiastic expression of approval, or **praise**—have come into English from Latin.

An Appraisal of *Praise*

The word *praise* comes from the Latin word *pretium,* meaning "price." **Appreciate** comes from this same Latin word, so it is appropriate for you to show **appreciation** when you receive praise. Price is sometimes associated with praise, as when people say they "can't buy a compliment." **Appraise** is derived from *praise;* you can appraise a person to see if he or she deserves a compliment, or you can appraise a house to decide what price it's worth.

accolades!

Two Words from Greek

Two words not included in the first paragraph have a different history: Their origins are Greek. A **eulogy,** a speech in praise of someone, is usually given only after a person has died. **Kudos,** meaning "honor, glory, acclaim," is a singular noun, although it looks plural. It's a very tricky word to use correctly. Learn how to use it, and you will merit nothing but kudos.

encomiums!

Your Turn Sing Your Praises

Write a song or a poem praising the things you like most about yourself.

Chapter 31

Expanding Your Vocabulary

"Well, Brian, your tryout has received nothing but plaudits. Your debating skills are estimable. I have decided that your participation would ameliorate our team's performance."
"Oh well, thanks anyway. Maybe I'll try again next year."
COACH

Grasping the Meaning

Have you ever been in a situation in which you weren't sure what someone was saying because you didn't understand some of the words? See if you can figure out what the debate coach is telling Brian in the illustration above.

Building a strong vocabulary can help you avoid embarrassing situations like the one Brian is experiencing. Many people will judge you by how well you use and understand language. Improving your vocabulary also can help you do well on standardized tests.

Write Away: The Word Escapes Me
Write two paragraphs about a time when misunderstanding a word created an embarrassing situation for you. When you are finished, put your writing in your **Working Portfolio.**

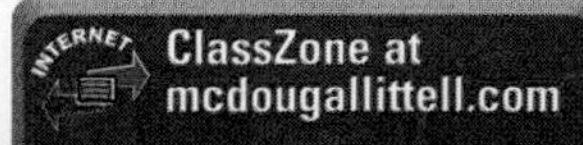

Using Vocabulary Strategies

Here's the Idea

The best way for you to learn new words is to draw on a variety of strategies. The following model shows how one student used different strategies to determine the meanings of unfamiliar words.

PROFESSIONAL MODEL

Tadpoles have a stinky way of warning each other to hunker down when a predator looms, according to a new study.

Like many aquatic species, tadpoles use their keen **olfactory** sense to identify danger, locate good food, and recognize family. Scientists also know that the amphibians, when captured, send out chemical distress signals. Now, researchers have learned that tadpoles that are merely harassed also release such distress signals. . . .

In the recent study, Joseph M. Kiesecker of Yale University and his colleagues put two groups of tadpoles of red-legged frogs in an aquarium **partitioned** by a screen that blocked visual and **acoustic** communication between the groups. Water, however, flowed freely through the partition.

When a wooden heron stalked the tadpoles in one compartment, those on the other side slowed down, moved from the divider, and ducked under a shelter, the researchers report. . . . Undisturbed tadpoles did not elicit those defensive behaviors in their neighbors. The researchers conclude that the **beleaguered** tadpoles released a chemical signal that penetrated the screen.

—*Science News*

STRATEGIES IN ACTION

Olfactory comes before *sense,* so it must have something to do with the five senses. I'm not sure which sense, though, so I'll check the dictionary.

Partitioned contains the word *part,* and here it involves a screen that blocks communication between the two groups. I guess *partitioned* means "divided into parts."

Acoustic is some type of communication that isn't visual—maybe sound?

The paragraph talks about undisturbed tadpoles and then beleaguered tadpoles. *Beleaguered* must mean "disturbed."

By using word parts, context clues, and dictionaries, you can master new words and improve your reading comprehension.

LESSON 2 Understanding Word Parts

Many words can be broken into smaller parts. These **word parts** include base words, roots, prefixes, and suffixes. Knowing common word parts and their meanings can often help you figure out the meaning of an unfamiliar word. In the following example, see how knowing the parts of one difficult word can lead to understanding the word as a whole.

amorphous = a + morph + ous
WITHOUT FORM HAVING

By studying the meaning of the parts, you can make an educated guess about the meaning of *amorphous.* The actual definition is "not having a definite form." The following sections will help you develop a better understanding of word-part analysis. Word-part analysis is closely related to **etymology**—the history of words.

1 Base Words and Roots

A **base word** is a word part that by itself is also a word.

part	**ition**

Partition has the base word *part* and means "to divide into parts."

A **root** is a word part that is used to form other words. A root by itself usually is not a word.

hiero	**glyph**

Hieroglyph has the root *hiero* and the root *glyph. Hiero* means "sacred," and *glyph* means "carving." *Hieroglyph* means "a carved symbol in the sacred writing system of ancient Egypt."

Some Common Greek and Latin Roots

Root	Origin	Examples
anthrop	Greek *anthrōpos,* "human being"	**anthrop**ology ("study of human beings") mis**anthrop**e ("hater of humankind")
phon	Greek *phonē,* "sound"	homo**phon**e ("word that sounds like another word") **phon**etics ("study of speech sounds")
sol	Latin *sōlus,* "alone"	de**sol**ate ("having no inhabitants") **sol**iloquy ("speech made while alone")
umbr	Latin *umbra,* "shadow"	ad**umbr**ate ("to give an outline of") pen**umbr**a ("partial shadow")

VOCABULARY

English words that have the same base word or root often have related meanings. When they do, they make up what is called a **word family.** Knowing the meaning of the base word or root can help you figure out the meanings of the words in the family. The diagrams below show two word families.

Word Families Formed from a Base Word and a Root

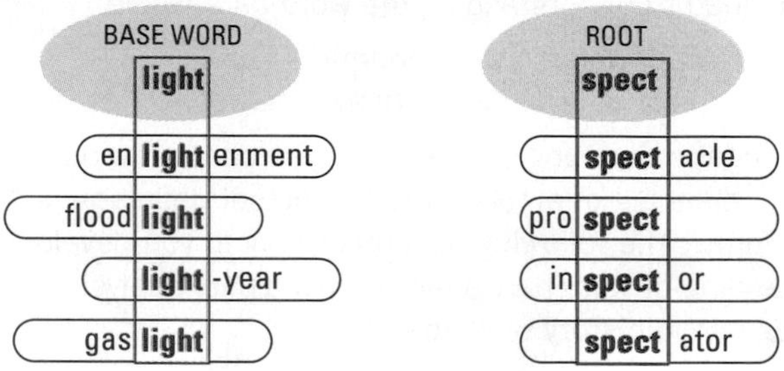

2 Prefixes

An **affix** is a word part of one or more letters that is attached to the beginning or end of a base word or root. An affix at the beginning of a word is called a **prefix.** Adding a prefix to a base word or root creates a new word with a different meaning. Most prefixes come from Greek, Latin, or Old English. (Old English is sometimes called Anglo-Saxon.) The following chart shows some examples of prefixes.

Common Prefixes

Prefix	Origin	Examples
be-	Old English *(be-)* for "completely"	**be**calm **be**grudge **be**siege
hydro-	Greek *(hudōr)* for "water"	**hydro**electric **hydro**foil **hydro**ponics
peri-	Greek *(peri)* for "around"	**peri**meter **peri**phery **peri**scope
pre-	Latin *(prae)* for "in front of, before"	**pre**meditated **pre**historic **pre**dict
sub-	Latin *(sub)* for "under, below"	**sub**atomic **sub**missive **sub**culture

❸ Suffixes

A **suffix** is an affix attached to the end of a base word or root. A suffix frequently indicates a word's part of speech. For example, the suffix *-arian* is often used to form a noun, such as *veterinarian.* The following chart shows some Greek, Latin, and Old English suffixes.

Common Suffixes

Suffix	Origin	Part of Speech	Examples
-ic	Greek; *-ikos* ("characterized by")	adjective	pedant**ic** sarcast**ic** volcan**ic**
-ion	Latin; *-iōn* ("process of")	noun	capitalizat**ion** rationalizat**ion** transformat**ion**
-ize	Greek; *-izein* ("to cause to become")	verb	familiar**ize** fossil**ize** homogen**ize**
-ness	Old English; *-nes* ("condition of")	noun	indebted**ness** porous**ness** uneasi**ness**
-ous	Latin; *-ōsus* ("characterized by")	adjective	igne**ous** monoton**ous** wondr**ous**

The etymologies included in the entries in many dictionaries show you any affixes and their meanings.

PRACTICE **Understanding Word Parts**

Use what you have learned about word parts to figure out the definitions of the highlighted words in the following paragraph. If a word part is not mentioned in this lesson, try to figure it out on your own.

Metamorphic rock is one of the three main kinds of rock on earth. Two of the best-known types of metamorphic rock are marble and slate. Heat or pressure forms metamorphic rock by producing new minerals through **recrystallization.** One way recrystallization can happen is through a **hydrothermal** process. The new minerals often form parallel layers within the rock.

VOCABULARY

LESSON 3 Using Context Clues

A **context clue** helps you to figure out the meaning of a word, based on information in the sentence or paragraph that contains the word. Context clues often involve definition, restatement, examples, or contrast.

1 Definition and Restatement Clues

In a **definition clue** or a **restatement clue,** a word is accompanied by a definition or restatement of its meaning. Commas, dashes, or words such as *or, that is,* or *in other words* can signal these clues.

DEFINITION

A lichen is an example of symbiosis, a relationship in which two living things live closely together and at least one benefits. A lichen is a combination of algae and a fungus.

The comma signals a restatement of the meaning of *symbiosis.*

2 Example Clues

Example clues use examples to show words' meanings. Example clues may be signaled by words such as *including, such,* or *like,* as in the following description of a type of living thing.

PROFESSIONAL MODEL

Prokaryotes, which **include** bacteria and blue-green algae, are among the oldest forms of animal life. Prokaryotes live alone or in colonies. They make up the kingdom Prokaryotae, which most scientists recognize as one of the five kingdoms of living things. In a prokaryote, the nucleus of a cell is not surrounded by a membrane. This makes it different from other types of living cells.

—Tom Klonoski

Knowing that bacteria and certain types of algae are examples of prokaryotes can help you figure out that prokaryotes are primitive one-celled organisms.

3 Contrast Clues

Contrast clues are words or phrases that have a meaning opposite that of the unfamiliar word. Contrast clues often are signaled by the words *although, but, however,* and *on the other hand.*

> **Most organisms need to have oxygen to survive, but many types of bacteria are anaerobic.**

An anaerobic organism is one that does not need oxygen.

4 General Context Clues

Sometimes you can infer the meaning of a word from a **general context clue**—general information that appears in nearby clauses or sentences. The following example comes from a satire that features farm animals, including a cow named Mollie.

LITERARY MODEL

> As winter drew on, Mollie became more and more troublesome. She was late for work every morning and excused herself by saying that she had overslept, and she complained of mysterious pains, although her appetite was excellent. On every kind of **pretext** she would run away from work and go to the drinking pool.
>
> —George Orwell, *Animal Farm*

The second sentence indicates that Mollie was always making excuses for missing work. You can conclude that a pretext is a type of excuse.

PRACTICE **Using Context Clues**

Determine the meanings of the highlighted words in the following passage by using context clues.

> Pacific salmon are born in fresh water but spend most of their lives in salt water. These fish have evolved in a way that allows their bodies to **acclimate,** or adjust, to changes in the **salinity** of water. A system of **membranes,** including skin and gill tissue, helps the fish adjust to the differing salt levels.

Using Vocabulary Reference Books

1 Dictionaries

To get a complete understanding of a new word, you should look the word up in a dictionary. A general dictionary will tell you not only the word's definitions but also its pronunciation, parts of speech, and etymology.

forage

1 **for·age** 2 (fôr′ĭj, fŏr′-) 3 *n.* 4 **1.** Food for domestic animals; fodder. **2.** The act of looking or searching for food or provisions. **—forage** *v.* **-aged, -aging, -ages.** *—intr.* **1.** To wander in search of food or provisions. **2.** To make a raid, as for food: *soldiers foraging near an abandoned farm.* **3.** To conduct a search; rummage. *—tr.* **1.** To collect forage from; strip of food or supplies: *troops who were foraging the countryside.* **2.** *Informal.* To obtain by foraging: *foraged a snack from the refrigerator.* 5 [Middle English, from Old French *fourrage,* from *forrer,* to forage, from *feurre,* fodder, of Germanic origin. See pā- in Appendix.] —6 **for′ag·er** *n.*

—*The American Heritage® Dictionary of the English Language,* third edition

1 **Entry word** shows the correct spelling of the word and how to hyphenate it.

2 **Pronunciation** uses special symbols to show how to say the word, including which syllables to stress.

3 **Part of speech** helps you to use the word properly by showing its functions. The entry also gives the principal parts of the word if it's a verb.

4 **Definitions** show all of the accepted meanings of the word, with the most common meanings usually listed first.

5 **Etymology** provides a deeper sense of the meaning of the word by showing where it came from.

6 **Derived word** shows a word that is formed from the entry word and is not listed separately in the dictionary.

Other types of dictionaries are available for more specific uses. An unabridged dictionary shows all the words that have ever been used in English and includes meanings that are no longer current. A specialized dictionary focuses on a topic such as medicine or computers.

❷ Thesauruses and Other Vocabulary References

Three other types of references that can help you learn new words are thesauruses, synonym finders, and glossaries.

A thesaurus is a dictionary of synonyms, or words that have a similar meaning. A thesaurus can be especially helpful when you find yourself using the same modifiers over and over again. Here is an example of a thesaurus entry.

> **forage,** *v.* — *Syn.* search, scavenge, scrounge, rummage; see **hunt** 2, **search, seek** 1.
>
> —*Webster's New World™ Thesaurus,* third edition

Notice that this thesaurus entry includes cross-references to related words whose entries have longer lists of synonyms.

The words in a thesaurus entry are not identical in meaning, so don't automatically substitute one for another. You can understand differences in the words' uses and meanings by looking them up in a dictionary.

A synonym finder is often included in word-processing software. It enables you to highlight a word and to display its synonyms. A synonym finder is similar to a thesaurus but includes less information.

A glossary is a list of specialized terms and their definitions. It is often found at the back of a book. A glossary sometimes includes pronunciations. Many textbooks contain glossaries. You will find glossaries useful when

- you cannot find a definition or a context clue for a key term
- you are studying for a quiz or exam
- you do not have a dictionary handy

The people who learn the greatest number of new words are those who read the most.

PRACTICE **Etymologies**

Use a dictionary to find the etymologies of the highlighted words in lesson 1: *olfactory, partitioned, acoustic,* and *beleaguered*. Write down the etymology of each word, and explain how it is related to the word's meaning.

Exploring Shades of Meaning

To use new words effectively in your writing, you need to do more than just memorize their definitions. Understanding the shades of meaning that make words unique will allow you to use words precisely in their proper contexts.

1 Synonyms

Synonyms are words with similar meanings.

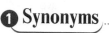

In the continuum above, each word is a synonym of the word or words next to it. As you move from left to right, however, the words express less intense feelings. The meaning of the word at the left end of the continuum, *ecstatic,* is quite different from the meaning of *satisfied,* the word at the other end.

Reading widely can help you learn the context in which writers use a particular word. For example, the parent of a newborn baby is more often described as joyful than contented.

2 Denotation and Connotation

A key part of learning a new word is to understand both its denotation and connotation.

Denotation is the dictionary definition of a word—its literal meaning apart from any greater context.

Connotation covers the additional meanings given to a word based on the greater context in which it is used.

rascal

Denotation
An unethical, dishonest person

Connotation
A mischievous person who is hard to dislike

scoundrel

Denotation
A villain

Connotation
An immoral person who is hard to forgive

Notice how the denotations of the words *rascal* and *scoundrel* are much more similar than the connotations are.

When studying words, watch out for **homophones.** These are words that sound alike but have different meanings and spellings. Some homophones, such as *stationary* and *stationery,* are frequently mlsused.

PRACTICE **Connotation**

Look at the five pairs of synonyms below and explain how their connotations differ. Use strategies you have learned, such as using a dictionary and analyzing word parts, to come up with your answers.

man—gentleman
disappointed—frustrated
protector—savior
sad—desolate
rumor—scandal

3 Antonyms

Antonyms are words with opposite meanings. Writers often use antonyms to create contrast or tension in their writing, as in this famous beginning of a novel.

LITERARY MODEL

It was the **best** of times, it was the **worst** of times, it was the age of **wisdom,** it was the age of **foolishness,** it was the epoch of **belief,** it was the epoch of **incredulity,** it was the season of **Light,** it was the season of **Darkness,** it was the spring of **hope,** it was the winter of **despair,** we had **everything** before us, we had **nothing** before us. . . .

—Charles Dickens, *A Tale of Two Cities*

Dickens used antonyms to show how people's attitudes toward the condition of their society could be very different.

VOCABULARY

Student Help Desk

Expanding Vocabulary at a Glance

Analyze word parts to see if an unfamiliar word is related to one you already know.

Look for context clues to see if adjacent words or sentences provide information about a word's meaning.

Consult a dictionary for a word's exact meaning, pronunciation, and etymology.

Learn the connotation of a word to understand the best time and place to use it.

When in Rome. . .

Some Common Prefixes from Latin

Prefixes That Reverse Meaning

Prefix	Meaning	Example
dis-	the opposite of	disoriented ("confused")
il-	not	illegible ("not readable")
im-	not	immobile ("not moving")
in-	not	intolerable ("not bearable")
ir-	not	irrepressible ("not controllable")

Prefixes That Show Relationships

Prefix	Meaning	Example
ante-	before	antebellum ("before a war")
circum-	around	circumnavigate ("to go around")
post-	after	postoperative ("after surgery")
re-	again	renegotiate ("to bargain again")
super-	over	superimpose ("to place over")

Assembling Word Parts

The Great Word-Making Machine

Prefixes	Base Word	Suffixes	New Words
pre-, inter-	view		preview, interview
	neighbor	*-hood, -ly*	neighborhood, neighborly
	honor	*-able*	honorable
	worth	*-less*	worthless
un-	improve	*-ed, -ment*	unimproved, improvement
de-	active	*-ate*	deactivate

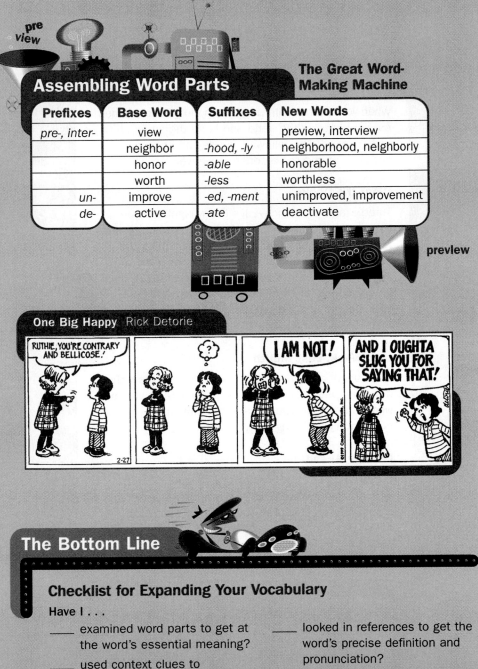

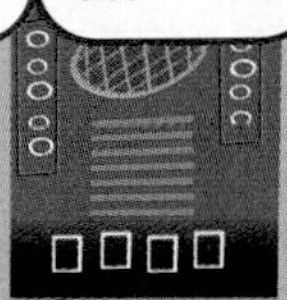

One Big Happy Rick Detorie

RUTHIE, YOU'RE CONTRARY AND BELLICOSE!
2-27

I AM NOT!

AND I OUGHTA SLUG YOU FOR SAYING THAT!

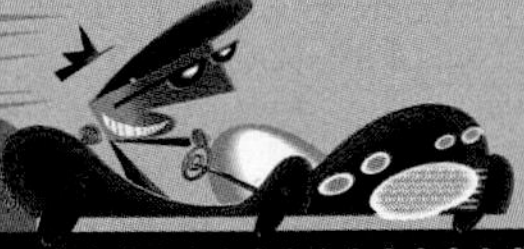

The Bottom Line

Checklist for Expanding Your Vocabulary

Have I . . .

____ examined word parts to get at the word's essential meaning?

____ used context clues to determine the meaning of the word?

____ looked in references to get the word's precise definition and pronunciation?

____ thought about how the word's denotation may differ from its connotation?

VOCABULARY

Power Words
Vocabulary for Precise Writing

Ready for Action?

When you're faced with a big exam, do you sometimes put your head in the sand and hope the situation will just go away? The following words can help you think about tests in a more constructive way.

Clear the Decks

Three exams on Monday? It's Friday night and you've got a busy weekend ahead. You'd better start **getting ready** to study. **Set your house in order! Clear the decks! Shorten the sails** and **batten down the hatches!** You'd better **limber up** and **get into shape; brace yourself** and **lay the groundwork. Roll up your sleeves** and **get in harness. Sharpen your tools, whet your knife,** and start hitting the books!

Last Week, Last Month

What about all of the evenings and weekends **before** now? the **prior** weekends? the **preceding** or **previous** weekends? Hope you did some **preliminary,** some **preparatory,** studying then.

Looking Ahead

Do you **expect** to do well on your exams? Do you **hope for, look forward to,** and **anticipate** good grades? (Well, of course you *hope* for A's. Who doesn't?) However, can you **predict** or **foresee** this positive outcome? Can you **assume** or **presume** it will turn out well? Can you **count on** it?

Your Turn Stress Test

With a group of classmates, discuss ways to prepare for tests. What are some key words you use to describe your techniques?

Chapter 32

Preparing for Tests

Testing the Waters

How do you feel the night before a test?

(a) Like I'm drowning and no one can save me
(b) Like I'm making my way slowly to the last lap of a race
(c) Like I can easily swim across the English Channel

Your answer is probably a reflection of how you prepare for tests. Do you wait until the last night and then cram until your brain is about to explode? Do you map out a study plan so that you cover a little of the material each night? Do you like to study with friends or alone? The skills and strategies in this chapter can help you sharpen your study habits as well as give you some tips for taking the many different kinds of tests you encounter.

Write Away: Changing Course

Think of your worst testing nightmare. Describe what happened before, during, and after the test. Then rewrite the scene so the experience becomes a successful one. Save your work in your **Writing Portfolio.**

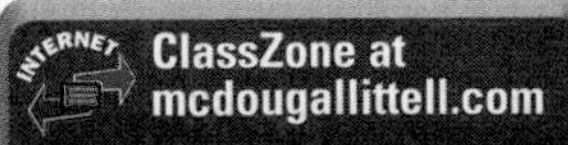

PREP. FOR TESTS

Studying in the Content Areas

Think of your time as money. You have only so much to spend so you want to spend it wisely. Use the content-area reading strategies in this lesson to get the most out of your study time as you prepare for tests.

1 Active Reading Strategies

Do you have trouble staying focused when you read your textbooks? Use these active reading strategies to stay alert and focus on the key concepts and facts in your texts.

Active Reading Strategies	
Previewing	Skim and scan the page, looking at key words, major heads, topic sentences, visuals, and captions.
Questioning	Ask and answer questions as you read. Jot down any questions you can't answer.
Using context clues	Use the words you know to help you infer the meaning of words you don't know.
Rereading	Reread paragraphs and sections that are especially important or parts that aren't clear the first time.
Taking notes	Jot down main ideas, related details, and key terms.
Using graphic organizers	Use a graphic organizer—such as a chart, Venn diagram, or time line—to organize your notes.

2 Reading and Studying Mathematics

A key to understanding math is studying the examples each time a new concept is introduced.

Example 2 ***Subtracting the Same Quantity from Both Sides***

Solve $-8 = n + 4$.

1 *Solution* On the right side of the equation, 4 is added to n. You can isolate n by subtracting 4 from both sides of the equation.

3

$-8 = n + 4$	*Rewrite the original equation.*
$-8 - 4 = n + 4 - 4$	*Subtract 4 from both sides.*
$-12 = n$	*Simplify.*

The solution is -12. Check this in the original equation. ■

1 **Preview:** Find the two basic parts of the example: the problem and the solution.

2 **Read and reread:** Read the problem to understand what is being asked and what is provided.

3 **Note the sequence:** Think about how each step leads to the next.

4 **Try it yourself.**

❸ Reading and Studying History

When reading history texts, you want to understand the major ideas so you can answer essay questions. You also want to focus on key facts and dates that might be part of an objective test.

Here's How **Reading History Texts**

1. **Preview.** Scan the page. Note the titles, subtitles, and visual elements to see what the page is about. Note any key terms in dark print.
2. **Look for and summarize main ideas.** Read any summaries that are provided. After reading each section, take time to summarize its main ideas.
3. **Make connections.** As you read, think about cause-and-effect relationships that may be stated or suggested. Note the sequence of events. Make a time line to keep track of what happened when.
4. **Interpret maps, graphs, and charts.** Key information is often presented in graphic aids. Use the keys to help you interpret what is being shown.

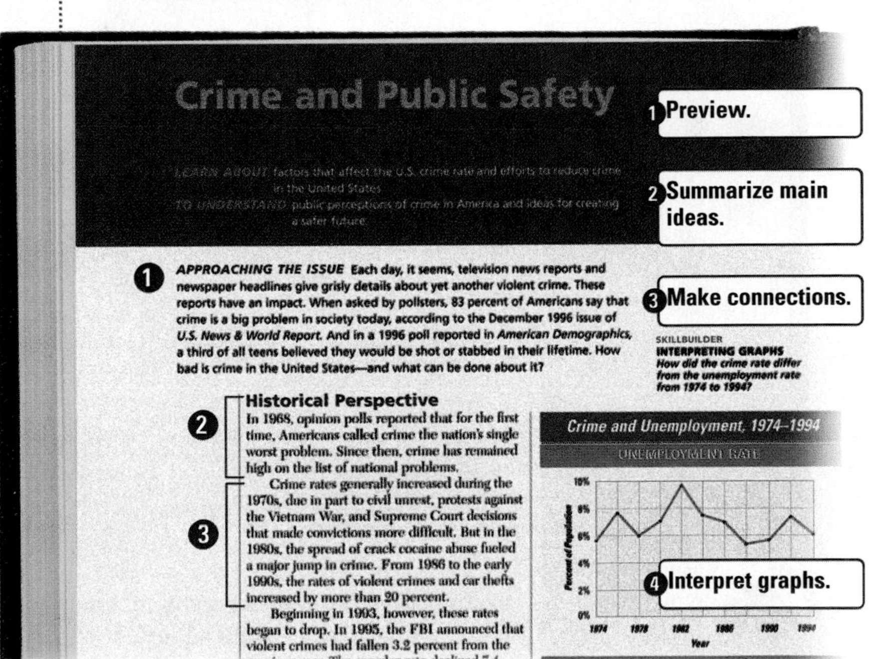

Crime and Public Safety

LEARN ABOUT factors that affect the U.S. crime rate and efforts to reduce crime in the United States
TO UNDERSTAND public perceptions of crime in America and ideas for creating a safer future.

❶ ***APPROACHING THE ISSUE*** **Each day, it seems, television news reports and newspaper headlines give grisly details about yet another violent crime. These reports have an impact. When asked by pollsters, 83 percent of Americans say that crime is a big problem in society today, according to the December 1996 issue of *U.S. News & World Report*. And in a 1996 poll reported in *American Demographics*, a third of all teens believed they would be shot or stabbed in their lifetime. How bad is crime in the United States—and what can be done about it?**

Historical Perspective

❷ In 1968, opinion polls reported that for the first time, Americans called crime the nation's single worst problem. Since then, crime has remained high on the list of national problems.

❸ Crime rates generally increased during the 1970s, due in part to civil unrest, protests against the Vietnam War, and Supreme Court decisions that made convictions more difficult. But in the 1980s, the spread of crack cocaine abuse fueled a major jump in crime. From 1986 to the early 1990s, the rates of violent crimes and car thefts increased by more than 20 percent.

Beginning in 1993, however, these rates began to drop. In 1995, the FBI announced that violent crimes had fallen 3.2 percent from the previous year. The murder rate declined 7.4

SKILLBUILDER
INTERPRETING GRAPHS
How did the crime rate differ from the unemployment rate from 1974 to 1994?

④ Reading and Studying Science

Reading science texts requires skills similar to those used in reading history texts. You need to recognize key terms and facts that support the basic concepts in the chapters. A science writer often poses a hypothesis and then provides research and data that prove or disprove the hypothesis.

Here's How Reading Science Texts

1. **Preview.** Scan the page. Note the titles, subtitles, and visual elements to see what the page is about. Note any key terms in dark print.
2. **Examine main ideas and conclusions.** Often the main idea is stated in the beginning of a section. The conclusion, usually stated at the end, is often a restatement of that main idea.
3. **Look for cause/effect relationships.** Scientific study depends on determining which causes produce which effects and then drawing valid conclusions from this evidence. Think about cause/effect relationships as you read.
4. **Use context clues.** Key terms are often defined or restated in the context. Examples of a concept can also provide clues to unfamiliar terms.

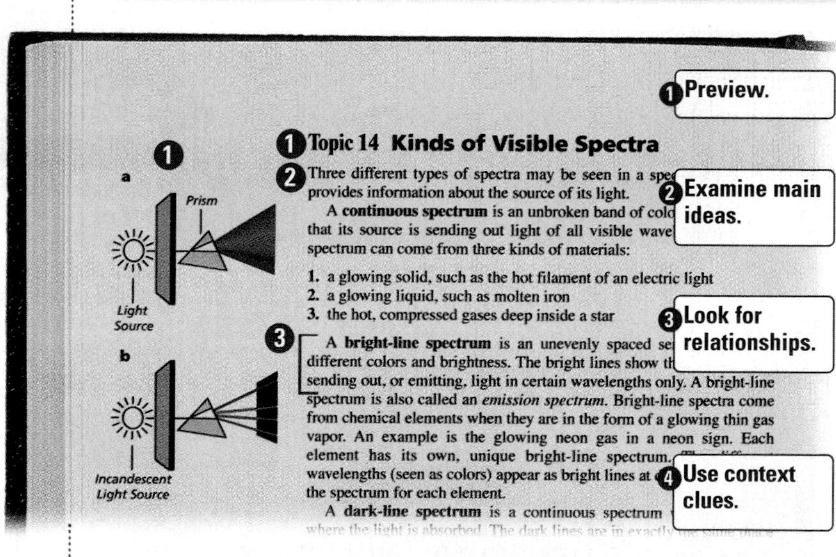

① Preview.
① Topic 14 Kinds of Visible Spectra
② Three different types of spectra may be seen in a spe
provides information about the source of its light.
A **continuous spectrum** is an unbroken band of colo
that its source is sending out light of all visible wave
spectrum can come from three kinds of materials:
1. a glowing solid, such as the hot filament of an electric light
2. a glowing liquid, such as molten iron
3. the hot, compressed gases deep inside a star
② Examine main ideas.
③ Look for relationships.
③ A **bright-line spectrum** is an unevenly spaced se
different colors and brightness. The bright lines show th
sending out, or emitting, light in certain wavelengths only. A bright-line spectrum is also called an *emission spectrum.* Bright-line spectra come from chemical elements when they are in the form of a glowing thin gas vapor. An example is the glowing neon gas in a neon sign. Each element has its own, unique bright-line spectrum.
wavelengths (seen as colors) appear as bright lines at
the spectrum for each element.
A **dark-line spectrum** is a continuous spectrum
④ Use context clues.
①
a
Prism
Light Source
b
Incandescent Light Source

Match your reading rate and style to the material. For new or difficult material, slow down and reread sections that don't make sense to you. Take notes and try to restate important concepts in your own words.

CHAPTER 32

LESSON 2 Test Preparation

An important part of preparing for tests is knowing what to expect. Use the tips in this lesson to help you do your best on objective tests.

Objective Tests

True-False Questions

True-false questions test your ability to recognize what you've learned when information is presented as a statement of fact.

Directions: Indicate whether each statement is true or false.

All birds can fly.

Answer: False

Tips for Success

- For an answer to be true, the entire statement must be true.
- Words such as *all, none, always, never, every,* and *only* often signal a false statement. In the statement above, your clue is the word *All.*
- Similarly, words such as *generally, sometimes, may, most,* and *few* often signal a true statement.

Fill-in-the-Blank Questions

You may be asked to supply missing words or phrases for a fill-in-the-blank type of question.

Directions: Supply the missing word or phrase.

Europe and North America are separated by ________.

Answer: the Atlantic Ocean

Tips for Success

- Your answer must fit grammatically into the sentence.
- Your answer should be the best possible answer. In this example, *an ocean* would also complete the blank but it is not as specific as *the Atlantic Ocean.*

PREP. FOR TESTS

Matching Questions

Matching questions test your ability to recognize relationships between items in two columns and to pair the items accordingly.

Directions: Match each item in the left column with one item in the right column.

____	1. racket	A. skiing
____	2. stick	B. golf
____	3. club	C. hockey
____	4. bat	D. tennis
		E. baseball

Answers: 1D, 2C, 3B, 4E

Tips for Success

- Check whether an answer can be used more than once or may not be used at all.
- Match items first whose pairing you know with certainty. Cross out each answer as you find it.
- If you change one answer, decide if you need to change others.

Multiple-Choice Questions

Multiple-choice questions test your ability to choose the correct answer from several alternatives. In a well-written test, each of the wrong answers represents an error in thinking that you might make if you are careless or don't know the material.

Directions: Write the letter of the correct answer.

Soil erosion is caused by

A. wind C. ice

B. water D. all of the above

Answer: D

Tips for Success

- Read the question carefully.
- Try to answer it before looking at the possible choices.
- Cross out answer choices that you know are wrong.
- Use word clues in the question, such as *except, unless,* or *never,* to help you answer.
- Read all the choices. Don't just pick the first answer that fits—pick the best answer.

Standardized Testing: Vocabulary

1 Synonyms and Antonyms

Synonym questions require you to find the word that is nearly the same in meaning as a given word. Antonym questions require you to find the word that is nearly the opposite in meaning.

Directions: Choose the synonym for the underlined word.

ominous

A. all-knowing C. omen
B. threatening D. inviting

Answer: B

Directions: Choose the antonym for the underlined word.

indispensable

A. unnecessary C. require
B. current D. vital

Answer: A

Tips for Success

- Make sure you know whether you're being asked for a synonym or antonym.
- Watch for antonyms among the answer choices in a synonym question (and vice-versa) and eliminate them. (In the second sample question, *vital* is a synonym for *indispensable.*)
- Eliminate any answers that are not the same part of speech as the given word. (In the first sample question, because *ominous* is an adjective, you can eliminate *omen,* a noun.)
- Don't fall for trick answers such as words that sound like the original word or have some other association with it.

PRACTICE A Antonyms

Write the antonym for each boldfaced word.

1. specific	particular	rare	general
2. eccentric	weird	central	normal
3. candid	dishonest	sour	sincere
4. liberate	release	imprison	generous
5. prohibit	forbid	protect	permit

2 Analogies

An **analogy** compares two sets of relationships. On a test, an analogy item prompts you to find a pair of words that are related in the same way as a given pair of words.

Directions: Select the pair of words that expresses a relationship most like that expressed in the original pair.

KITTEN : CAT: :
A. poodle : dog
B. bear : cub
C. lamb : sheep
D. robin : bird
E. lion : cat

Answer: C

Tips for Success

- Read the question as a sentence: *Kitten is to cat as **what** is to **what?***
- Determine the relationship between the pair of words and create a sentence that expresses the relationship: *A kitten is a young cat.*
- Mentally plug the answer choices into your sentence, for instance, *A poodle is a young dog.* Does the sentence work?
- If two pairs fit the sentence, choose the pair that is most like the original pair.
- Don't fall for analogies in the wrong order. For instance, in *KITTEN : CAT : : bear : cub,* the second pair has the same relationship as the given pair, but it is in the wrong order.
- Don't fall for alternatives that are only superficially related. For instance, don't select *lion* and *cat* just because a lion is a cat.
- Look for alternatives that are the same parts of speech as the original pair.

The more precisely you state the relationship, the better your results will be. For example, if you are given WHEEL : BIKE, you might create one of the following sentences:

vague: A bike has a wheel.

better: A wheel is part of a bike.

WATCH OUT

Watch out for words that have more than one meaning and could therefore suggest more than one relationship.

Some analogies are unique; many others belong to one of the categories shown below.

Common Relationships in Analogies	
Relationship	**Example**
Synonyms	FUN : AMUSING : : boring : tedious
Antonyms	REMOTE : NEAR : : casual : formal
Part to whole	STEM : FLOWER : : keyboard : computer
Cause to effect	RAIN : FLOOD : : drought : dust
Tool to user	HAMMER : CARPENTER : : brush : painter
Product to source	BREAD : BAKER : : bouquet : florist
Action to object	DRIVE : CAR : : watch : television
Connotative differences	CHEAP : FRUGAL : : skinny : lean

PRACTICE B **Recognizing Analogies**

Write the pair of words that expresses a relationship most like that expressed in the original pair.

1. SUN : DAY : :
- **A.** stars : sky
- **B.** hot : bright
- **C.** moon : night
- **D.** summer : winter
- **E.** planet : Earth

2. FAMOUS : PROMINENT : :
- **A.** unknown : noted
- **B.** foolish : silly
- **C.** wander : lost
- **D.** celebrity : wealthy
- **E.** generous : stingy

3. DIG : SHOVEL : :
- **A.** cut : knife
- **B.** mend : sew
- **C.** pencil : draw
- **D.** water : drink
- **E.** dirt : ditch

4. HAND : GLOVE : :
- **A.** ring : finger
- **B.** head : neck
- **C.** warm : cold
- **D.** foot : shoe
- **E.** glove : mitten

5. BOOK : WRITER : :
- **A.** story : poem
- **B.** chef : meal
- **C.** editor : writer
- **D.** worker : boss
- **E.** suit : tailor

6. CONFIDENT : UNCERTAIN : :
- **A.** offensive : rude
- **B.** assured : convinced
- **C.** amazed : astonished
- **D.** lean : fat
- **E.** unabridged : dictionary

Standardized Testing: Reading

Reading Comprehension

Reading-comprehension sections test your ability to read a passage, understand it, and correctly answer questions about it. Read the following strategies and then use them to test your knowledge in the practice exercise.

Reading Strategies

- **Skim** through questions first, but do not spend time on the answers. Try this strategy a couple of times in practice situations and decide whether you find it helpful.
- Quickly **review** the passage for its main idea and for the key points in each paragraph.
- **Read** through the passage thoroughly only once. Remember, you are not trying to become an expert on the content.
- **Mark the passage**—underline key words and phrases; circle dates of events, and number events in sequential order; write the words *cause and effect* or *pro and con* on margins where these concepts apply .
- Do not spend too much time on one question.

Read each question carefully so that you are sure you understand what is being asked. Then look through the answer choices and eliminate those that fall into any of the following categories:

- **Incorrect**—Contradicts the reading.
- **Irrelevant**—May be true, but doesn't answer the question.
- **Incomplete**—Only provides part of the answer.
- **External**—Presents facts that aren't covered in the reading.

PRACTICE **Reading Comprehension**

After reading the passage, select the best answer to each question.

> Many people feel that the design of the telephone is very complex, but in reality, it is one of the simplest devices used in the home. In fact, if you had a phone from the early 1900s, you could plug it right into your wall jack, and it would work fine. After all, a basic telephone consists of only three basic parts: a switch, a speaker, and a microphone. The switch connects and disconnects a phone from its network. The speaker allows you to hear. And the microphone allows you to talk. Additional things found in a telephone are a duplex coil, which blocks the sound of your voice from reaching your ear, and a touch-tone keypad.

1. **What would be the best title for the passage?**
   a) Alexander Graham Bell and His Famous Invention
   b) Household Necessities
   c) A Simple Plan: The Basic Components of the Telephone
   d) The Dramatic Changes of the Telephone

2. **Which sentence best states the author's main idea?**
   a) The telephone is used more frequently today than it was in the early 1900s.
   b) Although the telephone appears to be a complex device, its design is actually uncomplicated.
   c) The telephone has three basic parts: a switch, a speaker, and a microphone.
   d) The invention of the telephone is the most important invention in history, yet it is a simple device.

3. **In the passage, the word *network* refers to**
   a) a group of people with similar interests
   b) a chain of radio or television broadcasting stations linked together by wire or microwave relay
   c) a system of computers interconnected by telephone wires
   d) a system of lines, channels, cords, threads, or wires that cross or are interconnected

Answering Essay Questions

An essay test measures your knowledge of a subject and your writing skills. It determines whether you can think logically, plan and organize coherent paragraphs, and support your topic with appropriate facts.

1 Analyzing the Prompt

Tips for Success

- If you have a choice of questions, take a moment to decide which one you can answer best.
- Read the question carefully. Underline important content words. Also circle words that signal how to present or organize your answer.

Directions: Write an essay to answer the following question.

1. Compare and contrast the features of an opera and a musical.

Key content words are *opera* and *musical*. The words *compare* and *contrast* signal that the essay needs to cover the similarities and differences between an opera and a musical.

Key Terms in Essay Prompts

Term	Strategy
Discuss	Examine a topic in detail and also consider the big picture.
Compare/ contrast	Explore similarities and differences.
Explain	Clarify a problem, relationship, concept, process, or term so that a reader can understand it.
Analyze	Break something down into its parts, then explain how the parts are related and how each contributes to the whole.
Persuade	Clearly state your position and use logical arguments to convince the reader that it is correct.
Prove	State a fact, then support the fact by citing evidence and building logical arguments.
Summarize	Present a condensed version of an event or a process.
Define	List the distinguishing characteristics of a subject, or describe it exactly.
Synthesize	Formulate a general idea from diverse facts.
Interpret	Give your opinion and support it with reasons and details.

❷ Planning and Writing Your Answer

Once you understand what type of question is being asked, you can plan your answer. Use these tips to help you as you write your essay.

Tips for Success

- Jot down or outline key points in the order in which you want to present them. Include specific details that demonstrate your knowledge of the subject.
- Estimate your time limit and plan accordingly. Save some time to proofread your answer. Look for grammar, spelling, or punctuation errors.

Look at the following sample question and student model. Notice how the student jots down key points as a quick reference for the essay.

Sample Question:
Compare and contrast the features of an opera and a musical.

Intro: *Brief definition*
1st paragraph: *Compare*
• performed on stage
• use music to tell a story
2nd paragraph: *Contrast*
• musical often includes dance
• all dialogue is sung in opera
Conclusion

❸ Evaluating Your Work

As you reread your essay, recall the six traits of effective writing—ideas and content, organization, voice, word choice, sentence fluency, and conventions. Similar guidelines will be used by those who evaluate your essay.

For more on the six traits, see p. 309–311.

PREP. FOR TESTS

Student Help Desk

Preparing for Tests at a Glance

Before the Test

- Plan your study time to avoid cramming.
- Know the format of the test.
- Use the review strategies that work for you.

During the Test

- Read the directions and questions carefully.
- Circle key words in the questions or writing prompts.
- Plan your time.
- Don't waste time on questions you can't answer.

Reading in the Content Areas

Taming the Texts

Math

- Study the examples.
- Read and reread the problem carefully.
- Think about the sequence of the solution.

History

- Scan for key terms, main ideas, and summaries.
- Think about causes and effects and note the sequence of events.
- Interpret maps, graphs, and charts.
- Summarize main ideas and draw conclusions.

Science

- Scan for key terms and definitions.
- Think about the facts and how they relate to one another.
- Use context clues to help you understand new terms.

Analogies

It's All About Relationships

Don't get tangled up in tricky analogies. Use these simple steps.

1. Build a short sentence that uses the sample pair of words and tells how they are related.

   brick : wall (A brick is part of a wall.)

2. Plug each answer choice into your sentence. If the sentence is a strong one, only one answer will fit.

   tree : forest (A tree is part of a forest.)

3. If more than one answer fits, make your sentence more specific.

Checklist for Essay Questions

☑ **Topic**

Did you address the topic identified in the prompt?

☑ **Purpose**

Did you respond directly to the question?

☑ **Content**

Is your content strong?

☑ **Organization**

Do your ideas flow logically? Did you use an appropriate type of organization?

☑ **Elaboration**

Did you develop and expand on your ideas?

☑ **Support**

Did you use reasons and examples to support your claims?

☑ **Tone**

Did you write in an objective and impartial voice?

Peanuts by Charles Schulz

"TRUE AND FALSE" TESTS ARE EASY
I FIGURE I HAVE A FIFTY-FIFTY CHANCE ON EVERY QUESTION...

WHAT SCORE DID YOU GET, SIR?

The Bottom Line

Checklist for Test Preparation

Have I . . .

— learned what material will be covered on the test?

— become familiar with the test format?

— used appropriate study techniques?

— used active reading techniques to analyze the questions?

— carefully planned the use of my time?

— left time to check my answers?

Student Resources

Exercise Bank

1 The Parts of Speech

1. Nouns (links to exercise A, p. 8)

➜ **1.** *Rock and Roll Hall of Fame:* proper, concrete, singular; *Cleveland:* proper, concrete, singular; *visitors:* common, concrete, plural; *world:* common, concrete, singular
3. *building:* common, concrete, singular; *I. M. Pei:* proper, concrete, singular; *architect:* common, concrete, singular; *designs:* common, concrete, plural

Write each noun. Identify it as common or proper, concrete or abstract, singular or plural.

1. Like other forms of jazz, swing allows musicians the freedom to improvise.
2. Bandleaders like Glenn Miller, Artie Shaw, and Duke Ellington popularized the sound.
3. The popular bands that played this music were known as "big bands" because they had many musicians.
4. Today, young people have rediscovered the music and dances of swing.
5. They are doing the lindy hop, a popular swing dance named after Charles Lindbergh, the famous aviator.

2. Personal and Possessive Pronouns (links to exercise A, p. 10)

➜ **1.** *them:* personal **2.** *he:* personal; *his:* possessive

Write each pronoun and tell whether it is personal or possessive.

1. *La Bohème,* an opera, is loved for its unforgettable characters and their romantic lives.
2. The opera focuses on Rodolfo, a poor poet, and Mimì, the woman who loves him.
3. When Rodolfo learns Mimì is dying, he can do nothing to help her because of his own poverty.
4. They are friends with the other main characters—Marcello, a struggling painter, and Musetta, his fickle sweetheart.
5. Mimì dies in the final scene, but only after she and Rodolfo have declared their love.

3. Other Kinds of Pronouns (links to exercise A, p. 13)

➜ 2. *that:* experience 3. *Someone:* none

Write each pronoun and identify its antecedent, if it has one.

1. Anyone in the market for a violin made by Antonio Stradivari can expect to pay close to a million dollars.
2. Stradivari, who lived from 1644 to 1737, was one of the greatest violinmakers in the history of music.
3. What makes a Stradivarius violin worth a million dollars?
4. Each of the instruments produces a sound unequaled even by those manufactured today.
5. Music lovers or musicians who can afford the price should treat themselves to the finest instrument money can buy.

4. Verbs (links to exercise on p. 16)

➜ 2. *might scare:* action, *is:* linking

Write each verb or verb phrase and identify it as an action or a linking verb. Underline any auxiliary verbs.

1. All sounds are simply vibrations.
2. Place your hand on your throat as you speak.
3. Can you feel the vibrations?
4. Vibrations travel through the air as invisible sound waves.
5. When the sound waves are a certain frequency, they vibrate the eardrum and the bones in your ear.
6. Nerve endings in your inner ear sense the vibrations, which are sent to your brain as electrical signals.
7. Scientists measure the loudness of sounds in decibels.
8. The units were named in honor of Alexander Graham Bell, who was the inventor of many communication devices.
9. The noise level in a school cafeteria might be rated at about 80 decibels, which sounds almost painful.
10. The loudest rock concerts can produce sound of more than a hundred decibels, which can be harmful to your ears.

5. Adjectives (links to exercise A, p. 18)

➔ **1.** *major:* trend
2. *Japanese:* invention

Write each adjective that is not an article in these sentences, along with the word it modifies.

1. For many years, Ravi Shankar has played the sitar.
2. The sitar, a musical instrument with strings, is used to play Indian music.
3. Since 1995 Shankar's talented daughter, Anoushka, has been attracting worldwide attention.
4. She made her professional debut in India at the age of 13 and has since performed in many countries.
5. In 1998, the British Parliament honored Anoushka with a medal for her outstanding contributions to Asian arts.

6. Adverbs (links to exercise A, p. 21)

➔ **2.** often, late   **4.** terribly

For each sentence below, write each adverb.

1. For some rock 'n' roll fans, February 3, 1959, will always be "the day the music died."
2. On that particularly stormy day, Buddy Holly and Ritchie Valens died tragically in a plane crash.
3. Valens and Holly had extremely popular rock 'n' roll hits, and they were traveling together on a bus for a concert tour.
4. They were due next in Fargo, North Dakota, and Holly decided to hire a small plane instead.
5. Valens had originally planned not to be on the fatal flight, but, unluckily, he won a seat from another musician in a coin toss.

7. Prepositions (links to exercise A, p. 25)

➔ **1.** of (music)   **2.** to its (birth)

For each sentence below, write each prepositional phrase and underline the preposition. Then circle the object of the preposition.

1. Rock 'n' roll got its start in the 1950s and captured fans when it was played on the radio.
2. A few disc jockeys at radio stations across the country began playing rhythm and blues and rock 'n' roll.
3. Rhythm and blues, created and performed by African Americans, was known throughout the South.

4. Without this style of music, rock 'n' roll might never have existed in the form we know today.
5. Chuck Berry, Little Richard, Bo Diddley, and many other early rock 'n' roll stars got their start in rhythm and blues.

8. Conjunctions (links to exercise A, p. 28)

➔ **1.** when, and **4.** but

For each sentence below, write the conjunctions.

1. In the late 1800s and early 1900s, songwriters had neither radio nor TV to help them sell their songs.
2. In those days, composers and songwriters worked full-time for music publishers.
3. After a song was published as sheet music, stores sold copies to the public.
4. A song's popularity was judged both by how many copies of sheet music it sold and by how much it was sung in theaters and elsewhere.
5. When we talk about hit songs today, we are referring not to the number of copies of sheet music sold but to the number of CDs or cassettes purchased.

9. Interjections (links to exercise on p. 29)

➔ **1.** Great!

Choose the better interjection in each sentence.

1. (Say,/Ouch,) which kind of music do you think cats prefer—classical or disco?
2. (Yuk!/Wow!) How could anyone tell which music they like?
3. (Alas,/Well,) a Japanese researcher measured some cats' heartbeats while the animals listened to different kinds of music.
4. Just tell me the result, (OK?/aha!)
5. (Hey,/Anyway,) the cats preferred soothing music, like classical and New Age, to loud music, like disco or rock.

2 The Sentence and Its Parts

1. Simple Subjects and Predicates (links to exercise A, p. 39)

1. Hurricane Andrew, struck **2.** storm, destroyed

Write the simple subject and simple predicate of each sentence.

1. Lighter-than-air gas lifts airships, or dirigibles, into the air.
2. These aircraft differ from balloons in one important way.
3. Powerful engines move these "ships" through the air.
4. People called large, rigid airships "zeppelins," after their inventor, Count Ferdinand von Zeppelin.
5. This German engineer had designed several zeppelins in the early 1900s.
6. Many passengers traveled overseas on airships before the age of the airplane.
7. Several tragedies ended airship passenger service.
8. On May 6, 1937, the *Hindenburg* exploded in New Jersey.
9. The terrible accident killed 35 of the 97 people aboard.
10. The event remains one of the most famous air disasters of all time.

2. Complete Subjects and Predicates (links to exercise A, p. 42)

3. The special effects crew
5. The real challenge

Write the complete subject and complete predicate of each sentence.

1. Socialite Molly Brown showed remarkable courage at the scene of the *Titanic* tragedy.
2. The sailor in charge of the lifeboat turned out to be unfit for the job.
3. The outspoken and courageous Brown supposedly ordered everyone to start rowing or bailing water.
4. This vigorous work kept the women and children alive in the frigid night air.
5. This courageous act earned Brown the nickname "the unsinkable Mrs. Brown."

3. Compound Subjects and Verbs (links to exercise A, p. 44)

➔ 1. Children and adults
2. signals and triggers

Write the compound parts in each sentence below. Underline the compound subjects once and the compound verbs twice.

1. Matthew Henson and Robert E. Peary reached the North Pole on April 6, 1909.
2. Earlier, Peary had traveled to and explored the polar regions near Greenland.
3. In the 1890s Peary met and hired Henson, an African American, as his personal assistant.
4. Henson organized and went on several of Peary's expeditions.
5. Henson and four Inuit men made it to the North Pole with Peary.
6. The weather and terrain almost defeated the explorers.
7. The resourceful Henson had studied and learned the Inuit language.
8. Both fame and controversy surrounded Peary on his return.
9. Eventually, experts and fellow explorers acknowledged Peary's discovery of the North Pole.
10. Though never as famous as Peary, Henson deserved and received recognition for his role in the expedition.

4. Kinds of Sentences (links to exercise A, p. 46)

➔ 1. interrogative 2. declarative

Identify each of the following sentences as declarative, imperative, interrogative, or exclamatory.

1. Wildlife photographer Jim Brandenburg followed a pack of arctic wolves for three summers.
2. Have you ever seen pictures of these beautiful animals?
3. Notice their large ears and sharp eyes.
4. A wolf's sense of smell is thousands of times keener than ours!
5. How did Brandenburg get along with the wolves?
6. He was careful to learn and respect their code of behavior.
7. Did the wolves accept the stranger in their midst?
8. They even seemed sad when he left!
9. Locate Ellesmere Island on a map or globe.
10. This island is where Brandenburg lived as the lone human in the wolves' territory.

5. **Subjects in Unusual Positions** (links to exercise A, p. 49)

1. ships, were   2. storm, sprang

On a separate sheet of paper, write the simple subject and the verb of each sentence below. Be sure to include all parts of each verb phrase.

1. There is amazing biodiversity within the Amazon rain forest.
2. Does the forest really cover about a third of South America?
3. In this lush environment live countless species.
4. Consider the different layers of the forest.
5. From the top layer, or upper canopy, come the cries of parrots and of the forest monkeys.
6. Below the canopy are slender trees resembling poles.
7. Is the bottom level called the forest floor?
8. In this zone reside many grazing mammals.
9. Think about the importance of the Amazon rain forest.
10. There still exist many undiscovered species in its midst.

6. **Subject Complements** (links to exercise A, p. 51)

1. mountain, PN
2. risky, PA

On a sheet of paper, write each subject complement and identify it as a predicate adjective (PA) or a predicate nominative (PN).

1. Kentucky's Mammoth–Flint Ridge cave system is a popular tourist site.
2. This network of caves is the world's longest.
3. One of California's fascinating sites is Death Valley.
4. To some, the valley looks desolate and lifeless.
5. However, it has become a tourist magnet thanks to its warm climate.

7. **Objects of Verbs** (links to exercise A, p. 53)

1. height, DO
2. Mount Everest, IO; name, DO

Each sentence below contains at least one complement. Write each complement and identify it as a direct object (DO) or an indirect object (IO).

1. Caves fascinate many people.
2. Scientists known as speleologists study these natural formations.
3. Amateur spelunkers explore caves as a hobby.
4. The underground passages offer scientists glimpses of the earth's interior.

5. The bizarre landscapes give spelunkers a special thrill.
6. Every year, thousands of tourists visit these underground worlds.
7. Guides show visitors the spectacular limestone pillars.
8. Electric lights illuminate the underground chambers.
9. The lights give the caves a dramatic air.
10. Sunlight never enters a cave's eerie interior.

3 Using Phrases

1. Prepositional Phrases (links to exercise A, p. 68)

➜ 1. of outdoor competition, type 2. in this sport, participate

Write each prepositional phrase, along with the word or words it modifies.

1. Orienteers are people who compete in woods or across open country on foot.
2. Checkpoints are marked along the course with colored flags.
3. The winner of the contest is the person who reaches all the checkpoints in the fastest time.
4. People without any experience can enjoy orienteering.
5. If anyone is lost for three hours or more, rescue teams start searching.

2. Appositives and Appositive Phrases (links to exercise A, p. 70)

➜ 1. another championship sprinter, Wilma Rudolph
2. polio, disease

Write the appositives and appositive phrases in these sentences, along with the words they rename or identify.

1. The sprinter Wilma Rudolph became the first American woman to win three gold medals in a single Olympics.
2. Rudolph grew up in a large family in Tennessee, the Volunteer State.
3. Polio, a viral illness, left the young Rudolph unable to walk.
4. She had also suffered from the illnesses pneumonia and scarlet fever.
5. The Rudolphs, a loving and determined family, helped Wilma overcome her disability.
6. At Tennessee State University, Rudolph joined the women's track team, the Tigerbelles.
7. Her hometown, Clarksville, honored Rudolph with a big parade after the 1960 Olympic Games.

8. During her track career, Rudolph set world records in the short-distance races—the 100-meter and 200-meter runs.
9. Rudolph was "born to inspire," according to her Olympic teammate Isabelle Daniels Holston.
10. The 1977 television movie *Wilma* told the dramatic story of Rudolph's life.

3. Verbals: Participial Phrases (links to exercise A, p. 73)

➔ 1. steadily declining, interest

Write the participial phrase in each sentence. Then write the noun modified by the phrase.

1. Many teenagers playing on high school football teams have had to quit because they must work after school.
2. Also, parents worried about their children's grades insist that their teenagers concentrate on academics, not sports.
3. In some schools, severely strained budgets have forced administrators to drop their football programs.
4. As a result, National Football League (NFL) officials say they may have to create special academies promoting high school football.
5. Many future professional players may learn their skills at these football academies established by the NFL.

4. Verbals: Gerund Phrases (links to exercise on p. 75)

➔ 1. Olympic swimming, OP
2. having her children learn to swim at an early age, PN

Write the gerund phrase in each sentence. Then tell if the phrase functions as a subject (S), an object of a preposition (OP), a direct object (DO), an indirect object (IO), or a predicate nominative (PN).

1. Swimmer Pablo Morales's goal was making the 1992 Olympic team.
2. Watching Pablo swim at the Olympics was difficult for Pablo's father.
3. Mr. Morales coped with the tension by clutching a picture of his late wife.
4. Spectators applauded Pablo's winning of two gold medals.
5. In 1998 Morales returned to the limelight by heading a list of swimmers to be inducted into the International Swimming Hall of Fame.

5. Verbals: Infinitive Phrases (links to exercise A, p. 77)

1. *to help people in need:* adverb
2. *To give something back to society:* noun

Write each infinitive or infinitive phrase, indicating whether it functions as an adjective, an adverb, or a noun.

1. After the 1997 Masters golf tournament, Tiger Woods was ready to do something for golf.
2. Woods loves to teach at his golf clinics for children.
3. He is involved in First Tee, a project to build affordable golf facilities.
4. First Tee was created to expand children's opportunities in golf.
5. To make golf more popular and ethnically diverse is the project's ultimate goal.
6. At first, Woods didn't plan to inspire people.
7. Even as a small child, he had a goal to be a championship golfer.
8. In August 1996, Woods sought to win a third consecutive U.S. Amateur Championship.
9. To compete for prize money is one reason Woods turned professional.
10. He became the only rookie in golf history to finish among the top five in five consecutive tournaments.

6. Placement of Phrases (links to exercise on p. 79)

1. Correct
3. Competing for Stanford University, Lambert was awarded the most-valuable-player trophy at the 1997 NCAA championship.

Rewrite these sentences to eliminate misplaced and dangling phrases. If a sentence has no errors in phrase placement, write *Correct.*

1. To be good at volleyball, many skills are required.
2. A player in several different ways must be able to hit the ball.
3. Three of the most common ways of hitting the ball are "digging," "setting," and "spiking."
4. To make a dig, the ball is hit just before it reaches the floor by a player who lunges or squats.
5. For a set, the ball is hit high in the air so that another player can spike it.
6. Making a spike, the ball is hit hard by a player who jumps high, near the net.

7. Having a height of seven to eight feet, it is difficult for young players to spike over a volleyball net.
8. Consisting of six players, good chemistry is required for a volleyball team.
9. Called the forwards, the three players who stand near the net focus on spiking and on blocking the other team's spikes.
10. Called the backs, digging and setting for the forwards is the focus of the other three players.

4 Clauses and Sentence Structure

1. Kinds of Clauses (links to exercise on p. 93)

➜ 1. independent
2. subordinate

Identify the underlined clauses as subordinate or independent.

1. While some scientists map the human genome, others map the genes of simpler animals.
2. They started with viruses and with bacteria, which are single cells.
3. Some biologists study a worm called *Caenorhabditis elegans*, which has a nervous system like that of complex animals.
4. This worm has a transparent body, which makes it easier to study.
5. The biologists, who thought the worm would have about 6,000 genes, found that it had nearly 20,000.
6. The scientists had to sequence 97 million bases, which are the chemical building blocks of DNA.
7. After they had worked for a number of years, scientists had sequenced 99 percent of the worm's genes.
8. That this was a challenging project is clear.
9. Scientists can learn much from this particular worm because it shares many genes with humans.
10. Whatever scientists learn about the *C. elegans* genome may help in finding cures for some diseases.

2. Adjective and Adverb Clauses (links to exercise A, p. 97)

2. when the U.S. Army Air Force bought the first Sierra Sam, started
5. that humans could ride, anything

Write the adjective and adverb clauses in the following sentences. After each clause, write the word or words that it modifies.

1. Many diseases, even those that are not hereditary, have a genetic component.
2. After scientists learned how genes work, they found that more than 5,000 diseases are caused by a change in one gene.
3. More than half the people who are living in the world today will probably suffer from some form of genetic disease.
4. One such disease is cancer, which starts when the genetic instructions in cells go wrong.
5. Cancer is often caused by cell mutations that occur late in life.
6. The environment can be a factor in certain kinds of cancer, since exposure to toxic chemicals and radiation can affect cells.
7. Some cancer drugs are called "magic bullets" because they are aimed directly at tumor cells.
8. Another genetic disease is sickle cell anemia, which is caused by a recessive gene.
9. Only a person whose parents both carry the sickle cell gene can get the disease.
10. Although scientists still have a lot to learn, they have made much progress in fighting genetic illnesses.

3. Noun Clauses (links to exercise A, p. 99)

1. That birth order influences personality, S
2. that first-born children tend to be more conservative and traditional, DO

Write the noun clause in each sentence. Indicate whether the clause is a subject (S), a direct object (DO), an indirect object (IO), a predicate nominative (PN), or an object of a preposition (OP).

1. Many adoptive parents have feared that their children could suffer from being adopted.
2. Therapists looked for certain problems in whoever was adopted.
3. They thought that adopted children would be more likely than other children to have problems at home and in school.

4. What the therapists overlooked was the large number of adopted children who are well-adjusted.
5. They studied whoever was adopted and ignored other factors.
6. The reason some children are adopted is that they were abused or neglected by their birth parents.
7. That abuse and neglect hurt children is clear.
8. Most adopted children recover from whatever affected them early in life.
9. That is why they are as successful as their peers.
10. What researchers have found in several studies of adopted teens is good psychological health.

4. **Sentence Structure** (links to exercise A, p. 103)

2. CD 4. CX

Identify each of the following sentences as simple (SS), compound (CD), complex (CX), or compound-complex (CC).

1. Your first name can be a blessing or a curse, depending on what your parents chose.
2. Some people claim that your name affects your relationships, career, and self-esteem.
3. Whoever has an odd name can overcome it or change it.
4. Every first name has conscious or unconscious associations.
5. Many names have literal meanings; for example, the name Margaret comes from a Greek word meaning "pearl."
6. Frederick means "peaceful," and Kevin means "kind" or "gentle," while Herman means "warrior."
7. Many names can be translated into other languages, so the English "John" becomes "Sean" in Gaelic and "Ivan" in Russian.
8. Some parents name their children after relatives, while others choose names that sound good with their last name.
9. Others can't resist a joke, which is how people have been given the names Candy Barr, Mac Aroni, and Merry Christmas.
10. A couple with the last name Beach named their children Rocky, Coral, Sandy, and Pebble.

5 Writing Complete Sentences

1. Sentence Fragments (links to exercise A, p. 119)

Answers may vary.

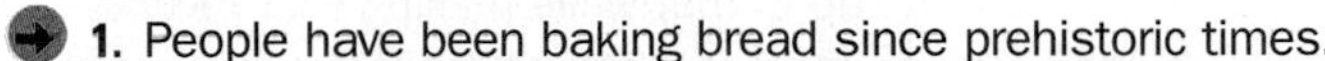

1. People have been baking bread since prehistoric times.
2. About 4,600 years ago, bakers in Egypt learned how to use yeast to make bread rise.

Rewrite the numbered fragments as complete sentences. You may add words to the fragments or combine them with sentences.

Baking soda is used as an ingredient in batter and dough. The soda reacts with acids in various other ingredients, such as milk or lemon juice, and produces carbon dioxide bubbles. **(1) Cause the batter or dough to expand.** Because of its chemical properties, baking soda has many other uses. **(2) Apart from baking.** It neutralizes acids, including stomach acids. **(3) That can cause acid indigestion.** Because many odors can be traced to acids, baking soda can often be used to neutralize the acids and eliminate the odors. **(4) Have probably seen people using baking soda to absorb odors in refrigerators, closets, and litter boxes. (5) To deodorize a locker filled with sneakers and gym clothes!**

2. Run-On Sentences (links to exercise A, p. 121)

Answers may vary.

1. Julia Child originally had not prepared for a career in the food industry; in fact, she majored in history in college.
2. During World War II, Child served with a secret intelligence agency. Her assignments took her around the world.

Correct the run-ons below. (There may be more than one way to fix each run-on.) If a sentence is not a run-on, write *Correct.*

1. Fannie Farmer occupies a special place in the history of food writing, in the late 1800s she invented the modern cookbook.
2. Before Farmer created a recipe format that gave exact measurements, cooks used recipes that advised them to add a "pinch" or a "handful" of an ingredient.
3. Farmer's method ensured that a recipe gave the same results each time, it did not matter who did the cooking.

4. Her approach was an immediate success with the American public, the *Boston Cooking School Cook Book,* her first published work, became a bestseller in the United States and was soon translated into French, Spanish, and Japanese.
5. Think of Fannie Farmer the next time you measure out a teaspoon of this or a cup of that while making your favorite recipe!
6. Irma Rombauer was another groundbreaking cookbook author; her book, *The Joy of Cooking,* is generally considered a classic of the genre.
7. Over the years, three generations of Rombauers have been involved in producing various editions of the book, Rombauer's daughter Marion coauthored a major revision that was published in 1951, and her son Ethan was in charge of the revision that came out in 1997.
8. Perhaps cooking is not exactly your cup of tea, perhaps your taste in reading tends toward humor.
9. If this is the case, you might enjoy the essays of Calvin Trillin.
10. Trillin is an author and humorist who has a keen interest in food he clearly enjoys searching out memorable foods, unusual food facts, and remarkable food rituals to share with his readers.

6 Using Verbs

1. The Principal Parts of a Verb (links to exercise A, p. 133)

➜ **1.** made **2.** seeking

Choose the correct form of the verb in parentheses.

1. Night has (fallen, fell) in Florida.
2. The amateur astronomers (prepared, preparing) their gear carefully before coming outside.
3. Everyone has (bringed, brought) binoculars, a telescope, and insect repellent.
4. They (wear, worn) the stinky salve to ward off mosquitoes.
5. In the past, they had been (ate, eaten) alive by the bloodthirsty attackers.
6. They are discussing their sightings when suddenly a shout (rings, rang) out.

7. One observer has (seen, saw) Jupiter and its moons.
8. At 11 P.M., he (swinged, swings) his telescope around to Jupiter again.
9. He (spotting, spots) something strange.
10. Later, he will (found, find) out that two of Jupiter's moons had (make, made) a rare double shadow on the planet.

2. Forming Verb Tenses (links to exercise on p. 136)

➜ 1. open 2. is reading

Write the correct tense or form of each underlined verb in the passage below.

(1) In this day and age, flying around the world was no big deal. **(2)** However, could a person do in the 20th century what Jules Verne's character does in 1872? **(3)** In 1989 Michael Palin and a BBC TV crew accepted the challenge and are attempting to go by land and sea around the globe in 80 days.

(4) Verne's Phileas Fogg and his servant Passepartout have left on their journey from Charing Cross Station. **(5)** Palin and his crew started in London on a train that leaves from Victoria Station. **(6)** In Saudi Arabia, bureaucrats had restricted train travel, so Palin drives through the desert, but his TV crew flew. **(7)** While they will be crossing the Persian Gulf in a small ship called a dhow, Palin became seasick. **(8)** On their trip across the United States by train, they stop in Colorado and went for a ride in a dogsled.

(9) They return to London at the end of 80 days but missed their station because of a bomb scare. **(10)** In the 21st century, probably some traveler will have tried the trip again, keeping the spirit of adventure alive.

3. Using Verb Tenses (links to exercise on p. 140)

➜ 1. wonder *or* have wondered 2. know

Write the correct tense of each underlined verb.

1. As I am reading, I kept wondering what else could happen to Yossi Ghinsberg.
2. He survives the terrors of the river, but he faced other problems on land.
3. It was growing dark, and Ghinsberg has needed food and shelter.
4. He didn't know whether Kevin is looking for him.

5. At one point, when a deadly snake was within striking distance, Ghinsberg becomes angry.
6. He had been keeping his frustration in check, but he suddenly vents his anger against the snake.
7. Driven by hatred, he has picked up a rock and killed the snake with it.
8. As I eagerly turned the page, I wonder—by morning, will he have eaten the snake?
9. I have never been so hungry that I will think of eating a snake.
10. However, I am never in a fight for survival, so I don't know what I would be capable of doing.

4. Shifts in Tense (links to exercise on p. 143)

➔ **1.** saw **2.** was traveling

For each sentence below, choose the correct verb from the pair shown in parentheses.

1. Did the creators of the Iditarod know that their race (inspires, would inspire) other races?
2. Crossing Alaska in a dogsled sounds crazy, but a bike race in the snow (seems, seemed) even crazier.
3. Nevertheless, the classic Alaskan race (has given, gives) birth to other races that are run on the Iditarod trail.
4. People call these races the Iditasport; besides biking, they (include, included) running, skiing, and snowshoeing.
5. The snowshoe race covers 75 miles, whereas the bike race (is, was) twice as long.
6. Monique Cole never (races, had raced) until she entered the Iditasport bike race in 1995.
7. The bike race (has become, will become) an obsession for Cole, who has been living in Hawaii.
8. She even (moves, moved) to Colorado, where she trained in the mountains.
9. During the race, she (is pushing, pushed) herself hard and rode the last 60 miles in 19 hours without a break.
10. The winner (has completed, completed) the race only 2 hours sooner than Cole did.

5. Active and Passive Voice (links to exercise on p. 145)

➡ **1.** In 1986, the Russians launched the first section of the space station *Mir.*
2. Years later, Gene Roddenberry created another space station in *Star Trek: Deep Space Nine.*

Rewrite each sentence, changing the verb from the passive voice to the active voice. Change other words as necessary.

1. The International Space Station (ISS) is considered by scientists to be the starting point for future space travel.
2. Space colonies on our moon and on Mars will someday be established by astronauts.
3. In the meantime, the ISS is being built by people from 16 countries.
4. Work on tools and facilities has been done by engineers and designers.
5. Seventy-five space walks to put the station together have been scheduled by NASA.
6. For these walks, special space suits are being made by scientists.
7. An astronaut will be protected from extreme temperatures by the space suit.
8. Because the space gloves are bulky, special tools have been developed by technicians for use by the astronauts.
9. Eventually, the ISS will be lived in by six astronauts.
10. Everything will be recycled by them in order to cut down on the supplies they will need from our planet.

6. The Mood of a Verb (links to exercise on p. 147)

➡ **1.** subjunctive **2.** indicative

For each numbered item, identify the underlined verb as indicative, subjunctive, or imperative mood.

Dear Ms. I. Knowitall,

(1) You have no idea how hard it <u>is</u> to be a teenager today. **(2)** I wish I <u>were</u> living in the 1800s. **(3)** The principal says, "<u>Wear</u> a uniform," and "Don't arrive at school wearing T-shirts with slogans." **(4)** At the same time, my friends <u>tell</u> me to get tattoos like theirs. **(5)** All of them want me to be like they are, but I just <u>want</u> to be myself. What should I do?

Independent in Idaho

7. Commonly Confused Verbs (links to exercise on p. 149)

➜ **1.** sit **2.** teaching

Choose the correct verb from the pair shown in parentheses.

1. The lookout (rose, raised) the spyglass and couldn't believe his eyes.
2. (Laying, Lying) beyond the sand dunes was a lagoon filled with hundreds of whales.
3. The captain of the whaling ship couldn't (let, leave) the whales in peace.
4. As he (sat, set) down his spyglass, he ordered the ship to proceed.
5. When the sailors entered the lagoon, they (lay, laid) their lives on the line.

7 Subject-Verb Agreement

1. Agreement in Number (links to exercise A, p. 159)

➜ **1.** The play's setting is a farmhouse in the early 1900s.
4. Her motive remains a mystery, however.

Rewrite the incorrect sentences so that the verbs agree with the subjects. If a sentence contains no error, write *Correct.*

1. Since the late 1980s, forensic scientists has used a remarkable technique to help solve crimes.
2. The technique is called DNA fingerprinting.
3. DNA "fingerprints" is not the same as the prints made by a person's fingertips.
4. Technicians use cells from a drop of blood, a strand of hair, or another part of the body to develop a DNA fingerprint.
5. The initials DNA stands for deoxyribonucleic acid.
6. This chemical is found in the nucleus of every human cell, and it is the key to each individual's genetic code.
7. Like the fingerprinting long used by police in crime detection, DNA testing have been used to establish a link between a suspect and a crime scene.
8. Some people has been cleared of crimes thanks to DNA fingerprinting.
9. Scientists even uses DNA analysis to help with historical research.
10. For example, one scientist were able to determine that a woman who had for many years claimed to be Anastasia, the

daughter of the last tsar and tsarina of Russia, was not in fact related to the royal family.

2. Words Between Subject and Verb (links to exercise A, p. 161)

3. are **5.** join

Correct the subject-verb agreement errors in the sentences below by writing the correct verb forms on a separate sheet of paper. If a sentence contains no error, write *Correct.*

1. The real-life cases of Di Renjie has served as inspiration for detective novels featuring Judge Dee.
2. Di, a Chinese government official, lived during the seventh century A.D.
3. Historical records from the distant past reveals his remarkable detective skills.
4. Robert van Gulik, the creator of the Judge Dee stories, were an avid student of Chinese history.
5. Gulik's portrayal of Judge Dee and his adventures are both entertaining and informative.

3. Indefinite-Pronoun Subjects (links to exercise A, p. 163)

2. involves **5.** points

Correct the subject-verb agreement errors in the sentences below by writing the correct verb on a separate sheet of paper. If a sentence contains no error, write *Correct.*

1. Most of Agatha Christie's murder mysteries feature a detective who investigates and solves a crime.
2. In this story, someone invite ten people to a rocky, isolated island.
3. Nobody in the group, it turns out, know why this mysterious person has brought the ten strangers together.
4. All seems to have terrible secrets in their past, however.
5. After dinner on the first night, each are accused of murder by a voice on a phonograph record.
6. Shortly afterward, several of the characters watch as one guest dies of poisoning.
7. Another are found dead the next day.
8. Everyone are terrified when one more murder takes place; eventually, only two people are left on the island.
9. Both now know who the murderer is.
10. Few guesses the surprising twist before it is revealed at the end of the story.

4. Compound Subjects (links to exercise A, p. 165)

➜ **1.** have **3.** has

Write the verb form that agrees with the subject of each sentence.

1. Chester Himes and his detective novels featuring Grave Digger Jones and Coffin Ed Johnson (has, have) paved the way for other African-American detective writers.
2. Neither the detectives nor their creators (is, are) dull or predictable.
3. Marti MacAlister and Blanche White (is, are) two fictional female African-American detectives.
4. Eleanor Taylor Bland and Barbara Neely, the authors who created them, (knows, know) how to tell exciting stories.
5. Problems at home and pressure from colleagues often (causes, cause) stress for MacAlister, the mother of two and the only African-American female detective in her department.
6. Her toughness and intelligence (help, helps) her succeed.
7. Neither her complicated personal life nor her difficult and dangerous cases (overwhelm, overwhelms) her.
8. Intellect and resourcefulness (enables, enable) Blanche White to solve crimes that baffle others.
9. Blanche's job as a cook and housekeeper and her work as an amateur sleuth (expose, exposes) her to all sorts of people and problems.
10. Either the unusual plots or the exploration of social issues within Bland's books (is, are) bound to capture your interest, whether or not you are a devoted reader of mysteries.

5. Other Problem Subjects (links to exercise A, p. 168)

➜ **1.** begins **4.** is

Write the verb form that agrees with the subject of each sentence.

1. "Art and Authenticity" (is, are) an article you might enjoy if you are interested in the subject of art forgery.
2. *The Art of the Faker* also (provides, provide) a wealth of information on this topic.
3. News of forgeries occasionally (makes, make) headlines.
4. The majority of art forgers (fakes, fake) works of art.

5. These days, 10 million dollars (is, are) not an unheard-of price for a painting by a famous artist.
6. Of course, the majority of art forgeries (duplicates, duplicate) the most valuable works.
7. To fight forgery and theft, the staff of a modern museum (spends, spend) a great deal of time, energy, and money on security.
8. Sometimes, two-thirds of a budget (goes, go) toward such security-related expenditures as insurance and the salaries of security personnel.
9. "Famous Forgeries and Fabulous Fakes" (is, are) the title of a lecture series that the university art museum is currently sponsoring.
10. The audience (seems, seem) fascinated by stories of notorious forgeries.

6. Agreement Problems in Sentences (links to exercise A, p. 170)

➡ 2. criminals, appear 3. example, is

Write the subject of each sentence. Then write the verb form that agrees with the subject.

1. From books and television shows (comes, come) stories of criminals who make incredibly stupid mistakes.
2. There (is, are) many dumb crooks out there, according to these sources.
3. Here, for your amusement, (is, are) two of their stories.
4. Into a pen holding several homing pigeons (sneaks, sneak) one unthinking thief.
5. There (is, are) a dealer in town who is willing to buy the birds.
6. (Does, Do) this man and the thief have any brains?
7. Back to their home (flies, fly) the pigeons the very next day!
8. (Is, Are) a thief who leaves obvious clues behind any smarter?
9. Inside one burglarized office, for example, (was, were) a speeding ticket belonging to the burglar, a recently fired employee.
10. (Do, Does) it surprise you to learn that someone would actually use a speeding ticket to prop open the door during a burglary?

8 Using Pronouns

2. Nominative and Objective Cases (links to exercise A, p. 183)

➜ 2. they 5. him

Choose the correct form from the pronouns in parentheses.

1. Though most people watch television, (they, them) may not know how a television show is put together.
2. When my friend and (I, me) went to see a show being taped, we learned a lot about how a TV show works.
3. Before the show, we saw workers scurrying around and learned that it is (them, they) who put the scenery, props, and lights in place.
4. We talked to one worker who told us that (she, her) and other technicians were responsible for controlling the lights.
5. (She, Her) explained that just one televised scene may require as many as 20 different lighting instruments.
6. (Us, We) and the others in the audience watched as microphones and cameras were put in place.
7. We saw a man rushing off to the side of the filming area and learned that (he, him) and others worked behind the scenes, in the control room.
8. The director seemed to be everywhere at once; the one responsible for coordinating everyone and everything on the show is (she, her).
9. Before the taping began, makeup was applied to each performer so that (he or she, him or her) would look natural on camera.
10. After a show is taped, the tape is reviewed by the director, corrected by editors, and stored until the time you and (me, I) will see it on our screens.

3. The Possessive Case (links to exercise A, p. 186)

➜ 2. their, our

Write the possessive pronouns in the following sentences.

1. Residents of the state of Washington are proud of its natural beauty—the rugged mountains, stately evergreen forests, and sparkling lakes and rivers.
2. No one can blame the residents for their boasting.
3. If you like to hike, fish, or ski, you should consider going to Washington for your vacation.
4. Because we live in Washington, many opportunities for

recreation are ours all year long.

5. A recent visitor to Washington expressed her curiosity about Washington's motto, *Alki,* which is an Indian word for "by and by."
6. When settlers landed at Alki Point—now Seattle—they called it "New York Alki" because they hoped that "by and by" their town would be the New York of the West Coast.
7. The people of Stampede Pass, Washington, claim the record for the snowiest town in the United States as theirs; the average yearly snowfall there is 431.9 inches.
8. A favorite fact of mine is that Washington's Grand Coulee Dam is built with enough concrete to pave a four-lane highway from Seattle to New York!
9. What is your favorite fact about Washington?
10. Everyone has a favorite sight, and mine is the snowy slopes of Mount Rainier as seen from an airplane.

4. Using *Who* and *Whom* (links to exercise A, p. 189)

➔ 1. who 3. whom

Choose the correct pronoun in parentheses.

1. (Who, Whom) doesn't know at least something about circuses?
2. Few people know much about the remarkable man for (who, whom) the most famous circus is named.
3. P. T. Barnum's life would interest (whoever, whomever) has seen a circus.
4. Barnum, (who, whom) was from Connecticut, moved to New York City when he was in his early 20s.
5. In 1841, his American Museum began drawing many people, (who, whom) came to see such attractions as Jumbo the giant elephant and a mermaid (fake, of course).
6. The museum was successful, but it could be seen only by (whoever, whomever) could travel to New York.
7. (Whom, Who) had Barnum failed to reach?
8. He was sure that if his show could travel, it would attract those (who, whom) were unable to get to New York.
9. In 1871, Barnum took off on a railroad tour, bringing his show within reach of (whoever, whomever) lived in towns along the route.
10. Now the circus comes to many towns, thanks to Barnum, without (who, whom) the show might never have gone on the road.

5. Pronoun-Antecedent Agreement (links to exercise A, p. 192)

➔ **1.** their **2.** his

Choose the correct pronoun in parentheses.

1. Mount Everest divides Tibet from Nepal, with Nepal situated on (their, its) south side.
2. Mount Everest was formed about 60 million years ago, but until May 29, 1953, no one had ever climbed to (his, its) highest point.
3. Sir Edmund Hillary and Tenzing Norgay became the first men to do so when (they, he) reached the summit on that date.
4. Hillary, a beekeeper from Auckland, New Zealand, and Tenzing, the son of a farming family from Nepal, first met when (he, they) joined an expedition to climb Everest.
5. When the men began the expedition, (it, they) all dreamed of being the first to reach the summit.
6. Other members turned back, but neither Hillary nor Tenzing wanted to give up (his, their) dream.
7. Either Hillary or Norgay put (his, their) foot on the summit first, but neither would say who did so.
8. Hillary and other climbers have written books about (his, their) experiences conquering the world's highest monutain.
9. Jon Krakauer describes the natural beauty of Mount Everest in (its, his) book *Into Thin Air.*
10. The mountain was named for Sir George Everest in 1865, but (its, his) name in Nepal is Sagarmatha, which means "ocean mother," while in Tibet it is called Chomolungma, or "mother goddess of the universe."

6. Indefinite Pronouns as Antecedents (links to exercise A, p. 195)

➔ **1.** their **3.** their

Choose the correct word or words in parentheses.

1. Everyone who values freedom should pay (their, his or her) respects to Harriet Tubman, a onetime slave who became an American hero.
2. In the years before the Civil War, many who escaped slavery owed (his or her, their) freedom to Tubman.
3. Each of the people who traveled on the Underground Railroad was willing to risk (their, his or her) life for the sake of freedom.

4. Several of the people who were abolitionists risked (his or her, their) lives to help slaves reach the north and freedom.
5. After Tubman made her own escape, she joined forces with some of the abolitionists, working with (them, him or her) to liberate others.
6. Each of the 18 trips she made along the Underground Railroad had (its, their) dangers.
7. Most of the journey was fraught with peril up until (their, its) end.
8. Of the more than 300 slaves Tubman guided along the Underground Railroad, no one lost (his or her, their) life or was recaptured.
9. Both of Tubman's parents, whom Tubman helped escape in 1857, owed (his or her, their) freedom to their daughter.
10. Abolition and women's rights were critical issues to Tubman, and both took (its, their) share of her time and energy.

7. Pronoun Reference Problems (links to exercise A, p. 198)

➜ 1. Before Xena became a heroine, she honed her warrior skills, but her human skills were lacking.
2. She paid the price for leaving her army by going through the gauntlet.

Rewrite the following sentences to correct instances of indefinite, general, and ambiguous pronoun reference. (There may be more than one way to rewrite a sentence.)

1. In stories and songs, you get the idea that pirates were dashing, elegant characters.
2. Pirates were desperate men who turned to a life of robbery on the high seas, which paints a less romantic picture than the stories.
3. However, as our history book explains, they often chose the outlaw's life because of the cruel and unfair treatment they received working as honest seamen.
4. A rough form of democracy allowed them to choose their own captains and set up rules.
5. In one nonfiction book, it says that pirates set up free colonies of their own, such as Libertatia on the island of Madagascar.
6. The pirates of Libertatia held all the goods in a shared treasury, which they had stolen.
7. Some pirates became national heroes and patriots, which is the subject of an interesting book I read.

8. In the book, they tell how Sir Henry Morgan became commander of English forces in Jamaica and how Jean Laffite helped American forces in the War of 1812.
9. Sir Frances Drake committed acts of piracy. That surprises people who know him only as a famous explorer and navigator.
10. Not only men became pirates; Anne Bonney and Mary Read were pirates along with Captain Kidd and Blackbeard, who were women.

8. Other Pronoun Problems (links to exercise A, p. 201)

➜ **3.** him

Choose the correct pronoun in parentheses.

1. (Us, We) students were interested in finding out the origins of the English names for the days of the week.
2. A trip to the library helped (us, we) researchers find out that four of the seven days are named for characters in Norse mythology.
3. That Wednesday was named for Odin, ruler of the Norse gods, was a surprise to (we, us) students.
4. Tuesday is named for Tyr, a son of Odin, though a less well-known character than (him, he).
5. Thursday was named for Thor, the god of thunder, so two days were named after Odin's sons, (he, him) and Tyr.
6. Friday was named for Frigg, the wife of Odin; when their son Balder died, no one was sadder than (her, she).
7. It was (she, her), Frigg, who was goddess of marriage.
8. If you read about gods in Greek mythology, you may conclude that Norse gods were not as powerful as (they, them).
9. In fact, Balder, (him, he) who was most beloved of ail the gods, was killed in one story.
10. Although no one believes in the Norse gods anymore, (we, us) students still like to read stories about them.

9 Using Modifiers

1. Using Adjectives and Adverbs (links to exercise A, p. 212)

1. *superstitious:* adjective; *still:* adverb
2. *some:* adjective; *accidentally:* adverb

On a separate sheet of paper, write each italicized word in these sentences, indicating whether it is used as an adjective or an adverb.

1. Youngsters gather *eagerly* around the *respected* elder.
2. For *three* days, they have waited to hear about the *great* thunderbird.
3. The elder speaks so softly that the children can *barely* hear.
4. *Outside,* a storm rages, and everyone is startled by a *deafening* thunderclap.
5. The *patient Sioux* elder smiles *knowingly* and continues the story.
6. The thunderbird must be sitting in its *mountain* tipi and giving *its* approval.
7. The thunderbird has huge, *powerful* wings and an *extremely sharp* beak.
8. The *loudly* rumbling thunder is made by the flapping of the thunderbird's *gigantic* wings.
9. It wears *enormous* robes made of *dark* clouds.
10. It may seem *mysterious,* but the *thunder* being is the guardian of truth.

2. Problems with Modifiers (links to exercise A, p. 216)

3. badly 5. has

For each sentence, write the correct choice of the words in parentheses.

1. While in a department store, a woman (sudden, suddenly) became very sick.
2. She hadn't been doing (anything, nothing) except trying on a fur coat.
3. The doctor examined her (good, well) and found tiny punctures.
4. He (could, couldn't) hardly believe what he was seeing.
5. Her wounds (strong, strongly) indicated that she was a snake-bite victim.
6. Later the store found a coral snake trapped in the sleeve of (that, that there) fur coat.

7. You may have heard a story like (this, this here) one before.
8. It is one of (them, those) urban myths that seems to have an element of truth.
9. It (has, hasn't) never been disputed that coral snakes are poisonous and strike quickly.
10. A story about a deadly snake in a coat sleeve seems (possible, possibly).

3. Using Comparisons (links to exercise A, p. 219)

➜ 2. best 4. colder

For each sentence, write the correct comparative or superlative form.

1. Many squabbles break out among wild horses, but the (fiercer, fiercest) battles are between stallions.
2. The dominant stallion has been the (more victorious, most victorious) one in battle.
3. In the herd, survival of the (fittest, more fit) is the law.
4. In the competition between two stallions, often only the (stronger, strongest) one survives.
5. When a stallion senses a battle, its instincts become (most acute, more acute).
6. Since the dominant stallion has (greater, greatest) strength than a young stallion, the contest is uneven.
7. But a fight to the death against an equal is the (more challenging, most challenging) contest of all for a stallion.
8. A stallion must fight (better, more well) than his challenger.
9. The (less, least) sign of hesitation could cost him his life.
10. His senses are heightened as his challenger comes (closest, closer).

4. Problems with Comparisons (links to exercise on p. 221)

➜ 1. the scariest film
2. than any other actor

Correct the illogical or double comparisons in these sentences. If a sentence contains no error, write *Correct.*

1. Can a teenage girl turn into one of the most deadliest monsters?
2. At first Nancy, the newest student at a school for girls, seems no different from any student.

3. Miss Branding, the chemistry teacher, is much more kinder to her than the other teachers are.
4. In truth, she uses Nancy in the most evilest experiment.
5. In her possession is an amulet that is more powerful than any charm.
6. She uses it to put Nancy in a hypnotic trance, which grows more deeper.
7. While under the spell, Nancy is transformed into a vampire, but later she has no memory of even her most worst deeds.
8. Unlike any vampire, Nancy isn't affected by sunlight.
9. She also sleeps in the same kind of bed as everyone in the dormitory.
10. Yet, like other vampires, she dies when a stake is driven through her heart—the most surest way to stop a vampire.

10 Capitalization

1. People and Cultures (links to exercise A, p. 232)

➜ 2. Ms. Malaika Fisher 3. religion

Identify and rewrite the words that contain capitalization errors in the following sentences.

1. My Uncle believes that few people have equaled benjamin Franklin.
2. He was one of the most famous and respected americans of his day.
3. While still in his teens, Franklin wrote a number of newspaper articles under the pen name mrs. silence Dogood.
4. He was famous for scientific research, and his writings on electricity were translated into french and other european languages.
5. During the American Revolution, the United States sought support from France and received it after the defeat of British forces under general Burgoyne at Saratoga.
6. Franklin was chosen to be a Diplomat who would represent the United States in Paris.
7. During his time in Paris, Franklin was an effective negotiator and very popular with the french people.

8. Franklin's son also achieved a position of importance, becoming Governor of the colony of New Jersey.
9. However, governor Franklin sided with the British during the American Revolution and eventually was forced to flee to England.
10. Some of Franklin's best-known writing appeared in his popular series of books called *Poor Richard's Almanack,* which i may read someday.

2. First Words and Titles (links to exercise A, p. 235)

➜ **1.** Each **2.** *Gettysburg*

Identify and rewrite the words that contain capitalization errors in the following sentences.

1. "Who can tell me," asked the teacher, "The author of these lines?"
2. "Shall I compare thee to a summer's day? thou art more lovely and more temperate."
3. "I'll tell you," she said. "they were written by William Shakespeare, who may have been the greatest writer of all time."
4. We learned that Shakespeare is especially famous for his plays, such as *the tempest.*
5. There are many movie versions of Shakespearean plays, including a new one of *Romeo And Juliet.*
6. I read a review of that movie in *The Los Angeles times.*
7. I wrote a fan letter to the director of the movie; "Dear sir," it began.
8. I closed the letter by writing "Sincerely Yours," and signed my name.
9. Did you know that the musical *West side Story* is based on that play?
10. We'll read the play this year in school, and we'll also read a novel by Charles Dickens, *the Pickwick Papers*.

3. Places and Transportation (links to exercise A, p. 238)

➔ 1. Liberal, Kansas; United States of America
4. Buckinghamshire

For each sentence, write correctly the words that contain capitalization errors. If a sentence is correct, write *Correct.*

1. The Eiffel tower Is one of the most remarkable buildings in the world.
2. Its designer, Alexandre Gustave Eiffel, also designed the framework for the statue of Liberty.
3. In addition, he was responsible for the design of the locks of the Panama canal.
4. The Eiffel Tower stands in the heart of paris, france.
5. At 984 feet, it was the world's tallest building until 1930, when the Chrysler building topped it.
6. It is located just South of the Seine river.
7. It is probably the most widely recognized monument in Europe.
8. It may be the best-known structure in the western hemisphere.
9. Tourists can get to it by using the municipal subway, called the Metro.
10. This monument is among the most popular tourist attractions in the City.

4. Organizations and Other Subjects (links to exercise A, p. 241)

➔ 1. April, Purdue University, Bug Bowl 2. Correct

For each sentence, write correctly the words that contain capitalization errors. If a sentence is correct, write *Correct.*

1. If you like dogs, you might be interested in an organization called basset hound rescue.
2. The organization looks for caring owners for homeless basset hounds and publicizes its efforts with special events called basset waddles.
3. For example, in Milford, Ohio, the Ohio branch of the organization participates in the Frontier Day parade.
4. In 1999, the Parade took place on Thursday, June 3.
5. In Williamsport, Maryland, the Great Basset ramble began at 11:00 a.m., and more than 100 floppy-eared bassets were present.
6. None of these dogs are apt to win the American Kennel Club Best-of-Breed Award, but many people love them anyway.
7. During the Summer of 1999, Ellicott Creek park in Buffalo, New York, was the setting for the Basset picnic.

8. Carolina Basset Hound rescue, or cbhr for short, raises money and collects dog food at its annual events.
9. Dogs and human beings have been living together since the Stone Age.
10. Someday you might want to contribute a few cans of Happy Snappy dog food to feed a hungry basset hound.

11 Punctuation

1. Periods and Other End Marks (links to exercise on p. 251)

1. Can a child learn to play chess at three years of age?
2. Bobby Fischer, the first American to win the world championship, learned the moves of chess at the age of six.

Write these sentences, inserting periods, question marks, and exclamation points as needed.

1. The TV sports announcer said, "The game of squash has been played since the 1700s"
2. Do some research to see if you can find out what squash used to be called
3. You should be able to find out that it was called racquets
4. Do you already know that squash is played with a long-handled racquet and a small ball inside a fully enclosed court
5. Squash was first played by prisoners in London's Fleet Prison, where they bounced the ball off the prison courtyard walls
6. Do you think it's odd that the next group of people to begin playing squash was the British upper class
7. From the prison yard to the elite clubs of the upper class—that's quite a jump
8. A list of sports similar to squash would look like this:
   1 racquetball
   2 jai alai
9. Racquetball was invented in 1949 in Greenwich, Conn, by an American, Joe Sobek
10. Jai alai, which is popular in Mexico and other Spanish-speaking countries, is played on a much larger court and with a 3-ft-long "basket" strapped to each player's arm

2. Commas in Sentence Parts (links to exercise on p. 254)

➜ 1. yo-yo, brain-squasher 2. invention

Write the words that should be followed by a comma.

1. Cricket the game that has been a part of village life throughout England for centuries may have begun as early as the 13th century.
2. In fact it is believed to have developed from a game in which country boys bowled a rock at a tree stump or at the gate of a sheep pen.
3. The original bat probably was a long heavy tree branch resembling a hockey stick.
4. Today cricket is played with a straight wooden bat.
5. At first the cricket wicket had two stumps or upright poles; later a third stump was added.
6. In the 1800s in England the modern style of overarm bowling gained popularity.
7. Throwing quickly a bowler can send the ball at a very high speed.
8. Yes cricket has long been popular with women as well as men.
9. For about 100 years cricket has been enjoyed as an international sport by countries that were once colonized by the British.
10. In the history of international cricket there have been only two tied matches: first in 1960 when Australia played the West Indies; second in 1986 when India played Australia.

3. More Commas (links to exercise A, p. 257)

➜ 1. Scottsdale, Arizona 2. Correct

Write each word that should be followed by a comma. If no commas are needed in a sentence, write *Correct.*

1. My teacher said "The bow and arrow are believed to have been invented by prehistoric people."
2. By the 900s the Turks had developed a more advanced bow and by the 1100s the crossbow was used extensively in Europe.
3. Although there is evidence that recreational archery was practiced by the ancient Egyptians and Greeks, the bow and arrow were used primarily for hunting and warfare until the late 1500s.
4. In England, archery societies came into being in the 16th and 17th centuries and archery was practiced as a sport by both royalty and the general public.

5. In 1844 the Grand National Archery Society held its first meeting in York England.
6. The first American archery organization founded in 1828, was the United Bowmen of Philadelphia.
7. The National Archery Association, which held its first national tournament in the year of its founding, was established in 1879.
8. The number of people involved in the sport of archery grew tremendously after 1930 and today more than 10 million Americans participate in archery.
9. The world championships which take place every two years began in 1931.
10. Archery contests which can take place at both indoor and outdoor ranges are also part of the Olympic Games.

4. Semicolons and Colons (links to exercise on p. 259)

➜ 1. Greece;

Write each word that should be followed by a semicolon or colon. If a sentence is correct, write *Correct.*

1. Roman ruins excavated in London provided early evidence of ice-skating: leather soles and blades made of animal bones, which date back to 50 B.C.
2. It is believed that the Scandinavian people used ice skates for transportation as early as A.D. 1100 however, the blades of their ice skates were not made of metal, either.
3. Their skate blades were made from shank or rib bones from the following animals: reindeer, oxen, and elk.
4. Ice-skating for recreation is believed to have begun in the 1100s in England prior to that ice skates were used only as a means of transportation.
5. Metal blades were the next breakthrough in skate technology iron blades came first, in 1250, followed by steel blades on wooden soles in about 1400.
6. The first all-steel skates were developed around 1850 by E. W. Bushnell these skates were lighter and stronger than iron skates.
7. The development of the all-steel skate was a turning point for ice-skating: skating clubs opened as the popularity of ice skating increased.
8. Around 1870 an American ballet dancer named Jackson Haines introduced the idea of blending dance movements with ice-skating he is responsible for introducing this approach in Europe as well.

9. The year 1892 was very important in the history of ice-skating the International Skating Union was founded, and the first international speed-skating and figure-skating competitions were held.
10. Both figure skating and speed skating have been included in the Winter Olympics since 1924 however, women were not included in the speed-skating competition until 1960.

5. Quotation Marks (links to exercise A, p. 262)

➜ 1. "Whoever wants to know the heart and mind of America," one famous educator wrote, "had better learn baseball."
2. "Most young Americans learn about this game, and they delight in stories about legendary players like Babe Ruth and Joe DiMaggio," said my teacher, Mr. Richards.

Write the following sentences, inserting quotation marks and commas where necessary. If the sentence is correct, write *Correct.*

1. Has anyone ever had a coach who was crazy about using motivational quotations? Mindy asked her friends.
2. Mark answered, My football coach used to quote Vince Lombardi and say, Coaches who can outline plays on a blackboard are a dime a dozen. The ones who win get inside their players and motivate.
3. Michael Jordan was my basketball coach's favorite, said Sarah.
4. She continued, He used to tell us how Michael once said, You have to expect things of yourself before you can do them.
5. My wrestling coach liked to quote Muhammad Ali, added Joe.
6. Coach told us that Muhammad Ali said, It's a lack of faith that makes people afraid of meeting challenges, and I believed in myself, which is pretty similar to what Michael Jordan said, quipped Joe.
7. Some coaches use motivational quotes to get you to work better together as a team, Karl said.
8. He continued, My baseball coach liked to quote Babe Ruth, who reportedly said, The way a team plays together as a whole determines its success. You may have the greatest bunch of individual stars in the world, but if they don't play together, the club won't be worth a dime.
9. When my tennis coach wants us to watch videos, added Ryan, he even quotes the skier Jean-Claude Killy, who said, The best and fastest way to learn a sport is to watch and imitate a champion.
10. Mindy couldn't help but laugh as she said, Well, now I don't feel so strange about my coach using quotations!

6. Other Punctuation (links to exercise on p. 267)

➜ **1.** (heavenly bodies that move in large elliptical orbits about the sun)

2. a comet's characteristics

Proofread the following sentences for punctuation errors, inserting hyphens, apostrophes, dashes, and parentheses where necessary. If a sentence is correct, write *Correct.*

1. The roller skate may have been invented by the Belgian inventor and musical-instrument maker Joseph Merlin in the 1760s.
2. However, in 1863, James Plimpton of Medford, Massachusetts, designed the first practical four wheel skate.
3. Plimptons skate caused quite a stir both at home and abroad.
4. It led to the first great roller skating craze to spread over the United States and western Europe.
5. Many rinks most of them used for recreation were built at this time.
6. The late 1900s saw a change in the materials used to construct roller skate wheels.
7. In the mid-1970s, the traditional wooden or metal wheels gave way to lightweight polyurethane wheels. Some still prefer the old metal wheels.
8. Skaters wishes for wheels that were quieter than wooden or metal wheels and that would allow them to move more smoothly were granted with the invention of the polyurethane wheel.
9. During the 1980s, skates with in line wheels gained popularity.
10. In this type of skate, a single row of wheels is used in place of the standard four wheeled rectangular design.

7. Italics (links to exercise A, p. 269)

➜ 1. *marathon*

Write these sentences, underlining words that should be italicized. Also, indicate which words, if any, are incorrectly italicized. If a sentence is correct, write *Correct.*

1. Rodeo is a sport that involves a series of contests and exhibitions derived from the skills of cowboys and cowgirls of the *Old West.*
2. The word rodeo also refers to a rodeo contest.
3. Although mainly confined to the United States, Canada, and Mexico, *rodeos* are also held in Australia.
4. Rodeos came into being when cowhands got together at the end of cattle-drives and competed for various unofficial titles (best roper, best bull rider, best bucking horse rider, *etc.*).
5. A *paid spectator rodeo* was first held in Denver, Colorado, in 1887.
6. The five main rodeo events are steer wrestling, bareback bronc riding, saddle bronc riding, calf roping, and bull riding.
7. Steer wrestling is also known as *bulldogging.*
8. A bronc, also known as a bronco or bucking bronco, is an unbroken range horse.
9. *Barrel racing,* in which a saddle horse races around a series of barrels, is a women's event at most rodeos.
10. An interesting book to read in order to learn more about rodeos is American Rodeo: From Buffalo Bill to Big Business by Kristine Fredriksson.

Model Bank

Personal Narrative (links to Writing Workshop on p. 396)

The Sound of My Name
by Kris Schultz
from *Twins* magazine
November/December 1998

RUBRIC IN ACTION

I heard something last week that touched me in a way no one would understand unless they had lived my life. It was not a philosophical anecdote or a piece of advice from a wise elder. It was much more simple than that.

It was my name. Someone said my name.

> ❶ Begins with a provocative statement that captures attention

Growing up as the younger (by two minutes) of twin girls, my name was not a sound I heard often. Fearing to call out the wrong name, people referred to me as "one of the twins." Sometimes I would simply be called, "Twin," as in, "Hey, Twin." Often I would summon laughter by replying, "Yes, Singlet?" but beneath the laughter, it tore at me.

> ❷ Gives important background information

After all, no one said "Hey, Tall Person." No one said, "Hey, Singlet," but "Hey, Twin," seemed as common as the word "hello."

Our mother always told us twins were special, and at a young age I realized the friendship and bond I had with Kirsten was one of the most important of my life. No one understood me as Kirsten did, and I trusted her above all others.

But still, I often felt like a traveling freak show, with people staring or asking questions. . . .

I tried telling people how I felt. They usually returned to calling me "Twin," until they eventually admitted their fear of using the wrong name. I would explain that I would rather be called the wrong name and know they were trying, than to be recognized by a generic term on a daily basis. . . .

> ❸ Makes the significance of this topic clear

In second grade, we met an intuitive boy who understood the importance of hearing our names. He knew we appreciated those who acknowledged our separate personalities and he was determined to set straight those who failed to recognize our differences. Life was simple when he was fighting for our cause, but at 14 we drifted apart and he disappeared from our lives, leaving us to defend ourselves. At first, we did this diligently. But soon we realized it required too much energy to constantly explain ourselves, and I fell into an identity crisis just in time for those tumultuous teen years.

I was not a classic rebellious teen. I got along well with students and teachers alike and stayed busy with athletics. But if I didn't think someone recognized me as the individual I was, I would make it known in a big way. I spoke with a Swedish accent during the first weeks of home economics in seventh grade, and in high school I tested my Spanish teacher by throwing off-the-wall phrases at her using vocabulary words she assigned.

❹ Uses descriptive details to show how much the topic means

After high school, Kirsten went to a college in southeastern Kansas to play basketball, and I accepted a javelin scholarship at Kansas State University. For the first time, we met people who knew us separately. Although I missed my sister and, as our parents can attest, we generated a monstrous phone bill, I do not regret that year apart. I finally had a name of my own and would silently rejoice at its sound. . . .

I began to take it all for granted. These last few years, the sound of "Kris" had become a common occurrence. But recently I visited friends in Austin, Texas. One friend has a habit of repeatedly saying the name of the person to whom he's speaking. As he spoke to me, I felt as though I were hearing my name for the first time, noticing the power of the syllables bouncing through the air, falling on my ears. . . .

❺ Concludes by returning to the incident described in the introduction

For more on writing a personal narrative, see pp. 396–403.

Character Sketch (links to Writing Workshop on p. 404)

Sadie Delany, Witness to a Century, Dies at 109
by Richard Severo
from the *New York Times*
January 26, 1999

Sarah (Sadie) Delany, [who died recently at the age of 109,] . . . was the oldest survivor of one of America's most remarkable families, the daughter of a man who had been born a slave, and the first colored woman—the term she preferred—ever permitted to teach home economics in white New York City schools.

Miss Delany and her younger sister, Dr. A. Elizabeth (Bessie) Delany, were always celebrated in Harlem, where they lived and flourished from 1916 to 1957, after leaving their native Raleigh, N.C.

Dr. Delany, who received her doctorate in dental surgery from Columbia in 1923, was the second black woman licensed to practice dentistry in New York State. She had an office in Harlem and was known to thousands of people only as "Dr. Bessie." She charged $2 for a cleaning and $5 for a silver filling and never raised her rates in 27 years of practice.

RUBRIC IN ACTION

❶ Introduction provides necessary background information and begins to establish personality characteristics.

The sisters gained widespread fame after the publication in 1993 of a memoir they called "Having Our Say; the Delany Sisters' First 100 Years." They wrote it with Amy Hill Hearth as an oral history from their early days in the Jim Crow South to their arrival in New York City during the Harlem Renaissance to their life in a white suburb. . . .

❷ Places the sisters in a context to help readers understand

The sisters liked to say that Dr. Bessie was the acerbic one, who was convinced it was her duty to tell people the truth, whether it concerned race relations or their molars. Sadie would say to her, "Bessie, don't you realize that people don't want to hear the truth?"

❸ Uses dialogue and descriptions to establish a main impression of each person

If Dr. Bessie was the vinegar, then Miss Sadie was the molasses, with an uncommon talent for getting along and for being as sweet as the candy she used to make for extra money as a young teacher.

The Delanys were a mix of hard-working African, white and American Indian stock, a family that was rich in everything but money, reserved, aristocratic and irrepressible even as they suffered through segregation. . . .

Sadie Delany liked to say that when she got her master's degree in education from Columbia in 1925, a white teacher there observed, "That Sarah Delany. You tell her to do something, she smiles at you, and then she just turns around and does what she wants anyway." . . .

Toward the end of her life, Sadie Delany did not want anybody to think that she and her sister were just a couple of old women letting life slip by as they sat in their rocking chairs. "Why, we don't even own a rocking chair," she said.

She said she woke up every morning at 6:30, smiled and said, "Thank you, Lord, for another day." Then she would wake up Bessie, a late sleeper, who would open her eyes and say, "Oh Lord, another day?". . . .

❹ Continues to present the sisters through their own words and the words of others.

They believed that their simple lives and good food contributed to their longevity. Bessie said another reason was they "never had husbands to worry us to death."

But Sadie Delany said, "Life is short, and it's up to you to make it sweet."

For more on writing a character sketch, see pp. 404–411.

Response to Literature (links to Writing Workshop on p. 412)

Within Reach: My Everest Story
by Mark Pfetzer and Jack Galvin
Review from *Publisher's Weekly*
September 14, 1998

In May 1996, Mark Pfetzer at age 16 was the youngest climber on Mount Everest to reach 26,000 feet, and his gripping autobiography focuses exclusively on his mountain climbing achievements. Recounted in diary format, Pfetzer's dense but taut story opens during the 1996 Everest expedition, then jumps back to a 1992 advanced camping trip, when his passion for climbing first ignited.

An advertisement for a mountaineering trip in Nepal sparks his imagination and determination (he must raise $5,000 for the excursion), and the experience starts Pfetzer off to the farthest (and highest) reaches of the globe, on to Peru, Ecuador, Tanzania and finally to Mount Everest. Even though he fails to reach the summit on either of his two Everest trips (the second of which takes place during the fatality-filled 1996 expedition described by Krakauer in *Into Thin Air*), Pfetzer does set an altitude record for his age. While some of his inspirational comments about going for one's dreams come off as a bit condescending, and a few of the descriptions and metaphors have an adult flavor, readers are sure to be fascinated by the suspenseful storytelling and the wealth of insider details. For instance, at high altitudes climbers can break a rib just by coughing; those who reach the summit often urinate on the peak to commemorate the event. Even readers with no interest in rappelling will likely be swept up in the details of people and places Pfetzer meets in his travels. A glossary and a chapter by chapter "Cast of Characters" will help readers unfamiliar with the world of climbing.

RUBRIC IN ACTION

1. Introduction identifies the literary work and indicates the reviewer's response.
2. Provides important background information
3. Gives clear reactions to the work
4. Reviewer uses specific details to support his statements.

For more on writing a response to literature, see pp. 412–419.

Process Explanation (links to Writing Workshop on p. 420)

Discover Your Family Tree
by Troy Corley
from *Parade Magazine*
November 29, 1998

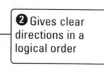

RUBRIC IN ACTION

Finding the roots of your family tree has never been easier than with today's technological tools, ranging from computer programs to genealogy Web sites. Here's how to get started:

❶ Begins with a clear statement of the topic and purpose

Learn what's involved

- Join a genealogy society, take a class, or start with one of the sources below. . . .

Talk with relatives

- Write down family stories that relatives tell you. If they have articles, obituaries, or letters, photocopy them. If they won't part with the documents, write everything down and note the source. "When I first started, I'd just scribble down bits of information," says John Corley of Fayetteville, N.C., who started tracing his roots in 1995. "I could kick myself for that."

❷ Gives clear directions in a logical order

❸ Uses an anecdote to emphasize a point

Collect all the data you can

- E-mail other researchers tracing the same surname. Find them on genealogy bulletin boards, mailing lists or Web sites.
- Refer to *Where to Write for Vital Records* on the Web *(www.pueblo.gsa.gov)* or find the book in libraries. Write to state vital-records offices.

Organize research materials

- Record the details you find on genealogy guide sheets. *Cyndi's List* (see box) offers printable research-record forms. Genealogy computer software also can keep your information orderly.

Check censuses

- Search U.S. census records for family clues from 1920 and earlier. The Censuses for each decade from 1850 to 1920 (except 1890, most of which was lost in a fire) are on microfilm. Contact the National Archives and Records Administration in Washington, D.C., or one of its 13 regional branches. Some libraries will let you rent microfilm copies.

❹ Continues to give instructions in a logical order

- Order or view microfilms of censuses and other records through one of the thousands of Family History Centers of the Church of Jesus Christ of Latter-day Saints, in Salt Lake City, Utah. The church runs the largest genealogical library in the U.S. and has all the censuses.

Genealogical Resources

- Consumer Information Center—www.pueblo.gsa.gov
- Cyndi's List of Genealogy Sites on the Internet—www.cyndislist.com (from the genealogist Cyndi Howells)
- National Archives and Records—www.nara.gov/genealogy/genindex.html
- National Genealogical Society—www.ngsgenealogy.org
- "Netting Your Ancestors," by Cyndi Howells (Genealogical Publishing Co., $19.95)
- Roots-L Home Page—www.rootsweb.com/roots-l
- The Church of Jesus Christ of Latter-day Saints' Family History Centers—1-800-346-6044
- Usgenweb Project—www.usgenweb.com

❺ Provides specific helpful information at the end

For more on writing a process explanation, see pp. 420–427.

Comparison-Contrast Essay (links to Writing Workshop on p. 428)

Overshadowed Sosa Equally Worthy of Acclaim
by Carol Slezak
from the *Chicago Sun-Times*
September 9, 1998

You may remember Mark McGwire, who set an all-time record hitting 70 home runs in the 1998 baseball season. His rival Sammy Sosa ended the season with 66 home runs and the National League's MVP Award. In the last month of that historic season, one sports columnist wondered who would win the race to the home run record, and who deserved it more.

It really doesn't matter that McGwire beat Sosa to 62 on Tuesday with his record-breaking blast against the Cubs. What matters is where they finish. So let's wait to anoint the new king.

If it's McGwire, he can be fitted for his crown then. America can celebrate his rare combination of brute strength and precise timing. . . .

I'll be happy for him, but I'll still raise my glass to Sosa. Because from the beginning of the great chase to wherever it might end, only Sosa has unfailingly demonstrated the meaning of grace under pressure. Only Sosa has consistently approached the game with unadulterated joy. . . .

Sosa's emergence as a full-fledged baseball hero is all the more impressive because it's come amid the real pressure of a pennant race. When McGwire fails, he lets only himself down. His St. Louis Cardinals have been out of pennant contention all season. But when Sosa fails, he lets 24 teammates down, not to mention an entire Cubs franchise and the most loyal fans in baseball. . . .

I'm happy that McGwire has found a way to graciously accept the attention his home runs have garnered. But I'm even happier that Sosa has never viewed America's interest as a burden.

RUBRIC IN ACTION

❶ This writer identifies the subjects being compared and clearly assumes her readers are familiar with them.

❷ Uses characteristics of the two subjects as the primary organizational pattern

Because, for all the drama, all the glamor and all the history that McGwire has provided, Sosa has given us something greater: a reminder that baseball is supposed to be fun. That's as important as all the home run balls in Cooperstown. . . .

Theories abound as to why most of America has been rooting for McGwire over Sosa in the home run chase. Tops among the theories are that McGwire, having been the home run king-in-waiting for several seasons, has paid more dues; that McGwire was born in this country, while Sosa was born in the Dominican Republic and speaks with an accent; that McGwire is larger than life, while Sosa is merely big.

It's simpler than all of that. Until recently, America just didn't know Sosa. My guess is that anyone who's been paying attention to his daily sound bites is rooting for Sosa now.

It's not just that Sosa always says the right thing, as in, "Mark McGwire is the man," and "Isn't this a great country?" . . . No, it's that Sosa has met every challenge this season, before an ever-growing throng of journalists, without a moment of "Woe is me."

❸ Supports the comparison with specific examples

Those who have been paying attention to the box scores also must be pulling for Sosa. For he's more than a one-dimensional player. He's hitting over .300. He drives in runs with singles as well as homers. He steals bases. He plays the outfield. He's the single biggest reason the Cubs are contending for postseason play. McGwire's home runs travel farther, but Sosa's win games. What's more important? . . .

❹ Provides background information to support the overall point

When the final count is in, McGwire might be America's new home run king.

But . . . Sosa has become baseball royalty.

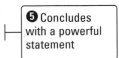

❺ Concludes with a powerful statement

For more on writing a comparison-contrast essay, see pp. 428–435.

Opinion Statement (links to Writing Workshop on p. 436)

Is Computer Gap Bad for Girls?
by Christine Loftus
from the *New York Times*
October 22, 1998

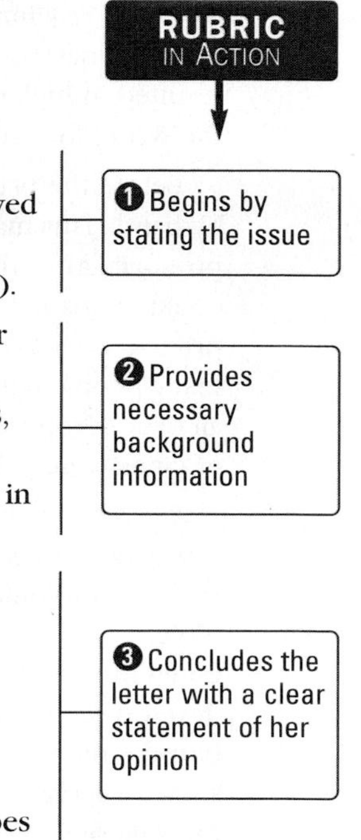
RUBRIC
IN ACTION
❶ Begins by stating the issue
❷ Provides necessary background information
❸ Concludes the letter with a clear statement of her opinion

To the Editor:

The release of a report showing that girls are less proficient in computer skills than boys is being followed by the usual concerns that this gender gap poses a danger to the future success of girls (editorial, Oct. 19).

The same study showed that boys are taking fewer English classes and are dropping out of school at a higher rate than their female classmates. Despite this, the study's finding regarding computer skills would seem to suggest that girls are the disadvantaged ones in our schools.

But who decided that computer literacy is to be valued above the ability to read and write well? Perhaps we are doing a disservice to young girls by telling them that their technical shortcomings are a problem. Instead, maybe teachers should be pulling boys back from their computer monitors and video games and instead helping them to decide on the types of skills that should be valued in life.

For more on writing an opinion statement, see pp. 436–443.

Writing for History

PROMPT: Briefly describe the effects of the invention of the printing press on European society.

The invention of the printing press had a revolutionary impact on European society. For the first time, ordinary people could afford to own books. This resulted in higher literacy and increased knowledge of the world for ordinary people.

❶ Strong introduction summarizes the answer.

Before the printing press, books could only be copied by hand. This made them very expensive and slow to produce. After the press was invented, exact copies could be made by the hundreds. Because of this, the price of books dropped enough so that for the first time many people could buy them. Printing became popular all over Europe, and by the 1500s, presses in hundreds of cities were printing millions of books.

❷ Shows effects on society, as the prompt directs

Since so many people now had books, and because it was now so easy to mass-produce papers, new ideas spread more quickly than ever before. For instance, the Bible was produced in many languages, so many people could now own and read it. When people began to develop their own interpretations of the Bible, they became more critical of the Church's authority and some of its practices. This eventually led to demands for religious reform.

❸ Details further effects using specific examples

<u>In addition</u>, printers published books on a wide range of subjects, such as travel guides and medical manuals, which led to a rise in the education level. People began to form clearer ideas of how the world around them worked and what their place was in it.

❹ Uses transitions to help connect the ideas

Generally, the new availability of books, made possible by the printing press, led to a rise in the literacy and involvement in society of the everyday people.

❺ Conclusion summarizes effects.

Writing for Science

PROMPT: Describe how the Earth's orbit and rotation affect the seasons.

Earth's seasons are created by the different distances between the Earth and the sun during the Earth's orbit, and by the tilting of the Earth on its axis.

❶ Introduction summarizes the answer to the prompt.

The Earth revolves around the sun once every 365 days, which is how we measure our year. At the same time, it rotates on its axis once every day. The Earth's orbit is oval, not round, so that at some times the Earth is closer to the sun, and at other times it is farther away. The Earth is closest to the sun in January and farthest away in July.

❷ Explains three key elements affecting the seasons

The Northern Hemisphere has winter when the Earth is closest to the sun because the Earth is tilted on its axis. When Earth is closest to the sun the Northern Hemisphere is tilted away, so it isn't getting the sun's rays directly. During this time, the North Pole is dark for six months because it is tilted completely away from the sun, and the South Pole has six months of sunlight. This is reversed in the other half of the year. Then, the Earth is farthest away from the sun and the Northern Hemisphere is tilted toward it. Now, the North has summer and the South has winter. Spring and autumn are the periods when the Earth is moving closer to or away from the sun.

❸ Gives specific details to explain the answer

If the Earth's orbit were a perfect circle, and if the Earth weren't tilted on its axis, we would have only one season and the Northern and Southern hemispheres would get exactly the same amount of the sun's energy.

❹ Conclusion illustrates the point by using a what if . . . question.

Business Letter

44 Tanglewood Trail
Noroton, CT 06904
May 25, 2002

Commercial Objects, Inc.
500 West Maple
Franchise, NC 40001

Dear Sir or Madam:

I am writing to complain to you about the Tune Tote 2000 CD carrying case I got for my birthday.

I've had it for only two weeks, and I have already broken three CDs by storing them in your case. The teeth that hold the center of the CD in place are too strong! I am unable to get my CDs back out again without their snapping in two.

I have been a fan of your products in the past, so I was very surprised and disappointed when the Tune Tote turned against me. I ask that you please refund me the price of the carrying case. I also would like some sort of compensation for the three CDs that were broken.

Thank you for your attention.

Sincerely,

Tom Taylor

Tom Taylor

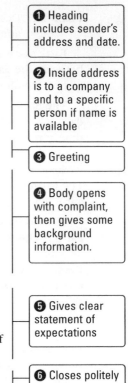

❶ Heading includes sender's address and date.

❷ Inside address is to a company and to a specific person if name is available

❸ Greeting

❹ Body opens with complaint, then gives some background information.

❺ Gives clear statement of expectations

❻ Closes politely

Résumé

Johnny Passat
1977 Alpha Blvd.
Darien, Connecticut 06820
(203) 555-1212
e-mail: jpass@domain.com

Job Objective

Part-time summer employment as a camp counselor

Experience

- Baby-sitting
- Caddy at local golf club
- Volunteer at Habitat for Humanity
- Assistant coach for Tadpole Swim Team

Education and Honors

- Darien High School, class of 2003
- Second place in 1999 science fair

Special Qualifications

- CPR certificate
- Outward Bound participant
- A/V knowledge, on staff at school A/V center
- Team leader in Nature Club
- Scout for five years

References

Phone numbers of parents I've baby-sat for available upon request

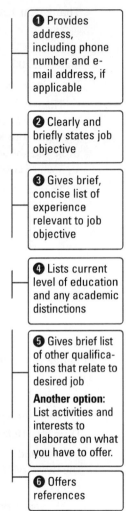

❶ Provides address, including phone number and e-mail address, if applicable

❷ Clearly and briefly states job objective

❸ Gives brief, concise list of experience relevant to job objective

❹ Lists current level of education and any academic distinctions

❺ Gives brief list of other qualifications that relate to desired job

Another option: List activities and interests to elaborate on what you have to offer.

❻ Offers references

Personal Letters

Thank-You Letter

March 4, 2002

Dear Uncle Pete,

Thank you so much for the excellent book of sheet music! I was getting sick of practicing the trumpet to the same four songs over and over again. I love all these old show tunes in the book, so practicing will be a pleasure again.

Thanks again, Uncle Pete. You really helped make my birthday special. I'll dedicate my next solo to you!

Love,

Kathleen

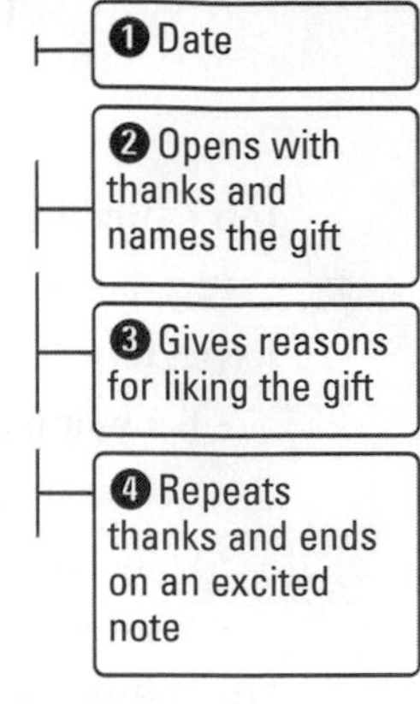
❶ Date
❷ Opens with thanks and names the gift
❸ Gives reasons for liking the gift
❹ Repeats thanks and ends on an excited note

Letter of Condolence

February 22, 2002

Dear Mrs. Deirdorf,

I wanted to tell you how sorry I was to hear about the death of Mr. Deirdorf. I know I will miss him for a long time.

He was especially generous to me when I would come over in the summer to mow your lawn. He would give me a couple of extra dollars and say it was money for gas, but it always seemed to me like it was an extra thank you.

I know that everyone in the neighborhood is thinking about you at this difficult time.

Yours truly,

Gerry Porter

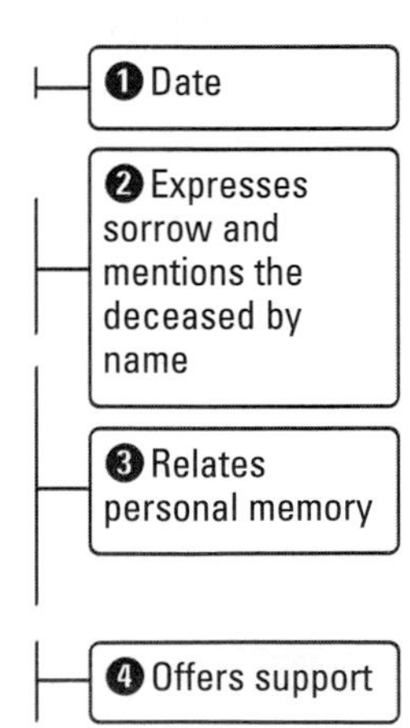
❶ Date
❷ Expresses sorrow and mentions the deceased by name
❸ Relates personal memory
❹ Offers support

Guidelines for Spelling

Forming Plural Nouns

To form the plural of most nouns, just add ***-s.***

prizes **dreams** **circles** **stations**

For most singular nouns ending in ***o,*** add ***-s.***

solos **halos** **studios** **photos** **pianos**

For a few nouns ending in ***o,*** add ***-es.***

heroes **tomatoes** **potatoes** **echoes**

When the singular noun ends in ***s, sh, ch, x,*** or ***z,*** add ***-es.***

waitresses **brushes** **ditches** **axes** **buzzes**

When a singular noun ends in ***y*** with a consonant before it, change the ***y*** to ***i*** and add ***-es.***

army—armies **candy—candies** **baby—babies**
diary—diaries **ferry—ferries** **conspiracy—conspiracies**

When a vowel ***(a, e, i, o, u)*** comes before the ***y,*** just add ***-s.***

boys—boys **way—ways** **array—arrays**
alloy—alloys **weekday—weekdays** **jockey—jockeys**

For most nouns ending in ***f*** or ***fe,*** change the ***f*** to ***v*** and add ***-es*** or ***-s.*** Since there is no rule, you must memorize such words.

life—lives **calf—calves** **knife—knives**
thief—thieves **shelf—shelves** **loaf—loaves**

For some nouns ending in ***f,*** add ***-s*** to make the plural.

roofs **chiefs** **reefs** **beliefs**

Some nouns have the same form for both singular and plural.

deer **sheep** **moose** **salmon** **trout**

For some nouns, the plural is formed in a special way.

man—men **goose—geese** **ox—oxen**
woman—women **mouse—mice** **child—children**

For a compound noun written as one word, form the plural by changing the last word in the compound to its plural form.

stepchild—stepchildren **firefly—fireflies**

If a compound noun is written as a hyphenated word or as two separate words, change the most important word to the plural form.

brother-in-law—brothers-in-law **life jacket—life jackets**

Forming Possessives

If a noun is singular, add **'s.**

mother—my mother's car **Ross—Ross's desk**

Exception: the **s** after the apostrophe is dropped after *Jesus'*, *Moses'*, and certain names in classical mythology (*Zeus'*). These possessive forms, therefore, can be pronounced easily.

If a noun is plural and ends with **s,** just add an apostrophe.

parents—my parents' car **the Santinis—the Santinis' house**

If a noun is plural but does not end in **s,** add **'s.**

people—the people's choice **women—the women's coats**

Spelling Rules

Words Ending in a Silent *e*

Before adding a suffix beginning with a vowel to a word ending in a silent **e,** drop the **e** (with some exceptions).

amaze + -ing = amazing **love + -able = lovable**
create + -ed = created **nerve + -ous = nervous**

Exceptions: *change + -able = changeable; courage + -ous = courageous*

When adding a suffix beginning with a consonant to a word ending in a silent **e,** keep the **e** (with some exceptions).

late + -ly = lately **spite + -ful = spiteful**
noise + -less = noiseless **state + -ment = statement**

Exceptions include *truly, argument, ninth, wholly,* and *awful.*

When a suffix beginning with ***a*** or ***o*** is added to a word with a final silent **e,** the final **e** is usually retained if it is preceded by a soft ***c*** or a soft ***g.***

bridge + -able = bridgeable **peace + -able = peaceable**
outrage + -ous = outrageous **advantage + -ous = advantageous**

When a suffix beginning with a vowel is added to a word ending in ***ee*** or ***oe,*** the final **e** is retained.

agree + -ing = agreeing **free + -ing = freeing**
hoe + -ing = hoeing **see + -ing = seeing**

Words Ending in *y*

Before adding a suffix to a word that ends in ***y*** preceded by a consonant, change the ***y*** to ***i***.

easy + -est = easiest **crazy + -est = craziest**
silly + -ness = silliness **marry + -age = marriage**

Exceptions include *dryness, shyness,* and *slyness.*

However, when you add ***-ing,*** the ***y*** does not change.

empty + -ed = emptied but **empty + -ing = emptying**

When adding a suffix to a word that ends in ***y*** preceded by a vowel, do not change the ***y*** to ***i***.

play + -er = player **employ + -ed = employed**
coy + -ness = coyness **pay + -able = payable**

Exceptions include *daily* and *gaily.*

Words Ending in a Consonant

In one-syllable words that end in one consonant preceded by one vowel, double the final consonant before adding a suffix beginning with a vowel, such as ***-ed*** or ***-ing.*** These are sometimes called 1+1+1 words.

dip + -ed = dipped **set + -ing = setting**
slim + -est = slimmest **fit + -er = fitter**

The rule does not apply to words of one syllable that end in a consonant preceded by two vowels.

feel + -ing = feeling **peel + -ed = peeled**
reap + -ed = reaped **loot + -ed = looted**

In words of more than one syllable, double the final consonant (1) if the word ends with one consonant preceded by one vowel or (2) if the word is accented on the last syllable.

be•gin´ per•mit´ re•fer´

In the following examples, note that when the suffix is added, the accent remains on the same syllable.

be•gin´ + -ing = be•gin´ ning = beginning
per•mit´ + -ed = per•mit´ ted = permitted

In the following examples, the accent does not remain on the same syllable; thus, the final consonant is not doubled.

re•fer´ + -ence = ref´ er•ence = reference
con•fer´ + -ence = con´ fer•ence = conference

Prefixes and Suffixes

When adding a prefix to a word, do not change the spelling of the base word. When a prefix creates a double letter, keep both letters.

dis- + approve = disapprove **re- + build = rebuild**
ir- + regular = irregular **mis- + spell = misspell**
anti- + trust = antitrust **il- + logical = illogical**

When adding ***-ly*** to a word ending in ***l,*** keep both ***l***'s. When adding ***-ness*** to a word ending in ***n,*** keep both ***n***'s.

careful + -ly = carefully **sudden + -ness = suddenness**
final + -ly = finally **thin + -ness = thinness**

Special Spelling Problems

Only one English word ends in ***-sede:*** *supersede.* Three words end in ***-ceed:*** *exceed, proceed,* and *succeed.* All other verbs ending in the "seed" sound are spelled with ***-cede.***

concede precede recede secede

In a word in which ***ie*** or ***ei*** is used to represent the long ***e*** sound, use ***ei*** after ***c*** and ***ie*** in all other cases (with some exceptions).

i* before *e:	**thief relieve piece field grieve pier**
except after *c:*	**conceit perceive ceiling receive receipt**
Exceptions:	***either, neither, weird, leisure, seize***

Commonly Misspelled Words

abbreviate
accidentally
achievement
amateur
analyze
anonymous
answer
apologize
appearance
appreciate
appropriate
argument
associate
awkward
beginning
believe
bicycle
brief
bulletin
bureau
business
calendar
campaign
candidate
certain
changeable
characteristic
column
committee
courageous
courteous
criticize
curiosity
decision
definitely
dependent
description
desirable
despair
desperate
development
dictionary
different
disappear
disappoint
discipline
dissatisfied
efficient
eighth
eligible
eliminate
embarrass
enthusiastic
especially
exaggerate
exceed
existence
experience
familiar
fascinating
February
financial
foreign
fourth
fragile
generally
government
grammar
guarantee
guard
height
humorous
immediately
independent
indispensable
irritable
judgment
knowledge
laboratory
license
lightning
literature
loneliness
marriage
mathematics
minimum
mischievous
mortgage
necessary
nickel
ninety
noticeable
nuclear
nuisance
obstacle
occasionally
occurrence
opinion
opportunity
outrageous
parallel
particularly
permanent
permissible
persuade
pleasant
pneumonia
possess
possibility
prejudice
privilege
probably
psychology
pursue
realize
receipt
receive
recognize
recommend
reference
rehearse
repetition
restaurant
rhythm
ridiculous
sandwich
schedule
scissors
seize
separate
sergeant
similar
sincerely
sophomore
souvenir
specifically
strategy
success
surprise
syllable
sympathy
symptom
temperature
thorough
throughout
tomorrow
traffic
tragedy
transferred
truly
Tuesday
twelfth
undoubtedly
unnecessary
usable
vacuum
vicinity
village
weird
yield

Commonly Confused Words

Good writers master words that are easy to misuse and misspell. Study the following words, noting how their meanings differ.

accept, except — *Accept* means "to agree to" or "to receive willingly." *Except* usually means "not including."
Did the teacher *accept* your report?
Everyone smiled for the photographer *except* Jody.

adapt, adopt — *Adapt* means "to make suitable" or "to adjust." *Adopt* means "to opt or choose as one's own" or "to accept."
The writer *adapted* the play for the screen.
After years of living in Japan, she had *adopted* its culture.

advice, advise — *Advice* is a noun that means "counsel given to someone." *Advise* is a verb that means "to give counsel."
Jim should take some of his own *advice.*
The mechanic *advised* me to get new brakes for my car.

affect, effect — *Affect* means "to move or influence" or "to pretend to have." *Effect* as a verb means "to bring about." As a noun, *effect* means "the result of an action."
The news from South Africa *affected* him deeply.
The band's singer *affects* a British accent.
The students tried to *effect* a change in school policy.
What *effect* did the acidic soil produce in the plants?

all ready, already — *All ready* means "all are ready" or "completely prepared." *Already* means "previously."
The students were *all ready* for the field trip.
We had *already* pitched our tent before it started raining.

all right — *All right* is the correct spelling. *Alright* is nonstandard and should not be used.

a lot — *A lot* may be used in informal writing. *Alot* is incorrect.

altogether, all together — *Altogether* means "completely." *All together* means "as a group."
The news story is *altogether* false.
Let's sing a song *all together.*

anywhere, nowhere, somewhere, anyway are all correct. *Anywheres, nowheres, somewheres,* and *anyways* are incorrect.
I don't see geometry mentioned *anywhere.*
***Somewhere* in this book is a map of ancient Sumer.**
***Anyway,* this street map is out of date.**

between, among are prepositions. *Between* refers to two people or things. The object of *between* is never singular. *Among* refers to a group of three or more.
Texas lies *between* Louisiana and New Mexico.
What are the differences *among* the four candidates?

borrow, lend *Borrow* means "to receive something on loan." *Lend* means "to give out temporarily."
He *borrowed* five dollars from his sister.
Please *lend* me your book.

bring, take *Bring* refers to movement toward or with. *Take* refers to movement away from.
I'll *bring* you a glass of water.
Would you please *take* these apples to Pam and John?

can, may *Can* means "to be able" or "to have the power to." *May* means "to have permission to." *May* can also mean "possibly will."
Vegetables *can* grow nicely without pesticides.
We *may* not use pesticides on our community garden.
Pesticides *may* not be necessary, anyway.

capital, capitol, Capitol *Capital* means "excellent," "most serious," or "most important." It also means "seat of government." A *capitol* is a "building in which a state legislature meets." The *Capitol* is "the building in Washington, D.C., in which the U.S. Congress meets."
Proper nouns begin with *capital* letters.
Is Madison the *capital* of Wisconsin?
Protesters rallied at the state *capitol.*
A subway connects the Senate and the House in *the Capitol.*

choose, chose *Choose* is a verb that means "to decide or prefer." *Chose* is the past-tense form of *choose.*
He had to *choose* between art and band.
She *chose* to write for the school newspaper.

desert, dessert	*Desert* (des´ ert) means "a dry, sandy, barren region." *Desert* (de sert´) means "to abandon." A *dessert* (des sert´) is a sweet, such as cake. **The Sahara in North Africa is the world's largest *desert.*** **The night guard did not *desert* his post.** **Alison's favorite *dessert* is chocolate cake.**
different from	is used to compare dissimilar items. *Different than* is nonstandard. **The hot sauce is very *different from* the yogurt sauce.**
differ from, differ with	*Differ from* means "to be dissimilar to." *Differ with* means "to disagree with." **The racing bike *differs* greatly *from* the mountain bike.** **I *differ with* her as to the meaning of Hamlet's speech.**
farther, further	*Farther* refers to distance. *Further* refers to something additional. **We traveled 200 miles *farther* that afternoon.** **This idea needs *further* discussion.**
fewer, less	*Fewer* refers to numbers of things that can be counted. *Less* refers to amount, degree, or value. ***Fewer* than ten students camped out.** **We made *less* money this year on the walkathon than last year.**
good, well	*Good* is always an adjective. *Well* is usually an adverb that modifies an action verb. *Well* can also be an adjective meaning "in good health." **Dana felt *good* when she finished painting her room.** **Angela ran *well* in yesterday's race.** **I felt *well* when I left my house.**
imply, infer	*Imply* means "to suggest something in an indirect way." *Infer* means "to come to a conclusion based on something that has been read or heard." **Josh *implied* that he would be taking the bus.** **From what you said, I *inferred* that the book would be difficult.**
its, it's	*Its* is a possessive pronoun. *It's* is a contraction of *it is* or *it has.* **Sanibel Island is known for *its* beautiful beaches.** ***It's* great weather for a picnic.**

kind of, sort of Neither of these two expressions should be followed by the word *a.*

What *kind of* horse is Scout?

What *sorts of* animals live in swamps?

The use of these two expressions as adverbs, as in "It's kind of hot today," is informal.

lay, lie *Lay* is a verb that means "to place." It takes a direct object. *Lie* is a verb that means "to be in a certain place." *Lie* and its past form *lay* never take direct objects.

The carpenter will *lay* the planks on the bench.

My cat likes to *lie* under the bed.

lead, led *Lead* can be a noun that means "a heavy metal" or a verb that means "to show the way." *Led* is the past-tense form of the verb.

***Lead* is used in nuclear reactors.**

Raul always *leads* his team onto the field.

She *led* the class as president of the student council.

learn, teach *Learn* means "to gain knowledge." *Teach* means "to instruct."

Enrique is *learning* about black holes in space.

Marva *teaches* astronomy at a college in the city.

leave, let *Leave* means "to go away from." *Leave* can be transitive or intransitive. *Let* is usually used with another verb. It means "to allow to."

Don't *leave* the refrigerator open.

She *leaves* for Scotland tomorrow.

The Cyclops wouldn't *let* Odysseus' men *leave* the cave.

like as a conjunction before a clause is incorrect. Use *as* or *as if.*

Ramon talked *as if* he had a cold.

loan, lone *Loan* refers to "something given for temporary use." *Lone* refers to "the condition of being by oneself, alone."

I gave that shirt to Max as a gift, not a *loan.*

The *lone* plant in our yard turned out to be a weed.

lose, loose *Lose* means "to mislay or suffer the loss of." *Loose* means "free" or "not fastened."

That tire will *lose* air unless you patch it.

My little brother has three *loose* teeth.

majority refers to more than half of a group of things or people that can be counted. It is incorrect to use *majority* in referring to time or distance, as in "The majority of our time there was wasted."
Most of our time there was wasted.
The *majority* of the students study a foreign language.

most, almost *Most* can be a pronoun, an adjective, or an adverb, but it should never be used in place of *almost,* an adverb that means "nearly."
***Most* of the students enjoy writing in their journals.** (pronoun)
***Most* mammals give birth to live young.** (adjective)
You missed the *most* exciting part of the trip. (adverb)
***Almost* every mammal gives live birth.** (adverb)

of is incorrectly used in a phrase such as *could of.* Examples of correct wordings are *could have, should have,* and *must have.*
I *must have* missed the phone call.
If you had played, we *would have* won.

principal, principle *Principal* means "of chief or central importance" or refers to the head of a school. *Principle* means "a basic truth, standard, or rule of behavior."
Lack of customers is the *principal* reason for closing the store.
The *principal* of our school awarded the trophy.
One of my *principles* is to be honest with others.

quiet, quite *Quiet* refers to "freedom from noise or disturbance." *Quite* means "truly" or "almost completely."
Observers must be *quiet* during the recording session.
We were *quite* worried about the results of the test.

raise, rise *Raise* means "to lift" or "to cause to go up." It takes a direct object. *Rise* means "to go upward." It does not take a direct object.
The maintenance workers *raise* the flag each morning.
The city's population is expected to *rise* steadily.

real, really *Real* is an adjective meaning "actual" or "true." *Really* is an adverb meaning "in reality" or "in fact."
***Real* skill comes from concentration and practice.**
She doesn't *really* know all the facts.

seldom should not be followed by *ever,* as in "We seldom ever run more than a mile." *Seldom, rarely, very seldom,* and *hardly ever* all are correct.

I *seldom* hear traditional jazz.

set, sit *Set* means "to place" and takes a direct object. *Sit* means "to occupy a seat or a place" and does not take a direct object.

He *set* the box down outside the shed.

We *sit* in the last row of the upper balcony.

stationary, stationery *Stationary* means "fixed" or "unmoving." *Stationery* means "fine paper for writing letters."

The wheel pivots, but the seat is *stationary.*

Rex wrote on special *stationery* imprinted with his name.

than, then *Than* is used to introduce the second part of a comparison. *Then* means "next in order."

Ramon is stronger *than* Mark.

Cut the grass and *then* trim the hedges.

their, there, they're *Their* means "belonging to them." *There* means "in that place." *They're* is a contraction of *they are.*

All the campers returned to *their* cabins.

I keep my card collection *there* in those folders.

Lisa and Beth run daily; *they're* on the track team.

way refers to distance. *Ways* is nonstandard and should not be used in writing.

The subway was a long *way* from the stadium.

whose, who's *Whose* is the possessive form of *who. Who's* is a contraction of *who is* or *who has.*

***Whose* parents will drive us to the movies?**

***Who's* going to the recycling center?**

your, you're *Your* is the possessive form of *you. You're* is a contraction of *you are.*

What was *your* record in the 50-yard dash?

***You're* one of the winners of the essay contest.**

MLA Citation Guidelines

Forms for Working Bibliography and Works Cited Entries

The following are some basic forms for bibliographic entries. Use these forms on the bibliography cards that make up your working bibliography and in the list of works cited that appears at the end of your paper.

Whole Books

The following models can also be used for citing reports and pamphlets.

A. One author

Liptak, Karen. Coming-of-Age: Traditions and Rituals Around the World. Brookfield: Millbrook, 1994.

B. Two authors

Dolan, Edward F., and Margaret M. Scariano. Illiteracy in America. New York: Watts, 1995.

C. Three authors

Rand, Donna, Toni Parker, and Sheila Foster. Black Books Galore!: Guide to Great African American Children's Books. New York: Wiley, 1998.

D. Four or more authors

The abbreviation *et al.* means "and others." Use *et al.* instead of listing all the authors.

Quirk, Randolph, et al. A Comprehensive Grammar of the English Language. London: Longman, 1985.

E. No author given

Science Explained: The World of Science in Everyday Life. New York: Holt, 1993.

F. An editor, but no single author

Radelet, Michael L., ed. Facing the Death Penalty: Essays on a Cruel and Unusual Punishment. Philadelphia: Temple UP, 1989.

G. Two or three editors

Langley, Winston E., and Vivian C. Fox, eds. Women's Rights in the United States: A Documentary History. Westport: Greenwood, 1994.

H. Four or more editors

The abbreviation *et al.* means "and others." Use *et al.* instead of listing all the editors.

Brain, Joseph D., et al., eds. Variations in Susceptibility to Inhaled Pollutants: Identification, Mechanisms, and Policy Implications. Baltimore: Johns Hopkins UP, 1988.

I. An author and a translator

Rabinovici, Schoschana. Thanks to My Mother. Trans. James Skofield. New York: Dial, 1998.

J. An author, a translator, and an editor

LaFontaine, Jean de. Selected Fables. Trans. Christopher Wood. Ed. Maya Slater. New York: Oxford UP, 1995.

K. An edition other than the first

Metcalf, Robert L., and Robert A. Metcalf. Destructive and Useful Insects: Their Habits and Control. 5th ed. New York: McGraw, 1993.

L. A book or a monograph that is part of a series

Simon, Rita James. The Jury System in America: A Critical Overview. Sage Criminal Justice System Annuals 4. Beverly Hills: Sage, 1975.

M. A multivolume work

If you have used only one volume of a multivolume work, cite only that volume.

Tierney, Helen, ed. Women's Studies Encyclopedia. Rev. ed. Vol. 2. Westport: Greenwood, 1999. 3 vols.

If you have used more than one volume of a multivolume work, cite the entire work.

Tierney, Helen, ed. Women's Studies Encyclopedia. Rev. ed. 3 vols. Westport: Greenwood, 1999.

N. A volume with its own title that is part of a multivolume work with a different title

Cremin, Lawrence A. The National Experience, 1783–1876. New York: Harper, 1980. Vol. 2 of American Education. 3 vols. 1970–88.

O. A republished book or a literary work available in several editions

Give the date of the original publication after the title. Then give complete publication information, including the date, for the edition that you have used.

Hemingway, Ernest. The Sun Also Rises. 1926. New York: Scribner, 1954.

P. A government publication

Give the name of the government (country or state). Then give the department if applicable, followed by the agency if applicable. Next give the title, followed by the author if known. Then give the publication information. The publisher of U.S. government documents is usually the Government Printing Office, or GPO.

United States. Dept. of Labor. Bureau of Labor Statistics. Perspectives on Working Women: A Databook. By Howard Hayghe and Beverly L. Johnson. Washington: GPO, 1980.

- - -. Dept. of Health and Human Services. U.S. Public Health Service. Centers for Disease Control and Prevention. The ABCs of Safe and Healthy Child Care: A Handbook for Child Care Providers. Washington: GPO, 1996.

Parts of Books

A. A poem, a short story, an essay, or a chapter in a collection of works by one author

Hawthorne, Nathaniel. "Young Goodman Brown." The Portable Hawthorne. Ed. Malcolm Cowley. Rev. ed. New York: Viking, 1969. 53–68.

B. A poem, a short story, an essay, or a chapter in a collection of works by several authors

Faulkner, William. "Race and Fear." Voices in Black and White. Ed. Katharine Whittemore and Gerald Marzorati. New York: Franklin Square, 1993. 83–94.

C. A novel or a play in an anthology

Cather, Willa. My Mortal Enemy. The Norton Anthology of American Literature. Ed. Nina Baym. 4th ed. Vol. 2. New York: Norton, 1994. 975–1025.

D. An introduction, a preface, a foreword, or an afterword written by the author(s) of a work

Bloom, Harold. Introduction. Modern Crime and Suspense Writers. Ed. Harold Bloom. New York: Chelsea, 1995. xi–xii.

E. An introduction, a preface, a foreword, or an afterword written by someone other than the author(s) of a work

Primack, Marshall P. Foreword. Phobia: The Crippling Fears. By Arthur Henley. Secaucus: Stuart, 1987. 1–4.

F. Cross-references

If you have used more than one work from a collection, you may give a complete entry for the collection. Then, in the separate entries for the works, you can refer to the entry for the whole collection by using the editor's last name or, if you have listed more than one work by that editor, the editor's last name and a shortened version of the title.

French, Warren G., ed. A Companion to The Grapes of Wrath. New York: Viking, 1963.

- - -. "What Did John Steinbeck Know About the 'Okies'?" French, Companion 51–53.

Steinbeck, John. Their Blood Is Strong. 1938. French, Companion 53–92.

G. A reprinted article or essay (one previously published elsewhere)

If a work that appears in a collection first appeared in another place, give complete information for the original publication, followed by *Rpt. in* and complete information for the collection.

Searle, John. "What Is a Speech Act?" Philosophy in America. Ed. Max Black. London: Allen, 1965. 221–39. Rpt. in Readings in the Philosophy of Language. Ed. Jay F. Rosenberg and Charles Travis. Englewood Cliffs: Prentice, 1971. 614–28.

Magazines, Journals, Newspapers, and Encyclopedias

A. An article in a magazine, a journal, or a newspaper

Allen, Jodie. "Working Out Welfare." Time 29 July 1996: 53–54.

"Dumping by the Coast Guard." Editorial. New York Times 6 Sept. 1998, late ed., sec. 4: 10.

Eisenberg, David M., et al. "Unconventional Medicine in the United States: Prevalence, Costs, and Patterns of Use." New England Journal of Medicine 328.4 (1993): 246–52.

B. An article in an encyclopedia or other alphabetically organized reference work

Give the title of the article, the name of the reference work, and the year of the edition.

"Storytelling." The World Book Encyclopedia. 1999 ed.

C. A review

Schwarz, Benjamin. "Was the Great War Necessary?" Rev. of The Pity of War, by Niall Ferguson. Atlantic Monthly May 1999: 118–28.

Miscellaneous Print and Nonprint Sources

A. An interview you have conducted or a letter you have received

Jackson, Jesse. Personal interview [*or* Letter to the author]. 15 July 1992.

B. A film

Star Wars. Screenplay by George Lucas. Dir. Lucas. Perf. Mark Hamill, Harrison Ford, Carrie Fisher, and Alec Guinness. 20th Century Fox, 1977.

C. A work of art (painting, photograph, sculpture)

Ward, John Quincy Adams. The Freedman. Art Institute of Chicago.

D. A television or a radio program

Give the episode name (if applicable) and the series or the program name. Include any information that you have about the program's writer and director. Then give the network, the local station, the city, and the date of the airing of the program.

"A Desert Blooming." Writ. Marshall Riggan. Living Wild. Dir. Harry L. Gorden. PBS. WTTW, Chicago. 29 Apr. 1984.

E. A musical composition

Chopin, Frédéric. Waltz in A-flat major, op. 42.

F. A recording (compact disc, LP, or audiocassette)

If the recording is not a compact disc, include *LP* or *Audiocassette* before the manufacturer's name.

Marsalis, Wynton. "Fuchsia." Think of One. Columbia, 1983.

G. A lecture, a speech, or an address

Give the name of the speaker followed by the name of the speech, if available, or the kind of speech (*Lecture, Introduction, Address*). Then give the event, the place, and the date.

King, Martin Luther. Speech. Lincoln Memorial, Washington, 28 Aug. 1963.

Electronic Publications

The number of electronic information sources is great and increasing rapidly, so please refer to the most current edition of the MLA Handbook for Writers of Research Papers *if you need more guidance. You can also refer to "MLA Style" on the Modern Language Association Web site <http://www.mla.org/>.*

Portable databases (CD-ROMs, DVDs, laser discs, diskettes, and videocassettes)

These products contain fixed information (information that cannot be changed unless a new version is produced and released). Citing them in a research paper is similar to citing printed sources. You should include the following information:

- Name of the author, if applicable
- Title of the part of the work used (underlined or in quotation marks)
- Title of the product or the database (underlined)
- Publication medium (CD-ROM, DVD, laser disc, diskette, or videocassette)
- Edition, release, or version, if applicable
- City of publication
- Name of publisher
- Year of publication

If you cannot find some of this information, cite what is available.

"Steinbeck's Dust Bowl Saga." Our Times Multimedia Encyclopedia of the 20th Century. CD-ROM. 1996 ed. Redwood City: Vicarious, 1995.

Eyes on the Prize: America's Civil Rights Years, 1954–1965. Prod. Blackside. 6 videocassettes. PBS Video, 1986.

Beowulf. Great Literature. CD-ROM. 1992 ed. Parsippany: Bureau Development, 1992.

"Jump at the Sun: Zora Neale Hurston and the Harlem Renaissance." American Stories. Laser disc. McDougal, 1998.

Online Sources

Sources on the World Wide Web are numerous and include scholarly projects, reference databases, articles in periodicals, and professional and personal sites. Not all sites are equally reliable, and therefore material cited from the World Wide Web should be evaluated carefully. Entries for online sources in the Works Cited list should contain as much of the information listed below as available.

- Name of the author, editor, compiler or translator, followed by an abbreviation such as *ed., comp.,* or *trans.* if appropriate
- Title of the material accessed. Use quotation marks for poems, short stories, articles, and similar short works. Underline the title of a book.
- Publication information for any print version of the source
- Title (underlined) of the scholarly project, database, periodical, or professional or personal site. For a professional or personal site with no title, add a description such as *Home page* (neither underlined nor in quotation marks).
- Name of the editor of the scholarly project or database
- For a journal, the volume number, issue number, or other identifying number
- Date of electronic publication or of the latest update, or date of posting
- For a work from a subscription service, list the name of the service and—if a library is the subscriber—the name of the library and the town or state where it is located.
- Range or total number of pages, paragraphs, or other sections if they are numbered
- Name of any institution or organization that sponsors or is associated with the Web site
- Date the source was accessed
- Electronic address, or URL, of the source. For a subscription service, use the URL of the service's main page (if known) or the keyword assigned by the service.

Scholarly project

Documenting the American South. Aug. 1999. Academic Affairs Lib., U of North Carolina at Chapel Hill. 11 Aug. 1999 <http://metalab.unc.edu/docsouth/>.

Professional site

American Council of Learned Societies Home Page. 1998. Amer. Council of Learned Societies. 13 Aug. 1999 <http://www.acls.org/jshome.htm>.

Personal site

Fitzgerald, Evan. A Students' Guide to Butterflies. 5 July 1999. Butterfly Farm. 11 Aug. 1999 <http://www.butterflyfarm.co.cr/farmer/bfly1.htm>.

Book

Poe, Edgar Allan. Tales. New York: Wiley, 1845. Documenting the American South. 16 Sept. 1998. Academic Affairs Lib., U of North Carolina at Chapel Hill. 13 Aug. 1999 <http://metalab.unc.edu/docsouth/poe/poe.html>.

Article in reference database

"Dickinson, Emily." Encyclopaedia Britannica Online. Vers. 99.1. Encyclopaedia Britannica. 11 Aug. 1999 <http://www.eb.com:180/bol/topic?eu=30830>.

Article in journal

Wagner, Diana, and Marcy Tanter. "New Dickinson Letter Clarifies Hale Correspondence." Emily Dickinson Journal 7.1 (1998): 110–117. 29 July 1999 <http://muse.jhu.edu/demo/emily_dickinson_journal/7.1wagner.html>.

Article in magazine

Swerdlow, Joel L. "The Power of Writing." National Geographic Aug. 1999. 28 July 1999 <http://www.nationalgeographic.com/ngm/9908/fngm/index.html>.

Work from a subscription service

"Cinco de Mayo." Compton's Encyclopedia Online. Vers. 3.0. 1998. America Online. 29 July 1999. Keyword: Compton's.

Weiss, Peter. "Competing Students' Science Skills Sparkle." Science News 30 Jan. 1999: 71. General Reference Center. InfoTrac SearchBank. Evanston Public Lib., IL. 16 Aug. 1999 <http://www.searchbank.com/searchbank/evanston_main>.

Glossary for Writers

Allegory a story in which the major events and characters have hidden or symbolic meanings. A quarrel between friends, for example, might represent a conflict between their native cultures.

Alliteration the repetition of beginning sounds of words in poetry or prose; for example, the "c" sound in "creeping cat"

Allusion a reference to a historical or literary person, place, event, or aspect of culture

Analogy a comparison used to explain an idea or support an argument. For example, an analogy for how a government works might be a family.

Analysis a way of thinking that involves taking apart, examining, and explaining a subject or an idea

Anecdote a brief story told as an example to illustrate a point

Argument speaking or writing that expresses a position or states an opinion with supporting evidence. An argument often takes into account other points of view.

Audience one's readers or listeners

Autobiography a biography (life story) told by the person whose life it is

Bias a preference to lean toward one side in an argument; to be unbiased is to be neutral

Bibliography a list of sources (articles, books, encyclopedias) in a paper or report used to document research or to recommend further study

Body the main part of a composition, in which its ideas are developed

Brainstorming a way of generating ideas that involves quickly listing ideas as they occur without stopping to judge them

Cause and Effect a strategy of analysis that examines the reasons for actions or events, and the consequences or results of those actions

Characterization the way people (characters) are portrayed by an author

Chronological organized according to time sequence

Clarity the quality of being clear and easy to understand

Classification a way of organizing information by grouping or categorizing items according to some system or principle

Cliché an overused expression, such as "quiet as a mouse"

Clustering a brainstorming technique that involves creating an idea or topic map made up of circled groupings of related details

Coherence connectedness; a sense that parts hold together. A paragraph has coherence when its sentences flow logically from one to the next. A composition has coherence when its paragraphs are connected logically and linked by transitional words and phrases.

Collaboration the act of working with other people on projects or to problem solve

Colloquial characteristic of conversational style in speech or writing; linguistically informal, the way people ordinarily speak in conversation

Comparison and Contrast a pattern of organization in which two or more things are related on the basis of similarities and differences

Conclusion a judgment or a decision that is reached based on evidence, experience, and logical reasoning; also, the final section of a composition that summarizes an argument or main idea with added insight, and points the reader toward action or further reflection

Connotation the meaning of a word that carries ideas and feelings, as opposed to the word's strictly literal definition (denotation)

Context the setting or situation in which something happens; the parts of a statement that occur just before and just after a specific word and help determine its meaning

Controversy — a disagreement, often one that has attracted public interest

Counter-argument — a refutation; an argument made to oppose (counter) another argument

Criticism — discourse (usually an essay) that analyzes something (usually a literary or artistic work) in order to evaluate how it does or does not succeed in communicating its meaning

Critical Thinking — what a writer *does* with information; thinking that goes substantially beyond the facts to organize, analyze, evaluate, or draw conclusions about them

Cubing — a method for discovering ideas about a topic by using six strategies of investigation (in any order): describing, comparing, associating, analyzing, applying, and arguing for or against

Deconstruction — the process of taking apart for the purpose of analysis

Deductive Reasoning — the process of deriving a specific conclusion by reasoning from a general premise

Denotation — the meaning of a word that is strictly literal, as found in the dictionary, as opposed to the ideas and feelings the word carries (connotation)

Descriptive Writing — an account, usually giving a dominant impression and emphasizing sensory detail, of what it is like to experience some object, scene, or person

Dialect — a form of a language (usually regional) that has a distinctive pronunciation, vocabulary, and word order

Dialogue — spoken conversation of fictional characters or actual persons; the conversation in novels, stories, plays, poems, or essays

Documentation — the identification of documents or other sources used to support the information reported in an essay or other discourse; usually cited in footnotes or in parentheses

Editorial — an article in a publication or a commentary on radio or television expressing an opinion about a public issue

Elaboration the support or development of a main idea with facts, statistics, sensory details, incidents, examples, quotations, or visual representations

Evaluation writing that purposefully judges the worth, quality, or success of something

Expository Writing writing that explains an idea or teaches a process; also called informative writing

Expressive characterized by expression; refers to descriptive discourse full of meaning or feeling, often used by writers in personal writing to explore ideas

Fiction made-up or imaginary happenings as opposed to statements of fact or nonfiction. Short stories and novels are fiction, even though they may be based on real events; essays, scientific articles, biographies, news stories are nonfiction.

Figurative Language language that displays the imaginative and poetic use of words; writing that contains figures of speech such as simile, metaphor, and personification

Formal Language language in which rules of grammar and vocabulary standards are carefully observed; used in textbooks, reports, and other formal communications

Freewriting a way of exploring ideas, thoughts, or feelings that involves writing freely—without stopping or otherwise limiting the flow of ideas—for a specific length of time

Gender Neutral refers to language that includes both men and women when making reference to a role or a group that comprises people of both sexes. "A medic uses his or her skills to save lives" and "Medics use their skills to save lives" are two gender-neutral ways of expressing the same idea.

Generalization a statement expressing a principle or drawing a conclusion based on examples or instances

Gleaning a method of picking up ideas to write about by observing events, by scanning newspapers, magazines, and books, and by talking to others

Graphic Device a visual way of organizing information. Graphic devices include charts, graphs, outlines, clusters, and diagrams.

Idea Tree a graphic device in which main ideas are written on "branches" and related details are noted on "twigs"

Imagery figurative language and descriptions used to produce mental images

Inductive Reasoning a method of thinking or organizing a discourse so that a series of instances or pieces of evidence lead to a conclusion or generalization

Inference a logical assumption that is made based on observed facts and one's own knowledge and experience

Informative Writing writing that explains an idea or teaches a process; also called expository writing

Interpretation an explanation of the meaning of any text, set of facts, object, gesture, or event. To interpret something is to try to make sense of it.

Introduction the opening section of a composition, which presents the main idea, grabs the reader's attention, and sets the tone

Invisible writing writing done with a dimmed computer screen or with an empty ballpoint pen on two sheets of paper with carbon paper between them

Irony a figure of speech in which the intended meaning is the opposite of the stated meaning—saying one thing and meaning another

Jargon the special language and terminology used by people in the same profession or with specialized interests

Journal a record of thoughts and impressions, mainly for personal use

Learning Log a kind of journal used for recording and reflecting on what one has learned and for noting problems and questions

Literary Analysis critical thinking and writing about literature that presents a personal perspective

Looping a repetitive process for discovering ideas on a topic through freewriting, stopping to find promising ideas, then producing another freewrite on that subject, and repeating the loop several times

Media various forms of mass communication, such as newspapers, magazines, radio, television, and the Internet; the editorial voice and influence of all of these

Memoir an account of true events told by a narrator who witnessed or participated in the events; usually focuses on the personalities and actions of persons other than the writer

Metaphor a figure of speech that makes a comparison without using the word *like* or *as.* "All the world's a stage" is a metaphor.

Monologue a speech by one person without interruption by other voices. A dramatic monologue reveals the personality and experience of a person through a long speech.

Mood the feeling about a scene or a subject created for a reader by a writer's selection of words and details. The mood of a piece of writing may be suspenseful, mysterious, peaceful, fearful, and so on.

Narrative Writing discourse that tells a story—either made up or true. Some common types of narrative writing are biographies, short stories, and novels.

Onomatopoeia the use of words (usually in poetry) to suggest sounds; examples are "the clinking of knives and forks," and "the trilling of a flute."

Order of Degree a pattern of organization in which ideas, people, places, or things are presented in rank order on the basis of quantity or extent. An example is listing items in order from most important to least important.

Paraphrase a restatement of an original passage in one's own words that stays true to the original ideas, tone, and general length

Parenthetical Documentation the placement of citations or other documentation in parentheses within the text

Peer Response suggestions and comments on a piece of writing provided by peers or classmates

Personal Writing writing that focuses on expressing the writer's own thoughts, experiences, and feelings

Personification a figure of speech in which objects, events, abstract ideas, or animals are given human characteristics

Persuasive Writing writing that is intended to convince the reader of a particular point of view or course of action

Plagiarism the act of dishonestly presenting someone else's words or ideas as one's own

Point of View the angle from which a story is told, such as first-, second-, or third-person point of view

Portfolio a container (usually a folder) for notes on work in progress, drafts and revisions, finished pieces, and peer responses

Précis a short summary or abstract of an essay, story, or speech, capturing only the essential elements

Proofreading the act of checking work to discover typographical and other errors; usually the last stage of the revising or editing process

Propaganda discourse aimed at persuading an audience, often containing distortions of truth; usually refers to manipulative political discourse

Prose the usual language of speech and writing, lacking the special properties of meter and form that define poetry; any language that is not poetry

Satire a literary form that ridicules or mocks the social practices or values of a society, a group, or an important individual

Sensory Details words that express attributes of the five senses—the way something looks, sounds, smells, tastes, or feels

Sequential Order a pattern of organization in which information is presented in the order in which it occurs, as in telling a story chronologically or describing the sequence of steps in a process

Simile a figure of speech that uses the word *like* or *as* to make a comparison. "Trees like pencil strokes" is a simile.

Spatial Order a pattern of organization in which details are arranged in the order that they appear in space, such as from left to right

Style the distinctive features of a literary or artistic work that collectively characterize a particular individual, group, period, or school

Summary a brief restatement of the main idea of a passage

Symbol something (word, object, or action) that stands for or suggests something else. For example, a flag can stand for or symbolize a nation; a withered plant may suggest or symbolize a failing relationship.

Synthesis the combining of separate elements to form a coherent whole

Theme the underlying idea or central concern of a work of art or literature

Thesis Statement a statement in one or two sentences of the main idea or purpose of a piece of writing

Tone the writer's attitude or manner of expression—detached, ironic, serious, angry, and so on

Topic Sentence a sentence that expresses the main idea of a paragraph

Transition a connecting word or phrase that clarifies relationships between details, sentences, or paragraphs

Tree Diagram a graphic way of showing the relationships among ideas; particularly useful in generating ideas; also known as an idea tree or spider map

Trite Phrase a phrase overused so much that it loses meaning and suggests a lack of imagination on the part of the user

Unity a consistent focus on a single writing purpose. A paragraph has unity if all its sentences support the same main idea or purpose; a composition has unity if all its paragraphs support the thesis statement.

Venn Diagram a way of visually representing the relationship between two items that are distinct but that have common or overlapping elements

Voice the "sound" of a writer's work determined by stylistic choices such as sentence structure, diction, and tone

Index

A

B

C

INDEX

D

E

INDEX

F

G

H, I, J, K

INDEX

RESOURCES

L

M

INDEX

N

O

P

INDEX

INDEX

Q

R

INDEX

S

T

U

V

W, X, Y, Z

Acknowledgments

For Literature and Text

Susan Bergholz Literary Services: Excerpt from *How the Garcia Girls Lost Their Accents* by Julia Alvarez. Copyright © 1991 by Julia Alvarez. Published by Plume, a division of Penguin USA Inc. Originally published in hardcover by Algonquin Books of Chapel Hill. Reprinted by permission of Susan Bergholz Literary Services, New York. All rights reserved.

Brandt & Brandt Literary Agents: Excerpt from "The Most Dangerous Game" by Richard Connell. Copyright © 1924 by Richard Connell. Copyright renewed © 1952 by Louise Fox Connell. Reprinted by permission of Brandt & Brandt Literary Agents, Inc.

Chicago Sun-Times: Excerpt from "Overshadowed Sosa Equally Worthy of Acclaim" by Carol Slezak, *Chicago Sun-Times,* September 9, 1998. Copyright © 1998 by the Chicago Sun-Times. Reprinted with special permission from the Chicago Sun-Times, Inc.

Houghton Mifflin Company: *The American Heritage Dictionary of the English Language,* 3rd ed., s.v. "forage." Copyright © 1992 by Houghton Mifflin Company. Reprinted by permission. All rights reserved.

James Hurst: Excerpt from "The Scarlet Ibis" by James Hurst. Copyright © 1960 by *The Atlantic Monthly* and renewed 1988 by James Hurst. Reprinted by permission of James Hurst.

Macmillan General Reference: *Webster's New World Thesaurus,* 3rd. ed., edited by Victoria Neufeldt and David B. Guralnik, s.v. "forage." Copyright © 1997, 1996, 1991, 1988 by Simon & Schuster, Inc. Reprinted with the permission of Macmillan General Reference, a division of IDG Books Worldwide, Inc.

Men's Fitness: Excerpt from "Marathon Man" by Michael Konik, *Men's Fitness,* October 1998. Copyright © 1998 by *Men's Fitness*. Reprinted by permission of *Men's Fitness*. All rights reserved.

The New York Times: Excerpt from "Sadie Delany, Witness to a Century, Dies at 109" by Richard Severo, *New York Times,* January 26, 1999. Copyright © 1999 by The New York Times. Reprinted by permission.

Parade: "Discover Your Family Tree" by Troy Corley, *Parade,* November 29, 1998. Copyright © 1998 by *Parade*. Reprinted by permission of *Parade* and Troy Kathleen Corley.

Publishers Weekly: Review of *Within Reach: My Everest Story* by Mark Pfetzer and Jack Galvin. From *Publishers Weekly,* September 14, 1998. Copyright © 1998 by Publishers Weekly. Reprinted by permission.

Rashmi Rathor: Excerpt from "A Fly Running on a Battery" (retitled "A Fly in the House") by Rashmi Rathor, *Illinois English Bulletin,* Fall 1997. Copyright © 1997 by Rashmi Rathor. Reprinted by permission of the author.

Reader's Digest: Excerpt from "Tales Out of School" contributed by Liz Bassett, *Reader's Digest,* November 1998. Copyright © 1998 by the Reader's Digest Association, Inc. Used by permission of Reader's Digest.

Scholastic: Excerpt from *365 Meditations for Teachers* by Greg Henry Quinn. Copyright © 1995 by Gregory H. Quinn. Reprinted by permission of Scholastic, Inc. All rights reserved.

Science News: Excerpt from "Besieged Tadpoles Send Chemical Alert" by S. Carpenter, *Science News,* June 12, 1999. Copyright © 1999 by Science Service. Reprinted with permission from *Science News,* a weekly newsmagazine of science.

Scribner: Excerpt from the essay "Neighbors" reprinted in *Pieces of My Mind* by Andrew A. Rooney. Copyright © 1984 by Essay Productions, Inc. Reprinted with the permission of Scribner, a division of Simon & Schuster, Inc.

Twins Magazine: Excerpt from "The Sound of My Name" by Kris Schultz, *Twins Magazine,* Nov./Dec. 1998. Copyright © 1998 by Twins Magazine. Reprinted by permission of Twins Magazine, 1-888-55-TWINS. All rights reserved.

Universal Press Syndicate: Excerpt from *The PreHistory of The Far Side* by Gary Larson.

Copyright © 1989 by Universal Press Syndicate. Used by permission. All rights reserved.

University of New Mexico Press: Excerpt from "The Great Taos Bank Robbery," from *The Great Taos Bank Robbery and Other Indian Country Affairs* by Tony Hillerman. Copyright © 1973 by Anthony G. Hillerman. Reprinted by permission of the University of New Mexico Press. All rights reserved.

University of Pittsburgh Press: Excerpt from "The Bass, the River, and Sheila Mant," from *The Man Who Loved Levittown* by W. D. Wetherell. Copyright © 1985 by W. D. Wetherell. Reprinted by permission of the University of Pittsburgh Press.

For Illustrations by Daniel Guidera

6, 11, 12, 13, 15, 16, 23, 29, 34, 35, 38, 45, 54, 56, 57, 62, 63, 66, 67, 71, 75, 80, 81, 82, 83, 89, 93, 97, 112, 113, 126, 127, 135, 142, 154, 155, 160, 163, 166, 176, 206, 220, 230, 238, 247, 252, 267, 275, 276, 279, 308, 317 *top left,* 320, 324, 325, 326, 327, 341, 347, 348 *top left,* 349, 355, 357, 358 *center left, center right, bottom left, bottom right,* 359, 360 *top, bottom,* 361, 363, 372, 373, 374, 376, 377 *top,* 381, 383, 384, 389, 391, 392, 402, 403, 480, 484, 489, 490, 498, 502, 503, 505, 507 *bottom,* 511, 512, 520, 521, 524, 525, 526, 531, 536, 540, 545, 550, 553, 565, 571, 580.

Art Credits

CHAPTER 1 **2, 3** © Ron Chapple/FPG International; **4** *background* Corbis/Henry Diltz; *top* © Copyright 1999 PhotoDisc, Inc.; **6** Photo courtesy of the Chicago Symphony Orchestra; **18** © PhotoDisc, Inc.; **19** Copyright 1997, Brooke McEldowney. Distributed by the Los Angeles Times Syndicate. Reprinted by permission; **21** *background* © Copyright 1999 PhotoDisc, Inc.; *foreground* © Joseph Stieler/Wood River Gallery/PNI; **25** Corbis/Robert Holmes; **30** © Copyright 1999 PhotoDisc, Inc.; **31** Photo by Sharon Hoogstraten

CHAPTER 2 **36** *background* © Copyright 1999 PhotoDisc, Inc.; **40** *Calvin and Hobbes* © 1989 Watterson. Dist. by Universal Press Syndicate. Reprinted with permission. All rights reserved; **42** © 1995 Dan McCoy/The Stock Market; **46** © 1985 FarWorks, Inc. All rights reserved. Reprinted by permission; **57** © Tribune Media Services, Inc. All rights reserved. Reprinted with permission; **58** © Copyright 1999 PhotoDisc, Inc.

CHAPTER 3 **64** © Copyright 1999 PhotoDisc, Inc.; **72** © Tribune Media Services, Inc. All rights reserved. Reprinted with permission; **84** Photo by Sharon Hoogstraten; **86** AP/Wide World Photos; **88** *left, right* © Copyright 1999 PhotoDisc, Inc.

CHAPTER 4 **90** AP/Wide World Photos; **92** Farkas family. From a private collection; **100** *Foxtrot* © 1995 Bill Amend. Reprinted with permission of Universal Press Syndicate. All rights reserved; **108** *background* H. Armstrong Roberts; *foreground* Copyright © L.L.T. Rhodes/Animals Animals.

CHAPTER 5 **114** *background* © Burke: Triolo/FoodPix/PNI; *foreground* Photo by Sharon Hoogstraten; **117** © PhotoDisc, Inc.; **122** *center* Photo by Sharon Hoogstraten; *top right* © 1997 Peter Menzel; **123** © 1998 Peter Menzel.

CHAPTER 6 **128** *background* © Archive Photos/PNI, *foreground* © Copyright 1999 PhotoDisc, Inc.; **137, 138, 139** © Luiz C. Marigo/Peter Arnold, Inc.; **141** © Tribune Media Services, Inc. All rights reserved. Reprinted with permission; **145** NASA; **148** *background* © F. Stuart Westmorland/AllStock/PNI; *foreground* © Copyright 1999 PhotoDisc, Inc.; **150** *foreground* Illustration by Nobee Kanayama © 1997 McDougal Littell Inc.

CHAPTER 7 **156** Tabletop by Sharon Hoogstraten; **171** © 1999 *Zits* Partnership. Reprinted with special permission of King Features Syndicate; **172** Photo by Sharon Hoogstraten.

CHAPTER 8 **178** *top left* Photofest; *top right* © Frank Connor/Photofest; **182** © Copyright 1999 PhotoDisc, Inc.; **184** Tournament in King Arthur's court. MS Douce 383, fol. 16r. The Bodleian Library, Oxford, England; **186** Photograph © Courtney Milne; **192** Corbis/Lindsay Hebberd; **194** Corbis/Hulton-Deutsch Collection.

CHAPTER 9 **207** *top* U.S. Treasury; **208** © Archive Photos/PNI; **212** *Calvin and Hobbes* © 1986 Watterson. Dist. by Universal Press Syndicate. Reprinted with permission. All rights reserved; **218** © Copyright 1999 PhotoDisc, Inc.; **222** *background*

Photo by Sharon Hoogstraten; *foreground* © Copyright 1999 PhotoDisc, Inc.; **223** Corbis/Bettmann; **226** © 1992 Thaves. Reprinted with permission.

CHAPTER 10 **228** AP/Wide World Photos; **232** *background* © SuperStock; **233** AP/Wide World Photos; **237** Culver Pictures; **240–243** © Copyright 1999 PhotoDisc, Inc.

CHAPTER 11 **256** *center left* © Terry E. Eiler/Stock, Boston/PNI, *bottom Peanuts* reprinted by permission of United Feature Syndicate, Inc.; **261** © Jim Cummins/FPG International/PNI; **268** © Christopher Morris/Black Star/PNI; **270** © Copyright 1999 PhotoDisc, Inc.; **271** *bottom right, bottom left* © 1998-1999 EyeWire, Inc. All rights reserved; *bottom center* © Copyright 1999 PhotoDisc, Inc.

CHAPTER 12 **300–301** © Frank Saragnese/FPG International; **302** *background, foreground* © Copyright 1999 PhotoDisc, Inc.; **303** © 1982 FarWorks, Inc. All rights reserved. Reprinted by permission; **304** *top right* © James Keyser/Contact Press Images/PNI; *bottom left* Courtesy, Arte Público Press; **306** AP/Wide World Photos; **307** © Archive Photos; **309** © Robert Foothorap/Black Star/PNI; **310** © Neal Preston/Corbis; **314** © Frank Capri/Archive Photos/PNI; **317** *Calvin and Hobbes* © 1988 Watterson. Dist. by Universal Press Syndicate. Reprinted with permission. All rights reserved.

CHAPTER 13 **318** *left* Corbis; *right* Corbis/Charles O'Rear; **319** Tabletop by Sharon Hoogstraten; *background, left* © Copyright 1999 PhotoDisc, Inc.; **323** © David Young Wolff/Tony Stone Images; **324** Illustration by Daniel Guidera, *background* © Copyright 1999 PhotoDisc, Inc.

CHAPTER 14 **334** © Copyright 1999 PhotoDisc, Inc.; **335** © Patrick Ingrand/Tony Stone Images; **348** *bottom, Foxtrot* © 1999 Bill Amend. Reprinted with permission of Universal Press Syndicate. All rights reserved.

CHAPTER 15 **350** © 1998–1999 EyeWire, Inc. All rights reserved; **352** Copyright © 1987 by David Sipress; **358** *top right* © Bill Aron/PhotoEdit.

CHAPTER 16 **362** © Copyright 1999 PhotoDisc, Inc.; **365** *Peanuts* reprinted by permission of United Feature Syndicate, Inc.; **370** © Copyright 1999 PhotoDisc, Inc.

CHAPTER 17 **378, 379** © Copyright 1999 PhotoDisc, Inc.; **380** *Calvin and Hobbes* © 1990 Watterson. Dist. by Universal Press Syndicate. Reprinted with permission. All rights reserved; **386** © 1999 Index Stock Imagery; **393** © Copyright 1999 PhotoDisc, Inc.

CHAPTER 18 **394–395** Corbis; **401** *left* Reproduced courtesy of Home Box Office and the United States Holocaust Memorial Museum. *One Survivor Remembers.* A film by Kary Antholis. Academy Award Winner 1995 Best Documentary Short Film. For more information: 310-636-8200; *top right* "Cover design" by Melissa Jacoby, from *Freedom's Children* by Ellen Levine. Copyright © 1993 by Ellen Levine. Used by permission of G. P. Putnam's Sons, a division of Penguin Putnam Inc. Photo by Euvester Simpson (1964), Jackson, MS; *bottom left* Photo © Renee Stockdale/Animals Animals. Reprinted with permission from the May 1998 *Reader's Digest.* Copyright © 1998 by The Reader's Digest Assn., Inc.

CHAPTER 19 **409** *top left* AP/Wide World Photos/The Cousteau Society; *top right, People* Weekly is a registered trademark of Time Inc. Used with permission. Photo © Jonathan Daniel/Allsport; *bottom left* Suzanne Dechillo/NYT Pictures; **410** © 1999 *Zits* Partnership. Reprinted with special permission of King Features Syndicate.

CHAPTER 20 **417** *top right* From *Within Reach: My Everest Story* Copyright © 1998 by Mark Pfetzer and Jack Galvin. Used by permission of Dutton Books, a division of Penguin Putnam Books for Young Readers. Photo copyright © 1998 Mark Pfetzer; *bottom right* From *Soldier's Heart* by Gary Paulsen. Copyright © 1998 by Gary Paulsen. Used by permission of Random House Children's Books, a division of Random House, Inc. Web page by Patricia C. Kindermann, www.embracingthechild.com; *bottom left, The Horn Book Magazine,* January/February 1999, reprinted by permission of The Horn Book, Inc., 56 Roland St., Suite 200, Boston, MA 02129. Taken from *The Only Outcast,* illustration by Julia Bell © 1998 published by Tundra Books.

CHAPTER 21 **425** *center* © Copyright 1999 PhotoDisc, Inc.; *bottom right* From *Newsweek,* November 30, 1998 © 1998 Newsweek, Inc. All rights reserved. Reprinted by permission. Copyright © Jan Sonnenmair.

CHAPTER 22 **433** *center* "Test Your Backpack" © 1997 by Consumers Union of U.S., Inc. Yonkers, NY 10703-1057, a nonprofit organization. Reprinted with permission from the September/October 1997 issue of *Zillions: Consumer Reports for Kids,* for educational purposes only; *bottom right* Sporting News/Archive Photos.

CHAPTER 23 **443** *top left* Public service announcement produced by the American Diabetes Association was created by Atelier Design, Inc., Washington, D.C.; *bottom* Photograph © Susan Reich. Brochure © 1999 Lincoln Park Zoo.

CHAPTER 25 **467** *Calvin and Hobbes* © 1989 Bill Watterson. Dist. by Universal Press Syndicate. Reprinted with permission. All rights reserved.

CHAPTER 26 **472–473, 474** © Copyright 1999 PhotoDisc, Inc.; **475** Illustration by Jenny Adams; *background* Tabletop by Sharon Hoogstraten; *center* Photo © Stockbyte; **479** *top, bottom right The 1999 Grolier Multimedia Encyclopedia*®Copyright © 1998 by Grolier Interactive, Inc. All rights reserved; *bottom left* © Stockbyte; **483** The Duplex © 1999 Glenn McCoy. Reprinted with permission of Universal Press Syndicate. All rights reserved.

CHAPTER 27 **488** Copyright © 1998–1999 EyeWire, Inc. All rights reserved; **495** © StockFood/Barrow; **500** © Copyright 1999 PhotoDisc, Inc.

CHAPTER 28 **504** Corbis/James L. Amos; **506** *left, right* © Copyright 1999 PhotoDisc, Inc.; **507** *top right* © 1982 FarWorks, Inc. All rights reserved. Reprinted by permission; **510** © 1997 David Woods/The Stock Market; **513** © Jon Riley/Tony Stone Images; **519** © 1997 Tom Stewart/The Stock Market.

CHAPTER 29 **522** *background, foreground* © Copyright 1999 PhotoDisc, Inc.; **523** © A. Ramey/PhotoEdit; **528** *left,* **529** *TV* © Copyright 1999 PhotoDisc, Inc.; **529** *inset* AP/Wide World Photos; **530** *left* © SuperStock; *right* © 1998 Jose L. Pelaez, Inc./The Stock Market; **532** Courtesy David R. Lee Animal Care Shelter. Photography © Bob Randall. Ad created by Charlie Propsom, copywriter, and Karl Anderson, art director; **534** Reprinted from the March 1, 1999, issue of *Business Week* by permission. © 1999 by The McGraw Hill Companies; **537** © Copyright 1999 PhotoDisc, Inc.

CHAPTER 30 **538** *background* © Copyright 1999 PhotoDisc, Inc.; *foreground* Copyright © 1998–1999 EyeWire, Inc. All rights reserved; **539** © Bob Daemmrich/Stock, Boston/PNI; **541** Courtesy of Habitat for Humanity International; **544** *left, right* © Index Stock Imagery; **549** © Copyright 1999 PhotoDisc, Inc., **551** *top,* Calvin and Hobbes © 1990 Bill Watterson. Dist. by Universal Press Syndicate. Reprinted with permission. All rights reserved.

CHAPTER 31 **552** *background* Corbis/George Lee White; *top right* Corbis; **559** © Copyright 1999 PhotoDisc, Inc.; **562** *top left, top right, bottom left, bottom right* © Copyright 1999 PhotoDisc, Inc.; **565** Copyright © 1999 Creators Syndicate, Inc. Reprint by permission of Rick DeTorie and Creators Syndicate.

CHAPTER 32 **566** *background, foreground* © Copyright 1999 PhotoDisc, Inc.; **567** *background* © Melchior Di Giacomo/The Image Bank/PNI; *foreground* © Copyright 1999 PhotoDisc, Inc.; **576** © 1997 Charles Gupton/The Stock Market; **581** *Peanuts* reprinted by permission of United Feature Syndicate, Inc.

McDougal Littell Inc. has made every effort to locate the copyright holders of all copyrighted material in this book and to make full acknowledgment for its use.